MANITOBA POLITICS
AND GOVERNMENT

MANITOBA POLITICS AND GOVERNMENT

Issues, Institutions, Traditions

Edited by Paul G. Thomas and Curtis Brown

University of Manitoba Press

© The Authors 2010

University of Manitoba Press
Winnipeg, Manitoba
Canada R3T 2M5

www.umanitoba.ca/uofmpress

Printed in Canada on chlorine-free, 100% post-consumer recycled paper.

All rights reserved. No part of this publication may be reproduced or transmitted in any form or by any means, or stored in a database and retrieval system, without the prior written permission of the University of Manitoba Press, or, in the case of photocopying or any other reprographic copying, a licence from ACCESS COPYRIGHT (Canadian Copyright Licensing Agency) 6 Adelaide Street East, Suite 901, Toronto, Ontario M5C 1H6, www.accesscopyright.ca.

Interior design: Karen Armstrong Graphic Design
Cover image: Joe Bryska/Winnipeg Free Press

The photograph on page vii is used courtesy the *Winnipeg Free Press*.

Library and Archives Canada Cataloguing in Publication

Manitoba politics and government : issues, institutions, traditions / Paul G. Thomas, Curtis Brown, editors.

Based on papers presented at the Roblin Professorship conference : Manitoba Politics, Government and Policy into the 21st Century, held at St. John's College, University of Manitoba, Winnipeg, Man. from Nov. 19–21, 2008.
Includes bibliographical references and index.
ISBN 978-0-88755-719-4

1. Manitoba—Politics and government. 2. Manitoba—Social conditions.
I. Thomas, Paul G. II. Brown, Curtis, 1981–

FC3361.M36 2010   320.97127   C2010-902853-8

The University of Manitoba Press gratefully acknowledges the financial support for its publication program provided by the Government of Canada through the Canada Book Fund, the Canada Council for the Arts, the Manitoba Department of Culture, Heritage, and Tourism, the Manitoba Arts Council, and the Manitoba Book Publishing Tax Credit.

CONTENTS

Introduction: Manitoba in the Middle
Paul G. Thomas and Curtis Brown 3

PART ONE
MANITOBA'S POLITICAL CULTURE

1. The Manitoba Political Tradition
   Gerald Friesen 21

2. Political Culture in Manitoba
   Jared Wesley 43

PART TWO
PARTIES AND ELECTIONS IN MANITOBA

3. The Success of the New Democratic Party
   Nelson Wiseman 73

4. Manitoba's Progressive Conservative Party: A "Great Renewal" Or Continued Disarray?
   Kelly L. Saunders... 96

5. Manitoba's Liberals: Sliding into Third
   Paul Barber 128

6. Realigning Elections in Manitoba
   Christopher Adams 159

PART THREE
GOVERNMENT INSTITUTIONS AND PROCESSES

7. The Manitoba Cabinet
   Paul Vogt 181

8. The Manitoba Legislature: A Personal Reflection
   Jean Friesen 205

9. The Evolution of Political Journalism in Manitoba
   Frances Russell 218

10. The Past, Present, and Future of the Manitoba's Civil Service
    Paul G. Thomas, with Curtis Brown 227

11. A Practitioner's Reflections on the Practice of Federalism
    Jim Eldridge 257

12. Leading from the Middle: Manitoba's Role in the Intergovernmental and Transnational Arenas
    Paul G. Thomas 265

PART FOUR
MANITOBA'S ECONOMY AND SOCIETY

13. Manitoba in the Middle: A Mutual Fund Balanced for Steady Income
    Derek Hum and Wayne Simpson 293

14. Manitoba Agriculture: Cultivating a New Approach Towards Sustainability
    Kerri Holland 306

15. Segregated City: A Century of Poverty in Winnipeg
    Jim Silver 331

16. "Closing the Gap" in Manitoba
    Harvey Bostrom 358

17. The Role of Aboriginal Political Organizations in the Policy Process
    Irene Linklater 372

18. Has the Manitoba "Advantage" Worked for Women?
    Joan Grace 382

19. Health Care Policy in Manitoba: The Past, Present, and Future of Regional Health Authorities
    Paul G. Thomas 404

20. Questions of Allocation: Resources and Degrees Awarded at the University of Manitoba, 1998–2005
    Rodney A. Clifton 434

Contributors 448

*This book is dedicated to the exemplary life of public service
and the enduring legacies of the
Hon. Duff Roblin, PC, CC, OM, 1917–2010*

MANITOBA POLITICS
AND GOVERNMENT

Introduction: Manitoba in the Middle

Paul G. Thomas and Curtis Brown

Manitoba might be considered the forgotten province of Confederation. Like the so-called "flyover" country of the American Midwest, the keystone-shaped landmass in the centre of the continental map rarely merits attention in a country's mass media and contributes very little to the popularized (though caricaturized) images of Canada as a land of snow-capped mountains, Mounties, and maple syrup. Even in the formal study of Canadian politics, Manitoba's social, political, and economic life tends to be ignored. As Jared Wesley notes in Chapter 2 of this book, undergraduate students of political science at universities across Canada learn that "Manitoba is a province without a distinctive political culture."[1] Lacking Quebec's cultural and linguistic distinctiveness, Ontario's traditional demographic and economic hegemony, or Alberta's combustible mix of prairie populism and oil wealth, Manitoba appears to blend into the background of the national family portrait, lacking the political importance, economic strength, or cultural effervescence of its larger and more colourful provincial cousins.

This, along with the dearth of academic analysis of Manitoba's politics and society, is what prompted the publication of this book, which resulted from a three-day conference at St. John's College at the University of Manitoba 20–22 November 2008. The conference was made possible by the financial support of the Roblin Professorship fund. Established in 1999 by Manitoba's former premier, the Hon. Duff Roblin, PC, OM, LLD, and his friends and admirers, the fund supports the position of the Roblin Professor of Government, two annual Roblin fellowships awarded to outstanding graduate students as well as to the sponsorship of events like the conference which led to this book.

As the co-editors of this volume, who also co-chaired the conference, we have benefited enormously from the generosity of the Roblin fund. Since 1999, Dr. Paul G. Thomas has served as the Roblin Professor of Government at St. John's College, University of Manitoba. And at the time of the conference in late 2008, Mr. Curtis Brown was a holder of a Roblin graduate fellowship. We are both exceedingly grateful to Mr. Roblin and the other contributors to the fund for enabling the conference to take place. And we were most honoured and pleased that Mr. Roblin was able to address the dinner opening the conference and agreed to provide a foreword to this volume.

To state that Mr. Roblin was a distinguished Manitoban who made an incredible contribution of leadership, innovation, and public service in this province qualifies as a gigantic understatement. Arguably, no other single public official contributed as much to the transformation of the province during the second half of the twentieth century. Entering the provincial legislature in 1949, becoming leader of the Progressive Conservative Party in 1954 and leading his party to office—first as a minority government in 1958, and then to majority status in provincial elections held in 1959, 1962, and 1966—Mr. Roblin's record of accomplishments and integrity is almost without parallel in Manitoba history. Successive Roblin-led governments reformed education on all levels, invested greatly in the health care system, made great improvements to social services, and engaged in important economic development initiatives. He is probably best remembered, especially outside of the province, for the foresight and political courage he showed in building the floodway which protects the city of Winnipeg, the population and economic centre of the province, against annual spring flooding. The costs at the time seemed prohibitive and the project was ridiculed by critics as "Duff's Folly," but the Red River Floodway has been used numerous times to avert hundreds of millions of dollars of property and other economic losses, as well as relieving the anxiety of Winnipeggers. And to demonstrate its necessity even further, the floodway has been expanded recently to protect Winnipeg and the surrounding area from potentially more cataclysmic floods, which have threatened the region periodically.

Roblin left provincial politics in 1967 to run unsuccessfully for the leadership of the national wing of his Progressive Conservative Party. In 1978 he was appointed to the Senate and made a further contribution to national public life as leader of the government in the Senate. After retiring from the Senate in 1992, he continued to provide leadership and ideas at the provincial, national, and international levels through service on many committees and by providing informal, wise, reasoned, and balanced advice to governments and others who would seek his counsel. Throughout his decades of public service he always commanded enormous respect across party lines and within all segments of Manitoba society. In light of these facts, it was no surprise that in 2008, the year of the conference, Duff Roblin was chosen by the readers of the *Winnipeg Free Press* as "the greatest Manitoban" in the history of the province.

The conference and book were meant to address the lack of material on various aspects of Manitoba society, politics, government, and contemporary policy issues. In a conference lasting only three days and whose proceedings are confined to a single book, it was not possible to fill all the gaps in our scholarly knowledge of the many important and intriguing areas of potential inquiry into Manitoba's rich and varied public life. Also, the conference (and this subsequent volume) sought to bring the scholarly research and findings of academics in several disciplines together with the experience and distinctive understandings of practitioners in government, the media, and other fields outside of the university. Hopefully this effort to bridge the gap which too often exists between theory and practice has enriched the final content of this volume. In total, fourteen formal papers were presented to the conference. They covered the history and political traditions of the province, its economy, the contemporary political culture, watershed elections, each of the three parties represented in the provincial legislature, the political executive consisting of the premier and the cabinet, the public service, the media, and public policy in several policy fields. In addition to the substantive papers, the decision was made, based on their importance and quality, to include addresses by several accomplished leaders in the public service and other fields. These include addresses by Jim Eldridge—considered the dean of the Manitoba government's "fed-prov" apparatus and a veteran of countless negotiations involving Manitoba and other federal, state, provincial, and municipal governments—who reflects on Manitoba's role in the various intergovernmental arenas. Harvey Bostrom, who has experienced policy making both as a senior public servant and as a minister of the Crown, deals with the improving circumstances and serious unmet needs of Manitoba's Aboriginal peoples, which is a topic that Irene Linklater of the Assembly of Manitoba Chiefs examines in her discussion of the role political organizations such as the AMC play in developing policies that affect First Nations people. As well, Frances Russell's observations on a lifetime in political journalism and the rapidly changing media environment prompts reflection on the significant changes that have taken place in terms of how Manitobans learn about their province's political processes and institutions.

With its multiple topics and authors, this book acts in part to address the paucity of scholarly research and contemporary study of Manitoba society, elections, political parties, the machinery of government, and some leading issues of public policy. One has to go back to 1963 and Murray Donnelly's *The Government of Manitoba* to find a reasonably comprehensive study of public life in Manitoba. Of course there have been other, narrower studies over the years. Political scientists such as James McAllister,[2] Nelson Wiseman,[3] and Ian Stewart[4] have evaluated particular political parties, government administrations or political events in the province. Some political actors, including Lloyd Stinson,[5] Russell Doern,[6] Sharon Carstairs,[7] Duff Roblin,[8] Sid Green,[9] Roland Penner,[10] and Herb Schulz[11] have published memoirs of political life in the keystone province, while others such as historian John Kendle have written biographies of particular political figures like former premier John Bracken.[12] Most recently, Dr. Christopher Adams, a contributor to this volume, has published an important full-length study of the history of Manitoba political parties. He examines their fluctuating fortunes in elections going back to the founding of the province in 1870 and the changing content of their appeals to voters, as well as shifting contours of their support in the contemporary period of Manitoba politics, which most observers date from the end of coalition government and the majority victory by the Progressive Conservatives led by Duff Roblin in 1958.

This volume seeks to assess what might be described as the main political institutions, their evolution in the responses to changing circumstances in the province and their impacts on the quality of life in Manitoba. In order to recognize the importance of the historical, economic, and social context, contributors were asked to analyze the past, present, and future of the institutions they were investigating. By drawing upon the insights of a wide array of scholars—political scientists, historians, sociologists, and economists, each with long-standing academic interests in Manitoba—as well as soliciting the perspectives of others, such as journalists and policy actors from the province, this book provides an informed and comprehensive analysis of many of the main features of Manitoba's political life.

Manitoba in the Middle

One recurring phrase throughout the literature on Manitoba politics and history that comes up frequently in this book relates to Manitoba being in the "middle." This is not only an obvious fact of geography—the longitudinal centre of Canada, 96°48'35" W, runs just east of Winnipeg through the town of Landmark—but it is also due to the fact Manitoba ranks among the middle tier of provinces both economically and demographically. With 1.18 million people as of the 2006 census[13] and a gross domestic product (as of 2006 and measured in 2002 dollars) of $40.3 billion,[14] Manitoba places fifth in both categories among the ten provinces.

Unlike provinces such as Alberta, which are prone to strong surges and periodic collapses in both population and economic activity, throughout most of its history Manitoba has made slow and steady progress, reaping small increases of both people and wealth while other provinces experience booms and busts. It is neither rich nor poor. It was the last Western province to qualify for equalization, but the amounts have been declining in recent years as the provincial economy has performed above the national average for all provinces. Manitoba was not immune to the recent global economic downturn, but its diversified "portfolio" of manufacturing, resource extraction, services, and primary industry such as agriculture generally make it less vulnerable to peaks and valleys. The theme of Manitoba's 2009 provincial budget—"Steady. Balanced."—speaks to this idea.[15] As Derek Hum and Wayne Simpson argue in Chapter 12, Manitoba's "mutual fund model" of economic performance belies the steady, cautious nature of its citizens and their province.

Manitoba can also be described as being in the middle in social and cultural terms. Its social realities mirror in many ways those of the country as a whole. For example, it has a bilingual past which was somewhat tumultuous, to say the least. Manitoba began in 1870 as a bicultural and bilingual province with a bicameral legislative assembly in which both English and French were recognized as languages of debate. The courts also operated in both languages. In 1890 an act of the legislature made English the official language of these institutions. There was in 1890 a dual school system of English and French instruction. Contrary to popular mythology, the 1890 legislation did nothing to change the language of instruction in schools; it remained English or French depending upon the decision of local school trustees. However, a subsequent bill passed by the legislature in 1916 made teaching in English mandatory, signalling the end of French schools until the 1970s.

In the early 1980s the leadership of the still sizable, but declining francophone population undertook a constitutional challenge—prompted by a unilingual parking ticket, of all things—to the 1890 legislation which had eliminated the status of the French language. As a result of Georges Forest's successful court challenge, all Manitoba's laws that were passed solely in English dating back to 1890 were declared invalid. In a tumultuous and emotional series of events too involved to be recounted here, the eventual outcome was a pragmatic compromise which involved the translation of laws dating only from 1970, the limited operation of the legislative process in both languages, the provision of provincial government services in French where numbers warranted, and the creation of a province-wide school division to oversee French language schools.[16] Today the issue of French language rights is submerged and the leaders of Manitoba's

French-speaking community seem to be firmly of the view that more progress in gaining services to protect and promote their language and culture will be obtained through quiet diplomacy than efforts to obtain constitutional recognition of the province as officially bilingual.

Manitobans probably think of their past as orderly and peaceable like the country itself, whose constitutional preamble declares the aim of "peace, order and good government." However, from the time European settlers arrived in the Red River Valley, violence and hardship have been the order of the day at regular intervals. Lord Selkirk's settlers, cleared from their ancestral homes in highland Scotland and seeking a new life in the New World, survived initial hostility and outright violence from the North West Company and the region's Métis residents—culminating in the 1816 Battle of Seven Oaks—only to have their fledgling settlement wash away during the great flood of 1826.[17] In 1869–70, Manitoba became the only province to enter Confederation under a cloud of conflict, as an armed resistance which formed a provisional government ultimately bargained with the national government on the province's terms of entry. In 1896, the debate over some of those terms—education and linguistic provisions for the province's French Catholic minority—dominated an election campaign and nearly tore the governing Liberal Party apart. As we just noted, the French-language controversy of the early 1980s shut down the province's legislature for months and in some ways presaged the tensions that would erupt during the coming round of "mega-constitutional" negotiations between the provinces and the federal government in the late 1980s and early 1990s, a period that included the dramatic episode of the Meech Lake constitutional package failing to pass the Manitoba Legislature in 1990.[18]

Religious and linguistic conflicts have also been eclipsed by socio-economic cleavages that for a brief moment in 1919 erupted into an all-out class conflict between Winnipeg's haves and have-nots. The city's workers effectively shut down the city during a weeks-long general strike, leading the federal government—at the urging of the city's business leaders—to use the North West Mounted Police to break the strike on "Bloody Saturday," 17 June 1919. The class divide, which Jim Silver argues in Chapter 14 persists to this day as "spatialized" poverty divides the city's haves from have-nots, is also expressed as a partisan divide, traditionally separating wealthier, middle-class supporters of the Progressive Conservative Party in south Winnipeg from working-class backers of the New Democratic Party in north Winnipeg, with support for the Liberal Party falling at narrow points in between these two halves.[19] The state of support for Manitoba's three major political parties is taken up by Nelson Wiseman, Kelly Saunders, and Paul Barber in Chapters 3, 4, and 5 respectively. These class divisions also extend beyond Winnipeg, as the residents of the "rock and water"-filled Canadian Shield[20] in the northern and eastern stretches of the province have traditionally held different political preferences and economic interests than those who live in the southern farm belt. Indeed, the issues facing prosperous cities and towns such as the province's second-largest city, Brandon, or burgeoning communities straddling the Red River Valley such as Morden, Winkler, and Steinbach, are quite different from the issues facing northern cities such as Thompson, Flin Flon, or The Pas. Just the same, the effects of rural depopulation, such as closing hospital emergency rooms and elementary schools, that are facing small farming communities in the southwest corner of the province bear some similarity, yet remain quite different from the challenges of isolation, poor transportation and communication links, economic underdevelopment, and systemic poverty facing remote northern Aboriginal communities.

As Gerald Friesen succinctly notes in Chapter 1, "Histories of Manitoba politics typically dwell on conflicts." Yet despite deep historic divisions, reflected somewhat in the polarized party competition within its legislature, the province largely eschews radicalism and extremism, aiming towards the safe middle ground. Manitoba is a place where political pragmatism is valued and where citizens expect their leaders not to be so hampered by their partisan differences or ideology that they become incapable of working together to solve common problems. Friesen, quoting Paul Vogt (whose contribution to this volume examines the role of cabinet in government decision making), uses the word "accommodationist" to describe the way in which legislators are able to overcome their differences to forge compromises. There is a long tradition of this in Manitoba, extending from former premier Thomas Greenway's compromise with then-prime minister Wilfrid Laurier on Catholic education to the rare and unprecedented period during the Second World War when all parties in the legislature participated in a coalition government with the Liberal-Progressive party (itself the product of an earlier agreement to govern co-operatively). In fact, before Roblin and the Progressive Conservatives came to power in 1958, party competition had waned due to the existence of coalition governments and acclamations to fill public office. The legislature is far more polarized today, largely divided between the New Democrats and Progressive Conservatives with a small Liberal presence, yet even there the atmosphere retains much of its collegiality, as historian and former deputy premier Jean Friesen notes in Chapter 8.

This tradition of compromise and accommodation is also present on the national stage: in the intergovernmental arena, Manitoba governments have typically adopted a constructive approach which seeks to support the national interest, which includes creating relatively equal opportunities for Canadians in less affluent regions. This has meant supporting a strong national government, especially one which has the financial capacity to equalize opportunities across the country through devices like equalization transfers and shared-cost programs. Unlike Quebec and richer provinces such as Alberta, Manitoba has not been hung up on the constitutional implication of federal spending in areas of exclusive provincial jurisdiction and—with the notable exception of the Meech Lake Accord—has generally supported the initiatives of the federal government rather than opposed them as a matter of course.[21] As Jim Eldridge, one of Manitoba's most experienced civil servants in the area of intergovernmental affairs, explains in Chapter 11, Manitoba has been an "active and enthusiastic participant and contributor" in the federal-provincial arena.

There is also a degree of hesitancy in Manitoba to bring about radical change: though Manitoba was one of the first jurisdictions to elect an openly neoconservative government, it rejected Sterling Lyon's Progressive Conservative administration after one term and only accepted reform of its government and public services in the form of "pragmatic incrementalism" during Gary Filmon's decade in power.[22] The effect of public sector reform in Manitoba—including, as Paul Thomas highlights in Chapter 17, in the implementation of the regional health authorities (RHAs)—illustrates how Manitobans generally strive for a middle way, free as possible from polar extremes and serious discord. Owing in some part to its history as a "quiet and traditional organization,"[23] the Manitoba civil service did not experience the more radical forms of reorganization witnessed in jurisdictions such as Britain and New Zealand yet still pioneered reforms to the way services are delivered to citizens. As Paul Thomas explains in his examination of the province's civil service (Chapter 10), Manitoba's civil service has evolved significantly by doing things that reflect the priorities of different administrations, but it has continually carried forward the legacies of previous administrations in earlier eras. Some would argue, however, that public sector reform in Manitoba was driven more by the need to save money than by a genuine desire to alter how citizens receive services.[24] The Balanced Budget law passed by Gary Filmon's Progressive Conservative government, which has been retained with only recent minor amendments by the current NDP administration, reflects a long-standing preoccupation with "affordable government." Manitoba spends the second-lowest amount per capita to operate the core departments of government. In a province known for its wholesale commercial culture, Manitobans appear to believe that they are entitled to cheap, reliable quality government.

Terms such as "middle" evoke the notion of "mediocre," which has a negative connotation. A better word, one certainly more fitting (though admittedly obscure) is *lagöm*, a Swedish word which has no direct English equivalent. *Lagöm* might be used to refer to the baby bear's porridge in the classic children's story—that is, something that is "just right." It is not too much or too little, reflecting Aristotle's idea of the "golden mean," or that "virtue lies in the middle point."[25] As Ester Barinaga puts it, in the Swedish context *lagöm* "mirrors the dilemma between personal freedom and social responsibility...between expressing one's emotions and avoiding open conflict through compromising and consensus."[26] This description fits Manitoba well, as it illustrates not only the province's tendency to strive for the middle, but also the strong overlap between individualism and collectivism that marks its politics and society. We hope this volume echoes that idea, showing that Manitoba is a place where many different cultures and traditions have created together a highly balanced society that accommodates several competing interests. The province faces many serious policy challenges, including (to name but a few areas): the needs of an aging population; the need to develop and retain a skilled workforce; the need to help an Aboriginal population that has long been economically and socially marginalized achieve its full potential; and the need to ensure rural and remote communities are not left behind in a rapidly urbanizing province dominated by a single city, Winnipeg. The historic ability of the province's people to overcome the handicaps presented by geography and nature, however, suggests that Manitobans will be more than able to address these problems and together build a stronger, well-balanced, and sustainable provincial community.

This book proceeds as follows. The first section addresses questions related to the province's overall political culture. In Chapter 1, Gerald Friesen assesses whether it is realistic to assume that the province has a single "political culture" to speak of. Based on his interviews with prominent Manitoba leaders as well as his analysis of what has been written about Manitoba's history, Friesen suggests that Manitoba's political culture is defined by "distinct groups battling for paramountcy" but also "an entire community agreeing on the rules of the political process." He further argues that the contours of this political culture have evolved during distinct periods: from the time Manitoba joined Confederation in 1870 to the outbreak of the First World War in 1914, from 1914 to about 1960, and from 1960 to the present, with each era bringing forth different dynamics of consolidation and division between class, ethnic, religious, and gender groups.

In Chapter 2, Jared Wesley further explores the conventional idea of Manitoba as a "middling" or "mediocre" province by examining a number of provincial symbols, including its flag, provincial motto, licence plate, and coat of arms. He argues that this notion of mediocrity is often misinterpreted and that Manitobans take pride—almost to the point of demonstrating immodesty—in their status as the "modest" middleman of Confederation. While this idea is denigrated by those who might view Manitoba as complacent, he contends that Manitoba's immodest form of modesty and aspiration towards the middle of the pack is a microcosm for Canada, which often plays a similar role on the world stage.

In the second section, the province's major political actors and institutions are examined. Chapters 3, 4, and 5 examine the three political parties that have been the major vehicles of electoral competition in the previous half-century. In Chapter 3, Nelson Wiseman looks at the leadership, performance, ideology, and policies of the New Democratic Party to consider whether the current governing party (as of 2010) can be described as the province's "natural governing party." While he contends that the NDP historically has been a party which places principles ahead of political expedience, he suggests that thanks in part to deft leadership and political circumstances, the NDP has remained successful by being able to pragmatically adjust to the province's socio-economic realities.

In Chapter 4, Kelly Saunders highlights the difficulties facing the Progressive Conservative Party since its own period of dominance during the 1990s and highlights some of the internal organizational and ideological challenges—including the long-standing tension between its "progressive" and "conservative" wings— that must be overcome in order for the party to form the government once again.

In Chapter 5, Paul Barber evaluates the slow decline of the provincial Liberal party since its period of shared dominance as part of the Liberal-Progressive coalition government of the 1930s, 1940s, and 1950s. In doing so, Barber evaluates the continued persistence of the Liberal Party in the Manitoba Legislature and weighs the circumstances under which the Liberals could experience a renaissance in their electoral fortunes once again.

Chapter 6, by Christopher Adams, analyzes the rises and falls of these respective parties. Specifically, he outlines how the electoral behaviour of Manitobans have changed since 1958 by highlighting, using V.O. Key's framework of "critical" or "realigning" elections,[27] when the political preferences of Manitobans have undergone significant shifts during the past half-century and uses this as a guide to assess what future electoral shifts may be in store in provincial elections.

In Chapter 7, the current clerk of the executive council, Paul Vogt, illustrates how the Manitoba cabinet makes decisions. Directly challenging the notion that the Manitoba government is ruled "from the centre" by the premier and the non-elected "courtiers" in his office, Vogt argues that the cabinet remains the locus of decision making within the provincial government.

In Chaper 8, former MLA and deputy premier Jean Friesen explores the place of the Manitoba Legislature based on her own personal experiences as a representative. From her own experience, she colourfully illustrates all of the aspects of being an MLA and shows how politics inside what Manitoba's political class refers to as the "Leg" is very much a team sport, with camaraderie and teamwork extending across party lines as well as within party caucuses.

In Chapter 9, veteran journalist Frances Russell reflects on the momentous changes that have taken place in the local media during the five decades that she has served as a reporter, commentator, and author. She vividly describes the way media outlets such as the *Winnipeg Free Press* and now-defunct *Winnipeg Tribune* comprehensively covered the provincial government during the 1960s. She laments the way media coverage of provincial politics is reflected by the dwindling numbers of journalists covering the legislature on a full-time basis and the fact their coverage focuses on the staged theatre of the daily question period.

In Chapter 10, Paul Thomas considers the reforms made to Manitoba's civil service by the former Progressive Conservative and current New Democratic Party governments. He contrasts the approach taken by the PC government to rationalize and "reinvent" service delivery (both of which were in vogue in many other jurisdictions during the period in which it was in power) with the NDP's emphasis on civil service "renewal" and its ongoing challenges to attract, develop, and retain the incoming generation of public servants.

Chapter 11, penned by Jim Eldridge, examines Manitoba's performance at the intergovernmental level, both as a province within Confederation and as a sub-national jurisdiction within North America dealing with the same issues as American and Mexican states. Based on his four decades of experience as a practitioner of intergovernmental relations, Eldridge illustrates the constructive role Manitoba has played in federal-provincial relations as well as highlights how a growing aspect of its intergovernmental relationships are with sub-national governments in the U.S., Mexico, and other countries. Chapter 12, by Paul Thomas, assesses many of these intergovernmental issues from an academic perspective, arguing that Manitoba "punches above its weight" in the intergovernmental arena through this collaboration with other jurisdictions.

The third section assesses some of the issues that define Manitoba's politics and society. In Chapter 13, Derek Hum and Wayne Simpson assess the province's economic performance, arguing that by sheltering itself from "the extremes of most volatile economic cycles," the province remains on an even economic keel, experiencing neither booms nor busts. This "mutual fund model" of economic growth, they argue, will continue into the future so long as the province retains a diversified mix of primary and secondary industry and avoids any type of short-term "forced growth" policies.

Chapter 14 features Kerri Holland's examination of agriculture, focusing on the inherent conflict within the concept of "sustainable development" and between modern farm practices and a desire for greater environmental stewardship. Holland suggests that the goal of sustainable development, prefaced on "economic prosperity, social stability and environmental maintenance," requires more inclusive dialogue between governments, industry (in this case, agricultural operations), and the broader public, with clear goals established to measure progress towards sustainability.

In Chapter 15, Jim Silver illustrates the evolving nature of poverty in Winnipeg by showing how it has been concentrated in the city's North End and adjacent inner-city neighbourhoods. While poverty has historically been rooted in racism and social exclusion, he argues that the nature of poverty has evolved along with the area, with the newly arrived "working poor" of the early twentieth century assimilated into mainstream society and replaced by a growing Aboriginal underclass that faces greater challenges related to chronic joblessness, racism, family breakdown, assimilation, and crime. In sum, these changes have created a form of poverty that Silver argues may be more spiritually and emotionally demoralizing than that experienced by recent immigrants a century ago.

In Chapter 16 and Chapter 17, Harvey Bostrom and Irene Linklater offer perspectives on some of the issues facing Aboriginal Manitobans today. In Chapter 16, Bostrom discusses some of the ways the Manitoba government is working to "close the gap" in several areas between Aboriginal and non-Aboriginal Manitobans, while in Chapter 17 Linklater describes the role played by the Assembly of Manitoba Chiefs (AMC) in improving the lives of First Nations people. Placing this discussion in the context of the treaties signed between First Nations and the Canadian government, Linklater describes the many ways in which the province's Aboriginal leadership uses this framework to work with local, provincial, and national governments and act upon the provisions contained in these treaties to better the lives of the province's growing Aboriginal population.

In Chapter 18, Joan Grace examines the record of the current New Democratic Party government on gender issues and evaluates whether the government's stated "Manitoba advantage" has been good for women. In particular, she examines their response to the advocacy strategies of feminist organizations advocating for women's concerns to be addressed in provincial budgets. While noting that marginal progress has been made, Grace suggests that substantive changes have not been made due to the fact these concerns must compete with other concerns in a "neo-liberal" policy environment.

Chapter 19 assesses an issue—health care—that is very personal and political in Manitoba and elsewhere. Paul Thomas evaluates the regionalization of health care governance in Manitoba, focusing upon the evolution of the regional health authorities as rational managers of primary health provision. While he argues these bodies have been moderately successful in delivering care more efficiently and effectively than before, he contends their operation has been affected a great deal by political considerations both at the provincial and local level and that they have not completely lived up to their original promise.

Finally, Chapter 20 focuses on the province's largest post-secondary institution, the University of Manitoba. Rodney Clifton examines the provision of degrees at the province's main university and provides several ideas on how universities can not only manage somewhat-scarce public funding, but also work to improve graduation rates among their student bodies. In the proposal he sketches, Clifton argues that decisions about funding specific faculties and programs must become de-politicized, with students able to pay tuition fees directly to their programs and university administrators facing a mix of financial incentives and penalties for student performance.

In summary, we would like to thank each of the authors, their discussants, and the conference participants for their lively and thought-provoking contributions to this volume. Their work helps erase a deficit of scholarly work on Manitoba and will enhance the knowledge of future scholars on this unique, diverse—and by no means mediocre—province.

Dr. Paul G. Thomas
Curtis Brown
University of Manitoba
27 February 2010

Notes

1. Rand Dyck, *Provincial Politics in Canada* (Scarborough: Prentice-Hall, 1996), 381.
2. James McAllister, *The Government of Edward Schreyer: Democratic Socialism in Manitoba* (Montreal: McGill-Queen's Press, 1984).
3. Nelson Wiseman, *Social Democracy in Manitoba: A History of the CCF/NDP* (Winnipeg: University of Manitoba Press, 1983).
4. Ian Stewart, *Just One Vote: From Jim Walding's Nomination to Constitutional Defeat* (Winnipeg: University of Manitoba Press, 2009). This book places the 1988 defeat of Howard Pawley's NDP government in a broader national context of constitutional negotiations and ponders whether the Meech Lake Accord might have passed had Pawley's government not been defeated by one of its own members, disgruntled backbench MLA Jim Walding.
5. Lloyd Stinson, *Political Warriors: Recollections of a Social Democrat* (Winnipeg: Queenston House, 1975).
6. Russell Doern, *Wednesdays are Cabinet Days* (Winnipeg: Queenston House, 1981).
7. Sharon Carstairs, *Not One of the Boys* (Toronto: Macmillan, 1993).
8. Duff Roblin, *Speaking for Myself: Politics and Other Pursuits* (Winnipeg: Great Plains, 1999).
9. Sidney Green, *Rise and Fall of a Political Animal* (Winnipeg: Great Plains, 2003).
10. Roland Penner, *A Glowing Dream: A Memoir* (Winnipeg: J. Gordon Shillingford, 2007).
11. Herb Schulz, *A View From The Ledge: An Insider's Look at the Schreyer Years* (Winnipeg: Heartland Associates, 2005).
12. John Kendle, *John Bracken: A Political Biography* (Toronto: University of Toronto Press, 1979).
13. Statistics Canada, Population by Year, By Province and Territory, http://www40.statcan.gc.ca/l01/cst01/demo02a-eng.htm (accessed April 21, 2009).
14. Statistics Canada, Real Gross Domestic Product, Expenditure Based, By Province and Territory, http://www40.statcan.gc.ca/l01/cst01/econ50-eng.htm (accessed April 21, 2009).
15. Manitoba Budget 2009, http://www.gov.mb.ca/finance/budget09/min_msg.html (accessed April 30, 2009).
16. For a more thorough analytical and historical treatment of debates over the status of the French language and bilingualism in Manitoba, please see Raymond Hébert, *Manitoba's French Language Crisis: A Cautionary Tale* (Montreal: McGill-Queen's Press, 2004); Frances Russell, *The Canadian Crucible: Manitoba's Role in Canada's Great Divide* (Winnipeg: Heartland, 2003); Lovell Clark, ed., *The Manitoba School Question* (Toronto: Copp Clark, 1968). For more personal accounts, please consult Russell Doern, *The Battle Over Bilingualism* (Winnipeg: Cambridge, 1985) as well as Penner, *A Glowing Dream*.
17. Jack Bumsted, "Early Flooding in Red River," in *Thomas Scott's Body* (Winnipeg: University of Manitoba Press, 2000), 78–80.
18. Peter Russell, *Constitutional Odyssey*, 3rd ed. (Toronto: University of Toronto Press, 2004), 151–152. See also Stewart, *Just One Vote*.
19. Chris Adams, *Politics in Manitoba* (Winnipeg: University of Manitoba Press, 2008), 8.
20. Ibid., 7.
21. See Nelson Wiseman, "In Search of Manitoba's Constitutional Position, 1950–1990," *Journal of Canadian Studies* 29, 3 (1994): 85–107.

22 Alex Netherton, "Paradigm and Shift: A Sketch of Manitoba Politics," in *The Provincial State in Canada: Politics in the Provinces and Territories*, ed. Keith Brownsey and Michael Howlett (Peterborough: Broadview Press, 2001), 226.
23 Ken Rasmussen, "The Manitoba Civil Service: A Quiet Tradition in Transition," in *Government Restructuring and Career Public Services*, ed. Evert Lindquist (Toronto: Institute of Public Administration in Canada, 2000), 350.
24 Ibid., 370.
25 Ester Baringa, "Swedishness through lagöm: Can words tell us anything about a culture?" *Centre for Advanced Studies in Leadership*, 1999, 10, http://www.hhs.se/NR/rdonlyres/1749CB67-FC33-4D3E-B498-29FF42C4F550/0/rp_1999_6.pdf (accessed April 21, 2009).
26 Ibid., 9–10.
27 V.O. Key, "A Theory of Critical Elections," *Journal of Politics*, February 1955, 11.

PART ONE
POLITICAL CULTURE

What makes Manitoba different from neighbouring Canadian provinces like Saskatchewan or Ontario, or nearby American states like North Dakota? Why do Manitobans typically vote for pragmatic, middle-of-the-road governments that eschew radicalism or excessive amounts of ideology? What do Manitoba's symbols—its flag, its coat of arms, and now the marketing "brand" it offers to the broader world—tell us about its government, its society, and its people? Where did they come from? Why do we have them? And how have these evolved since the time Manitoba joined Confederation in 1870 to today?

The answers to these questions are related to the "political tradition" or "political culture" of a particular place. These two controversial and difficult-to-define concepts are addressed by Gerald Friesen and Jared Wesley, respectively, in Chapters 1 and 2. Both chapters explore some of the underlying traditions that mark the province and its people, while looking at how other factors—critical events and critical perspectives, to name but a couple—challenge the dominant consensus that pervades the province's main institutions. In Chapter 1, Gerald Friesen evaluates the concept of political tradition and how it applies within Manitoba. In Chapter 2, Jared Wesley considers how Manitoba's political culture, which values "modesty" and "moderation," is reflected in symbols such as its flag, its coat of arms, its licence plate—and how trying to change these time-honoured symbols can lead to controversy.

The Manitoba Political Tradition

Gerald Friesen

The topic of the "Manitoba political tradition" was devised by Paul Thomas as a means of adding a little history and an historian to a discussion dominated by political scientists. But what does it mean? A tradition can be defined as a custom handed down from ancestors to posterity but, in the Manitoba case, no single statement of principles derived from experience has ever won widespread acceptance. Indeed, when I asked former premier Duff Roblin for his thoughts about a provincial political tradition he replied, "I don't think there is such a thing. You'll have to invent one."[1]

Where did the idea originate? The term "political tradition" enjoyed a brief flowering in the 1940s with the appearance of Richard Hofstadter's *The American Political Tradition and the Men Who Made It*. It has been used only rarely in the intervening decades, chiefly because it is regarded as elitist, simplistic, or both.[2] Critics have argued that the quest for a single approach to a community's public affairs fails to take into account the many differences that exist in any society. Hofstadter's defence was that, in "plac[ing] political conflict in the foreground of history," generations of observers had ignored a perspective at least as important as, and probably more important than the power of difference. Simply put, societies that have managed to stay united must have been able to transcend disagreements: "the fierceness of the political struggles," Hofstadter wrote, "has often been misleading."[3]

Hofstadter sketched what he believed were the conditions necessary for peaceful transitions in governments and fruitful debates about policy. The United States, he wrote, had achieved a consensus on economic matters: "The range of vision embraced by the primary contestants in the major parties has always been bounded by the horizons of property and enterprise." This range of vision included "the rights of property...the right of the individual to dispose of and invest it, the value of opportunity, and the natural evolution of self-interest and self-assertion, within broad legal limits, into a beneficent social order."[4] Hofstadter argued that societies in "good working order have a kind of mute organic consistency" and that the key political figures within those communities, whom he described as "practical politicians," may dispute particular points but "share a general framework of ideas which makes it possible for them to cooperate when the campaigns are over." These people of action were accountable to large followings and must be distinguished from "alienated intellectuals" who were not required to muster majorities in democratic contests. Studies of twelve such practical leaders and groups of leaders comprised the book.[5]

There is strength as well as weakness in Hofstadter's approach. Its merit lies in its emphasis on the compromise that must occur in any democracy if a government is to retain legitimacy and authority. Its weaknesses lie in the implied assumption that a single "tradition" can prevail over a long period of time and the explicit assertion that a community's eventual acceptance of political arrangements is accompanied by the erasure of profound differences. This paper contains both support for and opposition to Hofstadter's original approach. First, it surveys secondary literature in history and the social sciences to establish the range of academic views concerning the province's political culture and, in the process, to emphasize the power of *difference* in provincial life. Second, it reports on my interviews with some well-informed, politically experienced Manitobans, most of whom would respond sympathetically to Hofstadter's emphasis on consensus. And third, it outlines an historical approach that moves beyond difference and consensus, thereby establishing an inclusive interpretation of the provincial community's political tradition.[6] In short, it offers an historian's version of what students of politics label "political culture."

Manitoba's Scholarly Literature: The Power of Difference

Most observers of the Manitoba polity have focused on the differences that have shaped this diverse community. First among these is the population itself. Manitoba is home to Aboriginal people who can claim, directly and indirectly, 6000 years of connection to this place. They belonged to several different language groups, adopted several different economic strategies, and developed several different cultural perspectives. Manitoba is also a home to immigrants. The earliest migrations from Europe during the fur trade sustained widely dispersed communities of mixed European and Aboriginal heritage, French and English and Michif-speaking Métis. By 1870, when the western interior was annexed by Canada, and Manitoba became a province in its own right, the community had known important differences for some thousands of years.

A tiny polity measuring about 100 miles square, "the first new province of the Dominion" included fewer than 15,000 residents, four-fifths of whom were Métis. Migrants in the next three decades, including British Canadians from Ontario, German-speaking Mennonites from Russia, Icelandic Protestants, French-Canadian Roman Catholics, and a dozen other peoples swelled the population to about 250,000 at the beginning of the twentieth century. A tidal wave of immigration from Britain and Europe as well as other parts of the globe then multiplied the total to about 700,000 by 1930. This flow was reduced to a trickle during the Great Depression and the Second World War, but incoming Europeans pushed the provincial population to more than 900,000 by 1960. And a slow, steady influx of migrants, both from Europe and the so-called global south (including the Philippines and south Asia), raised the total to 1.2 million by 2010.[7] Manitoba is a community distinguished by these recurrent waves of immigrants and by its relatively modest population increases over the past century and a half.

In spatial terms, too, the province is constructed upon difference. It has customarily been divided into three zones based on geology, vegetation, and history. The largest area, the "North," is associated with the Precambrian rocks and boreal forests that extend diagonally from the southeast corner to the northwest and cover more than 80 percent of the territory. Home of Aboriginal people and resource development enterprises, its population is less than 100,000. A second zone is associated with the mixed-grass prairie and aspen parkland of the southern 15 percent. This is farm country, and its service towns, once numerous and now fewer in number, are linked by railways and highways to world markets for wheat, canola, hogs, cattle, and other farm products. Its population is less than 300,000. The third zone is a comparatively limited urban and suburban space, the area of the Red River settlement that became the province's administrative and economic hub, Winnipeg. Its population includes about 700,000 in the Winnipeg Census Metropolitan Area (CMA), with another 100,000 in the city's shadow, a diameter of about 100 km.[8] In sum, there is not now nor has there ever been uniform social composition or homogeneous economic structure in the territory of present-day Manitoba.

Histories of Manitoban politics typically dwell on conflicts. The list of such disagreements includes Catholic-Protestant differences over public funding of schools, French-English differences over official languages, British Canadian-continental European differences over school language policy, Jewish identification of anti-Semitism in public institutions, Aboriginal-Caucasian differences over matters of Aboriginal self-government, and differences between Caucasians and visible minorities over racist discrimination and anti-racist human rights legislation. This list could be extended to include rural-urban differences over public spending priorities (highways in rural areas versus urban infrastructure, for example) and provincial regulation of local affairs (including conflicts over such matters as land drainage and hog barns). Equally prominent are worker-management differences over such fundamental issues as industrial relations law, union organization, and workplace contracts. Strikes have constituted important moments in political life, particularly one crucial work stoppage, the Winnipeg General Strike of 1919. Gender differences and family matters, too, have been fundamental sources of dispute in public affairs, including women's right to vote, specific laws concerning spousal rights to property, provision for children's preschool daycare, and gender discrimination in education and the professions. This list is not complete but its very length, and the extended catalogue of academic references lying behind each item, establishes an important generalization: the academic literature on provincial politics has been especially focused on issues wherein two parties clearly disagreed.

In addition to the analyses of particular conflicts, academics have written several sweeping interpretations of Manitoba politics. A 1955 essay by the dean of Manitoba historians, William Morton, concentrated on formal party politics and relations between the two levels of government. Morton argued that the province, and the Prairie region, had experienced a period of colonial subordination between 1870 and the early twentieth century, during which time the national government controlled the keys to economic development, including public lands and natural resources, railway policy, and immigration regulations. This colonial era was succeeded by several decades of agrarian radicalism that reached a climax when farm communities, then accounting for over half the provincial population, elected an independent farmer government (it and its successors held power from 1922 to 1958), and sent farmer members of a third party, the Progressives, to the federal Parliament in Ottawa. Morton suggested that a third moment in political history commenced when electors turned to "utopian" parties, socialist and social credit groups, that embraced what he described as "untried methods" in their quest for "ideal ends." Morton's three-phase approach to prairie political history—colonial protest, agrarian protest, utopian protest—became a standard interpretation for a generation of students. It still stands as a plausible statement about aspects of Manitoba's past between the 1870s and 1950s.[9] His central arguments, concerning Prairie citizens' feelings of inferiority within Confederation, were repeated in many works in the following years. The differences between Manitoba and central Canada thus constituted another theme in academic treatments.

Tom Peterson, a University of Manitoba political scientist, published his masterly essay on provincial political life in the 1970s. He emphasized the cultural and economic differences within provincial society. He was especially preoccupied by what has been called the "fault line" separating elite British and northern European groups from less-favoured southern and eastern Europeans in the first half of the twentieth century.[10] He employed traditional Marxist language about classes and posited a circumstance in which the "lower classes," "the non-British," the "poorer class" faced off against "the Ontario British," the "prosperous," the "culturally more secure," "Manitoba's traditional ruling group." His interpretation, which is simplified here, was not crudely Marxist, though his presentation did embolden others to make bald statements about conflict between two classes in the province. Rather, Peterson posited an evolution—"a sequence"—of political cleavages which changed character (shifting from cultural to economic causes) between the late nineteenth and late twentieth century.

Peterson emphasized that the British-heritage citizens arrived earlier, whether from Ontario or the United Kingdom, settled on the best land in the province, built the major business institutions, and controlled the government; continental Europeans were left with the poorest land and deferred to British leadership. He believed that the main protests against the unfairness of this circumstance came not from leaders of the continental European-origin groups, despite their lesser share in provincial wealth, but from British workers who brought with them the experience of socialist and labour resistance movements in their homeland. Only in the 1960s, Peterson suggested, did the cultural factors recede in importance and local political practice begin to approximate what he described as "the British pattern." By this, he meant that political debate eventually focused on "hierarchy vs. equality," the most important political cleavage separated "rival income groups," and the goal of the rival groups was "to protect or improve their respective economic positions." It should be underlined that Peterson, a well-informed, critical observer, also noted that "articulate class consciousness was far from widespread" and that "there was no neat division in the electorate along class lines."[11]

A third influential interpretation, also by a political scientist, Nelson Wiseman, employs the same historical evidence but places greater emphasis on the ideological views of the various immigrant groups. Writing in 2007, and following Peterson in broad outline, Wiseman suggests a "collectivist ideology and culture" existed in a "distinctly coherent political region" called the "Midwest," an area embracing Saskatchewan and Manitoba. Wiseman says the latter province, which he calls "the Ontario of the Prairies," was shaped by migrating Ontarians who brought with them "their Tory-touched and liberal Grit biases...." Manitoba's "fundamentally liberal farmers" were British in orientation, he writes, not American. The same could be said for the two powerful factions in the province's major city. In Winnipeg's South End lived Ontario-origin business elites who were moneyed, well-connected, and British in their sympathies. In the West End, North End, and several poorer suburbs resided workers led by British labourists. Continental European migrants lived "on the periphery of the political system..." and often ended up in more radical movements, culminating in the founding of a branch of the Communist Party. If the British group, led by wealthier farm and business households, was able to control the provincial legislature for the thirty-six years after its first surprise election victory in 1922, it was because the constituencies were so skewed in distribution that one rural vote equaled two, three, or more city votes, and because Aboriginal people were "systematically disadvantaged."[12]

Saskatchewan's composition differed slightly from its Prairie neighbour in Wiseman's descriptions, but the two provinces also shared a great deal in common. Wiseman suggests that a social democratic consensus, a "collectivist ideology," was more successful in Manitoba and Saskatchewan than in other parts of the country, perhaps because its "collective ideal and culture...fits well with the co-op tradition in the Midwest." It was not just a Prairie phenomenon, he notes, because the NDP acted as an "integrated national and provincial party...linked to a broader national and international social democratic movement..." that trained workers and leaders for campaigns and for the jobs generated by election victories. He also argues that the focus of this collective ideal shifted significantly over the course of the twentieth century, as it moved from its roots in the "Social Gospel" in the first quarter to social planning in the second, social security in the third, and a wide variety of social movements in the fourth. He concludes that the Midwest's ideological composition was distinctive within the Canadian polity. Clearly, Wiseman regards social democracy as a fundamental aspect of the Manitoba political tradition.[13]

Political tradition, as concept, proposes the existence of legacies from past societies that shape behaviour, outlook, and institutions in the present. Morton, writing in the 1940s and 1950s and viewing the region on the national plane, suggested the Prairie provinces were shaped by Canada's region-based inequities. Peterson, who thought in terms of a provincial political system, argued that the cleavages within Manitoba society were initially ethno-cultural but evolved into money-based debates in the 1960s and '70s. Wiseman, both in 1981 and in his 2007 book, emphasized the immigrant composition of the Manitoba and Saskatchewan populations and depicted this "Midwest" as a bastion of social democracy in a country that contains a variety of political cultures. Each interpretation—Morton's regional, Peterson's class-related, and Wiseman's social democratic analyses—identifies a component of the Manitoba political tradition.[14] Each builds upon the work of many other scholars in the humanities and social sciences. And, in terms of the provincial political sphere, each emphasizes an aspect of difference: for Morton, between Prairie and other Canadians; for Peterson, between two groups of Manitobans; and, for Wiseman, between Midwest and other Canadian ideologies and between two social camps within Manitoba. Taken in conjunction with the picture of population, geography, and historical narratives, the academics' picture of Manitoba can only be described as one built upon the theme of difference.

Participant Observers and "Accommodationist" Influences

Richard Hofstadter built his picture of a political tradition upon the careers and actions of political leaders. To capture a similar perspective in Manitoba I interviewed five individuals connected to New Democratic Party governments (including a senior civil servant, two former premiers, and the directors of a survey research company), and five individuals who held leading roles in the Progressive Conservative and Liberal parties, including three former Progressive Conservative premiers. In employing this approach, I was particularly interested to discover what experienced individuals with differing political opinions might see as the underlying principles and conditions shaping public conversation and public arrangements in Manitoba.

The first theme that stood out in the observations of this diverse group was a surprising insistence upon the degree of consensus in Manitoba's public sphere, at least in the last half-century. Despite their experiences in vigorous and heartfelt disputes over a wide range of public policies, the interviewees did not see the provincial government as a forum of profound disagreements. Though they acknowledged the litany of conflicts that has preoccupied historians and political scientists, many of them were at pains to emphasize the importance of "conscious accommodation" in provincial political life. Duff Roblin, former premier, said: "I'm not sure that we are less extreme than other places but one thing I would say is that there's less political bitterness here, less acrimony between the parties. My experience is mainly with D.L. Campbell. And my policies were as different from his as they could possibly be, but we never exchanged a harsh word. We gave the other fellow credit for good intentions and we didn't make disagreements into personal quarrels. We stuck to policy." The then premier of the province, Gary Doer, pointed to specific occasions when leaders of labour and business were able to meet informally to discuss their differences before they became serious ruptures. Paul Vogt, head of the provincial civil service and secretary to cabinet, acknowledged that cultural and economic cleavages had been real in the past, and were reinforcing rather than cross-cutting, which ensured their roots went very deep. But, despite the possibility of continuing conflict, the various segments of the population had eventually been able to reach compromises. He used the term "accommodationist" to depict this aspect of provincial life.

Were there obvious principles to which Manitobans referred in resolving their differences? These are elusive matters but several of the interviewees did see identifiable tendencies in Manitoba's public life that differed from other provinces. Paramount among these leanings is a middle-of-the-road disposition among both citizens and political leaders. Virginia Devine of the survey firm Viewpoints Research said that "Manitoba is less tolerant of extremes." Her colleague Leslie Turnbull, also of Viewpoints, said: "In [former Progressive Conservative premier Mike] Harris's Ontario and [current BC Liberal premier Gordon] Campbell's BC the governments sought to change the culture [as Margaret Thatcher did] and to ensure that their perspective would dominate. In Manitoba, a government that followed that course wouldn't last long." Gary Filmon, former Progressive Conservative premier, shared this view: "I've always said that we're in the middle of the political spectrum, no matter who's in office. I can't recall any major swings in philosophy when governments changed." Jim Carr, a former Liberal member of the legislature and now executive director of the Manitoba Business Council, agreed: "In Manitoba, the polity hugs the centre. Neither east nor west, neither left nor right, neither boom nor bust, neither rich nor poor."[15]

An aspect of the Manitoba public sphere, these experienced observers said, is its relatively small size. In a community of just 1.2 million people, said Carr, leaders could be expected to know one another and members of one social group could be expected to recognize the interests and outlook of most other groups. Virginia Devine explained: "It's a smaller place, representatives of the various communities know each other, end up in the same restaurant, their kids meet in games, people work more on getting along, crossing lines of class and income and culture." Added Jim Carr: "I can't imagine anywhere in the world where the elites move more easily across all lines than in Winnipeg. The Aspers and Richardsons are an example. There was a time when the elites were far more isolated one from the other. This is a function, too, of the size of Winnipeg. It's small enough, and big enough, to enhance such possibilities.... Winnipeg is small enough that one can have access to everybody within a day. Not just the elites but anyone can talk to union presidents or CEOs. (Premier) Gary Doer will return (business executive) Hartley Richardson's call."

These observers also emphasized Manitoba's population stability across the generations, a degree of continuity that many other Canadian centres do not possess. As Leslie Turnbull said:

> What strikes me about Manitoba society is that most of the people who live here were born here and have chosen to stay here. (This isn't true in the same way for poorer people; they were born here and had little choice except to stay.) But the proportion of residents who were born here is very high—75–80 percent. This contrasts with British Columbia, for example, where only 45–48 percent of residents were born in the province. People go to BC from other parts of Canada and the world seeking financial improvement. People stay here because of family connections, other personal connections, friends, a strong sense of community—something that is more important than money. They are making a trade-off and economic well-being comes second. Except for people who are poor, who don't have such choices. If you put money first, you move. But family, roots, friends—that defines Manitoba more. Izzy Asper, when asked why he stayed, said "because it's home."

The continuity and the smaller size mean that people are familiar with each other but also that they are readier to make compromises for the sake of social peace. Virginia Devine said: "[There is] not a sharp divide between peoples." And Leslie Turnbull, who grew up in Montreal and then moved to Winnipeg, was more blunt: "It's a bit of a slog to live here. People recognize that it's a small place, that they have to rely on the public sector, have to find a way to get along, and that there's trade-offs in making such choices. The labour movement recognizes that they have to get along with business and vice versa. And in the NDP, labour and the party don't fight in the same way that they conflict in other provinces."

Gary Doer extended this argument when he emphasized the importance of "fairness" as a criterion by which Manitobans measure winners and losers in public debates. Fairness was not the same thing, he said, as equality. The French language crisis, which nearly caused the defeat of a government in 1983–4, he attributed to the fact that people would not permit French to be "more important" than other languages.

This list of characteristics, running from moderation to continuity to accommodation, may sound unappetizingly bland. But, as Nelson Wiseman's interpretation implies, many of the interviewees added an important qualifier to this picture of uniformity and temperance. Was the Manitoba political tradition merely centrist or was it consistently to the left of centre, whatever that might mean? Former premier Howard Pawley argued for the latter:

> Manitoba is more centre-left than most other provinces of Canada, with the possible exception of Saskatchewan. I think the 1919 strike was the earthquake that influenced the province's political culture. But even the coalition in the Second World War, when [CCF leader] S.J. Farmer was in the cabinet, reflected this centre-left orientation. And the governments of Schreyer [1969–77], Pawley [1981–88] and Doer/Selinger [1999–present] represent a long period of New Democrat governance. Some of the policies that Manitoba followed also were ahead of the rest of Canada. Schreyer's government was the first to go with home care, auto insurance. Mine was the first to introduce pay equity in the public service, and certain aspects of labour legislation. Even Roblin [1958–67] was very progressive. His government was not conservative in the usual sense of the term.... [It was] more centre-left in orientation. Campbell [1948–1958] was certainly more conservative. And Lyon [1977–81] deviated...[too], and therefore was only a one-term administration because he went well over to the right.[16]

Leslie Turnbull made a similar observation: "Manitoba is a centre-left province. If BC is 40/60 left and right, then Manitoba is 60/40. Saskatchewan has changed and is not as left as Manitoba is. The biggest BC win for the NDP was Bob Skelly's 46 percent and in the other elections it was much lower. Gary Doer won 50 percent in 2003 and 49.3 percent in 2007."

If the interpretation was offered only by New Democrats, one might dispute its validity. But Gary Filmon, in arguing for a continuity of policy between governments of either stripe, seemed to agree: "When you look at the province's Conservative party, it's still a *Progressive* Conservative group, not a Conservative one as it might be elsewhere. And when Doer came in, they compared themselves to [British Prime Minister] Tony Blair—it was the 'progressive' model that they wanted. There's a sense of Prairie populism in Manitoba governments, no matter what the actual governments say they do."

There is a perception among this group of political leaders that Manitobans follow public affairs attentively. They suggest it is normal in provincial life for a few citizens to belong to the established parties, to attend legislative committee hearings, and to read about public debates, as in any polity, but that the wider electorate also follows major issues closely. Duff Roblin related this attentiveness to an important practice of the legislature:

> I think political debate has to be vigorous, that the issues have to be worthwhile, and the positions taken on those issues have to be significant.... We had public hearings after second reading of a bill, and people could make any representation they liked. It seemed to me an eminently reasonable way to proceed. The school issues, for example, were hotly contested, and the debate was a good thing. Part of the secret of a democratic system is to let people have their say. Don't cut them off. The purpose of Parliament is to let people speak on public issues. There were half a dozen people who came out all the time—always had an opinion and wanted to talk, whatever the issue. Some of the members on our side said it was a waste of time when the same people came so regularly and wanted to throw them out. I didn't agree—we should hear them all—they're entitled to that.

Howard Pawley made a similar point:

> There was much more participation by the public in politics in Manitoba compared to Ontario, for example. I was surprised by the difference when I came to Windsor. We had the highest membership in the [Manitoba] New Democratic Party during my time, the early 1980s, when it was 25,000–30,000, I think. That's partly why we won government in 1981—the strength of our organization. I felt it was different in Ontario, fewer members in parties, and so on. It's possible that Saskatchewan might have been comparable. And there was much more involvement in rural areas as well as in the trade union movement.... And that was clear in Meech [the Meech Lake constitutional crisis] as well. We had hearings and public input and I told the other first ministers that we would go to the public for review, even if they did not. We were the only one to do so. The same with the Free Trade Agreement and the Marital Property Act: we held public hearings.[17]

The above comments paint the positive and the ideal because I had asked for a political tradition and my interviewees believed that they could see spheres in which a broad provincial consensus existed. But, inevitably, in focusing on the consensus, these leaders spent less time reflecting on the divisions and exclusions that plague every society. One who did pause to reflect on this absence was Leslie Turnbull, who said:

> Winnipeg is exclusionary. Aboriginal people and poor people aren't in the circles of those whom I describe as cooperating and getting along. There's a deep division between the North End and South End in the

city, and it has become even deeper in the time that I have been here [since the mid-1980s]. This is also true of Regina. The two cities share the title of "murder capital" [and] have high numbers of car thefts. This is a terrible circumstance and yet nothing seems to change, year after year—it's as if we put the North End in a box and close the lid. About 20 percent of the city's residents in Winnipeg are so poor. The present government has done a great deal—incremental things—but has it really changed much? Gary Doer [went] out of his way to be inclusive, to find Aboriginal candidates, and women candidates, and representatives of visible minorities as candidates. Does it make a difference? There are two ways to look at it: we've been in power and done a lot; or our values have not been put into practice.

Though they might appear to some observers to be gender-free viewpoints, much of the commentary failed to acknowledge the significance of women's alternative perspectives on public life. Howard Pawley understood this challenge in policy terms: "I thought Manitoba was ahead of the rest of the country on women's rights, starting with Nellie McClung and the right of women to vote. In 1976 we were the first province to undo the effect of the Supreme Court ruling vis-à-vis Murdoch on the division of property after marital breakdown. And in the 1980s we moved on pay equity—I think Manitoba was ahead of Ontario in its dealings on pay equity in the public sector, if not in the private sector." Again, though, it was Leslie Turnbull who identified the very different perspective that was necessary if one was to take women's participation into account: "The women activists I know seem less extreme here than in Ontario or BC. There's a tradition of women's rights and of being in the vanguard of rights for women. The NDP certainly targets women voters and seeks to present its case to them. Women, more than men, believe in the role that government can have in people's lives. They have the custodial consciousness that men are less persuaded by." But this was more than a generalized gender consciousness, as she explained when she addressed the influence of women in unions: "The public sector unions that are not in the MFL (Manitoba Federation of Labour) are an important force—the MGEU (Manitoba Government Employees Union), teachers, nurses—and have been successful in shaping the agenda. Because the public sector is used heavily here, and we have very little reliance on private health clinics or private schools, the workers in these sectors can drive the public agenda."

A political tradition is not just a matter of internal arrangements but also of external relations. Manitoba's position in Canada is unusual, Paul Vogt said, because the province's citizens have had experience with so many of the elements that affected other parts of the country. Manitobans have been dealing with ethno-cultural diversity since the beginning of the twentieth century; they know the pressures associated with Aboriginal policy and French-English bilingualism and they are now working to integrate thousands of immigrants from the global south. They live in a middle-ranking province in terms of individual income and public wealth. In economic composition, Manitoba combines manufacturing, resources, agriculture, and services. And, in geographical terms, it sits in the middle of the country. Vogt argued that Manitoba shows greater support for the powers of the central government than some other provinces (including Saskatchewan and Alberta), and is less likely to express regional alienation. Manitoba, he said, was "less a region than it is a broker, as in Doer's alliances with Quebec and New Brunswick, or as in Filmon's and Pawley's roles in federal-provincial relations."

Were there national circumstances that contributed to a Manitoba political tradition? Gary Doer's reply, which referred to his experience at federal-provincial discussions, is significant. He said:

> You don't start off saying that this is what I want to do—to play a middle role—but we sit between "plates"—north and south, east and west—we're at the "heart of the continent." And we shouldn't allow the situation to be factionalized and regionalized by TILMA [the Trade, Investment and Labour Mobility Agreement, concluded between BC and Alberta] and other such deals. Manitoba's role in the nation is to bring the plates together—to avoid the rigidities that come with TILMA in the Alberta-British Columbia deal, or the Ontario-Quebec arrangements. The cap-and-trade approach [to greenhouse gases and global warming] is such a bridge.

Doer cited the activities of three previous premiers in this context: "Maybe Lyon played the same role by contributing—through Jim Eldridge's words—to the equalization language in 1981–2, or Roblin in founding the premiers' meetings, or Bracken [premier 1922–42] in the work of the Rowell-Sirois Royal commission.... Location is obvious and an issue—Manitoba has a higher profile at U.S. and Mexican meetings when they are addressing north-south routes.... [Manitoba] Hydro is an on-ramp to the Midwest and western states. And north-south links, including Russia, could well be important in the future." In this perspective, an aspect of the provincial political tradition is Manitoba's interest in acting as a mediator and broker when regional and federal-provincial tensions develop within Confederation.

The interviewees suggested that Manitoba was a society of conscious conciliation, driven by a keen sense of what was fair and unfair. They saw the community as remarkably stable and its citizens as committed to collective well-being. They regarded it as a place of intersection because its central location in the nation and the continent enabled its representatives to act as mediators. These qualities, too, are part of a provincial political tradition.[18] But, as is evident, they offer a picture of the province that differs radically from the picture painted by academic researchers who have laboured diligently to uncover the conflicts that have erupted time and again. Instead, these practitioners concentrate on consensus. Richard Hofstadter would have approved. But which is the appropriate interpretive emphasis, difference or consensus?

A Social and Cultural History of Manitoba Politics

The province has been home to a number of community groups that possess sufficient coherence, historic depth, and political effectiveness to count as significant factors in its political history. And its 140-year history falls neatly into three eras which constitute identifiable phases in the story. These generalizations, which are based on social and cultural history approaches, sustain an inclusive interpretation that might be described as a series of "political traditions."[19]

Eight major groups constitute distinct and lasting forces in the political composition of Manitoba. These include two communities of Aboriginal people, the First Nations peoples and the Métis. Three others—rural residents, urban working people, and French Canadians—each occupy categories by themselves. Given the steady arrival of immigrants, a sixth category should be reserved for the most recent arrivals who now face the difficult task of making their way into the established order. Women may not have been central to the history of politics in the generation after Confederation but, because they did acquire greater power after the turn of the twentieth century and continue to shape political decisions today, belong in a seventh category. Finally, a separate category is necessary for what Tom Peterson called the ruling class and the culturally more secure. Each of these groups has developed means of internal communication and social interaction. Each is long-lived and has managed to establish among its members a clear sense of the group's place in the provincial past. All must be counted as parts of the provincial political story.[20]

Manitoba was founded by Métis peoples, groups of mixed Aboriginal and European ancestry. Their defining moment, the Resistance of 1869–70, remains a living part of the provincial story today. The Métis built an association, L'Union nationale métisse Saint-Joseph du Manitoba, sustained and published a work of history, de Trémaudan's *Histoire de la Nation Métisse dans l'Ouest canadien* (1936), struggled to adapt to changing circumstances in the mid-twentieth century (as witnessed by the Lagassé report of 1959), and then in 1982 won the decisive prize, the naming of their group in the Canadian Constitution as one of the three

Aboriginal peoples possessing distinctive Aboriginal rights. Whatever the difficulties of their political organizations, whatever the fortunes of specific legal claims, the Métis exercise an important influence in Manitoba political history.

The French community retains an equally strong group identity. From Archbishop Taché's invitation to four young Quebec professionals in 1870 to form a cadre of leaders and their subsequent entry into politics, there have been French-speaking representatives in the legislature. A weekly newspaper was founded as early as 1871 and its successors have continued to this day. In addition to the battles fought over confessional schools and official language rights, Franco-Manitobans have maintained a strong institutional presence in the province, including cultural production in theatre, book publishing, radio, and television. The language has been maintained in the face of considerable challenges. The French community maintains a significant presence in public life and also should be singled out as a political entity.

Business leader Arthur Mauro has argued there is "a thread of continuity, a sustained tension, between urban and rural Manitoba, producer and trader, throughout the province's history. This isn't a black and white story, because throughout this history there were variables that mixed the two." He makes a point that should not be forgotten: Manitoba was shaped by urban-based, British-Canadian business interests during the first two generations after Confederation. The railways, the fur trade, the land market, and the grain trade were, first and foremost, business operations. Their western operations were administered from Winnipeg, a city that possessed regional and even national metropolitan status for Canada's first century and remains the dominant urban community in the province. Business leaders, as the spokespeople for various economic interest groups, shaped public policy in city and province. Business power has been challenged many times, not least during the Winnipeg General Strike of 1919, but the business community's leaders have been consistent winners when they squared off with representatives of opposing groups.[21]

The other pole in Mauro's construct, the rural Manitoba group, consisted of farm families. They lost many struggles in the 1880s and 1890s, built their own organizations (Patrons of Industry, Grain Growers, United Farmers) that shaped government policy during the next two decades, and elected an administration in 1922 that survived for thirty-six years. It was a cautious, conservative government, particularly under Premiers Bracken and Campbell (though less so under Stuart Garson), but it expressed the outlook of its rural constituency perfectly. As Mauro said, "Campbell didn't spend a penny unless it was in the bank. To him infrastructure was an expense, not an investment with an anticipated return. His was the farm household's perspective of public finance; Campbell thought in terms of crop to crop. He had been shaped by the Depression, by the vagaries of farming. His great claim to having contributed to provincial development was rural electrification. But that aside, he consistently opposed 'the fat cats at the Grain Exchange, the CPR, and the Bank of Montreal.'" This rural constituency divided in political sentiment after the Second World War, with those south of the CPR tending to stay with the Pool and later the Keystone Agricultural Producers, while those to the north who were, as Peterson and Wiseman have pointed out, less likely to be British and to operate grain-only farms, moved to the newly formed Manitoba (later National) Farmers Union. There were many exceptions, of course, but the pattern did exist. Farmers and rural Manitobans have consistently constituted another element in provincial political history.

A militant critique of business leaders came from urban workers, especially those in Winnipeg and Brandon but also miners and other unionized employees in smaller centres. Their unions began in the late nineteenth century, became powerful organizations during the First World War and waged a remarkable confrontation with capital in the Winnipeg General Strike of 1919. If the strike itself must be counted labour's loss, the longer term proved that it had burned class consciousness into the minds of both sides and thereby ensured that labour itself would survive as a cohesive political force. Communist and social democratic civic politicians, union meetings and union campaigns, and eventual victory for a New Democratic Party provincial government communicated critiques of capitalism through the rest of the century. These institutions and the social networks they generated remain important forces in provincial and civic political life because the labour movement and its allies have been able to assemble funds, activists, and articulate spokespersons to represent the workers' cause.

Manitoba has been the recipient of waves of immigrants commencing in the 1880s, around 1900, shortly after the First World War, again after the Second World War, and in the generations after 1970. The waves differed in place of recruitment and in the cultures of the new arrivals. The host society also changed with the passage of time, especially when established citizens began, in the post-1945 generation, to receive newcomers in a more helpful manner. But every group of immigrants encountered racism and every group tried to influence the state in one way or another. Ukrainian-Canadians sought to maintain their language. Jewish-Canadians sought the abolition of various restrictive caveats such as the selective quotas in the University of Manitoba medical school. Japanese-Canadians sought redress for their wartime expulsion from their homes in BC and the government's expropriation of their property. The similarities of experience across so many decades underlie the thesis that immigrants, though a group constantly changing in composition, should be seen as another continuing factor in the Manitoba political tradition.

Women campaigned for the vote in the decade before the First World War and won their prize in 1916 after the victory of the T.C. Norris-led Liberals. They were not as assertive in provincial politics for the next generation, perhaps because their next crucial struggle concerned respect for their labour in the home. But women's issues accumulated again in the 1950s and 1960s as their increasingly prominent place in the professions, their share in the ownership of marital property, and the relation between their wage work and family roles became matters of public debate. Women's distinctive approach to political parties and platforms, and their place in the growing spheres of health care and public sector unions, also ensured their voices would be acknowledged in public life. As a consequence, women, as a group, influenced the course of public affairs throughout the twentieth century.

First Nations people, including both non-status individuals and those recognized as Indians under Canada's Indian Act, also represented a distinct and enduring force in provincial life. United in interest in the 1870s by treaties, the Indian Act, and disfranchisement, the first peoples were excluded from the province's political arrangements for several generations. Only after they organized and protested this exclusion were they recognized as having a legitimate grievance. They won the provincial franchise in 1952 and the federal franchise in 1960. As the 1988–91 Aboriginal Justice Inquiry attested, however, the right to vote did not mean that injustices would cease. Still, Elijah Harper's role in defeating the Meech Lake constitutional amendment and the remarkable success of Manitoba First Nations leaders, including Phil Fontaine and Ovide Mercredi, both of whom became national chiefs of the Assembly of First Nations, testified to the influence of first peoples in political life.

All of the groups listed above had roots deep in the past. All experienced defining moments that reinforced their self-conscious determination to survive and ultimately to prevail. To discuss each on its own, in the manner of Peterson and Wiseman, emphasizes the differences that divide Manitobans into distinct groups. But to lump Manitobans together in a single coherent community, as the political practitioners might seem to be saying (though this is not, in fact, their message), is to infer wrongly that dissenting groups represent mere tensions, enduring aberrations but not influential alternative views, within a single political tradition. This is not fair to groups that launched what they themselves regarded as profound challenges to a complacent provincial establishment.[22] Besides, each of these groups has endured for an extended time and influences contemporary political affairs. Each, in itself, seen from the perspective of social history, constitutes a significant political tradition.

Another approach to the question of political tradition falls under the broad rubric of cultural history, a branch of the discipline that inquires into communities' collective perspectives. From this vantage point, one might argue that Manitobans have experienced three quite different political conversations during the past 140 years, each of which constituted a local variation on international themes. The first was rooted in a British-Canadian imperial and colonial outlook between the province's founding in 1870 and, roughly, the outbreak of the First World War in 1914; the second was marked by multicultural and class conflict and endured until the decades after mid-century (the Roblin government of 1958–1967 can stand as the era of transition); the third, an era of integration and accommodation, began in the 1960s and continues to the present.

Manitoba's initial political conversation, or "political culture," was constructed on conflicts between the Métis and British-Ontarian newcomers, between French-speaking Catholics and English-speaking Protestants, and between a "West" possessing newfound economic interests and an "East" determined to shape the growing national economy as it saw fit. These battles were real, culminating in a ministerial crisis in 1879, a struggle over railway policy in the 1880s, a prolonged legal battle over public funding of Roman Catholic schools (1890–1897), and a contest over the status of the French language. The British Canadian, central Canadian, and English language victories were not inevitable but, when they came, they established the ground rules for succeeding generations.

Manitoba grew in population and social diversity during the opening decades of the twentieth century, acquiring the ethnic and class composition that drove its politics for the next two generations. The elections of 1914 and 1915, which saw the Conservatives challenged and then defeated by the Liberals, illustrated that farm, labour, and women's groups were no longer willing to abide by the consensus established after Confederation. Women won their campaign for the vote in 1916. But labour and farm groups discovered their concerns could not be resolved without long and difficult struggles. After the Winnipeg General Strike of 1919, unions lost influence and foundered over internal disagreements that preoccupied them for a generation. Farm groups won the provincial election of 1922 and maintained rural dominance in the legislature, but the Great Depression of the 1930s postponed their acquisition of hoped-for rural social amenities, including better access to health care facilities and to electric power. Immigrants from eastern and southern Europe lost the right to educate their children in their own languages in public schools, a measure adopted by the legislature in 1916, and endured British-Manitoban social leaders' reluctance to admit them to full membership in provincial society. Ethnic tension, rural-urban conflict, and labour-capital hostility marked this second era of Manitoba politics, just as Tom Peterson suggested.

Duff Roblin's government, 1958–1967, ushered in recognizably modern Manitoba political arrangements. Inherited tensions over women's status, First

Nations sovereignty, French-language rights, income distribution, ethnic cultural expression, and rural versus urban precedence made regular appearances in political debates. Though such issues constituted crucial policy distinctions at the local level, they did not constitute the organizing themes of political life. Rather, as Nelson Wiseman suggested, the international debate between neo-liberalism and social democracy shaped local political choices. In the language of the Manitoba legislature, "left-wing socialists" (said the Progressive Conservatives of the New Democrats) opposed "right-wing neo-cons" (said the New Democrats of the Progressive Conservatives). The Liberals were sandwiched between these two parties, losing saliency in the process. Around the parties and their debates, the pressures associated with integrating increasing numbers of southern-hemisphere immigrants and northern Aboriginal migrants into provincial society increased. Fortunately for the community, its multi-sector economy grew steadily, if very slowly, most Manitobans resisted the siren call of out-migration, and such flashpoints as the French-language dispute (1983–84) and the murders of Helen Betty Osborne and J.J. Harper (which provoked the establishment of the Aboriginal Justice Inquiry, 1988–91) did not result in irreparable breaches of public order.

To suggest that there are three distinct periods in the political culture of the province puts the comments of the practitioners whose views were outlined above in a different light. These experienced leaders stressed the importance of accommodation in provincial politics. Could they have ignored all the groups canvassed here? Surely not. Instead, one can see that their experience in the post-Roblin era, the years since the 1960s, differs dramatically from the circumstances of Manitoba's first century. Quite simply, these recent leaders have experienced a different political environment. This is the perspective that a cultural history can offer. As Tom Peterson argues, by the 1970s Manitobans had attained a "basic unity.... [and] in their second century appeared ready for a more straightforward competition between those inclined to reform and equalization and those who expressed the need for restraint and stability."[23]

Conclusion

The concept of "political tradition" is unconventional because it marries the academic disciplines of history and political science, perhaps intending to avoid thereby the assumptions and the rigour of both. As used by the late American historian, Richard Hofstadter, it was a liberating concept because it postulated the existence of a consensus beneath the obvious contestation in any society's public life. Is there a Manitoba political tradition?

The preceding pages have outlined disagreements as well as consensus. Students of Manitoba politics have typically concluded that important differences lay at the heart of the provincial political community. The political practitioners whom I interviewed suggest, in contrast, that the community operated on the guiding principles of accommodation and fairness. A historical approach offers a little of both: distinct groups battling for primacy—yes, each of which constitutes a "political tradition" in itself. And three cultural eras: in the first two, between 1870 and the 1950s, disagreements were profound; and, in the third, though the entire community accepted the rules of the political process, significant ideological differences over such matters as government's role in the economy, the maintenance of social safety nets, and the enforcement of rules related to reproduction and the family, suggest that political debate was far from over. Hofstadter's quest for a single "tradition" spanning this long history of 140 years is simplistic. It would be unfair to the dissatisfied, and complacent in the face of continuing inequality, not to recognize that privilege has been challenged many times by those who represent different interests and different outlooks.

Notes

1   Interview with Duff Roblin, 12 November 2008 (notes in author's possession)
2   One exception is the Canadian political science text edited by R.S. Blair and J.T. McLeod *The Canadian Political Tradition: Basic Readings* (Scarborough, ON: Nelson Canada, second edition, 1993).
3   Richard Hofstadter, *The American Political Tradition and the Men Who Made It* (New York: Alfred A. Knopf 1948, 1967), vii and viii.
4   Ibid., viii.
5   Ibid., ix, x.
6   I recognize that today's social scientists are accustomed to using such concepts as political culture, path dependency, and realigning elections when discussing such problems. Nelson Wiseman defines political culture as evanescent, elusive, but not a mirage – rather "a work in perpetual process" in *In Search of Canadian Political Culture* (Vancouver: UBC Press, 2007), 263.
7   A rough estimate of the ethnic origins of Manitobans, calculated from a Statistics Canada 2006 report which permitted respondents to declare multiple heritages: 57 percent British (including Irish), 58 percent European (not including British and French), 17 percent Aboriginal (including both first peoples and Métis), 6 percent Visible Minority (Filipino 39,000; South Asia 15,000; Chinese 18,000), in Statistics Canada, "Ethnic origins, 2006 counts, for Canada, provinces and territories—20% sample data," http://www12.statcan.gc.ca/english/census06/data/highlights/ethnic/pages/Page.cfm?Lang=E&Geo=PR&Code=46&Table=2&Data=Count&StartRec=1&Sort=3&Display=Page (accessed 8 January 2009).

8   Statistics Canada, "Population and dwelling counts, for Canada, census metropolitan areas, census agglomerations and census subdivisions (municipalities), 2006 and 2001 censuses," http://www12.statcan.ca/english/census06/data/popdwell/Table.cfm?T=303&SR=1&S=3&O=D&RPP=25&CMA=602 (accessed 10 November 2008).

9   W. L. Morton, "The Bias of Prairie Politics," in *Contexts of Canada's Past: Selected Essays of W. L. Morton*, ed. Brian McKillop (Toronto: Macmillan, 1980), 149–160; first published in *Transactions of the Royal Society of Canada* Series 3, 49 (1955): 57–66.

10 Tom Peterson, "Manitoba: Ethnic and Class Politics" in Martin Robin, ed., *Canadian Provincial Politics: The Party Systems of the Ten Provinces* (Second edition, Scarborough: Prentice-Hall of Canada 1978): 61–119. This is the second version of the article. The first, a shorter version, was published in the book's first edition, in 1972. Paul Vogt used the term "fault line" in our interview, 24 July 2008, and so did Gary Filmon in the interview of 12 November 2008.

11 Tom Peterson, "Manitoba: Ethnic and Class Politics," 102–3, 108.

12 Nelson Wiseman, *In Search of Canadian Political Culture*, 213–15, 218, 229, 235. Wiseman estimates the Aboriginal proportion of the population at 14 percent in the early twenty-first century. Wiseman wrote a slightly different version of this interpretation a quarter-century earlier, though this analysis, too, emphasized "ideology and ethnicity." See Wiseman, "The Pattern of Prairie Politics," first published in *Queen's Quarterly* 88, 2 (1981) and republished in R. Douglas Francis and Howard Palmer, eds., *The Prairie West: Historical Readings* (Edmonton: University of Alberta Press, 1992), 640–660. According to Wiseman, Manitoba's political parties reflected the province's divided social composition. The Citizens' League, defender of the middle and upper classes, was led by Ontarians; the moderate Independent Labour Party was led by British immigrants. In later decades, Wiseman suggests, following Peterson's line, continental European immigrants and their children who lived in rural Manitoba were more likely to align with the left-wing Manitoba Farmers Union; *In Search of Canadian Political Culture*, 221. Like many observers, Wiseman regards the 1969 election as constituting a realignment of political representation. The old farm-business alliance lost much of its strength, many of its voters going to the social democratic NDP, which became a mainstream, if left-leaning, alternative that spoke on behalf of such previously alienated groups as Unitarians, Jews, Slavs and Aboriginal people (223). It emphasized equality, the absence of discrimination, government-owned and cooperative economic institutions, investment in the public sector, public health insurance, and social welfare reform (231). In 2009, the Manitoba New Democratic Party quietly celebrated the fortieth anniversary of its first electoral victory in 1969. It had been in power in Manitoba for twenty-five of these forty years. Wiseman may exaggerate the strength of the left, and may also exaggerate the right's weakness, but his definition of a social democratic strain in Canadian political culture that relied heavily on Manitoba and Saskatchewan roots does ring true.

13 Wiseman, *In Search of Canadian Political Culture*, 229 and 235; David Laycock suggests that a "crypto-liberal" strain of thought was strongest in Manitoba in the first few decades of the twentieth century; Wiseman: 216. A concern for the "regional distribution of the benefits and costs of national growth" was prominent in Saskatchewan (217–8). Though he does not say so, one could conclude on the basis of Morton's work that the same concern motivated Manitobans. Wiseman notes that Manitoba, like Ontario, rejected free trade in both 1911 and 1988 (Alberta did not; 219). He adds that Rodmond Roblin criticized direct democracy tactics, a view that did not secure support in Saskatchewan or Alberta but was "marketable in Ontarianized, tory-touched, rural Manitoba" (219). Also David Laycock, *Populism and Democratic Thought in the Canadian Prairies, 1910 to 1945* (Toronto: University of Toronto Press, 1990).

14 The changing preoccupations of these three academic observers illuminate changes in Canada's intellectual foundations: note the shift from a concern with institutions

of government to social and then ideological differences. This shift can be viewed as a transition in conceptual frame from region to class to ideology. Note, too, the decline of interest in conflict between local, space-defined or space-based communities and the increasing interest in internationally recognized, idea-based sources of difference.

15   Interviews with Duff Roblin, Gary Doer, Paul Vogt, Virginia Devine, Leslie Turnbull, Gary Filmon, Jim Carr (notes in author's possession).

16   Interview with Howard Pawley (notes in author's possession).

17   Jim Carr linked this participation to geographical and social necessity: "Because of our isolation, we couldn't rely on nearby places for symphony concerts or performances of Shakespeare's plays. Manitoba is an act of will."

18   Shannon Stunden Bower, "The Great Transformation? Wetlands and Land Use in Manitoba During the Late Nineteenth Century," *Journal of the Canadian Historical Association*, New Series 15 (2004): 29–47, and J. Edgar Rea, "The Roots of Prairie Society," in *Prairie Perspectives: Papers of the Western Canadian Studies Conference*, ed. David P. Gagan (Toronto: Holt, Rinehart and Winston, 1970), 46–55.

19   Readers should be aware that several distinguished historians have distinguished two types of social analyst, the lumper and the splitter. These scholars would describe the Wiseman approach as "splitting" and the political practitioners' approach as "lumping." The subject is discussed in J. H. Hexter on Christopher Hill, in the *Times Literary Supplement*, 1975, and in Isaiah Berlin's essay, *The Hedgehog and the Fox: An Essay on Tolstoy's View of History*.

20   Leslie Turnbull's summary is interesting: "What groups make a difference in the political culture? One tightly knit, focused, active group is the Jewish community. Another in which everyone knows everyone else, and that is very aware of its interests and causes, is the French. But neither is exerting much pressure, as a group, on the rest of the community. The Jews are active within their own group. And the French constituencies have been migrating outward and are now more consciously 'suburban' rather than French. Aboriginal people, the First Nations, are an important group. I'm not sure that the Métis have the same impact. The Labour movement is influential. And the business community. Big businesses try to make things work; [they] see Manitoba as a whole and are less self-interested than the smaller businesses. Farmers are an active community that can be identified with particular constituencies." (Interview with Leslie Turnbull: notes in author's possession).

21   Interview with Arthur Mauro (notes in author's possession).

22   Richard Hofstadter asserted the merits of lumping as opposed to splitting in his book on the American political tradition: "It is in the nature of politics that conflict stands in the foreground, and historians usually abet the politicians in keeping it there." Hofstadter, *The American Political Tradition*, ix. Hofstadter emphasized consensus, in doing so becoming a leader among American historians in the postwar decades. "It seems to me to be clear that a political society cannot hang together at all unless there is some kind of consensus running through it, and yet that no society has such a total consensus as to be devoid of significant conflict. It is all a matter of proportion and emphasis, which is terribly important in history. Of course, obviously, we have had one total failure of consensus which led to the Civil War. One could use that as the extreme case in which consensus breaks down." Jack Pole, "Richard Hofstadter," in *Clio's Favorites: Leading Historians of the United States, 1945–2000*, ed. Robert Allen Rutland (Columbia: University of Missouri Press 2000), 73–4.

23   Peterson, "Manitoba: Ethnic and Class Politics," 109–110.

Political Culture in Manitoba[1]

Jared Wesley

Introduction

Compared with the popular impression of other Canadian provinces, Manitoba's political culture remains undeveloped in the minds of many observers. Saskatchewan is home to the country's collectivist, social democratic traditions, for instance, whereas Alberta is the bastion of Canadian populism, individualism, and Western alienation.[2] Even in the most trained minds, Manitoba enjoys no comparable identity. In the words of Rand Dyck,[3] the author of a leading undergraduate textbook on Canadian provincial politics,

> Manitoba is a province without a distinctive political culture. If Manitobans have a self-image, it is probably one of a moderate, medium, diversified, and fairly prosperous but unspectacular province. Many value its ethnic heterogeneity; others, its intermediary position on federal-provincial affairs, interpreting east to east and vice versa.[4]

Dyck is not alone. Many define Manitoba by its ambiguous mediocrity, rather than any unique political personality. These conclusions are drawn quite easily. Manitoba is the "keystone province," after all; it is the geographic centre of North America, the "Heart of the Continent," and the buffer between the "old" country of the east and Canada's "new west." Its population and economy are among the country's most diverse, and both are of average size. Relative to other major Canadian centres, even its capital city, Winnipeg, is viewed as a "balance between exotic and obscure."[5] In short, Manitoba *is* Canada's "middling" province, positioned between prosperous and poor, east and west, old and new, exciting and bland.

Yet, such views distort the notion of "political culture," and misconceive the precise nature of Manitoba politics. Indeed, the province "is more than a fuzzy middle ground where the East ends and the West begins."[6] It has its own, distinctive political ethos, which is grounded in the very concepts of *modesty* and *moderation* that make up its popular "middleman" image.

Modesty and Moderation

Some regard it as a form of prudent pragmatism—an unpretentious, unassuming, conciliatory approach to politics that holds as its principal goal the accommodation of diversity, the preservation of order and tradition, and the protection of Manitoba's median position in Confederation. Others view the province's culture as a brand of prudish pessimism—a sign of Manitobans' quiescence on divisive issues or reticence on the national stage. Some see humility and realism in Manitoba's political culture, where others see meekness and resignation.

Whatever the case, there is little doubt Manitoba has always been "a land of steady ways" in which "the simple, sturdy virtues of hard work, thrift and neighbourliness have been cherished and transmitted." As William Morton wrote four decades ago,

> if it is too much to assert that a Manitoban can be recognized abroad, it is still true that life in Manitoba forces a common manner, not to say character on all its people. It is the manner, or mannerism of instant understanding and agreeableness at meeting, and rises from the need for harmony in a society of many diverse elements. This superficial friendliness is common to all North Americans, of course, but in Manitoba, a truly plural society, it is a definite and highly conscious art.[7]

Reflecting these tendencies, Manitobans, "though driven to strike out in new ways in politics, [have] remained fast wedded to the old ways in manners and morals."[8] In this sense, Manitoba politics have featured a stronger strain of traditionalism than Canada's other two prairie provinces. This tendency is embodied in the province's political culture of modesty and moderation—a shared sense of identity that has both reflected and shaped the community's political evolution.

To elaborate on this view, this chapter begins by exploring the term "political culture," which is defined as a system of common values that determine a community's approach toward politics. Discussion then turns to the main characteristics of political culture in a community like Manitoba: its collective symbols. In its flag, mottos, logos, licence plates, institutions, and myths, we find that Manitoba's political culture is decidedly—and avowedly—modest and moderate. This raises the obvious question: How did Manitoba develop these tendencies? Three related explanations are offered, suggesting the province's political culture may be traced to its original settlement patterns, a series of formative (and transformative) events throughout its history, and the nature of the Manitoba economy. A concluding section explores the effects of Manitoba political culture on the province's politics, in general, noting its impact on individual residents and their elites. In the end, the modesty and moderation embedded in their shared ethos shape the way Manitobans define and solve their major challenges. They have a political culture, it is distinctive, and it matters.

Political Culture

Scholars have struggled to define a term as "popular," "seductive," and "controversial" as political culture.[9] The concept, itself, is by no means novel. In writing about the differences between the customs, mores, and habits of nineteenth-century Americans and Europeans, Alexis de Tocqueville became one of the first modern political culturalists. (Karl Marx's discussions of the capitalist superstructure, and Weber's exposition of the Protestant Ethic also qualify as early works in this genre.) Over time, the concept has become associated with a wide range of topics, from "political values" or "ideology," to "national character" or "mentalité." While many researchers feel that the concept is capable of evoking such "quick intuitive understanding" that they need not provide a definition at all;[10] for others, defining political culture is rather like "trying to nail Jell-O to the wall."[11] Precisely what is it?

For the purposes of this chapter, political culture is defined as a set of common values underpinning a given political system. In this vein, a community's political culture is akin to a guiding "ethos"—the spirit of a society that informs its political beliefs, customs, and practices. It is a collection of unstated, implicit assumptions about politics, a fact that distinguishes political culture from the more explicit and contested nature of "ideology."[12] This is what makes studying political culture so challenging: there is no single book or tract, author or philosopher, to which students may turn for the definition of a community's culture.

Instead, these guiding values are embodied in the polity's shared symbols, entrenched in its institutions, echoed in the attitudes of its residents and reflected in the behaviour of its citizens. Because it is so deeply embedded, political culture is an enduring feature of any political community. According to a popular analogy, political culture is to public opinion as climate is to weather—the former is long-term and stable, while the latter is short-term and ephemeral.

Political culture is thus a lens, screen or filter through which members of a community view the world around them. It helps to identify problems or challenges, and defines the limits of acceptability in terms of their solutions. Although it influences individuals in their opinions and actions, it is important to remember: political culture is a fundamentally *collective* phenomenon. Only groups may possess cultures; individuals cannot.[13] As Wiseman puts it, "Culture is a group activity, a shared experience. No person alone constitutes a culture."[14]

Before proceeding to the definition of Manitoba political culture, one further caveat is necessary. By presuming the boundaries of a particular society, we often overlook the existence of sub- or supra-cultures that exist within or transcend the borders of that community. There are two ways of defining a culture: from the "top down" (identifying the polity a priori, terming it a culture, and uncovering its values); or from the "bottom up" (searching for "commonality before bestowing the name 'culture' on a collectivity").[15] Given the nature of this volume, a focus on "Manitoba political culture" requires us to take the "top down" approach.

Readers should be mindful of the many subcultures within the Manitoba community (e.g., farmers, northerners, women, Aboriginal peoples, Métis, urbanites, seniors, and so on), and the fact that Manitoba is part of broader regional, national, continental, and global cultures.[16] Moreover, not every Manitoban may feel part of the province's political culture. In this sense, there are elements of a provincial "counter-culture," to which many of the groups above subscribe. Deep-rooted feelings of alienation and discrimination lie beneath the veneer of conciliation and accommodation, as other chapters in this book attest. The very nature of Manitoba's political culture masks these divisions under a layer of complacency. As Harvey Bostrom, Joan Grace, and Jim Silver suggest in their contributions in this volume, Manitoba's modest and moderate political culture makes addressing challenges facing Manitoba's Aboriginal community, women, and low-income populations extremely difficult. This is the dark side of political culture in Manitoba, and one that should not be overlooked.[17]

Yet, as Chilton tells us, the "existence of a political culture is not defined by all people liking the culture, or regarding it as legitimate. Rather, it is defined by the ways of relating that people actually use to coordinate their dealings with one another. Culture is what is publicly expected and subscribed to, not what is individually preferred."[18]

Symbols

In order to sketch the contours of Manitoba's political culture, it is crucial that we distinguish the *indicators* of the community's overarching values from their potential causes and consequences. This is a technical way of saying we must separate symptoms, on one hand, from sources and effects, on the other. Consider this example. As much as they may offer clues, a doctor would never diagnose her patient with the flu (the phenomenon) solely by asking whether he had failed to get a flu shot (a possible cause), or failed to attend class (a possible consequence). Rather, she would look for direct evidence (indicators) of the flu, including symptoms like fever, aches, chills, or tiredness. The causes and consequences of the flu may be useful to point her in the right direction, or to validate the doctor's verdict. But to establish the diagnosis, direct evidence is necessary.

The same principles apply to studying political culture. Political scientists must search for the indicators of the community's ethos—for the purest possible embodiment of these guiding norms and values. They cannot settle for settlement patterns, formative events, or economic forces, for instance. These are discussed in greater detail below as the *sources* of political culture. Individual attitudes, beliefs, and behaviours of residents and elites cannot be used as indicators, either; they may stem from culture, much as skipping class may result from the flu. (Recall that culture is a collective phenomenon that exerts its influence on these individual actors. A community, or culture, is more than a sum of it parts.) Such orientations are discussed later as *consequences* of culture. So, precisely where does political culture manifest itself most clearly?

For evidence, we must turn to a community's symbols.[19] As Johnson suggests, "culture consists of inter-subjectively shared symbols, deployed in ritual or other cultural practices, which actors invest with meaning in the process of imposing conceptual order on the social and political world."[20] In its broadest sense, culture may manifest itself, symbolically, in artifacts like folk songs, popular novels, children's stories, television shows, music videos, movies, school textbooks, contracts, greeting cards, popular leisure activities, or public prayers.[21] From this perspective, "the social," "fowl supper," and "potluck dinner" are indicative of collective spirit embodied in Manitoba's broader social culture.[22] Symbols like these both reflect and reinforce culture, in that, once the values become well established, they take on "a life of their own," independent of the forces and factors that contributed to their rise.[23]

Drawing on these principles, political scientists have identified a wide variety of indicators for political culture. These have included anthems, emblems, currency, constitutions, and the like. A close examination of Manitoba's political symbols reveals a political culture steeped in the principles of modesty and moderation.

Consider Manitoba's official emblems. Adopted in 1905, the Manitoba coat of arms signals the province's history of cultural conservatism, accommodation, and diversity (see Figure 2.1). As a tribute to its parent societies, British and

Canadian icons are displayed, including the royal crown, the Cross of St. George (of England), maple leaves, a beaver, and a Red River cart wheel. By the same token, Aboriginal bead and bone decorations adorn the pair of unicorns in the crest, paying homage to Manitoba's first peoples. Lily flowers (fleurs-de-lis) symbolize the province's French-Canadian heritage, rounding out the province's three founding cultures. The province's economic diversity is represented at the bottom of the arms, marked by the presence of wheat, timber, and water. Most prominent, however, are the province's primary figurehead—the bison—and the provincial motto, *Gloriosus et Liber* (Latin for "Glorious and Free"). Borrowed from one of the country's early anthems, "O Canada," the maxim reflects Manitoba's ties to Canadian culture, more generally.[24]

Figure 2.1. Manitoba Coat of Arms

Image Courtesy of the Government of Manitoba:
http://www.travelmanitoba.com/images_tr/visitors_info/big_coatofarms.jpg

Manitoba also has a provincial tartan, the pattern of which reflects similar principles. According to the government's description of the official plaid:

> Each colour has its own significance: Dark Red Squares—natural resources of the province; Azure Blue Lines—Lord Selkirk, founder of the Red River Settlement (Winnipeg); Dark Green Lines—the men and women of many races who have enriched the life of the province; and Golden Lines—grain and other agricultural products.[25]

Of note, Manitoba is the only province in Canada to make specific reference to the inter-mingling of cultures in its tartan—a sign of the extent to which ethnic diversity forms a unique part of Manitoba's political culture.[26]

While reflecting the community's values, these formal symbols are likely unfamiliar to most Manitobans. By contrast, the provincial icon, flag, slogans, and other prominent institutions enjoy greater visibility. The bison is by far Manitoba's most recognizable symbol. It appears on everything from the provincial coat of arms and flag, to official government stationery and licence plates, to sports jerseys and postcards. As with any object, tracing the symbolism of the bison is a subjective exercise. Historically, the bison epitomizes Manitoba's primordial roots as a plains society. It hearkens back to the time when the buffalo outnumbered humans in the region, or to the province's origins in the fur trade. More abstractly, the bison symbolizes Manitoba's stolid, yet vulnerable, presence in Confederation. The animal's own history speaks of scars, while its future remains optimistic if uncertain.

Yet, for anyone who has seen a herd up close, the bison carries a respectful and respectable air. As Morton indicated in the introduction to this chapter, this same sense of quiet confidence can be felt among Manitobans, in general. It is one you strain to hear even at the loudest Roughrider-Blue Bomber games in late summer. While Manitobans and their leaders may lack the bravado of their Western neighbours, their quiet confidence speaks volumes of the nature of their pride. Alberta has its cowboy and Saskatchewan its wheat farmer, just as Quebec has its fleur-de-lis and Ontario its maple leaf. As a community of communities, Manitobans cherish all of these symbols, yet stake their collective identity on none of them. If Manitoba has its own symbol, it is the bison.

While the bison figures prominently, it is not the only symbol of note on the Manitoba flag. As history reveals, the Union Jack is equally important. The province's present flag was adopted on 12 May 1966, amid a nationwide debate over symbols and heraldry. A year earlier, then prime minister Lester Pearson's government had adopted Canada's Maple Leaf flag, sparking resentment among those committed to retaining British symbols, particularly the Union Jack.[27] Galvanized by federal Progressive Conservative leader John Diefenbaker, opposition to "Pearson's pennant" was fiercest in (rural) Ontario and Manitoba.[28] Tory governments in both provinces endorsed this sentiment by adopting a Red Ensign template for their respective new provincial flags. Modelled on the Canadian Red Ensign—the country's unofficial flag prior to 1965—each features the Union Flag in the upper left corner (or canton), defaced by the provincial shield to the right (or in the fly) (see Figure 2.2).

Figure 2.2. Flag of Manitoba

Image Courtesy of the Government of Manitoba:
http://www.travelmanitoba.com/images_tr/visitors_info/big_mbflag.jpg

To some, the new Manitoba flag signified a form of loyalist protest against the severing of symbolic ties to the British Empire.[29] Whereas most other provinces abandoned the ensign in designing their new flags in the 1960s, Manitobans had it emblazoned on theirs.[30] To others, the new flag represented a more positive statement of the province's identity, rooted as it was in the trappings of its past. Either way, by endorsing the province's quasi-colonial roots and traditions, the Manitoba Ensign remains a symbol of the province's modest, "steady ways."

The province's penchant for moderation also finds its voice in its political slogans. Engraved on its licence plates since 1976, the moniker "Friendly Manitoba" serves as the province's unofficial motto.[31] Its capital city recently adopted a new official slogan, "Heart of the Continent," in reference to Winnipeg's geographic location and down-home character. As stated earlier, both phrases draw on Manitoba's reputation as a community of diversity, "understanding and agreeableness."[32]

Sceptics may doubt the extent to which such symbols really matter in defining Manitoba's political culture. Few people in the province could identify the coat of arms or provincial motto, let alone its provincial tartan. Yet, as manifestations of their culture, the importance of these symbols to average Manitobans should not be confused with their salience. For evidence, consider two recent episodes during which a pair of Manitoba's symbols came under threat: the Golden Boy, and the "Friendly Manitoba" slogan.

In the first case, prompted by an overwhelming outpouring of community support, the Manitoba government undertook a multimillion-dollar project to restore the famous "Golden Boy" statue in 2002.[33] During the restoration process, the Golden Boy was lowered from his perch atop the Manitoba Legislative Building for the first time since the First World War. Thousands of Manitobans visited the restoration site for an up-close glimpse of the statue, marking a pilgrimage of sorts for people of all walks of life, all regions, and all ages. To many, the Golden Boy not only represented a prized piece of Manitoba's history. As a popular provincial folk song indicates, the statue also symbolized a sense of quiet confidence that is found in the province's modest, moderate political culture:

> With his head way up high in the Manitoba sky
> He shines in the sun till your work is done.
> And he glows in the night as he proudly holds the light
> That brightens our happy way of life.
>
> *Chorus:* He's the symbol of success
> At the gateway to the west
> And he's our legendary pride and joy.
> He's an idol by acclaim
> May the good Lord bless his name.
> He's the famous Manitoba Golden Boy.
>
> When the blue skies are grey on a rainy, rainy day,
> He waits not in vain for the sunshine again.
> Then way up from the ground with a rainbow for a crown
> He brightens our happy days again.
> *Chorus*
>
> With a pose simply grand in our winter wonderland
> He waits for the spring, and bluebirds to sing.
> With his bundle of wide and the stride of no retreat,
> It makes everybody want to sing.
> *Chorus*[34]

The same "spirit" was expressed during Manitoba's recent corporate branding exercise. In 2006, the government launched "The Manitoba Image Project"—a highly publicized attempt to forge "a fresh, new image for Manitoba; a way of communicating our province's unique identity to raise our profile and tell the world that Manitoba is an exceptional place to live, work, visit and invest in."[35] Granted, this was primarily a marketing gambit, aimed at retaining and attracting businesses, youth, immigrants, and tourists. Nonetheless, the Manitoba Promotion Council claimed a much larger mandate:

> Manitoba's image is much more than a logo. Our image is not an advertising strategy, a tagline, or a sales message. Everything we do defines the way people think about and talk about Manitoba. Our image defines "who we are" and "who we are not." It incorporates our aspirations; it expresses how we want our province to grow.[36]

Moreover, the council argued:

> Manitoba's image is often based on our own self-deprecating attitudes. We need to change the way we see ourselves, so we can do a better job of selling ourselves to the world.... It's time we redefined who we are. It's time we told the world how proud we are to call Manitoba home. It's time to tell a new story, our story.[37]

In this vein, their choice of slogan—"Spirited Energy"—aimed to capture "the truth about our province, and the way we want everyday Manitobans, business people, and visitors to think about Manitoba." In particular, the brand was meant to embody

> Manitoba's rich history of diverse cultures, varied climate, and northern location [which] has instilled a unique energy that radiates in from the hearts and minds of our people. From the birthplace of many successful artists, musicians and entrepreneurs who compete on the world stage, to the natural resources that fuel our economy, Manitoba is a wellspring of energy. This mobilizing force and enterprising spirit is as transparent as it is contagious. Manitoba's spirited energy propels our province and its people, and drives our success. A rich past, a vibrant future—it's ours.[38]

While it evokes a greater sense of dynamism and vibrancy than the other, more established symbols, nonetheless, the new "Spirited Energy" brand was intended to draw on many of the same, core principles.

Manitobans' reaction to the new brand was mixed, at best, ranging from support to indifference to outright hostility. Among those in the latter category, some felt that the new slogan departed too drastically from the province's more modest, moderate unofficial motto: "Friendly Manitoba." Despite opposition from those whose position appeared grounded in the province's penchant for "steady ways," the Spirited Energy campaign suggested the province's identity lies in its accommodation of diversity, and its future retains strong links to its past. This is the very essence of Manitoba's ethos of "moderation and modesty."

Sources

The question remains: where did these values originate? Some students treat political culture as a primitive (or "primordial") element of each community, inherited a priori by its members.[39] Others treat political culture as being "manufactured" or "imagined,"[40] emphasizing its "constructedness" over its "givenness."[41] From the latter perspective, political culture is less a stable structure than a dynamic process through which political ideas are translated and transmitted within a community over time. According to these constructivists, political culture amounts to a "myth," created and propagated by select members of a political community, and imprinted in the minds of individual residents.[42]

The reality lies somewhere between these two extremes. Political cultures are neither entirely primordial, nor are they entirely constructed. They do not simply "exist," but require definition and cultivation by members of the community. By the same token, they are not entirely "invented." Would-be myth-makers do not have a blank canvas upon which to paint their visions of a society; when proselytizing, they must take into account their community's social, ethnic, geographic, economic, historical, and other characteristics. In short, political culture contains both structural elements that appear inherited, and agential elements that must be experienced.

Fragments

On the inherited side, one approach examines how early immigration patterns contribute to the development of a community's political culture. "Fragment theory" posits that, when settling a new society, dominant immigrant groups import certain values from their parent cultures.[43] By virtue of the new society's virgin ideological soil, the ideas achieve almost universal acceptance. The character of these values depends on both the point and time of the group's departure, such that the settlers will only transplant a "fragment" of their original political culture (the portion is determined both by the dominant values present among the group's members, as well as the point in the ideological evolution of the parent culture). Thereafter, the new society becomes severed from its parent, effectively "freezing" in its stage of ideological development, and spawning a unique political culture.

As John Ralston Saul convincingly argued, many of the values of conciliation, accommodation, and egalitarianism that pervade political culture in Canada, more generally, were "absorbed" by European settlers when they came in contact with Canada's first peoples.[44] The same is true in Manitoba, where many white pioneers were exposed to the principles (and necessity) of negotiation with the region's first inhabitants. In this sense, Manitoba's political culture may be seen to predate the formal establishment of European political institutions.[45]

In terms of European settlement, Manitoba's founding fragment was decidedly British. Beginning with the opening of the West in the late-nineteenth century, Manitoba drew the vast majority of its immigrants from the province of Ontario.[46] As Dyck puts it,

> Manitoba was initially populated largely by ex-Ontarians, and this dominant group laid the foundations for a basic value structure just slightly more progressive and politically experimental than central Canadian liberalism. Even in the period of agrarian revolt in the 1920s, the province's leading political figures, T.A. Crear and John Bracken, did not stray far from Ontario rural liberalism.[47]

This "progressivism" brought with it a penchant for social and political reform, including the extension of suffrage, individual rights, and temperance. Yet, these British-Ontario pioneers brought with them a "tory-touched liberalism" not found in other parts of the prairies.[48] This toryism—also known as "classic," "traditional," or "Burkean" conservatism—has a long, if disputed, history in Canadian politics.[49] Compared to the "new right" (or "neo-liberal") conservatism of today, toryism involves a higher level of deference to authority, a stronger preference for social order, a keener reverence for the past, a deeper affinity for the United Kingdom and a greater willingness to use the state to serve the public good. In addition to the many British symbols found in Manitoba's emblems, the presence of this tory strain helps to explain Manitoba's aversion to populism and radicalism, as holds currency elsewhere in Western Canada. If the province inherited its "progressive" streak from the Ontario Grits and Western Canadian farming community (by far the most dominant fragment), Manitoba inherited its "steady ways" from these early Ontario tories.[50] Thus, in the late-nineteenth century, its combination of western liberal-progressivism and eastern tory-conservatism made Manitoba a sort of ideological melting pot of Confederation.

Transformative Events

From the second perspective, we might interpret political culture as a product of the community's shared experiences. One school of thought suggests societies like Manitoba experience certain formative, and transformative, events throughout their history. As pioneers of this approach, Almond and Powell suggested "Certain events and experiences may leave their mark on a whole society. A great war or a depression can constitute a severe political trauma for millions of individuals who may be involved...[As a consequence they may] acquire new conceptions of the role of politics in their lives and new goals for which they may strive."[51]

Some of these episodes are exogenous to the community, or imposed on it by outside forces. Wars, global economic trends, natural disasters, and other occurrences may fall under this category. Others are endogenously created, fostered by forces or actors within the community, itself. These may include scandals, budget crises, social turmoil, or other, more localized events. Regardless of whether they originate from within or without, and regardless of their political, economic or social character, these transformative events leave a lasting imprint on the community's political culture.

Manitoba has experienced more than its share of such "critical junctures." Since its violent entry into Confederation in 1870, the province has played host to some of the country's most divisive political debates, many with lasting ramifications for the country as a whole. From the Riel Rebellions (a series of armed Métis uprisings that gave birth to responsible government in the province) and the Manitoba Schools Question (which pitted rival cultures against one another for control over the province's education system), to the periodic, but heated debates over biculturalism and the province's place in Confederation, Manitoba has been a "polity on the edge" at various points in its history.[52]

Nowhere is the importance of transformative events clearer than in the case of the 1919 General Strike. The violent suppression of the uprising constituted a major turning point in the province's history. The event helped to polarize, yet mute the radical elements of, the province's business and labour movements, and set the stage for the success of more moderate parties like the Liberal-Progressives, Progressive Conservatives and NDP.[53]

Numerous other episodes could be cited as pivotal in Manitoba's history, of course. The two world wars, the Great Depression, the Red River floods of 1950 and 1997 or the scandals surrounding the construction of the legislative buildings (1915) and the administration of northern election campaigns (1995) spring to mind. Each brought with it a spirit of sacrifice (modesty) and togetherness (moderation) in the face of steep challenges, be they to the security of Manitobans' way of life, the future of the provincial economy, or the quality of Manitoba democracy. Dark days, like the opening of the Panama Canal in 1914—which ended Manitoba's reign as the sole gateway to the Canadian West[54]—or the departure of the Winnipeg Jets in 1996—thus capping the city's era as a "major league" community—also served to reinforce Manitobans' humility and modesty

From this perspective, an understanding of modern Manitoba politics begins with an appreciation for the periods of intense confrontation and disappointment that punctuate its past. As discussed below, these episodes have left a lasting mark on Manitoba's elites. The result has been the development of a provincial "code" based on compromise and accommodation, and the avoidance of crisis and controversy. Indeed, from a cultural perspective, these transformative events have conditioned Manitobans to be wary of disruptive modes of political competition and discourse, and to avoid raising unrealistic expectations.

Economy

Finally, Manitoba's political culture may be linked to the nature of its economy. This connection may be drawn in several ways. On one hand, Manitoba's first economic activity—the fur trade—helped forge (and, in many ways, challenge) Manitoba's penchant for inter-cultural compromise. Since that time, its lack of ideological tilt may reflect the absence of a dominant economic activity, or "staple." (By contrast, the dominance of the oil industry in Alberta, and the agricultural sector in early Saskatchewan, may help to explain why the former developed a political culture conducive to free-market liberalism, while the latter adopted a more collectivistic ethos.)[55]

In a second, related sense, Manitoba maintains Canada's most diversified economy, "balanced among various primary industries and among primary, secondary, and tertiary sectors. Although this economy is not outstanding in any particular respect, the province manages to remain relatively stable and prosperous."[56] Besides creating a heterogeneous community of interests, classes, and occupations, the structure of its economy has insulated Manitoba from the boom-and-bust cycles experienced by other provinces. As a result, by avoiding the depths of the Depression or heights of economic growth experienced in Alberta and Saskatchewan, for example, Manitoba has not been subject to the same type of radical, "utopian sorties," led by parties such as Social Credit and the CCF.[57] In this sense, Manitoba's stable, diversified economy has contributed to its ethos of moderation.

Third, the average size and growth rate of the Manitoba economy places it consistently near the national mean. This means that, since the modern equalization program was introduced in 1957, Manitoba has maintained a "have-less" position relative to other, richer members of Confederation. Discussed in greater detail below, this fiscal status helps to explain Manitoba's moderate, cautious approach to either expanding or contracting social programs or its modest, conciliatory tack toward the balance of power between the provincial and federal orders of government.

Combined, these distinct settlement patterns, transformative events, and economic factors have all contributed to the development of Manitoba's modest, moderate ways. Those are the primary sources of the province's political culture, but what of its effects?

Constraints on time and space do not permit a full examination of its full impact. As others in this volume attest, political culture leaves its mark on all political institutions, including government programs and organizations, as well as political parties and party systems. Of note in this chapter, political culture also affects all members of a community, from those at the grassroots to those in the halls of power.

Impacts on Individual Attitudes

On the first count, according to two pioneers of the concept, Gabriel Almond and Sidney Verba, political culture is reflected in "the specifically political orientations—attitudes toward the political system and its various parts, and attitudes toward the role of the self in the system."[58] Thus, political culture manifests itself in community members' "psychological orientation toward social objects...as internalized in the cognitions, feelings and evaluations of [the] population."[59]

An examination of public polling data reveals this is certainly the case in Manitoba. While reliable province-wide surveys are difficult to come by,[60] existing data supports the notion that Manitobans' attitudes reflect a fundamentally modest and moderate political culture.

There is a noticeable strain of realism in Manitobans' orientation toward the economy, for instance. Findings from a spring 2008 Canada West Foundation (CWF) survey revealed that, compared with their Western Canadian neighbours, Manitobans were far more modest in their assessments of the health of their economies.[61] While positive, Manitobans were less likely to report that their local (60.2 percent), provincial (62.3 percent), or national (71.9 percent) economy is in "good or excellent" shape. By contrast, Albertans (81.4 / 88.3 / 75.9 percent) and Saskatchewanians (72.4 / 81.1 / 74.1 percent) were significantly more optimistic.[62]

Furthermore, according to a 2004 CWF survey, only 5.5 percent of Manitobans believed their province would be at least somewhat "better off economically if it separated from Canada." Granted, the same general sentiment was expressed throughout Western Canada and Ontario. Yet, the degree to which Manitobans doubted their province's economic autonomy is indicative of their modesty. By contrast, almost one-quarter of Albertans (24.5 percent), one-fifth of British

Columbians (19.4 percent), and 10 percent of Saskatchewanians believed they would be in a better economic position outside of Confederation.[63]

Some may argue that these views flow directly from the "realities" of Manitoba's diversified, consistent, steady, yet "unspectacular" economy (see above). Yet, Manitobans' perceptions of these "realities" are crucial; and this is where political culture plays a critical intervening role. Manitobans' could just as easily be more pessimistic (defeatist) or optimistic (delusional) about their economic prospects. Instead, and in large part, they have chosen to accept their economic standing. This economic realism is even reflected in Manitobans' attitudes toward reacquiring a National Hockey League franchise. A decade after losing the Jets, when asked if they were "generally in favour of Winnipeg getting an NHL hockey team," a full 41 percent said "no."[64] The modesty embedded in Manitoba political culture is the fount of these perceptions.

This sense of realism is connected to Manitoba's fiscal and political position within Confederation. Compared with other regional residents, Manitobans are less attached to "Western Canada" as a distinct political identity, for example, and are more content with their province's treatment in the federation. According to the results of a 2001 survey, slightly more than three in four Manitobans (76.1 percent) viewed "The West [as] a distinct region, different in many ways from the rest of Canada."[65] While this proportion rose to 83.5 percent in 2004, Manitobans were still significantly less attached to their regional identity than their neighbours in Saskatchewan (90.0 percent) and Alberta (88.6 percent) (see Table 2.1). In terms of "western alienation," Manitoba's distinctiveness is even clearer. In 2004, almost half of Manitobans felt that their province was treated with the respect it deserves in Confederation (47.1 percent), that it received its fair share in terms of transfer payments (44.4 percent) and that the rest of Canada demonstrates a concern for the West (44.2 percent). As illustrated in Table 1, in all of these areas, Manitobans sit "sandwiched between the highly satisfied Ontario and the highly dissatisfied Saskatchewan."[66] This lack of western alienation reflects the province's age-old penchant for moderation.

Even on topics on which most Western Canadians agree—including the desire for Triple-E Senate reform—Manitobans remain unique in their approach. A vast majority of residents in Alberta (86.9 percent), Saskatchewan (81.3 percent), and Manitoba (78.1 percent) feel that "Canada should replace the existing Senate with an elected senate with equal representation from each province."[67] Yet, when it comes to supporting the reform "if it required changing Canada's constitution," Manitobans were even more reluctant; only 61.2 percent of those in favour of a Triple-E Senate were willing to reopen the Constitution, compared to 65.1 percent of Albertan and 66.7 percent of Saskatchewanian reformers.[68] This reticence may be a result of Manitoba's first-hand experience with Constitutional turmoil. In addition to formative events like the Manitoba Schools Question, more recently, Manitoba played host to Elijah Harper's famous stand against the Meech Lake Accord in 1990.

Table 2.1. Attitudes Toward the West and Confederation, by Province, 2004

	AB	SK	**MB**	ON
Provincial interests adequately / well represented in Confederation	33.4	26.4	**43.4**	65.2
Province treated with respect it deserves in Canada	41.4	29.2	**47.1**	72.9
Province receives about its fair share of funding from the federal government	40.3	33.3	**44.4**	49.5
The West is a distinct region	88.6	90.0	**83.5**	71.5
The rest of Canada does not care about the West	52.7	64.3	**55.8**	26.2
Federal government should make a greater effort to address western alienation	68.6	72.6	**59.9**	45.1

Cell figures represent percentage of respondents agreeing or strongly agreeing with the statement. Adapted from: Canada West Foundation, "Looking West 2004 Survey" (Berdahl 2004).

In summarizing the results of recent public opinion polls, Berdahl suggests students "need to treat Manitoba as unique in research and analysis." Rather than grouping the province in with other "Western" communities, including neighbouring Saskatchewan, analysts "must recognize and respect the distinct perspectives of Manitobans." These unique outlooks owe much to Manitoba's unique political culture.

Impacts on Elite Politics

Beyond the grassroots, a community's shared values also affect the way elites approach politics. Specific cultural factors make a community more conducive to certain sets of ideas and their carriers, for example. A society originally populated by collectivist-minded settlers, encouraged to cooperate with one another amid harsh climatic and economic conditions, is likely to be more receptive to the appeals of social democracy than a fragment society of nineteenth-century American liberals; this is how many describe the political divide between Saskatchewan and Alberta.[69] By the same token, situational factors may also make a community more receptive to a given message or messenger. Discussed above, crises like the Great Depression or world wars may create the opportunity for a reevaluation of a society's leadership.

Overall, however, the presence of a stable, guiding ethos—like modesty and moderation—makes a community such as Manitoba more susceptible to certain types of leadership. As David Bell describes, political culture

> provides a range of acceptable values and standards upon which leaders can draw in attempting to justify their policies. Unless a culturally viable justification can be attached to a controversial policy, it will usually not be adopted. Thus, political culture shapes the perception of the politically relevant problems, thereby affecting both the recognition of these problems as issues requiring some sort of governmental action and the diagnosis of what sort of action is appropriate. Political culture influences beliefs about who should be assigned responsibility for solving problems and what kind of solutions are likely to work. This aspect of political culture is related to broader notions about the general purposes of government and the kinds of processes and substantive decisions that are seen as acceptable and legitimate.[70]

This is certainly true in Manitoba, where a political culture grounded in modesty and moderation has spawned an elite discourse based on three related principles: progressive centrism, pragmatism, and flexible partisanship.

"Progressive centrism" constitutes the foremost element of "high politics" in Manitoba. More than in any other Prairie province, leading politicians in Manitoba have consistently stressed the importance of avoiding extreme ideological positions in favour of pragmatic, "middle-of-the-road," incremental policies and programs.[71] This is not to say that Manitoba parties have been unprincipled, or devoid of ideological commitment. Recounted elsewhere, Manitoba parties have taken distinct left-wing and right-wing positions throughout history.[72] Yet, the differences between them have been much more subtle than those found in Saskatchewan and Alberta.

Ultimately, the persistence of this theme of moderation goes some way in explaining why—with the notable exceptions of Ed Schreyer and Sterling Lyon—most of Manitoba's party leaders have been praised for their competence and congeniality, as opposed to their vision and charisma. They have been viewed as both reformist—adopting change when necessary and where popular—and conservationist—standing by established ends and means, and relying on compromise and patience. As Morton put it, Manitoba leaders have tended to be "hard-headed, practical men who took life as they found it, were skeptical of reform and...indifferent to idealism."[73] Again, this places Manitoba in sharp contrast with Alberta and Saskatchewan, where leaders have been praised for their personal magnetism and boldness.[74]

The search for the progressive centre is related to the second component of Manitoba elite politics: pragmatism. Since Manitoba lost its status as the commercial and transportation gateway to the Canadian West with the opening of the Panama Canal at the turn of the last century, Manitoba politicians have adopted a modest, cautious view of Manitoba's economic and political future. In the province's dominant political narrative, there is little trace of the utopian visions of an ideal society embedded in the other two prairie societies. This practicality underlies the incrementalism that pervades major party platforms in Manitoba, both in terms of their policy pledges and their rhetoric. With few notable exceptions, the focus of party elites has been on convincing voters they offer a "better administration" of government, rather than a fundamentally "better way" of doing politics. This is not to say Manitoba leaders are pessimistic or defeatist, as others have implied—far from it.[75] The realism found in Manitoba elite discourse merely reflects a belief that, with its stable and diversified economy and society, a "better Manitoba" is more attainable and desirable than an unrealistically "ideal" one.

A final, related element of Manitoba "high politics" is flexible partisanship. In their campaign rhetoric, Manitoba elites have tended to promote a more fluid conceptualization of party interaction than their counterparts in Saskatchewan or Alberta. At times, the Manitoba narrative has defined politics as a "non-partisan" affair, as the efforts to create broad, formal coalitions in the early twentieth century attest; or as multi-partisan, as seen in during periods of negotiation over Manitoba's constitutional position in later decades.

Some attribute this partisan flexibility to a form of "politicophobia"—a concern over contesting controversial issues in the partisan arena for fear of dividing the province, or losing elections.[76] Others view the approach as placing provincial interests above partisan ones. Either way, this form of "stewardship"[77] has been practised by Manitoba's most successful premiers, beginning with John Norquay, who "believed that the government should represent not a party but a province, both to conciliate groups within it, and also to strengthen the province in negotiations with Ottawa."[78]

On the latter point, moderation in Manitoba has also extended to the realm of federal-provincial relations, where links between Winnipeg and Ottawa have been far friendlier than in other Western Canadian capitals.[79] Even prior to achieving provincehood, Manitoba had always held a central place in Canadian nation-building and its founding settlers, elites and institutions were drawn predominantly from Ontario. As a result of this, and its historic position as a have-not province, Manitoba has been more closely tied to central Canada than either of its Prairie neighbours.[80] Consequently, its elites have lacked the same "oppositional reflex" as found in Alberta[81] and, compared with either of its western neighbours, Manitoba election campaigns feature the lowest level of provincial patriotism.[82]

All three elements of Manitoba elite discourse speak to the same spirit of conciliation and accommodation embodied in the province's political culture. Notable breakdowns have occurred, of course. Tumultuous periods surrounding the Winnipeg General Strike, recessions in the 1970s and 1980s, and the Meech Lake Accord featured much more acrimony than so-called "normal times." But, due largely to Manitoba's political culture, these episodes have been exceptions to the rule. The province's guiding ethos, as cultivated by elites bent on stability, mitigates the intensity and duration of these "punctuations." This final point speaks to the two-way relationship between political culture and political leadership—politicians are shaped by their culture, but also help reinforce and recraft it through their rhetoric.[83]

Conclusion

Manitoba's "mediocre" image is well-earned, if undervalued or misinterpreted. Rather than being a default classification, the label reflects an ethos of "modesty" and "moderation" that is deeply ingrained in the province's political culture. These values are embodied in the province's core symbols, including its flag, logos, mottos, and slogans. They are rooted in Manitoba's early, tory-touched liberal settlement patterns and highly diversified economy, and have been tested and reinforced through several transformative events, ranging from the Riel Rebellions, to the Winnipeg General Strike and more recent debates over Manitoba's position in Confederation. This culture of modesty and moderation is not only reflected in Manitobans' attitudes toward the economy and the province's place in Confederation. It is also manifest in the behaviour of the province's elites, who have emphasized the importance of progressive centrism, pragmatism, and flexible partisanship throughout much of the province's history.

Ironically, these values of accommodation and humility are a sense of pride to many Manitobans. This suggests they are rather immodest in terms of their modesty. And not all people agree with the nature of Manitoba's political culture. To some, Manitobans' quiet confidence manifests itself in an unhealthy form of complacency. A self-image based on moderation and compassion can lead Manitobans to underestimate the challenges and discrimination that still face many members of their community. To others, Manitoba's moderate, modest predisposition is almost defeatist. By accepting the province's middling status, the culture holds Manitoba back from greater aspirations and progress as a society.

For better or worse, the story may seem familiar to students of Canadian politics, more generally. And it should. From the time of European settlement, and in many ways, Manitoba remains the "microcosm" of Canada: "it is both rural and urban, with urbanization being the trend; it contains an ethnic mosaic anchored by an internally diverse Anglo-Saxon charter group; its economic life and institutions reflect a hinterland status; and its politics are perhaps best noted for their typically Canadian moderation."[84] Manitoba is, in short, the "matrix" of Canada—

> the mould in which the disparate elements that bedevil this country could finally be shaped into an organic whole. For Manitoba is Canada in miniature. Imagine all our complex problems and potential—numbing distances, the untapped North, biculturalism and bilingualism, teeming cities and deserted farms, the need for investment capital and the concern about where it comes from—condensed and reduced to one twentieth of scale, you would have something that looks a lot like Manitoba.[85]

In these ways, Manitoba is the country's quintessentially Canadian province. Yet, this does not mean it lacks a distinctive identity. The province's modest and moderate ethos is derived directly from that image, and, as a result, its political culture is defined by its own unique symbols, sources, and consequences.

Notes

1. This chapter owes much to fascinating discussions held at the Duff Roblin Professorship Conference, co-chaired by the editors of this volume in November, 2008. In particular, the author owes much thanks to Nelson Wiseman, Gerald Friesen, David Stewart, and Paul Barber, whose insights are very much appreciated. Any errors remain the author's alone.
2. David Stewart and Keith Archer, *Quasi-Democracy? Parties and Leadership Selection in Alberta* (Vancouver: UBC Press, 2000), 13. See also Gregory P. Marchildon, "Why The Heavy Hand of History?" *The Heavy Hand of History: Interpreting Saskatchewan's Past* (Regina: Canadian Plains Research Centre, 2005), 4.
3. Rand Dyck, *Provincial Politics in Canada* (Scarborough: Prentice-Hall, 1996), 381.
4. "Manitoba has in many ways become Canada's median or average province. The 'gateway to the West,' it is centrally located and traditionally served as the location where eastern manufactured goods were exchanged for western raw materials. In modern times, the decline of railways, the advent of air travel and telecommunications, and the emergence of substantial manufacturing capacity in the West have reduced Manitoba's role in interprovincial trade. It is still the median province in terms of size, and is more advanced economically than the Atlantic region but behind the three richest provinces. It has a relatively balanced economy, not being identified with any particular industry, and is somewhat 'average' in terms of its ethnic distribution, with a medium-sized francophone community." Dyck, *Provincial Politics in Canada*, 373.
5. Chris Read, "From Scranton to Winnipeg: The Office Goes North," *CBC News Online*, 23 October 2008, http://www.cbc.ca/arts/tv/story/2008/10/23/office-winnipeg.html.

6   Douglas Marshall, "How Manitoba Turned 100 By Standing On Its Head," *Maclean's*, December 1970.
7   W.L. Morton, *Manitoba: A History* (Toronto: University of Toronto Press, 1967), viii–ix.
8   Ibid., 382.
9   David J. Elkins and Richard Simeon, "A Cause in Search of Its Effect, or What Does Political Culture Explain?" *Comparative Politics* 11 (1979): 127–128.
10   Ronald P. Formisano, "The Concept of Political Culture," *Journal of Interdisciplinary History* 31, 3 (2001): 394–396.
11   Russell Dalton, "The Decline of Party Identifications" in *Parties Without Partisans: Political Change in Advanced Industrial Democracies*, ed. R.J. Dalton and M.P Wattenberg (Oxford: Oxford University Press, 2000), 914.
12   Gabriel Almond, "Comparative Political Systems," *Journal of Politics* 18 (1956): 391–409. To some, political culture is little more than a popular (or dominant) political ideology—one shared by, or at least governing the political life of, an entire community. See Allan Kornberg, William Mishler and Harold D. Clarke, *Representative Democracy in the Canadian Provinces* (Scarborough: Prentice-Hall, 1982), 53–58. The relationship between political culture and ideology is more complicated, however. While there may be parallels between a particular ideology and a given political culture, the two concepts are not synonymous. "From the outset, political culture was intended as a broader concept with wider application than ideology. Political culture involves the study of all segments of society, including members of the general public whose ideas about politics are insufficiently coherent and programmatic to be called ideological. Moreover a single political culture could comprise several ideologies." David V.J. Bell, "Political Culture in Canada," in *Canadian Politics and the 21st Century*, ed. M. Whittington and G. Williams (Scarborough: Nelson, 2000), 279.

      Nelson Wiseman captures the primary distinction between cultures and ideologies. "Both deal with fundamental values and are related, but they are also fundamentally different. Culture is an ordered system of symbols; ideology is an ordering of symbolic terms. 'Left' and 'right,' conservatism and liberalism, are shorthand ideological categorizations. Ideologies or political philosophies may be defined, dissected and debated at a metaphysical level without reference to a specific group, society or nation. Culture is no less a mental construct than is ideology. It, however, cannot be explored solely on a theoretical plane, for it refers to real and specific groups, societies or nations." Nelson Wiseman, "Social Democracy in the Neo-Conservative Age: The Politics of Manitoba and Saskatchewan," in *Canada: The State of the Federation 2001*, ed. H. Telford and H. Lazar (Kingston: Institute of Intergovernmental Relations, 2002), 217; Nelson Wiseman, *In Search of Canadian Political Culture* (Vancouver: UBC Press, 2007), 13–14.
13   Elkins and Simeon, "*A Cause in Search of Its Effect.*"
14   Wiseman, *In Search of Canadian Political Culture*, 14.
15   Stephen Chilton, "Defining Political Culture," *The Western Political Quarterly* 41, 3 (1988): 428.
16   See Ailsa Henderson, "Regional Political Cultures," *Canadian Journal of Political Science* 37, 3 (2004):
17   See Gunnar Myrdal, *An American Dilemma: The Negro Problem in America*, vol. 1 (New York: Harper and Row, 1969).
18   Chilton, "Defining Political Culture," 429–430. See also Myrdal, *An American Dilemma*.
19   Clifford Geertz, "Ideology as a Culture System," *Ideology and Discontent*, ed. D.E. Apter (New York: The Free Press, 1964); Geertz, *The Interpretation of Cultures* (New York: Basic Books, 1973). Dittmer suggests political culture lay in the "system of political symbols," which, itself, "nests within a more inclusive system that we might term 'political

communication.'" Lowell Dittmer, "Political Culture and Political Symbolism: Towards a Theoretical Synthesis," *World Politics* 29 (1977), 566. For other examples, see Elisabeth Jean Wood, *Insurgent Collective Action and Civil War in El Salvador* (Cambridge: Cambridge University Press, 2003); James C. Scott, *Weapons of the Weak* (New Haven: Yale University Press, 1985), 28–47.

20   James Johnson, "Conceptual Problems as Obstacles to Progress in Political Science," *Journal of Theoretical Politics* 15, 1 (2003): 99.
21   See Chilton, "Defining Political Culture," 436; Robert Putnam, *Bowling Alone: The Collapse and Revival of American Community* (New York: Simon and Schuster, 2000).
22   Gerald Friesen, *The West: Regional Ambitions, National Debates, Global Age* (Toronto: Penguin Group/McGill Institute, 1999), 185.
23   Sheri Berman, "Ideas, Norms, and Culture in Political Analysis: Review Article," *Comparative Politics* 33, 2 (2001): 234.
24   *O Canada* did not become Canada's official national anthem until 1980, and the official English translation of the song was not written until 1908. Any reference to the terms "glorious and free" must have been adopted from popular versions of the song that were in circulation to that point.
25   Travel Manitoba, Manitoba Quick Facts—Official Emblems, http://www.travelmanitoba.com/default.asp?page=134&node=589&menu=436.
26   Canadian Heritage, Ceremonial and Canadian Symbols Promotion—The Symbols of Canada—Tartans, http://www.pch.gc.ca/progs/cpsc-ccsp/sc-cs/06_e.cfm.
27   For the record, many alternative flag designs included British symbols alongside French (e.g., the fleur-de-lis) or Canadian (e.g., the maple leaf) symbols.
28   Alaistair B. Fraser, "A Canadian Flag for Canada," *Journal of Canadian Studies* 25 (1991): 64–80.
29   In particular, some interpret the new flag as a partisan protest by Manitoba Progressive Conservatives, following Diefenbaker's defeat at the hands of the Pearson Liberals in Parliament over the national flag.
30   In 1960, prior to the national flag debate, British Columbia adopted its flag, which incorporates the Union Jack.
31   Prior to 1976, the provincial licence plate featured the slogans "100,000 Lakes" and "Sunny Manitoba," or featured a bison icon.
32   Morton, *Manitoba: A History*, viii–ix.
33   Aftab A. Mufti, "Restorational Health Monitoring of Manitoba's Golden Boy," *Canadian Journal of Civil Engineering* 30 (2003): 1123–1132.
34   While the lyrics for this song are widely published, its author is unknown.
35   Manitoba Promotional Council, *Manitoba's New Image*, 2008 (http://www.mbpromotion.ca/spirited_energy_message.php) and Manitoba Promotional Council, *Why Change Manitoba's Image?* 2008 (http://www.mbpromotion.ca/spirited_energy_why_brand.php). The effort was coordinated by the Premier's Economic Advisory Council (PEAC).
36   Manitoba Promotional Council.
37   Ibid.
38   Ibid.
39   Alexander Motyl, "Imagined Communities, Rational Choosers, Invented Ethnies," *Comparative Politics* 34, 2 (2002): 233–250.
40   Benedict Anderson, *Imagined Communities: Reflections on the Origin and Spread of Nationalism* (London and New Haven: Verso, 1991).
41   Formisano, "The Concept of Political Culture," 408.

42 Dale Eisler, *False Expectations: Politics and the Pursuit of the Saskatchewan Myth* (Regina: Canadian Plains Research Centre, 2006).

43 See Louis Hartz, *The Founding of New Societies* (New York: Harcourt, Brace and Jovavich, 1964). Space does not permit a detailed appraisal of fragment theory. Numerous scholars have criticized the model's applicability to the Canadian context. See H.D. Forbes, "Hartz-Horowitz Theory at Twenty: Nationalism, Toryism and Socialism in Canada and the United States," *Canadian Journal of Economics and Political Science* 20, 2 (1987): 287–315; Janet Ajzenstat and Peter J. Smith, "The 'Tory Touch' Thesis: Bad History, Poor Political Science," in *Crosscurrents*, ed. M. Charlton and P. Barker, 5th ed. (Scarborough: Nelson, 1998); Rod Preece, "The Myth of the Red Tory," *Canadian Journal of Political and Social Theory* 1, 2 (1980): 3–28; Kenneth C. Dewar, "Toryism and Public Ownership in Canada: A Comment," *Canadian Historical Review* 64, 3 (1983): 404–419; David V.J. Bell and Lorne Tepperman, *The Roots of Disunity: A Look at Canadian Political Culture* (Toronto: McClelland and Stewart, 1979); Carol Wilton, *Popular Politics and Political Culture in Upper Canada* (Montreal: McGill-Queen's University Press, 2000); Ian Stewart, "All The King's Horses: The Study of Canadian Political Culture," in *Canadian Politics*, ed. J.P. Bickerton and A.-G. Gagnon (Peterborough: Broadview Press, 1994). Others have employed the theory to explain aspects of Canadian political culture; for example, see Christian Ruprecht, "The Tory Fragment in Canada: Endangered Species?" *Canadian Journal of Political Science* 36, 2 (2003): 401–416; Nelson Wiseman, "Provincial Political Cultures," in *Provinces: Canadian Provincial Politics*, ed. C. Dunn, 2nd ed. (Peterborough: Broadview Press, 2006) and Gad Horowitz, "Conservatism, Liberalism and Socialism in Canada: An Interpretation," *Canadian Journal of Economics and Political Science* 32, 2 (1966): 143–171.

44 John Ralston Saul, *A Fair Country* (New York: Viking Press, 2008).

45 See Gordon Stewart, "The Beginning of Politics in Canada," *Canadian Parties in Transition*, A.-G. Gagnon and A.B. Tanguay, eds., 3rd Edition (Scarborough: Nelson, 2007).

46 Nelson Wiseman, *Social Democracy in Manitoba: A History of the CCF-NDP* (Winnipeg: University of Manitoba Press, 1983), 3–5.

47 Dyck, *Provincial Politics in Canada*, 381.

48 See also Walter D. Young, *Democracy and Discontent*, 2nd ed. (Toronto: McGraw-Hill Ryerson, 1978), 5; J.E. Rea, "The Roots of Prairie History," in *Prairie Perspectives*, ed. D.P. Gagan (Toronto: Holt, Rinehart and Winston, 1969); Morton, *Manitoba: A History*, viii.

49 Grounded in the semi-feudal, traditionalist tendencies of the country's Loyalist heritage, toryism represents Canada's "old right." As a unique mixture of seemingly disparate philosophical elements, toryism has attracted criticism as being non-ideological, (Forbes, "Hartz-Horowitz at Twenty"), politically expedient (Roger Gibbins and Neil Nevitte, "Canadian Political Ideology: A Comparative Analysis," *Canadian Journal of Political Science*, 18 [1985], 577–598), unscientific (Ajzenstat and Smith, "The 'Tory Touch' Thesis,'"), and even mythical (Preece, "The Myth of the Red Tory"). To some critics, for all its usage in political circles, mass media, popular culture, and academia, the term remains too vaguely defined (Rod Preece, "The Anglo-Saxon Conservative Tradition," *Canadian Journal of Political Science* 13, 1 [1980]: 3–32; Kenneth Dewar, "Toryism and Public Ownership in Canada." Despite these criticisms, the principles of toryism do conform to the characteristics of ideology employed in the present analysis. Granted, it may be a "recessive strain" in Canadian political ideology (see William Christian and Colin Campbell, *Political Parties and Ideologies in Canada*, 3rd ed. [Toronto: McGraw-Hill Ryerson, 1990], 9; Ian Stewart, "All The King's Horses," 78–80), but even its harshest critics have noted the continued resonance of toryism as a key theme in Canadian politics. Charles Taylor, *Radical Tories: The Conservative Tradition in Canada* (Toronto: Anansi Press, 1982), 115. See also Forbes, "Hartz-Horowitz at Twenty," 305; Ajzenstat and Smith 1998, 84.

50 This tory-touched fragment not only helps to explain the long-term survival of the Progressive Conservative Party in Manitoba. It suggests why socialism found a toehold in Manitoba in the form of the Independent Labour Party, CCF and, most recently, the NDP. According to fragment theory, when combined with the reform-minded philosophy of liberalism, the organic sense of community embodied in toryism produces an environment conducive to socialism. See Hartz, *The Founding of New Societies* 1964; Horowitz, *Conservatism, Liberalism and Socialism in Canada*; James McAllister, *The Government of Edward Schreyer* (Kingston: McGill-Queen's University Press, 1984), 90–93. British labourites, whose brand of Fabian socialism found a sympathetic ear among the province's working class population, seized this opportunity, establishing the partisan foundations for the modern New Democratic Party. Wiseman, *Social Democracy in Manitoba*, 4–9. In short, "Manitoba had enough Ontario in it to have sustained the only provincial Conservative party west of Ontario that has never collapsed. But it also had enough of modern Britain and Continental Europe to provide CCFer J.S. Woodsworth and Communist leader W.A. Kardash with parliamentary seats." Wiseman, *Social Democracy in Manitoba*, 149.

51 Gabriel Almond and G. Bingham Powell Jr., *Comparative Politics: A Developmental Approach* (Boston: Little, Brown and Co., 1966), 65. Seymour Martin Lipset is another pioneer of the formative events approach. His comparison of political cultures in Canada and the United States traces their origins to the American Revolutionary War. See Seymour Martin Lipset, *Revolution and Counterrevolution* (New York: Basic Books, 1968) and Seymour Martin Lipset, *Continental Divide: The Values and Institutions of the United States and Canada* (New York: Routledge, 1990).

52 Gerald Friesen, *River Road: Essays on Manitoba and Prairie History* (Winnipeg: University of Manitoba Press, 1996). 29. The phrase "polity on the edge," used by the authors to describe Canadian politics, in general, is borrowed from Harold Clarke et al., *A Polity on the Edge: Canada and the Politics of Fragmentation* (Peterborough: Broadview Press, 2000).

53 Wiseman, *Social Democracy in Manitoba*,: 8–9; Nelson Wiseman and K. Wayne Taylor, "Class and Ethnic Voting in Winnipeg during the Cold War," *Canadian Review of Sociology and Anthropology*, 16:1 (1979), 62. See also: Morton, *Manitoba: A History*, 362–372 and McAllister, *The Government of Edward Schreyer*, 89-90).

54 The opening of the Panama Canal in 1914 "sap[ped] the traffic that fed [Winnipeg's growth]," elevating Vancouver as the primary gateway to the West. Morton, *Manitoba: A History*, 308.

55 This contrasts with Alberta, for instance, whose agricultural and petroleum industries have contributed to the province's right-leaning political climate. The province's farmers and ranchers have been commercially oriented, independent commodity producers whose position within the Canadian economy and global markets has made them as supportive of free markets as their counterparts in the natural resource sector. Lewis G. Thomas, "Alberta 1905–1980: The Uneasy Society," in *The New Provinces: Alberta and Saskatchewan*, H. Palmer and D. Smith, eds. (Vancouver: Tantalus Research Limited, 1980), 28. Conversely, the pre-eminence of wheat in Saskatchewan has tended to isolate its farmers by creating a sense of uncertainty amid unpredictable climatic and international economic forces. See also John C. Courtney and David E. Smith, "Saskatchewan: Parties in a Politically Competitive Province," in *Canadian Provincial Politics*, ed. M. Robin (Scarborough: Prentice-Hall, 1972), 312–313; David E. Smith, "Saskatchewan Speaks: Public Documents and the Study of Provincial Politics," *Government Publications Review*, 20 (1993): 24; Seymour Martin Lipset, *Agrarian Socialism: The Cooperative Commonwealth Federation in Saskatchewan* (Garden City, NY: Doubleday, 1968), 47; Christopher Dunn and David Laycock, "Saskatchewan: Innovation and Competition in the Agricultural Heartland," in *The Provincial State: Politics in Canada's Provinces and Territories*, ed. Keith Brownsey and Michael Howlett (Mississauga: Copp Clark Pittman,

1992), 208–212. Despite diversification in recent decades, Saskatchewan's continued reliance on natural resources has perpetuated the "boom and bust" nature of its political economy. Dunn and Laycock, "Saskatchewan," 212–216; Ken Rasmussen, "Saskatchewan: From Entreprenurial to Embedded State," in *The Provincial State in Canada*, 241. For these reasons, Saskatchewan's economic environment has been most conducive to the collectivist thinking and cooperative endeavours at the heart of social democracy. See also Courtney and Smith, "Saskatchewan: Parties in a Politically Competitive Province," 311–313; Vernon Fowke, *The National Policy and the Wheat Economy* (Toronto: University of Toronto Press, 1946); Dunn and Laycock, "Saskatchewan," 208–212; Friesen, *The West*, 101–105.

56   Dyck, *Provincial Politics in Canada*, 374. Brett Gartner describes Manitoba's economy as featuring "Consistent Performance," and Todd Hirsch notes that, over the past decade, it has been "Holding Steady." See Brett Gartner, *Consistent Performance: Manitoba's Economic Profile and Forecast* (Calgary: Canada West Foundation, 2006) and Todd Hirsch, *Holding Steady: Manitoba's Economic Profile and Forecast* (Calgary: Canada West Foundation, 2007).

57   Wiseman, *In Search of Political Culture*, 217. See also W.L. Morton, "The Bias of Prairie Politics," in *Riel to Reform: A History of Protest in Western Canada*, ed. G. Melnyk (Saskatoon: Fifth House Publishers, 17); Dunn and Laycock, "Saskatchewan," 225).

58   Gabriel Almond and Sidney Verba, *The Civic Culture: Political Attitudes and Democracy in Five Nations* (Princeton: Princeton University Press, 1963), 10.

59   Almond and Verba, *The Civic Culture*, 13. It is crucial to note that Almond and Verba (and their many followers in the psycho-cultural school) consider political culture to *be* these attitudes. To them, culture is simply an aggregation, or average, of these individuals' beliefs and opinions. I take a theoretically different approach. In this chapter, we consider individual attitudes to be *consequences—not* indicators—of political culture. This is done for several reasons. First, as Durkheim argued, culture is more than simply an aggregation of individual behaviours. Rather, it lies in the broader social structure—what he terms the "collective conscience" of a society, or the "repository of common sentiments, a well-spring from which individual conscience draws its moral sustenance. Emile Durkheim, *Suicide: A Study in Sociology*, (New York: Free Press, 1965 [1897]), 16. By the same token, a community's culture—by definition, its *shared* values and norms—is more than a simple aggregation of individuals' beliefs. In technical terms, Almond and Verba fall victim to what is known as "false aggregation" or "the reverse ecological fallacy. Just as we cannot use macro-level data (e.g., census statistics) to make valid inferences about micro-level actors (e.g., individual residents of a census district), we cannot do the reverse. In short, as Johnson argues, analysts "gain little by treating the distribution of 'orientations' among a population as 'political culture' rather than, for example, simply as a 'mass belief system' or, more prosaically still, as 'public opinion.'" Johnson, "Conceptual Problems as Obstacles to Progress in Political Science," 99.

Second, political culture is less transitory than public opinion. Just as descriptions of the weather offer us only limited glimpses into the climate of a particular community, one-off surveys of individual residents offer us only a "snapshot" of a community's beliefs and orientations. Wiseman concurs, noting that the definition of 'culture' as an aggregation of individual attitudes misconstrues the term's true meaning, which "is rooted in a specific group or nation and is cross-generational. It does not come and go like fashion. It is relatively stable and enduring. Studies purporting to deal with political culture, therefore, must strive to bring an historic, dynamic perspective to their analysis." Nelson Wiseman, "The Use, Misuse and Abuse of the National Election Studies," *Journal of Canadian Studies* 21, 1 (1986): 31. Moreover, he notes, "'Political culture,' however defined, persists over a substantial period of time: hence the power and significance of the concept. Do variables such as 'efficacy' and 'trust' meet this test? The evidence suggests not." Wiseman, "The Use, Misuse and Abuse of the National Election Studies," 32–33.

For these reasons, individual attitudes are considered consequences, rather than indicators, of (group) culture. This is not to say that Almond and Verba's approach is useless in the study of political culture. While it may be misused as an indicator of political culture, their methodology is very valuable in terms of measuring the *effects* of political culture on individual attitudes.

60   Aside from a pair of diligent polling firms—Probe Research Inc. and NRG (formerly Western Opinion Research)—and an outstanding think tank in the Canada West Foundation, few surveys are conducted with enough consistency and significant sample sizes to allow for a close examination of Manitoba political attitudes (a notable exception is Adams, *Politics in Manitoba*, which draws upon Probe Research's polling data). The Canadian Election Study incurs just such a shortcoming. With sample sizes of just over 200 respondents in Manitoba, these surveys are difficult platforms from which to judge Manitoba political attitudes. For the pitfalls of this approach, see Wiseman, "The Use, Misuse and Abuse of the National Election Studies."

61   Brett Gartner, *State of the West 2008* (Calgary: Canada West Foundation, 2008). It should be noted, however, that since it was administered in January and February 2008, the survey was conducted prior to the global economic downturn.

62   Gartner, *State of the West 2008*, 17. For a similar assessment, see Probe Research Inc., *Economic Outlook and Job Security in Manitoba* (Winnipeg: Probe Research, 2008).

63   Loleen Berdahl, *Regional Distinctions: An Analysis of the Looking West 2004 Survey* (Calgary: Canada West Foundation, 2004), 13.

64   Probe Research Inc. *Public Attitudes on NHL Hockey in Winnipeg* (Winnipeg: Probe Research Inc., 2007). According to the poll, 47 percent of Manitoba adults were in favour, 6 percent were unsure, and 6 percent responded "it depends."

65   Berdahl, *Regional Distinctions*, 9.

66   Ibid.

67   Ibid., 8.

68   Ibid., 9.

69   Peter R. Sinclair, *Populism in Alberta and Saskatchewan: A comparative analysis of Social Credit and the Cooperative Commonwealth Confederation* (Edinburgh, University of Edinburgh, 1972); David E. Smith, "A Comparison of Prairie Political Development in Alberta and Saskatchewan." See also Ken Andrews, "'Progressive' Counterparts of the CCF: Social Credit and the Conservative Party in Saskatchewan, 1935–1938," *Journal of Canadian Studies* 17, 3 (1982): 58–74; R.T. Naylor and G. Teeple, "The Ideological Foundations of Social Democracy and Social Credit," *Capitalism and the National Question in Canada*, ed. G. Teeple (Toronto: University of Toronto Press, 1972); Ruth Woolsey Flores, *Alberta and Saskatchewan: A Contrast in Political Participation* (University of Alberta, Edmonton, 1983); Wiseman, *In Search of Political Culture*, 2007.

70   Bell, "Political Culture in Canada," 277. Kathryn Sikkink concurs, noting, "New ideas do not enter an ideological vacuum. They are inserted into a political space already occupied by historically formed ideologies. Whether or not consolidation occurs often depends on the degree to which the new model fits with existing ideologies." Sikkink, *Ideas and Institutions: Developmentalism in Argentina and Brazil* (Ithaca: Cornell University Press, 1991), 2. As Hall suggests, ideas "do not acquire political force independently of the constellation of institutions and interests already present there." Peter Hall, "Conclusion," in *The Political Power of Economic Ideas*, ed. P.A. Hall (Princeton: Princeton University Press, 1989), 390. To be adopted as codes, therefore, ideologies must work within the parameters of their host culture. Lipset, *Revolution and Counterrevolution*, 190–191. Also see Berman, "Ideas, Norms and Culture in Political Analysis," 236.

71   Timothy O.E. Lang, "Liberals in Manitoba: Provincial Decline and Resurgence" (M.A. thesis, University of Manitoba, 1991), 92.

72   See Jared Wesley, "The Collective Centre: Social Democracy and Red Tory Politics in Manitoba," paper presented at the Canadian Science Association Annual Meeting, Toronto, 2006, and Jared Wesley, "In Search of Brokerage and Responsibility: Party Politics in Manitoba," *Canadian Journal of Political Science* 42, 1 (2009): 211–236.
73   Morton, *Manitoba: A History*, 335.
74   See Bradford J. Rennie, *Alberta Premiers of the 20th Century* (Regina: Canadian Plains Research Centre, 2004); Gordon Barnhart, ed., *Saskatchewan Premiers of the 20th Century* (Regina: Canadian Plains Research Centre, 2004); Barry Ferguson, ed. *Manitoba Premiers of the 20th Century* (Regina: Canadian Plains Research Centre, forthcoming).
75   Gerald Friesen alludes to an "atmosphere of negativism" that has pervaded Manitoba since its gradual decline as the Gateway to the West began in the early-20th century. Friesen, *The West*, 127.
76   K.W. Taylor and Nelson Wiseman, "Class and Ethnic Voting in Winnipeg: The Case of 1941," *Canadian Review of Sociology and Anthropólogy* 14, 2 (1977): 176. Much like Canada as a whole, the province's politics have been defined more by the number of issues left in abeyance than by the depth of its cleavages. As Thomas (1997) said of federal politics, Manitobans and their elites have deliberately avoided or obscured issues that may lead to disunity within the community. As a result, divisive issues are left unresolved, producing a state of "unsettled settlement" on topics like language, ethnicity, religion, ideology, class, and the urban-rural divide.
77   The term "stewardship" is borrowed, in part, from Morton's description of the Liberal/Liberal-Progressive approach toward public ownership of hydro-electricity. Morton, *Manitoba: A History*, 459–460.
78   Ibid., 197.
79   See Paul G. Thomas, "Manitoba: Stuck in the Middle," in *Canada: The State of the Federation 1989*, ed. R.L. Watts and D.M. Brown (Kingston: Institute for Intergovernmental Affairs, 1989) and Paul G. Thomas, "Leading from the Middle: Manitoba's Role in the Intergovernmental Arena," *Canadian Political Science Review* 2, 3 (2008): 29–51.
80   Morton, *Manitoba: A History*, 420–421 and 470–471.
81   Friesen, *The New West*, 9.
82   Jared Wesley, *Solving the Prairie Paradox: Codes and Party Politics in Alberta, Saskatchewan and Manitoba* (Vancouver: UBC Press, forthcoming). This moderation may be a reflection or a source of the many examples of cross-level-jumping by Manitoba party elites. A number of Manitoba politicians have made careers at both the federal and provincial level. While the following list is by no means exhaustive, prominent examples of level-jumping among Manitoba politicians include: Conservatives Joy Smith, Rick Borotsik, Vic Toews, and Duff Roblin; Liberals T.C. Norris, Stuart Garson, Jon Gerrard, Gil Molgat, Lloyd Axworthy, Sharon Carstairs, and Reg Alcock; and New Democrats Bill Blaikie, Jim Maloway, Judy Wasylycia-Leis, and Ed Schreyer. Others have crossed not only levels, but party lines, most notably John Bracken.
83   Jared Wesley, "Code Politics and the Prairie Paradox: Party Competition in Alberta, Saskatchewan and Manitoba," paper presented at the Prairie Provinces Political Science Association Annual Meeting, Regina, 2008.
84   Wiseman, *Social Democracy in Manitoba*, 148.
85   Marshall, "How Manitoba Turned 100 By Standing On Its Head."

PART TWO
PARTIES AND ELECTIONS

Political parties articulate and establish the parameters for how public debates are carried out in a democratic society. Though there were no provincial parties represented in the first Manitoba Legislature, groups of politicians have come together into various factions to contest elections in an organized and cohesive fashion, with their respective fortunes and the dynamics of their competition in constant flux throughout the twentieth century and into the twenty-first.

Since the 1950s, three parties have been the predominant competitors in provincial elections—the New Democratic Party, the Progressive Conservative Party, and the Liberal Party. In this section, the histories, current status, and future projections for each of these three parties are considered by Nelson Wiseman (Chapter 3, regarding the NDP), Kelly Saunders (Chapter 4, regarding the PCs), and Paul Barber (Chapter 5, regarding the Liberals). Though each of these chapters evaluates the fortunes of each party on its own, obviously the contours of party competition are affected by the internal dynamics within each of these groups as well as the external pressures that are brought to bear on each party. In Chapter 6, Christopher Adams analyzes in greater depth the rises and falls in party support since the 1950s and pinpoints moments when voter preferences permanently "realigned" or deviated from the existing norms of party competition.

The Success of the New Democratic Party[1]

Nelson Wiseman

This chapter peers at the Manitoba New Democratic Party through the prisms of leadership, performance, ideology, and policy. It traces the party's development, membership, and changing bases of support. It probes the interplay of leader, party, and society, of biography and history. To understand the party, its ideas, and its leaders requires an appreciation of Manitoba's ever-evolving political sociology.

The provincial NDP's meteoric rise to power came on 25 June 1969, exactly fifty years to the day after the Winnipeg General Strike ended. The party's 1969 victory was remarkable because the NDP and its predecessor parties—the Independent Labor Party (1920–1936) and then the Co-operative Commonwealth Federation (CCF)—had never been more than third parties in the Manitoba Legislature. Within a few short years of the NDP's creation, however, the party catapulted into government and moved from the periphery to the centre of provincial power and from the margins into the mainstream of provincial society. The party has held office in every decade since its initial election, in twenty-seven of the last forty-one years, winning seven of eleven elections. This raises the question: What accounts for the NDP's success?

Consciously constructed as a mass party, it is principle, philosophy, and the membership that ostensibly drive the NDP rather than opportunism, expedience, and leaders. A major element in the NDP's successes and setbacks, however, has been its leaders' personal qualities. It has also benefited from the missteps of the other parties and the pratfalls of their leaders. Social and institutional forces have also shaped the party's fortunes. Ethnic integration, intermarriage, assimilation, and modernization transformed the provincial political culture during the twentieth century in directions favouring the NDP. More recently, the party has commanded a large, middle-aged, middle-to-upper class, urban support base. Institutionally, the party profited from periodic changes to the electoral map, the polarizing effects of a first-past-the-post electoral system, and public expectations of government in a "have-not" province.

Flagging CCF federal electoral fortunes—evident in 1958 with the CCF shut out in Manitoba for the first time—propelled the NDP's creation in 1961. Like the CCF, the federal NDP is a federation of provincial parties so it was critical to the new party's architects that the provincial CCFs dissolve and reconstitute themselves as provincial NDPs. In light of the Manitoba NDP's subsequent success, it is ironic that more opposition to the NDP project arose in Manitoba CCF circles than in any other province.[2]

Notwithstanding the effort to launch a "new party,"[3] the NDP's first federal convention evidenced partisan continuity and little "newness": no more than five of the Manitoba delegates would have been ineligible to attend had it been another CCF convention.[4] What was seemingly new about the NDP was that it represented a formal political alliance of the CCF and the Canadian Labour Congress and its provincial affiliates, in this case, the Manitoba Federation of Labour (MFL). However, most of Manitoba's union delegates at both founding federal and provincial NDP conventions had been CCF members and regular attendees at CCF conventions. Moreover, the CCF had provided for affiliated unions as well. Yet another sign of continuity was leadership: Russ Paulley, a member of the ILP's youth wing[5] and the last Manitoba CCF leader, became the NDP's first leader.

Despite the social democratic party's makeover, the fledgling provincial NDP's 1962 electoral debut was unimpressive; floundering, it garnered fewer seats and votes than the CCF had won in the 1958 and 1959 elections. By the 1960s, social democrats were struggling to differentiate themselves from the welfare liberals in the federal Liberal Party of Lester Pearson and Pierre Trudeau and from provincial "red tory" Conservatives such as Duff Roblin and George Johnson. In 1959, a prominent CCFer summed up the dilemma, which soon also confronted the federal NDP in Ottawa:

> Look at our position. The Roblin [federally, read: Pearson] government is putting in effect good legislation. The people want it: they need it, and they should have it. Are we going to defeat them and face the charge that we obstructed the very things we have been calling for over the years?

The only thing we can say is that they are not doing enough...On the other hand, we're supposed to be socialists. We believe in an entirely different system. We're supposed to want to change the whole order of things, not just vote for this improvement here and that one there.[6]

What changed in Manitoba in the late 1960s was a dramatic lurch to the right by the NDP's opponents. The Liberals' choice of a new leader, Bobby Bend—a former cabinet minister during the less-than-progressive Liberal-Progressive era—proved a boon to the NDP. Combined with the Progressive Conservatives' rightward shift in 1967 under Walter Weir after Roblin's departure, the ideological stage was set for an NDP upsurge. In confirmation of partisan repositioning, the consensus in a survey of Liberals who deserted their party in 1969 was that the NDP "was doing what the Liberals ought to be doing."[7] The party also benefited from a new regime for redistributing seats. It replaced a system based on the legal requirement that the votes of four rural voters equal the weight of seven urban ones, and edged closer to the principle of equality, boosting the urban-anchored NDP.

The media, too, helped the NDP: they generated an unprecedented level of public awareness of the party by televising for the first time its leadership convention, held in the midst of the election campaign. Even the *Winnipeg Free Press*, the NDP's nemesis, weighed in by endorsing Ed Schreyer for party leader.[8] The upshot was that the NDP displaced the Liberals as a major party. In moving toward the centre of the ideological spectrum under Schreyer, the NDP appeared to growing numbers of Manitobans as having entered the political mainstream. The NDP's ascent realigned and polarized the party system. The NDP and the Progressive Conservatives, secondary forces between the First World War and the Cold War, became its major protagonists. The Liberals suffered the NDP's earlier handicap as a third party in a single member plurality electoral system: the perception by many that a vote for them was "wasted."

The NDP's socio-geographic bases of support expanded dramatically. Essentially a party of native-born Manitobans, the NDP looked quite different than the ILP-CCF—a party led and supported by British-born immigrants concentrated in central and north Winnipeg.[9] Under Schreyer, the NDP became more representative of the province's people and places. Contrast, for example, Winnipeg's phalanx of twenty ILP-CCF aldermen elected between 1920 and 1945—the overwhelming majority of whom were British-born with nary a Winnipeg native or anyone of Ukrainian, Polish, or German descent[10]—with NDP cabinets of later decades. In 1969, for the first time in provincial history, Anglo-Saxons became a minority in the cabinet. By the time Schreyer's government left office, the cabinet—which contained unprecedented numbers of Unitarians, Catholics, and

Jews—had six Ukrainians, two Franco-Manitobans, a Métis, a Dutchman, and a German alongside six Anglo-Saxons.

Premiers

As a mass party, the NDP tenders its platforms as the democratic expression of its members' preferences as determined at annual conventions. Party leaders are, in principle, merely the party's spokespersons. In contrast, the Conservatives and Liberals, as cadre parties,[11] revolve around their leaders and their coteries. Their partisans look to them as shepherds and potential scapegoats. In practice, the NDP marketed Schreyer's and Gary Doer's qualities as major assets and favourably contrasted them with those of their opponents. An example is the NDP's 1977 campaign slogan, "Leadership you can trust." The party has had only four leaders since 1969 and each has served as premier. Durability of NDP leadership contrasts with the relative instability of Liberal and Conservative leadership. The Liberals contested the six elections between 1966 and 1986 under six different leaders. The Conservatives have had eight leaders, including an interim leader, since the mid-1960s. The NDP premiers, however, have reflected different currents in party thinking and their philosophical orientations and legacies have been distinctive. Each has also had a different relationship to the party.

Schreyer came closest to inspiring a personality cult. He appeared charismatic in comparison with Weir and Bend in 1969. Elected as a twenty-two-year-old CCF MLA, he had a "rural touch," a quality that escaped previous CCF-NDP leaders.[12] He proved to be the legislature's most independent MLA, often voting against his party. Evoking glee and awe in party circles, Schreyer appeared invincible at the polls despite his quiet, shy, introverted personality and dull speaking style. His philosophy was a blend of American New Deal liberalism and Scandinavian-style social democracy. He disavowed Marx but embraced Methodism's social ethic of a fairer distribution of wealth in the cause of man's spiritual betterment.[13] He also wanted a more "pragmatic party" with "more centrists." He was the sole respondent in a 1966 survey of 70 journalists, intellectuals, and politicians who viewed the prospect of a federal Liberal-NDP merger with equanimity.[14] He considered, but declined, overtures from Trudeau's Liberals to join them in 1968 although, unlike the federal NDP, he later endorsed Trudeau's invocation of the War Measures Act and wage-and-price controls.

A large part of Schreyer's appeal was his ability to combine a circumspect, cautious, and rural outlook with a reformist, progressive, urban image. He held three university degrees, taught political science, and was the son-in-law of CCF MP Jake Schulz, the Bessarabian-born founder of the Manitoba Farmers Union, a leftist organization that arose to compete with the Manitoba Federation of Agriculture, dominated by Anglo-Saxons of Ontarian origin "who were almost Liberal to the core."[15] A German Catholic who could communicate in four languages, Schreyer broke the Anglo-Saxon Protestant mould of provincial leadership at a time when Manitoba's ethnic minorities were ascending the socio-economic ladder. He was the only party figure who was capable of mustering the support the NDP captured in 1969 because, as David Orlikow put it, he was a "leader who personifies in himself, sort of, Manitoba."[16] "Schreyer," wrote James McAllister, "was the perfect candidate for the moment," and he won over former Liberals, Conservatives, and even Social Crediters.[17]

In power for 100 months, Schreyer exhibited shrewd political instincts in masterfully managing his caucus, his party, and public opinion. He nimbly converted a shaky minority government into a majority by wooing a Liberal MLA and scoring two byelection victories. The party "delivered itself into the hands of one man" according to an observer at its 1972 convention.[18] A 1973 survey showed Conservative and Liberal supporters preferred Schreyer as premier, their most common criticism of him being that he was "in the wrong party."[19] In 1974, *Time* magazine designated him as one of the "150 Faces for the Future"[20] and, in 1977, "[t]here were times on the campaign trail," reported a journalist, "when the premier was greeted almost as a figure of royalty."[21] Two years later, at Trudeau's invitation, he became Governor General. Schreyer's return to politics in the 2006 federal election revealed, again, societal and generational change since his political heyday; he appeared as a faint echo of the past to a younger electorate and lost.

Howard Pawley, like Schreyer, had been an active CCFer and also attended United College, the womb of Canada's social gospel tradition. The son of a CCF candidate, he married a Schreyer: Ed's cousin. Unlike Schreyer, however, Pawley ran and lost in five elections before 1969. While Schreyer accepted the 1956 reformulation of social democratic thinking known as the Winnipeg Declaration,[22] Pawley opposed it. He also led strenuous resistance to the CCF's dissolution and the New Party movement. His concerns were that union influence in the NDP would be excessive and would dilute the CCF's socialism. "I didn't think it would work. Philosophically, I thought it was wrong."[23] No one would have thought in 1969 that the lacklustre Pawley—sworn in as the last and most junior cabinet minister—would become Schreyer's successor a decade later. From his position in Schreyer's government, however, Pawley successfully piloted the NDP's most celebrated and bitterly contested bill, the creation of public automobile insurance (Autopac). It led to thousands of insurance agents and their sympathizers marching on the legislature, many waving signs reading "Pawley's Folly" and packing the legislative gallery for weeks. Autopac proved successful and immensely popular, boosting Pawley's stature.

Upon Schreyer's departure, Pawley won the caucus leadership by a narrow plurality (ten to eight), and a convention subsequently confirmed him as party leader, defeating two opponents. While Schreyer's coattails brought the NDP to power, the NDP's coattails elevated Pawley to the premiership. Unlike Schreyer, Pawley consistently trailed his party in the polls. He mismanaged and squandered a majority government and was defeated in a confidence vote on a budgetary matter in 1988 after two MLAs deserted him. One MLA left the caucus after Pawley ignored his dreams of a cabinet post; the other felt shabbily treated after a senior Pawley aide challenged his re-nomination and he was demoted from the speakership of the legislature. The upshot was the only instance in Canadian history of a majority government defeated by a vote of one of its own members.

Honest, decent, kind, compassionate, unassuming, and quiet-spoken, Pawley was also uninspiring. "Consensual to the point of immobility and tolerant to the point of feebleness," as a journalist with NDP sympathies described him. "He is no platform showman. His awkward syntax, frequent malapropisms and mixed metaphors left his audience bemused if not bewildered."[24] Where Schreyer exhibited a particular interest in energy policy, Pawley demonstrated a bureaucratic interest in the administration of Crown corporations.[25]

There is an ironic symmetry in the political paths of Manitoba's first social democratic leader, John Queen, and its most successful one, Gary Doer. Incarcerated for his role in the General Strike, ILP leader Queen won election to the legislature from his jail cell. Doer served as a corrections officer. A university dropout and the youngest-ever head of the province's largest union—the Manitoba Government Employees' Association—at the age of thirty-one, he criticized Pawley's government but co-operated with it too. At an international labour conference in 1981, Doer persuaded then-Swedish prime minister Olaf Palme to send Pawley a congratulatory telegram on his victory, but he later accused the Pawley government of bad-faith bargaining and practising "white wine socialism."[26]

Courted unsuccessfully by the Conservatives, Doer entered the NDP cabinet immediately after his election as an MLA in 1986. His public sector union background, in contrast to Queen's association with private sector industrial unions and Schreyer's membership in the Farmers Union, mirrored something of Manitoba's economic transformation as government came to constitute a larger share of the economy. As premier, Doer terminated the institutionalized funding links between organized labour and the NDP. The son of a German father and Welsh mother, he embodied the growth in the twentieth century of the number of ethnically intermarried Manitobans. Unlike Schreyer and Pawley, who came to the NDP via the CCF, Doer joined the party during Schreyer's first term and then resigned from it in 1975 to preserve, he said, his union's official neutrality.

Affable, bright, quick on his feet, and articulate, Doer had acquired a reputation as an astute mediator and consummate negotiator. Despite his managerial and organizational skills, however, he could not escape the burden of the NDP's unpopularity in 1988 after it raised Autopac premiums. The paradox was that the public had rewarded the party with re-election in 1973 for its Autopac initiative. In dramatically lowering premiums for most motorists, Autopac easily withstood Conservative fear-mongering; their deputy leader had likened its coming to the sound of jackboots approaching. In 1988, however, the Conservatives shrewdly championed Autopac's low premiums and trounced the NDP, punished for raising them. "There was a sense that the public had been betrayed by the party. We all knew," reflected Doer, "that we would be lucky to become the official opposition."[27] An internal party poll had its voter support as low as 6 percent.[28]

In 1969, the NDP had swept to power eighteen days after changing leaders; in 1988, the party suffered a resounding defeat twenty-seven days after changing leaders. Pawley resigned as party leader after losing the legislature's confidence but Doer, after winning the party's leadership in the midst of the resulting election campaign, astutely chose not to be sworn in as premier. Doer, therefore, did not appear opportunistic by grasping the premier's job without first gaining a mandate from the electorate. It meant that for the only time in Canadian history, a premier, Pawley, was not a party leader. The Liberal resurgence in 1988 occasioned by their leader Sharon Carstairs's popular assault on the Meech Lake Accord that Pawley's government had signed on to—an Accord unpopular with many in the party including ministers[29]—relegated the NDP to its older role as a third party. Schreyer, along with many others, believed the election spelled the end of the NDP as one of the two major parties.[30]

In the 1990 election, however, Doer's feisty performance in a televised leaders' debate, his talk of a "people's agenda," Carstairs's capitulation on Meech Lake, and momentum generated by the Ontario NDP's election a week earlier, helped the NDP overtake the Liberals and Doer become the leader of the opposition. Premier from 1999 to 2009, he insisted, unlike Schreyer and Pawley, that he was "non-ideological." *Maclean's* described his "knack for negotiating a middle way between the province's entrenched business and labour interests," and anointed him "Canada's most successful politician."[31] Annual polls between 2003 and 2006 affirmed that estimation.[32]

Greg Selinger, the fourth NDP premier and the first not elected to the position by the voters is the first of the party's leaders and the province's premiers to hold a PhD. A former professor of social work—a field long associated with social democracy—he is very much in Doer's self-proclaimed "non-ideological" mould, but his social concerns, however nuanced, are apparent: "We will govern with warm hearts and cool minds," he intoned upon winning the party leadership after Doer vacated it to become Canada's ambassador to the United States.[33] Unlike the other NDP premiers, Selinger had extensive municipal and financial experience as a member of the City of Winnipeg's executive policy committee and as chairperson of its finance committee. As minister of finance from his election in 1999 to 2009, he balanced ten consecutive budgets to undercut Progressive Conservative claims of the NDP's fiscal recklessness and kept the business community from launching a full-scale attack on Doer's government, unlike the experience of the Schreyer/Pawley governments. Like the other NDP leaders, he represented continuity as the favoured candidate of the party's unionists and its long-established officials.

Party and Performance

The NDP's initial electoral success proved transformative and magnetic. In 1962, the party had been dormant in about half of the fifty-seven constituencies; a decade later it was a relatively booming operation with organized party structures in every constituency. In 1964, it was so feeble that it dispensed with its annual convention; in 1976, its annual convention boasted more delegates, 721, than there had been CCF members two decades earlier.[34] In the aftermath of its impressive 2007 re-election, the party mustered 585 convention delegates, double the number at the convention preceding its 1999 victory.[35] This demonstrated that party strength, as measured by membership or convention size, are not necessarily related to success at the polls. Party and campaign finance are also weak indicators of electoral success. After winning the 1969 election with its central campaign spending a modest $45,000, the NDP's annual budget by 1976 grew to over $400,000 with a dozen full-time staff including six organizers.[36] Such relative wealth and resources did little for the party in the following year's election loss. "With 10,000 members," the party secretary noted, "we can raise more money than we did with 17,000."[37]

More pivotal to the party's fortunes than either membership or finances have been party leadership, strategic voting, and the ideological repositioning and occasional faux pas committed by the NDP's competitors. A vote-splitting scandal that broke in 1998, for example, revealed the Progressive Conservatives had recruited and funded some Aboriginals as bogus independent candidates with the intention of splintering the NDP vote among Aboriginals. The scandal implicated the Progressive Conservative premier's principal secretary, the secretary of the treasury board, and "others who stood at the height of the Manitoba establishment."[38] The revelations helped set the stage for the NDP's 1999 victory. Progressive Conservative leader Stuart Murray subsequently exhibited poor judgment in hiring a Tory operative implicated in the scandal[39] and in speaking in favour of the United States' invasion of Iraq.[40]

The print media, especially the *Winnipeg Free Press*, have historically been unsympathetic to the CCF-NDP, but the growth of television after the NDP's launch meant less editorializing and more neutral and wider reportage on the party. Viewers could see and hear the party's leaders, not merely read about them when the print media deemed it fit to cover them. The party also honed its ability to harness modern political communications techniques by massaging its messages to deflect media attacks. It adopted marketing methods and strategies common in the private sector and relied less on the educational meetings, debates, door-to-door canvassing, and the grassroots organizing of its ILP-CCF forerunners.

The Manitoba CCF-NDP has not been as vibrant a mass party as its sister Saskatchewan party[41] nor have its members been as militant as their British Columbia counterparts.[42] The party's constitution provides for an annual vote on the leadership, but party conventions—particularly when the party is in power—have mainly served as forums for the leadership rather than the membership. McAllister described the party's structures as "democratic showpieces for the electorate and as mechanisms for control and communication by the leadership."[43] Schreyer was sufficiently popular that his threatened resignation as leader convinced a largely reluctant convention, caucus, and cabinet to permit a free vote in the legislature on the issue of state aid to private and parochial schools, something the party had always rejected. He also won the membership's backing in convention to endorse the federal Liberals' wage-and-price controls policy of 1976, something fiercely attacked by the federal and other provincial NDPs.

One indicator of the party's distance from its ILP-CCF legacy was its faded Protestant social gospel tradition. That tradition—exemplified by J.S. Woodsworth's People's Mission, William Ivens's Labour Church, and clergymen such as Stanley Knowles and CCF leader Lloyd Stinson—was not wholly expunged, however. Transcona MP and United Church minister Bill Blaikie, the federal NDP's longest-serving MP and runner-up for its leadership, reflected it, for example. Nevertheless, societal secularization overtook the social gospel. Prodded by the ILP-CCF-NDP, provincial governments eclipsed churches' charitable roles. The party also served in the political forefront on abortion rights, a position at odds with many religionists including a cabinet minister, Joe Borowski, who left the NDP over the issue.

In another break with the past, the party severed its financial links to organized labour in 2000, a development greeted ambivalently by union leaders. This, however, did not weaken the affinity between them and the NDP, which launched initiatives in areas such as workplace safety and minimum wages and introduced a state-funded regime of election and party finance that the union movement supported[44] and which benefited the party. NDP labour laws contributed to union ranks declining proportionately less in Manitoba and Saskatchewan between 1981 and 2004 than in any other province.[45] It occurred in the context of a radically transformed, if shrunken, labour movement. Craft unions (such as Knowles's printers) which had backed the ILP, and industrial unions (such as Paulley's railroaders), who were partial to the CCF, gave way in size to public sector unions such as Doer's. Five of those unions, largely composed of government employees, nurses, and teachers, accounted for over 90,000 of the province's 167,000 unionists in 2007. They look more favourably upon the NDP than the other parties because it has the most positive disposition to expanding government services. Progressive Conservative criticism of NDP labour laws also contributes to keeping the unions in the NDP camp.

By the 1980s, the party's base and mobilization efforts had expanded beyond its traditional urban and union support. For example, the party pursued and was pursued by the women's movement. In the 1960s and well into the 1970s, women filled auxiliary roles in the party as they had in the CCF, serving tea and crumpets and holding fund-raising bazaars. Evidence of their subsidiary status was on display at the 1969 convention: an MLA organized a bevy of young women, outfitted them in miniskirts and red-and-white sashes, and labelled them the "Schreyer Dolls."[47] The image and role of women in both party and society soon changed dramatically, however. Myrna Phillips described how "The women's movement in the party congealed at the 1973 convention and mobilized after that.... We realized that just having an NDP government with NDP guys was not enough. We began to learn the process and get into the hierarchy of the party."[48] In 1977, Muriel Smith became the party's first female president and, two years later, she was runner-up in the leadership convention that elected Pawley. By the 1980s, the party's constitution provided for gender equality on its executive committee. Another turning point came in 1981 with the unprecedented election of seven female MLAs, five of whom were NDPers. Three of them appeared in the cabinet, including the deputy premier. Sidney Green, a party president who contested the leadership twice in the 1960s and served as a senior cabinet minister, attributed his marginalization in and departure from the party to the influence of so-called militant feminists and union leaders.[49]

Strategic voting now aids the provincial NDP and hurts its federal counterpart just as it now weakens the provincial Liberals and assists their federal cousins. Since its debut, the CCF-NDP has only bested the Liberals in Manitoba in four of 22 federal elections, those between 1979 and 1984 and in 2008. In contrast, the provincial NDP has outpolled the provincial Liberals in ten of the eleven contests since 1969, something the CCF had only managed to do once, in 1945, at the apex of its support. In retrospect, the 1990 election proved critical because in winning more seats and votes than the Liberals, the NDP regained its status as one of the two largest parties. This made it the logical alternative for those who wanted to defeat the Progressive Conservatives.

The 1999 election demonstrated the crossover between federal Liberal voters and provincial NDP supporters as the NDP pushed the Conservatives out of many of their traditional south Winnipeg redoubts, a pattern that has held ever since. The NDP to date has also escaped victimization by the Green Party, which only captured 1 percent of the vote in the 2003 and 2007 elections. In contrast, the Greens snared substantial support in recent provincial elections in British Columbia (12 percent in 2001, 9 percent in 2005) and Ontario (8 percent in 2007) at some expense to the NDP.

The NDP's change to party finance law, eliminating corporate as well as union contributions and capping individual ones, most adversely affected the Conservatives. They lost more than two thirds of their annual revenues between 2000 and 2001.[50] Benefiting the NDP, as the largest party, is the scheme for public funding of the parties on a per-vote basis. Such a regime is consistent with the NDP's statist orientation and contributes to consolidating its status as a major party at the expense of the smaller parties, the Liberals and Greens.

Surveys conducted during the 1999 and 2007 elections revealed the party's stable and shifting social bases of support. Women, the poor, the middle-aged (thirty-five to fifty-nine years), and urbanites, gravitated disproportionately to the NDP in 1999.[51] Women, who historically and cross-nationally have disproportionately preferred conservative parties to socialist ones,[52] are now more likely than men to support the NDP. They have greater sympathy than men do for the ensconced welfare state. Political socialization has also contributed to party fortunes; the more experience people have with an NDP government, the more willing they have become, it appears, to support it. In 1999, those over fifty-five years old preferred the Conservatives to the NDP by the gaping margin of 57 percent to 32 percent. By 2007, however, this age cohort disproportionately preferred the NDP.[53] On the other hand, the lifelong process of socialization also represents a looming threat to the NDP: it trailed the Conservatives in 2007 among young voters, those under thirty-five, after having had a substantial advantage among that group in 1999.

Perhaps the most illuminating and counterintuitive feature of the NDP's changing base of support is the weakening allegiance of those with lower incomes. Conversely, the party has newfound strength among the relatively well-to-do. Between 1999 and 2007, an 18 percent NDP advantage over the Conservatives among low-income earners shrank to 8 percent.[54] This occurred despite the NDP's identification with the less privileged and its characterization of the Conservatives as the party of the wealthy. Dramatically, these survey data point to an astonishingly refurbished NDP image among the well-to-do; it is now their preferred party. Among higher-income earners, a Conservative advantage of 16 percent in 1999 reversed itself to an NDP advantage of 7 percent by 2007 and made the party appear as that of the affluent.

The growth of the Aboriginal population aids the party too and may well continue to bolster it. In the 1981, 1990, and 2003 elections, for example, between 72 and 83 percent of those on First Nations reserves voted for it.[55] If the affinity between Aboriginals and the NDP persists, the party will benefit further; Aboriginals constituted 17 percent of Manitobans in 2001, but will account for 23 percent by 2017, and their children under fifteen years of age will make up 31 percent of that age cohort.[56]

One result of electoral success is that the NDP attracted many followers despite its ideology. A profound transformation of party membership resulted. Doer, who joined the party in the early 1970s, is a case in point. A study of the party's 1973 members revealed that fewer than five percent had been CCFers. Indeed, a remarkable 70 percent had not been members as recently as 1970 and over half joined in 1972–73.[57] The membership's ephemeral composition led one organizer to speculate about the ideological implications for the party:

> These figures suggest that the NDP is not broadening its base, but shifting in character, conceivably from the left to the right. The party base has been wholly transformed not only from what it was in 1969 but also from what it was in 1971. No definitive evidence of the ideological bias of those leaving the party is available yet it is the feeling of some observers within the party that as senior members exit quietly via the left door, the NDP is welcoming large numbers of novice members through the right door.[58]

This analysis implies, questionably, that the party has only two ideological doors.

Ideology and Policy

It is analytically important not to confuse ideology with policy. Vital at the ideological level is the rationale for a policy or program. Partisans of various parties and of different ideological orientations may embrace the same program, such as public education or medicare, but may do so on the basis of quite different motivations. A red tory Conservative might endorse medicare out of a sense of *noblesse oblige*, the belief that society's privileged classes are obliged to help underwrite the needs of less privileged citizens. A philosophic liberal might support it out of the belief that all individuals are entitled to an equal opportunity to get ahead, something compromised by an individual's illness or injury through no fault of her own. A socialist might embrace medicare because it manifests mutuality, our care for one another as equal members of a community in solidarity. A demonstration of policy convergence,[59] therefore, does not necessarily mean ideological convergence.

Discernible contrasts in parties' ideological orientations and their depictions of each other reveal more about the parties than policy convergences among them. The NDP's website, for example, continues to voice the party's socialist heritage: "Our society must change from one based on competition to one based on cooperation," reads its first enumerated party principle. The second conveys a decidedly radical leftist flavour: "We wish to create a society where individuals give according to their abilities, and receive according to their needs."[60] Autopac, ManOil, a crown corporation created for oil exploration, and the creation of Leaf Rapids—Manitoba's first government-planned mining community—demonstrated the NDP's willingness to wield government's instrumentality to redistribute goods and services. So too, did the party's opposition to the Progressive Conservatives' privatization of Manitoba Telephone Systems.

The NDP's ideological mellowing came with changing conditions and success. The party, like other social democratic parties all over the world, veered from the CCF's programmatic genesis by shedding much of the ILP-CCF's anti-capitalist, socialist crust. It forswore, for example, the nationalization of natural resource industries. A telling tale was the NDP's appointment of Eric Kierans—the ex-president of the Montreal Stock Exchange and former federal Liberal cabinet minister—to examine natural resource policy. Schreyer dismissed his report, which recommended the long-term takeover, with compensation, of the private mining industry. Schreyer characterized it as "too drastic and retrospective," and reassured the industry it had nothing to fear.[61] The NDP has remained on the left of the political spectrum as a party identified as committed to advancing the welfare of society's underclasses—the vulnerable, the weak, the less privileged, outsiders, and those facing discrimination—but it became less insistent, like social democracy everywhere, that this be at the expense of private capital.

The NDP also came to redefine and expand the older socialist notion of class politics by welcoming the new social movements of the twentieth century's last quarter—women, environmentalists, newer immigrant ethno-cultural communities, many of them visible minorities, and gays and lesbians. The party looks benignly upon the rise of identity politics, and although its posture is muted compared to the federal NDP, it is decidedly more sympathetic to this development than the Conservatives. The provincial NDP, for example, has taken a leadership role on Aboriginal rights and programs. Pawley's government was a staunch advocate for them at the four First Ministers Conferences of the 1980s that dealt with Aboriginals. It sent large delegations, outnumbered only by Quebec, and spoke of the need to "liberate Canada's aboriginal peoples from the remaining vestiges of colonialism."[62] This position reflected continuity in that the CCF had been the first party to seek out an Aboriginal candidate in the 1950s.[63] Schreyer appointed the province's first Aboriginal cabinet minister, funnelled money into labour-intensive northern programs, and contracted with northern First Nations bands for road and airport bush clearance. Pawley appointed another Aboriginal cabinet minister, Elijah Harper, and two Aboriginals served in Doer's first government.

With respect to gays and lesbians, the NDP incorporated sexual orientation into provincial human rights legislation in 1986 after having introduced pay equity in the public sector. More recently, the party's 2008 convention pressed Ottawa to reverse its ban on gay organ donors.[64] The NDP has also demonstrated sympathy for francophones, but Pawley's government paid a steep political price for its cosponsorship, with the federal government and the Société Franco-Manitobaine, of a 1983 tripartite constitutional accord on language rights.[65] It paralyzed the legislature for months and over 30 municipalities, including Winnipeg, held plebiscites that revealed about 75 percent opposition to the proposal. Pawley's support for francophone rights was belated, coming only after legal compulsion—the Supreme Court declared Manitoba's language regime unconstitutional[66]—and a change of mind. Pawley, as attorney general a decade earlier, had rejected French statutes on the peculiar logic that it would oblige the government to provide German and Ukrainian statutes since "we have more populous groups of people that speak" those languages.[67]

In social policy, the NDP moved squarely into the liberal world of social welfare by defining state intervention narrowly—maintaining a high reliance on family relations and the private market.[68] Nevertheless, its innovations often stand apart from and ahead of those in other provinces, a notable achievement for a relatively poor province. It introduced Canada's first provincial home care program for seniors, which served as a catalyst and model for similar programs in other provinces. Likewise, its childcare regime reflected a communitarian orientation "characterized by more social solidarity than in other English provinces."[69] Manitoba, despite its "have-not" status, spends more per capita on early childhood education and care than any other province with the exception of Quebec.[70]

On fiscal issues, the depiction of CCF-NDP governments as spendthrifts has always been ill-deserved. Conservatives and others have propagated an image of the NDP as profligate spenders. Jared Wesley, for example, characterizes Doer's government as "a drastic departure from the more programmatic, idealistic agenda of the Old Left [of Schreyer and Pawley]" and he defines that Old Left as "tax and spend."[71] Doer did retain Conservative legislation that requires a referendum to raise taxes. This, however, is consistent with the NDP's fiscal record: the Saskatchewan NDP government recorded fourteen consecutive balanced budgets and the Schreyer government's spending grew less as a percentage of the provincial economy than under the Roblin-Weir governments. Under its watch, Manitoba was accorded its highest-ever credit rating on the international bond market. Its taxation regime was less burdensome for the poor and the middle-class than those in relatively wealthy Alberta, British Columbia, and Ontario, leading the *Edmonton Journal* to declare, "Overtaxed? Move to Manitoba."[72] Wesley oddly associates affordable government with neo-liberalism,[73] yet Schreyer's government, like Doer's government, consistently generated balanced budgets while Sterling Lyon's Conservative administration generated Manitoba's largest budgetary deficit.

Intriguingly, Wesley argues that the ideological key to electoral success in Manitoba is to capture the province's "collectivist centre" and that "the trajectory of social democracy in Manitoba is closely associated with that of red toryism."[74] Deploying the triad of ideological constellations of classical conservatism, liberalism, and socialism, he adopts Gad Horowitz's dialectical ideational connection between toryism and socialism[75]—their common belief in the state's positive role for the "common good." Wesley contrasts that with neo-liberal and neo-conservative suspicion of the state and paints a picture of a primarily liberal provincial ideological landscape with tory and social democratic touches, reflected by the Roblin and NDP administrations. Both were committed to economic development—the Conservatives pursued mega-projects while the NDP looked to Crown corporations—but for different reasons: "the NDP used economic development as a means to achieving social justice, whereas, to the Progressive Conservatives, economic development was often a province-building measure."[76] From a political economy perspective, Alex Netherton has argued that a Keynesian modernization paradigm of the state's role drove both the Roblin and Schreyer/Pawley regimes, but that they offered alternative visions of it.[77]

With Keynesianism's unravelling, Gary Filmon's Conservatives and Doer's NDP similarly proposed competing visions of an emergent neo-liberal "globalization" paradigm. The NDP offered a more nuanced collectivist stance, however, in contrast to the Conservatives' greater faith in the free-enterprising individual. Doer supported the Conservatives' 1995 balanced budget legislation but also identified with Tony Blair's "Third Way" philosophy: state support for the market economy by cutting business, property, and individual income taxes in conjunction with public investment in human capital as a means of propelling economic growth. After Filmon's departure, the Conservatives shifted further to the right under a leader who, in a reverberation of the United States' Republicans and to the benefit of the NDP, stressed downsizing government. For example, Filmon's successor Stuart Murray called for workfare legislation, a welfare cheat hotline, and jettisoning a planned northern University College to pay for tax cuts.[78] This left the NDP to occupy the strategic "collective centre" by "striking a balance between liberal individualism and social democratic collectivism."[79] When their opponents on the right pulled too far from the centre, the NDP benefited from its default image as a moderate, centre-left party.

In Wesley's schema, ideological divisions among the parties complement intra-party differences within them. NDPers express an amalgam of "social democratic, reform liberal, 'New Left', and neo-liberal attitudes" with leftism defined as support for welfare, civil liberties, and the environment.[80] This wide net underplays social democracy's underlying egalitarian, communitarian ethic, and vision of social solidarity. The party's 2008 convention, for example, adopted resolutions that dealt with enhanced Aboriginal health programs, improved wage equity for women, investments in worker safety, support for rural businesses and apprenticeship programs, and maintaining the Wheat Board's marketing monopoly.[81] For some, however, the NDP's socialist credentials fall short. Cy Gonick, for example, a Schreyer-era backbencher, dismissed the party as an unreliable agent for social transformation and he labelled Doer "a quintessentially small-'l' liberal" who "doesn't have a socialist bone in his body."[82] This is a common critique of social democrats among more left-wing socialists. Gonick pointed to Manitoba's relatively high proportion of low-wage jobs, its relatively high rates of child and family poverty and, from his vantage point, inadequate social welfare allowances. His appraisal, however, does not acknowledge Manitoba's relative "have-not" status, broader national economic and social conditions, and the variety in provincial natural and human resource endowments. They shape the welfare of a province's residents as well as the stripe of the party in power.

The Future of the NDP

The proposition that the NDP is Manitoba's natural governing party, its political hegemon—in light of its electoral successes over the past four decades—is as questionable as it is plausible. The NDP's success in Manitoba is unremarkable in comparison to the success of strong parties in other provinces. Indeed, in elections since the late 1960s, the Conservatives' average share of the popular vote has exceeded that of the NDP and the two parties have won about the same number of seats. Manitoba, with its two-party-plus party system, may not have a "natural governing party," although by one measure of dominance—how many elections won since the late 1960s—the NDP has done remarkably well (64 percent) bettered only by the Progressive Conservative parties in Alberta, Nova Scotia, and Ontario.

The party's prospects in the rest of the twenty-first century are no less contingent on a variety of unpredictable factors than were its past fortunes. This paper has suggested that no single agent or element accounts for its success. The party has enjoyed a comparative advantage when it comes to leadership. Nevertheless, while the cases of Schreyer and Doer intimate that leadership has been important, Pawley's victories despite his flawed performance indicate that it has been incidental. Schreyer dwarfed Bend and Weir as a personality and tactician and Doer towered over Murray and his successor, Hugh McFadyen. The NDP also capitalized on mishaps and blunders of the Lyon and Filmon Conservative regimes. The party's fortunes will continue to be determined by both agency—the party's ideas, mobilization efforts, and the skills of its leaders—and conditions—Manitoba's shifting socio-economic realities.

Conditions surrounding every election are unique, however striking the parallels with other elections. The NDP's 1969 breakthrough was dependent on a number of coincidental factors that favoured the party. They included Schreyer's selection in the midst of an election campaign in which the party's opponents had swerved programmatically, and the NDP benefitting from the first-past-the-post electoral system in the context of a more equitable distribution of legislative seats. Urbanization, technological changes in communications, and Manitoba's greater political and social integration all aided the party. Once in power, its legitimacy grew: in losing office in 1977, it still secured more support than in its 1969 victory. Dangerously weakened in 1988, the party subsequently benefited from the Liberals' inability to maintain their official opposition status in 1990. This contributed to their subsequent marginality and the NDP's increased credibility as the only viable alternative government to the Conservatives.

Political vagaries—scandals, leaders' skills, and societal change—will continue to mould the contours of Manitoba politics. Past or repeated success and favourable economic conditions are no guarantors of continued success. Witness the Saskatchewan NDP's defeat in 2007 in the midst of prosperity while less affluent Manitobans were content to maintain their NDP government. After a long bout of one-party rule, some voters will feel that a partisan change in regime is democratically healthy. This represents a challenge to Selinger's NDP no matter how adroitly he conducts himself. If a future government adopts proportional representation, it would compromise the NDP's prospects. Proportional representation could resurrect the Liberals at the NDP's expense and provide incentives for new parties to form; some may splinter the NDP and, indeed, feed its demise.

Policy disjunction between NDP and Progressive Conservative governments is perhaps less striking than policy continuity. The NDP, however, has been more innovative. Policy convergence does not mean ideological conjunction. Both parties have an interest in drawing contrasts in how they view society. Progressive Conservative leader McFadyen charged in 2006 that the Pawley government "found its inspiration in socialist and communist ideas that were [once] in vogue in eastern Europe," presumably because it included former Communist Roland Penner.[83] In contrast, Doer found it useful to depict the Conservatives as "a party that only governs for a privileged few on every issue of priority."[84] The NDP's campaign slogan in 1973, "Keep Your Government Yours," similarly tried to brand the Conservatives by implying that they rule on behalf of the wealthy few. This is not the kind of partisan sparring common in most provinces. Both sides wrangle ideologically in Manitoba partly because they hope to keep the party system polarized at Liberal expense. In federal politics, the chronic issue of national unity historically benefited the Liberals; this factor does not obtain provincially where other issues are more salient. Manitoba's regional tensions, between city and countryside, favour the NDP and the Conservatives.

The NDP proved adept at transforming its ideology from one grounded in Old Left social democracy to New Left and "Third Way" thinking. CCF platforms drew heavily on those of the British Labour party and Doer identified with Blairite Britain's "new" Labour. A British template also informs the evolution of the Manitoba party system. NDPers, like CCFers before them, wished to see both Canada's and Manitoba's party systems simplified and crystallized. They envisioned one party clearly on the right and another unambiguously on the left engaged in a democratic class struggle of "haves" and "have-nots." The party's strategy, eventually successful, was to squeeze and then displace the centrist Liberals as had occurred in Britain in the early decades of the twentieth century. Lloyd Stinson, the CCF's leader in the 1950s and a New Party organizer, articulated this perspective for a foreigner: "If there is any logic in Canadian affairs, now is the time when there should be a good chance for a third party to slip in and take the place formerly occupied by the Liberals against the older Conservatives."[85]

Voters' separate strategic calculations in federal and provincial elections, if they persist, will continue to benefit the provincial NDP. It is in its interest to keep the Liberals marginalized in a polarized party system because the key to victory is to capture the votes of federal Liberals who see little prospect for their provincial counterpart. Continued Liberal feebleness aids both the NDP and the

Conservatives. Allen Mills writes of the unspoken, informal alliance between Doer and Filmon in the 1990s "to dish the Liberals."[86] The NDP's historical bastions in the poorer north, central, and east Winnipeg districts, and among Aboriginals and in the North, allude to socio-demographic and economic factors less influenced by leadership change. The ability of the party to project a non-threatening image to middle- and upper-class voters is important too for, although Manitoba is a "have-not" province, substantial middle-class support is a requisite to elect and keep any party in power.

A trend likely to continue is divergence in the policy postures of the federal and provincial NDP, especially when the provincial party is in power. An example is proportional representation, pursued aggressively by the federal party but not mooted by the Manitoba NDP for it does not serve its interests as it does those of the federal NDP. As provinces have expanded their technical and bureaucratic capacities since the 1960s and insisted on protecting and extending their jurisdictional spheres, NDP governments have been no exception. The CCF's nationally centralized public policy prescriptions[87] slowly gave way to accepting, accommodating, and defending provincial policy particularisms when the NDP, as in Manitoba, governs. As a "have-not" province reliant on federal largesse however, Manitoba—under whatever party is in power—will likely continue to look favourably upon Ottawa exercising national powers to implement policies to which other wealthier provinces object.

The federal NDP's constitution turns Manitoba's supplicant status in the federal-provincial governmental arena topsy-turvy. The federal party is a federation of its provincial parties and is dependent on them. There is no federal NDP membership per se; to join the federal NDP one must purchase a provincial membership. The federal party's subordinate organizational status is evident in elections. It is from the provincial party's office that federal as well as provincial elections are coordinated because it is responsible for federal electoral activities in the province. The federal NDP's inferior status is accentuated when the provincial party is in power.

Manitoba and Saskatchewan are English North America's social democratic heartland. Winnipeg, given its twentieth-century experience, is its spiritual hub. It is so by virtue of its connection to the social gospel, the General Strike, John Queen's tenure as its mayor, the electoral base it provided between the 1920s and 1980s for Woodsworth and Knowles, and as the location where the Winnipeg Declaration displaced the Regina Manifesto as social democracy's statement of principles. The relative wealth, power, and growth of Winnipeg, its steadily increasing share of the legislature's seats in the only province where a city accounts for more than half the population, have helped the provincial NDP grow in tandem with the city. These factors, along with the party's ideological repositioning and pragmatism, the deftness of its leaders, the decline of the Liberal party, and the steady growth of an Aboriginal constituency sympathetic to the NDP, have all contributed to the NDP's success.

Notes

1   I am grateful to Jared Wesley for his constructive comments on an earlier draft of this chapter.
2   Nelson Wiseman, *Social Democracy in Manitoba* (Winnipeg: University of Manitoba Press, 1985), chapter 5.
3   Stanley Knowles, *The New Party* (Toronto: McClelland and Stewart, 1961).
4   Wiseman, *Social Democracy in Manitoba*, 102.
5   Russ Paulley, interview with author, February 1972.
6   Wiseman, *Social Democracy in Manitoba*, 72.
7   Eric Wells, "Is Being Premier of Manitoba as Comfortable as Ed Schreyer Makes it Look?" *Saturday Night*, October 1969, 42.
8   Sidney Green, *Rise and Fall of a Political Animal: A Memoir* (Winnipeg: Great Plains Publications, 2003), 68.
9   Nelson Wiseman and K.W. Taylor, "Voting in Winnipeg during the Depression," *Canadian Review of Sociology and Anthropology* 19, 2 (1982): 215–236.
10 J.E. Rae, "The Politics of Class: Winnipeg City Council, 1914–1945," in *The West and the Nation*, ed. Carl Berger and Ramsay Cook (Toronto: McClelland and Stewart, 1976), 234–235.
11 Maurice Duverger, *Political Parties: Their Organization and Activity in the Modern State*, trans. Barbara and Robert North (New York: John Wiley and Sons, 1963), 63–71.
12 Magnus Eliason, interview with author, May 1972.
13 Ed Schreyer, interview with author, February 1972. See also Paul Beaulieu, *Ed Schreyer: A Social Democrat in Power* (Winnipeg: Queenston House, 1977), 187–211.
14 Gad Horowitz, "The Future of the NDP," *Canadian Dimension* 3 (July–August 1966), 23.
15 Fred Tufford, interview with author, March 1972.
16 David Orlikow, interview with author, April 1972.
17 James A. McAllister, *The Government of Ed Schreyer* (Montreal and Kingston: McGill-Queen's University Press, 1984), 14.
18 Tom Peterson, "Manitoba," in *Canadian Annual Review of Politics and Public Affairs*, ed. John Saywell (Toronto: University of Toronto Press, 1974), 185.
19 John Wilson, "The Decline of the Liberal Party in Manitoba," *Journal of Canadian Studies* 10, 1 (1975): 32, and Jo Surich, "Leadership and the Voting Decision in Manitoba and Ontario," paper presented at the Annual Meeting of the Canadian Political Science Association, Edmonton, 1975, 10–11.
20 "150 Faces for the Future," *Time*, 15 July 1974, 38.
21 Arlene Billinkoff, "The premier fights the ads," *Winnipeg Free Press*, 4 October 1977, 31.
22 Alan Whitehorn, *Canadian Socialism: Essays on the CCF-NDP* (Toronto: Oxford University Press, 1992), 45–50.
23 Howard Pawley, interview with author, February 1972.
24 Frances Russell, "Pawley gives NDP a chance," *Winnipeg Free Press*, 11 March 1988, 7.

25 Howard Pawley, "In The Public's Interest: The Governance of Crown Corporations," in *Provinces: Canadian Provincial Parties*, ed. Christopher Dunn (Peterborough: Broadview Press, 1996), 301–320.
26 Doug Smith, Jock Bates, and Esyllt Jones, *Lives in the Public Service: A History of the Manitoba Government Employees' Union* (Winnipeg: Manitoba Government Employees' Union, 1993), 231–3 and 239.
27 Gary Doer, interview with author, December 1988.
28 Richard Cleroux, "NDP faces long road back, Doer says," *Globe and Mail*, 29 April 1988, A8.
29 Len Evans, e-mail to James MacAllister, 31 May 2008. Gerald Friesen, "Manitoba and the Meech Lake Accord," in *Meech Lake and Canada: Perspectives from the West*, ed. Roger Gibbins (Edmonton: Academic Printing and Publishing, 1988), 53–57.
30 Christopher Adams, "Realignment in Manitoba: The Provincial Elections of 1999, 2003 and 2007," paper presented at the annual meeting of the Canadian Political Science Association, Vancouver, 2008, 4.
31 Brian Bergman, "Soccer Field Wisdom: Canada's most successful politician finds new ways to stay in touch," *Maclean's*, 5 August 2002, 36.
32 Paul Samyn, "Doer must be doing it right," *Winnipeg Free Press*, 7 September 2003, A1. See also Paul Samyn, "But Doer still Canada's most well-liked politician," *Winnipeg Free Press*, 19 November 2004, A1; Paul Samyn, "Doer nation's most popular premier: poll," *Winnipeg Free Press*, 25 April 2005, A1; Paul Samyn, "How Premiers Rate," *Winnipeg Free Press*, 5 March 2006, A3.
33 Mary Agnes Welch, "Selinger wins NDP leadership race," *Winnipeg Free Press*, 17 October 2009.
34 Wiseman, *Social Democracy in Manitoba*, 131.
35 Manitoba New Democratic Party, "Today's NDP: Forward, not Back," http://www.todaysndp.mb.ca/news07 (accessed 10 March 2008). See also "Doer fires up NDP prior to likely election call: warns convention delegates not to underestimate Tories," *Winnipeg Free Press*, 16 March 2003, A3.
36 "Statement of Income and Expenses for September 1, 1968 to August 31, 1969," Attached to Provincial Council minutes, 24 January 1969, Magnus Eliason Papers, Archives of Manitoba. See also "Election Expenses, June 25, 1969," NDP Papers, Archives of Manitoba; *Manitoba New Democrat* 6, 6 (June–July 1976).
37 "Report of the Provincial Secretary," 23 August 1974, NDP Papers, Archives of Manitoba.
38 Doug Smith, *As Many Liars: The Story of the 1995 Vote-Splitting Scandal* (Winnipeg: Arbeiter Ring, 2003), 10.
39 "Manitoba Tory Leader Stuart Murray may face leadership challenge," *Canadian Press*, 28 October 2005.
40 David Kuxhaus, "Pro-war rally draws 1,000," *Winnipeg Free Press*, 6 April 2003, A4.
41 R.K. Carty and David Stewart, "Parties and Party Systems," in *Provinces: Canadian Provincial Politics*, ed. Christopher Dunn (Peterborough: Broadview Press, 1996), 69.
42 W.D. Young, "A Profile of Activists in the British Columbia NDP," *Journal of Canadian Studies* 6, 1 (1971), 19–26.
43 McAllister, *The Government of Ed Schreyer*, 130.
44 Manitoba Federation of Labour, "Manitoba Federation of Labour Brief on Bill 37," 20 May 2008, http://www.mfl.mb.ca/pdfs/B-37-brf.pdf (accessed 25 July 2008).
45 Statistics Canada, "Diverging trends in unionization," *The Daily*, 22 April 2005, http://www.statcan.ca/Daily/English/050422/d050422c.htm (accessed 28 June 2008).

46 Mia Rabson, "Murray takes aim at unions," *Winnipeg Free Press*, 30 May 2008, A3.
47 Russell Doern, *Wednesdays Are Cabinet Days: A Personal Account of the Schreyer Administration* (Winnipeg: Queenston House, 1981), 44.
48 Kathy Brock, "Women and the Manitoba Legislature," in *In the Presence of Women: Representation in Canadian Governments*, ed. Jane Arscott and Linda Trimble (Toronto: Harcourt Brace, 1997), 186.
49 Green, *Rise and Fall of a Political Animal*, 159 and 167.
50 Mia Rabson, "Law will squeeze party fundraising: Move to further restrict political donations," *Winnipeg Free Press*, 10 April 2006, A5.
51 Adams, "Realignment in Manitoba," 8.
52 Seymour Martin Lipset, *Political Man: The Social Bases of Politics* (Baltimore: Johns Hopkins, 1981), 231.
53 Probe Research, "*Winnipeg Free Press*/Global TV Probe Research Inc. News Release," 18 May 2007, http://www.probe-research.com/2007%20%The%20Vote.pdf (accessed 28 July 2008).
54 Ibid.
55 Michael Kinnear, "Aboriginal Participation in Elections: The Effect of Expansion of the Franchise on Turnout," *Electoral Insight* 5, 3 (2003): 47.
56 Statistics Canada, "Projections of the Aboriginal populations, Canada, provinces and territories 2001 to 2017," http://www.statcan.ca/english/freepub/91-547-XIE/2005001/bfront1.htm (accessed 30 June 2008).
57 "Provincial Executive Minutes," 14 June 1975, NDP Papers, Archives of Manitoba.
58 Glen McRuer, "A Membership Profile of the Manitoba New Democratic Party, 1961–1973," *Mimeo*, n.d., 10.
59 Florence Cartigny, "The 2007 Manitoba and Saskatchewan Elections: Broken Electoral Destinies?" paper presented to the Annual Meeting of the Canadian Political Science Association, Vancouver, 2008, 1.
60 Manitoba New Democratic Party, http://www.todaysndp.mb.ca/new07/node/58 (accessed 18 March 2008).
61 Bob Lowrey, "Kierans Report Attacked," *Winnipeg Free Press*, 21 April 1973, 1.
62 Nelson Wiseman, "In Search of Manitoba's Constitutional Position," *Journal of Canadian Studies* 29, 3 (1990): 98.
63 Wiseman, *Social Democracy in Manitoba*, 86.
64 Bruce Owen, "Wheat Board gets vote of confidence," *Winnipeg Free Press*, 4 February 2008, A3.
65 Raymond M. Hébert, *Manitoba's French-Language Crisis: A Cautionary Tale* (Montreal and Kingston: McGill-Queen's University Press, 2004).
66 *Reference re Manitoba Language Rights* [1985] 2 S.C.R. 347.
67 Russell Doern, *The Battle over Bilingualism* (Winnipeg: Cambridge Publishers, 1985), 5.
68 Helga Hernes, ed., *Welfare State and Women Power: Essays in State Feminism* (Oslo: Norwiegan University Press, 1987).
69 Susan Prentice, "Manitoba's Childcare Regime: Social Liberalism in Flux," *Canadian Journal of Sociology* 29, 2 (2004): 193.
70 Martha Friendly et al., "Early Childhood Education and Care in Canada," Childcare Resource and Research Unit, University of Toronto, October 2007.
71 Jared Wesley, "The Collective Center: Social Democracy and Red Tory Politics in Manitoba," paper presented at the Annual Meeting of the Canadian Political Science Association, York University, Toronto, 2006, 15 and 20.

72 "Overtaxed? Move to Manitoba," *Edmonton Journal*, 2 June 1977, 10.
73 Jared Wesley, "Spanning the Spectrum: Political Party Attitudes in Manitoba," (MA thesis, University of Manitoba, 2004).
74 Wesley, "The Collective Center," 20.
75 Gad Horowitz, "Conservatism, Liberalism and Socialism in Canada: An Interpretation," *Canadian Journal of Economics and Political Science* 32, 1 (1966): 143–171.
76 Wesley, "The Collective Center," 9.
77 Alex Netherton, "Paradigm and Shift: A Sketch of Manitoba Politics," in *The Provincial State in Canada: Politics in the Provinces and Territories*, ed. Keith Brownsey and Michael Howlett (Peterborough: Broadview Press, 2001).
78 Daniel Lett, "Murray plans to revive work-for-welfare law," *Winnipeg Free Press*, 20 May 2003, A3; Mia Rabson, "School on Tory hit list," *Winnipeg Free Press*, 11 May 2003, A1.
79 Wesley, "The Collective Center," 13.
80 Wesley, "Spanning the Spectrum."
81 Manitoba NDP, http://todaysndp.mb.ca/new07/node/58 (accessed 18 March 2008).
82 Cy Gonick, "Gary Doer's Manitoba," *Canadian Dimension* 41, 4 (2007): 12–15 and 40–41.
83 Steve Pona, "Pawley: Tory leader has gone overboard," *Winnipeg Free Press*, 14 September 2006, A13.
84 Mia Rabson, "NDP, Tories not the same, Doer insists: Premier arms the faithful 'for the coffee shops and doorsteps,'" *Winnipeg Free Press*, 20 March 2005, A3.
85 Fred Alexander, *Canadians and Foreign Policy* (Toronto: University of Toronto Press, 1960), 59.
86 Allen Mills, "Gary Albert Doer," *Encyclopedia of Manitoba*, ed. Ingeborg Boyens (Winnipeg: Great Plains Publications, 2007), 168.
87 League for Social Reconstruction, *Social Planning in Canada* (Toronto: T. Nelson, 1935).

Manitoba's Progressive Conservative Party: A "Great Renewal" or Continued Disarray?[1]

Kelly L. Saunders

At the 2009 annual general meeting of the Manitoba Progressive Conservative Party,[2] leader Hugh McFadyen acknowledged that while it had had some disappointing setbacks, the PC Party was nonetheless on the verge of a great renewal. "We are a party that is optimistic about our future," he declared to the gathered crowd. In light of the party's diminishing fortunes over the past decade, and most recently in the May 2007 election when it suffered its worst electoral showing since 1953, McFadyen's attempt to instill hope in his party's members was understandable. Whether the party is simply experiencing the ebb and flow natural to all political organizations, or is suffering from a deeper, more serious malaise, however, remains disputable. What is clear is that the Progressive Conservatives, as they enter the twenty-first century, are at a turning point in their history. The extent to which the party is able to overcome its current woes, and be viewed as a credible and realistic alternative to the governing New Democrats by a wider proportion of Manitobans, is the fundamental question before the party today. It is also the focus of this chapter.[3]

In addressing the varied challenges confronting the PC Party at the beginning of the second decade of the new millennium, this chapter draws on interviews with party insiders as well as a variety of primary and secondary documents. The first part of the chapter focuses on the party under the leadership of Gary Filmon, who led his party to three successive electoral victories. In contrast to these past successes stands the Progressive Conservative Party of today. Once lauded by some as the natural governing party of Manitoba, the Tories have suffered a steady erosion in their electoral support over the past three general elections, notably in the crucial battleground of Winnipeg. The second section of the chapter examines some of the defining variables that led to the downward spiral of the PC Party over the past decade. Some of these factors include the negative fallout from the 1995 vote-rigging scandal; the successful re-branding of the NDP and its movement to the ideological centre; financial and organizational woes; and the Progressive Conservative Party's leadership struggles in the wake of Filmon's departure from the helm in 2000.

The third section of the chapter considers both the challenges and the opportunities before the PC Party as it attempts to rebuild under its current leader Hugh McFadyen. While much of the party's fortunes will depend on the future of the NDP (in particular, the extent to which new leader and premier, Greg Selinger, can continue to capitalize on the popularity of former leader Gary Doer), its biggest challenge will be clarifying what it stands for in the twenty-first century. In doing so it will need to reconcile its progressive and conservative wings that have tended to reflect the urban/rural divide within its membership base and reclaim the ideological centre that has been the source of much of the NDP's electoral success. In addition to these challenges, section three will also consider the opportunities currently before the party. The rebuilding of its organizational base, its ability to consistently maintain a core group of popular support, a worsening provincial economy, and demographic trends all point to an optimistic future for the Manitoba Progressive Conservatives. How the party will take advantage of these opportunities, or alternatively whether it will fall victim to the many challenges it must still overcome, remains to be seen.

I. The PC Party in Power

When we think of the Progressive Conservative Party of Manitoba in recent times, the figure of Gary Filmon still looms large. So central was Filmon to the fortunes of the party throughout the 1990s that his legacy continues to reverberate, more than ten years after his retirement from public office. Indeed, it would not be far off the mark to suggest that much of the party's misfortunes over the intervening decade can be attributed precisely to the strong leadership of Filmon, his political acumen, and his accomplishments in office. As leader of the party from 1983 until his announced departure at the Tories' 1999 defeat, the party came to be singularly personalized in his image.

Building the Filmon Machine

Gary Filmon's tenure as one of the strongest and most effective leaders of any political party in Manitoba was anything but a foregone conclusion in his early career. First elected to the Manitoba Legislature in 1979, Filmon later joined the cabinet of Premier Sterling Lyon in the Consumer and Corporate Affairs and Environment portfolios. Two years later, in the 1981 provincial election, the Lyon Conservatives went down to defeat at the hands of the NDP under Howard Pawley; Filmon, however, managed to get re-elected in the new Winnipeg riding of Tuxedo. When Lyon announced his plans to retire from the head of the PC Party in 1983, three contenders—Gary Filmon, Brian Ransom, and Clayton Manness—threw their respective hats into the ring. The party membership was faced with a choice between the urban, more progressive image of Filmon in contrast to the rural, conservative figures of Ransom and Manness. In the end the party chose the former, with Filmon managing to win on the second ballot by fewer than fifty votes.[4]

During his bid for the leadership Filmon displayed many of the characteristics that would propel him to his later successes both within the party and in Manitoba politics generally. His leadership victory was largely based on his ability to inspire personal loyalty, and to reach out to individuals who had not been members or even supporters of the Progressive Conservatives in the past. In Geoffrey Lambert's estimation, Filmon was "a street politician of the first rank."[5] A consummate organizer, he built his leadership base by visiting every constituency association personally; meeting one-on-one with delegates and selling them on his personal, folksy style. Believers in the cause became "Filmon Tories" rather than "Progressive Conservatives," and were encouraged to place their faith in Filmon even if they remained unsure about the party as a whole. As a Filmon supporter and delegate to the 1983 leadership convention described it, "We were part of the 'Filmon Team' and we took great pride in that. We felt that we were all in this together."[6] Much of Filmon's appeal also rested with his clear and single-minded message—that in order to move Manitoba forward, the economy needed to be brought in order. "Filmon said 'I have a plan, a vision for Manitoba and I want you to help me achieve it.'"[7]

The loyalty that Filmon's supporters developed towards him rather than the Progressive Conservative Party per se did not occur by happenstance. Rather, it was a calculated manoeuvre designed to neutralize opposition within the party—notably emanating from the rural, conservative wing that still commanded a great deal of clout within the organization. Many heavy hitters within the rural caucus, which included both of his chief rivals for the leadership, remained mistrustful of Filmon's more moderate and centrist approach to issues. He was perceived as too ideologically soft and insufficiently aggressive to be able to take on his NDP opponents. As described by one former Progressive Conservative MLA from this era, Filmon was seen as "weak and a five-star nerd,"[8] a perception that was to linger in some quarters until his majority win in 1990. And indeed, much of his early years of leadership was spent trying to ward off challengers from within his own party.[9] The circumstances weren't helped by the fact that Filmon's predecessor as leader, Sterling Lyon, remained an MLA until his retirement from provincial politics altogether in 1986. Not surprisingly, the powerful presence of a former premier within his own caucus appeared to inhibit Filmon's assertion of authority and his ability to take control of his own party.[10]

Mired in leadership disputes and beset by the unpopularity of Brian Mulroney's federal PC government in the wake of the CF-18 decision, the Progressive Conservatives narrowly lost the 1986 provincial election, securing twenty-six seats compared to the NDP's thirty.[11] The party was given another opportunity two years later, however, when it managed to bring the Pawley government down in a non-confidence motion. In an election that marked what Alex Netherton has described as "the shift to the contemporary globalization-neo-liberal policy paradigm marked by fiscal orthodoxy, attention to market competitiveness, deregulation and privatization,"[12] in April 1988 the Filmon Tories managed to win enough seats to form a minority government. Focusing largely on the troubled state of the Manitoba economy—which was not too difficult of a sell given the times—Filmon was, in many respects, "the perfect candidate for the moment."[13] With provincial debt levels more than doubling during a six-year period and a series of fee increases implemented in major Crown corporations, confidence in the NDP's ability to economically manage the province had gone into freefall.[14] Despite Netherton's assessment, however, the PC's moved slowly at first, continuing with the expenditure control program developed in the latter years of the Pawley administration but extending it to such policy areas as health and education. As one former cabinet minister described the thinking during the party's first mandate, "we knew that we somehow had to start down that road (of structural and economic change), but we also recognized the limitations of minority government."[15]

While trying to portray his administration as a fiscally responsible but moderate government, much of Filmon's first two years as premier was caught up in the debates surrounding the Meech Lake Accord. While a tumultuous time for the province as well as for the PC Party itself, which remained deeply divided on the issue, in the end Meech Lake proved to be extremely fortuitous for Filmon.[16] Inheriting the issue from the Pawley government, Filmon marshalled the mounting opposition in the province against the Accord, and its ultimate defeat at the hands of NDP MLA Elijah Harper, to his political advantage. Thanks to Harper's actions, Filmon avoided being held responsible for the death of Meech Lake, while at the same time successfully dodging criticism from Manitobans for allowing the Accord to pass despite many of their objections—all in one fell swoop. Positioning himself as a champion of Manitoba's interests, the "image of Filmon which resonated with public opinion was not his compliance or surrender, but his long-standing opposition to Ottawa and Quebec."[17] The political benefits that this would accrue to Filmon personally as a result of the tumult over the Accord were also abundantly clear. As a former senior advisor to Filmon commented, "it was after Meech that we knew Filmon was a leader. I said, let's call the election now."[18]

The gamble paid off. Filmon called a snap election for 11 September 1990, and moved quickly to take advantage of his newfound persona as a strong defender of the province.[19] Mindful of the continued downward slide of the federal Progressive Conservative brand, the provincial Tories became revamped as the "Filmon Team." Campaign signs and brochures had Filmon's name prominently displayed, with "Manitoba Progressive Conservatives" barely legible underneath. Focusing on the singular image of Filmon, the Tories ran a series of "feel good" ads featuring the premier paddling a canoe down a river and strolling along a Manitoba beach.[20] Successfully capitalizing on the massive boost to his popularity as a result of his deft handling of the Meech Lake issue, and a Liberal campaign that was a "disaster from start to finish,"[21] Gary Filmon and his Conservative Party were returned to power with a majority government of thirty seats.

During their next term in office, the Progressive Conservatives built on their reputation as competent fiscal managers. Freed from the constraints of minority status, the Tories were able to pursue a more traditionally conservative ideological agenda focusing on smaller government, tax cuts, and private sector entrepreneurship. As campaign material from the 1995 election screamed, "our top priority is economic security and more jobs!"[22] And on this front, the Filmon administration could certainly boast of its achievements. Despite going through the second worst recession of the century and dealing with substantial cuts in federal transfer payments, under the Tories' watch Manitoba was able to avoid the more extreme economic fallout experienced by other provinces. Indeed, in March 1995 the Tories even managed to introduce the first balanced budget in Manitoba in more than twenty years.[23] The government also brought forward a mandatory balanced budget law; at the time, the toughest legislation of its kind in Canada. Not only did the legislation prohibit deficit spending, but it also prohibited tax increases in the absence of a province-wide referendum.[24]

The Progressive Conservatives headed into the 1995 election with the central campaign theme of "making Manitoba strong." The party not only focused on its economic record during the previous seven years in office, but once again banked a great deal of its fortunes on the personal popularity of Gary Filmon. With Filmon consistently named in national opinion polls as the most popular head of government in the country, and his approval ratings in his own province running at 70 percent, this choice of electoral strategy hardly came as a surprise.[25] Candidates for the party were again identified as part of "Team Filmon." With the Progressive Conservative label rarely mentioned, some voters undoubtedly presumed that the party had officially changed its name. Yet once again the plan paid off. When the final votes were counted on 25 April 1995, the Progressive Conservatives had increased their seat count by one and secured the party's largest majority in more than fifteen years.

As the Filmon administration proceeded through what was to be its last term in office, it could lay claim to numerous successes. Certainly, its record on fiscal management had earned it high marks. In the face of recessionary pressures and heavy cuts in federal transfer payments, the province continued to enjoy levels of economic growth that outpaced the national economy as well as a low unemployment rate (at that point, the best in the country). The Progressive Conservatives had also balanced the books for five years in a row and through eleven consecutive budgets had maintained a freeze on major taxes—a claim that no other government in Canada or North America could make at the time.[26] The Tories were also already ahead of schedule in meeting their ambitious thirty-year debt repayment plan. These conditions—a strong economy, low unemployment, and moderate taxes—reflected the typical kinds of factors that would typically lead to re-election for an incumbent government.

Much of the smooth operation of the Tory machine continued to rest with its leader. While some quietly bemoaned his rather authoritarian and dictatorial behaviour behind closed doors, his public image remained immensely popular. With his third consecutive election win in 1995, Gary Filmon had established himself as "one of Manitoba's most successful politicians since the end of the Second World War."[27] It is no coincidence that the only other Manitoba premier who had been able to boast of a similar record was none other than former PC premier Duff Roblin. Filmon's achievements aside, Roblin has remained to this day the most highly revered and respected individual within the PC Party. Indeed, Roblin served as the personal inspiration and mentor to many of those who would subsequently sit in the Filmon caucus, including Filmon himself.[28]

However, as the government proceeded through its third mandate there were troubling signs that not all was well for the party. While the Filmon Progressive Conservatives had banked much of their success on their ability to convince Manitobans of the need for their brand of strong fiscal medicine, a number of controversial bills led some to perceive them as arrogant and power-hungry. The premier also appeared to have dispensed with the pragmatic incrementalism that had marked his early years in government, and seemed committed to creating a leaner and more efficient government. While not as ideologically radical as the Mike Harris and Ralph Klein Progressive Conservative governments in Ontario and Alberta respectively, critics nonetheless pointed to several legislative changes proposed by the Manitoba PCs that suggested a shift to the right.[29] These proposals included the privatization of MTS (which 75 percent of Manitobans had opposed); new governance structures for health care and post-secondary education (with the introduction of regional health authorities and the creation of the Council on Post-Secondary Education); as well as various amendments to the province's labour laws that would make it harder for unions to organize, spend members' dues, and hold votes on contract offers.[30]

It also appeared as if the Progressive Conservatives had become victims of their own economic success. While they had managed to balance the books, a decade of protracted restraint under their watch had led to nothing less than a social deficit in Manitoba. In the public's mind, the years of cuts had eroded the quality of care in many of the province's social services, most notably in the area of health care; a perception the NDP were capitalizing on with their repeated references to "hallway medicine." A 1998 poll conducted by Angus Reid showed that on the health care issue, the Manitoba Progressive Conservatives had an almost 70 percent disapproval rating—the highest disapproval rate across the western provinces.[31] The government's stated plans to privatize home care services and contract out hospital food services, and the union strikes and public outcry with which these measures were met, did little to ameliorate the Progressive Conservatives' credibility gap on the health care issue.

Nonetheless a fall election was called, and the Tories entered the campaign on a positive note. Focusing their message on the strength of the economy and the popularity of the premier, the centrepiece of the PC election platform was the 50/50 plan. Billed as a "solid and balanced approach" designed to "keep Manitoba strong," the five-year plan offered $500 million in tax cuts on the one hand and a $500 million infusion for social programs on the other.[32] For a regime that had long sold the merits of fiscal restraint and cautious government, this apparent spending spree to the tune of a billion dollars was seen as totally out of character. It was also more than the voters could credibly swallow. When the dust settled on 21 September 1999, the NDP had won thirty-two seats to the PCs' twenty-four. After eleven years in power, the Filmon machine had come to a grinding halt. As longtime Tory MLA and cabinet minister Harry Enns was to later comment, "we lost an election we ought to have won."[33]

II. The Party in Disarray

In assessing the decline of the Progressive Conservative Party from the heights of majority government to opposition status in the span of a decade, several factors can be highlighted. Certainly the Tories' 50/50 plan was itself problematic. An overly ambitious plan that seemed an ill fit for a government that had built its reputation on financial caution, it proved to be a tough sell even to the Progressive Conservative faithful. Even the Party's own internal assessment of the 1999 campaign highlighted the poor job it did in communicating and presenting the plan to voters.[34] But the issues that led to the Tories' defeat went much deeper than simply poor electoral strategizing—and in many ways represent some of the challenges that the party is struggling to overcome to this day.

The Vote-Rigging Scandal

Without question, the vote-rigging scandal constitutes one of the most damaging events in the modern history of the Progressive Conservative Party of Manitoba. The plan allegedly involved the fronting of three "independent" Aboriginal candidates in the 1995 provincial election campaign, in an attempt to siphon votes away from the NDP.[35] Implicated in the scandal and the subsequent cover-up were several individuals who stood at the height of the party establishment, including Taras Sokolyk, Filmon's chief of staff and manager of the 1995 campaign, and Julian Benson, secretary of the Treasury Board and former party treasurer.

When the scandal first broke in 1998, both Sokolyk and the premier denied any knowledge of the scheme. As opposition and media pressure continued to mount, Filmon called a public inquiry into the affair, which was headed by retired Manitoba Chief Justice Alfred Monnin. In his final report Monnin concluded that he found Filmon's testimony that he knew nothing of the plan "credible"; however, he went on to declare that "in all my years on the Bench I never encountered as many liars in one proceeding as I did during this inquiry."[36] After the release of the Monnin Report, Filmon took the additional step of commissioning Leonard Doust, an independent prosecutor, to review its findings and consider whether charges might successfully be brought against Sokolyk and Benson. Doust's report, released in August 1999, concluded that prosecutions would likely be successful. However, he recommended against charges on the grounds that the two men had suffered enough both personally and professionally.[37]

While Justice Monnin's findings cleared Filmon of any wrongdoing, the collateral damage caused to him and his party was unequivocal. Polls taken only months before the 1999 provincial election revealed that a majority of undecided voters (57 percent) and a third of Progressive Conservative supporters believed that the premier was not telling the truth about what he knew regarding the vote-rigging scheme. A third of those polled, in addition to 10 percent of those who identified themselves as Progressive Conservatives, also indicated that the scandal would likely influence their vote.[38] Filmon found himself in a Catch-22 situation. "Many thought that it was inconceivable that he would know nothing and that, therefore, he was tarred with the same brush as the other miscreants"; however, even if Filmon was indeed unaware of the plan allegedly cooked up by his senior staff then he clearly had "a poor eye for talent."[39] The fact that one of the individuals implicated in the affair, Julian Benson, was also a high-ranking government official was also worrying, revealing as it did the reach of the Filmon machine in controlling the most powerful levers of the civil service.

Despite this, however, many within the party failed to fully absorb the degree to which the public's trust in Filmon, and the organization he led, had been violated. At the party's 1999 annual general meeting, held just a month before Monnin released his report, a senior aide to the premier was quoted as saying that "there's no question the scandal hurt, but not so much that it will mean losing the election." Another party delegate maintained the whole thing was being "overblown."[40] In the end, the issue of broken trust proved to be too significant an obstacle for the Progressive Conservatives to overcome. For a party that had singularly put its future in the hands of one man, once voters began to question their confidence in Filmon the PCs had little else to fall back on. Hence, despite the Tories' solid economic record and their eleven years of competent and steady leadership, it was the credibility question that sunk them in the end. As one former MLA summed it up, "I think we could have won in 1999 if not for the vote-rigging scandal. Sure health care was an issue, but not enough to lose over. But when the trust is broken, you need time to recover from that."[41]

Re-Branding the NDP

A second factor that accounts for the struggles of the Progressive Conservatives over the past decade, and by extension the success of the NDP, was the leadership of Gary Doer. Doer's impressive re-branding of the Manitoba NDP, and his keen assessment that the best way to beat the Tories was to imitate them, was born out of necessity. As Nelson Wiseman cogently argues, "neo-conservatism has, with some success, identified itself with fiscal prudence and tarred social democracy with the brush of fiscal profligacy—an image and fact that does not correspond insofar as the prairies are concerned."[42] As he further notes, despite the fact that it was the Lyon Progressive Conservatives that were responsible for running up what was until then the largest public debt in the province's history, the NDP's defeat in 1988 imprinted an image in the public's mind of the New Democrats as the party of high taxes and incompetent financial administration.

This was an image that Doer, upon becoming leader of the NDP in March 1988, knew he had to overcome if his party were even to win office again in the foreseeable future. And overcome it he did. At the party's last annual general meeting before the 1999 provincial election, Doer unveiled "Today's NDP"; a party that didn't seem all that markedly different from the Progressive Conservatives.[43] Borrowing a page from Tony Blair's Third Way philosophy, Doer pledged that under his tenure an NDP government would be committed to following the same fiscally prudent path as the Progressive Conservatives (and which had resonated so well amongst Manitobans)—but at a slower, more compassionate pace. The NDP's 1999 platform, while "strikingly modest" in its simplicity, was clearly the right approach to topple the governing Progressive Conservatives.[44] In addition to a promise to continue with the Tories' balanced-budget law, Doer also pledged to fix hallway medicine, to freeze university and college tuition fees, to keep Manitoba Hydro as a Crown corporation, and to make communities safer.

To a large degree Doer's successful reinvention of the NDP rested with his pragmatic, as opposed to ideological, approach to politics, and his resulting ability to attract supporters from beyond the New Democrats' traditional core base. Many liberals and soft conservatives, notably in urban ridings, were consistently drawn to his "reasonable" and "common sense" style of governance. As Gary Filmon himself commented, "I think it's fairly well known that Gary Doer hasn't always been a committed New Democrat."[45] It was also apparent that Doer heeded well the lesson to be learned from the damage done to Filmon in the wake of the vote-rigging scandal. As he noted in a speech early in his premiership, "I am finding that substantive policy is very important. But while we debate policy—in our party, in caucus, and in cabinet—the public wants to get a sense of the character of the people they may vote for or against. Personality politics, as I refer to it, is more important with the public than when I first entered public office over ten years ago."[46]

Already halfway through its first term, the NDP had successfully fashioned itself as a centrist, incrementalist party that appealed to people from all walks of life, including those who normally didn't vote on the left. As Paul Thomas notes, the ability of the Doer administration to combine some of the right-of-centre policies of the former government (such as the balanced budget law) with new funding in such social policy areas as health and child care struck the right balance with Manitobans. "The overall policy stance of the NDP government, which combines fiscal conservatism with spending to create social opportunities, seems to fit with the provincial culture."[47] Since 1999, the party's grasp on the huge political centre has remained as tight as ever. Doer's steady approach to governance not only allowed the NDP to divert from the typical Manitoba pattern of two terms in office, but allowed it to consistently build upon its electoral strength in the past three provincial elections. The "Doer phenomenon" has remained a challenge for the Progressive Conservatives ever since.

The NDP have also benefited from what Chris Adams has described as the "long-term realignment within the provincial electorate, especially in Winnipeg" that occurred in the 1999 election.[48] Support for the province's two dominant parties, the NDP and the PCs, has traditionally broken down along urban/rural lines. While NDP support has historically been strong in the core areas of Winnipeg and the northern regions of the province, the Progressive Conservatives have long dominated the rural areas, particularly in southwestern Manitoba, and the growing suburban ridings of Winnipeg.[49] However, in the 1999 election the New Democrats were not only able to more efficiently translate their votes into seats than the Progressive Conservatives, but they were also able to increase their support throughout all of Winnipeg, including ridings that had been formerly held by the Tories. This realignment, Adams adds, appears to have held through the 2003 and 2007 elections.

The Challenge of Leadership

In hindsight, it is questionable whether Gary Filmon did his party a disservice with his announcement, even before the Monnin inquiry into the vote-rigging scandal began its public hearings, that he would lead the Progressive Conservatives into the 1999 provincial election. With this pre-emptive move the membership was denied the opportunity to decide whether it wanted Filmon to remain at the helm, or whether it preferred to take its chances on a new leader and possibly salvage a minority government. As one long-time party member suggested, "Maybe if Filmon had stepped down a year or so earlier, perhaps we would have had time to recoup."[50] Yet, given the degree to which the party had so fully delivered its fate into the hands of one man, few could contemplate the vacuum that would be left in the wake of his absence. And indeed, the fact that so few contenders would step up to replace Filmon upon his subsequent departure is indicative of just how much the party, as an organization distinct from its leader, had withered. As it was, it would take another seven years before the leadership issue would be brought to any kind of resolution.

Filmon's departure would come just a few months later. On election night in 1999 the Progressive Conservative Party, reeling from its defeat after eleven years in power, had to further contend with Filmon's abrupt announcement of his intention to step down as leader. While the sudden departure of a leader would be difficult for any political organization, in the Progressive Conservatives' case it proved to be nothing less than devastating. As a cadre-style party, leadership has played a particularly prominent role in the Progressive Conservative Party. As opposed to mass organizations, cadre parties are seen as extensions of their leaders, revolving around them and their coteries of advisors.[51] The party organization thus becomes transformed into a personalized machine to build and sustain a coalition of support for the leader's policies, with party conventions and policy conferences "serving more as democratic showpieces for the electorate and as mechanisms for control and communication by the leadership."[52]

The centrality of leadership in the PC Party was reflected in the confidential interviews conducted for this chapter, as well as in public comments of high-profile MLAs in the wake of the party's 1999 defeat.[53] Several party insiders and organizers pointed to how the Progressive Conservative Party had been redesigned in the image of Gary Filmon, and the impact that this had on its organization and grassroots. As one former party strategist described it, "Once we won a majority government in 1990, Gary Filmon was seen as the winning formula. And after that, the thinking of his staffers was that we didn't need the party or the membership anymore as long as we had Filmon at the top."[54] As the "Filmon machine" became increasingly professionalized and controlled by his political advisors, the balance of power shifted not only from the party to Filmon and his inner circle, but from caucus as well.[55] Cabinet minister and subsequent leadership contender Darren Praznik publicly admitted that in its final years, the Filmon administration had turned its back on party rank and file, while Harry Enns, considered by many at that time to be the "dean" of the PC Party, stated that "we were arrogant and we paid for it. We have to get out of that inner-circle crowd that has been running the Conservative Party of Manitoba."[56]

The transformation of the Progressive Conservative Party into a marketable brand based on the persona of its leader is not a phenomenon unique to Manitoba, but in fact describes the general evolution of the dominant parties in Canada.[57] It seems to chiefly hold when parties are in power, as studies in Canada and Britain have suggested.[58] As Réjean Pelletier maintains, there appears to be a natural life cycle for political parties.[59] When in power, the party organization withers; rather than a political vehicle, it is reduced to little more than an administrative shell for the processing of memberships and appeals for donations from the party faithful. It is only during times of opposition where party activists are again able to assume positions of prominence and push through reforms. Pelletier's examination of the national Liberal, Progressive Conservative, and New Democratic parties found that in each case, despite the organizational and ideological differences amongst them, "ascent to power is often marked by decline in the party's internal life."

While Filmon's announcement of his imminent departure was a blow to his party, the Progressive Conservatives were thrown into further turmoil when shortly thereafter Eric Stefanson, the former finance minister and the most likely replacement to Filmon, declared that he would not be contesting the leadership. The events that followed were to shape the PC Party's fortunes for the next several years, the scars from which the organization still bears. Rather than appointing an interim leader and delaying a leadership convention a year or two, the decision was made to forge ahead immediately with Filmon's replacement. The quick turnaround would mean that the Progressive Conservatives would have insufficient time to recover from their 1999 defeat while simultaneously attempting to rebuild their organizational base and forge a new identity. At the very least, the party would have benefited from a well-fought leadership campaign; one which would officially mark the break from the old regime to the new, and would re-energize the grassroots of the party as only leadership campaigns typically can. Yet this was not to be the case.

In the spring of 2000, Darren Praznik was the first candidate to officially throw his hat into the leadership race. Soon after Stuart Murray, a long-time Progressive Conservative Party strategist and insider, also announced his intention to run. As described by ex-Filmon cabinet minister Linda McIntosh, the race between Murray and Praznik would shape up to be "a contest between the establishment and the grassroots."[60] Despite Praznik's tenure as a cabinet minister within the Filmon administration, Murray was clearly the preferred choice of the party elite. While he had long served in a number of advisory roles, most recently as Filmon's director of communications in the 1999 election campaign, the fact that Murray had never actually run for office himself was considered an asset. Untainted by this kind of direct political baggage, he was seen by his supporters as the kind of fresh, new face needed to renew the party rank and file, and to convince voters that the Tories were once again worthy of their trust.

Given the party heavyweights that threw their support behind Murray, the race was over as soon as it began. With Praznik's subsequent withdrawal from the race a short time later (citing as mitigating factors a lack of funds and the exceedingly long length of the campaign—almost twice that of the 1983 leadership campaign), Murray remained uncontested in his bid for the Party's top job. Praznik's withdrawal was to turn the leadership race into nothing less than a public relations disaster for the Progressive Conservatives. In announcing that he was stepping down, Praznik suggested that the contest had been set up so as to favour Murray. The party executive needed to think long and hard about the campaign rules it set, Praznik added, and needed to ask itself why only one person in the province would seek to lead a political organization that had ruled for all of the 1990s. As he stated, "I think [my withdrawal] is an indication that the people putting this together haven't thought things through."[61] Indeed, the fact that no other members of the PC caucus were interested in leading their own party was telling.

With Praznik's withdrawal from the race, Murray was acclaimed as leader at the party's annual general meeting in November 2000. As Gary Doer was to quip, the fact Murray assumed the top job without a single vote cast confirming his leadership was "unusual in this province. Even Boris Yeltsin had a leadership vote."[62] The manner in which Murray assumed the helm of the PC Party, by acclamation rather than through a legitimately contested leadership race, continued to plague him throughout his tenure. Not only did the absence of a leadership campaign fail to give the PCs the shot of adrenaline that they so badly needed after their demoralizing loss the previous year, but it constrained Murray from ever being able to fully solidify his authority over his own caucus and party.

The Party under Stuart Murray

Murray's leadership was beleaguered from the start with a number of fresh scandals and challenges. In the spring of 2001, Elections Manitoba launched investigations against several high-profile Progressive Conservatives for allegedly engaging in smear tactics against an NDP candidate during the 1999 election campaign, as well as for spending irregularities in the 1995 and 1999 campaigns. Particularly damaging for Murray, however, were two events that led some within the party to question his political judgement. The first was his decision in October 2002 to hire Taras Sokolyk, the man at the centre of the vote-rigging scandal, on a three-month consulting contract. What was particularly troublesome was the fact that Murray had apparently failed to inform the party's executive, which was constitutionally mandated to approve all expenditures. Murray had also seemingly neglected to inform the majority of his elected caucus until a month after Sokolyk had been hired; indeed, the issue was only brought to light when Sokolyk submitted an invoice to party headquarters.[63] The issue subsequently sparked a firestorm and led to the resignation of the party's treasurer. Dubbed "Taras-gate" by the media, the scandal created rifts within the Tory caucus, and shook party members across the province. While Murray managed to escape calls for a subsequent leadership review,[64] the damage was done. As one Conservative commented, "Murray had tried to sell the fact that the party was under new management; that it had learned its lessons and could be trusted again. To go ahead and hire the one person many Tories still blamed for costing us government was seen as pretty questionable judgement."[65]

In hindsight, Taras-gate marked the beginning of the end for Murray; galvanizing as it did opposition forces within the party who still bore resentment over the loss of government in 1999 and the process that led to Murray's assumption of leadership. Despite attempts to address these criticisms and put his own stamp on the PC Party (including the unveiling of a new party name and logo and the adoption of a one-member, one-vote leadership selection process), grumblings within the caucus over Murray's seeming inability to lift the party out of its doldrums began to publicly surface.[66] Much of the blame was attributed to Murray's lack of experience as a politician, which was not helped by the fact that many of his closest staff members were also unseasoned. After the party's loss in the 1999 provincial election, there had been an exodus of not only Filmon's most skilled political and policy advisors, but also former cabinet ministers and MLAs who carried with them a wealth of experience and institutional knowledge.[67] A similar upheaval had also occurred over at PC Party headquarters, with the organization going through three executive directors within a two-year period.

The second event that was to cause Murray much personal damage was his mishandling of concerns surrounding the Crocus Investment Fund, a labour-sponsored venture capital corporation in Manitoba. While rumours had begun to surface in 2001 of financial mismanagement within the fund, Murray decided to not only back away from the issue and possibly score some much needed political points against the NDP, but he also stopped his finance critic from looking any further into the matter. In June 2005, the day after the Auditor General of Manitoba released a report affirming the fund was in trouble, Murray admitted in a live radio broadcast that he had been "shaken down" by high-ranking members of the PC Party who were themselves involved in the investment fund. As someone close to Murray at the time commented, "Stu never seemed to recover after that."[68]

The Progressive Conservative Party was also substantially wounded during this period by changes brought in by the NDP to the province's Elections Finances Act. These amendments, which took effect in January 2001, banned corporate and union donations to political parties in Manitoba, and set ceilings on individual donations of $3,000 per person. The PCs cried foul over these changes, arguing that it was an attempt by the NDP to financially cripple its opponents. And while all parties saw their donations drop as a result of these changes, the PC Party was by far the hardest hit. The Tories, who were more dependent on corporate donations for the bulk of their financial resources than the NDP, was plunged into nothing short of a financial crisis. Between 2000 and 2001, the PC Party lost more than two-thirds of its annual revenues; the largest drop of all the parties in Manitoba.[69]

The 2003 Election Campaign

When the Doer government called an election for June 2003, the prospects for the Manitoba Tories were anything but promising. Ongoing discontent within caucus, coupled with generally weak showings in the Manitoba Legislature, made it hard for voters to determine just what the PC Party stood for at the turn of the new century. Added to this was the fact that Murray remained a relatively unknown commodity to most Manitobans, with polls indicating that only 16 percent of voters could actually identify him as the leader of the Progressive Conservative Party.[70] As well, the party was still struggling on the financial front. Carrying a debt of over $350,000 with virtually no cash reserves, and having had already exhausted two lines of credit, the party was forced to borrow money from one of its supporters in order to fund its election campaign.[71] With little choice but to lay off staff, including the party's latest CEO, concerns began to surface over the extent to which the Progressive Conservatives would even be able to effectively compete in an election.

The result, to the say the least, was an austere election campaign, with a budget of only a quarter of what the party had spent in 1999.[72] The lack of resources meant the Conservatives were unable to launch either a significant advertising effort or leader's tour—and given the lack of name recognition and visibility that already existed where Murray was concerned, this did not help matters. The minimalist campaign the Tories were forced to mount undermined their ability to effectively sell their ideas (not helped by the fact that the campaign website was not active until almost two weeks into the writ period) and raised doubts whether they would actually be able to deliver on their key promises. Murray's growing unpopularity as a leader and perceived liability to the party was also reflected in the fact that some candidates did not even want him campaigning in their constituencies. In stark contrast to the re-branding of the PC Party that occurred under Filmon, Murray's picture was not portrayed in election brochures, nor was his name featured on candidates' signs. In an attempt to hang on to their own ridings, some incumbents even abandoned party-approved signs and brochures in favour of materials that were absent of references to the PC Manitoba team and Murray in particular.[73]

There was one distinct area where the 2003 campaign was reminiscent of the Filmon era, and that was the focus on the economy and taxes. As their central election plank the Progressive Conservatives promised to cut education property taxes to the tune of $200 million, while at the same time delivering balanced budgets. In the face of NDP attacks that dismissed it as reckless, the plan proved to be a hard sell. Voters remained skeptical about the Progressive Conservatives' ability to cut taxes that significantly without triggering deficit spending. In a larger sense, it also seemed that by returning to themes that had been well-worn during the Filmon years, the party had really nothing new to offer Manitobans. Unlike the recessionary climate of the 1980s, by this time the Manitoba economy was doing well, and most Manitobans were generally satisfied with the slow and steady approach of the Doer administration.

Yet despite these factors, the 2003 election was not the complete disaster for the Progressive Conservatives many had predicted. While it certainly was the party's worst electoral showing since 1953, the party still managed to hang on to twenty seats (down four from 1999), and garner a respectable 36 percent in popular support (a drop from 41 percent in 1999). Murray publicly noted that while the election result was a step backwards for the party, there was still reason for optimism. "The fact that we came back with twenty seats when everyone had written us off, I'm very, very pleased with that," he stated.[74] The Progressive Conservative Party's own post-mortem on the 2003 election, co-authored by Murray's campaign manager and director of communications, absolved the leader and the central campaign team for the loss of seats. Instead, blame was attributed to the lack of resources and volunteers, with the report noting that many Tories were "frustrated with the state of the party" and were hence "turned off."[75] As later events were to show, these findings would not endear Murray to his caucus and membership.

The Revolt Against Murray

As the party prepared for its first annual general meeting following the 2003 election, rumours abounded whether Murray's leadership would be challenged. While a last-minute motion that could have resulted in a leadership vote was almost unanimously defeated, it was clear to many in attendance at the 2004 annual general meeting that the issue was not going to go away. And indeed, it didn't. By the following October, despite the fact that the Tories had managed to not only retire $500,000 in debt but had begun to rebound in the polls, high-ranking members of the party were already openly discussing the need to remove Murray as leader.[76]

These plans became public when a motion calling for a leadership convention, to be brought forward at the party's 2005 annual general meeting, was seconded by a sitting member of Murray's own caucus. The timing of the motion, coming as it did on the eve of the opening of the fall session of the Manitoba Legislature, only led to the further division of an already fractious party. With no real contenders to replace Murray on the horizon, and with the next election looming closer, many Progressive Conservatives felt it was foolish to engage in internecine battles while the NDP continued to govern unchecked. As one party member commented, "It was all done in such poor taste. Despite whatever supposed faults he may have had, Stu was our leader, and we needed to respect that. Instead of fighting the NDP, we declared open war on our own leader."[77] On the other hand was the view, as expressed by one longtime Progressive Conservative member and former cabinet minister, that "Tories like to win, we haven't been winning, and somebody needs to account for that."[78] By this point it was evident Murray would not be able to contain the growing frustration within the PC Party. While the resolution was subsequently defeated by a 55 percent to 45 percent margin, Murray was left with little option but to call for a leadership convention. Two weeks later, he would bring his own political career to an end with the announcement that he would not be running as a candidate. As Ron Schuler, PC MLA and Murray supporter commented, "We've realized my greatest fear. We've overthrown the leader, we don't have a lot of time, there is no heir apparent and there's a government that needs our full attention."[79]

On a personal level, Murray was genuinely well-liked by many within and outside of the Progressive Conservative Party. However, in many ways his leadership was doomed from the start. He was never able to quite step out of the shadow of Gary Filmon, a leader who had brought the party a level of success not seen since the days of Duff Roblin more than thirty years earlier. He also inherited a caucus that seemed to never fully accept him as their boss, but rather saw him as some kind of temporary fix until their "real" leader returned.[80] In the final analysis, Murray fell victim to a common aspect of cadre parties. Intensely loyal to their leaders in times of success, these types of parties are just as quick to turn on them when they fail to deliver them to electoral victory—as Stuart Murray was to eventually discover.

III. The Party Rebuilds

Once again, the Progressive Conservative Party of Manitoba found itself in search of a leader. But now it had to contend with not only lingering resentment over the events which had resulted in the removal of Stuart Murray, but the realization that this time around there could be no quick fixes. If there was one thing that was abundantly clear, it was the need for a well-contested leadership race. The party executive banked on the hope that such a race, along with the new one-member, one-vote leadership selection process that had been implemented under Murray, would not only boost memberships but would also bring in some much-needed new energy. With a vote set for April 2006, three candidates stepped forward to replace Murray: Ron Schuler, MLA for Springfield; Ken Waddell, a longtime member of the party and the former mayor of Neepawa; and Hugh McFadyen, who had joined the PC caucus in a 2005 provincial by-election as the MLA for Fort Whyte.

While the party executive took pains to stress that this would be a truly open race, McFadyen quickly became the top contender. He was a rookie MLA, but McFadyen nonetheless had a long history with the PC Party. He had worked for a number of years behind the scenes in the Filmon administration, eventually replacing Taras Sokolyk in 1998 as Filmon's top advisor. A young, personable, and articulate lawyer, McFadyen had gone on to serve as the deputy campaign chair of the party's 1999 election campaign, and following the Tories' defeat had also worked as an advisor to Winnipeg mayor Sam Katz. Like Murray before him, McFadyen was clearly the preferred choice of the party establishment. Seen as a bit of a "golden boy," McFadyen amassed the support of an impressive array of former heavyweights from the Filmon era as well as a majority of sitting caucus members.

With the theme of renewal front and centre throughout the leadership campaign (not surprising, given the dismal state of the party at that point), McFadyen capitalized on his momentum and launched a polished effort to win over party members. In his speech at the party's leadership convention on 29 April 2006 McFadyen highlighted his plans to unite both the party and the PC caucus, recruit strong candidates, win back seats in Winnipeg, and keep young Manitobans at home. His slogan of "New day, winning day, join the winning way today," despite its awkwardness, clearly resonated amongst members. When the votes were counted that night he had won an overwhelming victory; securing 67 percent of the votes on the first ballot compared to 21 percent for Schuler and 12 percent for Waddell. An obviously pleased Gary Filmon (who had remained officially neutral throughout the race, as had Stuart Murray) commented, "It's a new generation and a new opportunity for the party."[81]

The 2007 Election Campaign

McFadyen was less than a year into his new job when the party was faced with a provincial election. Nonetheless, there were reasons to be hopeful heading into the campaign. Not only were the Progressive Conservatives confident that, in the natural order of things, it was "their turn" to govern, but they also had a new, young leader with a fresh outlook (in contrast to the considerably time-worn leaders of both the NDP and the Liberal Party). And indeed, the party had begun to rebound in the polls; shortly after McFadyen's win, the PCs had surpassed the governing NDP in the quarterly Probe Research-*Winnipeg Free Press* poll for the first time since 1999.[82] After eight years in power, the NDP government had also begun to fray around the edges, suffering a series of minor blows over issues related to the Crocus Investment Fund, problems within its handling of Child and Family Services which had resulted in the death of a young child, and the public's ongoing frustrations with the province's health-care system.

The Progressive Conservatives banked their electoral fortunes on several assumptions. The first of these was the idea that parties in Manitoba are entitled to only two majority governments after which the electorate will vote for change. Certainly, there was some historical justification for this assumption. Since the late 1960s, when the NDP under the leadership of Ed Schreyer became a major force in the province, Manitoba voters have typically alternated on a fairly predictable basis between the NDP and the Progressive Conservatives.[83] And it was a safe bet to assume that in the more volatile political climate that marked modern-day politics, voters would be less quick to give any political party a resounding blank cheque on governance, let alone an incumbent government that had already been in office for almost a decade. This was a common refrain heard not only within Progressive Conservative circles, but even NDP insiders admitted to hearing this view expressed in their party's internal research. "The scariest thing we heard in focus groups before the election was, 'Well, maybe we should give the other guys a chance,'" an NDP pollster explained after the election campaign.[84]

The Progressive Conservatives also assumed that a change of leadership would be enough to reinvent their party, in the absence of other changes to enhance their competitive position. As Stewart and Carty maintain, it has become conventional wisdom in Canada that changing leaders will pay an electoral dividend, since a new leader provides a fresh face for the easily jaded electorate. This is particularly the case for a party in trouble, since it is presupposed that "a new leader will represent new policy positions and establish a new persona and, in doing so, allow it to escape its record."[85] Despite the questionable validity of this assumption, however, it nonetheless reflected the thinking of many who had supported the call for a leadership review at the PC Party's November 2005 annual general meeting. Those members who had spoken out against the resolution had argued that the party should be focusing its energies on fighting the NDP, rather than squandering it on questions of leadership just a few short months before an anticipated election call; for others, a change in leadership was viewed as the panacea for the ills that plagued the party. As one party member put it: "The feeling going into the election was almost one of 'OK we've gotten rid of Stu, all of our problems are over now that we've got a new leader.'"[86]

It is possible the leadership gamble could have paid off for the Progressive Conservative Party of Manitoba in the 2007 campaign if it had also been accompanied by a renewed sense of what it now stood for. But the fact the party had still not done the heavy lifting in terms of clarifying its vision and establishing itself as a clear and viable alternative to the governing NDP was reflected in its inability to draw support during the campaign. As one party insider commented, "We failed on policy in the campaign. Not only did we not have a good platform, we didn't even have a core set of ideas to wrap around our supporters."[87] With the polls showing a virtual dead heat between the parties a month before the election was called, the Progressive Conservatives needed to give Manitobans a reason to vote for them; a clear ballot question that would have put the New Democrats on the defensive.[88] Despite some wear and tear, the general impression was that the NDP had provided competent government. Even the Progressive Conservative Party's internal polling was showing that most Manitobans still liked Doer, and were satisfied with the direction that his government was taking the province.[89]

McFadyen's campaign message of "together we can," derivative of Barack Obama's campaign theme that had resonated so well south of the border, failed to have the same kind of impact in Manitoba. When carefully elaborated and accompanied by strong leadership, this kind of message could inspire Manitobans to vote for change. When it is poorly articulated and not linked to a specific plan, however, it falls flat.[90] According to some, what was missing from the Progressive Conservative election platform was a clear message that would be reflected in all other policy statements. "We should have said, 'We're doing OK (as a province) but we could be doing better, OK is not good enough. Here's our plan, in our first four-year mandate we'll do this, and then we'll do that. But we have a plan, so just stick with us and we'll get there.' Instead, we got off track because people still liked Doer and we didn't know to sell it (the need for a new government)."[91]

The Progressive Conservatives also made the mistake of letting the NDP take the initiative in the campaign from the outset, and did not adequately go on the offensive to promote their policies. From the moment the writ was dropped, a few hours after the Winnipeg visit by Prime Minister Stephen Harper to announce funding for the Canadian Museum of Human Rights (during which Harper heaped praise on Doer for his leadership on the issue), the NDP set the tone for the rest of the campaign. This appeared evident already by the first week of the campaign. The PC strategy was based on five main planks, which would be released each week of the writ period. The first week they announced their plan to cut the PST by one percentage point. However, instead of defending the benefits of this proposal, "we just backed down. Doer said, 'It's not reasonable' and we didn't fight back."[92]

It was during the second and third weeks of the writ period, however, when the Tory campaign seemed to become irrevocably derailed. With the release of their crime and punishment platform, the Conservatives had hoped to tap into the fears of Winnipeggers regarding rising crime rates. As an NDP strategist commented, "if there was going to be an issue that brought us down, this was it."[93] But it appears the PCs panicked when the issue fell flat; as a way of spiking the polls, the party floated its idea to bring back the Winnipeg Jets hockey team.[94] The Jets announcement came to dominate the rest of the election campaign, and overshadowed any traction the party might have been able to pick up with the rest of its campaign announcements. As one party worker argued, in the aftermath policy making became developed on the fly. "Instead of spending ten days explaining and defending the Jets idea we got scared and ran away from it."[95] As such, the Jets issue effectively let the NDP off the hook from having to debate other issues, and defend their record on other important matters to Manitobans such as crime, taxes, and health care.

The end result was a historic achievement for Gary Doer and the NDP. On 22 May 2007, for the first time in the province's history, the Manitoba New Democrats won a third straight majority in the provincial legislature. Indeed, such a "three-peat" had occurred only once before in Manitoba, when Duff Roblin led his Progressive Conservative Party to three straight majorities in the 1960s. While keeping their hold on power was certainly accomplishment enough, the New Democrats also managed to pull off the seemingly impossible by actually increasing their number of seats by one. Having entered the election with thirty-five seats to the Progressive Conservatives' eighteen seats and the Liberals' two seats, by the time the votes were counted on election night the NDP had managed to increase its seats to a total of thirty-six.

While the election was historic for the NDP, it also represented a new record for the Conservatives—albeit a less than stellar one. While the party's popular vote increased slightly, the Conservatives went down to nineteen seats—the lowest number of seats for the party since 1953. At the same time, while the PCs' electoral strength dropped, whatever gains the party had made in Winnipeg through the 1990s collapsed. Not only did the New Democrats hold on to their traditional strongholds in the north and central regions of the city, but they also managed to pick up seats for the first time in such affluent suburbs as Southdale and Kirkfield Park, Winnipeg constituencies long considered safe for the Tories. The net effect of the 2007 election was a further shrinkage of the Progressive Conservatives' base of support down to the rural ridings outside of Winnipeg, where the party not only hung on to its existing seats but managed to return one seat, Brandon West, to the Tory fold (albeit by a scant fifty-eight votes).

A Great Renewal?

"Renewal" was the theme when PC Party members gathered in Brandon in April 2008 for the party's annual general meeting, the first such gathering of the membership since the party's disappointing showing in the 2007 election. In his letter to delegates, McFadyen proclaimed that the 2008 AGM would be "far different" than what had occurred in years past. "I believe that Manitobans want and deserve a government that sets out bold objectives, while mapping out a viable and sustainable path to meet those goals," he declared.[96] To this end, he added the 2008 annual meeting would mark the beginning of a two-year policy development process, designed to reinvigorate the membership and to guide the future direction of the PC Party and the province.

Yet despite McFadyen's enthusiasm, the future of the Progressive Conservative Party of Manitoba will depend on a number of critical issues, some of which lie beyond its immediate control. From a purely strategic point of view, the Progressive Conservatives must find a way to defeat at least ten NDP or Liberal MLAs in order to win a bare majority in the next election. Almost all of these seats are in Winnipeg, where thirty-one of the provincial legislature's fifty-seven seats are located. They are seats primarily held by the governing NDP. Hence, breaking through the NDP's so-called "Fortress Winnipeg" must remain a key objective for the Progressive Conservatives if they hope to appeal to more than just their traditional base of rural supporters.

The question, of course, is how to achieve this. Some argue the Progressive Conservative Party must take a more aggressive stand on issues if it ever hopes to break through in Winnipeg. As one party worker commented, "We don't realize the opportunities we miss to go after the NDP. We're not forcing their hand on anything; it's like we're scared of them."[97] At the same time, given that the road to political victory goes directly through the city, the party would do well to develop a strong urban platform. "We need to give Winnipeggers a reason to vote for us," declared another party member. This really hasn't happened yet, he added, because of the continued presence of a strong rural faction within the Progressive Conservative caucus. "Many of those guys don't know how to win Winnipeg, which is not surprising because that's not their frame of reference. But politics has changed from the old days when we could just rely on our rural base to win elections."[98]

Others point to what they view as the "identity crisis" that continues to plague the Progressive Conservative Party. There is still the lingering sense that the party, which had been so successfully re-branded in the image of Gary Filmon, has yet to figure out what it stands for in the wake of his absence. The lack of a clear party vision remained a challenge under Murray's leadership, and appears to have persisted thus far under McFadyen. In the words of one former political staffer from the Filmon days,

> It's not the 1990s anymore; we can't just talk about debt and the need to shrink government and cut taxes. That might have worked for Filmon, but the times were so different. People were more worried about jobs and the state of the economy then. Now things are basically good, Manitoba is doing well economically, the NDP have been seen as doing a good job. Sure things could be better, but there isn't a groundswell of Manitobans demanding change.[99]

The challenge for the Progressive Conservatives, then, is to find the issues that define them in the twenty-first century. However, in redefining itself the party must be cognizant of striking a balance between policies that maintain the support of its rural base while at the same time speaking to issues that appeal to urban and suburban voters. As Wesley's analysis of political party attitudes in Manitoba reveals, the Tories have always struggled in their attempts to balance out their more "progressive" and more "conservative" wings, which have tended to reflect the urban/rural divide within the party.[100] Spanning this spectrum, the party has historically swung between these two pillars depending on the ideological views of its leadership and the temper of the times. Indeed, to find evidence of this one need only contrast the progressive government of Duff Roblin, whereby "the state became an active partner in economic change," to the more conservative regime of Sterling Lyon, which was "clearly on the ideological right in fiscal, social, and constitutional matters."[101]

Finding this middle ground in the modern era, however, will be problematic. On the one hand, the party will be expected to continue to espouse the traditional values upon which it was built (and which continue to appeal to the right wing of the party), including fiscal management, individual freedom, smaller government, lower taxes, and law and order. Concomitantly, the party cannot afford to alienate or scare off potential voters in the urban areas that remain wary of the federal Conservative Party's brand. In terms of where the vast majority of Manitobans ideologically sit, the pragmatic centre appears to hold the best hope for improving the Progressive Conservative Party's electoral fortunes. As Paul Thomas argues, history along with economic, social, and political circumstances have combined to produce a moderate, small-c conservative political culture in Manitoba.[102] From the days of Duff Roblin, successful parties and premiers in the province have been pragmatic and cautious in their policy approaches.[103] Provincial elections are always close with the winning party usually having only a handful more seats than the opposition parties.

The difficulty, of course, is that in more forcefully staking out the middle ground, the Progressive Conservative Party will have to fight for ideological space that has already been successfully claimed by the NDP. Indeed, much of the Progressive Conservatives' fate rests with the fortunes of the NDP, and in particular the ability of the party to reposition itself in the wake of Gary Doer's resignation in the fall of 2009. Like Filmon in his time, Doer largely built the modern-day NDP in his image, and his persona continues to loom large over the party. While the first opinion poll released following Doer's departure showed the NDP maintaining a strong ten percentage-point lead over its Progressive Conservative rivals, Manitobans still have yet to form a strong opinion of new leader and premier Greg Selinger.[104] Despite having served for many years as minister of finance in the Doer administration, Selinger, like so many of his cabinet colleagues, was overshadowed by the charisma and popularity of his boss. In the absence of Doer's strong and steady leadership, there is the possibility that internecine battles amongst New Democrats could emerge, as the party's left wing seeks to reassert the traditional social democratic ideals of the NDP against those who would want to continue with Doer's centrist and pragmatic style. As Chris Adams articulates, the NDP also "faces a number of challenges as it moves towards the end of the current decade and beyond."[105] Precisely how the NDP will position itself as it moves forward, and the attendant opportunities that this might present for the Progressive Conservatives, remains to be seen.

Hugh McFadyen has used the intervening time since the last election to implement a number of initiatives designed to strengthen the PC Party, and to remedy some of the ills that have plagued it in recent years. Undoubtedly, these are also measures designed to ward off any leadership challenges, not surprising given the party's tendency to turn against its leaders in times of defeat. Central to these reforms has been a major overhaul of the party's organizational machinery; transforming it from primarily an administrative body into a more professional and political entity. As described by Doug Schweitzer, the PC Party's former CEO, these changes have been necessitated by the realization that indeed "politics [today] is different than it was in the 1990s."[106] Changes undertaken at the party's headquarters have included the hiring of new staff, the upgrading of database systems and the implementation of new fundraising mechanisms. In addition, the Progressive Conservatives have also invested considerable effort in transforming their communications infrastructure, and have recently unveiled a new interactive website. Combining multimedia, social networking, and the cleverly named "HughTube," the party is banking on its use of the Internet to be able to reach more Manitobans and convince them of its readiness to govern.

While the fortunes of the PC Party are difficult to predict, there are some positive signs on the horizon. The party has begun to rebuild itself financially; in recent years it has outpaced the NDP in donations, and in 2007 the party's total income reached the $2-million mark.[107] At the same time, the membership of the party has increased, considerably boosted by the growth in memberships that accompanied the 2006 leadership campaign.[108] More hopeful for the Progressive Conservatives are the demographic shifts occurring within the province; shifts which may provide them with further opportunities in the future.[109] In 1999 the NDP drew more of its support from younger and middle-aged voters, while a majority of those over the age of 55 supported the Progressive Conservatives by a ratio of almost two to one. By 2007, this pattern reversed somewhat, with the Conservatives pulling some of the 18–34 youth vote away from the NDP (41 percent for the Tories compared to 37 percent for the NDP). At the same time, older voters appear to be moving from the Tories and towards the NDP, from

34 percent to 51 percent respectively. The fluidity of the youth vote is a factor that McFadyen appears particularly well poised to capture. It is also a demographic the party is consciously targeting through its focus on the Internet and its aspirational messaging. "I think young people are far more engaged in politics and far more interested than what we give them credit for," McFadyen stated. "A big part of our challenge, and my mission, is to find a way to get them involved in what we're doing."[110]

As it looks ahead to the next election, which under provincial legislation is currently set to take place on 4 October 2011, McFadyen is likewise attempting to broaden the party's base of support with his message of hope and optimism. "The plan and the message that we're going to offer is going to be quite different," he indicated, than what the NDP has presented to the electorate in the past. As Manitobans we have been taught to believe that "we are mediocre, that we should never hope for the best" and that we should be content to remain where we are. "I just believe that we can do a lot better than that."[111] In particular, McFadyen is hoping to use the troubled national economy as a means of differentiating his party from that of the NDP. As he argues, while the Manitoba economy is anticipated to do better relative to other parts of the country, this has largely been due to the fact that the NDP have benefited from the unprecedented levels of revenue that have flowed from Ottawa. With Manitoba having become increasingly dependent on federal transfer payments, in McFadyen's estimation the last decade has been a story of missed opportunities. Referencing former leader Gary Doer, McFadyen stated "we [had] a premier who has made himself popular spending other people's money, which is really easy to do, and who has left us in a position where there's no flexibility, no room left now that that we're heading into difficult times."[112] Given that recessions typically hurt incumbent governments, the degree to which the Manitoba economy slides downward over the next couple of years could certainly play to the Progressive Conservatives' favour.

And despite some frustrated rumblings following the last election, it appears McFadyen's leadership, at least for the time being, is secure. With one election already under his belt, and no likely challengers waiting in the wings, many believe McFadyen will only continue to grow into the role of leader. At the very least, there appears to be the general realization the party would be foolish to repeat the mistakes of its past and put itself through yet another leadership crisis. As one long-time party member commented, "If he can continue to get himself known to Manitobans, and provide a better sense of who he is and what his party stands for, there's no reason why McFadyen can't be premier one day."[113]

It is also important to remember, as David Stewart rightly points out, the fact that support for the Progressive Conservative Party of Manitoba has remained remarkably stable over the past decade, even in the face of its seeming disarray. With a popular vote that has shifted by only 7 percent from their days in power to opposition status, the Progressive Conservatives have hardly been rendered to the dustbins of political history. The Manitoba Tories can also find great comfort in the results of the 2008 federal election, whereby their federal Conservative cousins managed to win four out of the eight ridings located in the City of Winnipeg. From 2006 to 2008, popular support for the federal Conservatives increased in every urban riding in Winnipeg, even in such traditional NDP ridings as Winnipeg North, Winnipeg Centre, and Elmwood-Transcona.[114] While there may have been intervening variables at play (namely, a weakened and fractious federal Liberal party), these results nonetheless indicate that conservatism remains a popular, and growing, force in the city.

At the end of the day, the best plan for the Progressive Conservatives may be to simply wait it out. If there is one guarantee that can be pointed to in Manitoba politics, it is that nothing is permanent. As Hugh McFadyen himself noted, "however infallible a party or a leader may appear at any point in time, with time all parties and all leaders eventually fall."[115] In terms of leading the party back to the corridors of power, this may prove to be the best strategy yet.

Notes

1 The author wishes to thank David Stewart and Nelson Wiseman for their thoughtful comments on an earlier version of this chapter.

2 For stylistic reasons, in this chapter the Progressive Conservative Party of Manitoba will alternately be referred to as the "PC Party," the "Progressive Conservative Party," the "Conservative Party," "the PCs," or the "Tories."

3 This chapter focuses on the fortunes of the PC Party of Manitoba during the past quarter century. For earlier discussions of Manitoba political history, see Murray Donnelly, *The Government of Manitoba* (Toronto: University of Toronto Press, 1963); Tom Peterson, "Manitoba: Ethnic and Class Politics," in *Canadian Provincial Politics: The Party Systems of the Ten Provinces*, ed. M. Robin (Scarborough: Prentice-Hall, 1978); Rand Dyck, *Provincial Politics in Canada: Towards the Turn of the Century*, 3rd ed. (Scarborough: Prentice-Hall Canada, 1996); Meir Serfaty, "Electoral Behaviour in Manitoba: The Convergence of Geography and Politics," in *The Geography of Manitoba: Its Land and People*, ed. J. Welsted, J. Everitt and C. Stadel (Winnipeg: University of Manitoba Press, 1996); Nelson Wiseman, "The Pattern of Prairie Politics," in *Party Politics in Canada*, ed. H. Thorburn (Scarborough: Prentice-Hall Canada, 1996); Duff Roblin, *Speaking for Myself: Politics and Other Pursuits* (Winnipeg: Great Plains Publications, 1999); and Alex Netherton, "Paradigm and Shift: A Sketch of Manitoba Politics," in *The Provincial State in Canada*, ed. Keith Brownsey and Michael Howlett (Peterborough: Broadview Press, 2001).

4 Chris Adams, *Politics in Manitoba: Parties, Elections and Leaders* (Winnipeg: University of Manitoba Press, 2008), 47.

5   Geoffrey Lambert, "Manitoba," in *Canadian Annual Review of Politics and Public Affairs 1991* (Toronto: University of Toronto Press, 1998), 210.
6   Confidential interview, Clear Lake, MB, 31 July 2008.
7   Ibid.
8   Confidential interview, Brandon, 13 August 2008.
9   Andrew Cohen, *A Deal Undone: The Making and the Breaking of the Meech Lake Accord* (Vancouver: Douglas and McIntyre, 1990); Geoffrey Lambert, "Manitoba," in *Canadian Annual Review of Politics and Public Affairs 1986* (Toronto: University of Toronto Press, 1990).
10 Geoffrey Lambert, "Manitoba," in *Canadian Annual Review of Politics and Public Affairs 1984* (Toronto: University of Toronto Press, 1987).
11 All election results are available on the Elections Manitoba website, http://www.electionsmanitoba.ca.
12 Netherton, "Paradigm and Shift," 225.
13 James McAllister, *The Government of Edward Schreyer: Democratic Socialism in Manitoba* (Montreal: McGill-Queen's University Press, 1984), 14.
14 Manitoba, *Framework for Economic Growth: Policy Directions for Manitoba* (Winnipeg: Manitoba Queen's Printer, 1993), 24.
15 Confidential interview, Winnipeg, 3 March 2005.
16 Geoffrey Lambert, *Canadian Annual Review of Politics and Public Affairs 1988* (Toronto: University of Toronto Press, 1995).
17 Nelson Wiseman, "In Search of Manitoba's Constitutional Position: 1850–1990," *Journal of Canadian Studies* 29, 3 (Fall 1994): 103.
18 Confidential interview, Brandon, 13 October 2005.
19 Sharon Carstairs, *Not One of the Boys* (Toronto: Macmillan, 1993), 176.
20 Jon Gerrard, *Battling for a Better Manitoba* (Winnipeg: Heartland Associates, 2006), 153.
21 Carstairs, *Not One of the Boys*, 175.
22 PC Party of Manitoba, *Manitobans and Gary Filmon—A Partnership that Works!* Election Platform, 1.
23 Manitoba Progressive Conservative Association Caucus, *The Filmon Government Record*, 17 March 1995, 4.
24 Manitoba Government, *The Balanced Budget, Debt Repayment and Taxpayer Protection and Consequential Amendments Act* (Winnipeg: Manitoba Queen's Printer, 1995).
25 Lambert, *Canadian Annual Review of Politics and Public Affairs 1991*, 210; Adams, *Politics in Manitoba*, 54.
26 PC Manitoba, "Our History," http://www.pcmanitoba.com.
27 Geoffrey Lambert, *Canadian Annual Review of Politics and Public Affairs 1995* (Toronto: University of Toronto Press, 2002), 160.
28 This comment was reflected in all of the interviews with various party figures.
29 This focus on the "conservative" as opposed to the more "progressive" end of the PC spectrum led Kevin Lamoureux, at the time the deputy leader of the Manitoba Liberal Party, to remark that this was "not the same Gary Filmon we saw eight years ago," *Winnipeg Free Press*, 12 March 1996, A8.
30 Paul Samyn, "Pragmatic? Undemocratic? Debate rages over Tory bills," *Winnipeg Free Press*, 12 March 1996.
31 Frances Russell, "PCs show wear and tear," *Winnipeg Free Press*, 23 January 1998, A10.
32 PC Manitoba, *Making Manitoba Strong*, 1999.

33 Dan Lett, "Tories feel strains of race to replace Filmon," *Winnipeg Free Press*, 15 May 2000, A8.
34 Tom Brodbeck, "Tory blames communication," *Winnipeg Sun*, 4 October 2000, 8.
35 Doug Smith, *As Many Liars* (Winnipeg: Arbeiter Ring, 2003).
36 Alfred M. Monnin, *Report of the Commission of Inquiry into Allegations of Infractions of the Elections Act and the Elections Finances Act during the 1995 Manitoba General Election* (Winnipeg: Manitoba Queen's Printer, 1999), 16.
37 CBC News, "Report says don't charge vote riggers," 12 August 1999, http://www.cbc.ca/news/story/1999/08/12/mb_doustreport081299.html.
38 William Neville, "Filmon may be Tory albatross," *Winnipeg Free Press*, 19 March 1999, A11.
39 Geoffrey Lambert, *Canadian Annual Review of Politics and Public Affairs 1999* (Toronto: University of Toronto Press, 2005), 175.
40 Doug Nairne, "Filmon does apology No. 2, pumps up Tory delegates," *Winnipeg Free Press*, 28 February 1999, A3.
41 Confidential interview, Brandon, 13 August 2008.
42 Nelson Wiseman, "Social Democracy in a Neo-Conservative Age: The Politics of Manitoba and Saskatchewan," in *Canadian Political Culture(s) in Transition*, ed. H. Telford and H. Lazar (Montreal: Institute of Intergovernmental Relations, 2002), 227.
43 Jared Wesley, "Spanning the Spectrum: Political Party Attitudes in Manitoba," paper presented to the Annual Conference of the Canadian Political Science Association, June 2005.
44 Lambert, *Canadian Annual Review of Politics and Public Affairs 1999*, 178.
45 J. Timm, "The Gary Doer phenomenon," *Maclean's*, 24 May 2007, http://www.macleans.ca/article.jsp?content=20070524_111541_5896. Indeed, Progressive Conservative Party lore has it that before he announced his intention to run for the leadership of the NDP, over the course of a weekend spent at Filmon's cottage in Gimli, Manitoba, Doer seriously contemplated joining the Progressive Conservatives.
46 Gary Doer, "Policy Challenges for the New Century: the Manitoba Perspective," speech presented at the 2000 Donald Gow Lecture at Queen's University, 2000, 7.
47 Paul Thomas, "Ottawa, Manitoba and Quebec: Leading from the Middle," *Some Lofty Thoughts on the 2007 Manitoba Election Campaign*, undated, 10.
48 Chris Adams, "Realignment in Manitoba: The Provincial Elections of 1999, 2003, and 2007," paper presented to the Annual Conference of the Canadian Political Science Association, June 2008, 9.
49 Dyck, *Provincial Politics in Canada: Towards the Turn of the Century*; Serfaty, "Electoral Behaviour in Manitoba."
50 Confidential interview, Brandon, 13 August 2008.
51 Maurice Duverger, *Political Parties: Their Organization and Activity in the Modern State* (London: Methuen, 1963). See also Nelson Wiseman's discussion of the role of party leadership in Chapter 3.
52 McAllister, *The Government of Edward Schreyer*, 130; Kenneth Carty, "Three Canadian Party Systems: An Interpretation of the Development of National Politics," in *Party Politics in Canada*, 7th ed., ed. H. Thornburn (Scarborough: Prentice-Hall, 1996), 138.
53 As evidence of this the durability of leadership in Manitoba's NDP, as a more mass-based organization, can be contrasted with the relative instability of leadership in the Manitoba Progressive Conservative Party. As Wiseman notes in Chapter 3, while the NDP has had only four leaders since 1969, with each of them serving as premier, the Progressive Conservatives have had eight leaders, including an interim leader, since the mid-1960s.

54 Confidential interview, Brandon, 16 July 2008.
55 Confidential interview, Clear Lake, MB, 31 July 2008.
56 Lett, "Tories feel strains of race to replace Filmon"; confidential interview, Winnipeg, 22 August 2008.
57 Reg Whitaker, "Virtual Political Parties and the Decline of Democracy," *Policy Options*, 16–22 June 2001; Steve Patten, "The Evolution of the Canadian Party System," in *Canadian Parties in Transition*, 3rd ed., ed. A. Gagnon and B. Tanguay (Peterborough: Broadview Press, 2007).
58 P. Woolstencroft, "The Progressive Conservative Party, 1984–1993: Government, Parties, Members," in *Party Politics in Canada*, ed. H. Thorburn (Scarborough: Prentice-Hall Canada, 1996); Reg Whitaker, *The Government Party: Organizing and Financing the Liberal Party of Canada, 1930–1958* (Toronto: University of Toronto Press, 1977); J. Wearing, *The L-Shaped Party: The Liberal Party of Canada, 1958–1980* (Toronto: McGraw-Hill-Ryerson Ltd, 1981).
59 Réjean Pelletier, "The Structures of Canadian Political Parties: How They Operate," in *Canadian Political Parties: Leaders, Candidates and Organization*, ed. H. Bakvis (Toronto: Dundurn Press, 1991), 271.
60 Tom Brodbeck, "Gang-up on Praznik?" *Winnipeg Sun*, 4 May 2000, 5.
61 Dan Lett and Doug Nairne, "Praznik drops out, knocks leader-selection process," *Winnipeg Free Press*, 20 May 2000, A6.
62 S. O'Connor, "Murray wins race of one to lead Tories," *Winnipeg Free Press*, 5 November 2000, A3.
63 Stuart Murray, in an interview with Chris Adams, denied this claim. See Adams, *Politics in Manitoba*, 57.
64 The PC Constitution calls for an automatic leadership review after an election in which the party fails to form government. A leadership vote can also be triggered in one of two other ways: by the leader himself, with a request to the party's executive council to hold a vote of confidence, or by a member of the party introducing a motion on a vote of confidence at an annual general meeting. In order to proceed, the resolution must be passed by a simple majority of the membership in attendance. See *Constitution of the PC Party of Manitoba*, 2008, 18.
65 Confidential interview, Brandon, 12 September 2008.
66 Helen Fallding, "Frustration, blunders plague PCs," *Winnipeg Free Press*, 14 March 2002, A12.
67 Adams, *Politics in Manitoba*.
68 Confidential interview, Winnipeg, 22 August 2008.
69 Mia Rabson, "Murray's campaign a complete disaster," *Winnipeg Free Press*, 4 June 2006, A5. In 2000 the PC Party raised $1.28 million; by January 2002, a year after the new financing law had come into effect, donations to the PC Party had dropped to $393,674. See Elections Manitoba, "Election Financial Returns 1995–2003," http://www.electionsmanitoba.ca.
70 David Kuxhaus, "Tory donations wither," *Winnipeg Free Press*, 7 May 2002, A1; Geoffrey Lambert, *Canadian Annual Review of Politics and Public Affairs 2001* (Toronto: University of Toronto Press, 2001).
71 Confidential interview, Winnipeg, 18 August 2008.
72 Elections Manitoba, "Party Financial Returns, 1999 and 2003," http://www.electionsmanitoba.ca.
73 Rabson, "Murray's campaign a complete disaster," A5; confidential interview, Brandon, 16 July 2008.

74 Dan Lett, "Murray throws down gauntlet to PC dissidents," *Winnipeg Free Press*, 5 June 2003, A4.
75 Editorial, "Mr. Murray must lead," *Winnipeg Free Press*, 23 August 2003, A14.
76 This was reflected in confidential interview, Brandon, 16 July 2008, and confidential interview, Winnipeg, 4 November 2005.
77 Confidential interview, Brandon, 12 September 2008.
78 Jim McCrae, "Delegates have lots to think about," *Brandon Sun*, 30 October 2005, A7.
79 Curtis Brown, "Murray Calls For Leadership Convention," *Brandon Sun*, 6 November 2005, A4.
80 Some party insiders suggested that Murray made a tactical error in not meeting the leadership issue head-on. As one observer noted, "I think Stu made the mistake of not calling for his own leadership review. He could have gotten his people in place and won, and that would have brought an end to all of the sniping" (confidential interview, Winnipeg, 22 August 2008).
81 CBC News, "McFadyen wins decisive victory in Manitoba's Tory leadership race," 29 April 2006, http://www.cbc.ca/canada/story/2006/04/29/manresuls-060429.html, 2
82 Dan Lett, "Support for Tories surging," *Winnipeg Free Press*, 6 July 2006, A6.
83 Dyck, *Provincial Politics in Canada: Towards the Turn of the Century*; Serfaty, "Electoral Behaviour in Manitoba."
84 Dan Lett, "Anatomy of an election," *Winnipeg Free Press*, 17 June 2007, B5.
85 David Stewart and Kenneth Carty, "Does Changing the Party Leader Provide an Electoral Boost? A Study of Canadian Provincial Parties: 1960–1992," *Canadian Journal of Political Science* 26, 2 (June 1993): 313.
86 Confidential interview, Brandon, 12 September 2008.
87 Confidential interview, Winnipeg, 20 August 2008.
88 Thomas, "Some Lofty Thoughts on the 2007 Election Campaign"; CBC News, "Parties and Leaders," 3 April 2007, http://www.cbc.ca/manitobavotes2007/parties/doer.html.
89 Confidential interview, Winnipeg, 18 August 2008.
90 Meir Serfaty, "The Manitoba Election Campaign of 2007: A Pre-Mortem," undated.
91 Confidential interview, Winnipeg, 18 August 2008.
92 Ibid.
93 Lett, "Anatomy of an Election."
94 Confidential interview, Winnipeg, 18 August 2008; confidential interview, Winnipeg, 22 August 2008.
95 Confidential interview, Winnipeg, 20 August 2008.
96 PC Manitoba, *Letter to Delegates*, April 2008.
97 Confidential interview, Winnipeg, 22 August 2008.
98 Confidential interview, Brandon, 16 July 2008.
99 Ibid.
100 Wesley, "Spanning the Spectrum."
101 Serfaty, "Electoral Behaviour in Manitoba," 183 and 185.
102 Thomas, "Some Lofty Thoughts on the 2007 Election Campaign," 9.
103 As Duff Roblin states in his memoirs, heading into the 1958 election campaign he saw the adoption of an ideologically centrist position as the best way for the Tories to win government. The thinking was that by combining elements of both conservative and progressive ideology, "we would fill the political vacuum and take up a strong position at the centre." See Roblin, *Speaking for Myself*, 78.

104 Probe Research Inc., "Provincial Party Standings in Manitoba," 15 December 2009, http://probe-research.com/2009/12/provincial-party-standings-in-manitoba.html. A poll conducted by the Angus Reid Group in December 2009 showed that while 29 percent of Manitobans approved of Selinger's job performance, fully 50 percent of provincial residents could not offer an opinion of the new premier. Larry Kusch, "Many of us can't rate new premier," *Winnipeg Free Press*, 17 December 2009, A5.
105 Adams, *Politics in Manitoba*, 131.
106 Interview with Doug Schweitzer, 2008.
107 Elections Manitoba, "Annual Financial Statements, 2003–Present."
108 Interview with Doug Schweitzer.
109 Adams, "Realignment in Manitoba," 18.
110 Interview with Hugh McFadyen.
111 Ibid.
112 Ibid.
113 Confidential interview, Brandon, 16 July 2008.
114 Elections Canada, "Past Elections, 2006 and 2008," http://www.electionscanada.ca. The increasing popular support of the federal Conservative brand in Winnipeg has not been lost on the provincial Tories. With the launch of its new website the PC Party also unveiled (yet another) party logo that is now remarkably similar to the federal Conservative Party logo.
115 Interview with Hugh McFadyen.

Manitoba's Liberals: Sliding into Third

Paul Barber[1]

Introduction

The key fact about Manitoba's Liberals is that they are a relatively weak third party. However, the party has deep roots in the province's history, including participation in a government that lasted three and a half decades in the twentieth century. This analysis will attempt to answer the question of why the Manitoba Liberals have arrived at their current diminished state: two seats in the legislature, just 12 percent of the vote in the 22 May 2007 provincial election.

When viewed from elsewhere in Canada there is much about Manitoba that suggests one could expect to find a strong Liberal presence here. For example, it has much of the urban, ethnically diverse character traditionally associated with Liberal strength in Ontario. Indeed, Nelson Wiseman characterized Manitoba as the "Ontario of the prairies" because the wave of immigrants from Ontario during Manitoba's first few decades had a formative impact on its political culture.[2] These Ontario migrants were British and prosperous, settling the good farmlands in Manitoba's south and west.

Indeed it helps to understand the state of Manitoba's Liberals by comparing their situation to that of the Liberal Party in Ontario—a party in a markedly different position than its Manitoba counterpart. The Ontario party has had considerable electoral success during the past few decades. Since 1987 it has won three decisive majority victories in Ontario elections, and by 2011 will have governed the province for thirteen out of twenty-six years. In Manitoba, by contrast, since 1969 the Liberals have generally won just a few seats in provincial elections—with the notable exception of 1988 when Sharon Carstairs achieved a dramatic breakthrough.

There are two critical junctures, 1932 and 1969, which determined the Manitoba Liberals' fate. The more recent is familiar to living Manitobans, but the roots of Liberal decline go back over several decades to longer-term historical developments. Most Manitobans recognize the importance of 1969, when Ed Schreyer's New Democrats relegated the Liberal Party to third place. There it remained firmly stuck until 1988 when the party rose phoenix-like from its electoral ashes and appeared briefly to be on the path to taking power. That upward bounce turned out to be short-lived, and the party slipped back within three subsequent elections to its diminished post-1969 state, where mere survival seems to be the most it can expect.

The path the party followed earlier during the twentieth century set the stage for 1969.[3] Premier John Bracken's administration originally came to power in 1922 as the United Farmers of Manitoba (UFM). By 1927 Bracken's party was known as the Progressives. Bracken merged his party with the Liberals in 1932, creating the Liberal-Progressive coalition that would continue to hold power until 1958, a period of twenty-six years.

The Liberal Party's 1932 decision to abandon its status as an independent party led to the transformation of what had until then been a party with an important urban wing into a rural conservative political force. The party's subsequent failure in the 1960s to remake itself into an urban-friendly party led directly to its slide into third place in 1969.

In Manitoba politics, it can be easy to confuse nomenclature with ideology. One should not be misled by the term "progressive." Widely used as self-description today by American small-l liberals, progressivism is perceived as synonymous with liberalism. However, American liberals adopted the "progressive" label to give the philosophy a different brand name. Liberals felt the need to do so because of the success of American conservatives during the Reagan era and after in demonizing their liberal opponents.

The capital-p Progressive Party of Canada started out as an agrarian radical party in federal politics focused on issues like freight rates and the tariff. As a provincial party in Manitoba it reflected the outlook of its rural, small-c fiscally and socially conservative activists and voters. The Progressive Party disappeared from the national political landscape during the 1930s but in Manitoba the Progressives had an enduring impact on Manitoba's Liberals through the coalition experience. By the 1950s, the Liberal-Progressive party was clearly a party on the right.

The argument of this analysis is that because of the coalition with the Progressives the Manitoba Liberals emerged initially as a small-c conservative party entering the modern era. By itself this might not have mattered to the party's fate. Equally important was that the Liberals then failed to adapt to changing times. The party was imprisoned by its past and failed to modernize. The result was disaster.

The Liberal Party of Manitoba dropped the Progressive suffix in 1961 but the party's lingering conservatism was too deeply embedded. It would be the key factor in pushing it to the political margins in 1969, setting the stage for long-run decline. The party needed to shed its "Progressive" heritage in the '60s and change with the times, yet it failed to do so. Some in the party recognized its dilemma but failed to alter its course. Although the Manitoba Liberals could not adapt to changing circumstances, during the same decade the federal Liberal Party was able to renew and transform itself sufficiently to assure continued political strength and viability into the twenty-first century.

The Manitoba Liberal Party today is a small-l liberal party similar to the moderate, centre-left federal Liberal Party. However, this transformation arrived too late to save it from third-party status. Nevertheless, forty years on it remains an important player in provincial politics, contesting every constituency in the 2007 election while retaining a somewhat distinctive character and outlook. An explanation of how the Liberals ended up where they are today must begin with an understanding of Manitoba's economic geography and demographics and their relationship to the province's politics.

I. Geopolitical Context and Historic Roots

The geopolitical context for Manitoba's politics shaped by the province's history was summarized this way following the 1969 election: "if one had stood on the corner of Portage and Main in downtown Winnipeg and faced north-west, he would have been upon a line that divided the whole province from the Lake of the Woods to the Swan River Valley. To the south and west of this line lay the older more prosperous urban and rural districts tracing their ancestry to Ontario in the 1880s. On the north and east of this dividing line were the non-British and relatively poorer areas."[4] The diagonal line describes the dominant geographic expression of politics in Manitoba post-1969—NDP seats north and east, PC seats in the south and west, and the few Liberals generally in between. Thomas Peterson has summarized this divide in Manitoba's politics as follows:

> The development of party politics in Manitoba has been influenced by the interaction of two social and economic classes. One of these has

generally been more prosperous and generally more secure. Most of its members were of British origin and many of them originally came from Ontario. For a hundred years this group controlled political and economic power. The second or lower class was more heterogeneous, comprised of several cultural groups including working class immigrants from Britain, various other immigrants of non-British origin and the province's native Indians and Métis.[5]

The Liberal Party, both in the Thomas Greenway and T.C. Norris administrations in Manitoba's early decades and during the era of Liberal-Progressive coalition, was rooted in the prosperous British group described by Peterson. When the province polarized along class lines in the 1969 election, the Liberals, having been largely displaced by Duff Roblin's Progressive Conservatives in the south and west in 1958, found themselves squeezed into a weak third position. Instead of polarization, the party needed a politics that would permit it to do well on both sides of the diagonal line. They should have become a moderate, centrist party that could appeal to both the affluent and the less well-off. But this was not to be, and to discover why one must first trace the party's evolution from its origins in the 1880s.

The first Manitoba Liberal Premier was Thomas Greenway, who would come to represent "the triumph of Ontario democracy."[6] With origins in Huron County, Ontario, Greenway was a champion of "provincial rights." He would become known best to Canadian historians for the Laurier-Greenway compromise that preserved limited minority educational rights, which followed Greenway's elimination of the dual system of French and English language rights in Manitoba that was a legacy of the province's entry into Confederation. Greenway's Liberal Party represented prosperous British Manitoba, and to a modern eye his opposition to federal power and coolness to French rights resembles more the rural, conservative forces of the former Reform Party and the Canadian Alliance than the twentieth-century Liberal Party of Pearson, Trudeau, and Chrétien.

At the same time as partisan politics took root in Manitoba, in the United Kingdom the Liberal Party began to evolve into a fully formed political party. British Liberals combined support for free trade with sympathy for the emerging needs of labour and the working class. They championed institutional reforms such as the extension of the franchise and the secret ballot along with social reforms such as universal state-provided education. They made an effort to win votes from the working class with changes sought by the labour movement around trade union rights, wages, and hours of work.[7] British liberalism integrated the promotion of free trade with advocacy of equality of the human condition plus an interest in institutional reforms, reflecting openness to changes that transform antiquated practices to modernize society. Canada's Liberals have a similar reformist tradition that has been central to the party's appeal for many decades. T.C. Norris, the second Manitoban to become Liberal leader, achieved high office in 1915 by linking himself closely to the burgeoning reform movement in Manitoba in the early part of the twentieth century.

If Greenway represented a right-leaning tradition for Manitoba Liberals, T.C. Norris was quite his opposite. Between the Greenway and Norris administrations, the Conservative Party ruled Manitoba for over fifteen years, mostly under former premier Rodmond Roblin. A tumultuous period featuring strong population and economic growth,[8] the era produced social strains that led to the creation of a powerful reform movement. Pressures came from suffragettes pressing for women's votes and a related temperance movement seeking to curb the abuse of alcohol. A growing labour movement wanted to combat the ills of an urbanizing and industrializing society including working conditions, "safety at work, hours of labour and compensation for injury."[9] Various groups supported direct legislation (the referendum), tax reform, and greater integration of immigrants.

These stresses, in combination with a general revulsion at the scandal surrounding the construction of the Manitoba Legislature, created a political tsunami that swept the Roblin Conservatives from office in 1915 and installed the reform Liberal administration of T.C. Norris with the second-largest electoral majority in Manitoba history.[10] During the seven years of its existence Norris's administration went on to enact a comprehensive reform program, described later as "breathtaking" in scope.[11] But Norris's political support gave way amidst the post–World War I economic crisis. The cost of the Norris government's program plus postwar inflation produced a perceived fiscal crisis that would be up to Norris's successor, John Bracken, to tackle. As Lionel Orlikow put it, the "achievement of short run objectives and the strain of wartime" brought the reform movement to an end by 1922 when the United Farmers of Manitoba swept the Liberals from office.[12]

Liberals and Progressives—The Path to Coalition

After the UFM victory, their leaderless but victorious caucus soon persuaded John Bracken, then president of the Manitoba Agricultural College, to become premier. Bracken's outlook on politics suited the farmers well, as he was sceptical of party politics. Bracken was both cautious and a fiscal conservative. His government also enacted a series of measures we would now characterize as socially conservative— for example, the introduction of film censorship.[13] Over the course of the next five years the government, known first as Brackenites and later as the Progressives, was sufficiently successful to win re-election in the 1927 election while the Liberal party fell to third place. Their weak position post-election and the evolving political situation in Ottawa soon put coalition on the Liberal agenda.[14]

Originally, the Progressive party was the vehicle in federal politics for a Prairie farm revolt against a political system that farmers viewed as stacked against them. Western farmers saw the federal parties as captive to central and eastern Canadian business interests that benefited from high tariffs. Moreover, partisanship itself was equated with the traditional party system.

The Mackenzie King Liberals in Ottawa spent much of the 1920s coaxing the Progressives to join with the Liberals. Some, such as T.A. Crerar, had originally been Liberals who had broken away from the national party over specific issues such as the tariff. Crerar and others eventually found it easy to return to the fold. The precarious character of the King minority governments of the '20s, which depended on Progressive support, meant the federal Liberals had a powerful incentive to encourage Liberal cooperation with the Progressive government in Manitoba. The Manitoba Liberals won just eight of fifty-five seats in 1922 and seven in 1927, but their support was important to the UFM/Progressives who won narrow majorities in those two elections and sought Liberal support to ensure the government's stability.

II. The Coalition Years

Faced with political as well as economic calamity, Bracken forged the coalition with the Liberals in 1932 to ensure his governing majority would continue. A more secure majority also enabled him to tackle the Depression on his own terms. Bracken had faith in the idea that non-partisan government was essential to achieve the efficiency and economy in government he believed was the right way to respond to the fiscal consequences of the Depression. Non-partisanship had purely political benefits too: coalition helped Bracken remain in office by defeating the provincial Conservatives in the 1932 election and proved effective in warding off defeat in later years.[15]

Despite Liberal weakness in the 1920s, the party might have been able to stage a comeback as a consequence of the politics of the Depression—most incumbent governments during the 1930s in Canada, both federal and provincial, did not survive. Instead, the coalition with Bracken enabled the renamed Liberal-Progressive government to survive. Bracken the fiscal conservative was also Bracken the adept opportunist: he survived the Depression politically in part by continuously expanding the coalition, eventually enticing all the opposition parties—the Conservatives, Social Credit, even briefly the Co-operative Commonwealth Federation—into its fold.[16]

Bracken's cautious conservative character along with his provincial political success would lead to his selection as the leader of the federal Conservative Party in 1942. Just as he turned the Manitoba Liberals into Liberal-Progressives, so he would insist that the national Conservative Party rename itself Progressive Conservative before he would agree to be its leader. By then, he had put the stamp of the Progressives on the Manitoba Liberals.

By joining a farmers' movement with its emphasis on fiscal frugality, the Manitoba Liberals put themselves on a course that would leave them vulnerable in a modern urban world that wanted a more activist state than their inherited beliefs would permit. When the idea of coalition first arose in the twenties some Liberals believed it would enable the party to absorb the Progressives.[17] Mackenzie King succeeded in doing so in Ottawa, but in Winnipeg, coalition with the Progressives led the Liberals to be ideologically dominated by their new partners, even if it was the Liberal label that would eventually prevail.

The coalition government throughout its reign remained staunchly fiscally conservative. For much of this period among Canada's provinces, "Manitoba had the lowest per capita levels of both public expenditures and public debt."[18] When confronted with the onset of the Depression, the Bracken government's instinct was to slash expenditures wherever possible. No detail was too small to escape their attention. Thomas Peterson cites this example: "When the stock market crashed, Premier Bracken was away on a European tour. He returned shortly and instituted a program of paring costs everywhere possible to the extent of cutting the *per capita* daily bread allowance of mental patients from 11.99 to 11.68 oz."[19] The Bracken government also raised taxes and pressed the federal government for assistance. One federal response to Bracken's pressure was to appoint the Rowell-Sirois Commission on Dominion-Provincial Relations.[20]

In 1942 Stuart Garson replaced Bracken as premier in Manitoba upon the latter's decision to move on to federal politics. Garson, originally elected in 1927 as a Progressive, made the full transition from Progressive to Liberal when he entered the St. Laurent government in 1948 and became Canada's justice minister.[21]

The last premier in the Liberal-Progressive regime that governed for more than three decades was Douglas Campbell, who assumed office in 1948. In contrast to Garson, Campbell explained that he always thought of himself as a Progressive rather than a Liberal.[22] Historian John Saywell, in the 1961 edition of the *Canadian Annual Review*, noted that Campbell "was reported several years ago to have said the only three conservatives left were [former U.S. president Herbert] Hoover, [former Conservative prime minister Arthur] Meighen and himself."[23] The Progressive regime, built originally on the United Farmers of Manitoba victory of 1922, drew its support primarily from the farm community, particularly in the Anglo-Saxon southwest, but also from Winnipeg's business community.[24] Ironically, the Liberal-Progressive Party would eventually be defeated by the *Progressive* Conservative Party—the descriptive adjective used by both parties came from the same roots.

Although one could justify retrenchment during the lean years of the Depression, Campbell, who had been one of Bracken's ministers, failed to recognize the changed circumstances after the Second World War. The government was proud of its investments in rural electrification, which appealed strongly to its rural constituency.[25] Yet even these efforts followed by a decade rural electrification in the United States under the New Deal.[26] The coalition also failed to invest adequately in many other public services and infrastructure such as education and highways. An account of the 1949 legislative session, when the CCF led the opposition, observed the following: "The low level of provincial government services was the focus of the opposition attack. The conditions and teaching standards in Manitoba schools, the poor quality of the province's roads and limited health care facilities were the issues constantly raised. The Government response was always the same: that the administration was spending the maximum possible consistent with its policy of rapid retirement of the provincial debt."[27]

In 1949, the Progressive Conservatives were still a part of the Campbell government. The PCs broke up the broader coalition in 1950 when they left to become the official opposition. Their exit from the coalition came partly from the prodding of Duff Roblin, who entered politics precisely because of his frustrations with the coalition. The mood of the time is reflected in Duff Roblin's memoirs. Elected to the legislature in 1949, Roblin's view was that the days of war and Depression were over and it was time for the province to be more expansive. In his memoirs he declared: "We could see better days ahead and wanted to be part of it. Manitoba was ready to move. The coalition responded but poorly, to the hopes of the public."[28] Despite having the word "Conservative" in its name, Roblin viewed his party as a centrist force in provincial politics falling between "the far-right views of the Liberal-Progressive government and muted radicalism of the minority CCF."[29]

Perhaps the single most important event in the province's postwar history was the 1950 Winnipeg flood. The coalition government's weak response provoked a negative reaction. An article on Roblin's role in politics states: "Even the *Winnipeg Free Press*, which consistently supported the coalition, declared that the mishandling of the flood crisis demonstrated the need for an alternative to the government in power. Premier Campbell compounded his problem when he balked at paying compensation for flood damage once the rivers were within their banks. By the time the premier gave in on the question Roblin and CCF leader Lloyd Stinson had been very effective in using the issue against the government."[30]

The government requested engineering and flood control studies but deferred any action on flood prevention pending the results from a commission appointed to investigate the cost-benefit ratio of the proposed works. This tepid response meant flood control would be a major PC plank in 1958. It aptly symbolized Campbell's approach to governance, a tight-fisted approach extending to all government programs. Manitoba had the lowest expenditures, measured as a percentage of personal income, of any province in Canada even though it had the revenue to spend more: "From 1950 to 1957 the government ran substantial surplus budgets every year but one; its net revenues exceeding expenditures for the period by $48.3 million—some 11% of total net expenditures for the period."[31] Campbell's governance was also inconsistent with the Keynesian policy approaches then emerging in Ottawa.[32]

III. Liberals in the Sixties: the Failure to Renew

In Canada the 1950s brought significant political change to both Canada and Manitoba. Two long-running Liberal dynasties crashed in the latter part of the decade. The King-St. Laurent era ended in 1957 when the minority government of John Diefenbaker took office in Ottawa. The defeat of the federal Liberals was not lamented by Campbell who later commented (in an apparent reference to 1922), "I never did run as a Liberal. I helped turn the Liberals out of office."[33]

The federal Liberals' hopes of a quick return to office were crushed in Diefenbaker's landslide victory in the 31 March 1958 general election. The political drama in Ottawa was soon echoed by developments in Manitoba. The Liberal-Progressives lost office to Duff Roblin's Progressive Conservatives less than three months later. The federal pattern repeated itself as Roblin's minority was turned into a majority triumph the following year. The PC Party held the political centre, fighting, as Roblin put it, "one campaign against the Liberals on the right, strange as it may seem, and another against the CCF on the left in the city."[34]

For their part the federal Liberals rebounded by 1963 and formed the federal government for thirty-three of the following forty-five years while Manitoba Liberals experienced continuing futility. Comparing the response of Manitoba Liberals to their federal counterparts following election losses less than three months apart helps explain why the fates of the two Liberal parties diverged so completely.

After their devastating loss, the federal Liberals recognized they needed to renew themselves. The organizational drive of what was known as "cell 13" and the Walter Gordon Toronto Liberals are now part of Liberal mythology.[35] A key aspect of this process of renewal was a rethinking of the cautious business liberalism of such figures as St. Laurent and C.D. Howe. This took place at gatherings such as the Kingston thinkers' conference in September 1960 and a policy convention called the National Liberal Rally. As Christina McCall-Newman put it: "The ideas discussed at both conventions were wide-ranging, as befitted such loosely constituted ideological groupings, but the overwhelming impression that emerged for public consumption was one of newness, vitality, and progressivism."[36]

Then-federal Liberal leader Lester Pearson also recruited a Manitoban in 1959 as part of this renewal. Tom Kent, a recent British immigrant, was editor of the *Winnipeg Free Press* at the time. Kent strongly advocated fundamental policy renewal. In his autobiography *A Public Purpose*, he quotes from a letter he wrote in 1959 to British Liberal leader Jo Grimond about Canada's Liberals:

> In Canada it is necessary to explain why the Liberal Party today, without being any less concerned about freedom, would extend public expenditures on education, health (including medical insurance and sickness benefits), housing and urban renewal. This has to be combined with a national policy for securing more equality among our regions.... Primarily, I would say that Liberals need to shift the emphasis of their thinking a good many notches (in our case) towards egalitarianism.[37]

Here one can see the reforming impulses of the Pearson era that would result in fundamental changes to the Canadian welfare state, including universal public health care, the Canada Pension Plan and many other reforms. Kent would play a key role as a policy advisor to Pearson once he became prime minister in 1963.

While some Winnipeg Liberals early on saw the need for rebuilding and renewal,[38] the post-1959 history of the Manitoba Liberal Party stands in marked contrast to the federal experience. The party organization had languished in the long years of the coalition.[39] It needed to revitalize and renew.

The Roblin government had demonstrated a reforming zeal, undertaking investments in infrastructure such as highways as well as proceeding, over considerable Liberal opposition in the legislature, with construction of the Red River Floodway.[40] There were also reforms to education and municipal government. The contrast with the provincial Liberals was striking. Historian W.L. Morton remarked:

> Here was the real clash with the policy of the administration it had displaced: the core of Campbell's policy was to expand expenditure as revenues allowed, but to abstain rigidly from all borrowing, provincial and municipal.[41]

The Liberal-Progressive Party that emerged from decades of coalition rule continued into the early 1960s as a small-c conservative party. Its outlook accurately reflected its rural, conservative base, but would be an obstacle to political success as the City of Winnipeg was emerging to become the dominant geographic and demographic fact in provincial politics.

After his defeat in 1958, Douglas Campbell carried on as party leader for a further two years, losing the 1959 general election. Despite stepping down as leader in 1961, he remained the MLA for Lakeside constituency until 1969, and continued to exercise influence within the caucus and party. As the 1961 leadership and policy convention to replace him got underway, the Liberals found themselves being lectured by the pro-Roblin *Winnipeg Tribune*, which editorialized that Manitobans would "no longer vote for the old 1922 platform. They will no longer buy the story that Manitoba can no longer afford a reasonable level of public services. Policies of retreat and retrenchment will no longer win elections in Manitoba."[42]

While the Manitoba Liberals selected Gil Molgat as their new leader in 1961 and dropped the name Progressive, it was about as much renewal as was accomplished. Molgat supporters were reported as believing "a swing to the left was in the cards."[43] However, in a convention that needed to move the party towards the centre and left, the Liberals opted for a keynote guest speaker, the outspoken Saskatchewan Liberal leader Ross Thatcher, who was conservative in outlook and who devoted his speech to excoriating the policies of the "New Party," the fledgling organization shortly to become the NDP.[44]

As early as 1959, responding to Roblin's successful occupation of the political centre, the Liberals had made an effort to capture lost ground. Their platform that year edged towards the centre, including a pledge to increase the minimum wage, build more roads and offer a medical benefit plan—though it cautioned nonetheless it would not be "state medicine." However, the Liberals adhered to their traditional fiscal approach, calling for "a sane, practical policy of paying for current expenditures out of current revenues and borrowing for capital expenditures on a sound repayable basis, thus avoiding tax increases and a sales tax."[45]

Molgat made an effort "to emphasize social issues but there remained some stubborn resistance in the party."[46] He recognized that the Roblin Progressive Conservatives had outflanked the Liberals, noting "the problem was that Roblin has moved into traditional Liberal territory, and it was difficult to be more liberal than Roblin."[47]

The result was a decade of ideological ambiguity. Molgat considered himself a Pearsonian Liberal.[48] However, his attempts to move the party to the centre were frustrated by a caucus that included not just Douglas Campbell but other rural members like him, some first elected before Roblin changed the tenor of Manitoba politics. This forced the party to bridge the differences within. During the 1966 election, for example, Liberals campaigned under the slogan: "The Job to be Done Can Be Done."

It is instructive to review the accounts of government and politics in Manitoba found in the *Canadian Annual Review* covering this period.[49] Tart comments by authors Thomas Peterson, Murray Donnelly, and John Saywell reflect the dilapidated state of Manitoba Liberalism during the sixties. John Saywell commented on the events of 1961:

> The Liberal Progressive Party led by D.L. Campbell continued the schizophrenic behaviour that had characterized it for some years. The most visible division came on April 14 when the members split 6–5 on a CCF housing motion. It was this left-right division on policy and the related replacement of Mr. Campbell by a younger man that dominated the April 19–21 Liberal convention in Winnipeg.[50]

The party's choice of Molgat meant, in Saywell's words: "it had at least moved back to the centre of the road." In 1965 Donnelly said of the Liberals that they "floundered in a mire of ineffective scandal mongering."[51] The following year, Peterson observed dryly that Molgat's critique of the 1966 Throne Speech could be characterized by the comment "Why wasn't more of this done earlier?"[52]

One episode illustrated that there was some recognition within the Liberal party of the failure to renew. Calling themselves the "ginger group" (after a breakaway faction of the Progressive party in the House of Commons in 1924) eight urban Liberal candidates articulated an urban reform platform during the 1966 provincial election as an effort to create a more urban presence in a party defined by its rural roots. More broadly, however, the "ginger group" reflected a growing dissatisfaction with the state of the Manitoba Liberal Party.

Although publicly the "ginger group" was said to have "the blessing of Molgat"[53] it led to the public impression, as the *Winnipeg Tribune* put it, that "it would leave the Liberal party...with two distinct factions: one urban and one rural."[54] In the end all eight members of the "ginger group" were defeated in the June 23, 1966 election, in which, Molgat acknowledged, the NDP hurt the Liberals "substantially."[55]

Lloyd Axworthy, a key founder of the "ginger group," agreed there was "a general trend to the NDP," which he thought unjustified: "there's no reason why there should be. Our policies are just as good but perhaps we [the ginger group] got into the race a little late."[56] Another defeated "ginger group" candidate admitted the existence of rural-urban divisions, blaming the problem on the party's leadership.[57]

The failure in Winnipeg meant the Liberal caucus from 1966 to 1969 still had holdovers from the coalition era, almost all representing rural constituencies. All members dating from the coalition era except for Molgat would finally lose in 1969. After the 1966 election, the Manitoba Progressive Conservatives moved decisively to the right. In 1967 they chose a rural conservative, Walter Weir, to replace Roblin. This ideological shift by the PCs helped them extinguish the rural wing of the Liberal Party for good.

Today, Winnipeg is fairly represented in the legislature with thirty-one out of the province's fifty-seven seats. However, for much of the twentieth century this was not the case. In 1914, despite having one-third of the province's population, the city was represented in the legislature by just six members out of forty-nine.[58] By the time Roblin came to power in 1958 Winnipeg still had just twenty of fifty-seven—35 percent of the members in the legislature but 48 percent of the province's population.[59] However, one institutional reform put in place by the Campbell government contributed to the Liberals' undoing. Manitoba was the first Canadian province to appoint an independent commission to revise constituency boundaries. The initial redistribution favoured rural areas by a statutory 7:4 ratio, but the second exercise, completed in 1968, allowed only a 25 percent tolerance in riding size, and this narrowed the rural advantage considerably.[60] Combined with urban growth, this meant that by 1969 close to half the ridings were in Winnipeg.

Gil Molgat resigned his leadership in early 1969 following four byelection losses in which the Liberal vote slumped badly. The growing unpopularity of the federal Liberals was perceived to be a key factor. Molgat cited a backlash against Trudeau's language policies, an anti-French public mood, and his own French-Canadian ancestry as reasons why he could no longer be party leader. In the end Molgat's efforts to move the party to the centre encountered too much resistance from the party's conservatives. At best the Liberal brand was indistinct as the 1960s drew to a close, setting the stage for a clash of the party's urban and rural wings during the contest to replace Molgat.

A leadership convention was called for early May. R.W. "Bobby" Bend, a former cabinet member in the Campbell era who described himself as "right of centre," was selected as leader over urbanites Duncan Edmonds and Bernie Wolfe. Although it was a large convention, the mood was bleak:

> Beneath the bubbling optimism of the Liberal leadership convention is a disquieting undercurrent of discontent.
>
> Top Liberals are suggesting that the wrong choice at the ballot box today spells the end of Manitoba Liberalism and others say privately any choice is the beginning of the end.

A party member of long standing said bluntly in the third floor bar at the Winnipeg auditorium that if the predicted favourite came out on top his party card was as good as burned.[61]

In choosing Bend the party rejected two urban candidates and made a choice that symbolized and confirmed the absence of renewal after 1958. Unduly impressed by the byelection results, they misread the public mood. They chose a leader who resembled in background and outlook Premier Walter Weir. As Nelson Wiseman notes in his history of the Manitoba CCF-NDP, *Social Democracy in Manitoba*: "In effect the Liberals chose a fiscal conservative to fight another fiscal conservative (Weir). The shift of both the older parties to the right permitted the NDP to make an effective appeal to Liberal and Conservative supporters who considered themselves progressives and reformers."[62] The result was Liberal catastrophe: the party dropped to just five seats in the legislature, losing support in the city to the NDP and in the country to the Progressive Conservatives. Despite the Carstairs upsurge in 1988, the party has never recovered from this event.

Many younger urban Liberals found Ed Schreyer's moderately left-of-centre image sufficiently attractive that the outcome of the leadership contest caused many to defect from the Liberals to the NDP during the 1969 campaign, some declaring as they did so that they saw Schreyer's NDP as representing true small-l liberalism.[63] The PC Party's rightward shift consolidated its support throughout rural Manitoba at the expense of the Liberals. Just three Liberals, including Molgat, were re-elected in 1969 in rural Manitoba (compared to twelve in 1966). By 1973 there were no Liberal members outside Winnipeg.

It was the 1969 election that drew the province's diagonal line as Manitoba politics polarized along the southeast to northwest ethnic-economic axis that separates the more British, prosperous southwest from the poorer, more ethnically diverse north and east. The Liberals represented neither class and were squeezed out. In contrast, one finds Liberals in Ontario representing constituencies of both the highly affluent and the very poor.[64] When the Manitoba Liberals eventually did achieve some success in the 1988 election, they successfully straddled Manitoba's diagonal line.

Part of the Manitoba Liberals' failure to renew, as the "ginger group" recognized, was its inability to see the political implications of demographic change. Following the Second World War, citizens living on Canada's farms migrated in large numbers to cities such as Winnipeg. The Liberal-Progressive Party of Manitoba was, because of its roots in the United Farmers of Manitoba, an agrarian party. There were parallels to its experience among the agrarian parties in Western Europe. As Arend Lijphart notes: "Where agrarian parties are found, mainly in Nordic countries, they have tended to become less exclusively rural and to appeal to urban electorates too, prompted by the decline in rural population. A clear sign of this shift is that the Swedish, Norwegian, and Finnish agrarian parties all changed their names to 'Center Party' between 1957 and 1965."[65]

In Manitoba the Liberals implicitly acknowledged rural decline when they dropped the Progressive prefix in 1961. The European parties described by Lijphart all had the advantage of competing in electoral systems based on proportional representation. No such advantage helped sustain Manitoba's Liberals as the province became more urban.

IV. Disintegration in the Seventies

In a first-past-the-post electoral system, there is a world of difference between second place and third, especially if one of the two major parties overlaps ideologically with the party in third place. In this context the third party can vault itself into major party status only when at least one of its two major opponents suffers a catastrophic political loss sufficiently great to permit a breakthrough. Initial success must subsequently be consolidated in order to endure. This is what happened in 1969 for the NDP, which went on to win two critical byelections in 1971 (one in a formerly Liberal-held seat) and then won the 1973 general election. The problem for the Liberals in the years that followed was finding an opportunity comparable to the one seized that year by Ed Schreyer and the NDP.

"I took the party to the right, Charlie [Charles Huband, Manitoba Liberal leader from 1975 to 1978] took it to the left and neither strategy worked."[66] This comment by I.H. "Izzy" Asper, the Winnipeg tax lawyer who replaced Bobby Bend as Liberal leader in 1970 after the electoral debacle of 1969, summarizes the eroding fortunes of the Liberals during the 1970s. The party had lost members and support to the NDP on its left, especially in the city of Winnipeg. Asper, chosen at a convention in October 1970, was an urban leader, but he was ideologically on the right.

Asper had previously published a book attacking a federal Liberal tax reform white paper. In a leadership campaign speech he denounced the white paper for "its punitive capital gains taxes, its confiscatory estate taxes and its crushing taxes on farmers and small business men, and its incentive-destroying taxes on those wage earners who rise to the middle-income level."[67] Asper briefly flirted with the idea of coalition with the Progressive Conservatives just after becoming leader, but was dissuaded by opposition from within the party.[68]

The Liberals won five seats in 1969 and repeated this performance in 1973 when Asper campaigned under the slogan "Self Control or State Control." The party finally moved left when it selected Charles Huband as its leader in 1975. Huband declared that, for the Liberals, the chances of "surviving hinge upon the

Liberal Party's ability to win votes from the New Democratic Party."[69] The effort to recapture the centre soon proved futile. Huband was never able to secure a seat in the legislature, being defeated twice—first in a byelection, and again in the 1977 general election when the Liberal Party was reduced to a single member, Lloyd Axworthy, who represented the urban riding of Fort Rouge. Within two years Mr. Axworthy departed the legislature to commence his long career in federal politics, while Mr. Huband resigned the leadership and abandoned political life.

Provincial Liberals and Federal Liberals

The provincial Liberals survived as a party throughout the 1970s and into the 1980s in part because the federal wing of the party was in power during most of this period. It was a source of strength both in terms of inspiration and in the less venerable aspects of politics—honours and appointments to boards and commissions, to the Senate, and to political jobs.

In a preface to a history of the Manitoba Liberals written by current party leader Jon Gerrard, Lloyd Axworthy writes this candid assessment of the impact of the federal Liberals in Manitoba:

> In a small province there is only a limited quantum of men and women who will run for office, contribute to a campaign, and become poll workers. That quantum gets divided amongst various parties and is further subdivided between federal and provincial wings—though there are many who do double duty. In the case of the Manitoba Liberals, the attraction of becoming a "fed," with the possibility of holding office, achieving policy results, and somewhat more crassly, gaining appointments, honours and acknowledgement, often works to the disadvantage of the provincial party. I know whereof I speak.[70]

The federal party, however, was simultaneously a source of weakness. For provincial Liberals, being branded with the same name as the federal party that controlled the government in Ottawa frequently proved to be a liability. Accounts of the Manitoba Liberals from the 1970s on cite a number of specific federal actions that had political costs for the provincial party. Some examples included:

- In 1969 federal Liberal popularity dropped throughout western Canada as a consequence of the federal government's new bilingualism policies and incidents such as Prime Minister Trudeau's appearing indifferent to Western farmers when media reports quoted him at a Winnipeg fundraiser in December 1968 as saying, "Well, why should I sell the Canadian farmers' wheat?" (In fact, his remarks were taken out of context as he was actually justifying the role of government in selling wheat.)[71] These developments hurt

Liberal prospects in the byelections held early in 1969 that led to the resignation of Gil Molgat.[72]

- In 1973 the Liberals' provincial election campaign was hurt by a federal budget that raised taxes.[73]
- In 1975 an increase in the federal gas tax days before a byelection in Crescentwood contributed to the defeat of Charles Huband.[74]
- Later, the introduction of federal gun control legislation during the 1995 Manitoba election had an adverse impact on the Manitoba Liberals' campaign.[75]

Both the federal and provincial Liberals reached a low point in western Canada in the late 1970s. By the end of 1979, there was just one elected provincial Liberal, June Westbury, who had won the byelection to replace Axworthy in the Manitoba Legislature after his election to the House of Commons in 1979.[76] After the 1980 federal election, Axworthy was one of just two elected Liberals at the federal level from western Canada.[77]

The provincial Liberal leadership remained empty for more than two years following Huband's departure. It was finally filled in 1980 by Doug Lauchlan, one of Axworthy's assistants. More recently, Manitoba's Liberals have created a separate federal party structure as a consequence of the provincial NDP government's reforms to election finance laws.[78] Despite the formal separation, the personnel involved in the two organizations are largely interchangeable.

Lauchlan led the party in the 1981 provincial election as it reached its post-1969 nadir when not a single member was elected, and the party's share of the popular vote dropped to 6.7 percent. It is clear that Liberal voters defected in the city to the NDP, while the residual rural Liberals still around from the Campbell era moved to the Progressive Conservatives. NDP support in 1981 rose to 47 percent, almost nine percentage points greater than the party had secured when winning its first government in 1969. In losing, the Progressive Conservatives obtained 44 percent, about eight points more than in 1969.

V. From the Ashes—the Carstairs Insurgency

Sharon Carstairs was raised in a Nova Scotia family steeped in Liberal politics. Her father, Harold Connelly, was a member of the Nova Scotia Legislature and served briefly as that province's premier before being appointed to the Canadian Senate.[79] Carstairs inherited his interest in politics as she became a Liberal activist. When she moved to Alberta in the 1960s and later to Manitoba in 1977, it was natural to involve herself with the Liberal Party in both provincial and federal politics. While the provincial scene in both provinces was bleak for the Liberals, the federal

Liberals were enjoying their sixteen years in power in Ottawa (save for the brief Joe Clark interregnum). Carstairs was a strongly committed Trudeau Liberal who, as she put it, "had fought the battles for bilingualism in Alberta and had the flat nose—from doors being slammed in my face—to prove it."[80]

Having demonstrated her willingness to embrace seemingly hopeless political struggles, Carstairs assumed the leadership of the Manitoba Liberals in early 1984 at a time when party fortunes were about to rebound. In a meaningful coincidence, the convention that elected her leader commenced just three days after Pierre Trudeau announced his resignation. The transition from Liberals to Conservatives in Ottawa later that year helped the provincial Liberals. Instead of an unpopular federal Liberal government weighing on the popularity of the provincial wing, it would soon be the provincial Tories who would have to cope with unpopular federal relations. When the Mulroney government awarded a maintenance contract for the CF-18 fighter jet to Canadair of Montreal rather than to a bid judged technically superior from Winnipeg's Bristol Aerospace, the scandal hurt the Manitoba Progressive Conservatives.[81]

It is evident from the account in her autobiography that the party's revival over the next four years owed a great deal to Carstairs's prodigious energy.[82] Her efforts were successful enough that by 1986 the party was able to run a full slate of candidates for the first time since 1969. While she was the only candidate to secure a seat, the party more than doubled its vote share to 14 percent. The NDP won the election by a narrower than anticipated margin, with some New Democrats blaming their shortfall on the Liberal surge in support.[83] The Manitoba Liberal Party's membership, which had dropped below 2000 in 1981, nearly doubled to 3717.[84] The narrowness of the NDP win permitted the single vote of backbencher Jim Walding to bring down the government on its budget in 1988, triggering the campaign that made Sharon Carstairs Leader of the Opposition in the Manitoba Legislature in the wake of the 25 April election.

Many factors contributed to the Liberal success. Of critical importance were some unpopular actions by the NDP government of then premier Howard Pawley, in particular the announcement of large increases in public auto insurance rates. The government's doomed budget had also proposed tax increases on tobacco, alcohol, and some fuels.[85] Pawley took the unprecedented step of resigning as party leader at the same time as the election was called, being replaced by Gary Doer at a convention held mid-campaign.

One campaign issue that assumed importance because of Sharon Carstairs was the Meech Lake Accord. Strongly opposed to the Accord, Carstairs made it a central campaign theme even if some observers felt it wasn't of great interest to the provincial electorate.[86] Seen as "a fresh face," she gained exceptional popularity during the election period.[87] Her appeal was strong enough that it clearly contributed to a much stronger voter turnout in 1988 than 1986.[88]

When the votes were counted the Liberals had won twenty seats with 35.5 percent of the popular vote. They finished a strong second to the Progressive Conservatives of Gary Filmon, who formed a minority government despite winning a smaller share of the vote in 1988 than in 1986.[89] For her part, Sharon Carstairs declared at her press conference the next day: "Meech Lake is dead!" She believed that Meech had been a key to her success and that public opinion in Manitoba meant it would not proceed.[90]

The 1988 Manitoba election produced highly contrasting results in Winnipeg and elsewhere. In the city, the Liberals won a landslide victory, gaining 42 percent of the popular vote while winning nineteen of twenty-nine constituencies. But outside Winnipeg, the Progressive Conservatives won most rural seats while the NDP swept the northern constituencies.

Figure 5.1. 1988 Provincial Election Vote Share by Region

	NDP	PC	Liberal
Winnipeg	23.0%	33.2%	42.3%
Rural	20.8%	47.5%	27.5%
North	52.5%	28.9%	18.6%
Manitoba	23.6%	38.4%	35.5%

The Liberals drew support from both sides of the diagonal line inside the city's boundaries, winning seats in the northern and southern sections of the city, in both affluent and poorer areas. In the party's traditionally strongest area, south Winnipeg, nine constituencies collectively cast 48 percent of their ballots for the Liberals.[91]

However, the Liberal gains would not be consolidated and did not endure. There are several explanations for this. The Liberal advantage over the NDP was lost two years later in the 1990 election when the NDP edged out the Liberals in popular vote, 28.72 percent to 28.02 percent, yet the NDP won twenty seats to the Liberals' seven. The NDP has benefited from a highly efficient, concentrated vote since 1969, never more critically than in 1990. The party also had the good fortune to be led by the highly effective Gary Doer at the point of the NDP's greatest post-1969 weakness.

Another key factor was that the Liberals' failure to form a government meant 1988 votes cast for the Liberals by disenchanted NDP voters were not transformed into the positive enduring support that might have been secured by a successful and effective Liberal government.

Despite the many kilometres travelled by Sharon Carstairs all over rural Manitoba, the party only won the constituency of Selkirk outside the city of Winnipeg in 1988, although it did register large gains in vote share in some rural constituencies. Ironically, for a party with roots in the Liberal-Progressive era, this rural failure kept the party out of government in 1988. For a party to be successful in Manitoba politics it must demonstrate some ability to win in both city and country. When the NDP won in 1969 based largely on victories in the city, it also made gains outside Winnipeg, both in rural areas and the far north.

Carstairs made various mistakes as leader. In particular, her preoccupation with federal issues, especially Meech Lake, proved costly. She devoted considerable time and energy to the issue from 1988 to 1990. Despite strong support among the public for her position, concentrating on Meech meant she did not build a profile on provincial issues. When she accepted a compromise during negotiations in Ottawa in the spring of 1990, it muted differences among the party leaders on the issue, and opposition to Meech in Manitoba came to centre on NDP MLA Elijah Harper rather than Carstairs. Carstairs paid the greatest political price since she no longer seemed to be quite the "fresh face" that the electorate had found so attractive in 1988. The "lady in red" who had appeared to be a strong leader on this issue instead appeared "indecisive and weak."[92]

VI. Post-Carstairs—Third-Party Status Again

The Liberals still had a caucus of seven after the 1990 election. However, Sharon Carstairs departed in 1993 after campaigning against the Charlottetown Accord and was replaced by Paul Edwards.

The Liberals entered the 1995 contest in a strong position in the polls, though the pre-election polling may have been influenced by the overall popularity of the federal Liberal government at the time. Respondents can confuse federal with provincial politics in answering polling questions so the Liberals' apparent initial strength could have been an illusion. Regardless, Paul Edwards stumbled early in the campaign. He could not articulate a clear position on the abortion issue when a campaign event happened by the Morgentaler abortion clinic, prompting the media to question him on the subject. Other missteps followed as divisions within the party revealed themselves on federal gun control and the question of a new hockey arena for Winnipeg's NHL franchise.[93]

The 1995 campaign, coming eleven years after the party began to revive under Carstairs, was beset with organizational and logistical difficulties that suggested the party's weakness after long years in the wilderness remained despite its earlier gains.[94] The Liberals managed to field a full slate of candidates in 1995 and did hold on to three seats but Paul Edwards lost in his constituency. Their vote share continued to decline from 28 percent to 23.6 percent.

It proved to be the last gasp of the revival begun under Carstairs. By the 1999 election the party was no longer able to field a full slate of candidates. Although enjoying stable leadership from former federal MP and cabinet minister Jon Gerrard (no small matter for a third party), since 1998 the Liberals have won no more than two seats while averaging 13 percent of the vote over the course of the 1999, 2003, and 2007 elections.

Voting NDP and Voting Liberal—Federal and Provincial Politics

A key reason for Liberal weakness provincially has been the growth of strategic voting by centre-left voters in Manitoba and Canada. Strategic voting has entered the vocabulary of Canadian politics in the last couple of decades because Canadian conservatives, who had views relatively close to the political centre in the 1960s, have gradually shifted to the right. Roblin could position the Manitoba Progressive Conservatives as a centre party to the left of the Liberal-Progressives in the late 1950s because Canada's Progressive Conservatives as a whole were close to the political centre.

The shift of Canadian conservatives to the right was documented in a study by one-time federal Liberal pollster Martin Goldfarb and former prime minister Pierre Trudeau's principal secretary, Thomas Axworthy.[95] Based on surveys of delegates to the 1967–1968 Progressive Conservative and Liberal leadership conventions that chose Robert Stanfield and Pierre Trudeau, and the 1983–1984 Progressive Conservative and Liberal leadership conventions that elected Brian Mulroney and John Turner, the authors argued: "As Canada moved from the affluent sixties to the recession of the eighties, the Liberal party stayed liberal or even became a little more progressive or left of centre. This minor shift in Liberal policy values contrasts with a dramatic change in Conservative party beliefs....The new right-wing agenda of American conservatives has entered Canada through the Conservative party."[96]

The result of this growing gap between the right and centre-left has been that voters with moderately left-of-centre views have found it easy to switch from the Liberals to the NDP and back, beginning in Manitoba with putting Ed Schreyer and the NDP into office in 1969. There has been an inverse relationship between support for the NDP and support for the Liberals that one can trace all the way back to 1958—higher support for the NDP has meant weaker Liberal support and vice versa. This pattern has been especially clear since 1969 as one can see in Figure 5.2.[97]

Manitoba's Liberals: Sliding into Third   149

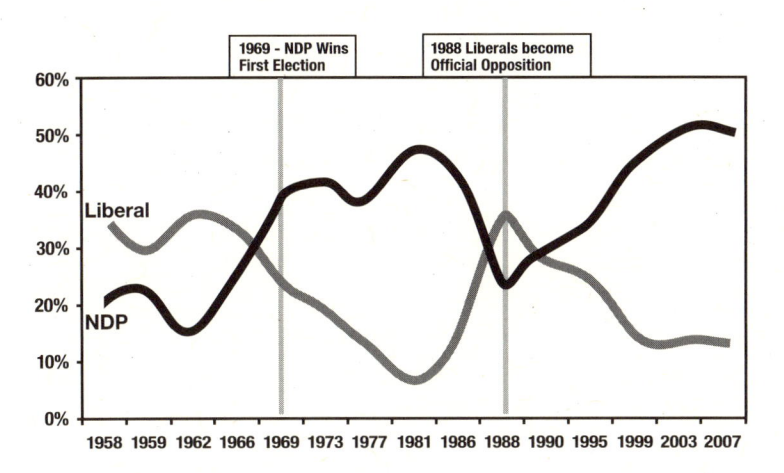

Figure 5.2. Patterns in Provincial Party Support in Manitoba

The provincial pattern is also visible in federal politics. Figure 5.3 illustrates support levels for the two parties since 1980 in federal elections in Manitoba (with the Green support added for 2004, 2006, and 2008).

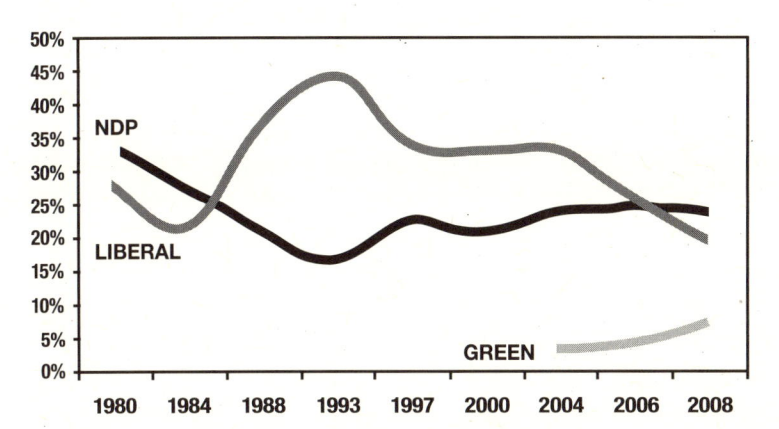

Figure 5.3. Patterns in Federal Party Support In Manitoba

A more recent illustration has been delivered as part of the unprecedented success of the current NDP administration in winning progressively larger majorities over the course of the past three provincial elections. The heartland of Liberal support has always been in Winnipeg's south end. As noted earlier, when Sharon Carstairs won 35 percent of Manitoba's popular vote in 1988 she secured 48 percent in the nine provincial constituencies in south Winnipeg. The NDP picked up only 17 percent of the vote in that area. However, if we compare that to the total vote covering the elections of 1999, 2003, and 2007 in the eleven constituencies that now represent approximately the same area we find that the NDP received 45.4 percent of support, the PCs 35 percent, and the Liberals 17.7 percent.[98]

These eleven constituencies approximately overlap the boundaries of the federal ridings of St. Boniface, Winnipeg South Centre, and Winnipeg South. If we total the votes for the 2000, 2004, and 2006 federal elections in these ridings, those nearest in time to the provincial contests in the table above, we get the following outcome: the Liberals received 43.5 percent of support, the Conservative Party 38.4 percent, and the NDP 15.1 percent.[99]

Overall, the linkages and inverse voting pattern strongly suggest an ideological affinity between federal Liberal and provincial NDP voters. In Winnipeg's North End the NDP has long dominated both federally and provincially. It is the south end results that clarify the relationship between the two.

VII. The Dilemma of Manitoba Liberalism

The core rationale for any political party is that it offers a distinctive voice and approach to governance that it hopes voters will prefer to the alternatives. Political parties have been transforming themselves in response to such contemporary trends as technological change and the growth of new institutions.[100] Public opinion polling has been of growing importance as parties seek out public views and shape their platforms to conform as best they can to public perceptions. Responding to the perceptions gives parties an incentive to re-shape their public profile and image in a manner that blurs their respective differences. This makes it increasingly difficult for a party such as the Manitoba Liberals to create a profile that is at the same time politically attractive and unequivocally distinct.

Since 1975 the Manitoba Liberals have generally been positioned as a centrist small-l liberal urban party. In the 2007 election, its extensive and detailed platform offered improvements in health care, education, the environment, the justice system, and social services as well as prescriptions for the economy that had the goal of making Manitoba a so-called "have" province by 2020. The party also offered a wide-ranging and detailed program in 2003.[101]

If one looks at Manitoba Liberal commitments offered over time, one finds a centrist but fluid ideological orientation, similar to the NDP but not identical. The Liberal Party's struggles to define its character distinctively are complicated by the differing interpretations party activists apply to its outlook. Jared Wesley finds influences in the Liberals' 2003 platform from the "neo-liberal" right and the "reform liberal" left, but notes that the platform as a whole had a "dual nature."[102]

It left the party "wavering on either side of the political centre." The party's opponents, the NDP and PCs, found the Liberal platform was both "ambiguous" and "eclectic."[103]

Wesley surveyed the Liberals' 2003 candidates and found that while the Liberals on the whole were clearly "centre-left," there was a significant division between older and younger Liberals:

> Namely, younger Liberal respondents tended to identify more closely with the tenets of the New Right, whereas the attitudes of those born prior to 1960 could be more accurately described in terms of reform liberalism. Younger Liberals were more populist and individualist than their elder counterparts, for instance. While the former supported continentalism, privatization and tax relief, the beliefs of the latter were located on the opposite side of the spectrum entirely. Older Liberal candidates, instead, were in favour of protectionist measures, increased funding for public services, and the public provision of health care in the province. And while younger Liberals preferred "economic growth, even at the cost of damage to the environment," older candidates opted for "protection of the environment, even at the cost of economic growth."[104]

Depending on historical circumstances a centre party can move to the right or left to seek political advantage. For the most part Canada's federal Liberals, especially in recent decades, have been a left-of-centre party, overlapping and competing with the CCF-NDP and more recently the Greens. However, they have also shown a capacity to move to the right when it is deemed advantageous.

During the mid-1990s the federal deficit became an increasingly important political issue. In 1995, the federal Liberals slashed spending while increasing some taxes and the deficit quickly became a surplus. The success of deficit reduction in the context of the strong economic growth of the 1990s gave the idea of balanced budgets considerable popularity.[105] Prior to the economic crisis that emerged in the fall of 2008, which dramatically altered this paradigm, one could find support for the idea across the political spectrum. For Jon Gerrard this means that Manitoba Liberals emphasize "responsible financial management and the creation of a compassionate and caring society."[106] The problem for the Liberals is that this mix of compassion and fiscal responsibility differs little from the NDP.

Looking at the last few decades, perhaps the clearest Manitoba Liberal consensus has been with respect to the constitution and individual rights, issues generally seen as being in the federal sphere. Sharon Carstairs regards one of her "proudest moments as a Liberal" as the day the Charter of Rights and Freedoms was enshrined in the constitution.[107] Devotion to Trudeau's constitutional vision made Carstairs and other Manitoba Liberals fierce opponents of the Meech Lake agreement. Indeed, the party adopted a resolution at its convention held during the 1988 election unanimously rejecting the Meech Lake Accord.[108]

Apart from their constitutional vision, the Manitoba Liberals' overall lack of coherence in their ideas and their overlap with the NDP means the party needs one of the major parties to discredit itself in a manner similar to the Pawley NDP of 1988. The Liberals have grown stronger since the 1999 election, at which time they could not field a full slate of candidates. Despite energetic campaigns in both 2003 and 2007 and full slates of candidates, the party's popular vote increased marginally. Changes to party finance enacted by the NDP government also suggest the party faces greater financial challenges in the future.[109] Nevertheless, the Liberal organization is currently sufficiently strong financially that as of April 2008 the party no longer charged a membership fee.[110]

Some political scientists in Canada have seen the path followed by the British Liberal Party as a precedent for Canada's Liberals. Shattered by tensions within its coalition generated by the First World War, the British Liberals were supplanted by the Labour Party over the space of three elections in the 1920s as the party of the political centre and left. In addition to social scientists, many CCF-NDP activists and leaders also saw in the British experience a natural evolution of democratic politics towards a two-party system where one party embodied the labour movement and progressive social reform while the other party represented conservative elements in society including support for the market, leaving little or no room for centre parties like the Liberals. Manitoba after 1969 became a focus of this attention for its potential as a precedent that would show up elsewhere in Canada.[111] While this phenomenon can be seen in Western Europe, it did not become a feature of Canada's national politics, nor did it happen in Ontario, where the NDP's only electoral success proved short-lived and the Liberals remain a major party.

The ideological congruence of the NDP and Liberals in both federal and provincial politics exists in the context of an increased ideological gap between the Conservatives and the other parties. The gap creates an ongoing incentive for strategic voting, a threat to third parties[112] while assisting the fortunes of the major party that is the preferred alternative in a strategic voting scenario. This is true in both federal and provincial politics. Voters approaching the ballot box reason about their choices.[113] If they have strong feelings about seeing their values reflected in government, as many do, they will assess both which party best expresses their values, and, of the choices available, which party has a chance to win. The latter assessment weighed upon the Manitoba Liberals for the past four decades as many potential supporters, who supported the party in federal electoral contests, abandoned them in provincial elections to vote NDP. While few have perceived the Manitoba Liberal Party as a prospective winner in the past three provincial elections, an average of 13 percent have nonetheless said to themselves "this is the party that represents how I view politics and government, and is therefore my only rational choice." It is a number that appears sufficient to ensure survival if not success.

Liberal leader Jon Gerrard survived a challenge to his leadership in early 2009,[114] which suggests that no leadership change should be expected in the Manitoba Liberal Party in the near future. The Liberals had hoped to benefit from the departure of Gary Doer in 2009, as Doer became Canada's ambassador to the United States and was replaced as premier by former finance minister Greg Selinger.[115] However, a Probe Research poll released two months into the Selinger era on December 15, 2009 reported results not much different from those of the 2007 election.[116]

The central question perpetually confronting Manitoba's Liberals is: can they achieve a dramatic breakthrough comparable to that of Sharon Carstairs? Such a transformation requires certain conditions. At least one of the two major parties must be going through a damaging political crisis, such as that experienced by the Pawley government in 1988, and it helps if the other major party has troubles of its own. In 1988 the Manitoba PCs were damaged by the unpopularity of the Mulroney government at precisely the same moment as Howard Pawley confronted his troubles. There must also be a catalyst to spark major change, such as a new leader. The departure of Doer is a relatively routine affair if viewed in this context, not one that would alter political fundamentals.

The steep slide of Manitoba's Liberals to third place in 1969 transformed a three-party system in Manitoba into a two-and-a-half party system, the Liberals playing the part of the half-party.[117] Third place in a first-past-the-post system can be an electoral trap and that is where Manitoba Liberals now find themselves. Current ideological trends and tensions suggest the capacity of Manitoba Liberals to affect Manitoba political trends such as would permit them to escape their forty-year dilemma is limited. It would take a political earthquake on the scale of 1988 for the Liberals to escape their current status, and major political earthquakes, like the natural events, are exceedingly rare.

Notes

1. The author would like to acknowledge the assistance of several who reviewed drafts of the paper and provided numerous valuable comments. They include Professor Allen Mills who also acted as the discussant for the paper at the Roblin Professorship Conference. Others who read and commented on the paper were Kim Malcolmson, Nelson Wiseman, Daniel Schwartz, Phillip Hansen, Timothy Lang, David Walker, Agnes Hall, Doug Smith, Josh Hjartarson, Tim Lewis, and Richard Barry. Comments were also provided by Paul Thomas, to whom I wish to express my gratitude for asking me to participate in the conference.
2. Nelson Wiseman, "The Pattern of Prairie Politics," in *Party Politics in Canada*, 8th ed., ed. Hugh Thorburn and Alan Whitehorn (Toronto: Prentice-Hall, 2001), 352. See also T.E. Peterson, "Ethnic and Class Politics in Manitoba," in *Canadian Provincial Politics: The Party Systems of the Ten Provinces*, ed. Robin, Martin (Scarborough: Prentice-Hall of Canada, 1972), 70.
3. John Edward Kendle, *John Bracken: A Political Biography* (Toronto: University of Toronto Press, 1979), 124–125.
4. T.E. Peterson and P. Barber, "Some Factors in the 1969 NDP Victory in Manitoba," *Lakehead University Review* 3, 2 (Fall 1970): 122.
5. Peterson, "Ethnic and Class Politics in Manitoba," 69.
6. W.L. Morton, "The Triumph of Ontario Democracy, 1881–1888," in *Manitoba: A History*, 2nd ed. (Toronto: University of Toronto Press), 199–233.
7. Chris Cook, *A Short History of the Liberal Party*, 5th ed. (London: Macmillan Press, 1998), 2–4.
8. Population increased by 81 percent between 1901 and 1911 and then by another 32 percent by 1921. See Table A2-14: Population of Canada, by province, census dates, 1851 to 1976, http://www.statcan.ca/english/freepub/11-516-XIE/sectiona/sectiona.htm. See also Peterson, "Ethnic and Class Politics in Manitoba," 73–76.
9. Lionel Orlikow, "The Reform Movement in Manitoba 1910–1915," in *Historical Essays on the Prairie Provinces*, ed. Donald Swainson (Toronto: McClelland and Stewart, 1970), 222.
10. Morton, *Manitoba: A History*, 220.
11. Orlikow, "The Reform Movement in Manitoba 1910–1915," 228.
12. Ibid., 229.
13. See Peterson, "Ethnic and Class Politics in Manitoba," 85 and 86.
14. Kendle, *Bracken*, 63.
15. Ibid., 116.
16. Nelson Wiseman, *Social Democracy in Manitoba* (Winnipeg: University of Manitoba Press, 1985), 24–36.
17. Kendle, *Bracken*, 64.
18. Harold Chorney and Phillip Hansen, *Toward a Humanist Political Economy* (Montreal: Black Rose Books, 1992), 46.
19. Peterson, "Ethnic and Class Politics in Manitoba," 89.
20. See Kendle, "Manitoba's Case," in *Bracken*, 147–163.
21. James A. Jackson, *The Centennial History of Manitoba* (Toronto: McClelland and Stewart, 1970), 239–240, and Mark E. Vajcner, "Stuart Garson and the Manitoba Progressive Coalition," *Manitoba History* 26 (Autumn 1993): 12.
22. Interview with Nelson Wiseman, May 1977.
23. John Saywell, "The Provinces: Manitoba," in *Canadian Annual Review of Politics and Public Affairs, 1961*, ed. John Saywell (Toronto: University of Toronto Press, 1962), 60.

24　Kendle, *Bracken*, 41.
25　Jon Gerrard, *Battling for a Better Manitoba: A History of the Provincial Liberal Party* (Winnipeg: Heartland Associates, 2006), 111.
26　For an account of rural electrification in the hill country of Texas, the result of efforts by Lyndon Johnson, then a member of the U.S. House of Representatives, see Robert Caro, *The Years of Lyndon Johnson, The Path to Power* (New York: Knopf, 1982) 502–528.
27　David McCormick, "The Dissolution of the Coalition: Roblin's Rise to Leadership," *Historical and Scientific Society of Manitoba Transactions*, Series III, 28 (1971–72): 37.
28　Duff Roblin, *Speaking for Myself* (Winnipeg: Great Plains Publications, 1999), 53.
29　Ibid., 77.
30　McCormick, "Dissolution of the Coalition," 38.
31　Harold Chorney, "The Political Economy of Provincial Economic Development Policy 1950–1970" (MA thesis, University of Manitoba, 1970), 37.
32　Timothy Lewis, *In the Long Run We're All Dead: The Canadian Turn to Fiscal Restraint* (Vancouver: University of British Columbia Press, 2003), 38–41.
33　*Winnipeg Free Press*, 28 June 1957, cited in David E. Smith, *The Regional Decline of a National Party: Liberals on the Prairies* (Toronto: University of Toronto Press, 1981), 69.
34　Roblin, *Speaking for Myself*, 86.
35　Christina McCall-Newman, *Grits: An Intimate Portrait of the Liberal Party* (Toronto: Macmillan of Canada, 1982), 14–19.
36　McCall-Newman, *Grits*, 36.
37　Tom Kent, *A Public Purpose* (Montreal: McGill-Queen's University Press, 1988), 76–77.
38　Ibid., 45 and 46.
39　Smith, *Liberals on the Prairies*, 69.
40　Liberal Elman Guttormson, in opposing the floodway, complained that "All over the province people were becoming 'tax poor.'" *Winnipeg Free Press*, 14 March 1961. See also Roblin, *Speaking for Myself*, 166–173.
41　Morton, *Manitoba: A History*, 485.
42　*Winnipeg Tribune*, 19 April 1961, 6.
43　*Winnipeg Tribune*, 20 April 1961.
44　Ibid.
45　J.F. O'Sullivan, Memo to Liberal Candidates 30 April 1959 in Gerrard, *Battling for a Better Manitoba*, 200.
46　Timothy Lang, "Liberals in Manitoba: Provincial Decline and Resurgence" (MA thesis, University of Manitoba, 1991), 42 and 43. Quote is from interview with thesis author, 29 October 1990.
47　Ibid.
48　Ibid., 51.
49　*Canadian Annual Review of Public Affairs*, ed. John Saywell (Toronto: University of Toronto Press, 1961–1969).
50　Saywell, *Canadian Annual Review*, 1961, 60.
51　Donnelly, *Canadian Annual Review, Manitoba*, 1965, 160.
52　Peterson, *Canadian Annual Review, Manitoba*, 1966, 131.
53　*Winnipeg Free Press*, 5 May 1966.
54　*Winnipeg Tribune*, 21 June 1966.
55　*Winnipeg Free Press*, 24 June 1966.
56　Ibid.

57   *Winnipeg Tribune*, 24 June 1966.
58   Three other constituencies might now be considered part of the city. Orlikow, "The Reform Movement in Manitoba 1910–1915," 226.
59   Statistics Canada, *Canada Year Book 1957–58*, http://www66.statcan.gc.ca/cdm4/document.php?CISOROOT=/eng&CISOPTR=3386&REC=19 (accessed 26 August 2008), 124 and 125.
60   Peterson and Barber, "Some Factors in the 1969 NDP Victory in Manitoba," 124 and 125.
61   *Winnipeg Free Press*, 10 May 1969, 1.
62   Wiseman, *Social Democracy in Manitoba*, 120.
63   Ibid., 120 and 121.
64   For example, in the 2006 election the federal Liberals won the Ontario constituencies of Don Valley West and Davenport. The latter has an average family income of $53,687 while the former has an average of $136,032, compared to the Ontario average of $73,849. Statistics Canada. 2001. Federal Electoral District Profile (2003 Representation Order) Data for Don Valley West and Davenport: http://www12.statcan.ca/english/census01/products/standard/fedprofile/selectFED.cfm?R=FED03 (accessed 31 August 2008).
65   Arend Lijphart, *Democracies: Patterns of Majoritarian and Consensus Government in Twenty-One Countries* (New Haven and London: Yale University Press, 1984), 136.
66   Former Manitoba Liberal Leader Izzy Asper in conversation with the author the day after the 11 October 1977 provincial election.
67   Quoted by Peterson, *Canadian Annual Review, Manitoba*, 1970, 261.
68   Lang, "Liberals in Manitoba," 60.
69   *Winnipeg Free Press*, 21 June 1977, cited in ibid., 65.
70   Lloyd Axworthy, preface to Gerrard, *Battling for a Better Manitoba*, 8 and 9.
71   Anthony Westell, *Paradox: Trudeau as Prime Minister* (Scarborough, ON: Prentice-Hall, 1972), 67.
72   Lang, "Liberals in Manitoba," 48.
73   Axworthy, preface, 8.
74   Gerrard, *Battling for a Better Manitoba*, 141.
75   Three rural Manitoba Members of Parliament actually voted against the legislation. Robert Andrew Drummond, "Liberal Party Organization and Manitoba's 1995 Provincial Election" (MA thesis, University of Manitoba, 1996), 66 and 67.
76   Lang, "Liberals in Manitoba," 71.
77   Howard Penniman, ed., *Canada at the Polls, 1979 and 1980* (Washington and London: American Enterprise Institute for Public Policy Research, 1981), 405.
78   David Stewart and Jared Wesley, "Electoral Financing Reform in Manitoba: Advantage Doer?" paper for presentation at the Conference on Party and Election Finance: Consequences for Democracy, 13.
79   Sharon Carstairs, *Not One of the Boys* (Toronto: Macmillan, 1993), 4.
80   Ibid., 63.
81   Trevor Harrison, *Of Passionate Intensity: Right-Wing Populism and the Reform Party of Canada* (Toronto: University of Toronto Press, 1995), 103.
82   Carstairs, *Not One of the Boys*, 82–96.
83   Lang, "Liberals in Manitoba," 82.
84   Ibid., 79.
85   Geoffrey Lambert, *Canadian Annual Review, Manitoba*, 1988, 253.
86   Carstairs, *Not One of the Boys*, 120.

87 Lang, "Liberals in Manitoba," 87 and 88.
88 Lambert, *Canadian Annual Review, Manitoba*, 1988, 255.
89 Elections Manitoba, *Historical Summaries 1870 to 2003*. http://www.electionsmanitoba.ca/pdf/2007_statvotes_history.pdf (accessed 30 August 2008), 269 and 271.
90 Carstairs, *Not One of the Boys*, 128.
91 The ridings included here were Fort Garry, Fort Rouge, Niakwa, Osborne, Riel, River Heights, St. Boniface, St. Norbert, and St. Vital.
92 Drummond, "Liberal Party Organization and Manitoba's 1995 Provincial Election," 17 and 18.
93 Ibid., 66–70.
94 Ibid., 100–107.
95 Martin Goldfarb and Thomas Axworthy, *Marching to a Different Drummer: An Essay on the Liberals and Conservatives in Convention* (Toronto: Stoddart, 1988). For an account of comparable (although far from identical) American developments, see Paul Krugman, *The Conscience of a Liberal* (New York: W.W. Norton, 2007), 101–123.
96 Ibid., 89.
97 Graphic created from elections results by author.
98 The ridings were Fort Garry, Fort Rouge, Fort Whyte, Lord Roberts, Riel, River Heights, Seine River, Southdale, St. Boniface, St. Norbert, and St. Vital.
99 For the 2000 election the votes of the Canadian Alliance and the Progressive Conservatives were combined. 2000 vote results based on Elections Canada. 2003. Electoral Districts: Ranking of Political Parties, by Electoral District, Following Transposition of Valid Votes, 2003. http://www.elections.ca/content.asp?section=cir&dir=tran&document=index&lang=e&textonly=false (accessed on 13 September 2008).
100 John Meisel and Matthew Mendelsohn, "Meteor? Phoenix? Chameleon? The Decline of and Transformation of Party in Canada," in *Party Politics in Canada*, 8th ed., ed. Hugh Thorburn and Alan Whitehorn (Toronto: Prentice-Hall, 2001), 164.
101 Jared Wesley, "Spanning the Spectrum: Political Party Attitudes in Manitoba" (MA thesis, University of Manitoba, 2004), 142.
102 Ibid.
103 Ibid., 148.
104 Ibid., 153.
105 See Timothy Lewis, *In the Long Run We're All Dead* (Vancouver: University of British Columbia Press, 2004), for an account of the decline in influence of Keynes in the federal Finance Department during the 1980s, particularly pp. 117 and 118.
106 Gerrard, *Battling for a Better Manitoba*, 185.
107 Carstairs, *Not One of the Boys*, 111.
108 Ibid., 105.
109 David Stewart and Jared Wesley, "Electoral Financing Reform in Manitoba," 13.
110 MLP Newsletter, July 2008, http://mlp.manitobaliberals.ca/?page_id=64 (accessed 6 September 2008).
111 John. M. Wilson, "The Decline of the Liberal Party in Manitoba Politics," *Journal of Canadian Studies* 10, 1 (1975): 28 and 29.
112 Andre Blais, Robert Young, and Martin Turcotte, "Direct or indirect? Assessing two approaches to the measurement of strategic voting," *Electoral Studies* 24 (2005): 163–176. The authors argue that the net number of strategic voters is small but drawn disproportionately from the third party. In the case under consideration by the authors,

the 1999 Ontario Election, this meant the NDP was most affected. The percentage of the electorate estimated by the authors to have voted strategically in 1999 was four to six percent (173).

113 Samuel L. Popkin, *The Reasoning Voter: Communication and Persuasion in Presidential Campaigns*, 2nd ed. (Chicago: University of Chicago Press, 1994), 7.

114 *Winnipeg Sun*, 22 March 2009, http://www.winnipegsun.com/news/winnipeg/2009/03/22/8845126.html (accessed 16 January 2009).

115 Jon Gerrard in his blog said, "It is the start of major change in Manitoba," http://www.manitobaliberals.ca/2009_09_06_archive.html (accessed on 16 January 2010).

116 Probe Research Poll, 15 December 2009, http://probe-research.com/2009/12/provincial-party-standings-in-manitoba.html (accessed 16 January 2010).

117 Christopher Adams, "Realignment in Manitoba: The Provincial Elections of 1999, 2003, and 2007," paper presented at the Annual Meeting of the Canadian Political Science Association, Vancouver, BC, 4 June 2008, 16 and 17.

Realigning Elections in Manitoba[1]

Christopher Adams

Introduction

In his 1955 *Journal of Politics* article regarding the study of American presidential elections, V.O. Key described a specific type of electoral event, which he titled a "critical election."[2] A critical election marks the fact that a "realignment, both sharp and durable" is occurring within the electorate.[3] While such elections are located at a specific point in time, Key argued these events are also part of "a stream of connected antecedent and subsequent behavior." To demonstrate this, Key revealed how shifts to the Democrats could already be discerned in 1928, four years prior to Franklin D. Roosevelt's 1932 presidential victory and the beginning of a new political era that lasted until Dwight Eisenhower's Republican Party victory in 1952. As such, identifying electoral realignments and critical elections is essentially an historical enterprise. It is only after watching a series of electoral outcomes that one is able to label with confidence the triggering event as a "critical" realigning election, and not simply a temporary shift in partisan support.

Of course, there are many types of elections and, building on the work of V.O. Key, three main categories of elections can be used to generally classify voter behaviour within the context of party support:

1. A "maintaining election" is one in which partisan support remains generally stable. Changes in government can occur with these types of elections, yet

these would be due to relatively minor shifts in partisan preference, or changes occurring in "swing" regions.
2. A "deviating election" is one in which partisan loyalties are disrupted by such factors as an economic downturn or a leader's charisma. As a factor's importance recedes, voters in subsequent elections revert to their original partisan positions. Deviating elections can precipitate a change in government, or even an electoral landslide, and are sometimes confused with realigning elections.
3. A "realigning election" is a critical election that signals a significant and long-lasting shift within the electorate. Such elections often reflect major social changes or upheavals: for example, a long-term economic depression, post-war prosperity, or shifting class divisions.[4]

Following in the steps of Key, Walter Dean Burnham outlined four major characteristics of critical elections and electoral realignment in his work *Critical Elections and the Mainsprings of American Politics*. The first is that a critical realignment is marked by "short-lived but very intense disruptions of traditional patterns of voting behavior." Secondly, this intensity "typically spills over" into other parts of the political system and manifests itself in intra-party power struggles and increases in voter turnout. Third, critical elections tend to occur periodically and at regular intervals. Fourth, and perhaps more significantly, critical elections and electoral realignment reflect a disconnection between existing party arrangements and major changes occurring in society. Therefore, a critical election will result in "significant transformations in the general shape of policy."[5]

This chapter examines four significant electoral periods that triggered long-term changes in Manitoba's government during the past half-century, and the extent to which these periods were produced by realigning elections.[6] The four periods studied are as follows:

1. Duff Roblin's Progressive Conservatives (PC) won a minority victory in 1958 which was followed with a majority breakthrough in 1959. The PCs remained in power until 1969.
2. Under Edward Schreyer, the New Democratic Party (NDP) won a minority victory in 1969 which led to a new political era for the province. With the exception of four years in which Sterling Lyon and the PCs held power (1977–1981), the NDP formed the government from 1969 to 1988.
3. Gary Filmon and his PCs won a minority victory in 1988. The election also produced twenty seats for the Liberals and temporarily forced the NDP into third-party status. This victory was followed by a majority PC victory in 1990 and, again, in 1995. The PCs held power until 1999.
4. In 1999, Gary Doer and the NDP won a majority victory which was followed by majority government victories in 2003 and 2007. It was the first time since

Duff Roblin that a Manitoba provincial party won three successive majority victories.

The Duff Roblin Breakthrough of 1958–1959

The Progressive Conservative minority government victory in 1958 closely fits the realigning election category. This election was followed by a 1959 majority victory for the party, and signaled the passing of the Liberal-Progressive era.[7] The 1958 victory was produced by a rejuvenated PC Party organization under a more urban-oriented leader who was willing to expand the province's role in the economy, health care, education, and social welfare programs, in contrast to the rurally oriented Liberal-Progressive government, which had been in power since 1922.

Duff Roblin, the grandson of former premier Rodmond Roblin, was first elected in 1949 as one of four MLAs in the multi-member riding of South Winnipeg. In contrast to other Conservatives who, under Errick Willis, had supported the Liberal-Progressive coalition government, Roblin was elected as an "Independent PC" and was only one of four elected Conservatives who served in opposition. The 1953 provincial election produced for Willis and the PCs only twelve out of fifty-seven seats, while thirteen seats went uncontested by the party. Of the twelve who were elected, only three PC MLAs represented Winnipeg constituencies,[8] with the other nine spread out across southern Manitoba. The stage was set for electoral realignment in Manitoba when, in 1954, Duff Roblin became the leader of the PCs. Roblin appealed to party delegates as both an urban candidate and someone who could win over rural voters. He defeated Willis on the second ballot in a hard-fought leadership race, with 137 out of his 160 votes coming from rural delegates.[9] With the exception of a brief period in the 1930s, when the party was led by Sanford Evans, Roblin was the first Winnipeg-based MLA to lead the party since Hugh John Macdonald's brief tenure from 1899 to 1900.

After winning the leadership and in preparation for his first provincial election, the new leader's strategy contained three straightforward elements: (1) attract new and qualified candidates, (2) reach beyond the party's predominantly Anglo-Saxon/Protestant upper-income and rural base of support (based chiefly in South Winnipeg and southern Manitoba) and (3) rejuvenate local constituency associations with new funds. This was implemented by recruiting candidates who were well-regarded in their local communities—as demonstrated by Roblin's ability to recruit Dr. George Johnson, who was elected in Gimli and later became minister of health—and by obtaining funds from the Ontario PCs in order to help build an effective campaign war chest.[10] Roblin's efforts dovetailed with John Diefenbaker's PCs, who won a minority victory in the 1957 federal election, and then a landslide the following year. Of the 208 of 245 seats won by the PCs across the country, all fourteen of Manitoba's federal ridings went to PC candidates. It was only three months after this event that, in the June 1958 provincial election, Roblin's PCs won their minority government victory with 40 percent of the vote and twenty-six seats out of fifty-seven. The Liberal-Progressives, which had held power under a number of party labels since 1922,[11] took nineteen seats while the Cooperative Commonwealth Federation (CCF) took eleven seats.

The realignment in Manitoba was completed with the 1959 provincial election. Voter turnout was at 65.6 percent, the highest level since 1936, which produced a majority victory for the PCs with thirty-six out of fifty-seven seats going to the party based on 46 percent of the vote. The shift occurred across the province with the PCs winning four of the five northern ridings (Rupertsland, Churchill, Swan River, and The Pas), southern ridings outside Winnipeg (which were divided between the Liberal-Progressives and the PCs), and in Winnipeg where support came from across all parts of the city, including Winnipeg Centre and even parts of the working-class North End (St. Matthews and Wellington).

Fitting Burnham's assertion that a realigning election often triggers a new era in policy-making, the 1958–1959 realignment brought to Manitoba a governing party that contrasted strongly with the tight-spending Liberal-Progressives. The new PC government tripled public spending, with much of the funding going to health care, social welfare, and education.[12] From 1958 to 1967, the PC government built 225 new schools, of which more than half were built between 1959 and 1961.[13] New efforts were also put into developing the northern frontier, including the ill-fated Manitoba Development Fund (MDF) which was established in 1958 to promote foreign investment.[14]

One way by which the 1958 realigning election can be examined is by using a tool that V.O. Key used to chart a number of critical elections in his *Politics, Parties, and Pressure Groups*. This tool was used to examine shifting support towards the Republicans in the elections of 1900 and 1904 in Indiana and California, and the 1904 and 1908 elections in New York and Ohio. He did this by charting, on a county-by-county basis, changes in the percentage in Republican Party support from the first election (using the x-axis) to the second (on the y-axis).[15] A county where support increased, such as from 20 percent to 25 percent, would appear above a diagonal line in the chart, while a county where a party's support dropped, such as from 33 percent to 30 percent, would appear below the same line in the chart.

By using Key's approach to chart electoral realignments in Manitoba based on aggregated voting data, a picture can be drawn showing what occurred between 1953 and 1958, and then 1959. In Figure 6.1, instead of using counties (which Key uses for studying American results), support for the PCs in each riding in 1953 is plotted on the x-axis (based on calculations from the number of PC votes cast in each riding out of the total votes cast in each respective riding). Plotted on the y-axis are the percent figure results for the party in these same ridings as they occurred for the 1958 election.[16] Northern ridings are marked with a triangle symbol, southern non-urban ridings are marked with a diamond, and Winnipeg ridings are marked with a square.[17] Because all three four-member ridings in Winnipeg were replaced by single-member constituencies between 1953 and 1958, it is not possible to chart riding-by-riding shifts for the city. Therefore, in order to make the results in Winnipeg comparable, votes for the PCs across all three Winnipeg ridings in 1953 have been merged to create a hypothetical single riding for the entire city. This has also been done for the newly created Winnipeg ridings that appeared in the 1958 election. The results are marked with a "W" symbol. It should be noted that the two-member riding of St. Boniface was converted into a single member riding for the 1958 election. Therefore, 1953 voter support for the two candidates has been totaled and then divided by the total vote cast. This riding is marked as a "B."

Figure 6.1. PC Support, 1953 to 1958 Elections

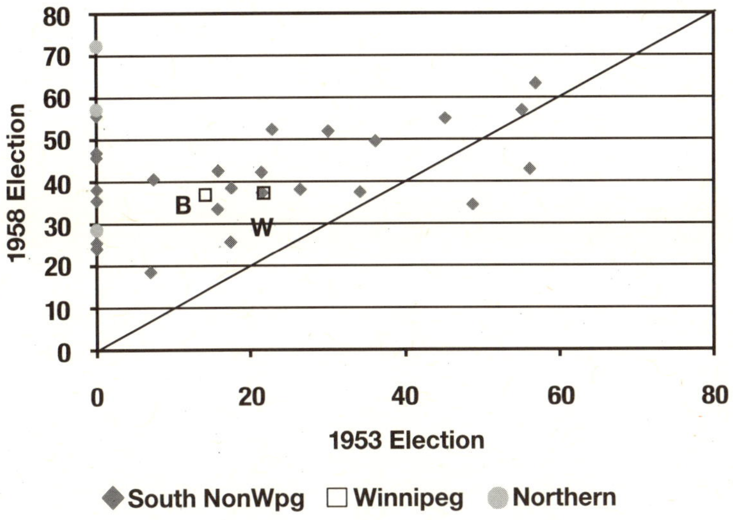

◆ South NonWpg □ Winnipeg ● Northern

Source: Calculated from Elections Manitoba data.

Riding-by-riding results (shown in Figure 6.1) reveal that a major across-the-board shift to the PCs occurred in 1958. With the exception of two non-urban ridings in the southern half of Manitoba (marked by diamonds), support for the PCs increased in all parts of the province. This includes Winnipeg (with the total vote percentage change marked with a "W"), St. Boniface (marked with a "B"), and in the North (marked with triangles), where the party was unable to run candidates in 1953.

As part of the realignment of 1958, the subsequent election of 1959 "locked in" the realignment of the previous year. Although not shown here, riding-by-riding results revealed that most ridings in 1959 hovered close to the line, including Winnipeg ridings, northern ridings, and most ridings across the south.

In keeping with Key's definition of critical elections and how they demonstrate a long-lasting impact on the party system, the 1958–1959 realignment endured to the PCs' benefit in the subsequent 1962 and 1966 provincial elections. As the election results that are provided in this chapter's appendix demonstrate, the realignment also signalled the beginning of a long-term decline for the Liberals, both in the form of popular support and, more significantly, in the number of seats in the legislature. Between 1953 and 1966, popular support for the PCs increased from 21 percent to 40 percent, and from twelve seats to thirty-one seats, while popular support for the Liberal Progressives (and later as the Liberals) declined from 43 percent to 33 percent, and from thirty-six seats to fourteen seats.

Ed Schreyer, the NDP, and the 1969 Election

A combination of factors produced the critical election of 1969. The first was that the postwar baby boom had produced many new voters who, upon reaching voting age, held a different political outlook than did their parents. Second, in part due to the policies of the Roblin government, Winnipeg now contained a new white-collar middle class with a better educated citizenry, many of whom were now employed as educators, health-care workers, and civil servants. Just one demonstration of how society was changing is found in the fact that between 1950 and 1970 the number of full-time university students in Manitoba grew from 4585 to 16,941.[18]

A third factor was that both the PCs and the Liberals were operating with new leaders who appeared out of touch with the changing nature of Manitoba society. Upon taking the leadership helm, both steered their parties towards the ideological right. The PCs chose Walter Weir to serve as their new leader and premier after Duff Roblin departed for federal politics. First elected in the riding of Minnedosa in 1959, and a funeral director by trade, Weir was closer to the party's rural roots and thereby re-oriented the party towards "small government, low tax" policies. In the meantime, Robert "Bobby" Bend replaced Gildas Molgat as Liberal leader and immediately put forward his own rurally oriented anti-welfare and pro-business platform.

While the PCs and Liberals were undergoing a change in leadership, the NDP's Ed Schreyer was about to enter the provincial arena equipped with a winning record as a federal MP and an ability to reach out to a wide range of social groups, including workers, farmers, those of eastern European ancestry, Métis, and First Nations. The party held its leadership convention during the provincial election, and Schreyer received a high level of visibility through a series of widely televised leadership debates. In contrast to Weir and Bend, the NDP appeared better suited to the age of television (see Illustration 6.1).

Illustration 6.1. *Winnipeg Free Press* **Advertisements**

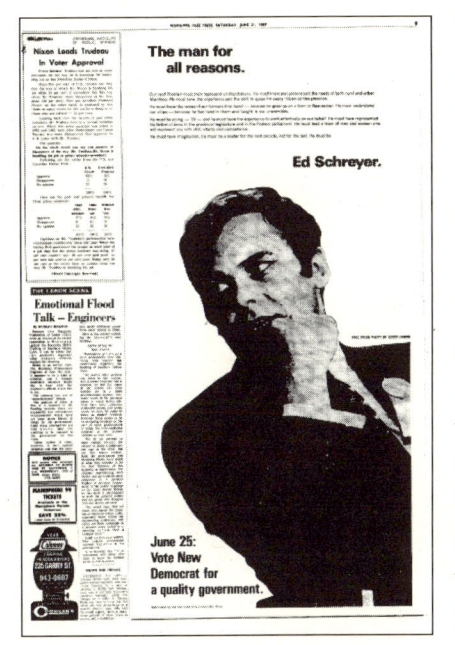

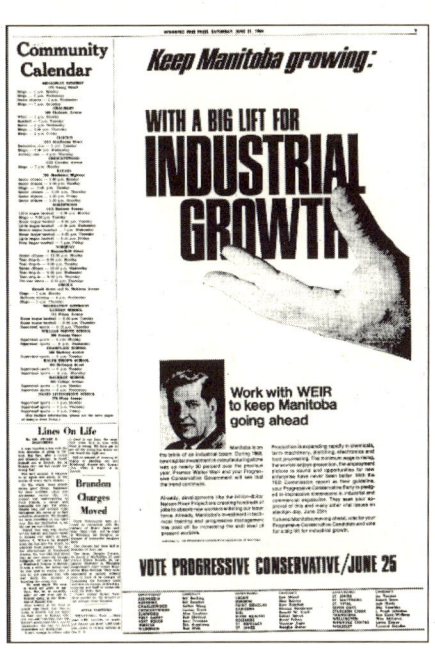

Source: *Winnipeg Free Press*, 21 June 1969.

The fifth and perhaps most important factor for the NDP, a party with roots in urban labour, was that in 1968 the provincial system underwent electoral redistribution thereby increasing the number of seats for the Winnipeg region while decreasing the power of the southern farm vote. As James McAllister points out in his work, *The Government of Edward Schreyer*, Manitoba's urban voters were for the first time electing almost half of Manitoba's MLAs.[19] In a 2006 interview, Schreyer was asked if he could have won the 1969 provincial election without the electoral redistribution. The retired premier responded after a moment of hesitation with a "probably not."[20]

At 64.4 percent, voter turnout was almost identical to the 1966 election, in which 64.3 percent turned out to vote. However, the results were very different. The NDP made inroads in Winnipeg, especially among younger voters, as well as in the less prosperous farm regions of the province, and, for the first time, much of northern Manitoba, including First Nations communities. The party also replaced the Liberals as one of the province's two major parties and, by 2010, had held government power in twenty-six of the previous forty-one years. While support for the NDP grew from 15 percent to 42 percent between 1962 and 1973, Liberal Party support declined from 36 percent to 19 percent. While the PCs demonstrated their ability to recuperate and win the provincial elections of 1977, the Liberals never recovered.

The riding-by-riding results (Figure 6.2) shows that NDP support grew across the entire province, with gains made both inside and outside Winnipeg and across both northern and southern regions. In the four northern ridings that appear for both elections (marked as triangles),[21] where 1966 support ranged from 0 percent (no candidate) to 27.7 percent, party support increased in 1969 with ranges of 21.1 percent to 40.8 percent. Among most southern non-Winnipeg ridings (marked as diamonds) where the growth was insufficient to unseat PC or Liberal candidates except in the less prosperous farm areas such as in the Interlake or the Dauphin region, here too there were increases in support for the NDP. It is in Winnipeg where the growth in support had the most significant impact on who would be chosen to lead the government. NDP candidates in Winnipeg drew support in the 15 percent to 30 percent range in 1966, whereas in 1969 this jumped into the 30 percent to 50 percent range. In fact, every Winnipeg riding[22] underwent a shift towards the NDP in 1969, many of which produced large shifts.

The long-term impact of the 1969 provincial election can be seen by examining the election results provided in the appendix to this chapter. With the exception of the 1988 provincial election when the Liberals cut deeply into NDP support, for the past quarter-century the NDP has served as one of the two main provincial parties. Since 1969, there were only two periods in which the NDP has sat in opposition. First, from 1977 to 1981, Sterling Lyon's PCs were elected on the strength of a neo-conservative agenda, but were defeated after only a single term by Howard Pawley and the NDP, signalling that the 1981 Pawley victory can be interpreted as an extension of the 1969 realigning election. Compared to the single term defeat of the NDP in 1977, the NDP's defeat in 1988 was more significant in that it temporarily reduced the NDP to third-party status—behind the Liberals—while the PCs won a minority victory which was then converted into two successive majorities in 1990 and 1995. It is to the rise of Gary Filmon and his PCs that the discussion now turns.

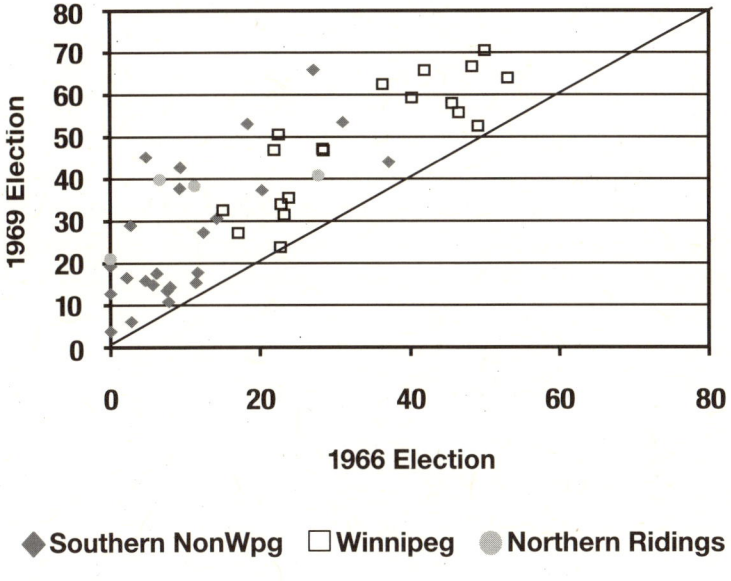

Figure 6.2. Shift in NDP Support, 1966 to 1969 Elections

◆ Southern NonWpg   ☐ Winnipeg   ● Northern Ridings

Source: Elections Manitoba Historical Summaries.

Gary Filmon, the PCs and the 1988 and 1990 Elections

To what extent did the Progressive Conservative Party's 1988 minority victory and their follow-up majority victory in 1990 signal electoral realignment? Are there parallels to the PC victories of 1958 and 1959s? In contrast to the placid 1950s, when the Liberal-Progressives had dominated the legislature for decades, in 1988 the provincial scene was in flux. The governing NDP under Howard Pawley was exhausted from dealing with budget deficits, a stagnant economy and an ongoing and bitterly divisive battle over French language rights. At the same time, Gary Filmon replaced Sterling Lyon as PC leader. Filmon put forward a more moderate image than that of his predecessor which, in turn, led many of the more right-wing elements in his caucus to believe he was unsuitable to lead the party.

The 1988 election was peculiar in that there was an exceptionally high level of turnout (74.0 percent) driven by competitive three-party races in parts of Winnipeg. Led by Sharon Carstairs, Liberal Party candidates were able to steal votes from both the NDP and PCs, leaving the NDP in third place and reliant for its survival on voters living on the northern edge of downtown Winnipeg, the eastern half of Brandon and the North. Watching the results come in on the evening of the election, many, including retired premier Edward Schreyer, believed the results to be the outcome of electoral realignment, and therefore the end of the NDP as one of the province's two major parties.[23]

But was it a realigning election? Did it signal a shift to the PCs which led towards their subsequent majority victories? The answer is no. Unlike Roblin's 1958 minority victory, no major shift towards the PCs occurred, and in fact PC support *dropped* in most parts of Winnipeg as well as in many non-Winnipeg ridings in the southern half of the province. Furthermore, even when the PCs won a majority two years later, most ridings straddle the 45° line when shifts in vote are compared from 1988 to 1990. A better fit for describing the 1988 election would be to categorize it as a "deviating election," with the 1990 election categorized as a "maintaining election." The 1988 results signalled what turned out to be a temporary collapse in NDP support with large shifts to the Liberals. Following this was a return in the 1990s to the more usual competition for power between the PCs and the NDP.

Even when the ridings were examined over a longer four-year period, between the 1986 NDP victory and the 1990 PC majority victory, there is no indication an electoral realignment occurred, as again, in most constituencies PC support straddled the 45° line. However, this is not to say that the impact on the provincial political scene was insignificant during the late 1980s and the 1990s. For a number of reasons, including his ability to competently handle federal-provincial pressures during the divisive debate over the Meech Lake Accord, Filmon was able to solidify his reputation as both a capable party leader and premier. He maintained his stature through much of the 1990s while leading the government during a period of fiscal restraint, thereby helping his party obtain two successive majority victories.

Gary Doer, the NDP and the 1999 Election

There were two campaign issues dogging Premier Filmon and his party leading up to the vote in 1999. The first involved health care and what was termed "hallway medicine" (i.e., patients being left in the hallways). The problem was rooted in federal rather than provincial government cutbacks,[24] but was worsened by the PC government's commitment to balance provincial budgets without increasing taxes. The second issue was perhaps more critical in that it involved high-level party strategists who were implicated in an illegal vote-splitting scheme that occurred during the previous (1995) election.[25] While the PCs took a hit on the issues of health care and integrity, the NDP and its leader Gary Doer positioned themselves as fiscally prudent pragmatists, even supporting the PC government's balanced budget legislation. The NDP's 1999 election platform contained five simple commitments that were aimed at middle-class voters: improve the health-care system, make college and university studies affordable, make communities safer, provide balanced provincial budgets, and work with the private sector to promote the province's economic well-being.[26]

There is no doubt that 1999 was a breakthrough election for the NDP, but was it a realigning election? Did it bear the same characteristics as the NDP's 1969 success? In the previous election (1995), Gary Doer and his NDP had gone down to their third defeat in a row. With only a third of the electorate (33 percent, up from 29 percent in 1990) and twenty-three seats going to the NDP, compared to the PCs who were able to take 43 percent of the vote and thirty-one seats, it appeared that the NDP would remain far from power for many years to come. However, an important factor in play with regard to the NDP's future was the Liberal Party. Under Paul Edwards, the Liberals were reduced to three seats based on 24 percent of the vote in 1995. Following Edwards' resignation, the party slipped into a period of intra-party squabbling and was forced to hold two leadership conventions prior to the 1999 election. With the Liberals continuing to deteriorate, in 1999 the NDP were left with only one major opponent in most ridings: the PCs.

Polling data collected just prior to the 1999 election revealed that NDP support was located in three significant social groups: middle-class voters (as measured roughly by household income), middle-aged voters, and women.[27] Table 6.1 reveals that among those residing in middle-income households ($30,000 to $59,999), the NDP were almost tied with the PCs with only three percentage points separating the two parties (while maintaining an expected lead among lower-income households). Among middle-aged voters (those aged thirty-five to fifty-four), and women, NDP support was a full ten percentage points higher than the PCs'.

Table 6.1. 1999 Party Support – Pre-Election Poll

	Totals (1010) %	Gender Men (494) %	Gender Women (516) %	Age 18-34 (339) %	Age 35-54 (370) %	Age 55+ (292) %	Household Income <$30K (279) %	Household Income $30K-$59K (480) %	Household Income $60K+ (250) %
Liberal	13	12	14	18	11	10	15	12	12
PC	42	47	37	35	39	57	32	45	49
NDP	42	38	47	44	49	32	50	42	33
Totals	100	100	100	100	100	100	100	100	100

Source: Christopher Adams, *Politics in Manitoba*, 127.

The 1999 election was remarkable for its high turnout. Sixty-eight percent of eligible citizens cast their ballot, compared to 69 percent in both 1990 and 1995. However, the results produced a majority NDP victory with thirty-two seats based on 44 percent of the popular vote, compared to the PCs' twenty-four seats based on 41 percent of the popular vote. At the same time the Liberals mustered only 13 percent of the popular vote, which was a drop from 24 percent in 1995. But did this NDP 1999 breakthrough signal an across-the-board provincial realignment? Or was the electoral shift restricted to specific ridings or particular regions of the province? An examination of riding-by-riding results show that with the exception of four out of fifty-seven ridings, the NDP experienced growth across the entire province. This includes virtually all ridings where NDP support was less than 50 percent in 1995, with growth occurring even in constituencies where support was less than 20 percent. In other words, the 1999 election was more than a breakthrough victory in the number of seats won: it was an event that signalled widespread provincial growth for the NDP. In addition to holding their traditional seats in the north, the northern edge of the farm belt (i.e., the constituencies of Swan River, Interlake, and Dauphin-Roblin) and the northern parts of Winnipeg, the NDP added ridings in the southern half of the province (including Brandon West and La Vérendrye in southeast Manitoba) and portions of south Winnipeg.

Fitting with V.O. Key's definition that critical elections have a long-lasting impact on the party system, since 1999 the NDP has increased its hold on power by winning thirty-five seats in 2003 (based on 49 percent of the vote to the PCs' twenty seats and 36 percent of the vote). Not since 1953 had the PCs dropped below twenty-one seats. In 2007, the NDP took thirty-six seats based on 48 percent of the vote to the PCs' nineteen seats and 38 percent of the vote. The NDP was able to build on its 1999 success due to four main factors: (1) a growing economy which helped the government to produce surplus budgets while delivering on its promises to support health care and post-secondary education, (2) a leader who proved to be both a charismatic and capable administrator, (3) a Progressive Conservative Party in disarray following Filmon's retirement, and (4) the continuing marginalization of the Liberals. Support for the NDP continued to grow from 1999 to 2003 across most ridings, especially in the critically important 30 percent to 50 percent support range (i.e., in ridings that are deemed neither "unwinnable" or "safe" for any particular party). In contrast to Doer and the NDP, the PCs under leader Stuart Murray appeared out of step with the times by campaigning in 2003 on cuts in government spending and taxes. The party was also hampered by new provincial party financing laws introduced in 2001 that prohibited corporate and union contributions while reducing annual individual contributions to $3,000. The impact was felt particularly by the PCs, who saw their party's revenues drop from $1.28 million in 2000 to just under $400,000 in 2001.[28] As a result, the party was unable to launch an effective advertising campaign and faced shortages in other areas of the election campaign.

Urban Realignment – 1999

A critical component in the provincial realignment has been Winnipeg, and it is to the urban electorate that this discussion now turns. An examination of the outcome in 1999 shows that with the exception of swing seats close to the city's centre (two of which were newly created from other ridings and two previously held by the PCs[29]), voters in most southern Winnipeg ridings elected PC candidates while northern Winnipeg ridings elected New Democrats. This reflected the long-standing North End vs. South End split in provincial politics within Winnipeg. However, when each of the Winnipeg ridings is studied in a longitudinal fashion, a more dynamic trend emerges. Except for two safe ridings (these are in the North End ridings of Burrows and Point Douglas, where support dropped for the NDP candidates with little effect on the outcome), in 1999 the party increased its support across the entire city and in many PC-held ridings.

When looking at the 2003 election outside Winnipeg, the provincial electoral map continued to feature the rural south painted Tory blue, while NDP orange prevailed in more northerly areas. In Winnipeg, however, the urban North-South line of cleavage was clearly deteriorating in the NDP's favour as the NDP captured the southern Winnipeg ridings of Fort Garry, St. Norbert, and Seine River and held the seats it gained in 1999. At the same time, support for the NDP increased throughout most of the city—even in seats the NDP did not win.

The 2007 Provincial Election

Early in 2007, it appeared the upcoming election would be close. The governing NDP was facing a reinvigorated PC Party led by an energized new leader, Hugh McFadyen. The PCs put forward a redesigned and more urban-oriented platform which shared a number of features with the NDP's platform. This included a promise to fight crime (a top issue in publicly released polls), keep college and university tuition fees frozen (a reversal of the PCs' 2003 platform), reduce provincial sales tax, promote downtown development and capital investments, and keep young people in the province. Along with this, the party now had the financial resources to get its message out to voters, having raised more than $1 million in 2006.[30] However, the PC campaign stumbled badly when senior strategists unexpectedly launched a mid-campaign promise to bring the Winnipeg Jets NHL team back to the city. The idea was intended to make Winnipeggers "think big,"[31] and on the day of the announcement both the NDP and Liberals appeared flat-footed with "us too" responses made to the media. The PC strategy soon turned into a fiasco, with many voters apparently wondering if they would have to experience a rerun of the failed fundraising campaign to "Keep the Jets," which occurred in the mid-1990s under the watch of the Filmon government.[32] The other two parties quickly distanced themselves from the PCs on the Jets issue, and when the votes were counted a few weeks later the PCs proved neither able to overcome NDP Premier Doer's widespread popularity nor to make significant inroads among women and urban middle-class voters. The NDP's hold on two important groups was demonstrated by a pre-election poll in which 46 percent of those in middle-income households ($30,000 to $59,999) supported the NDP compared to 38 percent for the PCs. Furthermore, 48 percent of women reported a preference for the NDP compared to only 34 percent for the PCs.[33] In the end, the NDP took thirty-six seats, based on 48 percent of the vote, to the PCs' nineteen seats on 38 percent of the vote, while the Liberals held onto their two seats and won 12 percent of the vote.

At least on the surface, the 2007 NDP victory was a repeat of the 2003 election, with the NDP winning a similar share of the popular vote and gaining an additional seat in the legislature. Manitoba voters had not produced a third successive majority victory for any party since Duff Roblin's PCs were re-elected in 1966. An examination of ridings in 2007, compared to 2003 results, revealed that the province-wide realignment towards the NDP commencing in the 1990s had crested. Based on shifts from 2003 to 2007, and compared to 1999 and 2003, the NDP vote in most ridings changed very slightly. Had the NDP realignment finally stalled? Was 2007 what can be termed a "maintaining election"? In part, yes. The traditional north-south cleavage in non-urban Manitoba remained intact, with the NDP holding ridings in the northern half of the province and the PCs holding the southern half (excluding Brandon, where the PCs regained one of the two seats from the NDP).

In 2007, the PCs were punished seriously in Winnipeg, where they took just 29 percent of the urban vote and four seats: one on the city's northern fringe (which required a recount) and three seats in the southwest corner.[34] The PCs failed to retake those Winnipeg ridings they lost to the NDP in 2003, and lost what were thought to be two "safe" suburban seats in Southdale and Kirkfield Park. The NDP not only held a majority of Winnipeg's ridings, after 2003 it also held a majority of south Winnipeg ridings. At the same time, NDP support growth continued in most Winnipeg ridings, especially in ridings where support had ranged from 35 percent to 55 percent in 2003. Outside Winnipeg, support for the NDP dropped in most southern ridings, signaling a growing provincial urban-rural split. However, the NDP's deterioration among non-urban southern ridings is less pronounced when riding-by-riding results are examined for the entire 1999 to 2007 period, as shown in Figure 6.3.

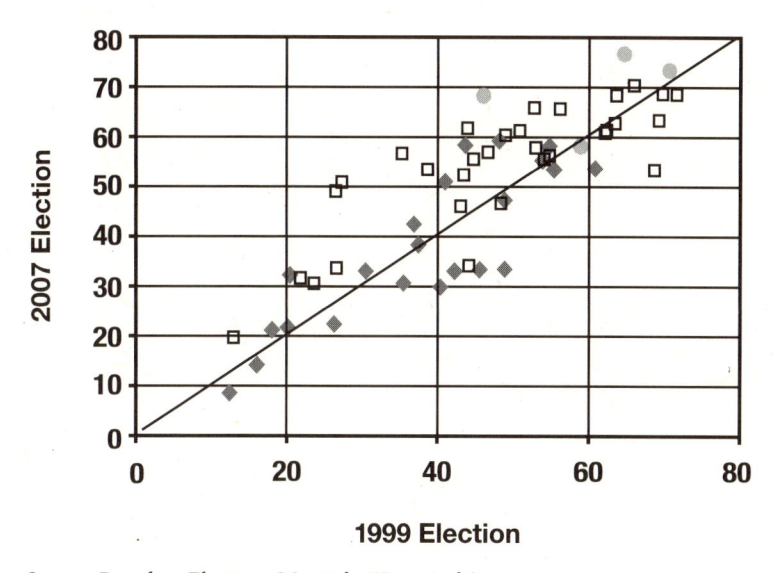

Figure 6.3. NDP Support, 1999 to 2007

Source: Based on Elections Manitoba Historical Summaries.

NDP Support: A Demographic Shift?

So far the focus of this chapter has been on shifts occurring within the electorate at the constituency level, but what about shifts within specific demographic groups? A large part of the NDP's success in Manitoba has been built on its ability to attract female voters. Based on a Probe Research poll of 800 Manitobans conducted for the *Winnipeg Free Press* and Global TV just prior to the 2007 election, 48 percent of women preferred the NDP compared to 41 percent of men. In contrast, 40 percent of men and 34 percent of women preferred the PCs. This pattern appears in most of Probe Research's quarterly polls since they began in 1999.

Opinion data also show that an age-related shift has emerged since 1999. The NDP drew higher levels of support among younger and middle-aged voters in 1999, with only 32 percent of those aged 55 or over supporting the NDP. This is shown in Table 6.2. It now appears that young people are becoming more drawn to the PCs while the NDP attracts older voters. In 2007, more than half (51 percent) of those aged 55 or over supported the New Democrats while only 37 percent of those under the age of thirty-five supported the party, down from 44 percent in 1999. At the same time, for the PCs, older voters appear to be moving away, while support increases from 35 percent to 41 percent among those under thirty-five.

Table 6.2. 1999 and 2007 Polling Data and Age Cohort: Manitoba

	\multicolumn{6}{c}{Age Categories}
	18 – 34		35 – 54		55 plus	
	1999	2007	1999	2007	1999	2007
NDP	44%	37%	49%	45%	32%	51%
PC	35%	41%	39%	37%	57%	34%
Liberal	18%	18%	11%	16%	10%	14%
Other	3%	4%	1%	2%	1%	1%

Source: Christopher Adams, "Diverging Paths? Why Manitoba Still Likes the NDP, and Saskatchewan Doesn't," *Inroads: The Journal of Opinion*, Spring 2008.

Conclusion

A number of provincial elections in Manitoba have produced a change in government during the past five decades, some of which had long-term consequences for the major parties. Yet only three of these significant elections should be labelled "realigning elections." These are the 1958 Duff Roblin PC minority victory, the 1969 Edward Schreyer NDP minority victory (which shortly transformed into a majority due to a defection from the Liberal caucus) and the 1999 Gary Doer NDP majority victory. In contrast to these three elections, Gary Filmon's PC minority victory in 1988 was linked to electoral dealignment as many voters fled to the Liberals, much to the detriment of the governing NDP. Furthermore, results from the subsequent 1990 election produced a majority PC victory, yet riding-by-riding results revealed that this outcome was due to the PCs winning key swing seats rather than some form of major realignment across the province. It would not be until 1999 that a clear realignment occurred, and this was to the NDP's benefit. The critical election of 1999 triggered a long-term shift towards the NDP across the province, especially in Winnipeg.

To what extent can we say that the realigning elections of Roblin, Schreyer, and Doer were marked by Burnham's four characteristics that were described at the beginning of this chapter? First, both the 1958 and the 1969 elections revealed disruptions in voting behaviour, especially with regard to the impact of social change in the 1950s and 1960s and the growing importance of urban voters. It is less clear that the 1999 election fits this pattern, especially in light of the NDP's move towards adopting many of the same fiscally conservative policies as the governing PCs they replaced. However, as did 1958 and 1969 reflect the importance of urban voters, so too did the 1999 realigning election.

The second characteristic—that the intensity of the divisions that are linked to realignment will spill over into "intra-party power struggles" and other parts of the political system was discernible in 1958 and 1969. Both Roblin's victory over Willis for the PC leadership in the early 1950s and Schreyer's successful leadership bid during the 1969 election moved their respective parties toward the ideological centre. Furthermore, both leaders represented the social changes of their day, including the declining importance of rural Manitoba, the growth of a new middle class, greater engagement with First Nations communities in the north, the impact of television, and demographic shifts within the population, including the "growing up" of the baby-boom generation.

Burnham's third characteristic, that realigning elections happen with regularity, does appear to fit the history of electoral politics in Manitoba. That is, if we include Filmon's 1988 minority breakthrough (in spite of it being more suited to the "deviating election" category), during the past half-century four out of five decades have produced elections demonstrating major changes in electoral behaviour: those of 1958, 1969, 1988, and 1999. It is beyond the scope of this paper to explain this periodicity, but perhaps it is due to parties and leaders losing their energy and effectiveness the longer they remain in power. For their part, the PCs must hope that a change is imminent with Gary Doer's appointment to Washington as Canada's new ambassador in 2009 and the selection of his longtime finance minister, Greg Selinger, as his replacement. And yet, polling results released at the time that this chapter was being finalized (in early 2010) reveal virtually no change in the NDP's popularity as the torch passed from Doer to Selinger.[35]

The fourth characteristic, that electoral realignments produce "significant transformations in the general shape of policy" was very apparent with the election of Roblin's PCs and his government's activity with regard to state spending across a number of important policy sectors, including health care and education. With the shift to the right under Walter Weir following the departure of Roblin to federal politics, Ed Schreyer's NDP government redirected policy back to the path initially cleared by Roblin, while also developing a greater policy focus on First Nations and the north. The 1999 election of Gary Doer and his NDP brought about a shift away from prioritizing low taxes and small budgets, but they were able to do so under conditions of relative prosperity which enabled expanded spending while providing balanced budgets and no new taxes. If a shift occurred under Doer, it was in providing a policy environment that was positively geared towards the middle class, which in turn reciprocated by generating an urban realignment from 1999 through to 2007. Now that what might be called "the age of prosperity" has been replaced by a recession, which necessarily accompanies the need for government cutbacks and deficit financing, it is unclear what impact this might have on the fortunes of Manitoba's parties. For this reason the study of politics is often a study of the unpredictable.

APPENDIX 6.1
Manitoba Elections, 1953 to 2007

Election Year	Progressive Conservative % Votes	Seats	CCF / NDP % Votes	Seats	Liberal-Progressive / Liberal % Votes	Seats	Other % Votes	Seats
1953	21%	12	16%	5	43%	36*	19%**	4
1958	40%	26	20%	11	35%	19	4%	1
1959	46%	36	22%	10	30%	11	1%	0
1962	45%	36	15%	7	36%	13	3%	1
1966	40%	31	23%	11	33%	14	4%	1
1969	35%	22	38%	28	24%	5	2%	2***
1973	37%	21	42%	31	19%	5	-	0
1977	49%	33	38%	23	12%	1	-	0
1981	44%	23	47%	34	7%	0	-	0
1986	40%	26	41%	30	14%	1	-	0
1988	38%	25	24%	12	35%	20	-	0
1990	42%	30	29%	20	28%	7	-	0
1995	43%	31	33%	23	24%	3	-	0
1999	41%	24	44%	32	13%	1	-	0
2003	36%	20	49%	35	13%	2	1%	0
2007	38%	19	48%	36	12%	2	1%	0

*Includes Independent Liberal-Progressives (3 seats)
** Includes 13 percent for Social Credit (1 seat)
***Includes 1 Independent and 1 Social Credit
Figures compiled by the author based on riding results provided by Elections Manitoba, "Historical Summaries."

Notes

1. The author wishes to thank Jared Wesley for his very detailed and insightful comments regarding this paper. His valuable insights will be used as this ongoing research project moves forward into a later phase. All shortcomings in this paper remain the author's.
2. V.O. Key, "A Theory of Critical Elections," *Journal of Politics*, February 1955.
3. Ibid., 11.
4. Numerous political science works deal with this typology. A succinct description is provided in Angus Campbell, Philip Converse, Warren Miller, and Donald Stokes, *The American Voter: An Abridgement* (New York: John Wiley, 1964), 274–276.
5. Walter Dean Burnham, *Critical Elections and the Mainsprings of American Politics* (New York: W.W. Norton, 1970), 6–10.
6. The author wishes to insert one major caveat here with regard to terminology. As does Key examine "realignment" in the context of voter shifts, rather than changing partisan identities, this is how the term will be applied in this essay regarding Manitoba politics. However, it is recognized that this is a liberal use of the term, in that vote-switching might not signify a change in partisanship or long-term preferences. See Harold Clarke et al., *Absent Mandate: Interpreting Change in Canadian Elections*, 2nd ed. (Toronto: Gage, 1991).
7. A summary of provincial election results dating back to 1953 is appended to this chapter.
8. At the time, Winnipeg consisted of three multi-member ridings, of which four MLAs were elected from each.
9. This is chiefly based on coverage in *Winnipeg Free Press*, 16 June 1954 and Duff Roblin's autobiography, *Speaking for Myself* (Winnipeg: Great Plains Publications, 1999), 62.
10. Roblin, *Speaking for Myself*, 68–73; Murray Donnelly, *The Government of Manitoba* (Toronto: University of Toronto Press, 1963), 67.
11. In 1922 the United Farmers defeated the Liberals under T.C. Norris. The party subsequently was renamed the Progressive Party and then amalgamated with the Liberals in 1932 to become the Liberal-Progressive Party. Christopher Adams, *Politics in Manitoba* (Winnipeg: University of Manitoba Press, 2008), Chapter 3, passim.
12. William Neville, "Climate of Change," in *Manitoba 125: Volume 3, Decades of Diversity*, ed. Gregg Shilliday (Winnipeg: Great Plains Publications, 1995), 103.
13. Figures are derived from Manitoba Department of Education Annual Report, reports for 1958–59 to 1966–67, and reported in Shaun McCaffrey, "A Study of Policy Continuity Between the Progressive Conservative and the New Democratic Party Governments of Manitoba, 1958–1977" (MA thesis, University of Manitoba, 1986), 12.
14. Unfortunately, $92 million of MDF funds were lost to the Churchill Forest Industries (CFI) project when its Austrian investors disappeared with the money, a problem that Schreyer's NDP government was later to inherit in 1969. Cy Gonick, "The Manitoba Economy since World War II," in *The Political Economy of Manitoba*, ed. James Silver and Jeremy Hull (Regina: Canadian Plains Research Center, 1990), 29–30.
15. V.O. Key, *Politics, Parties, and Pressure Groups*, 5th ed. (New York: Thomas Y. Crowell, 1964), 528.
16. The reader should note that only those ridings that existed in both elections are displayed. The same rule applies for other charts provided in this paper. Because there would only be a small impact on the overall results as they apply to shifting patterns of popular support across regions and the province as a whole, no adjustments are made for boundary changes that might have occurred between elections.
17. Included in the category of northern ridings are those north of the Canadian Shield line and devoid of functional farmlands. Due to its proximity to Winnipeg, Gimli and the Interlake

region have not been included in this category. With regard to the southern ridings, and in order to avoid making the charts overly complicated, Brandon is classified here with non-urban ridings. This is due to its strong link to the farm community and having a population which has only recently surpassed the 40,000 mark.

18 M.C. Leacy, ed., *Historical Statistics of Canada*, 2nd ed. (Ottawa: Statistics Canada, 1983), Table W340-438.
19 James McAllister, *The Government of Edward Schreyer: Democratic Socialism in Manitoba* (Montreal: McGill-Queen's University Press, 1984), 116.
20 Ed Schreyer, interview with author, 7 September 2006.
21 These are Churchill, Flin Flon, Rupertsland, and The Pas. The northern riding of Fisher was redistributed out of existence prior to the 1969 election. There was no Thompson riding in 1966, but the shift was clear even here in that the NDP won 50.7 percent of the vote in 1969.
22 The riding shown straddling the line is Assiniboia which contained a mixture of rural and suburban voters. Even here voters increased their support from 22.7 to 23.8 percent in 1969.
23 Ed Schreyer, interview with author, 7 September 2006.
24 See James Rice and Michael Prince, "Martin's Moment: The Social Policy Agenda of a New Prime Minister," in *How Ottawa Spends: 2004–2005*, ed. G. Bruce Doern (Montreal: McGill-Queen's University Press, 2004), 118. For an historical overview of federal cash transfers from 1983 to 2003, see Allan Maslove, "Health and Federal-Provincial Financial Arrangements: Lost Opportunity," in *How Ottawa Spends: 2005–2006*, ed. G. Bruce Doern (Montreal: McGill-Queen's University Press, 2005), 27–28.
25 Alfred Monnin, *Report of the Commission of Inquiry into Allegations of Infractions of The Elections Act and The Elections Finances Act during the 1995 Manitoba General Election* (Winnipeg: Manitoba Queen's Printer, 1999). For more background detail on the scandal, see Doug Smith, *As Many Liars: The Story of the 1995 Manitoba Vote Splitting Scandal* (Winnipeg: Arbeiter Ring, 2003).
26 *Maclean's*, 4 October 1999.
27 The surveys were conducted by Probe Research between 9 September and 15 September 1999, among 1010 Manitobans. The question was as follows: "Which party's candidate are you most likely to support in this provincial election?"
28 See *Winnipeg Free Press*, 10 April 2006, as well as Jared Wesley and David Stewart, "Electoral Financing Reform in Manitoba: Advantage Doer?" paper presented at the Party and Election Finance: Consequences for Democracy Conference, Calgary, Alberta, 2006.
29 These were St. Vital, Lord Roberts, Riel, and Fort Rouge.
30 *Winnipeg Free Press*, 20 August 2007.
31 Worth noting is that political insiders have remarked that this is the second time that "thinking big" has backfired on Hugh McFadyen, who was widely regarded as the chief architect of the "billion-dollar plan" in the 1999 election.
32 For an overview of the demise of the Winnipeg Jets see Joel Trenaman, "Winnipeg Jets," in *The Encyclopedia of Manitoba*, ed. Ingeborg Boyens (Winnipeg: Great Plains Publications, 2007).
33 Probe Research, press release, May 2007.
34 These constituencies were River East, Tuxedo, Charleswood, and Fort Whyte.
35 A Probe Research poll taken in December 2009 showed that the NDP was still the first choice of 47 percent of decided voters compared to 37 percent for the PCs and 11 percent for the Liberals. Probe Research, "Provincial Party Standings in Manitoba," news release, 15 December 2009, http://probe-research.com/2009/12/provincial-party-standings-in-manitoba.html (accessed 22 February 2010).

PART THREE
GOVERNMENT PROCESSES AND INSTITUTIONS

Canada's provinces have similar institutions—representative legislatures, cabinet governments, professional and non-partisan civil services, and free and independent media. Yet throughout the country, the way that each of these institutions functions varies depending on the particular contexts and realities of the province. Manitoba is no different in this regard, and its main public institutions are considered in this section.

In Chapter 7, current Clerk of the Executive Council describes how the traditions of the cabinet remain largely unchanged fifty years after their last major reforms and challenges the thesis that premiers govern "from the centre," with little regard to the opinions of cabinet ministers (and others, for that matter). Chapter 8 features historian and former deputy premier Jean Friesen's personal recollections of her thirteen years in the Manitoba Legislature, with colourful descriptions offered on the work of an MLA in government and in opposition. In Chapter 9, Frances Russell describes life on the other side of a microphone from an election official, reflecting on her career with two (one now defunct) Winnipeg newspapers and the incredible changes that have swept the media during the past half-century. In Chapter 10, Paul Thomas describes the evolving role of the provincial civil service, comparing the recalibration of the civil service's role during the Filmon Progressive Conservative era to the efforts of "renewal" during the New Democratic Party's time in power. In Chapter 11, veteran intergovernmental affairs practitioner Jim Eldridge describes what role Manitoba plays beyond its borders, as it engages the federal government, other provinces, American states, and other international actors on important issues facing the province. In Chapter 12, Paul Thomas offers an assessment of how Manitoba collaborates with other states and provinces on important policy issues facing these jurisdictions.

The Manitoba Cabinet

Paul Vogt

Introduction

At the end of 2008 the Manitoba cabinet of then-premier Gary Doer consisted of eighteen ministers.[1] This was only a third larger than the cabinet presided over by former premier Duff Roblin fifty years earlier, and many of the ministerial portfolios were unchanged from that time.[2] The main difference, noted by Roblin himself in an interview,[3] is that the faces at the table in the Doer cabinet reflected the ethnic and regional diversity of the province. Among the eighteen ministers in 2008 there were three from the North (two of whom were Aboriginal), three from rural Manitoba and six women. The Manitoba cabinet of Premier Greg Selinger of early 2010 included one minister from the North (who is also Aboriginal), four ministers from rural Manitoba, eight women (including Rosann Wowchuk, the province's first female minister of finance) and the first Filipino-Canadian cabinet minister in Manitoba history.

The procedures of the Manitoba cabinet have hardly changed at all in the past fifty years. Despite the growth in government responsibilities during the past half-century, cabinet still meets just once a week, usually for about two hours, and works through an agenda that ranges from minor board appointments to major policy initiatives. At the heart of the operation, today as in Roblin's day, is a balance between the responsibilities of individual ministers and the collective responsibility of cabinet. Each item on the cabinet agenda must be introduced and defended by a minister, and each must pass the "test of consensus" at the table. It is the prerogative of the premier, as chair, to declare the will of cabinet (although votes are regularly taken at some Cabinet tables, they are a rare event in Manitoba's experience[4]). But Manitoba premiers invariably observed the rule that any Minister may speak to any item, and that cabinet discussions are not closed until all voices have been heard.

Because cabinet meetings are held in camera, discussions at the table are frank and move easily from the technical details of proposals to considerations of political strategy. The "signature" commitments comprising the government's electoral mandate are recurring topics at the weekly meetings, and for that reason cabinet often has the character of an ongoing dialogue in which long-term goals are assessed in the light of emerging issues and pressures.

This practice of *collegial deliberation* ensures that, in addition to their departmental responsibilities, ministers remain focussed on the challenges facing government as a whole. It reinforces ministers' collective responsibility for all decisions taken at the table and adds a strong compulsion to work towards consensus. Typically, a cabinet proposal that encounters serious objections from one or more ministers will be sent back—and the minister who introduced it will be asked to work out a resolution with his or her colleagues.

While supporting a practice of collegial deliberation, it is also necessary that cabinet function as an *executive board*, in which every issue raised is worked through and every proposal brought to a decision. Most Manitoba premiers, Doer included, have used their chairing role to enforce a brisk pace, dispensing quickly with routine matters and saving discussion time for matters of real substance (Roblin, who exemplified the premierial trait of impatience, recalled that in his final term he took to scheduling cabinet meetings just two hours ahead of his weekly squash games).[5] The minutes of cabinet are written in an "executive" format that doesn't capture the breadth of deliberations but only the resulting decisions. Cabinet minutes are normally circulated to deputy ministers within days of each meeting, providing regular and authoritative direction to the public service.

Cabinet's practices are little known to the public yet they lie at the heart of provincial politics. Since its founding in 1870, Manitoba has enjoyed a form of *cabinet government*, in which the executive council of ministers dominates over the legislative assembly—so that decisions taken at the cabinet table stand, in almost all cases, as the final decisions of government. In fact, the conventions that make cabinet government possible predate the Manitoba Legislature by over a century. They are features of the so-called "Westminster model," and they had a long gestation in Britain before they were adopted (virtually *in toto*) by Canada's national and provincial governments.

One of the most important Westminster conventions supporting cabinet government is the enforcement of party discipline in the legislature. This practice ensures that the will of the executive, once formed, is rarely altered by the assembly (at least not when the government enjoys a serviceable majority—an outcome that another British inheritance, the first-past-the-post electoral system, tends to produce). The internal workings of cabinet are also framed by Westminster conventions, including, most importantly, the conventions of ministerial responsibility and cabinet solidarity. Where these are observed (as they generally have been in Manitoba) they create a condition of trust that allows cabinet deliberations to be at once frank, wide-ranging, and decisive.

While none of these traditions originated in Manitoba, what is remarkable is that they remain virtually unchanged by a century and a half of hard use. Indeed, the single comprehensive change of cabinet practices in Manitoba's history, the cluster of modernizing reforms introduced by former premier Roblin over his nine years in government (1958–1967), had the effect of reinforcing cabinet government and the conventions on which it rests. The explanation for this pattern of stability, I will suggest, is the value all sitting governments in Manitoba have placed on the two functions of cabinet: as a *deliberative body*, able to maintain a continuous dialogue on the ruling party's core commitments; and as an *executive body*, able to provide clear and detailed direction to government as a whole.

To argue for the virtues of cabinet government is to stand against the current of recent commentaries on the Westminster system. For several decades, political scientists in Britain and Canada have detected a worrying transfer of decision-making power from cabinets to first ministers. Focussing on Canada's national Parliament, Donald Savoie argues that "cabinet government" has been replaced by a new form he calls "court government" in which the central role once played by the executive council of ministers is usurped by unelected "courtiers" attached to the office of the First Minister.[6] The polemical title of Savoie's newest book links this trend to a "collapse of accountability" in Canadian government and it places him in the company of a long line of academics, parliamentarians and commission heads who lament that Canada's political system is becoming less "democratic"—not only less accountable to citizens, but less responsive and transparent. In fact, Savoie has taken these familiar criticisms a step further. Where earlier diagnoses of a "democratic deficit" seized on the dominance of cabinet over the legislature, Savoie contends that with the rise of the courtier class, cabinet itself has become irrelevant.[7]

Although the main purpose of this chapter is to explain how cabinet government functions in Manitoba, I will also argue for the continuing vitality of the institution. In Manitoba the cabinet has retained its central role and importance.[8]

Its essential structure has endured, even as other institutions of government have expanded and changed. The dynamic of the weekly cabinet meeting–the principle of collegiality and the balance struck between ministers' individual and collective responsibilities–has also endured, adapting to broader trends that have affected the role of the premier and the role of line ministers. The Manitoba experience is for that reason a challenge to the conclusions reached by Savoie, attesting to the resilience of cabinet traditions and the continued relevance of the institution.

I. The Cabinet Process

On the face of it, it would appear there is wide latitude for experimenting with the structure and processes of cabinet. It is a notorious feature of the Westminster model that it provides no written or binding rules for the operation of the executive branch. Indeed, the British and Canadian constitutions are silent even on the roles assigned to ministers and first ministers, leaving the executive decision-making process to be governed by an evolving set of conventions. Further, because cabinet meetings are held in camera, and the substance of what happens at the table is exempt from public disclosure (at least within the lifespan of any government),[9] no cabinet could be called to account for departing from "traditional" practice.

Yet what is most striking in Manitoba's experience is the deference shown to existing cabinet practice by successive governments. The pattern has been one of gradual and incremental change, save for the set of reforms introduced by former premier Roblin. During his three terms in office, Roblin modernized the procedures of the Manitoba cabinet, bringing them in line with the procedures that had already been adopted in Ontario and Saskatchewan. In so doing, he strengthened and renewed the institution—ending the era of what is called the "unaided cabinet," which extends back to the province's founding, and inaugurated a new era, that of the "institutional cabinet," which has lasted to the present day.[10] In effect, Roblin ended one long period of institutional stability only to begin another.

From 1870 on, Manitoba's cabinet has mimicked the practices of Westminster, the "mother Parliament," holding regular meetings of ministers in a designated "cabinet room," and using printed "Orders in Council" to record and implement executive decisions. These formal trappings aside, for the first eighty years of its existence the provincial cabinet was a casual operation, with few fixed protocols or supports. There was no dedicated cabinet office and, for the most part, no staff were present when the premier and his ministers met. Decisions were normally made without benefit of written proposals or supporting documents; meeting agendas were seldom circulated in advance; and minutes were not taken at the table (although some premiers would dictate minutes, in memo form, after the fact).[11]

The major change came with the election of Duff Roblin's government in 1958.

It was Roblin who, shortly after he assumed office, hired the first clerk of cabinet and introduced the practice of recording cabinet minutes. By the end of his final term the requirement of formal submissions for every item on the cabinet agenda (the institution of the "Cabinet Book") was in place, and a set of cabinet committees and a central planning secretariat had been established.

Roblin's new arrangements proved to be as lasting as those they replaced. From 1958 to 2010, a period encompassing three Progressive Conservative and three New Democratic Party governments, changes in the procedures and structure of the Manitoba Cabinet were so slight as to be negligible.

Roblin's ambitious policy agenda was the principal motive for his cabinet reforms. He wanted to greatly accelerate the modernization of the province's economy, infrastructure, and educational institutions. For that task he needed a central decision-making body that was efficient and properly resourced. When he came into office, however, he found he had inherited from his predecessor, Douglas Campbell, a core of very competent deputy ministers, who oversaw the line departments, combined with an executive branch that was informal and understaffed. This decentralized structure was in keeping with the prevailing philosophy of governance up to the 1950s. The period of the "unaided" cabinet in Manitoba, as in all provinces, coincided with a style of government that was focused on dispensing local patronage.[12] Public services were for the most part designed and delivered at the local level. The relationships between local officials and cabinet ministers tended to be personal in nature, and the idea of a *provincial* policy agenda rarely came into play. Roblin's modernizing reforms might be characterized as an assault on this tradition of "localism"—replacing one-room schools with school divisions; replacing local road maintenance with a provincial highways network; and, above all, using the resources of the provincial government to accelerate the pace of economic development across all regions of the province.

Roblin recalled that he not only wanted cabinet to be the initiator and driver of government policies, but also the means to focus his ministers' attentions on central priorities—and to draw them away from the parochial views of their departments. In an interview, he forcefully restated his view that ministers operating in isolation from their colleagues are prone to "believe their departments are always right." Cabinet, he asserted, "is the instrument to stop that nonsense" by imposing a government-wide view on policy.[13] In strengthening cabinet's capacity for collective deliberation, Roblin also wanted to ensure it provided comprehensive direction to the public service. He was the first premier to insist that all important decisions be brought to cabinet by his ministers and that all recommendations must pass "the test of consensus" (his phrase) at the cabinet table.[14]

The fact that the procedures Roblin put in place to centralize decision making have proved equally serviceable to subsequent Manitoba governments, both Progressive Conservative and New Democrat, "activist" and "restraint-minded," raises some interesting questions about the connection between party programs and the institutional imperatives of government. Among Roblin's successors were premiers who espoused a philosophy of "limited government" or who embarked on programs of fiscal restraint. Former premiers Walter Weir (1967-69) and Sterling Lyon (1977-81) fall into the first category, while the second includes Lyon again and former premier Gary Filmon (1988-99) from his second term forward. Although they came from the same party as Roblin, these leaders did not share his belief that the provincial cabinet (or the provincial government, for that matter) should play a lead role in bringing about economic development and social reform. Yet, as Christopher Dunn has shown in his careful examination of cabinet operations in Manitoba from the 1950s to the 1980s, no premier has been able to dispense with the structures and procedures of the "institutional" cabinet—which were created to implement Roblin's activist agenda.[15]

A possible explanation for this finding is that even those who seek to curtail government's reach need an effective instrument of central control. "Big government conservatism" is a phrase coined by political scientists in the U.S. for administrations, such as those of former president Reagan, committed to "reining in" the public sector yet quite willing to use state authority to achieve key policy objectives. It is also true that in Manitoba's recent history philosophies of limited government have been applied only at the margins. Former premier Lyon's 1977 promise of "acute, protracted restraint" was the most emphatic declaration of such a philosophy; and yet provincial expenditures and public sector employment grew under Lyon's term in office just as they grew through the terms of *every* Manitoba government since the 1950s. This points to a larger explanation, which is that, by significantly expanding the *scope* of government action, Roblin brought about an irrevocable change in Manitoba politics—such that public expectations of "government" were recalibrated and elected leaders were compelled to assume responsibility for a widening array of services and social outcomes (a change which took place in all Canadian provinces during the same period). Although it helped bring about this epochal shift, the institutional cabinet has to a large extent become its creature. It would be impossible to manage today's complex systems of health, education, and social service delivery—and provide the kind of responsiveness demanded by citizens—without an efficient and highly centralized executive.

To return to our main theme, however, it is important to note that the growth of government as a whole has not altered cabinet procedures and has in fact significantly outpaced the growth of the Manitoba cabinet and its supports. Roblin's cabinet started with nine ministers but grew to thirteen by his third term. Percentage-wise, this was the largest increase in the Manitoba cabinet under a single government. Roblin's successor, Walter Weir, kept the cabinet at thirteen. Ed Schreyer's cabinet started with fifteen ministers and grew to seventeen in his second term. Sterling Lyon's cabinet had eighteen ministers; Howard Pawley's cabinets had between nineteen and twenty; and Gary Filmon's between seventeen and eighteen. Gary Doer started with a cabinet of sixteen ministers in 1999 and and a decade later had eighteen.[16] The growth in the provincial public service and service provision has followed an altogether different trajectory. In 1958, at the start of Roblin's first term, the provincial workforce was fewer than 5000 employees and the provincial budget was just $27 million. Today's numbers are nearly 30,000 employees (if the same entities are counted) and an operating budget of more than $10 billion.

It is remarkable that roughly the same number of ministers meeting for about the same number of hours each week can give executive direction to such a vastly larger and more complicated government operation. A possible explanation (one that might lend support to Savoie's thesis) is that the expansion of central staff and agencies has relieved cabinet of some of its decision-making responsibilities and in that way kept ministers' workloads manageable. In Manitoba's history there is at least one period, at the start of Schreyer's first term, when there was a marked expansion in central staff and a seeming proliferation of new central agencies. Taking a longer view, however, we have not seen an ongoing increase in cabinet staff, to match the steady growth in the provincial workforce, but an accordion-like pattern of expansions followed by contractions—which by 2008 brought us back to a point very close to where Roblin had left off. When he resigned his premiership in 1967, Roblin's executive council—the Manitoba equivalent of the federal Prime Minister's Office (PMO) and the Privy Council Office (PCO) combined—had forty employees. In 2008 it was barely larger, with thirty-six on payroll and another dozen who, at any one time, were assigned to executive council on secondment from other departments.

A similar story can be told about the evolution of cabinet's committee structure. Treasury Board, which is the key financial management committee of Manitoba's cabinet, has been in existence since 1887. As part of his efforts to strengthen central policy direction, Roblin significantly increased Treasury Board's staffing resources, giving it an enhanced capacity to evaluate departmental spending plans. At the same time, Roblin created the Manitoba Development Authority, a new cabinet committee with a broad mandate to lead the modernization of the provincial economy. These were the two "key" cabinet committees, although over his three terms Roblin created several others which were given more focussed responsibilities.[17]

This committee structure has persisted since Roblin's time, with much of the change taking place in the "penumbra" of second-tier or single-sector cabinet committees. The number of such committees swelled under Schreyer, was radically cut back under Lyon, and then grew again under Pawley and Filmon. The pattern reflects an ongoing effort to balance between conflicting imperatives. All Manitoba premiers, from Roblin on, have valued the role cabinet committees play in working through policy details and saving cabinet's attention for top-level decisions; yet all have simultaneously worried about the potential for committees to usurp the central deliberative role of cabinet or (a more practical concern) to take up too much of their ministers' time and energies.[18] It was such worries that prompted former premier Doer in 1999 to limit the number of cabinet committees to Treasury Board, the Community Economic Development Committee (CEDC), and the Healthy Child Committee. He subsequently added a fourth committee to deal with Aboriginal issues, but even so remained with an articulated cabinet structure strikingly similar to Roblin's.

Premiers' conflicted feelings about cabinet committees have been most acute when it comes to Treasury Board. In overseeing the preparation and implementation of the provincial budget, Treasury Board comes close to rivalling the cabinet's role in determining cross-government priorities. Roblin, it is worth noting, at first served as his own finance minister, using the whole of cabinet to work through departmental estimates and drawing on the work of his Treasury Board officials on an "as needed" basis. By his third term, however, Roblin found this approach unworkable. He named Gurney Evans as his finance minister and allowed Treasury Board to play a more independent role in preparing cabinet submissions. In his first term of government, Schreyer emulated Roblin and served as his own finance minister; but although he continued to involve cabinet in the details of budget decisions, Schreyer also found it impractical to hold the finance portfolio himself. As a result, the two finance ministers who served under Schreyer, Saul Miller and Saul Cherniack, came to play a central role in his cabinet, just as Evans had in Roblin's cabinet.

In subsequent governments the pattern of strong finance ministers continued: with Don Craik and Brian Ransom under Lyon; Vic Schroeder and Eugene Kostyra under Pawley; Clayton Manness and Eric Stefanson under Filmon; and Greg Selinger under Doer. The pattern speaks to the balance of authority rooted in ministerial roles (a theme explored in more detail below), contrary to Savoie's thesis that first ministers have come to dominate their governments.

Of course, Savoie's thesis also points to the role played by unelected officials and advisors. In Manitoba's case, adding the role of senior policy advisors rounds out the description of cabinet operations but does not take away from the major themes of balance and stability. Although Roblin appointed a clerk of cabinet in his first term, it was not until his third term that he established the first policy unit within executive council. Under the Schreyer government, the unit was significantly expanded and a cadre of young, well-educated "planners" was recruited to Manitoba from across the country. Interestingly, Schreyer did not do away with the central agencies he had inherited from Roblin, nor did he replace the existing senior staff; in most cases he left the new planning and policy bodies to co-exist with the old. He was sanguine about the inter-agency rivalries that developed as a result of this parallel structure, believing it was healthy for cabinet to have the benefit of contending views.[19] Schreyer's attitude was in contrast to that of other modern premiers, who sought to reduce the rivalry between central bodies and to maintain a streamlined executive branch.

What is important to keep in mind, however, is that the cadre of staff in central offices (and, in particular, in the premier's office) has never grown to the point where it could develop or drive major policies without the support of the line departments. Manitoba premiers have typically looked for ways to supplement cabinet's policy and issue management functions from without, rather than create large agencies like the federal PMO and PCO. In 1977, Sterling Lyon dismissed most of the advisors who had been recruited under Schreyer, although he did not dispense with the means to assert central control over policy. In fact, it could be argued that Lyon assumed more direct, personal control over government policy than did Schreyer or any of his successors, relying on his convictions and his forceful personality, and taking full advantage of the authority granted to the premier at the cabinet table. Lyon also engaged external advisors to a greater extent than have other premiers in the modern period and, within government, relied less on his own central staff and more on the senior officials he had come to trust in the Treasury Board secretariat and the finance and the justice departments.[20]

In his first term, Premier Pawley's government restored a portion of the central planning resources dismantled by Lyon and, in so doing, inaugurated a period of relative stability for executive council, which has not seen dramatic changes in structure or staffing during the past twenty-five years. Pawley also encouraged the development of policy supports for Treasury Board and other cabinet committees. The Filmon government largely retained the structures it inherited in 1988 (albeit with the usual turnover of party loyalists who were housed in the central policy and communications units) and the Doer government did the same upon taking office in 1999. The stability of central roles during the past two and a half decades may well be something unique to Manitoba. It is possible to match up, almost position for position, the executive council staff charts from the 1980s through to the present day.[21]

II. Cabinet Roles

In strengthening cabinet procedures, Roblin's changes had the effect of reinforcing two of the most important conventions that undergird cabinet government in the Westminster model and frame the roles of ministers and first ministers: the convention of *ministerial responsibility* and the convention of *cabinet solidarity*.

The convention of *ministerial responsibility* holds that ministers are accountable for all policy and all administrative decisions in their departments. Much of the writing on this convention has focused on the accountability of ministers to the legislature and the electorate (and the importance of that principle for protecting civil service neutrality). Yet the convention also has a meaning at the cabinet table, where ministers are responsible for bringing forward for collective deliberation any major initiatives or challenges affecting their portfolios. At the same time, ministers are responsible for ensuring their departments follow through on cabinet decisions. This dual set of responsibilities—for what is brought to cabinet and for departmental delivery—is re-enforced in the weekly meetings of cabinet, occasionally, through pointed questioning of a minister by the chair but more regularly through the peer pressure that is part of the cabinet dynamic (I will describe this in more detail below).

The convention of *cabinet solidarity* is a necessary complement to the convention of *ministerial responsibility*. The convention holds that once a decision is reached in cabinet all ministers must publicly defend it. This is a key to the discipline of cabinet government, since debates at the table can be sustained and passionate, and yet once the "consensus" is declared even those ministers who argued on the other side must go out and defend it. If ministers cannot, in conscience, defend a cabinet decision, their only option is to resign their positions.

From an external view, it may appear the convention of cabinet solidarity facilitates the dominance of the premier over cabinet. After all, cabinet is not a democracy, and if the premier has the authority to declare the consensus by which all ministers are bound, it would seem he has all the power he needs to override dissent and impose his will. Yet all who have sat in the Manitoba cabinet room have witnessed the operation of a group dynamic that acts as a counterbalance to the premier's power. The group dynamic is bound up with the fact that, although it is not a democracy, cabinet nonetheless has the character of a collegial dialogue, in which the participants are united by common goals and shared public triumphs or battle scars and—in all likelihood—a shared fate in battles to come. In this context, the principle of solidarity contributes to a genuine quest for consensus. In practical terms, this means substantial deference will be shown to ministers arguing a minority position. Knowing that all must go out and defend cabinet decisions to their constituents and their stakeholders, ministers are reluctant to saddle a colleague with an outcome that he or she considers indefensible.

It is difficult to illustrate these points without breaking cabinet confidences. It is well known, however, that in the Pawley cabinet, one minister's strong views on reproductive choice were an effective counter to the views of the premier and most of his colleagues. In fact, all Manitoba cabinets are known to have been "hung up" by the need to placate internal dissent on major issues. Examples include the lengthy internal debates over the shared services issue in the Roblin cabinet; over independent school funding in the Schreyer cabinet; constitutional reform in both the Lyon and Pawley cabinets; over rural gasification in the Filmon cabinet; and over school division amalgamation in the Doer cabinet.[22] What is demonstrated in these cases is not the indecisiveness of cabinet but the elements essential to its vitality—the quest for consensus conditioned by a principle of collegial deference.

The dynamic at the cabinet table also reflects the representative roles of ministers. Each is expected to represent, first, their departments and areas of responsibility and, second, the regions or communities to which they belong. In the Doer government, for example, it was possible to identify a northern caucus, a rural caucus, an Aboriginal caucus and a women's caucus. There were individual ministers who were counted on to represent the views of major ethnic and linguistic communities. Speaking from their knowledge of these communities or interests, ministers have, at times, exercised what amounts to a *categorical veto*. A common intervention at the cabinet table is the objection that a proposed policy might work for, say, Winnipeg but will not address the needs in northern or rural Manitoba, for example. Objections of this kind are frequently show-stoppers at the cabinet table—resulting in a direction from the premier that the minister responsible for the proposal meet with the minister(s) raising the objection and return to cabinet with a solution.

To focus too much on ministerial disagreements would be to miss the real strength of cabinet deliberation, which is designed to incorporate a diversity of perspectives on the way to a decision that ministers can support. Without giving away cabinet confidences, it is possible to provide a few examples that capture the flavour of discussions in the Doer cabinet. The question, "What will this mean for Baba Ferren?" has acquired an almost legendary status over the years. Mrs. Ferren was a real person, a resident of Winnipeg's North End well known to Minister Dave Chomiak. At the cabinet table, however, she became something more: a composite of the average citizen and a touchstone used by all ministers to test the "real" impacts of policies submitted to cabinet. One week Baba Ferren was an ailing widow on fixed income, whose challenges in filling her prescriptions served as a reality check for proposed changes to the Pharmacare program. Another week her health would be restored and her husband resurrected, so that cabinet could assess home care options in cases where an elderly citizen is looking after an infirm spouse. The intimacy of cabinet discussions allows ministers to apply the sum of their political knowledge, including what they have been hearing in stakeholder meetings, on the doorsteps, and at their local hockey rink.

Over time, ministers become so familiar with one another's thinking that some interventions are unnecessary. Cabinet presentations will be crafted to address *anticipated* reactions. The form of power exercised in this instance is like that of the proverbial "sleeping dog" on the rug, who does not move a muscle but causes everyone to negotiate a new route through the living room. In the Doer cabinet, for example, ministers like Eric Robinson and the late Oscar Lathlin made sure the perspectives of northern and Aboriginal communities were present in the minds of their colleagues— to the point where reminders proved unnecessary (although they were sometimes offered anyway). In a similar way, Rosann Wowchuk and Stan Struthers ensured cabinet maintained a healthy appreciation for rural perspectives.

To speak of the group dynamic is not to take away from the authority of premiers in the "ultimate" sense. Like other features of the Manitoba cabinet, the powerful role of the premier is a result of conventions deeply entrenched in the Westminster tradition. It is the premier who appoints (and dis-appoints) all ministers, decides who chairs cabinet, and who declares the "consensus" on all items. It is also an accepted principle that the premier is the *keeper* of the government's core commitments—and certainly all Manitoba premiers in the modern period have assumed that role. While all ministers may be said to have a categorical veto arising from their portfolios or from their representative roles in cabinet, the premier's veto is applied more widely and more generously.

No doubt, a premier's style and personality come into play here, since the cabinet setting is an intimate one and the pressure of decision making brings all traits into the open. However, these traits do not account for a great deal of variation in Manitoba experience since virtually all premiers have been strong personalities and "active chairs" at the cabinet table. The notable exception (save for Walter Weir, who did not fully put his stamp on his government or his cabinet during his brief two-year tenure as premier) is Howard Pawley, who quite deliberately set out to foster a more collegial style in his cabinet. Among the modern premiers of Manitoba, Pawley is the one who allowed the greatest latitude to dialogue and the search for consensus at the cabinet table. Yet, as Pawley himself emphasized in a recent interview, he always reserved the authority to make the final decision.[23]

A second exogenous factor is the rise of executive federalism and the role given to premiers as, in effect, the "lead negotiators" of national policy on behalf of their governments. Paralleling this development is increased participation by premiers in international fora and, in particular, in dialogues and agreements with elected leaders in the U.S.—a trend that reflects the growing importance to all provinces of cross-border issues like trade, security protocols, and environmental policy. Here, too, the danger posed to the practice of cabinet government is the premier's latitude to personally negotiate commitments on behalf of the province. In practice, Manitoba cabinets have granted this latitude as a new prerogative of the premier, while maintaining a kind of *post facto* deference to cabinet's role by requiring that any agreements must be brought back to the table for discussion and that memorandums of understanding negotiated with outside parties must be formally approved by cabinet.[24]

While these factors have definitely worked to enhance the premier's powers vis-à-vis cabinet, they are offset in some ways by exogenous factors that enhance the role of ministers. Chief among these is the proliferation and the growing importance of stakeholder groups, or what sociologists call the "thickening of civil association." This trend is driven (on the one hand) by the growing sophistication of regional associations, commercial and interest groups; and (on the other hand) by the rise of "joined-up" or collaborative government, which grants to non-government organizations an active role in designing and implementing government policy. One practical consequence of the trend is that all ministers spend the better part of their working days meeting with stakeholder groups. In portfolios such as health and agriculture there are more than 100 such groups that expect—and receive—a regular audience with the minister. In the case of major groups like chambers of commerce, business or labour sector councils, the Aboriginal assemblies, and the province-wide municipal and agricultural organizations, ministerial meetings have acquired all the formality of intergovernmental summits. It is the knowledge gained from these meetings, rather than departmental knowledge per se, that provides something of a ministerial offset to the prerogatives of the premier. A minister who has a sure sense of what a key stakeholder will or won't accept has a formidable claim on cabinet's attention.

In Manitoba's experience there are also, of course, many examples of the type that Savoie calls a "courtier"—an unelected official who wields considerable influence across government. As noted earlier, however, there is nothing comparable to the swelling of central bodies like the PMO and the PCO in Ottawa that would provide an institutional support to a strong "courtier" class; and no figure comparable to, say, former Liberal prime minister Jean Chrétien's assistant Eddie Goldenberg or the British Labour Party's Peter Mandelson, whose public profile would rival that of a cabinet minister. It is also notable that in Manitoba's history the careers of some of the most influential officials have crossed several administrations—which suggests an institutional loyalty, or ethos of service, that outweighs loyalties to a particular government. Derek Bedson, the first cabinet clerk and a major figure in the development of Manitoba's modern public service, served in the same capacity through the Roblin, Weir, Schreyer, and Lyon governments. By contrast, the clerks who succeeded Benson and who exerted a comparable influence across the civil service (Michael Decter and George Ford, who served under Pawley, and Don Leitch, who served under Filmon) would be considered "partisans" because of their earlier work in government policy units. When Doer came into office in 1999, however, there was something of a return to past practice. He chose as his first cabinet clerk Jim Eldridge, the recognized "dean" of intergovernmental relations in Canada, who had been recruited into the public service by the Weir government and, like Bedson, had played a major role across several administrations.

Among the unelected officials who have exerted the greatest influence in the Manitoba government, there is a mix of central staff, department heads, and committee secretaries. The list includes the cabinet clerks mentioned above; the long-serving finance deputies, Stuart Garson and Charlie Curtis; Julian Benson, the secretary to Treasury Board under Filmon, and Eugene Kostyra, the secretary to CEDC under Doer.[25] No doubt, enjoying the complete trust of the premier is the sine qua non for such a role. Otherwise there is no evident pattern to the emergence of these figures and no institutional apparatus has developed by which a cadre of "courtiers" could entrench its influence. Indeed, with Savoie's thesis in mind, it is important to note that the influence of unelected officials in Manitoba stems from the roles they have assumed in relation to the decision-making process of cabinet—as clerks, deputy ministers, or cabinet committee secretaries. Nothing in Manitoba's experience points to a source of executive authority that exists separately from, or in opposition to, the provincial cabinet.

Conclusion

While the main intent of this essay is to describe the workings of the Manitoba cabinet, I have also argued, contra Savoie, that it remains an effective institution—capable, still, of maintaining a high level of internal deliberation while giving direction to government as a whole. Although the scope of premierial prerogatives has grown in recent decades, so too has the representative role of ministers. The two trends have offset each other and, together with the enduring features of the cabinet "dialogue" (its intimacy and its spirit of collegiality), have helped preserve the vitality of the Manitoba cabinet.

APPENDIX 7.1
Manitoba Cabinets, 1958–2008

25th Assembly 1958-1959

Duff Roblin—Premier; Provincial Treasurer
Errick Willis—Agriculture and Immigration; Public Works
Stewart McLean—Minister of Education
Gurney Evans—Mines and Natural Resources
George Johnson—Minister of Health and Public Welfare
John Carroll—Public Utilities
Sterling Lyon—Attorney General
Marcel Boulic—Provincial Secretary
John Thompson—Labour

26th Assembly 1959–1962

Duff Roblin—Premier; Provincial Treasurer
George Hutton—Agriculture and Conservation
Stewart McLean—Minister of Education
Charles Witney—Mines and Natural Resources
Walter Weir—Public Works
George Johnson—Minister of Health
John Carrol—Labour; Welfare
Sterling Lyon—Attorney General
John Thompson—Municipal Affairs
Gurney Evans—Provincial Secretary; Industry and Commerce

27th Assembly 1963–1966

Duff Roblin—Premier; Provincial Treasurer
George Hutton—Agriculture and Conservation
George Johnson—Minister of Education
Sterling Lyon—Mines and Natural Resources
Walter Weir—Public Works
Charles Witney—Minister of Health
John Carroll—Welfare
Stewart McLean—Attorney-General
Robert Smellie—Municipal Affairs
Maitland Steinkopf—Provincial Secretary
Gurney Evans—Industry and Commerce

Walter Weir—Highways
Obie Baizley— Labour

28th Assembly 1966-1969

Duff Roblin—Premier (to 1968)
Walter Weir—Premier (1968-1969)
Harry Enns—Mines and Natural Resources
Don Craik—Minister of Education
Thelma Forbes—Public Works
George Johnson-Minister of Health
John Carroll—Provincial Secretary; Welfare; Consumer and Corporate Affairs; Tourism and Recreation
Stewart McLean—Highways
Obie Baizley—Urban Development and Municipal Affairs
Sidney Spivak—Industry and Commerce
Gurney Evans—Provincial Treasurer
James Watt—Agriculture
Charles Witney—Labour
Sterling Lyon—Attorney General

29th Assembly 1969-1973

Edward Schreyer—Premier
Sidney Green—Mines, Resources and Environmental Management
Ben Hanuschak—Minister of Education
Russell Doern—Public Works
René Toupin—Minister of Health and Social Development
Larry Desjardins—Tourism, Recreation and Cultural Affairs
Peter Burtniak—Highways
Howard Pawley—Municipal Affairs
Len Evans—Industry and Commerce
Saul Cherniack—Finance
Sam Uskiw—Agriculture
Russ Paulley—Labour
Al Mackling—Attorney General
Sydney McBryde—Northern Affairs
Saul Miller —Colleges and Universities Affairs

30th Assembly 1974-1977

Edward Schreyer—Premier
Sidney Green—Mines, Resources and Environmental Management
Ian Turnbull—Minister of Education
Russell Doern—Public Works
Larry Desjardins—Minister of Health and Social Development
Ben Hanuschak—Continuing Education and Manpower; Tourism, Recreation and Cultural Affairs
Peter Burtniak—Highways
Bill Uruski—Municipal Affairs
Len Evans—Industry and Commerce
Sam Uskiw—Agriculture
Russ Paulley—Labour
Howard Pawley—Attorney General
Sydney McBryde—Northern Affairs
Saul Miller—Finance; Urban Affairs
René Toupin—Consumer, Corporate Affairs and Internal Services
Harvey Bostrom—Renewable Resources and Transportation Services
Bud Boyce—Minister responsible for Corrections and Rehabilitation

31st Assembly 1977-1981

Sterling Lyon—Premier
Don Craik—Energy and Mines
Ed McGill—Minister without Portfolio
Warner Jorgenson—Government Services
Bud Sherman—Health
Harry Enns—Natural Resources
Frank Johnston—Economic Development and Tourism
Jim Downey—Agriculture
Keith Cosens—Minister of Education
Robert Banman—Fitness, Recreation and Sport
Norma Price—Cultural Affairs and Historical Resources
Ken MacMaster—Labour and Manpower
Brian Ransom—Finance
George Minaker—Community Services and Corrections
Douglas Gourlay—Municipal Affairs; Northern Affairs
Don Orchard—Highways and Transportation
Gerald Mercier—Attorney General
Gary Filmon—Consumer and Corporate Affairs

32nd Assembly 1982-1985

Howard Pawley—Premier
Wilson Parasiuk—Energy and Mines
John Plohman—Government Services; Highways and Transportation
Larry Desjardins—Health; Urban Affairs; Recreation and Sport
Sam Uskiw—Natural Resources
Len Evans—Employment Services and Economic Security
Bill Uruski—Agriculture
Jay Cowan—Co-operative Development
Maureen Hemphill—Minister of Education
Eugene Kostyra—Culture, Heritage and Recreation; Industry, Trade and Technology
Al Mackling—Labour
Vic Schroeder—Finance
Muriel Smith—Community Services
Andy Anstett—Municipal Affairs
Roland Penner—Attorney General; Consumer and Corporate Affairs
Jerry Storie—Business Development and Tourism
John Bucklaschuk—Housing
Gerard Lecuyer—Environment and Workplace Safety and Health
Leonard Harapiuk—Northern Affairs

33rd Assembly 1986-1988

Howard Pawley—Premier
Wilson Parasiuk—Health; Energy and Mines
John Plohman—Highways and Transportation
Len Evans—Employment Services and Economic Security
Bill Uruski—Agriculture
Jay Cowan—Co-operative Development
Maureen Hemphill—Community Services
Eugene Kostyra—Finance
Al Mackling—Labour; Consumer and Corporate Affairs
Vic Schroeder—Industry, Trade and Technology
Roland Penner—Attorney General
Muriel Smith—Business Development and Tourism
John Bucklaschuk—Municipal Affairs
Gerard Lecuyer—Environment and Workplace Safety and Health
Harry Harapiuk—Government Services

Leonard Harapiuk—Natural Resources
Jerry Storie—Education
Elijah Harper—Northern Affairs
Gary Doer—Urban Affairs
Judy Wasylycia-Leis—Culture, Heritage and Recreation

34th Assembly 1988-1990

Gary Filmon—Premier
Harry Enns—Natural Resources
Don Orchard—Health
Albert Driedger—Highways and Transportation; Government Services
Glen Findlay—Agriculture
Charlotte Oleson—Family Services
Clayton Manness—Finance
Ed Connery—Co-operative, Consumer and Corporate Affairs
Jim Ernst—Industry, Trade and Tourism
Jim McCrae—Attorney General; Minister of Justice
Glen Cummings—Environment
Len Derkach—Education
Jim Downey—Northern Affairs
Gerald Ducharme—Urban Affairs; Housing
Bonnie Mitchelson—Culture, Heritage and Recreation
Jack Penner—Rural Development
Harold Neufeld—Energy and Mines
Gerrie Hammond—Labour

35th Assembly 1990-1995

Gary Filmon—Premier
Harry Enns—Agriculture
Jim McCrae—Health
Albert Diredger—Natural Resources
Glen Findlay—Highways and Transportation; Government Services
Bonnie Mitchelson—Family Services
Eric Stefanson—Finance
Jim Ernst—Consumer and Corporate Affairs
Jim Downey—Industry, Trade and Tourism
Linda McIntosh—Urban Affairs; Housing
Rosemary Vodrey—Attorney General; Minister of Justice

Glen Cummings—Environment
Clayton Manness—Education and Training
Gerald Ducharme—Minister Responsible for Seniors
Harold Gilleshammer—Culture, Heritage and Citizenship
Len Derkach—Rural Development
Don Orchard—Energy and Mines
Darren Praznik—Labour; Northern Affairs

36th Assembly 1995–1999

Gary Filmon—Premier
Harry Enns—Agriculture
Jim McCrae—Education and Training
Bonnie Mitchelson—Family Services
Frank Pitura—Government Services
Merv Tweed—Industry, Trade and Tourism
Linda McIntosh—Environment
Rosemary Vodrey—Culture, Heritage and Citizenship
Vic Toews—Attorney General; Minister of Justice
Glen Cummings—Natural Resources
Harold Gilleshammer—Finance
Len Derkach—Rural Development
David Newman—Energy and Mines; Northern Affairs
Darren Praznik—Highways and Transportation
Eric Stefanson—Health
Jack Reimer—Urban Affairs; Housing
Mike Radcliffe—Labour

37th Assembly November 1999–May 2003 (includes new portfolios)

Gary Doer—Premier and Federal-Provincial Relations
Eric Robinson—Aboriginal and Northern Affairs
Oscar Lathlin—Aboriginal and Northern Affairs
Rosann Wowchuk—Agriculture and Food
Oscar Lathlin—Conservation
Steve Ashton—Conservation
Ron Lemieux—Consumer and Corporate Affairs
Scott Smith—Consumer and Corporate Affairs
Diane McGifford—Culture, Heritage and Tourism

Ron Lemieux—Culture, Heritage and Tourism
Eric Robinson—Culture, Heritage and Tourism
Drew Caldwell—Education and Training; Education, Training and Youth
Ron Lemieux—Education and Youth
Tim Sale—Energy, Science and Technology
Tim Sale—Family Services and Housing
Drew Caldwell—Family Services and Housing
Greg Selinger—Finance
Dave Chomiak—Health
Steve Ashton—Highways and Government Services
Mary Ann Mihychuk—Industry, Trade and Mines
Jean Friesen—Intergovernmental Affairs
Gord Mackintosh—Justice and Attorney General
Becky Barrett—Labour; Labour and Immigration
Dave Chomiak—Sport
Ron Lemieux—Sport
Eric Robinson—Sport
Steve Ashton—Transportation and Government Services
Scott Smith—Transportation and Government Services

38th Assembly June 2003–April 2007 (includes new portfolios)

Gary Doer—Premier and Federal-Provincial Relations
Diane McGifford—Advanced Education and Training; Advanced Education and Literacy
Oscar Lathlin—Aboriginal and Northern Affairs
Rosann Wowchuk—Agriculture and Food; Agriculture, Food and Rural Initiatives
Scott Smith—Competitiveness, Training and Trade
Stan Struthers—Conservation
Steve Ashton—Conservation; Water Stewardship
Eric Robinson—Culture, Heritage and Tourism;
Peter Bjornson—Education, Citizenship and Youth
Ron Lemieux—Education and Youth
Tim Sale—Energy, Science and Technology
Dave Chomiak—Energy, Science and Technology
Drew Caldwell—Family Services and Housing
Christine Melnick—Family Services and Housing
Gord Mackintosh—Family Services and Housing
Greg Selinger —Finance

Dave Chomiak—Health
Tim Sale—Health
Theresa Oswald—Health
Jim Rondeau—Healthy Living
Theresa Oswald—Healthy Living
Kerri Irvin-Ross—Healthy Living
Scott Smith—Industry, Economic Development and Mines
Jim Rondeau—Industry, Economic Development and Mines
Mary Ann Mihychuk—Industry, Trade and Mines
Ron Lemieux—Infrastructure and Transportation
Rosann Wowchuck—Intergovernmental Affairs
Steve Ashton—Intergovernmental Affairs
Mary Ann Mihychuk—Intergovernmental Affairs and Trade
RosannWowchuk—Intergovernmental Affairs and Trade
Scott Smith—Intergovernmental Affairs and Trade
Gord Mackintosh—Justice and Attorney General
Dave Chomiak—Justice and Attorney General
Steve Ashton—Labour and Immigration
Nancy Allan—Labour and Immigration
Jim Rondeau—Science, Technology, Energy and Mines
Eric Robinson—Sport
Scott Smith—Transportation and Government Services
Ron Lemieux—Transportation and Government Services
Christine Melnick—Water Stewardship

39th Assembly December 2007

Gary Doer—Premier and Federal-Provincial Relations
Diane McGifford—Advanced Education and Literacy
Oscar Lathlin—Aboriginal and Northern Affairs
Rosann Wowchuk—Agriculture, Food and Rural Initiatives
Jim Rondeau—Competitiveness, Training and Trade
Andrew Swan—Competitiveness, Training and Trade
Stan Struthers—Conservation
Eric Robinson—Culture, Heritage and Tourism; Culture, Heritage, Tourism and Sport
Peter Bjornson—Education, Citizenship and Youth
Gord Mackintosh—Family Services and Housing
Greg Selinger—Finance (Premier as of October 2009)
Theresa Oswald—Health

Kerri Irvin-Ross—Healthy Living
Ron Lemieux—Infrastructure and Transportation
Steve Ashton—Intergovernmental Affairs
Dave Chomiak—Justice and Attorney General
Nancy Allan—Labour and Immigration
Jim Rondeau—Science, Technology, Energy and Mines
Eric Robinson—Sport
Christine Melnick—Water Stewardship

Notes

1   This essay was written in late 2008–early 2009, prior to former premier Doer's resignation in August 2009. I am grateful to a number of individuals who agreed to share their reflections, including former premiers Duff Roblin and Howard Pawley and former clerks of cabinet Don Leitch and Jim Eldridge. I am also grateful to Nick Kulyk, a management intern with the Manitoba government, who undertook a survey of the academic literature on cabinets, and to Peggy Barta, who compiled the material in Appendix 7.1.
2   See Appendix 7.1 for a list of ministerial responsibilities in Manitoba Cabinets from 1958 to 2008.
3   Personal interview with the author, 20 October 2008. Thanks are due to Jim Carr for arranging this interview.
4   Former premier Doer did not call a vote at the cabinet table in his eleven years as premier. Former premier Pawley recalls he sometimes asked for straw votes to test the strength of competing views; yet reserved to himself the authority to "declare the cabinet consensus" irrespective of the majority will (personal interview, 21 October 2008).
5   Personal interview, 20 October 2008.
6   Donald J. Savoie, *Court Government and the Collapse of Accountability* (Toronto: University of Toronto Press, 2008).
7   Ibid., 229–238.
8   Savoie does not deal with provincial governments in his book, focusing on Canada's national government and using the British (non-federal) government as a comparator. In fact, there are comparatively few studies of Canada's provincial cabinets and much of the debate in the academic literature is carried on without reference to provincial experience. This is unfortunate because provincial governments matter a great deal in Canada; collectively, they are responsible for a larger share of program delivery and public expenditures than the national government. In addition, as this essay suggests, a look at sub-national governments which follow the same 'Westminister model' as our national government may yield different conclusions about the inherent strengths or weaknesses of key institutions like the cabinet.
9   Manitoba Cabinet records are exempt from public disclosure for a period of twenty years (recently reduced from thirty years).
10 This terminology is used by Christopher Dunn, in his book *The Institutionalized Cabinet; Governing the Western Provincesc (*Montreal and Kingston: McGill-Queen's University Press, 1995).

11 I rely here on the recollections of Duff Roblin and of former clerks of cabinet, Jim Eldridge and Don Leitch—who relied in turn on their conversations with government leaders from an earlier era.
12 Dunn, *Institutionalized Cabinet*, 11–15.
13 Personal Interview, 20 October, 2008.
14 Ibid.
15 Dunn, *Institutionalized Cabinet*, 178 and 279.
16 The names and portfolios of each minister are listed in Appendix 7.1.
17 Dunn, *Institutionalized Cabinet*, 112–122.
18 See ibid., 84. This observation has been reinforced by the author's discussions with former premier Doer and in a personal interview with former premier Pawley.
19 Dunn, *Institutionalized Cabinet*, 148–154.
20 Personal interview with Don Leitch and Jim Eldridge, 24 July 2009.
21 This was a point that Premier Doer frequently made in defending the Estimates of Executive Council.
22 These examples are for the most part common knowledge, but confirmation was drawn from interviews with Roblin, Pawley, Leitch and Eldridge.
23 Personal interview, 21 October 2008.
24 This was the practice in the Doer cabinet and also (in Don Leitch's recollection) the Filmon cabinet.
25 This list is illustrative rather than comprehensive. It reflects the author's best guess at the names that would turn up in a "reputational survey" conducted among long-time observers of Manitoba politics.

The Manitoba Legislature:
A Personal Reflection

Jean Friesen

This essay offers a personal reflection on the Manitoba Legislature and its place, physical, metaphorical, and political, in our sense of ourselves and our province. This is not a historical view of the increasingly dominant place of provincial politics and legislatures in Canada, though as a historian I might be far more comfortable writing about that transition. Nor is it, most tellingly, the political science perspective of the companion pieces in this volume. Rather it is conceived as a personal reflection on "life in the Leg" from the perspective of an MLA. In particular, this paper will focus upon the less visible aspects of an MLA's life, including the importance of caucus, and the place of constituency work as well as the highly visible and often criticized theatre known as question period.

I was privileged, though admittedly initially shocked, to be elected as the MLA for Wolseley in 1990. I was re-elected in 1995 and spent nine years in opposition. In 1999 the New Democratic Party was returned to government and I was appointed minister of intergovernmental affairs and deputy premier. I chose not to run in 2003 and returned to the history department at the University of Manitoba. A senior Progressive Conservative minister, on his departure, claimed there are few "off-ramps" in politics and that fourteen years is a long time whether in opposition or in government. For once, I could agree with him.

Like most Manitobans I had not given much thought to the day-to-day life of an MLA. It is a job for which there is no training and no formal qualifications are required. A few of my university colleagues wondered how it could take up the whole day. Surely a question period of forty minutes, debate on a few bills, a Throne Speech or two were all that were required, leaving me with leisurely afternoons and evenings. One colleague pointed out that in any case the mandated ten days of formal debate on a Progressive Conservative budget beggared belief. "Ten days' debate on the invisible hand," he mocked. "There's a stretch for the imagination."

In fact nothing I had done before—not as a postal worker, psychiatric nursing aide, kindergarten teacher in an Inuit community, museum curator, civil servant, Cub leader, or professor of history—had prepared me to serve as an MLA. And yet, of course, like my new colleagues in the legislature, all of it had been a preparation for this role. And it was these new caucus colleagues who were to be my teachers, role models, critics, and supporters, and who offered a much-needed collective shoulder to lean on. I was, in fact, not just the member for Wolseley, but had joined a caucus of MLAs from all across Manitoba. Several were teachers, one or two had social work backgrounds, a few had farming backgrounds though only one still actively farmed. Others had worked on oil rigs or in industrial settings, two were lawyers, and two were ordained ministers. A few came from small-business backgrounds, some had been active in municipal government, and many had been involved in community politics or trade unions. There was considerable ethnic diversity, including four Aboriginal members, and although the majority were Manitoba-born there were several, like me, who had come here as adults from other provinces or from overseas. Eventually in my time, nine were women, which offered a strong contrast to my university department.

I know that for some parties at certain times caucus has been a place of much conflict, particularly during long periods in Opposition. Although our caucus was not without its disagreements, it generally was a place where frank opinions could be voiced but where a consensus could also be built. To walk into a caucus meeting, put an issue on the table, and hear it dissected by these men and women, representing different parts of Manitoba—from new Winnipeg suburbs, reserves, inner-city ridings, and rural and northern constituencies—was one of the most instructive and valuable experiences I had as an MLA. It was a daily seminar in the history, politics, and social perspectives of Manitoba, given by voices of experience and with immediate authenticity. What had seemed so self-evident from a Wolseley or university perspective now had to be examined through the eyes of someone from Dauphin, Swan River, Kildonan, and Flin Flon. One of my first unwritten tasks was to recognize the significance of the range of Manitoba opinion, to learn to predict it, and to incorporate it into my own understanding.

The range of experience was, of course, in striking contrast to that of an academic department. The diversity of opinion within a broad social democratic tradition was also remarkable and struck me quite forcibly. Often a consensus was possible; for some issues strong regional voices carried the day and on occasion what counted was leadership. A colleague in the Saskatchewan legislature once described the relationships within caucus as the closest and most intense she had experienced outside her family. Her words often came back to me.

During session caucus meets at least twice a day, once in the morning and once before question period. On Mondays we ate dinner together over a formal caucus meeting and lunches were usually taken with colleagues and staff. In fact once you arrived in the legislative building in the morning you would spend much of your day, inside and outside the chamber, engaged in some way with your caucus colleagues. In both opposition and government we also canvassed particular constituencies together. We travelled to each other's constituencies, met with citizens and groups, and spent many hours in each other's company "on the road" or in local coffee shops. Far from being wasted time, this offered a chance for longer policy and political discussions, the prospects in this or that riding, or political gossip. But it also gave rise to some of my most memorable recollections. On one occasion we drove ten miles past our destination because we were so engrossed in predicting the shape of the next leadership campaign (and this was years before there was a prospect of a leadership change). On another occasion I drove for thirty miles or so down Highway 59 listening with awe to one colleague explain how he and his brother captured whales in Churchill. Highway 8 will always remind me of another colleague describing both the daily life of an oil crew and the nature of Interlake politics. Another member, on a January journey to Gimli, explained patiently to me that the reason my feet had frozen was not because there was a hole in my floorboard but because my boots were far too tight. In fact I was not a popular driver in caucus—not only because my car had holes in it but because, as someone once put it, "if anyone is going with Jean they should have started yesterday." Highway speed was not my forte and was a distinct drawback for a politician in Manitoba.

I emphasize the intensity of caucus relationships for two reasons. Caucus, more than the legislature itself, was the seat of my learning. It was here where the toughest debates took place, where views were expressed most forcibly, and where shades of grey could be accommodated. The black and white of the legislative debates, necessary as they are to clear public policy, were in most cases the end of a process rather than the beginning of a dialogue. Second, I believe one of the reasons the NDP has been successful in opposition and in government is as a result of having a strong, well-functioning caucus that not only could see the forest for the trees but whose members were prepared to trust each other on significant issues. We also had the luxury of intensely dedicated staff and, it is no secret, an extremely focussed leader.

What I recognized as valuable in caucus—the ability to speak with confidence on the views of one's constituents—came, I was to learn, from a close attention to the MLA's role in the constituency. A small part of this is in the public eye. The MLA in Manitoba is invited to most events in the community. MLAs from older communities are expected to pour tea at church or seniors' events; others regularly attend to cook hot dogs at school picnics, give a short speech at graduations and turn sods for new construction, as well as attend powwows and community celebrations of all kinds. Attendance at these events eventually shapes the seasonal round of the MLA's year.

In the beginning I was quite uncomfortable with this "dignitary" (as it is termed in Manitoba) role and couldn't see my place in unfamiliar institutions or situations. Soon, however, I began to recognize that this was where the informal contacts were made that helped me understand both the lives and the perspectives of different communities. Constituents who would not normally pick up the phone to tell you of the problems encountered in their working week, or detain you at the doorstep with their perspective on a particular issue, would take a few minutes at a soccer game or over a pancake breakfast at a winter festival to discuss such matters. Over time I learned to predict the response of constituents to certain issues and also whom to contact for a particular perspective or information on any given issue. Most MLAs had a weekend routine of many such community events. This was what gave power and authenticity to the Monday morning caucus meetings where we shared the news and views we had encountered across the province.

Hidden from view, but forming a very significant part of an MLA's day, is what is known as casework. This takes many forms and since the late 1980s has been aided considerably by the ability of an MLA to hire constituency staff to help. Many of my university colleagues were surprised too by how much of my time this occupied. Academics are forceful, articulate, literate people with an expectation that their grievances and advice can be conveyed directly to their elected representatives. They are not intimidated by civil servants, lawyers, or the medical system. They are unlikely to run out of food or to be unable to pay for medications

My constituency, Wolseley, included part of the West End, West Broadway, and the Spence neighbourhood, as well as the neighbourhoods of Armstrong's Point and Wolseley itself. Many families lived "on the edge," from paycheque to paycheque. Their lives could be severely affected by bureaucratic delays, or seemingly arbitrary decisions by various levels of government. Others were new immigrants with language, housing, and educational challenges; still others were seniors, sometimes alone and facing difficult circumstances.

What they needed from me was both moral support and practical assistance. Some democracies have established "citizen advice" bureaus where staff and trained volunteers can help with a wide variety of these types of issues. In Canada, at both the provincial and federal levels, these functions of information, advocacy, and assistance are provided by the elected representative. Such a system has the advantage of bringing the elected official into close contact with the constituent and the issues that he or she might face. It has the disadvantage of perhaps adding a partisan overlay to the solution of many routine problems. And, one might add, even where citizen advice bureaus are established, the elected member is still required to act as an unofficial ombudsman or a "court of last resort."

It was at first a little astonishing that a phone call from the MLA would succeed where others had failed. Sometimes a clearly written letter from me on a constituent's behalf—stating the issue and suggesting the remedy—worked miracles. Sometimes it had no effect at all, though it normally did receive a courteous reply. Often what was needed was a phone call to exactly the right civil servant who actually had the authority to make a decision, find a solution or move an emergency cheque. If the matter were sensitive, a word with the appropriate minister after question period might get to the heart of the matter quickly, and allowed the minister to avoid the prospect of having it raised politically in the legislature.

Not all the personal and family issues could be solved, of course. In the beginning I had to learn the ways of the civil service and the range of government programs in departments as diverse as Culture, Labour, Tourism, Family Services, and Education. Constituents needed information and contacts. They needed links to others in the province who could help. In many cases the best I could do was enable people to connect to these community-based provincial networks of whose existence I was gradually becoming more aware as I attended their annual general meetings or listened as they made presentations to caucus. There are no manuals for this aspect of the job and each MLA, over time, builds up a store of knowledge and points of contact. This role of individual "advisor and advocate" took up a good deal of time on a daily basis for both me and my constituency assistant. It was frequently very frustrating work as we were often dealing with emergencies rather than enabling significant change for families. In retrospect I came to recognize that this strong practical link between an elected representative and some parts of the constituency helps, in part, to maintain Manitoba as a relatively close-knit society.

In opposition, an MLA is assigned a "critic" role in the legislature. The nature of this portfolio ensures that he or she becomes an advocate for associated groups and individuals across the province that need their problems resolved or their issues raised in the legislature. Over time these groups and individuals become the major source of questions for question period, both as generalized issues and as individual cases. The presence of the individual or group in the public gallery can add to the urgency of the matter. They usually make themselves available to the media outside the chamber, giving their case immediate public attention. As education critic for five years, I dealt with issues such as student loan difficulties, school discipline, special needs children, and apprenticeship matters on behalf of citizens from all parts of Manitoba. Casework is thus not confined to one's constituency and in portfolios such as health, family services, justice, and education, which affect many individuals and families, the workload is extensive and emotionally draining. Such wide public contact, however, offers the MLA a continuing insight into public policy issues in Manitoba. Its effect is to build an informed "loyal opposition" and, I believe, is one of the pillars of legislative experience that eventually makes for good government.

Each region of the province also has its own concerns, needs, and agenda. For northern constituencies, transport, resources, tourism, and Aboriginal issues are at the forefront. In Wolseley, beyond the individual and social issues, there were strong proponents of environmental concerns such as Dutch elm disease or pesticide use. Many had connections with art, film, music, theatre and dance and wanted those interests to be represented and celebrated in the legislature. In West Broadway and Spence in particular, there were activists involved in community gardens, landlord and tenant co-op programs, alternative justice circles, community policing, and other forms of community-based revitalization projects. I learned an enormous amount from them and carried those lessons into government to create Neighbourhoods Alive! and other programs in community economic development.

All of this is to underline the importance of the relationship between the MLA and the citizen. It extends beyond the constituency and has deeper implications for the development and formation of a government in waiting. At one level it can be viewed as essentially a form of social work. Cumulatively it is a very moving experience to be invited into the lives of so many, to be able on occasion to make that life a little easier and to ensure that those who see themselves as without a voice or influence have been heard.

It is sometimes said that politicians come to the job fully formed though not necessarily well formed. Proponents of this perspective argue that there is no time to read, to think, to develop intellectually while in office. It is true that constituency work, legislative business, and policy development are very demanding in time. But after four or five years the workload is more manageable, requiring large doses of common sense, personal flexibility, the ability to write a good letter, and a wide knowledge of people and programs at all levels of government.

Over time it also became clear to me that politics in Manitoba is primarily an oral culture. Books, reports and articles, newspapers, and annual reports fill every MLA's desk but I learned it was far more effective to be able make a case concisely in caucus than it was to write a precise memorandum for my colleagues. And equally, much of my learning about Manitoba came from caucus discussion, from speeches in the legislature by members of all sides of the chamber, and from citizens in small meetings across the province. The civil servant and the academic in me took time to recognize what now seems to be the blindingly obvious.

Question period of course institutionalizes this oral culture and as media legislative reporting has declined, it has become the most visible aspect of the formal work of MLAs. It's widely available on TV—the only part of legislative debate which is, although the home viewer sees a version that is mediated to some extent by the speaker's ability to switch off the proceedings at particularly noisy times. Hansard is easily available online and a visit to the public galleries of the legislature is a routine activity for students. Question period occurs every day of session and on each occasion involves a majority of the MLAs. It is dramatic and it can be theatrical and even MLAs refer to it on occasion as "showtime." Visitors to the legislative chamber will inevitably recoil from the robust, often hostile atmosphere of the forty-minute period and will frame their thinking about the role of the legislature from that experience. As many commentators have argued, this ignores the work done in committees, and diminishes the constituency role of the MLA.

But it is at question period, far more than in debates, that MLAs' political reputations are made and broken. Because it occurs on a daily basis, there is the opportunity for more frequent judgements. Opposition members whose research is inadequate, who are not forceful in pressing home their question or who appear to lack the enthusiastic support of their caucus are going to get brutal short shrift from government benches. And on the other side, the ministers who stumble early in their career over an issue, who appear on one or two occasions not to be in command of their departments or brief will find it difficult to re-establish themselves. Judgements are made daily, quickly, and are made to stick.

Yet question period, in my experience, more than debates or committee work, demonstrates that politics is not simply the expression of one individual but a collective endeavour—a team sport for those who think in sporting terms. In opposition the preparation of a question, although initiated by the individual MLA, owes its final form to the work of a team. I was astonished to read in one Canadian political science text that question period is largely unscripted. In my experience in nine years of opposition, I would say that it is highly scripted and carefully planned.

An issue for "QP" can emerge in several ways. It can be brought forward by a citizen—a phone call of complaint or concern, the proverbial brown envelope, a leak about something from someone, or a matter of local concern. Or it can be developed by MLAs' own research into public documents. The MLA for Brandon East, Len Evans, for example, prepared an annual list of economic indicators for the province which generated a series of questions based on long-term trends. Or questions can pick up on current media stories with the anticipation of the MLA becoming part of the story.

At the first caucus meeting of the day at 9:30 a.m., you must "pitch" your proposal, convince your colleagues of the cause, and take on board the several cautions that will come your way from those with long memories of similar questions or good strategic sense of what to emphasize or avoid. About six or seven questions are registered, of which one or two are likely to be the party leader's questions. Health, education, family services, and agriculture critics will have strong claims to the rest. If you are lucky enough to have your question on the board, the next two to three hours are spent on research—finding the statistics needed for evidence, the phone calls to confirm what might only have been rumour, or contacting the experts you might need to quote. At 1 p.m. caucus re-assembles, questions are examined more thoroughly, and an order is established. After half an hour you pull your wording together and work out the anticipated government response that you may need to respond to in your supplementary questions. In my time there was a particularly rigid format for questions in the House. All had to begin with the interrogative "Could the minister..." and were strictly timed to the second by the speaker so that the prospects for drama were somewhat limited.

Some political scientists have argued that there are better ways for MLAs to spend their time than in question period. They argue that both the time spent in preparation and the adversarial nature of the exercise are not conducive to a sensible or efficient political process. Although I am sure there are ways to improve the usefulness of question period I would argue that in general this daily exercise is a simple, easily understood way of ensuring a government is accountable both to the general public and to the media. It is effective in raising the issues of the day, plainly spoken in a formal and solemn setting. It is true that an answer is not necessarily forthcoming immediately. But a question raised in the House can result in quite fast action in order that a minister may claim the situation is under control. It can be more effective if one or more media outlets take up the issue. It can be particularly effective when the research is solid, and when the question is repeated frequently, perhaps daily, until policy change or action is undertaken. Even the anticipation of a question can be effective in ensuring the government takes action. The wrong can be righted and the citizens' needs dealt with quickly. Over a period of time, or sometimes over specific questions, an ideological divide between parties can be demonstrated that clarifies the voters' choices at the next election.

Because, it must be understood, that although the tasks of representation just described are undertaken responsibly as Her Majesty's Loyal Opposition, there is also in the role of opposition the *duty* to become government—to put before the voters the policies that you believe will make a better and fairer Manitoba. Question period is inevitably about the next election. It is about ideas and policies and personnel. It is not a tea party with a mutual exchange of slightly differing perspectives. It is not about exchanging pithy and witty academic memorandums. It is an oral culture that rewards plain language and forceful delivery. Most importantly, its unwritten rules force the daily presence of cabinet ministers in the House to hear the "complaints of the people." But it also comes at a cost, creating thick skins and rewarding the ability to thrive in a hostile atmosphere. In my time in opposition some ministers, though by convention not required to provide an answer, had some leeway and expertise in twisting the question, casting personal aspersions, and assuming unnecessarily aggressive responses. Others maintained the posture of a gracious desire to help the unfortunate member of the opposition understand the situation more fully and to explain patiently that the present policy was merely another example of why one of us was in government and the other was not. Yet in Manitoba we maintain a public culture with a moral narrative of working together, of consensus building, of government from the centre: a picture at odds with the almost literal cut and thrust of question period.

The "noise" of question period is not peculiar to the Manitoba Legislature. New South Wales's legislature has been described, affectionately, as akin to a Glasgow pub on a Saturday night. Manitoba's House hasn't come to blows in recent memory, but there is no doubt that to continue to fight elections on a daily basis requires and perhaps creates a strong team ethos and requires disciplined individuals with a well-developed sense of loyalty to each other. Such qualities are indispensable to both good government and effective opposition.

Visitors to the "Leg" or the "building" as it is known to its inhabitants are often quite disconcerted to see MLAs who have been enthusiastically attacking each other in question period walking together down the hall, metaphorically with arms around each other's shoulders. In my time it was a well-understood convention that outside of the chamber cross-party civility must rule. And in my own case I was quite specifically instructed by one of the senior MLAs from the North that that was what was expected. To carry such levels of hostility for long periods would be ultimately destructive to one's health, he explained. In opposition we need to be able to approach ministers on behalf of our constituents, he underlined, and the channels of communication have to be kept open. From a minister's perspective, too, the ability to discuss prospective legislation with the critic or to deal with one of their constituents' problems means that awkward public questions could be avoided.

Experienced members of caucus frequently repeated this message of co-operation. They believed the electorate expected it. The rules of the House, where one could cross the floor to speak to the other side after question period, reinforced this. On most days, during the debates following question period, there would be frequent private consultations across the floor on House business, constituent issues, or on forthcoming bills. In addition, the visible rancor of question period masks the fact that in some periods about eighty percent of legislation passes unanimously or with minor amendments.

Even ceremonially the legislature makes an effort to connect across party lines. In my early days MLAs were in the habit of attending each other's caucus Christmas parties, though I believe they have become more private of late. At the open house during the Christmas season there is a long-standing tradition of MLAs assembling on the main steps and singing carols together under the direction of the speaker. After serious political divisions, such as the debate over the sale of MTS, some sang through gritted teeth but nevertheless the traditional view of a cooperative legislative assembly was presented to the public.

This cross-party communication is viewed as vital in case of emergencies such as floods, or in some of the difficult issues we have faced in constitutional relations. All-party committees are desirable and necessary when dealing with, for example, agricultural crises, the Meech Lake or Charlottetown accords, or even smoking regulations. The will to make these all-party committees effective cannot be pulled from thin air. It must draw upon an experience of working together, a reservoir of goodwill, and a shared understanding of the benefit for all citizens of such cooperation.

This consciousness of the necessity of maintaining shared responsibilities across party lines has its institutional form in the ritual each session of "Condolences." This is time set aside in the legislative calendar for speeches from all parts of the House commemorating the death of a member or former member. Speeches are directed at the family but serve to remind old and new members of the values of service and representation that are common to all. "Condolences" is also the time when the caucus and House claim their place—their own kinship with the member. Nowhere was this more clearly and more poignantly evident than in the ceremonial farewell for Oscar Lathlin in the chamber and the rotunda. The speeches in the House of all three party leaders were dignified and eloquent.

Outside the chamber amidst the drumbeats of two Aboriginal drum groups and the honour guard of the Cross Lake cadet corps, Oscar's family accepted the chief's headdress from his legislative desk and with it the condolences of his legislative kin.

The great rotunda of the legislature, with its grand entrance flanked by two bronze buffalo, would not have heard the Aboriginal drums in such a way before. It is worth noting that as our population demographics change this building, designed on the classical lines intended to recall European ideals, continues to hold a special place in the political and social life of all Manitobans. Every MLA and civil servant who works at the legislature and most visitors recognize this is not only an institution, a house of representatives, similar to many others in the Commonwealth or the western United States, but that it holds a special place in the consciousness of our community. The Leg, as it is known across generations and social groups, a name spoken both in frustration and affection, is a place that is well-known to most Manitobans. Partly this is because almost seventy percent of Manitobans live close to Winnipeg, partly because it is the chosen site of public protest, memory, and celebration, and partly because as elsewhere it is a required visit for elementary and high school students. Manitobans view the "Leg" with an easy familiarity I have not encountered in other provinces. It was no surprise to find that Guy Maddin included in his tribute film *My Winnipeg* a dramatic scene in the rotunda of the legislative building.

One of the main reasons, of course, for the Leg's place in the Manitoba consciousness goes back to its design and construction and to the expectations of future greatness of that early twentieth-century generation. It is our largest public building, strategically situated facing both the Assiniboine River and the city. Its neoclassical design with grand staircase and fine allegorical mural provide a fitting setting for the chamber itself. It was intended to awe, to be imposing, and so it is. Since the 1950s the legislature and its grounds have become not just the house of assembly for a few, but the place of memory, the site of pilgrimage for the many. Vigils and demonstrations on issues sometimes unrelated to the province take place here. Inside the building are a number of plaques reminding us of the Mennonite and other migrations, the War Brides Association, the Royal Winnipeg Rifles, and the Winnipeg General Strike, among others. In the Manitoba Legislature the halls are thus lined with more than the portraits of premiers and speakers but reflect a broader historical presence. Outside in the spacious grounds are statues of Robbie Burns and Jón Sigurðsson, emblematic of two of the earlier groups of European settlers. In 1960 Ukrainian-Manitobans claimed their place at the legislature with a large statue of Taras Shevchenko, opened with great ceremony and enormous pride on the part of thousands of

Ukrainian-Manitobans. Over the years it has become the place to lay wreaths, to celebrate significant anniversaries, and to visibly demonstrate, to the whole community or to the president of Ukraine, the clear place of Ukrainians in Manitoba. More recently a new interpretation of Louis Riel, a Holocaust Memorial, a Women's Garden of Reflection, and a statue of Nellie McClung have taken their place in the grounds of the legislature as other communities have claimed a place in this, *our* garden of memories.

Manitobans have a personal as well as a collective sense of the legislature. At the weekends there is a heavy demand for the legislature as photographic location. So strong is the demand that there are scheduled rotations for wedding parties. The limousines line up at the front of the building as inside, beside the buffalo, the brides and grooms, the bridesmaids, and families pose for their formal commemorative photographs. It is an imposing setting and it is meticulously kept. Steamed, polished, and brilliantly maintained, it is one public building that shines its welcome. And not only wedding parties are welcomed. Musical performances are frequent and the acoustics particularly rewarding. Citizenship ceremonies and youth parliament are regular occurrences that use the chamber itself. International Women's Day, the Lieutenant-Governor's annual New Year's Day Levee, Seniors Day, the Christmas Open House, the Order of Manitoba ceremonies and the state dinner for the Queen are all occasions when hundreds are welcomed to *their* building. Such open and easy access is valued. In the twenty-first century, external events required changes in security measures, but both sides of the House were very conscious of the necessity of maintaining as much open access as possible to the building and to the galleries.

Perhaps it is not unexpected then that it is Manitoba that sends *every* bill to a legislative committee and asks for public comment and criticism. Increasingly, in quite large numbers, Manitobans respond to this opportunity. Many of the late-night sittings of committees are in fact to accommodate the many citizens who want to speak for their allotted ten or fifteen minutes on the impact of a particular bill on their lives. Manitobans' familiarity with and sense of "ownership" of the Leg has also contributed to their increasing interest in representing themselves in political debate in this way.

Critics of our present version of the Westminster system, usually surfacing at election time, propose changes to our first-past-the-post system based on several variants of a proportional representation system. Many of these advocate slates of candidates and some proposals are prepared to sacrifice the direct connection between the elected representative and the constituency. In my view, such a change would be a mistake and would undermine one of the great strengths of Manitoba's political system. In a population of slightly more than one million, with constituencies of 20,000 to 30,000 voters, it is possible to have political dialogue with individuals and for the MLA to build a close understanding of the views, needs and expectations of the constituency. It was this depth of understanding that made caucus discussions so significant. For the most part you were hearing the voice of a representative who lived in the constituency, whose children attended local schools and played on local teams, and whose family attended local churches. Both within Winnipeg and outside the city there is a strong attachment to place. This attachment to the Interlake and the "Valley" (Swan River) to the Kildonans, the North, St. Boniface, or Wolseley has in part been shaped by the boundaries of political constituencies and been served well by the creation and maintenance of such close ties to an MLA and to government.

Manitoba is changing, as the ceremonies honouring Oscar Lathlin demonstrated. And it will continue to change. This is not Ontario, nor is it Saskatchewan. This is a small province with moderate views but firmly held and long-lived political positions. The legislature has fierce caucus loyalties and raucous question periods, but it is consciously open and accessible, increasingly diverse in its composition, closely linked to its citizens, and able to articulate the shared ideals of public service.

The Evolution of Political Journalism in Manitoba[1]

Frances Russell

As a veteran of forty-eight years in journalism, I have witnessed one of the most profound and dramatic revolutions in the news business since Gutenberg invented the printing press.

I began my career at the *Winnipeg Tribune* in May 1962 after graduating with a Bachelor of Arts in history and political science. Back then, Winnipeg was a fiercely competitive newspaper market, boasting two broadsheet dailies representing the nation's two major newspaper chains: Southam, owned by the family of the same name and FP Publications, owned by the Siftons.

Both the Southam-owned *Winnipeg Tribune* and its bigger rival, the Sifton-owned *Winnipeg Free Press*, published a morning and up to three afternoon editions daily, re-plating the front page as necessary to carry breaking news. This was the era before computers, before tape recorders, before the Internet, before the BlackBerry.

Reporters scribbled their notes on copy paper using thick yellow newsprinter pencils. They pounded out their stories on blank sheets of newsprint wadded, along with carbon paper, into heavy black Underwood typewriters. Sometimes as many as four or five copies were required, the first for the all-important Canadian Press wire and the remainder for various editors.

If they were on deadline, reporters would rip each page out as soon as they had completed a paragraph, shout, "Copy!" and hand it to a "copy boy" who would rush one page to the city editor, another to his assistant and literally skewer a third on CP's long, very sharp metal spike resting on the city editor's desk. Its contents would be scooped up every hour or so throughout the day by a telegraph boy who would take the stories to the Canadian Press office in the *Winnipeg Free Press* building at 300 Carlton Street. From there, Winnipeg's and Manitoba's news would be tapped out to the nation and the world.

With four deadlines every day, a newspaper office was a noisy, frantic, and exciting place to work. You could hear, touch, and literally smell the news. I can still remember my first visit to the composing room on the floor above the "*Trib*" newsroom. The aroma of hot lead hung heavy in the air from the pots of molten metal hanging beside each huge, clanking linotype machine. Linotype operators took the words written by the reporters in the newsroom below and hammered them out into individual lead "slugs" that were then fitted into heavy metal-columned frames to create the "dummy" for each page of the newspaper. Immediately afterward, the lead slugs would be re-melted and readied for the next edition.

My first "beat" at the *Trib* was education. My *Free Press* counterpart and I covered the Winnipeg School Board. And I mean covered. Back at our respective newsrooms, we often stayed up all night writing as many as twelve or fifteen stories from every meeting. All, or nearly all, would run.

After two years, I won what to me was the lottery grand prize—the chance to cover the Manitoba Legislature.

It was the 1964 winter session. Duff Roblin's Progressive Conservatives were in power. I will never forget the short and succinct lecture I was given by my city editor and on-the-job journalism professor, Harry Mardon. A war correspondent with British United Press, Harry, as we all called him, was a proud Brit and an avowed Conservative. But here were his words to me: "Your job at the legislature is to level the playing field. The government of the day has all kinds of ways to get its message across to the public. We're there to make sure the opposition parties have an equal voice."

Researching my book on Manitoba's French language crisis, I had occasion to read some of Manitoba's earliest newspapers. From the 1870s to the 1970s, there really wasn't much difference in the way Manitoba newspapers—and indeed, newspapers everywhere in Canada—covered Parliament and legislatures. The coverage was wall-to-wall, from the daily opening prayer to the adjournment hour. In Manitoba's case—and in the case of the British Columbia and Ontario legislatures, which I also covered for the *Vancouver Sun* and the *Globe and Mail* respectively—the adjournment hour could be extended into the wee small hours of the next day in the drive to wrap up all business to break for summer.

Unlike today, when all media attention is focused solely on question period, political journalism in Manitoba until well into the 1970s involved writing stories not just out of question period, but on everything else debated in the House that day: estimates, bills, committee hearings, matters of privilege, private members' business, and so on. And all MLAs who spoke knew that at least a sentence or two of their comments would appear in the newspaper. It was gruelling work and the *Free Press* and the *Tribune* both maintained bureaus at the legislature numbering four or five journalists who would work in shifts. By the time I started in the press gallery, however, the newspapers had abandoned their earlier practice of reporting debates as though they were court stenographers and were applying news judgement to their coverage.

Still, Winnipeg's two daily newspapers—and, by this time, CBC radio and television, CKY radio and television, and CJOB radio staffed the legislature full time when it was sitting. In those days, the media, as it was by then being called, respected the fact that the legislature was Manitoba democracy at work. Its members were the representatives of the people and the people who had elected those fifty-seven MLAs had a right to know what they were saying and doing every day that they were tending to the public's business.

In keeping with the noisy, rough-and-ready nature of their craft in that era, journalists were a far cry from the well-paid, well-dressed, well-behaved, button-down professionals and TV stars of today. Winnipeg's newspapers and all of its television and radio outlets, with the exception of the CBC, were non-unionized and pay was, to put it mildly, poor. The "ink-stained wretches," as they were proud to call themselves, did not all go home to family and dinner at night. More often than not, they collected at the Winnipeg Press Club to raise more than a few prior to retiring for the day.

The St. Regis Hotel, favoured by rural MLAs during sessions, was another major watering hole. To this day among old-timers, there are many stories of well-lubricated evening sittings of the House when some MLAs were too drunk to speak and some reporters too drunk to write. There is even one famous yarn about a scion of the *Tribune* bureau being so inebriated one evening that he climbed up onto the gallery desk in the House to unleash a torrent of foul-mouthed criticism at the honourable member speaking below.

That dirty laundry aside, the era of spin was still a few years away. The government had an information office that drafted press releases and that was about it. There were no ministerial press aides, nor were there departmental communicators, let alone communication branches. In fact, the premier himself did not even have a full-time press secretary.

Individual journalists were on their own when it came to digging up news. It was tough sledding—and very competitive. Press gallery veterans had a distinct advantage over newcomers. They had years to establish not just contacts, but in many cases, close friendships with politicians and senior bureaucrats. As in most walks of life, who you know is all-important. Sometimes an MLA or minister would shun you simply because of the news organization you worked for. But most of the time it was just reality that the better you were known, the more information you were able to get.

The civil service was especially important to reporters and columnists back in the days before cabinet communications and press secretaries. They often knew a lot more about what was really going on regarding a certain issue than ministers themselves.

There used to be a saying in the press gallery, especially in the Roblin era: "The civil servant knows but can't say while the minister can say but often doesn't know." Manitoba was—and still is—a small enough province that government tends to be a one-man show. All roads led—and lead—to the premier's office. If the premier is open and professional with the gallery, the entire government tends to be the same. If not, the ship on Broadway can be very leak-proof indeed.

Back in the competitive era, if you were beaten on a story, you heard about it around 6 a.m. the next day from your irate city editor. Oblivious to the fact you may have been up half the night completing your assignments, he would be yelling down the phone at you, reading out the opposition's front-page story you had missed and berating you to get on it, post haste. A far cry from today when media outlets often simply ignore opponents' "beats," thus denying the public important information.

The *Free Press* vs. "The Socialists"

Perhaps not so surprisingly, Manitoba entered the modern era of politically polarized journalism with the stunning leap from third to first place by Ed Schreyer's New Democrats in the 1969 provincial election. The lead on the *Trib*'s front page the next day, written by veteran legislative reporter Chuck Thompson, said it all: "Nobody was more surprised than everyone."

The *Tribune*, nominally a Conservative paper, took the arrival of the socialist hordes with some equanimity. Over at the offices of the Liberal Old Lady of Carlton Street, however, such was not the case.

Free Press publisher and editor-in-chief Brigadier R.S. Malone set himself a mission—to rid Manitoba of the Schreyer government as quickly as possible. He used his editorial page to fulminate against virtually everything the NDP proposed—and the new government was not shy in offering lots to be upset about, from public automobile insurance to an end to health care premiums to the sequence of development of Manitoba Hydro's enormous Nelson River power plants to the unification of Winnipeg's sixteen area municipalities into one city.

I had occasion to run smack into the Brigadier's principal passion. I was by this time writing an editorial page column for the *Free Press* from the legislature. There had been many news stories denouncing public car insurance and I set up an interview with Sidney Green, then the minister responsible for MPIC. Green, who had run against Schreyer for the leadership and lost in 1969, never completely reconciled himself to his fate and seized any opportunity to if not openly defy the premier at least roil the waters.

In the interview, Green said the most important thing about Autopac was not that it was going to save Manitoba motorists a lot of money, as the premier kept emphasizing, but that Manitobans' car insurance premiums would be staying right here in this province helping to build hospitals, schools, nursing homes, and roads and not fattening the coffers of some big multinational insurance corporation in Toronto or Chicago.

I wrote the column and handed it in. In no time I received a telephone call from Peter McLintock, the editor of the editorial page. Peter was a kindly and very able newsman with moderate political views. He asked me how determined I was that the column be published. Naturally, I said I thought it was important information that the public should know. I could have it published, he said, but in the want ads section, not on the editorial page.

Malone never stopped taking runs at his socialist nemesis on Broadway.

Just before the 1973 provincial election, he, along with several other prominent Winnipeg businessmen, set up what they called the Group for Good Government. Its purpose was to identify, endorse, and financially support the Liberal or Conservative "free enterprise" candidate with the best chance of unseating the NDP incumbent in certain specified ridings. The GGG hired a polling firm and publicized its results, much to the chagrin of both opposition parties. In the end, the GGG effort only materialized in nine ridings.

Still, the GGG or single free enterprise candidate effort was spectacularly successful on two fronts. Despite a four-point increase in popular vote, from 38 per cent in 1969 to 42 per cent, the third highest since 1920, the New Democrats only netted thirty-one seats, two more than at dissolution but the same number they had a year earlier before the defections of northern MLAs Joe Borowski and Jean Allard to sit as independents. And the outcomes in five ridings—Wolseley, St. Boniface, Gimli, Crescentwood, and the premier's own riding of Rossmere—were either close enough or contentious enough to cast a pall of doubt over the election and the government for the next two years.

Herb Schulz, Schreyer's brother-in-law, provides a sardonic look at the wreckage of the GGG's 1973 electoral shenanigans in his 2005 book, *A View from The Ledge*: "We even knew who the two votes [that lost Wolseley election night] were. A couple, both good friends of the Schreyers' and strong NDP supporters, came home from work and decided to have a short nap before going out to vote. They awoke at 8:10 p.m. and realized the polls had closed."[2]

A measure of the antipathy towards the NDP and Schreyer in particular in certain quarters was the effort to controvert the premier's 600-vote win in Rossmere. Continues Schulz:

> Rossmere had the largest concentration of Mennonites of any constituency in Canada, many of them first or second-generation émigrés from the Soviet Union and [Progressive Conservative candidate Alfred] Penner played to the prejudices of his constituents. He billed his candidacy as offering "A Choice Between Freedom of Opportunity, or Socialism…We now have a government that stifles initiative, restricts freedom of choice, downgrades standards of decency and morality and compensates lawbreakers." Additionally, he wanted "studies of Socialist, communist and Marxist doctrines" in schools replaced with "the Bible and Christian principles."[3]

Nevertheless, Penner based his controversial challenge on the grounds the returning officer, an NDP appointee, was a Mennonite lay preacher and the Elections Act prohibited ministers, priests or ecclesiastics from acting in that capacity. After hearing lengthy arguments on both sides about whether and when a preacher is a minister, a Court of Queen's Bench judge threw out the case. Schulz concludes: "And so, after two years almost to the day after the 1973 election, after five electoral challenges, four judicial recounts, three by-elections and one court case, and after all the agonizing and the expenditure of time and staggering court costs which had drained some private pockets as well as that of the party, our representation in the legislature was exactly what it had been in June 1972."[4]

After all this, the bad blood the *Free Press* displayed towards the NDP was being returned with interest. In his address to the NDP's post-election convention, the premier, normally a low-key and at times ponderous speaker, was punching the air with his fists and roaring with fury at his newspaper tormentor while its journalists sat uncomfortably at the press table trying to overlook the hostile stares and rude remarks coming at us from the platform and the audience.

Relations between the province's government and its biggest newspaper normalized during Progressive Conservative Premier Sterling Lyon's years in power. But the hostility resumed after Howard Pawley brought the NDP back to power in 1981, consigning Lyon to the status of the only one-term premier in Manitoba history.

In 1986, the city editor of the day instructed one of the press gallery reporters that she had to "get" a cabinet minister before Christmas. Subsequently, the paper broke a story claiming Energy and Mines Minister Wilson Parasiuk, a Rhodes scholar and former senior economic advisor to Schreyer, was in a conflict of interest due to a business partnership. The province's retired chief justice, Sam Freedman, was appointed to inquire into the affair and cleared Parasiuk of all the paper's allegations.

Perhaps it was a matter of once bitten, twice shy—or just plain old political bias—but the paper was circumspect to the point of inaction when the Progressive Conservative government of Gary Filmon found itself immersed in the infamous vote-rigging scandal of the late 1990s.

As outlined in the 1999 commission of inquiry by retired chief justice Alfred Monnin, senior Progressive Conservatives created and funded a bogus political party to run Aboriginal candidates in selected ridings with large Native populations in an attempt to split the NDP vote and elect PCs in the 1995 provincial election. In that contest, Gary Filmon's Progressive Conservatives won a third term and a second majority.

Free Press senior legislative reporter Alice Krueger first got wind of the audacious attempt to buy an entire election in the dying days of the 1995 race. Pressed for time and working flat-out on the province-wide campaign, she was unable to write more than a single article outlining the NDP's allegations and the premier's denials the weekend before the vote. The paper's managing editor was as jumpy as a cat on a hot tin roof about running it, but finally did so under the bizarrely chatty headline, "Hey, whose side is he on?"[5]

Krueger continued to chase the story after the election, but met more and more resistance from the newspaper, a situation that became so intolerable for her that she finally resigned. Subsequently, CBC Radio's national affairs reporter in Manitoba, Curt Petrovich, pursued and broke the story, for which he won the Michener Award for public service journalism.

In his report on the affair, Alfred Monin wrote this damning indictment: "As a trial judge, I conducted a number of trials. As an appellate court judge I read many thousands of pages of transcript in a variety of cases: criminal, civil, family, etc. In all my years on the Bench I never encountered as many liars in one proceeding as I did in this inquiry."[6]

Trends in Ownership

The world of journalism changed forever in Canada on 27 August 1980 when Southam closed the *Winnipeg Tribune* and Thomson Newspapers closed the *Ottawa Journal*. Competitive broadsheet newspaper markets are now all but gone. Millions of Canadians in western Canada have been partially or wholly dependent on the Canwest Global newspaper chain for all their news. A Canwest executive never spoke a truer word than when he said privately "Freedom of the press belongs to the owners of the press."

Manitoba now boasts three daily newspapers. Two of these, the *Winnipeg Free Press* and the *Brandon Sun*, are owned by FP Publications Ltd., a partnership of businessmen Bob Silver of Winnipeg and Ron Stern of Vancouver. They also own the network of free community newspapers. Their only local competition is the Sun Media Group's tabloid, the *Winnipeg Sun*.

Following national and international trends, newsgathering is now largely infotainment, a commodity to help sell ads. Crime, celebrities, sports, and entertainment frequently drown out or sideline political and public affairs. As the saying goes, "If it bleeds, it leads."

The famous "Five W's"—who, what, where, when, and why—of basic news coverage is now harder and harder to find in newspapers now crammed with columns on everything from pets and lifestyle to civic, provincial, and federal issues. Journalism is personal and journalists are personalities—stars complete with pictures and their own blogs.

The use of the first-person pronouns "I" and "me," a journalistic capital crime in the past, is now ubiquitous. Reporters are expected to serve up the news with their own commentary. They don't cover the news any more. They tell you what you should think about the news.

Go to the Manitoba Legislature on most days and you will find the press gallery empty except for one or two *Free Press* reporters. It is largely ignored by the electronic media except for major news conferences and question period. Still, because political and legislative coverage is focused so narrowly on that one forty-minute legislative event, the media drives the agenda in ways that it did not when it covered the legislative function in its entirety. Indeed, it often functions as an informal research bureau for the opposition parties.

I will go out on a limb and say I do not think the revolution I have witnessed in my forty-eight-year career has been for the better, especially where politics is concerned. Our understanding, even our basic knowledge, of our provincial and national politics is more fragmented and sketchy than ever before, a fact eloquently demonstrated by the shockingly low voter turnout (58.8 percent) in the October 2008 federal election.[7] Technology is a liberator in many endeavours, but in news, both it and the arrival of giant, vertically integrated media conglomerates, have led to fewer voices, less diversity of opinion and, inevitably, a narrowing of democratic choice.

Notes

1   This paper is adapted from a speech delivered 21 November 2008 at the Manitoba Politics, Government and Policy Conference.
2   Herb Schulz, *A View from the Ledge* (Winnipeg: Heartland, 2006), 215.
3   Ibid., 216.
4   Ibid., 218.
5   Alice Krueger, "Hey! Whose Side Is He On?" *Winnipeg Free Press*, 22 April 1995. See also Doug Smith, *As Many Liars* (Winnipeg: Arbeiter Ring, 1995).
6   Justice Alfred Monnin, *Report of the Commission of Inquiry into Allegations of Infractions of The Elections Act and the Elections Finance Act during the 1995 Manitoba general elections* (Winnipeg: The Commission, 1999), 16–17.
7   Elections Canada, "Official Voting Results: 40th General Election 2008," http://www.elections.ca/scripts/OVR2008/default.html.

The Past, Present, and Future of the Manitoba Civil Service[1]

Paul G. Thomas, with Curtis Brown

Introduction

This chapter examines the role of the Manitoba civil service at the beginning of the twenty-first century. The civil service is not an island unto itself, it both reflects and shapes to some not easily measured extent the society and the political system in which it operates. Reflecting the small-c conservative nature of Manitoba society and the moderation of the province's most successful governing parties, the historical traditions of Manitoba's civil service can best be described as "institutional conservatism," which might be summed up by the phrase "change if necessary but not necessarily change." This orientation made Manitoba more of a follower than a leader when it came to civil service reform.

Until late in the twentieth century successive governments of various partisan backgrounds saw the civil service in strictly instrumental terms: it existed to carry out approved policies and programs and to do so in a financially prudent manner. There was little or no enthusiasm for bold, sweeping reforms based upon the prevailing, fashionable approaches to policy making and public management being embraced by larger governmental systems, such as the federal government and some provinces. When reforms were undertaken the preferred approach was pragmatic, limited, gradual, low-key, and affordable.

Particularly since the 1980s, the tradition of pragmatic gradualism with respect to civil service reform became more difficult to sustain as the changes both outside and inside government became more complex, rapid, and fundamental in their impacts on the role of government within Manitoba society. The responses of the Progressive Conservative government of former premier Gary Filmon (1988–1999) have been analyzed in some depth elsewhere[2] and accordingly that period in the recent history of the Manitoba civil service will receive less attention here. The Filmon reforms, however, help to shape the context in which the New Democratic Party (NDP) led by Gary Doer took office in 1999. It is the changes to the policy advisory and policy implementation roles of the civil services introduced during the decade that Doer was premier (1999–2009) that are the main focus of the chapter.

The integrating theme of the chapter is that the Filmon and Doer governments followed somewhat different approaches to public management reform. Facing difficult economic and budgetary circumstances, and imbued with neoconservative and new public management ideas, the Filmon government broke with provincial tradition by adopting a more ideological, top-down, aggressive and, critics would say, radical approach to public management reform In contrast, the Doer government was more pragmatic, consultative, gradual, and limited in its approach, exhibiting caution when it came to the adoption of the so-called "big ideas" of public management reform.

In setting forth this argument, the chapter speculates on the factors which might explain the differences in approach by the two governments. Three broad sets of factors are identified:

- **context** — the changing economic, financial, and political circumstances;
- **ideas** — the ideology of the governing party and the ideas ascendant in the public sector management field, both within the province and beyond;
- **leadership** — the leadership philosophy and style of the premier and, to a lesser extent, of senior public servants who actually design and implement civil service reforms.

While it is possible to separate these factors analytically, in practice they are clearly related and interdependent in their impacts. The comparison to be made between the two governments is therefore somewhat impressionistic. Also, care must be taken not to exaggerate the differences. The trends and conditions driving civil service reform were mainly the same, but the intentions, scope, and pace of the reform activities of the two governments were significantly different. It can be argued with some plausibility that if the Filmon government had not undertaken its budget cutting and civil service downsizing during the 1990s, the Doer government would have been forced to take more drastic actions during the subsequent decade from 1999 to 2009.

The analysis will proceed as follows. Section 2 will describe briefly the historical development of Manitoba's civil service and the sources of its influence in the contemporary policy process. Section 3 describes briefly the factors that contributed to the growing influential role of the civil service in the design and delivery of policy and programs as the scope and complexity of provincial government activities grew in the second half of the twentieth century. Section 4 analyzes the context, ideas, and reform approaches followed by the Filmon government. The Filmon approach was more about modernization and re-engineering than it was about civil service renewal per se. Sections 5, 6, 7, and 8 will examine the context and the reform initiatives adopted by the Doer government after it took office in 1999. In addition to strengthening the political direction provided to the civil service, the Doer reform agenda responded to the perceived necessity to renew the civil service to meet the policy and resource challenges it faced and to deal with a quiet crisis of professional identity among civil service after two decades of "bureaucracy bashing" in political and media commentary. Section 9 will draw together the various parts of the analysis and ask the question of whether Manitoba's civil service is better positioned to face the challenges of the twenty-first century.

The Historical Development of the Civil Service

A full history of the Manitoba civil service has yet to be written; the closest document we have is a multi-authored history of the Manitoba Government Employees' Union,[3] which tells the story of the main public sector union up to the early years of the Filmon government. Even without such a full history, it is clear that the role, size, and composition of the civil service have changed drastically from the time when the province was first created. The original postage-stamp-sized province of about 12,000 citizens was run almost single-handedly by the lieutenant governor. The provincial legislature and the cabinet were fledgling, rustic institutions without much independence from the representative of the Crown. This was true also of the civil service, with a small number of initial positions being filled part-time through appointments made by the lieutenant governor.

Manitoba's first Civil Service Act was passed by the legislature in 1885. It translated into law the existing distinction between "inside" and "outside" civil service workers. The twenty or so "inside" workers were the deputy ministers, senior and junior clerks, and messengers attached to the four departments of government, the largest of which was the public works department responsible for the settlement and development of the province.[4] Justice and agriculture were two other important departments. A far larger group of public employees were the so-called "outside" workers who served in such functions as tax assessment, surveying, road construction, and jails.

The fact the civil service was being developed at the same time party politics began to emerge in the legislature meant that political patronage dominated the appointment of civil servants, especially the larger outside group, which came and went with the party in power. New governments were expected to find jobs for their political friends and the wholesale replacement of large parts of the civil service became the pattern after each turnover in government. Individuals lobbied ministers and MLAs for government jobs. Civil servants also showed their gratitude to the governing party who appointed them by attempting to gerrymander elections.[5]

Political patronage remained the pattern in civil service appointments into the twentieth century. As Lionel Orlikow has documented, the political reform movement that emerged in the English-speaking world early in the twentieth century made its way during the decade from 1910 to 1920 to Manitoba, where it was reinforced by local developments.[6] Reflecting pressures from various community groups, T.C. Norris and the Liberal Party campaigned in the 1915 election against the spoils system, which involved government benefits of various kinds being provided to political friends in return for kickbacks to the governing party. Assisted by the scandal over the construction of the Legislative Building, the Liberals swept into office and passed major pieces of progressive legislation, including in 1918 a new Civil Service Act. The Act provided for the appointment of a single Civil Service Commissioner who could only be dismissed by a vote of the legislature. It defined six categories of employees, but the requirements for each job were determined by the cabinet. The commissioner certified candidates as qualified for jobs (based on background experience and tests) but it was the cabinet that made the final selection. Despite the beginning semblance of a merit system for appointments, ministers regularly hired people and set salaries without referring to the Civil Service Commission.[7]

Rural-dominated governments, including coalition governments from 1928 to 1958, ruled Manitoba on the basis of a philosophy of limited intervention in the economy. This meant the government response to population and economic growth, industrialization, and urbanization was reluctant and gradual. A government-owned telephone company was created in 1908 to ensure service to all segments of society. With the growth in automobile use, highways had to be built, but Manitoba roads remained notoriously bad into the 1960s. The transfer from the national government of responsibility for natural resource development in 1930 led to the creation of the new provincial department of Mines and Natural Resources. A federal-provincial health agreement in 1948 led to growth in provincial employment in that field. In 1949 a small department of Industry was created. While there was expansion, it was limited by political philosophy favouring balanced budgets. As late as 1958, total provincial spending stood at only $100 million and the civil service employed only 4417 people.[8]

Several decades of coalition government based on a philosophy of non-partisanship, and the efforts of the government employee association in calling for an end to patronage, led to the gradual entrenchment of the principle of merit in appointments and promotions within the civil service. In 1948 a new Civil Service Act was passed. It provided for the appointment of a three-person Civil Service Commission and the first part-time head of the Commission was a prominent, outside businessman.[9] The Act also created an Establishment Committee of Cabinet, which reviewed requests from departments for new staff and for reclassifications of existing staff. In the ensuing years the commission recruited and trained more competent staff for its own operations and these professionals began to apply recognized principles and standards of classification more widely throughout the civil service. By 1957, Scarrow writes, the practice of political patronage was largely eliminated as a basis for appointments to the core departments of government.[10]

It took major political change, however to transform the limited role of government favoured by rural-dominated coalition governments. The modernization of the Manitoba government really began with the end of the coalition and the election of the Progressive Conservative government of Duff Roblin in 1958. During the Roblin period (1958–1967) an acceptance of a positive role for government in fostering economic and social development became more widely accepted within Manitoba's political culture. New spending and programming was introduced in the policy fields of economic development, education, health, social services, and transportation. Total provincial expenditures increased fourfold in a decade and the civil service grew to 8882 employees in 1969. Not only was the civil service larger, it was also increasingly specialized and professionalized in terms of its composition.

The expansionary trend continued under the first New Democratic Party (NDP) government in Manitoba's history, elected in 1969 when Edward Schreyer became premier. The rate of growth of the civil service during the Schreyer governments (1969–1973 and 1973–1977) was approximately 5 percent annually, until the economic downturn hit in the mid-seventies and a restraint program was applied. Consistent with party priorities and its political bases of support, the Schreyer government introduced new programming and spending in education, health, northern affairs, and urban affairs. With its links to organized labour, the NDP government also granted binding arbitration rights in the collective bargaining process and political rights to civil servants.[11]

The defeat of the NDP in 1977 and the arrival of the Progressive Conservative government led by Sterling Lyon ushered in a more hostile environment for the civil service. The Conservatives had campaigned on the slogan of "acute protracted restraint" and they became forerunners of the neo-conservative movement which took power elsewhere during the 1980s. A task force on government efficiency led to downsizing in the public service (the number of jobs lost was in the 1300–2000 range) and to the privatization of several small Crown corporations. Sensing they would pay a political price for the zeal, as much as the extent, of their restraint efforts, the Conservatives backed off in the final year of their mandate. They still lost the 1981 provincial election and thereby became the first one-term government in Manitoba history.

The victory of Howard Pawley and the NDP in 1981 saw the pendulum swing towards an active role for the provincial government in the process of economic and social development. Facing an economic downturn, the Pawley government used Keynesian counter-cyclical budgeting to maintain demand for goods and services and to preserve jobs, including jobs in the civil service. This was also the real beginning of a continuing trend in which the civil service became itself the target of public policy. Under the Pawley government affirmative action supporting the entry and advancement of women in the civil service became an active concern, being adopted in 1983 on the basis of an agreement between the government and the Manitoba Government Employees Association. Later in 1996, during the Progressive Conservative government of Gary Filmon, the concept of employment equity was introduced into the civil service. The broader concept of diversity was part of the thinking of these earlier efforts to create a more representative public sector workforce, but a diversity strategy for the civil service was not officially adopted until 2003 when Gary Doer and his NDP government were in power. Diversity is a major focus of current civil service renewal efforts, as is discussed below.

By the mid-1980s, Pawley was leading the last NDP government in the country and in neighbouring Saskatchewan a Progressive Conservative government had begun privatizing Crown corporations and transforming its civil service based on new public management thinking. For Pawley and his key advisers, semi-independent Crown corporations were seen as more than pure business enterprises; instead they were regarded as public policy instruments to be used for economic and social development purposes. Scandals involving Crowns, especially the Manitoba Telephone System (MTS) and the Manitoba Public Insurance Corporation (MPIC) forced the government to introduce an elaborate framework of direction, control, and accountability for the Crown corporation sector.[12]

Not unrelated to problems with the Crowns, the Pawley government had been running annual deficits and increasing the debt during its first six years in office. When it moved to pay the bills by increasing taxes, a restive backbencher voted against the 1988 budget; the government fell and in the ensuing election the NDP became the third party in the legislature with just twelve seats.[13] For the next eleven years, then premier Gary Filmon and his Progressive Conservative government gave direction to the civil service. Before examining their record of public management, it is necessary to summarize briefly how the civil service had changed from the small, mainly operational organization of the nineteenth and early twentieth century to become in the Manitoba context a large institution which employs people in a wide variety of specialized fields, is the source of critical policy advice to ministers, and makes an important contribution to the quality of life in the province through the programs and services that it delivers.

The Civil Service at the End of the Twentieth Century

As the scope and complexity of government activity increased gradually during the twentieth century, governments come to rely more heavily upon the specialized knowledge and the management skills found within the evolving civil service, both to design public policy and to deliver programs in a professional manner. These developments led some commentators to suggest that the real policymakers no longer occupied the fifty-seven seats in the legislature or the fifteen to twenty seats in cabinet, but instead were to be found in the upper and middle ranks of the civil service. In support of this argument, they pointed to a number of trends of the second half of the twentieth century. In a changing communications environment, parties based their appeals to voters more on leadership and party images than on policy. As a result they came into office without a game plan and a clear electoral mandate. Policy experts in the upper and middle ranks of the civil service were obliged to fill the resulting void by drawing upon their institutional memories and the collective wisdom of departments concerning future policy directions. Increasingly, those same experts consulted outside stakeholder groups in advance, adding momentum and legitimacy to the policy advice they provided. There was also a small, but growing group of senior civil servants working within various intergovernmental arenas to advance Manitoba's interests. For these intergovernmental "diplomats" to be effective, governments had to grant them some freedom to negotiate agreements with other orders of government, deals which subsequently became the basis for policy and spending decisions. At the departmental level, the scope and complexity of activity, including the fact that many programs and services were delivered by other organizations (municipalities, regional health authorities, schools and colleges, etc.) meant that individual ministers could not be aware of, let alone be involved in, all the matters that went on within their portfolio. This made it harder to hold ministers accountable for actions and inactions that were controversial. Finally, most legislation passed by the legislature was general and vague and the real details of policy making were left to the regulations developed by departments and semi-independent boards and commissions of various kinds.

All of these developments led to a growing concern to ensure the responsiveness and accountability of the civil service to the premier and cabinet, while still preserving the independence and professionalism of the civil service to ensure that it was prepared to "speak truth to power" (as a popular slogan goes) and was able to administer programs in an impartial, objective manner. For several reasons, finding the appropriate balance was easier in Manitoba than in larger jurisdictions. Independence and impartiality was promoted by the disappearance of patronage and the application of the merit principle, overseen by the Civil Service Commission, in the vast majority of appointments to the regular civil service. On the other hand, with the growing number of non-departmental boards and commissions which were delegated regulatory, adjudicative, and advisory powers, "friends of the governing party" still had the inside track on appointment.

The fact that most regular departments remained relatively small meant that ministers had more opportunity for direct involvement with departmental matters. Manitoba has never had a huge policy apparatus so the risk of overwhelming ministers with specialized knowledge and expert policy advice was less than in larger governmental systems. Over the past four decades, total employment in the civil service has ranged from 12,000 to 15,000, but the vast majority of these individuals perform operational functions related to administration and delivery of programs. A report in 2001 from the Office of the Auditor General estimated that only 2 percent of civil servants were policy analysts, but this percentage was undoubtedly too low because by necessity many program managers are also required to do policy analysis. The recognition that the premier and cabinet needed access to countervailing advice to that flowing from the permanent civil service, led to the development of greater policy capacity at the centre of government in the Executive Council, a trend which began during the Schreyer era (1967–1977). However, Manitoba governments have generally been fearful of attracting criticism for building up a large policy advisory system serving the premier and other ministers. In addition to the small scale of government, face-to-face contacts daily between ministers and their deputy ministers is encouraged by their co-location in the Legislative Building.

To ensure reasonable responsiveness to the policy directions of the governing party, senior positions in the civil service are filled through cabinet appointment on the recommendation of the premier (referred to officially as Order-In-Council or OIC appointments). Chief among these positions is the Clerk of the Executive Council, who in the modern era of Manitoba politics has almost always had a partisan background. The clerk has a three-part job: to serve as deputy minister to the premier, as secretary to the cabinet, and as head of the civil service. In the latter role, he is the premier's chief advisor on the appointment of deputy ministers and tradition requires that he promotes non-partisanship in the senior civil service.

Manitoba's nineteen deputy ministers (as of March 2010) are also OIC appointments, as are assistant deputy ministers and directors above certain salary levels. Within the ranks of the deputies, there have usually been a small number of politically connected deputies, but most are neutral, career civil servants. The removal of senior and middle-ranked public servants when governments change has not taken place to the extent it has at times in other provinces. Before he became premier, Sterling Lyon (1977–1981) had promised to replace senior civil servants for reasons of political incompatibility and incompetence. In the end, three deputy ministers were fired and another forty-six senior managers were replaced, with approximately half of the replacements coming from outside the civil service.[14] In 1981, when Pawley replaced Lyon as premier, there was a reduction in the number of departments, three deputy ministers were removed and at least one deputy with clear political ties to the governing party was appointed.[15]

Even though wholesale purges of the civil service no longer occur, senior civil servants must be attuned to political realities and avoid, if at all possible, any actions that might be politically embarrassing. Civil servants up to the deputy minister level were granted limited political rights in the 1970s but they must be careful not to go too far in speaking their professional minds, especially in a public fashion. Creating a safe climate inside of government in which public managers are willing to speak their minds is easier said than done.

For many reasons the job of leading and managing in the civil service became more multi-dimensional and difficult during the final decades of the twentieth century. Externally, there were such forces as globalization and its impacts, economic downturns and budgetary restraint, the rise of neo-conservatism, leading to more ideological debates over the future role of governments, diminished trust and confidence in public office holders, greater insistence on transparency and citizen engagement and the spread on a global basis of new public management ideas. External scrutiny became more intense. The auditor general had been reporting on public spending problems since the nineteenth century, but by the twentieth century there were statutes and monitoring bodies on fairness in government action (the ombudsman), human rights, access to information, privacy and protection for civil servants who disclose serious wrongdoing in the public sector.

Internally, the civil service faced a series of challenges at the end of the twentieth century. There was, of course, the requirement to do more with less and to provide the assurance to ministers, the legislature, and the public that value for money in terms of effective programs and services were being delivered with the scarce tax dollars available. There were new performance measurement and reporting requirements to be met. There was also a quiet crisis developing in terms of human resource management issues. The baby boomers who had entered the civil service in the expansionary decades of the 1960s and 1970s were about to retire, taking with them their experience and knowledge. Finding the next generation of employees was made difficult by the poor image of the civil service and the need to compete with the private sector, especially in more specialized occupations where talent was in short supply. As revealed in employee surveys that began in 2001, a more professional civil service, with a higher proportion of so-called "knowledge workers," was looking for clear direction, meaningful work, autonomy, a supportive work environment, and a work/life balance. Creating a more diverse workforce and a respectful workplace was another expectation to be met by the leaders of the civil service. Finally, information and communications technology had major impacts on how public policy was developed, how programs and service were delivered and on the content and skill requirements of jobs in the civil service. Employee training and development became more important as both organizations and individuals in the civil service were expected to learn what works and to engage in continuous improvement.

This was the context of political, economic, social, and technological pressures that were driving public sector reform in the late twentieth century. The government of Manitoba and the civil service were obliged to cope with these changes. Arising from the "reinventing government" and NPM movements, there was a menu of public sector reform approaches and techniques from which the provincial government could choose. However, there were also the constraints of limited financial capacity, a public demand for affordable government, a relatively small civil service with less professional capability than larger jurisdictions, and an internal culture that favoured lower-key, more limited reforms over grand designs and rhetorical fanfare.

The Filmon Era

The civil service renewal initiatives of a series of Progressive Conservative governments (1988–1990, 1990–1995, and 1995–1999) led by Gary Filmon have been described in some detail elsewhere.[16] The purpose of this section is to interpret those public management developments in order to support a comparison to the approaches of the subsequent NDP governments (1999–2003, 2003–2007, 2007–

2009) led by Gary Doer. In comparing the approaches of the two governments, changed economic and political circumstances, the differences in the philosophy and leadership styles of the two premiers, and the changed intellectual climate in terms of the ascendancy of certain ideas of public management reform, all provide an explanation for the differences that are identified.

First elected as a minority government in 1988 and initially preoccupied with other issues, the Filmon government did not pay serious attention to civil service renewal until it gained majority status after the 1990 election. Then premier Gary Filmon was a university graduate in engineering and a businessman. He had served as a city councillor and briefly as a junior minister in the one-term government of Sterling Lyon (1977–1981). Elected leader of his party in 1983, Filmon was seen as an urban progressive in a party whose political centre of gravity was rural, fiscal, and social conservatism. His leadership was never fully accepted by right-wing elements within the party, especially after he lost the 1986 provincial election. As a self-described problem-solver, Filmon never felt comfortable in the opposition role which consisted mainly of criticism. Once in a majority position after 1990, he was able to apply his professional instincts as a planner and small businessman to the operations of government. Also, there was a gradual evolution in his thinking about the limits of government intervention and the need to operate public organizations in a more business-like manner. The story is told that he read the bestselling book by David Osborne and Ted Gabler, *Reinventing Government*,[17] and ordered copies for all ministers and deputies.

Changing economic and budgetary circumstances contributed to the emergence of Filmon as a political leader with stronger ideological convictions. During his time in opposition, he was critical of the NDP government for running up spending and being guilty of the politically motivated mismanagement of public organizations, especially Crown corporations. After the snap defeat of the Pawley government's budget in 1988, the Conservatives won a minority government in the ensuing election and in office they accepted the NDP tax increases, leaving them with an initial small surplus. However, the economic downturn of the early 1990s produced new budgetary challenges. These challenges were compounded by deep cuts to federal financial transfers (which comprised 30 to 40 percent of provincial revenues depending on which government was doing the calculation) arising from the deficit-fighting efforts of the national government; efforts Filmon supported in general but not with respect to transfers to the provinces.

Convinced that Manitobans wanted stricter financial management, the government passed a tough balanced-budget law in 1996 and froze personal income tax for seven consecutive years. In making the tough budgetary choices entailed with this fiscal policy stance, the Filmon government tried initially to protect the major provincial spending areas of education, health, and social services, but eventually the reality of limited revenues hit these program fields as well. Over the years Filmon escalated the rhetoric about the necessity for the provincial governments to withdraw from "non-core" activities, to rely upon the private sector more, to reduce federal-provincial "entanglements" and Manitoba's dependence on transfer payments, and to change the way that government "did business."

The responses by the Filmon government to the challenges of the 1990s were budgetary, structural, process, and cultural in character. Each category of reform initiative will be discussed briefly. Clearly the categories overlap and intersect in practice and there were some, not very successful efforts to align them in order to move the overall government system in the desired direction.

On the budgetary front, the Filmon government system began cautiously. Without much fanfare, it privatized in whole or in part several small Crown corporations and pocketed the revenues.[18] Once in a majority position after 1990 and facing an economic downturn, the government made selective cuts to the civil service and froze taxes, all done in the name of financial prudence and encouraging investor confidence. Employees who were laid off were placed on a redeployment list which meant that they had a slight advantage in applying as internal, rather than external, candidates when job openings were posted. Responding to a record deficit, the government legislated salary freezes for civil servants beginning in 1992. So-called "Filmon Fridays" were created in 1993 under legislation that forced employees of departments and Crown corporations to take ten unpaid days off each year. When the legislation ran out after five years, the unpaid days off were negotiated into the contracts with unionized workers. The government claimed that the reduced workweek saved $110 million and 500 civil service jobs. However, the unions claimed that "Filmon Fridays" were imposed without consultation and were followed by collective bargaining legislation which allowed the government to roll back public sector salary increases obtained through negotiation or arbitration awards.[19]

The 1995 budget was the first balanced budget in twenty-two years. Just as significant was the announcement of what was described as the toughest balanced-budget legislation (BBL) in the country.[20] The BBL prescribed a 20 percent salary cut for all cabinet ministers if the government failed to bring spending in line with revenues in any given year. It also required a province-wide referendum to increase personal, corporate, or sales taxes. Along with federal cutbacks in transfers, the BBL forced the civil service to follow the popular slogan of the day of "doing more with less."

In terms of structural reform, there were a number of initiatives. Privatization in the form of selling off Crown corporations and outsourcing the delivery of services gained momentum during the nineties. In 1996, without any discussion during the election of the preceding year which the Conservatives won, the Filmon government embarked on the highly controversial sale of the Manitoba Telephone System (MTS), a Crown corporation that had provided cheap, reliable telephone service to all parts of Manitoba going back to its founding in 1908. MTS was earning modest profits, which went into government coffers, but technology was forcing the company to face competition and a switch to stricter federal regulation was coming, making the future of the corporation in terms of dependable revenues less certain. The opposition NDP, the telecommunications unions, and citizen groups protested the privatization, but to no avail. The case for privatization—that a government enterprise required to carry public policy obligations could not survive in a dynamic, high-technology field like telecommunications—was not well presented by the Conservatives and undoubtedly the failure to prepare the public opinion for the MTS sale cost them votes in the 1999 election, which they lost.

Less political in inspiration, more bureaucratically driven and far less controversial was the decision to introduce Special Operating Agencies (SOAs). SOAs are a kind of hybrid which, depending upon the activity and structural features involved, reside halfway along a continuum between the traditional integrated department and use of the private sector to deliver public programs.[21] The aims of the SOA initiative were to reduce costs, to grant autonomy to managers and employees in order to encourage innovation, and to enhance service to either external or internal "customers." Agencies were usually created by separating part of an existing department, providing the small entities with focussed mandates, and insisting that, in return for a measure of freedom from central financial and administrative controls, agencies must demonstrate results, including "return on investment." The SOA experiment was led by the Treasury Board Secretariat (TBS), the management branch of the civil service. Departments were not compelled to adopt the concept, but they were encouraged to identify potential candidates for SOA status. Ministers and deputy ministers retained important levers of direction and control over SOA operations. Also, the employees of SOAs remained part of the civil service and members of the MGEU for collective bargaining purposes. In total seventeen agencies were created. Speaking to an international conference in 1999, former premier Filmon boasted that the SOA experiment had saved $13 million in efficiency gains and at the same time had improved service quality.

The NDP in opposition and the MGEU were not impressed. They saw the SOA experiment as driven by budgetary imperatives and as a stepping stone to the eventual privatization of existing public sector functions. In fact, only one activity moved fully from the public to the private sector. In practice, the independence of

SOAs from ministerial involvement and from central administrative controls was less than the theory of agencies implied, in part because ministers were still forced to answer for controversial agency decisions. Despite its earlier criticisms, when the NDP took office after the 1999 election, it kept the existing agencies, and created only one more agency in 2006. In 2008, the seventeen agencies collectively paid $21 million in "surpluses" to the Consolidated Revenue Fund, which explains in large measure why none have been eliminated.[22]

In the category of process reform, the major initiative of the Filmon government was called "Service First." It was inspired by the "reinventing" and "re-engineering" movements that had attracted the attention of then premier Filmon. During the nineties a number of projects based on these philosophies were launched, beginning with "Better Methods" (BM). Its objective was to overhaul the major internal processes of expenditure/revenue management, payroll/classification, procurement, and human resource management in order to achieve efficiencies, timeliness, and service quality. In conjunction with the SOA model, BM was meant to produce in the longer term a more "business-like" culture inside the civil service.

Using information technology to improve service delivery to businesses and individuals was another part of the Filmon agenda. In 1993 the Service First Initiative was launched. The initial focus was on improving the cost-effectiveness, timeliness, coordination, and integration of services delivered online, by telephone and in person, to business clients of government. Service improvements to individuals and the measurement of service satisfaction became the focus of subsequent efforts. Eventually, Service Manitoba, a division of the Civil Service Commission, assumed the lead role on the service modernization front and the SOA responsible for staff training began to offer courses on customer-focussed service delivery.

Unlike other areas of reform, this service innovation agenda was actually extended by the Doer government after it took office in 1999. In 2001, the department of Family Services and Housing began a service integration project, which led eventually to collaboration with the Winnipeg Regional Health Authority to provide a range of social and health services through community access centres in Winnipeg. A revamped government website, *At Your Service*, was launched in 2003 featuring clusters of services for designated users. In 2005 all three levels of government in Canada agreed to the creation of BizPal, a web-based service that allows businesses to obtain all the permits and licences they need from the different orders of government in one online location. By the end of 2009, the service involved the City Of Winnipeg and twenty-nine other Manitoba communities. Finally in 2007, Manitoba launched a Single Window Business Initiative to provide referrals and various levels of advice to business clients.

Performance measurement and performance reporting were strongly recommended in the new public management literature. In 1996, with a major speech by the premier, a framework for performance measurement and reporting called Manitoba Measures was announced. Based on a business planning model, there were three components to the framework:

- a set of government priorities, with which departments were expected to align their activities;
- business plans for each department outlining goals, strategies, resource requirements, and expected results;
- performance contracts which outlined specific "deliverables" at the departmental, program, and activity level.

The benefits claimed for the Manitoba Measures initiative were: improved strategic thinking, greater integration of policy and operations, better management of individual programs, and improved communication within and across departments.[23]

In opposition, the NDP expressed concern that Manitoba Measures meant "numbers" would drive budgetary cutbacks, especially to "softer" programs that were less amenable to quantitative measurement. They and the auditor general called for the publication of departmental business plans, but the government never agreed to such disclosure. Manitoba was following a growing performance movement across the world as governments sought to meet the demand of their publics that value for money be demonstrated. By the time that the NDP took office in 1999, the enthusiasm for performance measurement had waned, even in the leading jurisdictions, and the Doer government quietly replaced Manitoba Measures with the Priorities and Strategies program, which was tied more directly to the process for approving departmental spending plans. The slowing of the performance movement reflected, among other causes, the discouraging news that in most jurisdictions performance evidence was not being used to guide decision making.[24]

The Filmon reforms were inspired by the leading management ideas of the day and the "selling" of the reforms involved a fair amount of "hype." The premier's interest and enthusiasm for the ideas of reinvention, re-engineering, alternative service delivery, and a "customer friendly" public sector were shared by the Clerk of the Executive Council and a number of other senior civil servants who were frustrated by the cautious, gradual reform traditions of the civil service. Leading "gurus" of public management reform were brought to Manitoba, including on different occasions David Osborne and Ted Gaebler, the co-authors of the provocative bestseller *Reinventing Government*. On another occasion, a large meeting room was filled with senior and middle managers to hear Babak Armajani, the co-author of *Breaking Through Bureaucracy*. In June 1999, not long before it lost office, the government hosted a large and expensive "International Summit on Public Service Reform." Major corporate sponsors included the Deloitte and Touche Consulting Group, IBM Canada and SHL Systemhouse Corporation. A Nobel Prize winner and a dozen celebrity authors spoke to over 600 delegates representing fifteen countries. The majority of the speakers were converts to the reinvention movement, but there were also a few skeptics like the contrarian management thinker Henry Mintzberg. Then premier Filmon opened the event and Manitoba's renewal initiatives were featured very prominently throughout the two days. With generous government and corporate support, the conference made a modest profit and a follow-up event was planned, but the NDP government elected on 21 September 1999 cancelled those plans.

In summary, the combination of an economic downturn, budgetary stress, a premier whose convictions about a more limited role for government became stronger during his year in office, and the availability of new public management ideas, all contributed during the Filmon years to a reinvention and re-engineering agenda that was more ideological, radical, extensive, and aggressive than was the tradition of past Manitoba governments.

The Doer Decade (1999–2009): Leadership and Context

After serving a decade in opposition, the NDP under the leadership of Gary Doer won the provincial election of September 1999. Like all election outcomes, numerous long-term and short-term factors contributed to the NDP victory. The leader and senior party officials recognized that Manitobans trusted them least on matters of economic and financial management. Hard times during the nineties, combined with neo-conservative rhetoric, meant that many Manitobans had diminished expectations and confidence in government as an institution. The decision was made by the NDP party insiders to "under-promise" and hopefully to "over-deliver" in terms of their electoral commitments. Accordingly, the party made only five major commitments and then got a political break when the Conservatives promised a billion dollars of tax cuts and spending increases. Coming after a decade of austerity, the expensive Conservative promises seemed opportunistic to many Manitobans.

Over the decade that Doer served as premier, the province enjoyed, by historical standards, solid but not spectacular growth. In the second half of the decade, its annual growth rate exceeded the national average rate among provinces. Economic prosperity and population growth obviously improved the financial circumstances of the provincial government. It may also have been the case that the restraint measures introduced by the Filmon government had created more realistic expectations about the annual increases in spending than could realistically be expected. In addition, there were generous financial transfers from the national government, especially from the Liberal governments led by Jean Chrétien (1993–2003) and Paul Martin (2003–2006).

Upon taking office, the Doer government hired private consultants to review the province's finances and found $315 million in unbudgeted expenditures committed by the Filmon government prior to the changeover.[25] To comply with the Balanced Budget Law, which the NDP had promised during the election to retain, departments were ordered to practise strict financial control. Over the next ten years, Finance Minister Greg Selinger (who replaced Doer as premier in October 2009) produced ten balanced budgets comprised of modest tax cuts and spending increases targeted to strategic areas like education, health, social services, and Aboriginal budgets. "Living within its means" became a mantra of the Doer administration, which was determined to shed the tax-and-spend image of past NDP governments.

Gary Doer had stated during the election campaign that policy, not ideology, would be the focus when the NDP took power. This functional approach of creating a public sector which worked better and was affordable reflected the background of the new premier. Doer had undertaken some university studies before entering the juvenile correctional services field with the provincial government. In 1979 he became president of the MGEU, after having moved rapidly up the ranks in the union. Courted by both of Manitoba's main political parties, Doer chose the NDP and was first elected to the legislature in 1986. Appointed almost immediately as minister of urban affairs, he became known as a "problem solver" in the crisis-prone Pawley government. For example, in the wake of Crown corporation scandals, he took charge in creating a framework of direction and control over these semi-independent institutions. Following the surprise defeat of the budget in 1988 and the resignation of then premier Pawley, Doer became leader of the party (but declined to be sworn in as premier) at a point when it was so low in the polls that it finished third in the 1988 election. Eleven years in the opposition followed with the last nine spent as leader of the official opposition.

As premier after 1999, Doer's leadership philosophy and style was more pragmatic and transactional than visionary and transformational. His approach to policy making emphasized the importance of context, the feasibility of the actions being contemplated, and the necessity to mobilize support from the relevant stakeholders. As the leader of a relatively small governmental system, Doer did not see the necessity for radical restructuring, elaborate planning exercises, and the adoption of "best practices" which the "gurus" claimed were working elsewhere. Rather he preferred to provide clear political direction to the civil service based on a limited number of priorities and steady progress towards their achievement. Never too far ahead of public opinion, Doer created the appearance of governing on a consensus basis that left few openings for his political opponents to attack government actions.

This same approach was applied to the issue of civil service renewal. It was perceived by the premier and his key advisers that there was a lack of congruence between the budgetary policy of the Filmon government built upon cutbacks, layoffs, and privatization, and the rhetoric about transforming the civil service into a vital institution on the leading edge of change. To avoid such a perceived contradiction, the Doer government sought to create a renewal strategy that was aligned with the limits of available revenues. Money could not be spent on management consultants and conferences when money was scarce for health, education, and social services. To use a phrase popular with Premier Doer, "the optics" of spending " large" amounts of public money on civil service renewal would not be good politics. So if renewal was to take place it had to happen in an affordable and politically defensible manner.

In contrast to Gary Filmon who endorsed, at least rhetorically, the distinction (made popular by Osborne and Gaebler of reinventing government fame) between "steering" (policy) and "rowing" (operations), Gary Doer once described policy and operations as "two ends of the same stick."[26] He went on to emphasize that whatever the formal arrangements for dividing the work of government between ministers and civil servants, it is ministers who are ultimately answerable and pay a political price when something goes wrong. It was the role of the premier and cabinet to set priorities and to ensure coherence in policy making. It was the job of individual ministers and their departments to generate policy options, especially options which aligned with centrally determined priorities and fit within the constraints of the balanced budget law. Whereas Filmon's reinvention agenda was directed out of the offices of the premier and the Executive Council, Doer's renewal strategy for the civil service was directed mainly by the Civil Service Commission working with and through the deputy minister community.

Policy and Program Coordination

This approach was reflected in the structures and procedures of the Doer cabinet. Twice yearly there were cabinet and caucus retreats to discuss policy directions, legislation and spending issues. There were a small number of cabinet committees, including several that grouped ministers by policy sectors. Typically, committees were composed of five to six ministers, with provision at times for participation by backbench MLAS.

An innovation of the Doer era was the creation in March 2002 of the Healthy Child Committee of Cabinet, whose membership consisted of seven ministers representing portfolios that touched upon child development issues. A "mirror committee" of deputy ministers supports the committee. The cabinet committee approved a healthy child strategy, created the Healthy Child Manitoba Office with its own budget, and established a consultative network with partners in the community. A Healthy Child Manitoba Act, proclaimed in 2007, was intended to make these child-centred policy structures permanent in government. Similar structural arrangements for Aboriginal and poverty issues were also created to promote those government-wide priorities. However, given a cabinet of fifteen to twenty members, there is a limit to how many such committees can be created for these purposes.

An alternative strategy might be to create additional policy and coordination capacity at the centre in the Executive Council Office, which supports the premier and the cabinet. In fact, the size of that office has not grown over the past two decades, mainly because of a potential public backlash against an enlarged executive branch. Under the leadership of Paul Vogt, the clerk of the Executive Council since 2005, there has been a determined effort to communicate cabinet thinking and decisions to the group of nineteen deputy ministers at their weekly meetings. While there have been some changed assignments among the deputies, there has been relative stability in terms of the actual members of the group. One deputy minister with twenty-five years of experience, interviewed for this study, observed that he had never witnessed as much collegiality within the deputy group as existed at the end of the Doer era.

While acknowledging progress, Paul Vogt indicated in a 2009 interview the need for the civil service generally, not just at the senior level, to become less conscious of departmental boundaries.[27] One step taken to overcome "departmentalism" was the creation in June 2007 of the Cross-Departmental Coordination Initiatives Division (CDCI) which spans the departments of Family Services and Housing (FSH) and Health and Healthy Living (HHL). CDCI also works in partnership with the Winnipeg Regional Health Authority and community-based organizations to improve policy coordination, coordinate strategies, and integrate service delivery in areas such as housing, health, and social services, especially for mental health clients and seniors. Responsibility for leading the CDCI process has been assigned to an assistant deputy minister in HHL. A series of working teams have conducted stakeholder reviews and have become involved in the implementation of existing and new projects related to homelessness, mental health issues and seniors concerns. Given that resources exceed demand, a coordinated approach to resource allocation has been a challenge, which adds to the problem of merging different mandates, program responsibilities and cultures into a coherent, unified approach. As new as CDCI is, it would be premature to declare whether it is successful in terms of outcomes in society.

Policy capacity at the departmental level shrank during the Filmon years when policy and planning units across government were deemed expendable in the face of severe budgetary restraint. In 2001, a study by the Auditor General reported that 60 percent of senior managers identified a shortage of money, staff, and time to do policy development work. The potential consequences were poor policy advice and untimely responses.[28] The negative impacts of budgetary restraint on departments was uneven, with some being able to hold more of their policy capacity and others able to stretch their capacity through the establishment of informal policy networks. Looking forward, the clerk of the Executive Council suggested in 2009 that the solution to limited policy capacity was to have managers reach out to the delivery ranks to obtain policy ideas—another expression of the philosophy that policy and operations are two points on a continuum.[29]

A risk in terms of both policy and management capability is the fact that by 2016, almost 75 percent of senior leaders in the civil service will be eligible to retire. By the same year, almost 50 percent of the entire civil service will be in a position to retire. These statistics have profound significance for government-wide policy memory and the in-house capacity to formulate policy under more complex conditions. As mentioned earlier, the competition to attract and to retain talent has become stiffer, the government is committed to the creation of a more representative civil service at all levels, and civil servants were declaring in employee surveys that they wanted more autonomy and more meaningful work.

Civil Service Renewal: People and Values

Discussions on civil service renewal began upon the arrival of the Doer administration, but the process was slow to gain momentum. In July 2003, the clerk of the Executive Council appointed a nine-member deputy minister advisory committee on human resources which became the central forum to co-ordinate renewal activities. The committee continues to meet every three weeks to discuss renewal matters. Each of the eighteen departments was required to identify a senior official, called the Renewal Authority (RA), to serve as the point of contact with the committee. There were also interdepartmental project teams established to deal with various aspects of renewal. While the committee identified renewal initiatives, it was mainly left to the departments to translate them into action, largely according to their own pace with moral suasion serving as the main basis to bring laggards along.

The whole process was a lean, low-key affair, involving limited spending, few staff dedicated exclusively to the renewal strategy, and little fanfare. An employee survey conducted in 2004 found that fewer than 20 percent of respondents knew of the renewal strategy, suggesting there were communications challenges to be met.[30] In the 2005 budget, the renewal strategy was mentioned as being connected to the challenge of delivering quality services when money and talent were in short supply. The appointment of a new civil service commissioner, the establishment of the position of an assistant civil service commissioner, and the reorganization of that department in 2006 increased the momentum behind the renewal program. In 2009, the clerk of the Executive Council described the program as a "step-by-step" process scaled to the financial and organizational capacities of the government in order to ensure the long-term sustainability of the reforms.[31]

There were numerous renewal initiatives launched over the past ten years. Leadership development has been a major theme within the overall renewal strategy. There was a Leadership Development Initiative (for senior level succession), a Women's Leadership Program (to achieve better gender balance), a Leadership @ All Levels Program (to develop skills at working collaboratively), a Financial Management Development Program (to enhance financial skills), an Essentials of Supervision Certificate Program (for operational people moving into management roles), and a general Public Sector Management Certificate Program (for employees making career plans to move into management). The measures of progress for these various leadership initiatives were the number of participants and the career paths of graduates.

Under the theme of diversity in the civil service, there are a number of initiatives: recruitment campaigns targeted at underrepresented groups, internship programs (some of which came into existence in the latter years of the Filmon government), career assistance (for example, to disabled employees), an Aboriginal Management Development program, an Aboriginal Public Administration Program, a mentoring program, and an annual employment equity conference. The main measure of success has been the number of employment equity group members as a percentage of total employees and at different levels within the civil service. Creating a respectful workplace has also been a goal of the diversity program, which has been measured by the percentage of employees indicating in employee surveys whether their departments recognize the value of diversity. An annual conference on employment equity and diversity has been held to allow employees to discuss their work experiences.

Succession planning, along with the recruitment and retention of qualified, motivated, and loyal employees have been major components of the renewal process. Deputy ministers were expected to ensure that analysis of the future staffing needs of their departments were prepared, along with plans to fill gaps in terms of knowledge and skills. To overcome the image of the civil service as a hierarchical, rule-bound organization, new outreach activities and a new orientation program were introduced. To provide intellectual challenges and to promote innovation, a network of young professionals was established in 2005. By 2008, 370 employees were organizing and participating in regular learning events staged by the network. Along similar lines, employees were encouraged to develop and discuss with their supervisors individual learning plans to support the development of their careers. Beginning with a pilot project in the Education department, all departments were encouraged to develop corporate learning plans to be aligned with their general strategic plans and their succession plans. Departmental progress in terms of the preparation of these three types of planning documents was variable and "the centre" (the Executive Council and the Civil Service Commission) encouraged, rather than coerced, laggards into doing better.

The promotion of ethical awareness and behaviour was another component of the renewal program. Like other jurisdictions, Manitoba's civil service debated at some length the title, content, and tone of the document which would be used to promote a culture of integrity. It rejected a legalistic-sounding title such as a charter or code in favour of the lower-key phrase a "values and ethics guide." Whether providing advice or delivering program, civil servants were expected to act in the public interest, with integrity, respect for others, and with skill and dedication. Only five pages long, the guide was conversational rather than directive (it was not the more popular "Ten Commandments" model). It acknowledged the impossibility of having a rule for every ethically problematic situation, presented a series of questions for employees to consider when confronting such situations and identified sources where advice could be obtained. Underlying this approach was the intention to send a message that the ethical foundations of the civil service were sound and that the focus should be less on detecting wrongdoing and more on avoiding ethically problematic situations. The announcement of the values and ethics guide was low key. The guide is on the website, each new employee receives a copy, it has become part of the orientation for new civil servants, and training on the guide became mandatory for supervisors. Senior managers were encouraged to include the guide in all planning and performance management activity in their departments, but there is no formal monitoring of what departments are doing to promote high ethical awareness and standards of behaviour.

A similar philosophy informed the development of "The Public Interest Disclosure (Whistleblower Protection) Act," and a revised Conflict of Interest Policy, both of which came into effect in 2007. The whistleblower legislation applied initially to departments, four officers of the Legislative Assembly, agencies under the Financial Administration Act (e.g., Crown corporations), regional health authorities, child and family service authorities, personal care homes, and an assortment of other named public bodies. In 2007–2008, the coverage of the act was extended to universities, community health centres, residential care facilities, child care facilities, social housing units, and family violence crisis centres.

Employees have three avenues for disclosure: to their supervisor, to the designated office in their organization, or to the ombudsman. However, the legal structure of the act encourages employees to use internal channels of communication first, unless there are compelling reasons to go outside their departments with good-faith disclosures of serious wrongdoing. The Civil Service Commission oversees the administration of the act. The act offers protection against reprisal. Complaints about reprisals can be filed with the Manitoba Labour Board, who can order a number of remedies for proven reprisal, including the reinstatement of a demoted or dismissed employee. The whistleblower law is still very new and there have been only a couple of legitimate cases to date.

Resources and Results

One of the goals of renewal was "sustainability." The phrase meant that renewal would allow for quality services to be provided despite budgetary limits and turnover in the ranks of the civil service. Avoiding a contradiction between the budgetary and renewal policies was a lesson learned from the Filmon period. The fact that Doer's finance minister, Greg Selinger, also served as the minister responsible for the Civil Service Commission went a long way to ensuring that human resource initiatives would be strictly costed and affordable. In 2000, the Labour Relations Division (responsible for collective bargaining, classification, pay and benefits, etc.) was transferred from the Civil Service Commission to the Treasury Board Secretariat with the clear message that classification was more a budgetary than a human resource management issue.

Back in 1995 the Filmon government undertook a reduction and efficiency exercise involving the human resource functions of recruitment, selection, staffing, etc. Departments went from having their own human resources directors/branches to a sharing arrangement based on six sectors in which two to five departments shared human resources services. This meant that human resources directors reported to two or more deputy ministers within their sectors. Deputies in smaller departments complained of their needs being crowded out by the demands of larger departments within their sector. The sector approach continued until March 2010 at which time HR directors and their staff were assigned a reporting relationship to the Civil Service Commission. This realignment of HR functions was intended to address inconsistent practices across departments, a lack of coordination of human resource plans with government-wide priorities, and the uneven levels of training/development for HR specialists across government. Quantitative and qualitative measures to track progress under the realigned structure have been adopted. Along the same lines of strengthening the Civil Service Commission, the SOA called Organization and Staff Development was brought back into the administrative framework of the commission with the aim of integrating its activities into the renewal program.

Mention was made earlier of the Doer government decision to drop the Manitoba Measures program used by the Filmon government to discard or improve ineffective programs. During its initial years in office, the Doer government relied upon the annual estimates review process and strategic program overviews submitted by departments to integrate planning and budgeting. At the time, other jurisdictions that were once seen as leaders in the field were beginning to scale back their performance measurement efforts based on the recognition that too much was being measured, at too high a cost and with too little impact on decision making.[32] The decision was made in Manitoba to be more selective and relevant by focussing on outputs and outcomes that related to the government's commitments. A two-level approach was adopted. In 2005, a discussion paper (titled *Reporting to Manitobans on Performance*) was issued by the Manitoba Bureau of Statistics, presumably with the approval of government. This led to the production of a social indicators type of report on how government actions had affected the economy, environment, community, and people of Manitoba. This focus and content was quite different from the business-line reports produced during the Filmon years. *Reporting to Manitobans* was a public document, meant to promote understanding of the positive role of government, but it seems unlikely that many Manitobans have read the document.

There is a second level of performance reporting for individual departments. Beginning in 2005–2006 all departments were required to include a performance measurement section, in a standardized format, in their annual reports which are posted on line. In May 2008 the Treasury Board Secretariat issued a fifteen-page document on *Performance Reporting Principles and Guidelines* intended to assist departments. It was indicated that the frameworks for reporting would continue to evolve as problems changed and learning took place. There is a large amount of performance evidence being gathered within the civil service today, in response not only to the new policy but also to the requirement for the province to file data with the national government in connection with transfer payments and joint programs.

Creating a performance culture inside of any governmental system is a slow and uncertain process and the Manitoba government has a long way to go in terms of making performance evidence count in decision making of all kinds, but especially in the budgetary process. Like other jurisdictions, Manitoba has not mastered the dual challenges of developing logic models and causal analysis to link outputs to outcomes in society and creating the right incentives for politicians and civil servants to use performance evidence.[33]

Measurement of progress was also meant to be part of the renewal process. A small number of indicators for each of the renewal initiatives began to be published in the 2007 annual report of the Civil Service Commission. Another means of tracking progress were the random sample surveys of all government employees conducted every three years beginning in 1998. The surveys were designed, conducted, and analyzed by the Civil Service Commission. The 2007 survey contained 106 questions, many of which pertained to renewal, and many could be benchmarked to the three previous surveys.

Only some highlights of the 2007 survey as they relate to renewal can be presented in the space available here. The main drivers of employee satisfaction were identified as: authority/autonomy, clear directions, a supportive work environment, meaningful work, and work/life balance. These factors were prominent in similar surveys in other jurisdictions. Seventy percent of staff indicated they were satisfied with their job, down slightly from 77 percent in 2004. Approximately 60 percent of respondents felt they received the necessary training to do their work (the same percentage as 2004) and 59 percent said their departments supported work-related learning and development (up from 51 percent in 2004). Three quarters of respondents indicated their immediate supervisors provided clear direction, but almost half of respondents expressed frustration with the lack of a clear vision and shifting priorities at the top of their departments. Just over 40 percent felt confident in the leadership skills of senior managers and a similar percentage of employees felt senior managers communicated adequately and sought enough employee input. As part of a multi-jurisdictional initiative a series of common questions to measure employee engagement with their work were posed. Overall, Manitoba's engagement score was 60 percent, slightly less than the average of 63 percent for a number of provincial/territorial governments.

Communication about the renewal program during its first three years was limited, low-key, and uneven across departments. It became more extensive and promotional after the program was mentioned in the 2005 budget. Still in keeping with the quiet tradition of the Manitoba civil service, there was no elaborate, expensive fanfare used to promote the program. As a former deputy minister put it: "We prefer the whisper campaign over the big banner." The problem with whispering campaigns is the message may not be heard, especially at the outer reaches of a 14,000-person civil service that is mainly concentrated in Winnipeg but has a significant presence across the province. Awareness of the program is important, not only to ensure that all interested employees are able to take advantage of the various opportunities it presents but also to instill pride in them about being civil servants. In the 2004 employee survey, less than 20 percent of respondents were aware of the renewal initiative, but the 2007 survey registered progress with 42.5 percent indicating awareness. As this chapter is being completed (March 2010) a handbook on renewal is being developed and new leadership at the Civil Service Commission is putting a greater emphasis on getting the renewal message out. Since 1999 the provincial government has annually bestowed Service Excellence Awards on individual employees and teams who are recognized as having provided outstanding service to communities and citizens. The ministerial statements announcing such awards have often tied civil service efforts to economic growth in the province, another reflection of the government's view that renewal has to be defended in bottom-line financial terms, not just in terms of creating a happy, self-fulfilled workforce.

In an interview in May 2009, the clerk of the Executive Council, Paul Vogt, observed that the Doer government's approach reflected scepticism towards ideas of "revolutionizing" or "transforming" the civil service. He compared renewal to Manitoba's economy and culture in general: "We don't have a boom and bust economy, and when it comes to government programs and the public service, we look for improvements that are realistic and sustainable over time."[34]

A slow-and-steady approach (more tortoise than hare) may fit with Manitoba's economic, political, and administrative traditions, but whether it is adequately positioning the civil service to meet future economic, financial, social, and political realities is a question that needs to be discussed more extensively and openly. Diminished policy capacity in some key policy fields must remain a serious concern.

Conclusions

The Doer decade was a period of relatively good economic times, leading to fairly strong revenue growth for the provincial government, topped up by generous federal financial transfers in many major policy fields. Those favourable circumstances did not remove the necessity for choice and trade-offs in the provincial budgetary process. However, they did create more financial room to manoeuvre and allowed for spending increases and civil service hirings in priority areas like education, health, justice, and social services. The government could also afford wage increases to public sector employees that allowed them to recover ground lost during the prior decade of restraint and unpaid days off. Ten balanced budgets were produced between 1999 and 2009 through a financially and politically skillful combination of modest tax cuts and targeted spending increases that provoked little controversy.

Generalizations about the civil service have to be presented carefully because each of the eighteen departments and different occupational segments of the 14,000 civil service employees have dealt with both common and different circumstances over the past two decades. For example, the budget of Manitoba Health has grown at an annual rate of 6 to 8 percent, but most of its spending is done through regional health authorities and other outside bodies and the department must struggle to steer a complicated health system mainly by remote control. With health accounting for nearly 40 percent of total provincial spending, other departments like Agriculture and Industry were forced to absorb the rising costs of operations in their existing budgets and with existing or reduced staff levels. Mindful of their image as a "tax-and-spend" party, and of Doer's past as an MGEU president, the NDP in office wanted to avoid the charge that they were aggressively expanding the civil service, caving in to the wage demands of their public sector union allies and indulging individual civil servants with personal growth opportunities. There was never a large budgetary allocation for renewal. Most of the work was done by deputy ministers and other public managers designing and leading initiatives at the departmental level as part of their ongoing duties.

If a decade of prosperity created an opportunity to invest in civil service renewal, the end of the Doer era brought tougher financial circumstances. The worldwide economic downturn which began in 2008 was slow to arrive in Manitoba, but the government's reigning philosophy of financial prudence was reflected in the direction to departments to trim all non-essential spending. Gary Doer announced his resignation as party leader in August 2009 and a day later he was appointed as Canada's ambassador to the U.S. The leadership race to replace him culminated in the October 2009 election of Greg Selinger, minister of finance for the preceding decade. Given that Selinger was the designer of ten budgets, served as the chair of the Treasury Board committee of cabinet which reviewed all departmental spending, and also was the minister responsible for the Civil Service Commission, a major change of direction on renewal matters is not to be expected. Tight financial circumstances forecast for the next two to three years will force the Selinger government to take a tougher bargaining position with unionized employees across the public sector broadly defined. Initially, the new premier indicated that drastic actions such as wage freezes and layoffs were not on the table, but by early 2010 the MGEU, the main union representing civil servants, was being offered a choice between wage freezes and layoffs. Skeptics suggested that the government's stance was to avoid any public impression that the NDP was too cozy with its union allies. The severity of the present economic and financial circumstances do not rival those faced by the Filmon government during the nineties. Even if the context was comparable, it is more likely that an NDP government would emphasize job retention in the public sector than would a Progressive Conservative government.

It is now widely recognized that the ideas of reinvention and NPM which were fashionable during the 1990s no longer have the resonance and appeal with governments that they once had. In part, this is because in practice those ideas did not live up to the hype which initially supported their adoption. Gary Filmon was a gradual convert to transformational approaches to modernization of the public sector whereas Gary Doer was from the beginning a pragmatic skeptic about sweeping public management reform initiatives. He saw his mandate as providing Manitobans with what they have always wanted: an affordable government that works effectively to add value to society. Currently there is no ascendant paradigm in the public management field which might inspire transformational approaches to the design and delivery of public policy. The notion of "New Public Governance" probably comes closest to such status.[35] In a complex, interdependent, rapidly changing world, NPG involves governments working extensively with other institutions and actors to steer society in new directions. A collaborative, networked approach was central to Doer's leadership over his decade in office so senior and middle-range civil servants have become familiar with and more skilled at leading and managing across jurisdictional organizational boundaries.[36] This trend is likely to continue as Manitoba governments seek new policy ideas outside of the civil service, look for more efficient and effective ways to deliver programs and services through third parties, and seek to bolster citizen involvement and confidence in government.

Notes

1. The author would like to thank Curtis Brown for his excellent research assistance, including the conducting of a series of not-for-attribution interviews with senior civil servants involved with the Renewal Strategy. Thanks and appreciation must also be extended to those anonymous civil servants who shared information and insights on a confidential basis. The chapter would have been much weaker without their contribution. Also to be thanked are four people who read the first draft of the chapter, provided helpful factual and interpretative advice, and can be named: John Cumberford, Christopher Dunn, Kenneth Rasmussen, and Doug Smith. The author is responsible, of course, for any misinformation or misinterpretation that remains.
2. Donald Leitch and Guy Gordon, "Collaborative Partnerships: A New Model of Central Agency-Departmental Cooperation," in *Collaborative Government: Is There a Canadian Way?* ed. Susan Delacourt and Donald G. Lenehan (Toronto: Institute of Public Administration of Canada, 1999), 49–59; Ken Rasmussen, "The Manitoba Civil Service: A Quiet Tradition in Transition," in *Government Restructuring and Career Public Service in Canada*, ed. Evert Lindquist (Toronto: Institute of Public Administration of Canada, 2000), 349–73.
3. Doug Smith, Jack Bates, and Esyllt Jones, *Lives in the Public Service: A History of the Manitoba Government Employees' Union* (Winnipeg: Manitoba Labour Education Centre, 1993).
4. Murray Donnelly, *The Government of Manitoba* (Toronto: University of Toronto Press, 1963), 120.
5. Smith, Bates, and Jones, *Lives in the Public Service*, 7.
6. Lionel Orlikow, "The Reform Movement in Manitoba, 1910–1915" (Winnipeg: Manitoba Historical Society Transactions Series, 1959), 3, http://www.mhs.mb.ca/docs/tranasctions/3/reformmovement.shtml (accessed 1 April 2010).
7. Smith, Bates, and Jones, *Lives in the Public Service*, 22–23 and 89–90.
8. Ibid., 138–139.
9. Howard Scarrow, "Civil Service Commissions in the Canadian Provinces," *Journal of Politics* 19, 2 (1957): 243.
10. Ibid., 245.
11. Smith, Bates, and Jones, *Lives in the Public Service*, ch. 7.
12. Howard Pawley, "In the Public's Interest: The Governance of Crown Corporations," in C. Dunn (ed.) *Provinces: Canadian Provincial Politics*. Peterborough, Ont: Broadview Press, 1996), 301–20; Paul G. Thomas, "The Governing of Crown Corporations: The Role of Boards of Directors," *Public Sector Management*, Fall 1990, 18–20.
13. See Ian Stewart, *Just One Vote: From Jim Walding's Nomination to Constitutional Defeat* (Winnipeg: University of Manitoba Press, 2009), for a detailed account of these events.
14. Ian Wilson, "Derek Bedson: Clerk of the Executive Council of Manitoba, 1958 to 1981" (MA thesis, University of Manitoba, 2001), 114.
15. Levin Benjamin, *Managing Change Under Restraint: Post-secondary Education Reform in Manitoba* (Toronto: IPAC Case Study Program, 1988)
16. Leitch and Gordon, "Collaborative Partnerships"; Rasmussen, 2003.
17. David Osborne and Ted Gabler, *Reinventing Government* (Reading, MA: Addison-Wesley, 1992).
18. Smith, Bates, and Jones, *Lives in the Public Service*, 260–266.

19 Ibid., 278.
20 Patrick Gannon, "Manitoba's Balanced Budget, Debt Repayment and Taxpayer Protection Act," *Canadian Review* 19, 2 (1996): 70–75.
21 Paul Thomas and John Wilkins, "Special Operating Agencies: A Culture of Change in the Government of Manitoba," in *Alternative Service Delivery: Sharing Governance in Canada*, ed. Robin Ford and David Zussman (Toronto: KPMG/IPAC, 1997).
22 See the website of the Treasury Board Secretariat of Manitoba, http://www.gov.mb.ca/finance/treasury.
23 Leitch and Gordon, "Collaborative Partnerships."
24 Paul G. Thomas, "Why Is Performance-Based Accountability So Popular in Theory and So Difficult in Practice?" in *Holy Grail or Achievable Quest? International Perspectives on Public Sector Performance Management*, ed. John Herhalt (Brussels: KPMG International, 2008), 169–92.
25 Joan Grace, "Cabinet Structure and Executive Style in Manitoba," in *Executive Styles in Canada: Cabinet Structures and Leadership Practices in Canadian Government*, ed. Luc Bernier, Keith Brownsley, and Michael Howlett (Toronto: University of Toronto Press, 2005), 174.
26 The occasion was a meeting in 1987 of board chairs and CEOs of Crown corporations at which Doer explained the Pawley government's new framework for the governance of Crown corporations.
27 Paul Vogt, "Reflecting Manitoba," *Canadian Government Executive*, May 2009, 16–18.
28 Office of the Provincial Auditor of Manitoba, *A Review of the Policy Development Capacity within Government Departments* (Winnipeg, 2001), http://www.oag.mb.ca.
29 Vogt, "Reflecting Manitoba."
30 Service Manitoba, 2004.
31 Vogt, "Reflecting Manitoba."
32 Thomas, "Why Is Performance-Based Accountability So Popular in Theory and So Difficult in Practice?"
33 Ibid.
34 Vogt, "Reflecting Manitoba."
35 Peter Aucoin, "New Public Management and New Public Governance: Finding the Balance," in *Professionalisms and Public Service: Essays in Honour of Kenneth Kernaghan*, ed. David Siegel and Ken Rasmussen (Toronto: University of Toronto Press, 2008), 16–33.
36 See Paul Thomas's chapter "Leading from the Middle" in this volume.

A Practitioner's Reflections on the Practice of Federalism[1]

Jim Eldridge

Readers should be warned that the text that follows is what's sometimes called a "high altitude" overview. It touches on many events and personalities, but does not do proper justice to any of them. Students are advised to look to other sources for more complete information on the subjects mentioned here.

I started working for the Manitoba government more than forty years ago, in February 1968, in the Federal-Provincial Relations and Research Division of the Treasury Department. This department was the fiscal and economic policy unit in the department, and also the place where most of the government's staff work on intergovernmental relations was done. Walter Weir was the premier, having been chosen by his party the previous year to succeed Duff Roblin. Then, as now, financial issues generally dominated the agenda of federal-provincial relations, and finance departments were the focal point for coordination.

When I walked in the office door, situated on the main floor of the Legislative Building, I was delighted to see Paul Thomas already well established there. In fact, Paul was heavily engaged in two major projects—helping prepare the Manitoba government's response to the Benson White Paper on Tax Reform, and helping draft the province's position on constitutional reform. I did not realize it at the time, but I was coming into the federal-provincial relations field as the sun was setting on the so-called "golden age" of cooperative federalism, which happened to coincide with the Pearson years of minority government. In the previous year, under the direct leadership of former Manitoban Mitchell Sharp, then Canada's finance minister, the federal government had passed the 1967 Fiscal Arrangements Act, which brought in the comprehensive, ten-province national average equalization system, along with revenue stabilization arrangements and a new post-secondary education financing system. Meanwhile, the federal government was also putting the finishing touches on the Medicare Act and the financing arrangements that went with it, complementing the Hospital Insurance Act of a decade earlier. In the previous year, it had implemented the Canada Assistance Plan, and, of course, the Canada Pension Plan and the Quebec Pension Plan were beginning at the same time as well. There were also shared-cost programs for capital investments in health and post-secondary education, for economic and regional development, and for a great many other priorities. The Manitoba government was heavily involved in all the relevant negotiations. In fact, as far back as the 1930s and early 1940s, Manitoba's then-premier, John Bracken, had been a leading advocate of a National Adjustment Grant or equalization system to address provincial economic and fiscal disparities resulting from national policies such as tariffs and freight rates which favoured growth in central Canada. These positions were articulated at length in the province's submission to the Rowell-Sirois Commission.

In the late 1960s, all the large-scale arrangements were managed by a series of federal-provincial technical committees which met regularly under the oversight of ministers, and especially the ministers of finance and provincial treasurers and their deputies, who met as the Continuing Committee on Fiscal and Economic Matters.[2] Those were heady times for those with an interest in intergovernmental relations. The mechanisms for consultation and cooperation seemed to work pretty well, and new ones were also being developed. Executive federalism was alive, well and growing, and Manitoba was an active and enthusiastic participant and contributor. The provincial government recognized the major significance of federal policies, programs, and financial arrangements for Manitoba's development, and often played the role of positive consensus-builder or honest broker, looking for common ground between larger and smaller provinces and between east and west.

At the start of that decade, in 1960, the premiers of Quebec, Ontario, and Manitoba (with Duff Roblin serving as premier, of course; vision, intellect, and personality do matter) led in the establishment of the annual premiers' conferences. These were created to develop strategies and help build consensus among provinces for dealing with Ottawa, as well as to cooperate in their own areas of responsibility.[3] In 1965, premiers Roblin, Ross Thatcher of Saskatchewan, and Ernest Manning of Alberta began the Prairie Economic Council to deal with regional cooperation. In 1967, the premier of Ontario hosted the Confederation of Tomorrow conference, giving momentum to a new look at federal institutions. Around the same time, the finance ministers started working intensively, as the "Tax Structure Committee," to try to realign roles, responsibilities and revenues in a rational way. Manitoba contributed to virtually every aspect of this work.

It is little wonder that period was seen as the "golden age." The federal treasury was comparatively healthy and most of the provinces were in relatively good financial shape as well. One obvious conclusion is that good economic and fiscal times are conducive to dialogue and cooperation—probably not a surprise to even the most casual observer. Challenging or bad times can also foster positive joint action, but not always, as will be noted later.

By the late 1960s, partly because of growing attention being focused on the division of powers and other constitutional issues, some of the provinces—Ontario and Quebec in particular—were starting to increase the number of staff who specialized in non-financial intergovernmental work, although these bureaucrats continued to work within their finance departments. TEIGA, Treasury, Economics and Intergovernmental Affairs, was one of the departmental acronyms in Ontario. It was not until 1972 that the first free-standing provincial intergovernmental department—Federal and Intergovernmental Affairs (FIGA)—was established in Alberta when the Lougheed government came into office. Alberta's department, which also had important system-wide policy and coordination responsibilities, had its own minister, as did the intergovernmental affairs departments in other provincial governments throughout the years. Now, though, most premiers are their own intergovernmental ministers, a practice which remains in place in Manitoba at present.

Within a decade or so, most provinces had intergovernmental units outside finance departments, some of which were fairly large (Quebec, Alberta, and Ontario) and some quite small, such as Manitoba's. As an aside, I should note that Paul Thomas has often asked me if I think the practice of Canadian federalism has been improved or worsened because of the involvement of a new cadre of intergovernmental relations professionals. On reflection and on balance, I believe the answer is yes. While intergovernmental staffers may be inclined to find problems in relations between governments, they are also well-placed to find solutions and quite experienced in ways to help implement them.

By the end of the 1960s, the "golden age" was over, and some fairly tumultuous times were ahead for the federation. The economy was slowing down and so was revenue growth. Prime Minister Trudeau had declared there would be "no more Medicares," and, soon after, the federal government started efforts to get out from under at least some of its health care and social service cost-sharing obligations. At the same time, a major constitutional reform effort, the Victoria Charter, ended in failure, and the oil price shocks began, with major impacts on the fiscal arrangements and the locus of growth. The tone of federal-provincial dialogue was deteriorating, and confrontation and unilateralism were becoming more common.

Between 1969 and the end of 1972, all four western provinces elected new governments led by new premiers: Ed Schreyer in Manitoba, Allan Blakeney in Saskatchewan, Peter Lougheed in Alberta, and Dave Barrett in British Columbia. In the same period, the federal government under Mr. Trudeau experienced a major electoral setback, especially in the West, and, in an effort to help restore popular support, it proposed a special Western Economic Opportunities Conference (WEOC) to involve the prime minister and the western premiers and to focus on western priorities. In March of 1973, with then-premier Schreyer in the chair, the first Western Premiers' Conference was held in Winnipeg to prepare for the meeting with the prime minister a few months later in Calgary. The Western Premiers' Conferences have continued annually since then. These gatherings have played a major role in shaping the national agenda, with the territories now participating as full members. Manitoba has been a strong contributor to the WPCs throughout their existence and played an important role in encouraging the territories to join the group.

In the same year, 1973, federal urban policy initiatives led to a full-scale national "Tri-Level" Conference in Toronto, which brought together elected federal, provincial, and municipal representatives. It was the first and last such conference ever held, although tri-level partnerships are alive and well in Manitoba. In fact, the tripartite Winnipeg Core Area Initiative agreement in 1981 became the prototype for many subsequent agreements in Manitoba and across the country.

Other issues in which Manitoba played a major role around this time included a comprehensive national review of social security and changes in the fiscal arrangements to relieve equalization cost pressures for the federal government as a result of the oil and gas boom and its unprecedented revenue consequences for the producing provinces. Manitoba also signed a "publicity-sharing" agreement with the federal government in the mid-1970s which was designed to ensure the contributions of both governments to joint programs were portrayed fairly in public information campaigns. The agreement also provided for a unique, joint federal-provincial public inquiry service, which continued to operate, with a modest budget, for a quarter century.

The mid-1970s also saw the emergence of severe inflationary pressures and the federal Anti-Inflation Program, into which provinces were able to have fairly substantial input. In 1976, the Lévesque government took office in Quebec, and a major change occurred in the fiscal arrangements, with the replacement of cost-sharing with block funding for health and post-secondary education, something the provinces asked for and received. Manitoba was a proponent of the block funding change, believing it would facilitate health program improvements by allowing greater flexibility in program design. However, some in the province later regretted the change, as subsequent limits on federal support undercut provinces' abilities to direct funds toward new, potentially more effective service options.

In the late 1970s, as the Trudeau government headed toward another election, it convened televised First Ministers' Conferences on the economy with agreed-upon records of decisions. The new Manitoba government under Sterling Lyon participated fully in these conferences, with then-premier Lyon leading discussions on regulatory reform and later introducing a formal process of before-the-fact regulatory review and consultation which became a model for other jurisdictions. The federal experiment with covering the costs of provincial sales tax reductions took place around the same time. The election of the short-lived Clark government followed relatively soon after. Mr. Clark's only formal First Ministers' Conference earned considerable praise from the premiers but his government fell on a budget vote soon after. When Mr. Trudeau returned to office, the constitutional patriation process resumed in earnest, with extensive but manipulated "consultations" (the famous Kirby memorandum is worth a read for any who have not seen it) and intense media attention. The results, the Charter, the "constitutionalization" of equalization, which former premier John Bracken might have approved, and the refusal by Quebec to sign on to the final package have all had lasting impacts. Premier Lyon and his government were among the central participants on the provincial side in these negotiations, raising serious concerns about the patriation process, the implications of the Charter, and other proposals. At the same time, the premier supported the inclusion of Section 36 (2) of the constitution on equalization, which was drafted in Manitoba, as well as the "notwithstanding clause" and others. The Lyon government did not sign off formally on the constitutional package before premier Howard Pawley took office following an election in the fall of 1981; however, the Pawley government later endorsed the package.

Brian Mulroney's Progressive Conservative government came to power federally in 1984 and committed itself, under the Regina Accord the following year, to regular First Ministers' Conferences. For a time, Mr. Mulroney's government more than lived up to the Accord and its spirit, offering discussions of key economic and fiscal priorities, including women's priorities, plus continuing conferences on Aboriginal issues as required under the 1982 constitutional amendments. Manitoba played a leadership role in these conferences and later on Meech—"eleven men at at least two tables"—as well as on the Canada-U.S. Free Trade Agreement and NAFTA negotiations, with the prime minister and premiers meeting as often as every three months. This coincided with much more international activity by the provinces focussed on trade, energy, the environment, and other priorities. This is one of the most significant changes I have observed in the last quarter-century. Premier Pawley signed Manitoba's first formal cooperation agreement with a U.S. state, North Dakota, in 1985. He also attended at least one National Governors Association meeting to discuss trade issues. Pawley's successor, Gary Filmon, signed cooperation agreements with Minnesota and Kansas, as well as with several other sub-national governments in Mexico, China, eastern Europe, and South Africa. Working closely with then-governor George Sinner of North Dakota, Filmon also helped open the door for annual meetings of western premiers and western U.S. governors. His successor, Gary Doer, added several more U.S. state agreements (Texas, California, Wisconsin, Georgia) and became the most active Canadian premier in international relations, advancing both Manitoba's and Canada's interests on several key economic, energy, and environmental files.

Other noteworthy developments in the latter half of the 1980s included the federal government's decision on the CF-18 repair contract, with its negative impact on Manitoba and on federal political fortunes in parts of the West, and, as a partial attempt to make amends later, the establishment of the Level-4 National Microbiology Laboratory and the International Institute for Sustainable Development in Winnipeg. As well, the federal government created the Department of Western Economic Diversification (WD), and its eastern counterpart, the Atlantic Canadian Opportunities Agency (ACOA).

The "save-Meech" and Charlottetown processes followed these initiatives, and were designed to try to address the criticisms of the original 1987 process, which began almost immediately after the constitutionally mandated round of discussions of Aboriginal priorities had come to an abrupt and unsuccessful conclusion. Again, Manitoba played a significant role, including advancing positive proposals developed through an all-party committee chaired by Professor Wally Fox-Decent. Another important development was the Canada Assistance Plan court case, and the eventual replacement of CAP, which removed another important federal stabilizer for periods of economic downturn, with direct relevance to current circumstances.

The Jean Chrétien Liberal era brought noteworthy developments too: some early "normal" first ministers' meetings, followed by meetings that took place only when success was guaranteed and later "flying FMM's" or "travelling federalism" on

Team Canada trade and investment missions. Then-premier Filmon encouraged the prime minister to introduce the Team Canada model for trade missions and was a regular participant, with numerous provincial business representatives. Starting in 1994, the design and implementation of the then-new federal-provincial infrastructure program involved useful consultations, with Manitoba's joint priority-setting and administration system becoming the national model. However, provinces reacted negatively to other developments, such as major transfer cuts and the spread of so-called "boutique" federalism, where Ottawa offered program support to third parties contingent on provincial matching support, often with little or no prior consultation with provincial governments. The Social Union Framework Agreement (SUFA) negotiations, in which Manitoba also played a major role, and the SUFA document itself, were aimed at addressing these kinds of federal unilateralism, but the outcome was discouraging.

While there was some consultation between the federal government and the provinces in advance of the Quebec referendum of 1995, it was seen as far from adequate in light of the potential consequences for the country of an outcome that could have led to separation. Later, two provinces, Manitoba and Saskatchewan, led by premiers Filmon and Romanow, and the two then-territories of the Yukon and Northwest Territories provided important support to the federal government in the secession case and the Clarity Act.

In the early years of the twenty-first century, a primary focus of provinces was the restoration by the Chrétien and Paul Martin Liberal governments of the mid-1990 federal transfer cuts. Their efforts to mount a focussed campaign and assure better coordination of their priorities led the premiers to establish the Council of the Federation, as proposed by Premier Jean Charest of Quebec, and to pursue greater support for Aboriginal services and development through the Kelowna Accord. The Kelowna Accord was especially important to Manitoba because of the significant and fast-growing proportion of Aboriginal residents in the province. Gary Doer, who became premier in October 1999 and who hosted and chaired both the Western Premiers' and Annual Premiers' conferences within the next year, played an important part in these developments. He also helped re-energize and strengthen relations with the western U.S. governors and established ongoing relations with the Australian premiers, who formed their own Council of the Federation based on the Canadian premiers' model. On bilateral, federal-provincial relations issues, then-premier Doer placed considerable importance on developing, where possible, private sector and multi-party support for initiatives of major importance to the province. These efforts were reflected in positive negotiations with the federal government on several key priorities, including expansion of the Red River Floodway, locating the National

Microbiology Laboratory in Winnipeg, establishing the Canadian Museum for Human Rights and funding the new CentrePort inland port initiative. They were also instrumental in responding to major challenges in agriculture and other industries, and in Canada-U.S. trade in general.

As has been well reported, first ministers' meetings with Prime Minister Harper were initially few and brief, but as the global and domestic economic situations deteriorated in the latter half of 2008, the frequency of first ministers' meetings increased and there was widespread recognition of their value in focussing and coordinating federal and provincial stimulus efforts and in shaping strategies for addressing impediments to international trade. Indeed, it is possible to conclude that Canada's comparative success in addressing the global economic crisis is a testament to the responsiveness and value of its existing mechanisms for intergovernmental cooperation. Divisions remain, however, on other major issues such as climate change and energy strategies, harmonization of the GST with provincial sales taxes, securities regulation, Aboriginal services and development, and a host of others. Prime Minister Harper's commitment to move ahead with a Charter of Open Federalism, based on respect for jurisdiction, and his efforts to promote Senate reform are among the works in progress. Whether our existing institutions will facilitate positive collaboration and consensus on these issues, as well as on the challenges presented by the budgetary after-effects of the recession on all governments in Canada remains to be seen. There is every reason to believe, however, based on the experiences of the past half-century and more, that Manitoba's governments will continue to contribute actively, practically, and positively in federal-provincial, interprovincial, and international relations, both in the province's interests and in the national interest.

Notes

1. This paper is an updated version of an address delivered 22 November 2008 at the Roblin Professorship Conference on Manitoba Politics, Government and Policy into the Twenty-first Century. The speech outlined some of the major events and trends in federal-provincial and international relations, and the author's perspectives on Manitoba's involvement in them from the Walter Weir Progressive Conservative government (1967–1969) to the present day.
2. One of the definitive pieces on this is A.R. Kear, "Co-operative Federalism: A Study of the Federal Provincial Continuing Committee on Fiscal and Economic Matters," *Canadian Public Administration* 6 (March 1963): 43–56.
3. In 1990, Mr. Roblin wrote a first-hand account of the start-up of the APCs that is essential reading for students of federal-provincial relations. See also J. Peter Meekison, "Council of Federations: An Idea Whose Time Has Come," *Institute for Research on Public Policy* 9 (2003), http://www.irpp.org/miscpubs/archive/federation/meekison.pdf.

Leading from the Middle: Manitoba's Role in the Intergovernmental and Transnational Arenas

Paul G. Thomas

I. Introduction

This chapter uses the concepts of leadership, influence, political friendship, and trust to examine the role and impacts of successive governments of Manitoba within Canada's federal system and in transnational arenas. Studies of individual provincial governments in the intergovernmental arena are not that common in the vast literature on Canadian federalism. Most of the available studies focus on federal-provincial relations in general or on the impacts of federalism in particular policy fields. The place of regions—the West and the Atlantic provinces—is also the focus of many studies. However, with the exception of Quebec and to a lesser extent Ontario, there are not many case studies of how individual provinces approach and carry out their activities in federal-provincial, interprovincial, and transnational forums across a variety of policy fields. In presenting a case study of Manitoba's role in the Canadian federal system and in its transnational relations, this chapter makes the case that the provincial government has historically and in the contemporary period relied upon so-called "soft power" and collaborative approaches to increase its influence and to obtain benefits for Manitobans.

With this integrating theme in mind, the remainder of the chapter consists of four main sections. First, the concepts of leadership, influence, political friendship, and trust are briefly examined. It is recognized that each of the four concepts is elusive, multidimensional, and controversial. Second, the notion of the West as a distinct, coherent political community is examined. It is argued that increasingly the West represents four different provincial societies, economies, and political cultures. Moreover, Manitoba cannot be seen as simply the most easterly and least affluent of four provinces which are often mistakenly taken to constitute a distinctive region with a shared outlook. Third, the historical and contemporary circumstances of Manitoba within the federal system are examined. In terms of geography, size, its economy, social makeup, and political culture, Manitoba can be described as "in the middle" among Canadian provinces. The basic circumstances of Manitoba, it is argued, contribute to the distinctive role played by its premiers and their governments within the federal system. Fourthly, it is argued that as premier of the NDP government, which has held office since 1999, Gary Doer achieved political influence within the intergovernmental system and in transnational arenas beyond what might be expected from a relatively small, less affluent province. The conclusion of the chapter draws its themes together and speculates on whether the October 2009 replacement of Gary Doer as premier with Greg Selinger will make a significant difference in terms of the approach and effectiveness of the government of Manitoba in working the networks of intergovernmental and transnational relationships.

The analysis to follow is based upon the academic literature, documentary, and newspaper reports and a small number (twelve) of elite interviews with politicians and public servants in Manitoba.

II. The Key Concepts

Each of the four concepts employed in the analysis to follow is vague and controversial. Huge volumes of literature exist on the topics of leadership, influence, friendship, and trust. Definitions, theories, models, and measures of these complex phenomena abound in multiple disciplines. In the space available here, it is only possible to set forth briefly the meaning and the use to be made of the four concepts within the remainder of the chapter.

Leadership has been described as one of the most studied and least understood phenomena in society.[1] Many theoretical approaches and applied models of leadership exist in the literatures of many disciplines.[2] At the risk of oversimplification, it is possible to identify two broad approaches to understanding leadership. The first suggests it is best understood by focussing on the personal attributes, qualities, behaviours, and situational responses of individuals who are given the title or claim to be leaders. In contrast, a second approach sees leadership primarily as a group process in which people work together to pursue a common goal and/or to resolve disagreements.[3] I favour mainly the latter approach of seeing leadership as something larger than the individual leader, but clearly the personal qualities, knowledge, and skills of individuals can make them potentially more suited to perform successfully in leadership roles, whether they are formally designated as leaders or play that role informally.

In government, leadership is dual, overlapping, and interactive, involving both elected politicians and appointed public servants. The roles, and therefore the knowledge, skills, and behavioural repertoires of political and administrative leaders are somewhat different. In principle political leaders play the main role in identifying policy direction, approving policies, and mobilizing support to carry them out. Public servants are meant to be experts in formulating policy advice and in implementing policy effectively once it has been decided. It has long been recognized that this simple dichotomy between deciding and carrying out policies does not capture the complexities of interaction and mutual dependence between politicians and public servants during the multiple phases of policy making.

Federalism has increased the role of public servants in the process of policy formulation and implementation because ministers must grant senior public servants considerable autonomy to negotiate with other orders of government and with interest groups of various kinds. Deals worked out in intergovernmental meetings and committees eventually come before ministers and cabinets for approval, but by then there is considerable momentum in favour of adoption.

While leadership is to some extent shared and collective within the conduct of federalism, the key role played by the prime ministers and premiers (also referred to collectively as first ministers) is a central fact of political life. The concentration of power in the office of the first minister is said to result from the prerogatives of being leader of the governing party, the responsibilities for creating and leading cabinets and the fact of being the focal point of media attention for policy announcements and events taking place.[4] First ministers usually assume the lead role on the most sensitive federal-provincial matters.

Talk of one-person rule to describe the power of first ministers is probably an exaggeration.[5] Even with larger political and bureaucratic staffs serving them, first ministers cannot know all the issues and arrange to be present when all the important decisions are being made within their governments. Power within individual governments may have become more centralized in recent decades, but there are still pressures on first ministers to respect the traditions of collective cabinet decision making and to ensure that there is political support within cabinet and the caucus of the governing party for their actions. Probably the greatest constraint on the freedom of a first minister to single-handedly set and to manage the agenda of his/her government is the need in an unpredictable world to anticipate, and/or to respond creatively to, unforeseen events, including the actions of other orders of government. Because the environment outside of government has become more complex and turbulent, first ministers actually have less control over which issues will receive attention within government. Furthermore, the fact more pressure groups are active around various issues, and citizens generally are less trusting of public officials, combine to make it harder for leaders in government to mobilize consent and support for their actions.

The size of a particular government and its financial circumstances will affect the power of the prime minister or premier. In larger, sprawling jurisdictions such as the government of Canada or the Ontario government, the capacity to achieve unified direction, control, and coherence will be a challenge, no matter how greatly power is concentrated in the office of the first minister. In smaller governments such as Manitoba's there is more opportunity for face-to-face dealings between the premier and other cabinet ministers, as well as with senior civil servants, and the premier can play a personal role on more files. Often the cabinet in the provincial setting represents two-thirds of the governing party caucus so there are more elected followers who owe a position of influence to the premier. Resource scarcity imposes focus and discipline on less affluent provincial governments making centralization of power in the hands of the premier more justified. Smaller public services may be limited in terms of their policy analysis and networking capacities and they also allow for more direct control and involvement by the first minister.

Regardless of their size, all governments serve diverse societies and therefore are obliged to identify and accommodate in their decision making divergent values, interests, ambitions, and goals. Conflict is inevitable. This means that leaders in government, both politicians and public servants, must be skilled at conflict resolution and the management of power.

Power is a contentious term. In popular discourse, it carries negative connotations of coercion, manipulation, and ego gratification. In the vast literature on the topic, however, there is a recognition that influence, rather than coercion, is the most widely used form of power. Jeffrey Pfeffer defines power as "the potential ability to influence behaviour, to change the course of events, to overcome resistance and to get people to do things they otherwise would not do."[6] Defined in this way, understanding the nature, potential, and limits of power is essential for making things happen within government and with other orders of government. Bolman and Deal identify the "wellsprings" of organizational power as position power (authority), expertise (information and knowledge), rewards (patronage, budget control), coercion (threats and penalties), agenda setting (formally and informally), meaning framing (ideas and metaphors), and personal power (charisma and leadership style).[7] The first four "wellsprings" represent a "one-way" vision of leadership power which involves the use of "resources" of various kinds to bring others into line with one's intentions. The latter four wellsprings involve "power with" rather than "power over" others—they represent a persuasive model of leadership based upon cooperation toward shared goals. The two forms of power involve both formal and informal dimensions in their operation.

Measuring the influence of leaders in various contexts has proven to be difficult for social scientists in various disciplines.[8] There is no single approach or set of indicators which precisely captures the influence of individual leaders when complicated events and multiple actors are involved. A structural approach to the measurement of influence is based on the position occupied by a leader, along with the opportunities and resources to exert influence that come with a strategic location. A reputational approach asks others to rank the effectiveness of leaders based upon explicit criteria or their more general impressions of whether leaders are able to persuade others. A third approach is based on outcomes. This involves identifying what a leader sets out to achieve, determining what actually happened and attributing influence based on what appears to have occurred within the process. This approach often recognizes that influence may involve not only the achievement of a desired outcome, but also the prevention of an unwanted development. Different approaches will capture different dimensions of the complex and elusive phenomenon of leadership and influence.

First ministers must manage relationships of power both inside and outside of the governments. Internally they have all the power resources identified by Bolman and Deal: authority, rewards, knowledge, threats, agenda-setting, and coercion. Leadership can involve the use of both "hard" and "soft" power.[9] Soft power is the ability to obtain results through attraction, persuasion, and reputation, whereas hard power involves the use of authority or payments of various kinds to induce compliance. Ideally, first ministers prefer to rely upon persuasion and influence to bring their cabinet colleagues and others to their side. Shared goals—including re-election—and loyalty to the leader and the party will cause their followers to limit their challenges and dissent, especially in public.

In terms of external leadership, first ministers are involved with activities and events in numerous intergovernmental arenas covering various policy fields. In such processes first ministers relate to one another more as peers than as superiors and subordinates. Whatever the formalities, it must be recognized that some governments have more power than others. This means that a smaller provincial government such as Manitoba's must rely more on soft power approaches to advance its interests in intergovernmental arenas of various kinds. More is said on this point later in the chapter.

First ministers vary in their understanding and skills at exercising hard and soft forms of power, both inside their own governments and in their interactions with other governments. Some adopt more active leadership styles than others, although no leader can be completely passive and surrender the initiative completely to others. The success and influence of individual first ministers will vary over time, depending upon a wide range of factors such as their electoral mandates, the economic and social circumstances in their jurisdiction, the issues on the governmental agenda at the time, and their personal popularity with their party followers and other segments in society.

Historically, the prime minister and the government of Canada have controlled the agendas for federal-provincial meetings. However, the rise of stronger provincial governments with more bureaucratic capacity has reduced unilateral federal control, particularly since 2003 when the premiers created the Council of the Federation to promote interprovincial/territorial cooperation and to support their collective leadership role within the federal system. In short, compared to power relationships inside of particular governments, leadership, and power in the intergovernmental arena is more dispersed and collective, and fluctuates according to the issues and actors involved.

In academic and media analysis, the processes of intergovernmental relations are interpreted almost exclusively in terms of the exercise of power and calculations of how leaders can maximize the benefits for their individual governments, the people they represent, and their own reputations as skillful power brokers. Talk about the role that political friendships might play in terms of conditioning the dynamics and outcomes of the federal-provincial process is seldom mentioned. In the current cynical era towards politics, the suggestion that political friendship based on personalities, compatibility, mutual respect, and a commitment to shared public policy goals would invite ridicule from many observers. There is no doubt that first ministers must defend the fundamental interests of the governments they lead and the societies they serve. Re-election is always a background consideration, which is appropriate in a democracy. In short, the argument being made here is that political friendship will never trump either fundamental jurisdictional and/or political interests, but having close personal relationships with other leaders can make a significant marginal difference in the dynamics and outcomes of various intergovernmental processes.

Political friendship is meant to connote mutual knowledge, understanding, respect, compatibility, affection, and trust. The last of these relationship qualities, namely trust, has become a popular topic in a wide range of disciplines, including political science.[10] Most of the writing in the political science field has focused on external trust by the public in governments. There is close to unanimity on the view that such trust has been declining over the past three decades and, according to some writers, the rising levels of cynicism are undermining public support for and the legitimacy of the actions of governments.

Interpersonal trust among public officials who operate the federal system is different from the wider public trust towards governments in general. Trust among leaders is based upon more direct experience working over time with one another. Interpersonal trust among "insiders" is closely related to friendship, but it is not exactly the same. In this context, trust refers to positive, confident expectations about the motivations, intentions, behaviours, and competence of other actors.[11] There is an element of uncertainty and risk involved in placing trust in others that they will not act to harm one's interests if it can be avoided. Trust is seen to reduce ambiguity and unpredictability in interactions because one can anticipate some of the behaviour of other actors. Additionally, trust can facilitate the exchange of information, ideas, and intentions. It can facilitate cooperation and contribute to the constructive resolution of disagreements. Positive perceptions about the competence of actors to achieve desired outcomes will enhance the levels of trust among actors. In trusting relationships, there is a greater willingness to believe that a breach of trust is not the fault of a "friend," but can be attributed to the situation or the actions of others.

The relationship between trust and power is complicated and problematic. In some situations trust can be a substitute for power when others both identify with the goals a leader is seeking to obtain and have confidence in their leader's capacities. In such circumstances attempts to influence may be unnecessary. On the other hand, if power is used opportunistically and unethically, it can reduce or destroy trust. It is usually argued that the building of trust is a gradual, incremental process whereas the loss of trust can result from a single, dramatic event.

While it was necessary to introduce briefly the key concepts to be used in the analysis to follow, the point needs to be reinforced that each of the concepts is complex, multidimensional, difficult to measure, and controversial. In drawing attention to the "softer," more elusive dimensions of intergovernmental relationships, it is not being argued that such factors determine processes and outcomes. Leadership, trust, and friendship matter, but they do not override the pursuit of fundamental interests. How much they matter is contingent on the issues at stake and the alignment of the different interests, both governmental and non-governmental, which are involved in policy processes which are varied, complex, multi-tiered, and dynamic.

The analysis to follow of Manitoba's role within the intergovernmental and transnational arenas will use the above concepts in a qualitative way to speculate, hopefully in an informed way, about how they intersect with the changing context of Manitoba's role in the wider world.

III. Manitoba and the West

Historically the West—consisting of the three Prairie provinces and British Columbia—has been thought of as a distinctive political region bringing a shared set of concerns into the federal-provincial arena. Politicians, the media, and scholars still talk about the need to address "western alienation," the longstanding feeling of being excluded from the national policy process and the perception that central Canada uses the ample natural resources of the region while blocking its aspirations to diversify economically. Over many decades the West has given rise to many protest movements and third parties which have expressed the discontents of the region. There have also been attempts over the years for interests and individuals from western Canada to work within the two main parties at the national level and to reform policy and parliamentary processes to make them less majoritarian and dominated by the claims of Quebec and Ontario. Most recently, during the past three decades, the leading cause of western reformers has been the creation of a "Triple E" Senate—one that is elected, equal, and effective—as a way to ensure the growing populations and increased economic strength of the West (mainly Alberta and British Columbia) are reflected in increased political power in the national policy process. A related development is the insistence by provincial governments in the West (again led by Alberta and British Columbia) that the national government follow a stricter approach to federal-provincial relations that respects provincial jurisdiction, especially over issues of resource development.

These are familiar themes. They reflect an historical record and established political tradition which cause people to think of the West as a distinct political community with a shared set of expectations and demands.[12] The concepts of region and regionalism are inherently complex and subjective, which means that people disagree on their meaning and significance. There are geographic, economic, social, psychological, and symbolic dimensions to the concept of region. The argument here is that over time the West has become increasingly four distinct provincial societies, economies, and political cultures and less a homogeneous region which approaches the national government and participates in intergovernmental processes on the basis of a shared agenda and common set of concerns. Today the notion of the West is more psychological, cultural, and symbolic than it is economic and political.[13] Reflecting their separate geography, histories, traditions, social composition, economic circumstances, and political traditions, each of the four western provinces has its own distinct identity, including somewhat different perspectives on its role within the federal system. In all four provinces, a large majority of the population live in large cities with different economic strengths and tremendous social diversity. These "city regions" probably have more in common with one another and with similar centres elsewhere in the country than do the western provinces, in general, with one other.

There is no disputing the place of "the West" in the political consciousness of the region and the country. However, opinion surveys have confirmed that the differences between western Canadians and respondents in other parts of the country on major public policy issues are not great.[14] The greatest differences show up on symbolic issues involving the perceived nature of the country, the place of the region within Confederation, and the fairness of the political process towards regional interests. The general public's perceptions and feelings that the West has not been fairly treated are not supported by a great deal of knowledge about the basic features of the political system, including the federal system, about the actions of different governments or about the outcomes of those actions. In short, there is an undercurrent of regional grievance in the consciousness of Canadians in the West which is uneven in its breadth and depth, being strongest in the provinces of Alberta and British Columbia, and the knowledge base among the general public for feelings of regional alienation is limited. In fact, public opinion polls which claim to tap into regional protest may in fact be measuring more general alienation from the political system which has other causes, such as poverty or broken promises to Aboriginal peoples.[15]

In addition to the level of public opinion, regionalism could find expression on the elite level, particularly among politicians, public servants, and interest group representatives. The evidence of this type of regionalism is spotty and mixed, but there are some indications that among elites within the four western provinces there is less regional thinking and action than there used to be. During the 1970s there were conferences and reports devoted to the topics of "One Prairie Province" and to ways of strengthening the place of the West within Canada as its resource wealth brought prosperity and population growth. A Western Economic Opportunities Conference in 1973 led eventually to the creation of the annual Western Premiers Conference. This last institution still exists, but its level of activity and the willingness of premiers to take joint action has dissipated over time.[16]

A senior intergovernmental official from Manitoba with more than forty years of experience observed in a 2009 interview that cooperation among the four western provinces was at an all-time low and that increasingly the two westernmost provinces have focussed mainly on their own agendas. When the four provincial economies were more agricultural and resource-based, the provincial governments had more in common, whereas today they are more competitive as they seek to attract investment in the "knowledge" industries of the future. In the energy field, Alberta has become an exceptionally fast growth province with abundant revenues. This has caused significant disequilibrium in the complex system of federal-provincial financial transfers. Three of the four provincial governments in the West no longer receive equalization payments, making Manitoba the last "have less" government.

There are different historical experiences and traditions which factor into the contemporary political cultures of each of the four provinces in some not easily discernible way. Socially the four provinces are all becoming increasingly diverse, but the population of "new Canadians" is urbanized and does not represent a cohesive segment in the way rural interests did in the past. Aboriginal issues are found on the government agendas in all four provinces, but they loom larger in Manitoba and Saskatchewan because of the percentage of the population of Aboriginal heritage and the existence of strong political organizations representing Aboriginal peoples. The ideology of the ruling parties does not often supersede the fundamental interests of a given province in terms of their willingness to cooperate, but partisan differences across the West probably account in part for the relative lack of regional unity compared to the past. At the time of writing (March 2010), Manitoba had the only NDP government in Western Canada and the other three provinces were ruled by right-of-centre parties. Finally, the leadership philosophy and style of individual premiers reflect and shape the political culture of their province. On climate change policy, for example, Premier Campbell in British Columbia and former premier Doer have taken a more aggressive policy stance, both, it appears, because of the environmental circumstances of their provinces and the development of personal convictions about the importance of the issue. When they interact in the intergovernmental arena the leadership styles of premiers can be more or less compatible, leading to greater or lesser collaboration.

Over the past four decades there have been "defining moments" that symbolize the loss of regional unity among elites. One such event was the CF-18 controversy in 1986. When the government of Canada decided to place a fighter aircraft maintenance contract with a Quebec firm rather than the one in Manitoba, which had been rated superior on technical grounds, an all-party delegation from the Manitoba Legislature along with provincial business representatives went to Ottawa to protest the actions of the Conservative government of Brian Mulroney. Even though this seemed to be a clear case of the West being shut out again by political favouritism towards Quebec, there were no strong protests from premiers or the legislatures in the other three western provinces.

There have been more recent examples. Even though Manitoba's former premier Gary Doer had been the acknowledged leader among all ten premiers on the need to reduce internal trade barriers, in 2004 the governments of Alberta and British Columbia announced their own bilateral deal, apparently without giving serious thought to the inclusion of all four western provinces. In September 2009, the Alberta government hosted a meeting of trade ministers for the three westernmost provinces, to which Manitoba was not invited. Premier Brad Wall explained that it was easier to hold frank conversations among the three "have" provinces without the last equalization recipient province in the West being present. Of course there are counter-examples where the West in the form of the four provincial governments has spoken with one voice to obtain benefits for the region.

IV. The Case of Manitoba: "Stuck in the Middle"

Having suggested that the notion of a cohesive West can easily be exaggerated, this section of the paper examines the recent role of Manitoba governments in the intergovernmental arena based upon the integrating theme that the province is in several ways "stuck in the middle" of national political life. Occupying this distinctive political space has caused most Manitoba governments to adopt a conciliatory and constructive approach in their dealings with the national government, other provincial governments, state, and national governments in the United States and with business and non- governmental organizations.[17]

Geographically, Manitoba is clearly in the middle of the country, which means it looks both east and west in terms of conducting relations with other parties. Historically, the province was settled by migrants from Ontario during the late nineteenth century and later by successive waves of immigrants from other parts of the world. As a consequence the province is socially diverse. In many ways it mirrors the diversity of the nation itself. It has a large and fast-growing Aboriginal population, with as many as 70,000 Aboriginal citizens living in the capital city of Winnipeg. The province has a significant and politically active francophone population and it practises a limited form of official bilingualism at the provincial level and within the city of Winnipeg.

Manitoba is a one-city province with Winnipeg representing 60 percent of the provincial population and the capital region (Winnipeg and fifteen adjacent municipalities) representing close to 70 percent of the provincial economy. Thirty-one of the fifty-seven seats in the provincial legislature are located within the city of Winnipeg. The provincial government has experimented with the design of the urban political system (Unicity, 1971), and is the only provincial government to adopt vertical provincial-municipal tax sharing on so-called "growth taxes," to promote sustainable development and land use planning for the capital region, to collaborate with the city of Winnipeg and the government of Canada in tri-level projects to revitalize downtown Winnipeg, and to prominently pursue the so-called "cities agenda" at the national level on such issues as the gas tax transfers to support urban infrastructure upgrades. In short, Manitoba has been at the centre of national debates over how to support city regions as the focal points for future growth.

In economic terms, Manitoba can also be seen to be in the middle among provincial economies. It is western Canada's most diversified economy. Historically the economy has demonstrated slow but steady growth based upon agriculture, resource development, hydroelectric power, small to medium manufacturing, a growing service sector, and a significant role for public sector investment and employment, especially through Crown corporations. In recent years, Manitoba's economy has grown at rates slightly above the national provincial average, but below fast-growth provinces such as Alberta and Saskatchewan. Out-migration to other provinces had been the historical pattern, but it has slowed in recent years and net population gains in recent years have been achieved on the basis of federal-provincial programs to attract international immigrants. In terms of the sectors represented in the economy and its mixed private/public characteristics, Manitoba comes closest among the four western provinces in terms of mirroring the overall national economy.

Among provincial societies and provincial governments, Manitoba is neither poor nor rich, more like lower-middle class. It is the only province in western Canada currently eligible for equalization payments from the government of Canada. Such payments are intended to enable "have less" (a term preferred by a former Manitoba premier over "have not") provinces like Manitoba to provide approximately comparable public services without having to impose undue tax burdens on its citizens. Equalization, combined with the Canada Health and Social Transfer and other transfers, accounted for approximately 33 percent of provincial revenues in 2008.[18] Dependence on federal financial transfers has recently been portrayed by the business community and the editorial board of the leading provincial newspaper as a failure by the provincial government to create the competitive economic conditions necessary for prosperity which at least matches that of Saskatchewan. As is discussed below, the NDP government, which has been in office since 1999, does not reject the goal of becoming a "have" province, but argues that policy and financial support from the national government will be needed to complement provincial efforts.

Manitoba's party systems on both the federal and the provincial levels involve competition among three parties—the Conservatives, Liberals, and NDP—although the Liberals have not been a real contender for power at the provincial level since the late 1960s. In national politics, three-party competition means that, unlike Alberta, there have always been Manitoba MPs in the cabinet and the caucus of the governing party. Manitoba's regional ministers and the provincial caucus have enjoyed success in obtaining benefits for Winnipeg and the province. So successful was Lloyd Axworthy as a Liberal regional minister in the early 1980s that the subsequent Conservative government led by Brian Mulroney felt justified in limiting special payouts to the province for several years after 1984.[19]

Adding to Manitoba's voice in Ottawa and promoting intergovernmental collaboration at the bureaucratic level has been the little-noticed Manitoba Federal Council, which consists of senior federal public servants working in the province.[20] With the support of a small secretariat, the role of the council is to coordinate national policy and program initiatives and to gather intelligence on the needs and demands of the provincial government and other sectors of Manitoba society. By reputation the Manitoba Federal Council is rated the best or one of the best among such councils across the country in terms of achieving support for policies and projects that benefit the province.

Assisting regional ministers and federal public servants to serve provincial goals is the fact that much of the time the economic and social concerns within Manitoba society have matched up closely with those on the national policy agenda. In other words, there have not been wide gaps in public opinion on major policy issues between Manitoba and the national picture. According to public opinion surveys, Manitobans are the least alienated among citizens of the four western provinces. Based upon a Peripheral Regional Alienation index constructed by Shawn Henry, Alberta scored the highest while Manitoba's score was much lower, indeed the lowest of all but one of the Atlantic provinces.[21] In general, Manitobans do not judge the national policy process to be severely and permanently "rigged" against them as do Albertans and British Columbians.

History, economic, social, and political circumstances have combined to produce a moderate, small-c conservative political culture in Manitoba. In the modern era of Manitoba politics which dates from the victory of the Progressive Conservatives led by Duff Roblin in 1958, successful parties and premiers have been mainly pragmatic and cautious in their policy approaches. Provincial elections are always close, with the winning party usually having only a handful more seats than the opposition parties. This has encouraged centrist policies designed not to polarize voters. The exception to this pattern involved the only one-term government in the modern era led by the Conservative premier Sterling Lyon (1977 to 1981), who adopted the anti-government rhetoric and some of the policy stances of the neo-conservative movement that was beginning to make headway in Canada. In contrast, Gary Doer won a third general election in 2007 after transforming the NDP platform to resemble the "Third Way" made popular by Tony Blair in the U.K., by retaining some of the right-of-centre policies of the former Conservative government (such as a balanced-budget law) and generally heeding the call of the business community to make Manitoba more competitive by cutting taxes gradually. On the other hand, Doer spent substantial amounts of money on health care, child care, Aboriginal concerns, and public sector investments such as hydro development and projects in downtown Winnipeg. The overall policy stance of the NDP government, which combines fiscal conservatism with spending to create social opportunities, seems to fit with the provincial political culture. In 2007 then-premier Doer had a personal approval rating in the 70 percent range and he increased his majority in the May 2007 election based on capturing 49 percent of the popular vote and winning thirty-six of the fifty-seven seats in the legislature.

In summary, this section has suggested that geography, history, economics, and the political traditions of Manitoba have combined to produce a somewhat distinctive view of the role of the provincial government and the approaches it should follow in the various intergovernmental arenas.

Going back to the Depression era of the 1930s—when the government of Manitoba presented a voluminous document called "Manitoba's Case" to the royal commission studying dominion-provincial financial relationships—the tradition has been for all provincial parties in Manitoba to support a strong national government which has the policy and financial capacity to equalize opportunities across the country. With a few notable exceptions, Manitoba governments have accepted a policy leadership and program-standard-setting role by the national government. They have not been offended by intrusions into policy fields which under the Constitution are exclusively or primarily provincial responsibilities. This has caused them to resist proposals intended to place constitutional limits on the use of the so-called federal spending power. Even when non-constitutional limits on the use of the spending power have been proposed, Manitoba governments have insisted that such restrictions should not apply to bilateral deals with the national government. For Manitoba, there should be no constitutional prohibition or even strict limits on generosity by the national government, even if that generosity comes with strings attached, provided those strings can be negotiated.

Up to a point, Manitobans share the suspicion of other western Canadians that "central Canada" calls most of the shots in national policy making. This attitude is crystallized and reinforced by events like the aforementioned CF-18 decision to send the maintenance contract to Quebec. Like other provincial governments, Manitoba has complained about unilateral decisions by the national government to launch new shared-cost programs, to modify or terminate existing programs, or to cut back on federal financial transfers. Generally, however, Manitoba has not endorsed the idea, popular with more "provincial rights"-minded jurisdictions, of "disentanglement" leading to a stricter form of federalism in which each order of government has clearly delineated taxing powers and spending responsibilities.

An exception to Manitoba's usual orientation took place in the mid-1990s when former Conservative premier Gary Filmon (1988–1990, 1990–1995, 1995–1999) and his finance minister called for Ottawa to cede more tax room to the provinces and for a reduction in the interlocking activities of the two orders of government. This shift reflected the anger among provincial officials arising from the drastic cuts to federal transfer payments made as a result of the Program Review exercise (1994–1996) that had taken place at the national level under the Liberal government of then-prime minister Chrétien. The Manitoba government was already facing financial stress as a result of slow economic growth, tax cuts it had introduced, and the balanced budget law it had adopted. Strong language about breaking a bargain and a betrayal of trust was used by Manitoba officials to describe the actions of the national government. An examination of the more recent stance of the NDP government led by Gary Doer illustrates a return to the more traditional approach followed by the province.

V. Premier Gary Doer and Soft Power, 1999–2009

Gary Doer became leader of government only after serving eleven years in opposition in the Manitoba legislature. He was first elected in the provincial election of 1986 when the NDP government of Premier Howard Pawley was re-elected to a second term. Prior to his election, Doer had served since 1979 as president of the Manitoba Government Employees Association and held prominent positions in the Manitoba Federations of Labour and the National Union of Provincial Government Employees. This experience helped Doer develop and refine his leadership skills of strategic thinking, communication, negotiation, and conflict management. Appointed as minister of urban affairs in 1987, he was required to maintain harmonious relations with the city of Winnipeg and as the minister responsible for the government-owned Manitoba Telephone System he dealt with a scandal involving a failed investment in Saudi Arabia. Within two years in office he had the reputation of being a "fixer," working as a troubleshooter on the difficult issues, and was being mentioned as a future leader. When the NDP government suffered a surprise defeat on its budget in March 1988, Howard Pawley resigned as leader, an election was called, and a rushed leadership race saw Doer emerge as leader. At the time, the party's fortunes were at a low ebb and it ended up winning only twelve seats, while the Progressive Conservatives formed a minority government with twenty-five seats and the Liberals won twenty seats.

The dominant issue during the minority government period which lasted from 1988 to 1990 was the Meech Lake Accord, which proposed to recognize Quebec as a distinct society and to devolve powers from the national government to the provinces. Doer was part of an all-party panel which held public hearings on the accord and he was part of the Manitoba delegation which participated in a compromise deal brokered by then prime minister Brian Mulroney. For Doer and his NDP colleagues, restrictions on the use of the federal spending power was a greater concern than recognition of Quebec as a distinct society, although that provision within the accord did become a lightning rod for protest across the province, especially among Conservative Party supporters. Eventually the resolution to approve the accord failed to pass in the Manitoba Legislature when an Aboriginal member of the NDP prevented a vote. Doer described the MLA's action as a matter of conscience and blamed the defeat of the Accord on the unprincipled negotiating tactics of then prime minister Mulroney. Doer would bring his party back to the status of official opposition in the 1990 election, but would fail to capture power then and again in the 1995 election. So it was not until after the 1999 election that Gary Doer became the twenty-first premier of Manitoba. After eleven years in opposition he was better prepared in terms of knowledge and skills to lead the provincial government and to assume an effective role on the national stage.

Gary Doer's approach to intergovernmental relations reflected his style of governing in Manitoba. It was pragmatic, problem-specific, cautious, and driven by the political dynamics of the issue under consideration rather by some overarching theory of federalism. As a naturally gifted politician, Doer exhibited what has been called "contextual intelligence."[22] In other words he has excellent, intuitive diagnostic skills to understand an evolving environment and to "read" situations, issues, and people. For Doer, solutions are to be found less in abstract theorizing and more on the basis of what is feasible in terms of the nature of the issue, the policy knowledge available, the administrative capacities of governments, the budgetary requirements and, most importantly, the prospects for agreement among governments and the other actors involved.[23] Understanding the level of conflict a proposed action will arouse and whether a consensus can be found is a key requirement in successful policy making. Networking, negotiations, the mobilization of support, and the creative accommodation of differences are central to this approach. Avoidance of strong, fixed initial positions and of personalizing disputes are also features of the approach.

As practised by a smaller province, the approach requires intelligence gathering, policy analysis, the identification of potential allies, and trade-offs. The development of friendships and trust relationships on the political and bureaucratic level is also crucial to the success of this approach. These processes are time-consuming and uncertain. They tend to produce incremental changes, not dramatic policy shifts. Influence depends on a wide range of factors: what is at stake, the positions of the parties involved, past precedents, the capacities of politicians and public servants to identify compromises, the credibility and trustworthiness of leaders, and timing, particularly in terms of where different governments are in the electoral cycle. It is also the case that influence is a two-way street; attempting to influence others leaves the government of Manitoba open to the influence of others. Success does not necessarily mean always achieving the province's goals. It can involve blocking harmful actions, mitigating potential negative consequences, achieving partial victory, creating the opportunity to revisit issues, and not forsaking longer-term influence for the immediate gratification of attacking other parties involved.

Gary Doer's first major appearance on the federal-provincial stage as Premier of Manitoba took place at the Annual Premiers Conference (APC) in Winnipeg in August 2000. As host for the event, Doer chaired the meeting as a rookie premier, having been sworn into office in October 1999. Media accounts suggested that despite his inexperience he did well. According to Peter Meekison's analysis, the agendas for the APCs had shifted since the 1980s from interprovincial matters to more of a focus on federal-provincial issues.[23] Often described in the media as a chance for the provinces to gang up on Ottawa, the APC has been used over the years by Doer to develop the case for a pan-Canadian approach to issues and to deal with unilateral actions by the national government. He has found allies in these causes among other premiers including Bernard Lord (Progressive Conservative) of New Brunswick and Jean Charest (Liberal) of Quebec.

In 2001–02 Doer was very active in promoting the creation of the Premiers Council on Canadian Health Awareness, a body with a small budget and staff. Its purpose was to make Canadians aware of reductions in federal financial support ("the 14 cent campaign") and of innovations in the health field at the provincial level. According to Quebec journalist Chantal Hébert, Doer also played a key role in persuading other premiers to support a proposal from Quebec Premier Jean Charest for a Council of the Federation.[24] Established in 2003 the Council was intended to promote interprovincial/territorial cooperation and a more constructive and cooperative federal system. It brings together the premiers of the ten provinces and the three territories twice a year, with the premiers taking turns acting as chair for one year. A small secretariat supports the Council. It subsumed the responsibilities of two existing bodies: the Canadian Council on Health Awareness and the Secretariat for Information and Cooperation on Fiscal Imbalance. In 2004 the Council agreed on a list of priority areas, with federal funding for health being one of the most important. In calling for federal funding for a national pharmacare program, the Council acknowledged Quebec's right to opt out and receive full financial compensation—a compromise Premier Doer had promoted. Doer has argued that the new cooperative mechanism of the Council would enable the provinces and territories to participate more effectively in national decision making to promote a stronger economic and social union and to avoid a strict "go-it-alone" approach to federalism.

Mechanisms like the Council of the Federation have their limits in terms of resolving fundamental disagreements and achieving consensus. In its first three years, the Council maintained an appearance of unity, even if it only amounted to agreement on carefully crafted, ambiguous communiqués. The issue of fiscal imbalance—including problem definition and its resolution—divided provincial governments into "have" and "have not" camps and led to the creation of an expert panel to find a compromise. Eventually, at their 2006 meeting the premiers were forced to acknowledge a lack of agreement on the fiscal imbalance and on equalization. At the 2007 meeting the divisive issues were climate change and a proposal for a "cap and trade" system for greenhouse gas emissions. Led by Alberta, the four provinces with oil and gas reserves opposed the system whereas the three provinces with hydroelectric power (British Columbia, Manitoba, and Quebec) came out in favour. Ontario, where the auto industry is concentrated, could accept a cap-and-trade system, but only if Ottawa subsidized the development of "clean cars."

In addition to participating in interprovincial forums, former premier Doer conducted extensive bilateral relations with other premiers and their governments. Despite having a national image as a province that periodically exhibits intense anti-French and anti-Quebec sentiments, Manitoba's political and administrative elites probably collaborated more with their Quebec counterparts than with any other province. The basis for those close relationships begins with the similar structures of the two provincial economies. Both are resource-based economies, with significant hydroelectric sectors. There is a significant aerospace industry in both provinces and they have targeted similar "knowledge industries" for the future such as biotechnology and nutraceuticals. As equalization recipients, both provinces are dependent on financial transfers from Ottawa. Both provinces have sizable Aboriginal populations and Manitoba has one of the most concentrated francophone communities outside Quebec. In addition to these shared economic and social characteristics, the premiers were friends who respected and trusted one another.

The friendship between the two premiers dated back to the Meech Lake process when Jean Charest, then a Conservative MP, led a parliamentary committee to Manitoba to conduct public hearings and met Gary Doer, then opposition leader. They discovered a shared belief in a new style of politics that abandoned traditional left/right debates and searched instead for governing approaches that would work better and were affordable. When Charest gained power as a Liberal leader in Quebec his first visit outside of the province was to Manitoba. Over the years since, they were often allies in the intergovernmental process. Some examples of their collaboration are the following:

- the creation of the Council of the Federation in 2003;
- the 2006 compromise arrangement reached with then prime minister Paul Martin and the other premiers that would accommodate Quebec's distinctive circumstances by allowing for "asymmetrical federalism" in the health care field;
- the climate change issue which saw the two premiers write a joint "op-ed" piece in *The Globe and Mail* and co-host an international summit on the topic (December 2006);
- shared leadership in the Federal-Provincial/Territorial and Aboriginal policy process leading to the Kelowna Accord signed by then prime minister Paul Martin in 2005 (and subsequently rejected by the Harper government);
- child care issues and federal money for early childhood development programs at the provincial level;
- the promotion of the biotechnology industry in Canada by joint attendance at the BIO conferences in Philadelphia (2005) and Chicago (2006);
- the sharing of policy ideas and administrative practices at the political and bureaucratic levels on topics such as Aboriginal employment, hydroelectric development, lotteries, and government auto insurance;
- on the Western Hemisphere Travel Initiative intended to deal with cross-border security issues, the two governments jointly hired a lobbyist in Washington and offered Ontario and New Brunswick an opportunity to join the campaign to limit negative impacts.

Based on this pattern of interaction, a Manitoba official observed, "If you asked Quebec officials which provincial government they felt closest to in the West—indeed in all of Canada—they would likely say Manitoba."

Friendship and trust means that the two premiers supported one another whenever possible. For example, in 2006 when Prime Minister Harper had Parliament pass a resolution recognizing Quebec as a "nation" and promised to give that province a "unique" role at UNESCO (the cultural arm of the United Nations), Doer defended the actions as leading to more positive relationships between Ottawa and Quebec City. Even when the historical positions of the two provincial governments clashed, as for example on the use of federal spending power in areas of provincial jurisdiction, there was a strong inclination to search for a compromise. Manitoba has opposed constitutional limits on the spending power, but has been prepared to accept non-constitutional requirements to prevent unilateral federal intrusions. It has also opposed restrictions on the right of provincial governments to negotiate bilateral deals with the national government.

A Manitoba intergovernmental official with decades of experience observed in 2007 that over the past ten years the province more often looked east than west to find allies on intergovernmental issues and to engage in "policy borrowing" from other jurisdictions. Quebec was the leading example. However, former premier Doer also had a personal friendship with former premier Bernard Lord of New Brunswick (1999–2006) and there have been good working relations among public servants from the two provinces. Not surprisingly, given its proximity, the many issues in common, and the presence of another NDP government, there have also been frequent contacts at the political and bureaucratic level with Saskatchewan. Being a careful strategist, Doer would never deliberately antagonize another premier, but from the interviews conducted and the newspaper accounts reviewed, he shared fewer views with, and had less trust and confidence in, former premier Ralph Klein of Alberta and premiers Danny Williams of Newfoundland and Labrador, Gordon Campbell of British Columbia, and Dalton McGuinty of Ontario. One might infer that he saw those provincial governments as too self-interested in their stance on national issues and too opportunistic and unreliable in their behaviours.

VI. The Harper Government and "Open Federalism"

In the short time Paul Martin was leader of the Liberal Party and prime minister of Canada (2004–2006), Manitoba was successful in advancing a number of its priorities on the federal-provincial agenda (such as child care and the Kelowna Accord on Aboriginal issues), as well as gaining federal financial support for a range of projects. Doer and Martin got along well on a personal level, but there was also the fact that Martin had trouble saying no to provinces generally when they approached the national government with their wish lists. With this most recent positive experience working with the national government, Manitoba's politicians and senior public servants were a bit leery about what to expect when Stephen Harper and the Conservative Party of Canada took office after the 2006 election.

The first throne speech of the Harper government in 2006 announced a commitment to the concept of "open federalism." There is inadequate space here to discuss in detail this new direction by the national government. The essence of open federalism is a stricter, "respectful" approach to federal-provincial relations which will clarify the roles of each level of government, respect areas of provincial jurisdiction, place limits on the use of the federal spending power, tackle the fiscal imbalance between the spending responsibilities of the provincial governments and their revenue raising capacities, and recognize the distinctive place of Quebec in Confederation.[25] The declaration of open federalism, along with the government-sponsored resolution passed by Parliament to recognize the Québécois as a nation within Canada, was clearly designed to support the Charest government in Quebec and to build on the limited Quebec breakthrough of Harper's Conservative Party (ten seats) in the 2006 election.

In their initial dealings with the Harper government, Manitoba officials found it to be tightly controlled, secretive, and unresponsive, especially compared with their most recent dealings with the short-lived Liberal government of Paul Martin. It was acknowledged that a new government with minority status needed to be cautious and ministers need time to settle into their jobs, but Manitoba public servants working the intergovernmental networks complained initially about a lack of consultation by the Harper government, even in areas of provincial jurisdiction. Progress on a number of bilateral issues was slow, but by the second half of 2007 there was renewed momentum on issues such as the Devils Lake diversion, the future of the Port of Churchill and the issue of urban crime. More recently there has been less progress on issues important to Manitoba, such as Aboriginal programmimg, child care, and climate change

Despite having quite different personalities and working styles, Doer and Harper gradually came to know, understand, and respect one another. Doer recognized Harper's tendency to make provincial premiers who opposed him publicly pay a price in terms of ongoing access to or benefits from national decision makers. Unlike the premier of Newfoundland and Labrador, Doer would spend his "political capital" with the prime minister in order to gain political points back in Manitoba. Doer also supported Prime Minister Harper when there was a potential weakening of the leadership role of the national government, including on the national unity file. For example, when Prime Minster Harper had Parliament pass a resolution recognizing the Québécois as a "nation," the other premiers in the West spoke about the dangers of any appearance of favouritism to Quebec. Doer made no such comments; in fact, he applauded the efforts to strengthen federalist forces in that province.

Re-elected to his third term in June 2007, Gary Doer had became the most experienced premier in the country and he saw himself as a national statesman promoting pan-Canadian causes. While his government insisted on respect for provincial jurisdiction, he was not a strong provincial rights advocate. He favoured a more principled, collaborative approach to dealing with the undoubted interdependence between the two orders of government. For example, Manitoba was prepared to accept a more rules-based approach to the calculation of equalization payments, rather than the deal-making negotiations with individual provinces that has been the pattern in recent decades. A similar approach was seen in the province's approach to the Social Union Framework Agreement (SUFA) signed in 1999. Intended to restrict the use of the federal spending power in provincial fields, the SUFA has not been effective in part because Quebec had refused to sign the deal. Manitoba would accept negotiated rules to regulate the spending power, but would oppose enshrining such rules in the Constitution because of the loss of flexibility that would cause.

Strengthening post-secondary education and training was a priority for Doer and he was active in staging a summit of premiers with education authorities. The form that future federal policy and financial involvement in the post-secondary policy field should take is contentious. Under open federalism, Harper has demonstrated a preference for withdrawing from direct federal spending in favour of direct benefits to people, mainly through tax credits, who can then have choices to make. This approach supposedly reduces intergovernmental wrangling over joint program spending and clarifies accountability in terms of who raises the taxes and spends the money.

Tax cuts at the national level have been the main way that the Harper government has addressed the so-called "vertical fiscal imbalance" between the national government which, before the economic downturn of 2008, was running small surpluses or deficits. Reducing corporate, personal, and GST taxes would supposedly create room for the provincial governments to raise their own tax rates in order to solve their more pressing deficit/debt problems. As a "have less" province, Manitoba insisted that any future approach must deal with not only the vertical fiscal imbalance between the federal and provincial governments, but also with the horizontal fiscal imbalance between the rich and poorer provinces. This caused the Doer government to insist that not all federal financial transfers should come in the form of tax room.

Also, under Mr. Doer's leadership, Manitoba stuck to the philosophy that there are national policy goals and even program standards which cannot be achieved by having each level of government operate in isolation from one another. Having each provincial government pursue its own self-interest and hoping national policy direction will arise mainly out of interprovincial cooperation is not a realistic option given the history of intergovernmental relations in Canada.

VII. Manitoba's Cross-Border Links

Manitoba has applied the networking approach to expand the range of its activities in the international arena. Most of these activities are in the United States and the premier is usually the lead in dealing with officials in Washington, D.C., governors' offices, and state legislatures and regional associations, such as the Western Governors' Association. Former premier Doer has also participated in Team Canada and Western Team Canada trade missions to the United States and other parts of the world. In November 2003 the Department of Intergovernmental Affairs and Trade was created to develop a coherent strategy (Reaching Beyond

Our Borders) for Manitoba's international activities and to provide a single point of access to the provincial government by international actors. It was hoped that the new department would lead to greater effectiveness with available financial and staffing resources. The most extensive and continuous relationships maintained by the province are in the various policy fields among working level public servants. Memoranda of Understanding are the most widely used instruments to ratify arrangements.

Water diversion, flooding, and environmental damage in the Red River system flowing from North Dakota into Lake Winnipeg led to acrimonious disputes involving national and sub-national governments in both countries. Doer was successful in garnering support at all levels in Canada to block the Devils Lake diversion project, even persuading then–prime minister Martin to raise the issue at a joint press conference with then U.S. president George Bush in 2005. Doer has teamed up with other premiers to advance Manitoba's trade agenda; for example, conducting joint trade missions to Chicago, Atlanta, and Huston with then premier Lord of New Brunswick. In 2001 Doer outmaneuvered the premiers of Alberta and British Columbia by gaining a personal audience with the Republican governor of Texas while the other premiers were limited to working the state legislature. Manitoba was the first Canadian province to join the North American Supercorridor Coalition, which brings together public and private partners to address critical national and international transportation, trade, security, and environmental issues. Doer also developed close ties with Arnold Schwarzenegger, governor of California, particularly on climate change issues, and he was invited to speak at the annual meeting of Republican governors. In May 2006 when the western premiers held their annual conference in Manitoba, they were joined by governors from across the United States and Mexico, as well as by the ambassadors to Canada from those two countries, and the agenda's main theme was the region's future in an increasingly global economy. Manitoba is not alone in expanding the range of its international activities; all provinces have done so. However, as a smaller province, Manitoba benefited from the energy and leadership skills of former premier Doer to gain meetings with the key actors in the United States who affect Manitoba's economic future

As noted earlier, leadership in government is usually shared and collective, so that even as capable a political leader as Gary Doer could not achieve what he has without experienced, capable, and committed intergovernmental public servants. Mutual understanding, trust, and confidence between the premier and senior public servants have been an important basis for the scope of activity and degree of influence achieved by Manitoba. Larger provincial governments, such as Quebec, Ontario, and Alberta, have long maintained offices outside of Canada and sizable divisions within their public services to plan and coordinate their international strategies and activities. In comparison, the Manitoba government does not operate any full-time office outside the country. In 2003, Doer brought the areas of federal-provincial relations, intergovernmental financial matters, trade issues, and the emerging area of international activity under a designated assistant deputy minister in order to consolidate the government's policy making and operational efforts in a growing range of cross-jurisdictional activities. As of March 2010, the strategic bureaucratic centre for planning and coordinating the government's overall approach to intergovernmental and transnational relationships is found in a Federal Provincial Relations Branch and a Canada-U.S. Relations Branch, both of which report to the premier but are housed in the department of Entrepreneurship, Training and Trade. Neither of the branches involves a large number of employees, but the presence of experienced, skilled "intergovernmental diplomats" has been crucial to the past success of Manitoba in achieving its objectives in its dealings with other governments and private actors.

It bears repeating that activity and effort do not necessarily equal influence and results. However, the available evidence suggests that skilled leadership, friendships, and trust relationships can make a significant difference to the success of a smaller provincial government like Manitoba. Also, given the limits of its economic, financial, political, and bureaucratic resources, the reliance upon the philosophy and techniques of soft power represented pragmatic necessity as much as a coherent philosophy developed over time by Premier Doer.

VIII. Conclusion: Doer's Departure and Manitoba's Future Role in the Wider World

Under Gary Doer's leadership Manitoba was able, in boxing terms, to "punch above its weight" in the intergovernmental and transnational arenas. Two years into his third-term government, and still the most popular premier in the country, Doer made the surprising announcement in August 2009 that he was leaving partisan politics. A day later Prime Minister Harper announced Doer would become Canada's next ambassador to the U.S. There was almost universal praise for the selection of this skilled, networking politician who understood power and how to use it creatively to make things happen. It was also noted that over his decade in office Doer had established close trust ties with many leading actors at the national and state level in the U.S. so he could walk right into the job knowing many of the personalities and issues he would be dealing with.

At a leadership convention in October 2009, Greg Selinger, who had been finance minister for the preceding decade and had produced ten balanced budgets, was elected to replace Doer as party leader and premier. Giver that the annual budget is such a crucial political document affecting the full range of government activity, Mr. Selinger had at least general knowledge of the issues across many policy fields. As a PhD graduate and a former university professor, his leadership approach is more conceptual than that of his predecessor. Instinctively, he is more left of centre than Doer, having served as a city councilor who worked with social advocacy groups to create opportunities for marginalized groups. His approach to change is likely to be more planned than the improvised approach preferred by Doer, who emphasized the political need to move forward on the basis of smaller steps that were politically acceptable to the public.

At this stage in his development as a leader, Greg Selinger is probably not as good as Doer at what the professionals call "retail politics," which refers to the selling of oneself and one's ideas. In fairness, Selinger delivered ten balanced budgets, defended them ably, none of them occasioned any political uproar and, to the extent budgets matter in a small, open economy, the province enjoyed a decade of relative prosperity. Being preoccupied with managing provincial finances, Selinger has not developed the extensive network of contacts and friendships outside of the province that Doer possessed by the end of a decade in power. However, having worked closely with Doer for ten years it is not likely that Selinger will change the consultative, collaborative approach which has brought reasonable success and seems to fit with the political culture of a province that is "in the middle" in several ways.

Notes

1. James MacGregor Burns, *Leadership* (New York: Harper Torchbooks, 1978).
2. Gill Robinson Hickman, ed., *Leading Organizations: Perspectives for a New Era* (Thousand Oaks, CA.: Sage, 2003).
3. Robert C. Tucker, *Politics as Leadership* (Columbia, MO: University of Missouri Press, 1995).
4. Donald J. Savoie, *Governing from the Centre: The Concentration of Power in Canadian Politics* (Toronto: University of Toronto Press, 1999).
5. Paul G. Thomas, "Governing from the Centre: Reconceptualizing the Role of the PM and Cabinet," *Policy Options*, Dec.-Jan. 2004.
6. Jeffrey Pfeffer, *Managing With Power: Politics and Influence in Organizations* (Boston, MA: Harvard Business School Press, 1992), 35.
7. L. Boleman and T. Deal, *Reframing Organizations: Artistry, Choice and Leadership*, 2nd ed. (San Francisco: Jossey Bass, 1997).
8. Pfeffer, *Managing With Power*; James G. March, "An Introduction to the Theory and Measurements of Influence," *The American Political Science Review* 49, 2 (1955): 431–451.
9. Joseph S. Nye Jr., *The Powers to Lead* (Oxford: Oxford University Press, 2008).

10. J. Edenbos and E. Klyn, "Trust in Complex Decision-Making Frameworks: A Theoretical and Empirical Explanation," *Administration and Society* 39, 1 (2007): 25–50; Paul G. Thomas, "Trust, Leadership and Accountability in Canada's Public Sector," *Canadian Public Administration* (2008).

11. Paul G. Thomas, "Trust, Leadership, and Accountability in Canada's Public Sector," in *The Evolving Physiology of Government: Canadian Public Administration in Transition*, eds. O.P. Dwivedi, Tim Mau, and Byron Sheldrick (Ottawa: University of Ottawa Press, 2009), 215-248

12. Gerald Friesen, "Space and Region in Canadian History," in *Defining the Prairies: Region, Culture and History*, ed. Robert Wardhaugh (Winnipeg: University of Manitoba Press, 2001); Roger Gibbins, *Prairie Politics and Society: Regionalism in Decline* (Toronto: Butterworth, 1980); R. Gibbins and L. Berdahl, *Western Visions, Western Futures: Perspectives on the West in Canada*, 2nd ed. (Peterborough, ON: Broadview Press; 2003); Bill Waiser, "Introduction: Place, Process and the New Prairie Realities," *Canadian Historical Review* 84, 4 (2003): 509-516; L. Young and K. Archer, eds., *Regionalism and Party Politics in Canada* (Don Mills, ON: Oxford University Press, 2002).

13. H.D. Clarke, J.H. Pammett, and M.C. Stewart, "The Forest for the Trees: Regional (Dis) Sililarities in Canadian Political Culture," in *Regionalism and Party Politics*, eds. Lisa Young and Keith Archer (Don Mills, ON: Oxford University Press, 2002).

14. Richard Johnston, *Public Opinion and Public Policy in Canada* (Toronto: University of Toronto Press, 1985).

15. Shawn Henry, "Revisiting Western Alienation: Towards a Better Understanding of Political Alienation and Political Behaviour in Western Canada," in *Regionalism and Party Politics in Canada*, ed. Lisa Young and Keith Archer (Don Mills, ON: Oxford University Press, 2002).

16. J. Peter Meekison, "The Western Premiers' Conference: Forging a Common Front," in *Canada: The State of the Federation, 2002, Reconsidering the Institutions of Canadian Federalism*, ed. J. Meekison, T. Hamish, and H. Lazar (Montreal: McGill-Queen's University Press, 2004), 183–209.

17. Paul G. Thomas, "Manitoba: Stuck in the Middle," in *Canada: The State of the Federation*, ed. Ronald L. Watts and Douglas M. Brown (Kingston, ON: Institute of Intergovernmental Relations, 1989).

18. Manitoba Budget, 2008.

19. Herman Bakvis, *Regional Ministers: Power and Influence in the Canadian Cabinet* (Toronto: University of Toronto Press, 1991).

20. Herman Bakvis and Luc Juillet, *Horizontal Management in the Canadian Government* (Ottawa: Canadian Centre for Management Development, 2007).

21. Henry, "Revisiting Western Alienation."

22. Nye, *Powers to Lead*.

23. Hon. Gary Doer, MLA, "Policy Challenges for the New Century: The Manitoba Perspective," Gow Lecture, Queen's University, Kingston, ON, 2000.

24. Meekison, "The Western Premiers' Conference: Forging a Common Front."

25. Chantal Hébert, *French Kiss: Stephen Harper's Blind Date With Quebec* (Toronto: Knopf Canada, 2007).

26. Adam Harmes, "The Political Economy of Open Federalism," *Canadian Journal of Political Science* 40, 2 (2007): 417–437.

PART FOUR
MANITOBA'S ECONOMY AND SOCIETY

This section explores several features of the province. Chapters 13 and 14 look closely at important characteristics of the provincial economy, while Chapters 15 through 20 explore some of the important social challenges facing the province, including its growing Aboriginal population, its poverty-stricken urban neighbourhoods, gender and racial discrimination, and the health outcomes and educational attainment of its citizens.

Following up on the theme of Manitoba as "modest" and "moderate," in Chapter 13 Derek Hum and Wayne Simpson describe how Manitoba's economy performs like a "mutual fund," creating modest returns for citizens through a balanced, diversified economic portfolio. In Chapter 14, Kerri Holland describes the continued importance of the province's agricultural sector and considers some ways by which urban and rural Manitobans can strike a balance that respects both agriculture's economic importance and environmental concerns related to this section.

In Chapter 15, Jim Silver compares and contrasts the "spatialized" poverty that has affected Winnipeg's North End and the inner city for the past century, concluding that the deprivation (and related discrimination) hampering the area today is more pervasive and more challenging to overcome than the poverty that recent immigrants endured a century ago. In Chapter 16, Joan Grace considers whether Manitoba's attempts to create a simultaneously robust and redistributive economy have been beneficial to women, whom she argues have suffered during the recent era of "neo-liberal" economic restraint. In Chapters 17 and 18, Harvey Bostrom and Irene Linklater offer differing (albeit often similar) perspectives on how progress has been made in Manitoba to address the pressing challenges facing Aboriginal citizens by "closing the gap" with the non-Aboriginal population while overcoming the problems caused by the ugly legacy of colonialism, residential schools, and systemic discrimination.

In Chapter 19, Paul Thomas examines the past, present, and future of the province's regionalized model of health care delivery, assessing some of the benefits, challenges, and remaining drawbacks of having regional health bodies oversee health care delivery in the province. And finally, Chapter 20 features Rod Clifton's assessment of how the province's largest post-secondary institution, the University of Manitoba, has allocated its resources and to what extent it is making use of those funds to educate Manitobans in a fair and equitable manner.

Manitoba in the Middle:
A Mutual Fund Balanced for Steady Income[1]

Derek Hum and Wayne Simpson

Introduction

Canada is a country with immense natural resources. Much of its early history in nation-building can be viewed as securing and extending the "commons" and establishing the necessary infrastructure to accommodate "staples development." Indeed, the iconic image of the Canadian railway is bound up with immigration and raw materials. Canada has always taken its resource wealth for granted—an attitude that still shapes our cultural identity and self-image of our nation's proper work. However, "peace, order, and good government" is not enough to guarantee prosperity, and each successive generation must manage its economy to put bread on the table, produce electricity for our microwaves, fabricate bus coaches for public transport, and provide health care and education for our children. Manitoba is a small part of the Canadian economy, a smaller portion still of North America's economy, and a miniscule fraction of the global economy. The material prosperity of Manitoba, like every other small and open economy, is consequently tied to its size, location, resources—and of course, the talents of its people.

This chapter concerns Manitoba's recent performance and future prospects rather than a recounting of its historical fortunes. In other words, details outside Manitoba are extremely abbreviated, and Manitoba's economic past is painted with very broad strokes. The central theme, however, can be briefly stated as follows. Manitoba is sheltered from the extremes of most volatile economic cycles, neither suffering wholesale industrial decline nor enjoying exuberant heady booms. This has been characteristic of its postwar past, and will likely be its foreseeable future, arising from matters of geography, size, and natural endowments. These factors will likely trump any and all feasible short-term government attempts at "forced growth" type policies. Manitoba should therefore adopt a long-term vision of its place, display quiet patience, and maintain a realistic demeanour when contemplating its economic aspirations.

How did the Manitoba economy arrive at this state of affairs?

Manitoba's Staple Past: A Missing Heritage Minute

An economy's structure cannot escape its past. For this reason alone, some sense of history—however revisionist—is required to place Manitoba's present circumstances in perspective. But where to start? We arbitrarily begin with the wheat economy.[2] In 1870, agriculture was the largest sector in all of Canada, accounting for more than 40 percent of GDP (manufacturing only accounted for 22 percent). But from that point forward, this sector's relative importance continuously declined. The Prairie wheat boom is probably the most dramatic and most studied of economic developments in Canadian history, with Manitoba at its very centre. Further, the wheat economy exemplifies the "staples theory of growth," often suggested as the single uniquely Canadian contribution to economic understanding.[3]

The staples approach is variously interpreted as a growth model or a regional development model. It is also a useful schema for untangling the complexities of metropolis-hinterland; namely, a hierarchical conception of economic functions distinguished by industrial activity (manufacturing or staple production) or location (urban centre or periphery). Manitoba—a province with Winnipeg as its sole, large city—is tailor-made for application. In brief, the staples approach gives importance to staples production (in Manitoba's case, wheat). Domestic consumption of the staple is negligible so the staple is primarily sold in international markets at terms of trade dictated by external demand. The production of the staple for export, in turn, influences the entire structure of the domestic economy through its various "backward" and "forward" linkages in the form of transportation networks, service provision, and any ancillary inputs required to accommodate staples product for an export market.[4] Hum and Phillips demonstrate mathematically that a staple-producing region's growth rate depends on a weighted average of the growth rates of the staple and non-staple sectors. Consequently, with the continuous decline of wheat as an important staple, and absent the emergence of another staple (such as oil or potash), Manitoba's decline from the heady days of the wheat boom was inevitable. Today, agriculture in Manitoba accounts for less than 5 percent of GDP; realized net farm income is a meagre $25 million, and the value of wheat production in Manitoba has even lost its first-place ranking to canola.[5]

The outbreak of the First World War, the Great Depression, and the province's post-Second World War experience are also chapters that require examination in chronicling Manitoba's economic development, but we leave that task for others.[6] Our purpose here is simply to "locate" the benchmark of the staple economy for Manitoba, and note its high point. At the turn of the century, Canada was a major player in the wheat market, and as Norrie and Owram note, "in 1909, Winnipeg handled more wheat than any other centre in the world."[7] Thus, if Manitoba is no longer a province of agricultural workers, how should it be viewed today? It is fair to say its workforce is slow-growing but mostly fully employed, with labour force participation rates (approximately 79 percent) above the Canadian average. However, Manitoba's net population loss is sizable (8600 persons in 2006) and has increased of late. Immigration to Manitoba has also increased slightly, with more than 10,000 persons entering Manitoba in 2006. Given low birth and fertility rates for all of Canada, Manitoba's labour force growth is heavily reliant on immigrants for its meagre growth, since Manitobans have never been reluctant to leave the province for opportunities elsewhere. The rising net outflow of workers to Alberta is a mere reprogramming of the GPS for Manitobans, giving directions to "Go West!" rather than "Go East!" particularly since Manitoba's wages tend to be below the Canadian average. *Plus ça change, plus c'est la même chose.*

What can the staples approach tell us? Manitoba, once the centre of a dominant staple to the world economy, eventually became a more subdued hinterland to an Ontario-centred industrial and manufacturing enterprise, mainly by reason of geography and population size, and perhaps even "National Policy." Now, it finds itself cast again in the same handmaiden role to Alberta's oil-generated economic expansion and British Columbia's Far East linkages. But is Manitoba's destiny determined entirely by "place"? Cannot Manitobans affect its economy through purposeful action with a combination of individual resolve and public policy?

Manitoba's Economy: Characteristics and Structure

Manitoba's present-day economy is unrecognizable against the heady days of the wheat boom. We can glimpse its present-day structure through a recent report that details its features.[8] Manitoba's 2006 GDP (in real terms, 1997 dollars) was $37.1 billion, and has been growing at about its long-term historical rate of 2.2 percent since 1981 (the Canadian rate is about 2.7 percent between 1981 and

2004). In terms of the standard categories customarily employed by economists, consumption expenditures by households comprise about 60 percent, business non-residential investment is about 15 percent, and government expenditures about 25 percent. These proportions are not unusual. But focus now on how much Manitoba currently relies on the kindness of strangers. Exports from Manitoba in 2006 were valued at $23 billion, and about evenly split between exports to other countries and exports to other provinces. Imports typically exceed exports for Manitoba and reached $26 billion in the same year.

Economists typically portray the "openness" of an economy by calculating the sum of exports and imports divided by GDP. For Canada as a whole, this figure is 0.67 in 2007, that is, two-thirds.[9] For Manitoba the figure is $(23 + 26)/37 = 49/37 = 1.33$, or four-thirds. This is a very high number. In other words, the value of exports and imports significantly exceeds the value of Manitoba's entire GDP, demonstrating numerically the small and open nature of Manitoba's economy and all that this implies, particularly its vulnerability to economic trends, shocks, and events beyond its provincial borders and control.[10] None of this is either new or startling, but it is perhaps worrisome to note that, since 2001, there has been a marked deterioration in both the interprovincial trade balance as well as the international trade balances.[11]

One question commonly asked of a mutual fund, with or without international exposure, is whether the portfolio is balanced and diversified. What are the "weightings" of its different components? One might ask similar questions of the Manitoba economy itself. Two present-day features highlight the "casting against type" of our earlier historical experience. First, the service sector dominates the Manitoban economy—accounting for 72 percent of total provincial GDP. Second, agriculture comprises less than 5 percent of provincial GDP. Manufacturing accounts for 12 percent of GDP, construction accounts for 5 percent, mining together with oil and gas, and utilities each account for 3 percent.

The service sector is extremely diverse, comprising retail and distribution services as well as knowledge-intensive scientific research and health delivery so generalization is extremely hazardous except to note that Manitoba is now better described as a "service-oriented" economy than an agricultural producer. To underscore this point, consider this calculation: Manitoba farmers earned $3.7 billion in 2006. However, operating expenses were $3.27 billion, leaving only $417 million as net annual cash income for agricultural producers. Subtracting depreciation charges of $405 million from this amount (resulting in what is termed "realized net income") leaves only $25 million—a fairly small sum.[12] Therefore, the point is simply that Manitoba is no longer an economy dominated by agricultural production in terms of GDP but rather an immensely diverse, service-oriented economy. This is not to say agriculture is not influential; it is just no longer the main staple driving economic growth these days. In fact, we have moved well beyond the post-staples economy to a more knowledge-intensive structure. The model worker in Manitoba is now in the services sector, probably has a computer with a high-speed MTS connection, lives in an urban centre and goes to Tim Hortons for coffee breaks. The amount of wheat in two Timbits is inconsequential as a fraction of the total value of a day's gross provincial output.

Manitoba's Economic and Fiscal Prospects

Manitobans went to the polls in the spring of 2007 and gave then-premier Gary Doer's NDP government a resounding vote of confidence for a rare third majority government. Without a major issue to divide the electorate, voters appeared to be satisfied Manitoba is sharing in Western Canadian expansion while avoiding the economic malaise on its eastern border. Voters apparently thought it better to go with the steady course set by the Doer government during the previous eight years rather than risk the uncharted waters of an unproven and inexperienced opposition. But is such complacency justified? In a variety of respects, it is. Manitoba is in a familiar position between economies to the east and west that are moving in different directions. Manitoba shares the remnants of a once-thriving Prairie grain economy with Saskatchewan and Alberta, and a modest amount of the resource riches, but it also has a more diversified economy that includes manufacturing and service industries that compete directly with Ontario and Quebec. The manufacturing sector in Canada has struggled with a rising dollar and declining economic fortunes in the U.S. which has had significant implications for the economies of Ontario and Quebec. Yet the malaise in manufacturing has not spread to Manitoba, where shipments grew by 8 percent in 2007, the second-highest growth rate among provinces and far above the Canadian average of 0.3 percent.[13] Although economic prospects have declined sharply recently, all indications are that Manitoba's economy will do relatively well in virtually all sectors, particularly in comparison with its neighbours to the east.

This performance, even in a deteriorating economic climate, will keep Manitoba tax revenues relatively healthy, although Manitoba's performance may continue to lag behind at least some of its western neighbours, assuring continuing pressure for tax reductions to make Manitoba more competitive.[14] Saskatchewan, buoyed by petroleum revenues and world demand for potash, moved in the fall of 2006 to reduce its sales tax by 2 percent, to index its personal income taxes, cut corporate income tax, eliminate its corporate capital tax, and cut small business taxes. Meanwhile, Alberta has significantly and steadily raised its basic personal exemptions to nearly twice the level of provinces to the west and east. Yet in many respects, despite repeated claims to the contrary, Manitoba's current tax position is competitive. Economists like to focus on marginal effective tax rates (METR), which affect decisions about additional investment, output, and work. On the business tax side, analysis of the METR on capital by the C.D. Howe Institute show Manitoba's rate of 38 percent in 2006 lies below Ontario's, is roughly on par with Saskatchewan and BC, and is above only Quebec's and Alberta's rates of about 30 percent. Moreover, the 18 percent METR in Manitoba's largest industrial sector, manufacturing, is below all its competitors'.[15] Thus, while there will be some movement on business taxes in Quebec and in Saskatchewan, Manitoba does not appear vulnerable in general. Indeed, the Survey of Mining Companies conducted by the Fraser Institute has consistently ranked Manitoba near the top and, in its 2005–06 report, ranked Manitoba first among sixty-five jurisdictions around the world when it comes to creating a healthy policy environment for mining investment and exploration, ahead of Alberta (second), Saskatchewan (tenth) and BC (thirtieth).[16] Many view Manitoba's payroll tax as a "job killer," but Ontario has a comparable tax and Quebec a higher one. Provinces to the west have no payroll tax, but Alberta and BC charge employer health premiums that amount to a tax per employee.

Personal income tax rates in Manitoba are often thought to be high, but tax regimes are complicated and should take into account tax rates by income bracket, deduction levels, and tax credit programs when making comparisons. Recent calculations by Finn Poschmann for one-earner couples with two children suggest that the METR in Manitoba on taxable income in 2007, including GST and other refundable tax credits, is not out of line with other provinces.[17] The METR in Manitoba reaches 60 percent at $30,000 and falls to a range of 40–45 percent thereafter. At the lower end, this compares quite favourably with Alberta (70 percent at $30,000), BC (50–70 percent between $20,000 and $40,000), Ontario (60 percent at $30,000 and over 70 percent at $40,000), and Quebec (80 percent at $30,000). At the upper end, rates in Alberta and BC are lower by about 5 percent, while rates in Ontario are comparable and rates in Quebec are about 5 percent higher. Since higher-income labour is more mobile, there is some room for personal income tax reductions to attract professional and managerial talent but, again, only if Manitoba focuses on competition from the west and ignores Manitoba's distinct cost-of-living advantage, particularly Winnipeg's affordable housing. Annual reports by the Frontier Centre for Public Policy, comparing average salaries and home prices, place Winnipeg housing as the most affordable in the country, well ahead of cities such as Vancouver, Calgary, Saskatoon, Toronto, and Montreal.

So what exactly is the problem? If we look deeper at Manitoba's performance, particularly its labour market performance, complacency is not justified. With a relatively free flow of workers and capital across regions, it is not unreasonable to expect improvements in output and productivity to translate into increases in employment, earnings, and in investment per worker. In these areas, however, Manitoba has not done well, regardless of the standard. Between 2001 and 2006, Statistics Canada reports total employment growth of only 2.8 percent for Manitoba, dead last among all provinces from Quebec (4.3 percent) to Alberta (16 percent) and British Columbia (12 percent) and well below the Canadian rate of 7 percent.[18] As one might expect, this sluggish job growth translates into average weekly earnings levels that are also at the bottom of this provincial heap, not only 18 percent below Alberta but also 15 percent below Ontario. Although Manitoba's performance on employment growth and wages improved in 2007 relative to other provinces, this stands out as an area of concern for a province hoping to retain its best and brightest, even when housing costs are substantially lower in Manitoba. People typically try to find a good-paying job in a promising career and search for an affordable house; they do not generally pick out a house first, and then hope a good job will appear close by. Moreover, although capital spending is expected to remain robust, investment per worker in Manitoba continues to lag behind its immediate neighbours to the west. Robson and Goldfarb found investment per worker in Manitoba to be only one-third of Alberta's and 80 percent of Saskatchewan's, albeit 10 percent above investment per worker in Ontario and British Columbia and 20 percent above the figure for Quebec.[19]

There is sufficient concern about the sluggish labour market performance in Manitoba that it will remain an important economic as well as political issue. Prior to the last election, the NDP government announced a plan to introduce a new tax credit for post-secondary graduates who stay in the province after graduation, but this initiative cannot be expected to have much impact on its own in the absence of robust growth in good jobs. And there appears to be little in the current, cautious approach in Manitoba that offers substantial optimism in that regard.

On the labour market dossier, there are a few bright spots as well as some glaring challenges. The most obvious challenge, which is also the most difficult, concerns the integration of Aboriginals into civil society at large, but particularly their participation in Manitoba's economy. Given the fact that labour shortages can pose significant bottlenecks to further expansion, this large pool of untapped potential manpower is key.[20] It will be, at once, either a formidable challenge or an opportunity foregone.

A bright and positive note concerns immigration, and Manitoba's leadership and unqualified success with its provincial nominee program. Given Manitoba's low fertility and birth rates, and past practice of significant out-migration of its talent to other parts of Canada, Manitoba's labour force capital is currently augmented chiefly by immigration. For example, immigrants to Manitoba in 2007 increased 9 percent over levels in the previous year, 76.1 percent of whom were in the economic class. Putting it slightly differently, Manitoba received, in 2007, a higher proportion of total immigrants to Canada than its population share. While Ontario, Quebec, and British Columbia do receive large numbers of immigrants on an absolute basis, Manitoba is clearly "punching above its weight" in accepting and integrating immigrants, and Manitoba intends to double its annual immigration levels over the next ten years.[21] Manitoba's success is undoubtedly attributable to its provincial nominee program. Manitoba alone accounts for almost one in every two Canadian immigrants (49.9 percent in 2006; 45 percent in 2007) in this category.[22] At the same time however, Manitoba attracts only 5.9 percent of immigrants in the economic class, while the comparable all-Canada figure is 48.2 percent. In sum, Manitoba's leadership with its provincial nominee program is commendable, but its success may be masking fundamental weaknesses in the province's ability to attract economic class immigrants on a "non-recruited" or "voluntary" basis. Why don't more economic class immigrants choose Manitoba on their own? Is the Prairie landscape truly an acquired taste? Or maybe seasonal flooding and block heaters simply take some getting used to.

Despite Manitoba's current success with its active and selective approach to immigration, its strategy towards skills development and post-secondary education will be critical to economic prosperity in the long run. In the parlance of economics, this amounts to questions concerning the scope and amount of human capital investment. Are Manitoba's youth being given the right amount, and the right kind, of education and training? Manitoba's population aged 17–29 is expected to rise to a peak in 2014, and then fall fairly steadily to 2017. Alberta and British Columbia to the west, and Ontario to the east, will experience roughly the same overall pattern of change, but their decline will be more moderate than Manitoba's.[23] In other words, Manitoba's youth cohort will grow less quickly than the customary provincial magnets that attract our graduates and trainees.

Passionate calls for more post-secondary funding as well as entreaties to improve standards and the ranking of Manitoba's universities will not be discussed here, except to note that from the perspective of satisfying Manitoba's thirst for skilled labour, the marginal public education dollar might be better directed, in our opinion, to vocational training and the skilled trades rather than expansion of first-year general undergraduate slots. Using recent CAUT figures compiled from Statistics Canada, we calculate community college qualifications awarded as a percentage of the provincial population aged 18–24. For Manitoba, the figure is 0.015. The comparable statistics for Ontario, Saskatchewan, and Alberta are, respectively, 0.021, 0.018 and 0.020. In other words, a smaller percentage of Manitoba's population in this age group has received community college qualification. On the other hand, with respect to undergraduate qualifications awarded, the Manitoba proportion is 0.020, which is well above the corresponding figure for Saskatchewan (at 0.013) and Alberta (at 0.018).[24] Again, this suggests to us that Manitoba's education dollar is relatively biased towards university undergraduates and against community college students.

Forestalling further emotional discussion, we would only observe that waiting times for admission to apprenticeships and training slots in almost all trades are lengthy. On the other hand, capacity and waiting times for enrolment in undergraduate classes are not problematic by comparison. Not everyone would accept that "queuing" lengths mean anything; however, for economists, it is a "time price" and indicative of an unmet demand for skills training and apprenticeships that is not being satisfied in Manitoba.[25]

Present Challenges and Policy Directions

Every mutual fund prospectus is careful to warn that past returns are no guarantee of future performance. How can Manitoba dramatically improve its economic prospects? There is no question that a boom in exports would do it, as the resource boom in Alberta and now Saskatchewan attests. Export of staples have clearly provided a fiscal advantage for these provinces that will make it difficult for Manitoba to compete with them in terms of tax reductions and public spending. Natural resource revenues and investment income now account for a whopping 47 percent of revenue in Alberta, 20 percent in Saskatchewan and 17 percent in BC, compared to only 10 percent in Manitoba, 4 percent in Ontario, and 7 percent in Quebec.[26] Thus, Alberta need rely on income and consumption taxes for only 30 percent of its revenue compared to 43 percent for Saskatchewan, 46 percent for Manitoba and BC, 55 percent for Quebec, and 75 percent for Ontario. Fully 30 percent of Manitoba's revenues are derived from government transfers, far more than the common range of 16 to 18 percent in BC, Saskatchewan, Ontario, and Quebec, and 10 percent in Alberta. It is therefore hardly surprising that Manitoba is cautious about any discussion of rebalancing federal transfers. This dependence on largely federal transfers distinguishes Manitoba's "have-not" status among all its competitors and, perhaps of more concern for the future, generates an effective tax that provides a disincentive to any revenue growth that reduces federal transfer entitlements.

There is some significant room for expansion of hydroelectricity revenues where Manitoba, like Quebec, has chosen to forego substantial resource revenue to maintain low electricity prices for its citizens, something petroleum consumers in Alberta and Saskatchewan have never enjoyed and something that is difficult to justify on efficiency or energy conservation grounds. This may yet become an issue as Manitoba presses its potential to export hydroelectricity as a cleaner energy alternative, particularly to Ontario.[27] However, a "staple" of hydroelectricity is harder to export than either oil or potash. Policies could also focus on increasing investment in priority areas, as Manitoba has accomplished in mining. Increasing capital investment per worker would be expected to lift worker productivity, raise earnings prospects, and expand the labour force, particularly if coupled with improved training opportunities for workers, including the rapidly growing young Aboriginal population. Manitoba could also improve the regulatory environment for prospective investors, introducing "one stop" investing by streamlining and combining regulatory agencies, and work to reduce interprovincial investment and trading barriers with neighbouring provinces.

Much of the modern emphasis on regional growth strategies—unlike the staples approach—concentrates on creation and accumulation of knowledge through investment in research and development. This approach attaches great importance to the quality of the post-secondary education system, not only to provide a well-trained and qualified workforce but also to provide a basis for the creation and transformation of knowledge to produce a competitive advantage. Although a seven-year tuition freeze and subsequent limits on tuition increases in Manitoba appear to have been politically popular, these were not entirely offset by increases in provincial grant funding and did little to enhance the research and teaching capacity of the post-secondary system. Manitoba could therefore focus on improving post-secondary funding to improve the quality of its institutions and to enhance the linkages with the provincial economy.

On many issues, then, Manitoba can look good or bad, depending on the provincial comparison used, leaving Manitoba resolutely in the middle of the pack. In several crucial areas, however—including transfer payments, employment growth, earnings, and investment per worker—Manitoba lags behind Ontario and Quebec as well as the West, leaving little room for complacency. The danger appears to be that the Manitoba government will continue to move cautiously, with modest or negligible tax cuts and some significant investments in hydroelectricity and infrastructure, on the dodgy notion that things are going pretty well if you don't look too carefully.

Conclusion

The entry on the provincial economy in the *Encyclopedia of Manitoba* describes it nicely: "The well-diversified nature of the economy has allowed Manitoba to avoid many of the ups and downs of the business cycle, settling for a more even—albeit slower—rate of growth than the rest of Canada."[28] In more pithy language, this means Manitoba's economy grows "steady but slow" in the good times, and "slow but steady" during the bad.

Manitoba's economy is "extremely small," and "extremely open"; but "small" need not mean "powerless" and "open" doesn't have to be "vulnerable." The province's *belle époque* as an agricultural producer or gateway staging area is long gone. At the same time, a slow-growing workforce more than willing to relocate in response to economic opportunity elsewhere continues to be an encumbrance. Manitoba is not a nouveau riche province; it is also not obsessed with a false sense of entitlement. Neither envious of provinces with greater riches nor jealous of those with more political voice, the province is made up of hard-working immigrant stock that cherishes economic stability alongside dependable government.[29] They are, on the whole, content to *gagner la vie* in friendly Manitoba—relishing diversity and gathering at weekend socials, a uniquely Manitoban community event. They are exactly the sort of people who buy balanced mutual funds for steady income growth.

Notes

1   The authors would like to dedicate this chapter to their longtime colleague, Paul Phillips (1938–2008), who maintained a steadfast interest in the staples approach to Canadian economic history as well as the Manitoba economy.

2   It is also well known that the fur trade played a pivotal role in the economic development of the west, particularly Manitoba. We will start the story after increased immigration and completion of the transcontinental railway in 1885 allowed wheat to displace furs as the dominant staple.

3   For more details on Canada's economic history during this period, see Kenneth Norrie and Douglas Owram, *A History of the Canadian Economy* (Toronto: Harcourt Brace Jovanovich, 1991).

4   The staples approach is mainly the preserve of economic historians. However, Hum and Phillips provide a general mathematical formalization of the staples model based upon two key assumptions: (1) domestic consumption of the staple export is "small" relative to total production, and (2) propensity to produce the exportable staple is "large" relative to total output. With these assumptions they are able to derive a number of mathematical results respecting regional growth rates and the like. See Derek Hum and Paul Phillips, "Growth, trade, and urban development of Staple Regions," *Urban History Review* 10, 2 (1981):13–23.

5   Fletcher Baragar, *Report on the Manitoba Economy: 2007* (Winnipeg: Canadian Centre for Policy Alternatives–Manitoba, 2007), 20–22, http://nl1097.policyalternatives.ca/publications/reports/report-manitoba-economy-2007.

6   For a capsule treatment of Manitoba, see Michael Benarroch, "Economy of Manitoba," in *Encyclopedia of Manitoba* (Winnipeg: Great Plains Publications, 2007), 187–92. See Norrie and Orwam, *A History of the Canadian Economy* for a general economic history of Canada. For a book-length examination of Winnipeg's economic history, see Ruben

Bellan, *Winnipeg First Century; An Economic History* (Winnipeg: Queenston House, 1978), as well as Derek Hum, Frank Strain, and Michelle Strain, "Fiscal Imbalance and Winnipeg: A Century of Response," *Urban History Review* 15, 2 (1986).

7   Norrie and Orwan, *History*, 321.
8   Baragar, "Report on the Manitoba Economy: 2007."
9   Our calculation. Statistics Canada, CANSIM Tables 228-0003 and 384-0002.
10 In addition to the lack of control over external demand, a small economy such as Manitoba cannot influence the national exchange rate, national interest rates, or even head office decisions of national firms operating in Manitoba.
11 Baragar, "Report on the Manitoba Economy: 2007," 10.
12 This calculation is reported in ibid., 22.
13 Manitoba Government, "Manufacturing Week Proclaimed March 10 To 14," Manitoba Government News Release, 10 March 2008, http://news.gov.mb.ca/news/index.html?archive=2008-3-01&item=3279.
14 Saskatchewan and Alberta's fortunes are closely tied to currently volatile oil prices, although at least Saskatchewan was expected to outperform Manitoba in 2008.
15 Duanjie Chen and Jack Mintz, "Business Tax Reform: More Progress Needed," C.D. Howe Institute e-brief 31, 20 June 2006, http://www.cdhowe.org/pdf/e-brief_31_SI_.pdf.
16 See the Fraser Institute website, http://www.fraserinstitute.org/researchandpublications/publications/search.aspx, and search under "Survey of Mining Companies" for various reports from 2002–03 to 2007–08.
17 Figures are supplied by Finn Poschmann of the C.D. Howe Institute using Statistics Canada's Social Policy Simulation Database and Model, Release 14.1. For specific tax rates, see the Canada Revenue Agency website at http://www.cra-arc.gc.ca/tx/ndvdls/fq/txrts-eng.html
18 Ernest Akyeampong, "Canada's Unemployment Mosaic, 2000 to 2006," *Perspectives on Labour and Income*, Statistics Canada Catalogue No. 75-001-XIE, 2007, 5–12.
19 W. Robson and D. Goldfarb, *Canadian Workers need Better Tools: Rating Canada's Performance in the Global Investment Race*, C.D. Howe Institute e-brief, June 2006.
20 We regard it as unnecessary to catalogue the many economic disadvantages faced by Manitoba's Aboriginals vis-à-vis the general population with respect to education attainment, health, job market skills, labour force participation, employment, earnings, future prospects, and the like. For a more detailed discussion, see chapter 17 of this volume.
21 Manitoba Labour and Immigration, "Manitoba Immigration Facts: 2007 Statistical Report."
22 The provincial nominee program "recruits" immigrants for their potential economic contribution; it is designed to allow flexibility to local labour and business needs. Manitoba is clearly the leader as it accounts for 45 percent of all immigrants in this category in 2007. The second ranked province is British Columbia, which accounts for 14.7 percent.
23 Darcy Hango and Patrice de Boucher, *Postsecondary Enrolment Trends to 2031: Three Scenarios* (Ottawa: Statistics Canada, 2007), Cat No. 81-595-MIE2007058.
24 Manitoba's proportion of undergraduate qualifications awarded lies below Ontario's 0.025, but we suspect that the "double cohort effect" is an important and temporary factor in Ontario's number. See Canadian Association of University Teachers, *CAUT Almanac of Post-Secondary Education in Canada 2007–2008*.

25 We recognize that our comments do not give complete justice to the issues. But, what is the marginal benefit to Manitoba (not to the individual) of educating an additional undergraduate in general arts against the marginal benefit to the Manitoba economy of an extra apprentice? Do they also have the same propensity to out-migrate from Manitoba? Statistics reported in the main text and footnote are our calculations of numbers compiled by CAUT, *CAUT Almanac*, using Tables 3.15 and 7.1.

26 The source for these and subsequent figures is Statistics Canada's website, http://www40.statcan.ca/l01/cst01/govt08b.htm and http://www40.statcan.ca/l01/cst01/govt08c.htm. For data definitions see http://www.statcan.ca/english/sdds/document/1735_D9_T9_V1_E.pdf

27 Hum and Thomas earlier commented on Manitoba's equalization circumstances, pointing out the "uneasy" stance that Manitoba must tread respecting hydro revenues. That comment still stands. Derek Hum and Paul Thomas, "Less Equal than Others," *Policy Options* 6, 4 (1985).

28 Benarroch, "Economy of Manitoba," 189.

29 Simpson Cameron and Derek Hum contrast Manitoba with other provinces in the "West" on their economic positions respecting the Canadian federation. Paul Thomas reminds us that Manitoba's political culture also sets it apart from the other western provinces in intergovernmental relations. Norman Cameron, Wayne Simpson, and Derek Hum, "The View from the Less-Affluent West," in Norman E. Cameron et al., *From East and West: Regional Views on Reconfederation. The Canada Round*, no. 6 (Toronto: C.D. Howe Institute, 1991). See also chapter 12 in this volume.

Manitoba Agriculture: Cultivating a New Approach Towards Sustainability

Kerri Holland

As the resource economy in western Canada has considerably grown in recent years, so too have concerns over the environmental impact of such development. The environment is steadily gaining ground as one of the most important issues amongst Canadians, with discussion taking place at all levels of government to address short and long-term objectives, especially pertaining to economic development. However, in the attempt to find manageable steps that will effectively address environmental stewardship, industry cannot be solely targeted as the "problem," nor should it be disregarded as part of developing a "solution." Furthermore, given that both economic stability and environmental management are related to the quality of life that citizens enjoy, it is necessary that considerations be given to both through the phases of policy debate, decision making, and implementation.

The creation of environmental policy is not an easy task. As environmental impacts transcend provincial and national borders, there are often multiple pressures and complex considerations. As governments attempt to address the linkage between economic production and environmental degradation through policy action, the term "sustainable development" has become part of a popular discourse in many academic fields. The conception of sustainable development has been focused on achieving a perceived balance between economic activity and environmental stewardship. It is this ideal of reaching a "balance" which has drawn both criticism and support. As such, a central component of this chapter will not only be to put forth an alternative conception of sustainable development, but also to illustrate what challenges and opportunities there are for a new approach towards "development" that establishes short and long-term considerations for both Manitoba's agricultural producers and those concerned about the environment.

Agriculture has been, and continues to be, one of the most vital industries to rural communities and the province of Manitoba. There are a number of clear economic indicators of the industry's contribution to provincial employment, spin-off business, and general export revenue. In recent years, Canadian agriculture has gone through significant changes, which reflect financial pressures, dramatic decreases in the farm population, and in relation, an increasingly consolidated primary industry. The trend raises two central concerns for sustainable development in Manitoba. First, whether the continued growth and intensification of many agricultural sectors is environmentally sustainable. Second, whether agricultural producers who are dealing with financial anxieties will be able to meet changing consumer demands and government standards with regard to food quality, environmental management, and product safety. Therefore, policy initiatives that establish restrictions or incentive programs towards environmental objectives are critically important to ensuring environmental and economic stability. Moreover, it is imperative to understand that when conceptualizing the connection between agriculture and the environment, there are multiple and complex linkages between economic, ecological, and social goals. It is with this consideration that policy creation must include input from a range of policy actors in the attempt to create a long-term vision, while defining and measuring short-term manageable steps.

To provide a comprehensive analysis of this research topic, this chapter will explore a number of interrelated themes. The first two sections will examine the concept of sustainable development and explore some of the challenges and opportunities that are present within the Canadian political context for creating and implementing effective policy measures. The third section will analyze the linkage between a sustainable agricultural industry and a sustainable ecological system. The final section will summarize the chapter's main themes and explain the advantages of adopting a more broadly conceived "sustainable development" approach. It will be argued that aspirations towards economic prosperity, social stability, and environmental maintenance are possible if the integrating focus for the future encapsulates government coordination, industry cooperation, public support for incentive programs, and clear goals to measure and evaluate success. Throughout the chapter, references to policy measures will be made in order to understand how Manitoba is making the transition.

I. Conceptualizing Sustainable Development

The term "sustainability" is widely used in the discussion of policy objectives. George Hoberg argues that "sustainable development" is advanced by a broad range of actors in environmental policy making largely due to the term's vagueness.[1] To environmentalists it offers the promise of a sustainable environment; to industry it offers the promise of continued economic growth. A common definition of "sustainable development" put forth in the 1987 Brundtland Report and which continues to be referenced by numerous academics is "development that meets the needs of the present without compromising the ability of future generations to meet their own needs."[2] Robert Morrison adds that "sustainable development, as a concept, seeks to build a future world by balancing three sets of factors over time: economic, environmental, and social. It sees these dimensions as complementary rather than competitive."[3]

The concept of sustainability rests on the belief that it is possible for government to support both economic development and environmental stewardship in a way that achieves a balance for short- and long-term objectives of a society. It is for this core assumption that Joel Novek and Karen Kampen strongly criticize what they believe is an attempt to "reconcile the contradiction between economic development and environmental preservation."[4] Instead, they argue that the relationship between economic expansion and environmental preservation remains fundamentally contradictory.[5] While there is some obvious truth to Novek and Kampen's argument, they seem to miss the main point of what sustainability implies. Economic production that relies on natural resources will undoubtedly impact the environment. However, it is essential to be mindful that resource-based industries like agriculture depend on the availability of natural resources so it is obviously in their best interest to support actions that protect the environment and repair the damage caused by their activities. Therefore, the key to the sustainability concept is that it means both a sustainable environment and sustainable industries.

In the discourse related to sustainability, Herman E. Daly makes an important distinction between growth and development. Daly explains that to grow means to "increase naturally in size by the addition of material through assimilation and accretion" while to develop means to "expand or realize the potentialities of; bring gradually to a fuller, greater, or better state."[6] Building on Daly's distinction, Jennifer Sumner explains, "Growth is quantitative increase in physical scale, while development is qualitative improvement or unfolding of potentialities."[7] Therefore, instead of conceptualizing sustainable development as the pursuit of a balance, it is better to understand sustainable development as a more holistic way of developing resource sectors, public policies and programs, research initiatives that produce new technologies, and the implementation of better management practices throughout society. When combined, these actions will produce a more coherent understanding of "development" as it relates to agriculture and the environment. As such, "sustainable growth" is only part of what "sustainable development" should encompass as it relates to agriculture.

Sustainability in agriculture is thought of in terms of farm profitability, environmental stewardship, and quality of life for agricultural producers, rural communities, and the general citizenry. As such, policy initiatives must account for considerations of broader economic, social, and ecological impacts. The complex nature of the political environment often presents many obstacles to coherent, consistent, and effective policy creation, administration, and evaluation. The challenges within the policy environment have led some academics to argue that one of the major problems of Canada's sustainable development approach is "the inability of governments in Canada to translate policy commitments into practice."[8] However, this is not to say that Canada's political system is incapable of producing effective measures for working towards a sustainable environment or sustainable resource industries; rather, it is with political will, cooperation, and a more holistic approach that the political environment holds enormous possibilities. The following section will outline a number of challenges and opportunities that exist for Manitoba's policy makers and will also analyze two significant policy attempts made by the provincial government towards adopting a new approach for sustainable development.

II. Pursuing Sustainable Development within the Canadian Political Context

Public policy is a general term that refers to a set of interrelated decisions in a particular area of government jurisdiction. While the precise definition of public policy often varies among academics, a generally accepted interpretation has been Thomas Dye's definition that it is the "collective action or inaction taken by government in a given area of public interest."[9] Michael Howlett explains that Dye's definition entails two key components—it identifies government as the principal agent of public policy, and it implies that government has a fundamental choice to act or not to act.[10] As such, it is the role of government to set direction, implement legislation, and develop general policy objectives. The result of this role is a framework for programs and regulations that work towards achieving set goals in a given area.

As the general public has become increasingly conscious of environmental issues, governments at all levels have been encouraged to react to public pressure through policy action. As the governing political parties decide how, and to what extent, issues of public policy are addressed, the theoretical "political agenda" of government develops. Agenda-setting implies that issues vary in importance according to the time and manner of how they are addressed by government.[11] In setting the political agenda, a number of policy actors contribute. Within the environmental policy network, governments (municipal, provincial, federal, international), industry, scientists, interest groups, media, and citizens all play an important role. While it is beyond the scope of this chapter to discuss each policy actor in detail, what can be noted is that given the range of policy actors, the political agenda is one that reflects varying capacities, commitment, and priorities. Therefore, policy initiatives are usually developed with the consideration of multiple factors including: economic prosperity, foreign policy, environmental thresholds, employment strategies, and the level of public support.

Every Canadian citizen is directly or indirectly affected by the stability of the agricultural industry through employment, food supply, or benefiting from a strong economy. The wealth that comes from rural communities stabilizes Manitoba's economy through business, investment, and exports (estimated at $3.3 billion in 2007).[12] When taking into account related activities (i.e., processing), the Manitoba government estimates that the agricultural industry accounted for approximately 12 percent of the provincial Gross Domestic Product (GDP) in 2007.[13] Agriculture is also a major generator of jobs in both rural and urban Canada through employment on farms, the production of agricultural inputs, the processing of farm products, and in the service sector. In Manitoba, agriculture and the agri-food system provides one in nine jobs, which translates to over 62,000 people employed directly and indirectly by the sector.[14] Therefore, policy makers must not only be cognizant of how environmental policy initiatives will impact production and supply, but also the larger economic and social impacts that are related to policy action.

Government and industry must work together to develop a long-term vision that addresses public concerns for environmental management in terms of repairing past damage and minimizing future degradation. Public concern towards the environment has proven to be very strong in Manitoba. In a 2006 survey, the Canada West Foundation reported that "protecting the environment" was considered a "high priority" by 67.6 percent of Manitobans.[15] In addition, a 2005 survey conducted by Prairie Research Associates on behalf of the Manitoba government showed that more than 80 percent of Manitoba's citizens believed that "both a strong economy and a clean environment can be achieved without picking one over the other" and that individuals, industry, and government all have a role to play in being part of a solution.[16] In Manitoba, a sustainable future can only be achieved through the collaboration of government, industry, and citizens to find common objectives.

The creation of effective public policy is by no means an easy or uncomplicated task. There are multiple considerations and challenges that come with constructing policies associated with economic and environmental sustainability. While broad goals can be identified, the means of achieving objectives through coordinated manageable steps and being able to measure their effectiveness is often the greatest obstacle for government. The pursuit of sustainable policy initiatives in the areas of agriculture and the environment are subject to a number of challenges within Manitoba and the larger Canadian political context. The following discussion briefly touches on five particular challenges to environmental policy creation, all of which are interconnected. Moreover, it is important to keep in mind that while it is easy to discuss the merits of each one in turn, it is impossible to isolate any particular one in its overall impact on effective policy making. While the challenges discussed do not represent all impediments to creating sustainability, the intent is to provide a foundational understanding of the political framework in which public policy is created.

The *first challenge* that is a central theme within Canadian political science discourse is the nature of the federal system and the influence it has on the policy process. It is important to understand that policy lines often intersect as both levels of government work together to achieve shared or similar policy goals. The constitutional jurisdiction over agriculture and the environment is considered to be a joint responsibility of the federal and provincial governments and as such, the political decisions that are made by both levels of jurisdiction establish the overall picture of what sustainable policy constitutes.[17] Paul G. Thomas and Robert Adie explain that the relations between the federal and provincial governments vary across time and policy fields and that relations between the two levels of government reflect "the historical nature of the relationship, the wealth and size of the province, the distributive nature of the provincial society, the political parties in office in the two capitals, and the relative bureaucratic capacity and competence of the provincial government."[18] In relation, Grace Skogstad argues that effective environmental public policy making in Canada has often been hampered by Canada's federal system through "delays, incoherence, and conflict."[19] However, Skogstad does acknowledge that the federal system has not been the only institutional factor that has served as an obstacle but that it has been "weak or ineffective intergovernmental mechanisms to coordinate environmental and developmental issues and interests" that have also presented a serious test to policy making.[20]

A *second challenge* arises when policy makers focus on trying to achieve a sustainable "balance" between the economy and environment, as there is an implication of associating values to each. The development of resource industries is relatively easy to measure in terms of economic statistics, which indicate how many jobs are created, the amount of revenue generated, and the amount of spinoff industries within the local economy, among others. Conversely, placing value on nature and its preservation is extremely difficult because it may not be measurable in strictly economic terms and policy actors may adamantly disagree on their interpretation of value. Given these realities, environmental disputes frequently involve "intense value conflicts."[21] However, as this chapter previously noted, policy actors must attempt to go beyond a conception of sustainable development as simply a balancing of economic and environmental considerations.

A *third challenge* is that effective policy creation requires horizontal and vertical coordination between governments, as well as within a government. Horizontal coordination refers to the overlap that often exists within areas of public policy. Many of the prominent issues that relate to sustainability in the agricultural industry often require the inclusion of multiple government departments (e.g., Health, Environment, Energy, etc.) in addition to Agriculture. It is for this purpose that a clear strategy must be in place to ensure taxpayer dollars are being used in the most effective and efficient way.

With regard to vertical coordination, policy in the areas of agriculture and the environment requires a substantial amount of agreement and flexibility between jurisdictions to achieve positive results. This is because any initiative that transcends borders, such as climate change or water pollution, necessitates collaboration between municipalities, provinces, the federal government, and even foreign governments. One example of this is the concern over the water quality in Lake Winnipeg, which has experienced damaging levels of eutrophication in the last decade due to increasing levels of nitrogen and phosphorous. Despite actions taken by the government of Manitoba to impose regulations within the province, the fact remains that Lake Winnipeg's watershed extends over four Canadian provinces and two U.S. states (Figure 14.1). In fact, the majority of nitrogen (64 percent) and phosphorous (59 percent) is contributed by jurisdictions outside of Manitoba's borders.[22] This means that in order for Manitoba to effectively deal with the environmental problems under its provincial jurisdiction, it must work with other governments. Therefore, the challenge remains that environmental policy and implementing initiatives are increasingly dependent on the involvement of multiple jurisdictions that must establish common goals, provide resources, collaborate, and coordinate.

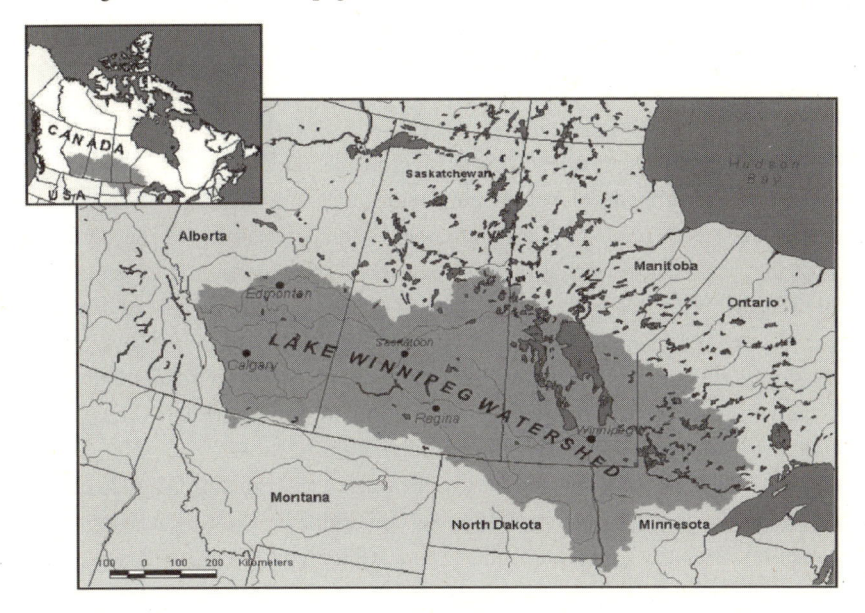

Figure 14.1. Lake Winnipeg Watershed

Lake Winnipeg is the tenth largest body of freshwater in the world, covering 24,000 square kilometres, and the second largest watershed in Canada. The Lake Winnipeg watershed is home to approximately 20 million livestock, 5.5 million people (80 percent live in eight urban centres).
Source: Manitoba, Water Stewardship, "Lake Winnipeg: Quick Facts."

Despite the challenges to creating policy measures, it is unfair to assume the Canadian political system is incapable of innovative and effective policy creation. First, the federal system allows for provinces to essentially be "laboratories for innovation," and there are numerous examples from across Canada of provinces and local communities developing successful programming. Second, given the executive-dominated nature of policy decisions, strong leadership can serve to support bold policy vision and legislative support. If common goals are supported with government commitment, there are significant benefits to joint federal-provincial initiatives, including the potential to combine resources, prevent overlap and conflict of regulations and programming, share research, and allow for national standards while at the same time tailoring initiatives to address the particular impacts on individual provinces. Furthermore, while there are a number of arguments that advocate either a provincial or federal leadership role in dealing with the environment,[23] it is essential that some type of shared direction be defined.

A *fourth challenge* to policy creation, especially as it relates to the environment, is the fact that it is best viewed with a long-term scope. In attempting to prioritize issues within the policy agenda, governments at all levels are often shortsighted as they seek maximum political advantage. This poses a problem in developing environmental policy because it is not one particular policy or program that will effectively deal with pressures facing the natural environment caused by economic development, but a multitude of interrelated policy endeavours—legislation, regulation, programs, educational initiatives, etc. Second, as it relates to economic growth, the benefits of economic expansion are often visible in the short term, while ecological impacts of such growth are best understood over a long-term period. In relation, most meaningful attempts by government to address existing environmental damage or to prevent further degradation will require long-term commitment, as well as time to fully assess whether specific policy and program initiatives achieved measurable results.

The *fifth challenge* is the difficulty in measuring and evaluating policy effects. To ensure the objectives of a specific policy endeavour are working, it is important to not only identify progress through manageable steps, but also to assess, redesign, and reallocate resources if necessary. Thus, performance measurement can be a useful tool for public policy creation, reinforcing government accountability (and action) on a particular issue, and making the most efficient use of taxpayer dollars. As Doris Graber explains, "Policy evaluation involves identifying the goals of a policy, devising a means for measurement, targeting a population for feedback, and assessing policy goal attainment, efficiency, and effectiveness."[24] Performance measurement is not a simple task because it first requires political will and commitment to establish steps towards a larger strategy within the policy area.

Admittedly, many elements of evaluating whether policy initiatives are contributing to reduce environmental degradation are difficult to fully appreciate given the time period required. Howlett explains policy evaluation is often complicated, given that: "Any emphasis on examining the extent to which policy objectives are accomplished by a program must contend with the reality that policies often do not state their objectives precisely enough to permit rigorous analysis of whether they are being achieved."[25] Despite this challenge, the dialogue that results from reviewing policy/program "effectiveness" creates a positive first step that can help work towards the end goal of improving public policies. As Paul G. Thomas argues:

> There is no technical procedure available to rank and to combine different types of measures to reach a judgement about the relative worth of different policies and programs. Such judgments must ultimately be

left to the political process. The real value of performance measurement (i.e. assessing policy and program outcomes/outputs in order to improve their results) and reporting comes not from providing the "right" answers, but by helping to frame questions and to structure a dialogue about how to improve public services.[26]

As a result of a policy process that encourages evaluation and associated improvements to legislation, regulations, and programming, it is hoped that governments that exercise the necessary political will and commitment can work towards sustainable development.

Despite the many challenges inherent in the policy process, the province of Manitoba has demonstrated its commitment to making steps towards intergovernmental coordination, innovative programming, and a more holistic conception of sustainability. Two policies that are especially noteworthy are the Alternate Land Use Services project and the Agricultural Policy Framework/Growing Forward initiative.

Alternate Land Use Services (ALUS) Project: An Innovative Manitoba Approach

The Alternate Land Use Services (ALUS) project, often referred to as "the farmers' conservation program,"[27] represents an innovative policy concept within Canada. It links the environmental demands of Manitobans to the farmers who provide ecological goods and services such as clean air and water to society as a whole. ALUS has shown enormous potential by demonstrating it is possible for industry groups, conservationists, landowners, and various levels of government to work together to find shared goals and workable solutions that reflect both economic and environmental considerations. The Manitoba Keystone Agricultural Producers (KAP) state: "ALUS is an agriculturally focussed conservation program that was developed by farmers, for farmers. It provides incentives for farmers and landowners to maintain and improve the environment on behalf of all Canadians...ALUS is unique because it is drawing together all of these groups to work together on a program that meets a common goal: Farmers being recognized and rewarded for the environmental services they provide."[28]

ALUS was developed by and presented to government by KAP in 1999 and has been fully supported by their umbrella organization, the Canadian Federation of Agriculture. The federal and provincial governments agreed to test the concept by establishing a pilot project in the Rural Municipality of Blanshard in November 2005. The purpose of the pilot project was to determine how farmers would respond to a voluntary, incentive-based program in addition to understanding how environmental goals could most effectively be met on the agricultural landscape.

The three-year initiative is delivered through the Manitoba Agricultural Services Corporation and received national, provincial, and local funding. The payment level is based on the service provided and the level of agricultural use that takes place on the land. ALUS Project Manager Steve Hamm says that response to the pilot project has been excellent.[29] In 2008, approximately 20,000[30] acres had been enrolled within the rural municipality and more than 75 percent[31] of local landowners are involved in the program. Through the ALUS project, farmers received $5 to $25 per acre[32] to maintain and protect wetlands, riparian areas along waterways, natural areas such as grasses or brush, or other sensitive lands that were prone to erosion, salinity, or other ecological damage.

The main principle of ALUS has been that "land provides ecological goods and services such as clean air and clean water to society as a whole, and that owners of the land should be paid for maintaining those services."[33] Alberta's Wild Rose Agricultural Producers president, Humphrey Banack, argues that the merit of such a program is that "it provides a bottom end support for farmers in tough economic times."[34] By promoting the adoption of beneficial management practices (BMPs) through economic incentives, it is expected to also encourage better rotation of crop land, which will reduce disease and promote soil fertility (reducing pesticide and fertilizer use), and will also allow for maintaining land for biodiversity.

ALUS is an excellent example of how the agricultural industry has not only supported innovative government programming for sustainable development, but also that the industry itself is pushing for better environmental management. Incorporating industry's input greatly benefits policy creation because farm groups have the firsthand expertise to know what will or will not work within the farm gate. In addition, farm groups can also invoke grassroots support among the farming community to promote understanding, acceptance, and compliance for BMPs to be implemented and maintained. The success of the ALUS project has been recognized on a national scale and similar programs have since been established in Prince Edward Island, Saskatchewan, Alberta, and Ontario. Farm organizations, conservation groups, and governments from across Canada have looked to the project in Blanshard as an example of the potential that exists to involve the agricultural industry in working towards environmental objectives (clean air, water, wildlife habitat, and biodiversity).

Conceptualizing a new approach towards sustainable development that realizes the intrinsic link between agriculture and the environment and develops manageable steps that promote both economic viability and environmental stewardship is extremely important for Manitobans. Industry must not be disregarded in finding workable solutions to environmental stability because the sustainability of the agricultural industry is in turn very much dependent on the condition of the environment as well. In addition, the Agricultural Policy Framework/ Growing Forward has been a federal-provincial initiative, which has also recognized the important linkage between stability in agriculture and the capacity for environmental management.

The Agricultural Policy Framework: A Positive Step Towards Sustainability

Decisions based on the conceptualization of sustainability were understood by those within the agricultural industry long before the term was popularized within the policy network. The discourse on sustainability as it relates to the agricultural industry was formally acknowledged by the Parliamentary Standing Committee on Agriculture in its 1992 report *The Path to Sustainable Agriculture*. The committee recognized that the industry's long-term viability was dependent not only on economic and social factors but also ecological conservation. The report made a number of recommendations, including the creation of educational and incentive programs, which would assist agricultural producers with environmental stewardship and address the economic hardships being felt by individual producers. Unfortunately, despite the merits of these suggestions, government commitments towards sustainable policies came at the same time as extensive budgetary cuts to reduce budget deficits at both the federal and provincial levels of government in the 1990s.

Mark Winfield explains that between the years 1993 and 1998 almost all of the Canadian provinces significantly reduced their budgets in the area of the environment. These cuts ranged from 30 percent in the case of Alberta to more than 60 percent in the case of Newfoundland.[35] As Winfield argues, these budgetary reductions translated to a loss of capacity especially in terms of enforcing environmental regulations.[36] At the national level, the governing Liberal Party made a number of cuts to department budgets and expenditures as part of the National Program Review process beginning in 1994. Agriculture was one of eleven departments singled out for the greatest cutbacks and many long-standing farm programs and subsidies were eliminated, including freight rate assistance (the Crow's Nest Benefit), inspection services, and research programs. The overall budget for Agriculture Canada was decreased by more than 30 percent and the affiliated staff reduced by 20 percent.[37] With budgetary reductions in both the areas of agriculture and the environment, the objective of sustainability seemed to be eclipsed by a focus on increasing production in the resource sectors with little policy action devoted towards developing a long-term strategy for sustainable development.

In 2002, a decade after *The Path to Sustainable Agriculture* report was released, the federal and provincial governments finally made a significant step with the creation of the Agricultural Policy Framework (APF). The policy initiative included five pillars,[38] which combined to form a strategy for ensuring a more stable agricultural industry—one of which was the central tenet of ecological capacity and stewardship. The joint federal-provincial agreement acknowledged the economic pressures faced by agricultural producers and established the Farm Stewardship Program, which provided financial, technical, and educational assistance to identifying, implementing, and measuring environmental practices. The incentives provided by the program have since proven to be extremely successful within the farming community as producers have demonstrated their commitment to environmental management when they are made aware of beneficial management practices and have the support to implement them. Given the volatility of export markets that many agricultural sectors depend on, it is critical that government initiatives towards environmental objectives place minimal financial stress on individual farm operations. The APF has demonstrated the potential of an intergovernmental initiative that encourages compliance to changing standards through incentives and education rather than the alternative of harsh regulations and penalties.

In April 2008, the APF was renewed under a new name with some minor modifications. The new framework, Growing Forward, still maintains two important components. Firstly, the Farm Stewardship/Environmental Farm Plans Program, which are a result of the positive response of the agricultural industry to become involved with the cost-shared initiatives for making improvements to their environmental management. Secondly, the policy framework is still based on the concept that economic, ecological, and social elements all combine to create sustainability. After a year of intense discussion, federal funding commitments were finally reached in April 2009 for the new framework agreement. A total of $1.3 billion has been committed over a five-year period for Growing Forward programs, which represents an additional $330 million compared to the APF and is cost-shared on a 60:40 basis between the Government of Canada and the provincial and territorial governments.[39] To explain in more detail why programs like ALUS and the Growing Forward framework are so important for Manitoba as a whole, the following section will discuss the interconnection between economic stability and environmental stewardship.

III. Linking a Sustainable Agricultural Industry to a Sustainable Environment

If we accept that the quality of life that citizens enjoy is a product of both economic and environmental stability, focusing on the agricultural industry presents an interesting perspective on the interconnection between the management of economic production and environmental stewardship. Government policy must consider the nature of the agricultural industry and what is needed to ensure long-term viability of the industry within a framework of broader economic, social, and environmental goals.

Many sectors within Manitoba's agricultural industry are subject to unpredictable and often volatile export markets. As such, fluctuations in income levels have created extended periods of economic instability within the farming community. Agricultural producers are constantly under pressure to meet changing consumer and market demands, while at the same time trying to ensure a reasonable profit for their operations. In order to be competitive in the long term, the agricultural industry must continue to implement production methods that improve environmental stewardship.

In producing agricultural products, farmers rely on the environment to sustain their practices. Concerns over the ecological system's ability to accommodate growing pressures of production are at all-time highs, which are related to the increased demands from a growing global population and diversion of grain crops towards such areas as biofuel production. The focus on agriculture's environmental impact is centred on four main areas: water (nutrient surpluses, spread of pathogens, entry of pesticides, water conservation), air (emissions, greenhouse gases, odours), soil (erosion, loss of organic matter), and biodiversity (habitat availability, species at risk, impact on wildlife). It is undeniable that agricultural production impacts the natural environment, as the very nature of the industry utilizes the land to produce raw commodities for manufacturing consumer products. Furthermore, it is unrealistic that agricultural production could be halted or even significantly reduced without far-reaching economic and social consequences. Therefore, as farmers respond to production pressures by increasing their outputs, the management skills employed through environmental standards are key in continuing to provide a safe, stable, and high-quality food supply, as the industry itself is highly dependent on the long-term ability of the ecological system on which it depends (i.e., balanced soil for crops, clean water for livestock, etc.). However, problems are more likely to occur when environmental goals are eclipsed by production pressures or if BMPs fail to be implemented because producers are unaware of new methods or cannot afford them.

In a report released by Statistics Canada in 2001, it was concluded that regardless of the size of farm, farmers are spending significantly more than they were in the mid-1990s to make the same level of income.[40] As farms have been getting larger, the industry has become more capital-intensive as farmers rely on getting the highest yield from their crops just to afford the increasingly expensive inputs and high freight rates. Agricultural economists Andrew Schmitz, Hartley Furtan, and Katherine Baylis argue that the high cost of agricultural production is as much a part of the farm problem as are low commodity prices.[41] In 2001, for every dollar Canadian grain farmers earned, 87 cents went to pay for operating expenses, and inputs are even higher for beef cattle producers at an estimated 94 cents for every dollar of revenue.[42]

The increasing cost of inputs has not been parallel to prices for raw commodities. For example, between the years 1999 and 2005, the cost of farm fuel (purple gasoline/purple diesel) escalated 84.1 percent and 99 percent respectively.[43] By comparison, the prices for wheat and canola, over the same period only witnessed marginal increases of 2 percent and 20 percent respectively.[44] When many agricultural sectors depend on fluctuating markets, farming operations can experience years of high commodity prices followed by difficult periods as a result of trade disputes, weather disasters or flooded markets. In the recent decade, Canadian farmers have been subject to both extremes. For example, between the years 2003 and 2005, the average farm in Canada had an annual realized net income of $3,734—one of the worst ever recorded in Canadian history.[45] As a result, Canadian farm debt reached a record high of $50.96 billion at the end of 2005.[46] In an unpredictable resource economy, the pressure to increase production is escalated when commodity prices are good and trade levels are stable. In the spring of 2008, the market demand for grain and oilseeds was producing relatively high prices after consistent years of minimal return. As a result, it was expected that grain farmers across Canada would be attempting to produce more to make up for debt incurred in recent years. However, it is important to be mindful that price increases for agricultural commodities are still small in proportion to the continually increasing costs of farm inputs (pesticides, fertilizer, fuel, machinery, etc.).

Canadian farms are becoming larger and more consolidated as the farm population declines.[47] Table 14.1 highlights the extent to which Manitoba's agricultural industry has experienced these trends during the past three decades.

Table 14.1. Manitoba's Farm Statistics 1976–2006

	1976	1981	1986	1991	1996	2001	2006
Number of Farms	32,104	29,442	27,336	25,706	24,383	21,071	19,054
Total acres in production	19,026,255	18,819,365	19,126,517	19,088,868	19,106,531	18,784,407	19,073,005
Total Hectares in production	7,699,651	7,615,926	7,740,226	7,724,990	7,732,138	7,601,779	7,718,570
Avg. Acres per farm	593	639	700	743	784	891	11,001

Source: Statistics Canada, "Farm land area by tenure, census years 1976 to 2006: Manitoba," 11 December 2007.

From Table 14.1 we can observe that the average size of a Manitoba farm was 1001 acres in 2006, up 12.3 percent from 891 acres in 2001. However, it is important to be mindful that these statistics take into account all types of farm operations and that many grain/oilseed farms are substantially larger in size. Regardless, the fact is that farming has become more intensified to produce larger amounts of products as a response to not only market demands, but also the necessity for farm income stability. For example, grain producers now rely on increased use of pesticides and application of fertilizers to boost productivity and maximize production.

It is with good reason that increased production levels have provoked a number of contentious environmental issues, specifically with regard to harming biodiversity as well as air, soil, and water pollution. Consequently, it is important to note that farmers have encouraged better environmental practices from within the industry. However, the fact remains that when farmers must produce more to make a profit, farmland is not being rotated properly, livestock numbers are concentrated in small areas, and ecological systems are under stress. As such, sustainable development requires that beneficial management practices be researched and implemented to help minimize the ecological impact and reduce past damage. Moreover, governments must address the financial anxieties faced by agricultural producers when it comes to responding to changing standards. Bob Friesen, past-president of the Canadian Federation of Agriculture, explains that "farmers recognize they are using the environment to produce food; they are willing to be accountable and responsible if they can afford it" and taking into consideration the last few years of difficult economic times in the agricultural sector "farmers need financial help in fulfilling society's environmental expectations."[48] Therefore, to enable agricultural producers to use better techniques to reduce their respective operation's negative impact on the environment, the issue then becomes finding initiatives that establish necessary capacity and encourage implementation.

Beneficial management practices (BMPs), which promote methods that help mitigate harmful impacts caused by production, can actually improve a farmer's bottom line in the long term. Not only is maintaining environmental integrity part of a viable operation over a long period, but also developing new techniques that lead to more efficient practices and the reduction of costly inputs can contribute to economic stability for farm families. To be competitive in the years to come, the agricultural industry must ensure it is meeting domestic and international standards for food safety and supply, animal welfare, and environmental management.

With specific regard to environmental concerns, farm organizations and their members have largely supported efforts to implement BMPs for their operations. The Canadian agricultural industry has responded positively to the National Farm Stewardship and the related Environmental Farm Plans (EFP). EFP certification workshops have allowed individual farmers to identify environmental risks and benefits from their own operations and develop an action plan. The EFPs are administered at the provincial level while adhering to national standards and objectives, which has enabled a consistent approach across the country with the goal of achieving environmental objectives in the areas of air, soil, water, and biodiversity.[49] It was anticipated that more than 75 percent of the farm operations in Canada would implement EFPs by the end of 2008.[50] As of September 2008, 6,530 Manitoba producers had completed an EFP workshop and 5,611 received their Statement of Completion.[51] The EFP certification allows producers to apply for a cost-shared program,[52] which promotes the implementation of beneficial management practices. What is significant is that farmers have shown great interest in improving their management practices despite personal financial costs associated with participating.

The Farm Stewardship Program, which provides a funding formula between producers and the government, has proven to be a positive step forward. Producers can invest in their operations, while having financial assistance to achieve environmental goals. Incentive programs serve to specifically help smaller farm operations adapt to changing standards as opposed to regulations that impose financial penalties. As agricultural economist Ed Tyrchniewicz explains,

"Tighter environmental regulations will impact small-scale farm operators more negatively than large-scale farm operators. Large farm operations are in a better position to have the financial resources, technical knowledge, and human resources to know and follow increasingly complex regulations."[53] For the agricultural industry, adopting management practices that incorporate environmental considerations that ensure long-term profitability and public support are essential. Government must find a way that enforces necessary regulations, encourages good management practices through incentives, and funds research to develop new methods of production.

Agriculture in Manitoba produces many economic and social benefits for citizens. In this regard, the environmental stewardship that producers execute is also significant to the quality of life all citizens enjoy. Support from the public is critical for the continuation of government action and the public should be made aware of the linkage between farm operation stability and environmental stewardship. In addition, development through research (scientific understanding of the environment, BMPs, and pollution data), policy implementation, and continuing dialogue among stakeholders is critically important to reaching economic, social, and environmental objectives. If, by creating a more stable economic environment for agricultural producers it helps to reduce negative impacts on the environment, the costs for the benefits all citizens enjoy should not become the burden of a declining farm population often faced with a multitude of financial pressures.

It is important to keep in mind that the environmental impact of the agricultural sector is only one part of a larger problem. For example, agriculture is estimated to have contributed to 5 percent of the nitrogen increase and 14 percent of the phosphorus totals in Lake Winnipeg.[54] There are a number of contributing sources to air, water, and soil pollution in Manitoba beyond the agricultural industry (for example, city sewage, small-town lagoons, manufacturing sectors, lawn fertilizers, etc.). Despite the many sources, the provincial government has directed the bulk of its efforts to reduce nutrient loading in Lake Winnipeg towards the agricultural industry by introducing increased regulations and even a moratorium on the hog industry's expansion in three regions of the province.[55] While it is significant that steps have been taken in protecting valuable water resources of the province, it is crucial that policy attempts reach beyond the industry to other major sources.

When governments choose to implement policies that enforce penalties, "command and control" regulations, and moratoriums, the financial burden is placed directly on individuals. Unlike most industries, the primary agricultural sector is comprised of individual producers who are unable to pass on to consumers their increased costs of production. Conversely, if the City of Winnipeg made a decision to invest in improving its water treatment facilities, the cost would be shared among the broader population of city taxpayers. For measurable progress to be made on the Lake Winnipeg issue, all Manitobans must be willing to do their part and support government initiatives that help to relieve the financial burden from being placed on one particular group of individuals. Despite the potential the government of Manitoba has shown in taking steps that create better environmental stewardship through incentives and research/development programs, the overwhelming blame and subsequent penalties placed on the agricultural industry for the condition of Lake Winnipeg demonstrates there is still ground to cover in transitioning to a more holistic understanding of sustainable development. The agricultural industry has an important role to play and must strive to continually practise better environmental management; however, by devoting the lion's share of attention to targeting farm operations it will not produce significant progress towards economic, social, and ecological objectives that Manitobans hope to achieve in the long term.

There are many misconceptions of agricultural practices propagated by a lack of knowledge about the industry through the media and the rhetorical "spin" of some politicians. Fertilizer application, pesticide use, and tillage practices are just a few of the topics not often fairly portrayed or well understood. Consequently, agricultural producers are often placed in a defensive position about their operations. It is for this vital reason that government should include industry representatives who not only contribute their expertise but can also help educate the public on the steps that farmers are taking to protect the environment. For improved water quality throughout Manitoba, there must be a collaborative approach between all sources and government. Progress must be monitored and education and incentives must be part of the overall initiative. By encouraging better standards through long-term vision and the defining of short-term manageable steps, progress towards sustainable development can be realized.

IV. Conclusion: Transitioning to a New Approach for Sustainability

> *Any fact facing us is not as important as our attitude toward it, for that determines our success or failure.*[56]
>
> —Norman Vincent Peale

The complexity and challenges that exist in the pursuit of sustainability are multifaceted. However, with the political will and long-term commitment by government, industry, and citizens, manageable steps to meet larger objectives will have benefits seen within and outside of Manitoba's borders. The efforts of all stakeholders must be coordinated and reinforced by communication, education, aligning values, and seeking mutual benefits. A holistic approach in which each major actor assumes some responsibility in the problem and the solution is needed. Ultimately, how environmental stewardship and economic development fit into broader social goals should be reflected in government policy endeavours and neither should be taken for granted in terms of the quality of life that citizens enjoy.

There are many challenges that are present in sustainable policy making, including value measurement, intergovernmental relations, short-and long-term judgments, and performance evaluation. These challenges all contribute to the overall complexity of addressing the somewhat contradictory nature of economic development and environmental stewardship. Despite these challenges, it does not mean that objectives should not be pursued, or that goals cannot be realized. The fact remains that economic development and the environment are ultimately interconnected and as such, policy makers should not consider one without fully appreciating the impact on the other. Sustainability is based on the ability to find common ground and workable solutions so that citizens can still benefit from a stable economy and a stable environment for generations to come. Governments and industry must play leadership roles, but success in these broad ventures will require a high level of public understanding about the importance of sustainable development and in the legitimacy of the solutions being proposed.[57] Therefore for citizens, the required role is one of engagement in trying to understand how their daily lives are affected by the agricultural industry—economically, environmentally, and socially.

The environmental impact of Manitoba's industrial sectors is a valid concern. The ecological systems that are utilized through resource production not only affect the quality of life of citizens, but also determine the viability of many industries in the long term. As such, higher standards of management should be continually adopted to reduce environmental degradation and ensure competitiveness for sectors of the economy. Agriculture is a distinctive industry for a number of reasons. Compared to other resource sectors such as forestry, energy, or mining, manufacturers of agricultural goods and services are still very much dependent on independent farmers to supply raw commodities. Furthermore, society is also dependent on how these individuals are able to implement changing production standards to guarantee a safe and stable food supply while maintaining ecological systems. With the financial instability that can often be a reality within many agricultural sectors, farmers cannot always be expected to have the necessary capacity to accommodate production demands and beneficial management practices.

Investment into the agricultural industry in terms of researching new technologies, measuring environmental impacts and creating programs that promote economic stability will allow for new markets to be accessed, progress to be evaluated, BMPs to be identified and implemented, and a more stable economic sector and a more stable environment to be created. When conceptualizing sustainable development as advancing both the agricultural industry and environmental management, it promotes the idea that industry can be part of the solution to the challenge of environmental conservation and not simply the source of the problem.

Establishing a long-term vision for sustainability requires leadership and initiative by multiple levels of government. Addressing the problems that the primary agricultural producers continue to face will produce many short- and long-term benefits for the entire nation, and therefore warrants meaningful political consideration. Government coordination is not an easy task within a federal system that must allow for varying capacities, commitments, and priorities of governments. However, recent federal and provincial attempts in the field of agricultural policy deserve some recognition. Of course, shortcomings can be identified, but significant steps have still been made towards promoting a more holistic understanding of the industry and its connection to broader social, economic, and ecological objectives. This transition from conceptualizing "sustainable development" simply in terms of sacrifices, balances, or compromises between economic stability and environmental protection, to an approach that acknowledges the interconnection between the two, has allowed for the incorporation of a national strategy with clearly defined goals and innovative programming.

The dialogue on sustainable development that continues to be a part of many academic fields, policy circles, and industry leaders is an important part of translating goals into reality. Furthermore, it is also critical that our vision of sustainability be periodically redefined, policies should be evaluated and modified, and new research should be applied so that a clearer understanding of manageable steps can be continued.

Ronald Mazur argues that public policies are more than solutions to problems; they incorporate a society's shared beliefs about the ends to which it is striving collectively, as well as the means to achieve these goals.[58] Moreover, despite the attempt to present an alternative approach to sustainable development, the concept may still be criticized for its idealism. However, in setting policy goals that seek to reduce decades of environmental damage from a range of contributors across the globe, in addition to outlining objectives for future ecological protection, ideals are not necessarily a disadvantage. The challenge remains on how to achieve manageable steps towards meeting environmental ideals, while also being considerate of economic and social issues. In this regard, by presenting an analysis of the agricultural industry, which seems to reflect a level of encouraging results for the benefits of promoting a greater understanding and need for widespread "development," it is hoped that some sense of optimism can be felt about the future of sustainability in Manitoba.

Notes

1. George Hoberg, "Environmental Policy: Alternative Styles," in Michael Atkinson, *Governing Canada: Institutions and Public Policy* (Toronto: Harcourt Brace Jovanovich, 1993), 317.
2. Robert W. Morrison, "Energy Policy and Sustainable Development," in G. Bruce Doern, ed., *Canadian Energy Policy and the Struggle for Sustainable Development* (Toronto: University of Toronto Press, 2005), 84. Also see World Commission on Environment and Development, *Our Common Future* (Oxford: Oxford University Press, 1987).
3. Ibid.
4. Joel Novek and Karen Kampen, "Sustainable or Unsustainable Development? An Analysis of an Environmental Controversy," *Canadian Journal of Sociology* 17 (1992): 2.
5. Ibid.
6. Herman E. Daly, "Toward Some Operational Principles of Sustainable Development," *Ecological Economics* 2 (1990): 1.
7. Jennifer Sumner, *Sustainability and the Civil Commons: Rural Communities in the Age of Globalization* (Toronto: University of Toronto Press, 2005), 117.
8. O.P. Dwivedi, Patrick Kyba, Peter J. Stoett, and Rebecca Tiessen, *Sustainable Development and Canada: National and International Perspectives* (Peterborough, ON: Broadview Press, 2001), 235.
9. Thomas R. Dye, *Understanding Public Policy* (Englewood Cliffs, NJ: Prentice-Hall, 1972), 2.
10. Michael Howlett and M. Ramesh, *Studying Public Policy: Policy Cycles and Policy Subsystems*, 2nd ed. (Don Mills, ON: Oxford University Press, 2003), 5.
11. Stuart N. Soroka, *Agenda-Setting Dynamics in Canada* (Vancouver: University of British Columbia Press, 2002).
12. Manitoba, Agriculture, Food, and Rural Initiatives, "Agri-Food Exports, 1998–2007."
13. This percentage is a compilation of both direct and indirect revenue generated by the agricultural industry as projected by the Manitoba government. Manitoba, "Agriculture: Climate Friendly Farms," *Beyond Kyoto: NEXT STEPS: 2008 Action on Climate Change*, 2008.
14. Manitoba, Agriculture, Food, and Rural Initiatives, "Grow in a Growing Industry," July 2006.
15. Loleen Berdahl, *Consistent Priorities: An Analysis of the Looking West 2006 Survey* (Calgary: Canada West Foundation, 2006), 6.
16. This survey conducted by Prairie Research Associates contacted 1104 Manitobans between 23 March and 4 April 2005. The survey is considered accurate to plus or minus 3 percent,

nineteen times out of twenty. Manitoba, "Poll Puts Water Quality at top of Manitobans' Environmental Concerns," news release, 12 August 2005.

17 Jurisdiction over environmental protection in Canada is shared between the provinces and the federal government, although the written constitution is silent on the issue. The provinces have taken primary responsibility for environmental protection, acting on their jurisdiction over natural resources, municipal institutions, and "matters of a local and private nature." For a more in-depth account of the historical development of division of powers over the jurisdiction of the environment please refer to F.L. Morton, "The Constitutional Division of Powers with Respect to the Environment in Canada," in *Federalism and the Environment*, ed. Kenneth M. Holland, F.L. Morton, and Brian Galligan (Westport: Greenwood Press, 1996), 37–54.

18 Robert F. Adie and Paul G. Thomas, *Canadian Public Administration: Problematic Perspectives*, 2nd ed. (Scarborough, ON: Prentice-Hall Canada, 1987), 456.

19 Grace Skogstad, "Intergovernmental Relations and Politics of Environmental Protection in Canada," in *Federalism and the Environment*, ed. Kenneth M. Holland, F.L. Morton, and Brian Galligan (Westport: Greenwood Press, 1996), 125.

20 Ibid.

21 George Hoberg, "Environmental Policy: Alternative Styles," in *Governing Canada: Institutions and Public Policy*, ed. Michael Atkinson (Toronto: Harcourt Brace Jovanovich Canada, 1993), 311.

22 A. Bourne et al., "A preliminary estimate of total nitrogen and total phosphorus lead to streams in Manitoba, Canada," *Interim Report: Reducing Nutrient Loading to Lake Winnipeg* (Manitoba, Water Stewardship, Lake Winnipeg Stewardship Board, January 2005).

23 For an outline of the basic arguments, please refer to Kathryn Harrison, "Federal-Provincial Relations and the Environment," in *Canadian Environmental Policy: Context and Cases*, 2nd ed., ed. Debora L. VanNijnatten and Robert Boardman (Oxford: Oxford University Press, 2002), 123–125.

24 Doris Graber, Denis McQuail, and Pippa Norris, eds., *The News of Politics* (Washington, DC: Congressional Quarterly Press, 1998), 227.

25 Michael Howlett and M. Ramesh, *Studying Public Policy: Policy Cycles and Policy Subsystems*, 2nd ed. (Don Mills, ON: Oxford University Press, 2003), 213.

26 Paul G. Thomas, "Performance Measurement, Reporting and Accountability: Recent Trends and Future Directions," Saskatchewan Institute of Public Policy, Public Policy Paper No. 23, February 2004.

27 Keystone Agricultural Producers, "Alternate Land Use Services: National Update 2006," November 2006.

28 Lenore Smaldon, "ALUS: Changing attitudes and gaining speed," Keystone Agricultural Producers, *Farmers' Voice*, Fall 2006. The ALUS research project receives its funding from the Advancing Canadian Agriculture and Agri-Food (ACAAF) program, the Delta Waterfowl Foundation, the Manitoba Rural Adaptation Council, Manitoba Agriculture, Food and Rural Initiatives (MAFRI), and the Rural Municipality of Blanshard, with technical expertise provided by Manitoba Habitat Heritage Corporation, LSRCD, MAFRI, and Agriculture and Agri-Food Canada–Prairie Farm Rehabilitation Administration (PFRA).

29 Ibid.

30 Keystone Agricultural Producers, "Alternate Land Use Services: National Update," November 2006.

31 Manitoba. "Agriculture: Climate Friendly Farms," *Beyond Kyoto: NEXT STEPS: 2008 Action on Climate Change*. 2008.

32   Ibid.
33   *Manitoba Co-operator*, "Paying farmers to protect the planet is future—UN," 22 November 2007.
34   Bonnie Baltessen, "ALUS recommended cure for farm ills," *Manitoba Co-operator*, 17 April 2008, 13.
35   Mark S. Winfield, "Environmental Policy and Federalism," in *Canadian Federalism: Performance, Effectiveness, and Legitimacy*, ed. Herman Bakvis and Grace Skogstad (Don Mills, ON: Oxford University Press, 2002), 132.
36   Ibid.
37   Barry Wilson, "Budget kills Crow, slashes Ag Canada," *Western Producer*, 2 March 1995.
38   The five integrated pillars of the APF were Business Risk Management, Food Safety and Quality, Science and Innovation, the Environment, and Renewal.
39   Canada, Agriculture and Agri-Food, "Growing Forward: The New Agricultural Policy Framework," April 2009.
40   Statistics Canada, *Farming Facts 2002*, Ministry of Industry, Catalogue no. 21-522-XPE, 2003.
41   Andrew Schmitz, Hartley Furtan, and Katherine Baylis, *Agricultural Policy, Agribusiness, and Rent-Seeking Behaviour* (Toronto: University of Toronto Press, 2002), 335.
42   Ibid.
43   "Farmers' expenses soar higher," *Russell Banner*, 10 May 2005, 20.
44   Ibid.
45   These figures cover all Canadian farms, including supply-managed ones, and include all government payments. Ron Friesen, "CFA paints grim farm picture," *Manitoba Co-operator*, 17 March 2005, 7.
46   Saskatchewan. Agriculture and Food, "2005 Farm Debt," *Finance-StatFact*, 5 May 2006.
47   The farm population is decreasing because of an aging population within the primary sector, financial pressures, and consolidation. The average Canadian farm grew by almost 12 percent, increasing from 608 acres to 728 acres in the period 1996 to 2006. Statistics Canada, "Canadian farm operations in the 21st century," *2001 Census*, and Statistics Canada, "2006 Census of Agriculture: Farm operations and operators," 16 March 2007.
48   Bob Friesen, "Farmers ahead of the environmental trend," *Keystone Agricultural Producers, Farmers' Voice*, Summer 2007, 28.
49   Canada, Agriculture and Agri-Food Canada, "Environment Pillar: Securing Our Natural Resources for Today and the Future," 2008.
50   Ibid.
51   It is estimated that over 8.9 million acres in Manitoba are managed by producers who have received their EFP certification. Wanda McFayden, executive director of the Farm Stewardship Association of Manitoba, e-mail correspondence, 10 October 2008.
52   Once a project was approved, program funds were provided to producers that covered 30 to 50 percent of the total cost.
53   Ed Tyrchniewicz et al., "Acceptable Phosphorus Concentrations in Soils and Impact on the Risk of Phosphorus Transfer from Manure Amended Soils to Surface Waters" (Manitoba, Manitoba Livestock Manure Management Initiative, 1 May 2003).
54   Bourne et al., "A preliminary estimate of total nitrogen and total phosphorus lead to streams in Manitoba, Canada."
55   While the moratorium was in effect as of fall 2007, it was formally passed into legislation on 24 September 2008. The three regions of Manitoba impacted by the moratorium are the Red River Valley, Interlake, and the Southeast. It is estimated that these three regions

contain approximately two-thirds of hogs in Manitoba. *Manitoba Cooperator*, "Pork producers offer moratorium alternative," 18 September 2008, 3.
56 *Western Producer*, "Quote," 13 July 2006, 5.
57 Robert W. Morrison, "Energy Policy and Sustainable Development," in *Canadian Energy Policy and the Struggle for Sustainable Development*, 85.
58 Grace Skogstad, "Globalization and Public Policy: Situating Canadian Analyses," *Canadian Journal of Political Science* 33, 4 (2000): 806.

Segregated City:
A Century of Poverty in Winnipeg

Jim Silver

Introduction

Poverty has been a constant presence in Winnipeg throughout the twentieth century and into the twenty-first. No adequate understanding of historical or contemporary Winnipeg is possible without understanding the remarkable persistence, on a large scale, of this damaging and often soul-destroying phenomenon. Winnipeg has been about railways and industry, about boosterism, about remarkable local cultural achievements, about organized labour and its conflicts with employers, about a bewildering variety of political ideologies...and about poverty, deep and unrelenting poverty. Yet relentless though it has been, the character of poverty has changed in the past quarter-century, and not necessarily for the better. One could say about poverty in Winnipeg during the past century that "it's the same, but it's different."

In this chapter I examine the constant but changing character of poverty in Winnipeg throughout the twentieth century and into the twenty-first. I describe the poverty of the first half of the twentieth century, concentrated disproportionately among Eastern European immigrants in Winnipeg's North End. I describe the dramatic post-Second World War changes in Winnipeg, and especially the suburbanization that emptied the North End and broader inner city of many of the descendants of those Eastern European immigrants, and the post-1960s changes to the labour market that modified the character of poverty—contributing to its becoming, it will be argued, deeper and more complex. And I describe the transformation of poverty in the last quarter of the twentieth century and beyond, into the entrenched and complex form in which it now manifests itself, and which has become such a prominent feature of Winnipeg's socio-economic, demographic, and spatial landscapes.

I will argue both that many of the characteristics of poverty in Winnipeg today are the same as they were 100 years ago, and that poverty today is different in important respects. Poverty in Winnipeg continues disproportionately to be spatially concentrated in Winnipeg's North End and the broader inner city; it continues to be associated with—indeed, inextricably bound to—a deeply-rooted albeit seldom-acknowledged racism. It continues to be associated with and plagued by inadequate housing; it continues to be associated with the stigmatization, stereotyping, and social exclusion of those who are poor; and it continues to be associated with, and continues to be an important causal factor of, high rates of poor health, lower-than-average rates of educational attainment, and various forms of street crime.

Yet there are differences between the poverty of yesteryear and that of today. I will argue that the following are among the most important.

First, the poverty of early twentieth-century Winnipeg was overwhelmingly a poverty of the working poor: it was a working-class phenomenon. Today, because of dramatic global economic shifts, a much higher proportion of those in poverty are the jobless poor: largely outside of and in many cases with little or no experience of the paid labour market.

Second, in the case of a very high proportion of the poor early in the twentieth century, two-parent families were intact, and ethnic cultures were a source of strength and pride. Today, a much higher proportion of those who are poor are in families and communities that for various reasons are less strong and resilient than was the case in the past, and in many cases the historical cultures of those families and communities have been seriously damaged. In the case of Aboriginal people, this is the result of the historic and contemporary process of colonization.

Third, the presence of a disproportionate number of Aboriginal people among today's poor is evidence both that the racialization of poverty persists, and that its character has changed. The assimilation of Aboriginal people into the dominant culture is a much different issue than the rapid, post-Second World War assimilation of the descendants of early Eastern European immigrants. In short, in the absence of significant changes, the path taken out of poverty by the descendants of early Eastern European immigrants from the North End may not be as open to the high proportion of today's Winnipeg poor who are Aboriginal.

Fourth, while poor health, relatively low levels of educational attainment and relatively high levels of street crime continue to characterize Winnipeg's North End and broader inner city, the character and consequences of the street crime, while still causally connected to poverty, have changed in significant and negative ways.

Fifth, I will attempt to make the case that while poverty always has damaging psychological and emotional effects—and even "spiritual effects," that is, it affects the human spirit—and that while such was certainly the case in the early twentieth century, the psychological and emotional damage caused by today's poverty is qualitatively different, and perhaps even more debilitating.

I. Poverty in Early Winnipeg

Winnipeg was built around the railways and related industries. The CPR yards were among the world's largest; "dozens of trains passed through every day, belching smoke and cinders."[1] The rail yards cut the city in half. North of the yards became the North End, the "Foreign Quarter," home to tens of thousands of immigrants—many from Eastern Europe, speaking Ukrainian, Yiddish, Polish, Russian, Hungarian, German—who poured into the booming city after 1896.

Living conditions were hard. Developers, seeing easy profits, hastily erected cheaply built houses north and immediately south of the tracks. More than half were not connected to the city's water supply system. Infant mortality in the North End was 248.6 per 1,000 births in 1913, more than double the rate in the western and southern areas of the city.[2] Typhoid and smallpox were concentrated in the North End; in 1904 and 1905 Winnipeg had more cases of, and more deaths from, typhoid than any city in North America.[3]

In the early twentieth century poverty-level wages were common in the North End. J.S. Woodsworth, then director of the All Peoples' Mission on Stella Avenue, conducted a study in 1913 showing that "a normal standard of living" in Winnipeg required an income of at least $1,200 per year. Few in the North End earned that much: "large numbers of workmen are receiving under $600 per year, many under $500, half of what is necessary."[4]

Housing was inadequate, and overcrowding was common. The 1908–09 annual report of All Peoples' Mission described an area of Euclid Street in the North End where "in 41 houses there were 120 'families,' consisting of 837 people living in 286 rooms," with more than twenty people per house.[5] With overcrowding came unsanitary conditions and health problems, made worse by undernourishment related largely to low wages. Artibise describes the North End of the pre-1914 era as characterized by "overcrowded houses and tenements, lack of sanitary installations, dirty back-yards, muddy, foul-smelling streets, and poor lighting conditions."[6] Woodsworth himself described an inner-city dwelling as follows: "Shack—one table and a lean-to. Furniture—two beds, a bunk, stove, bench, two chairs, table, barrel of sauerkraut. Everything very dirty. Two families lived here. Women were dirty, unkempt, bare-footed, half-clothed. Children wore only print-slips."[7]

Typically, these conditions were blamed on the moral failings of the poor. In their 1908–09 annual report All Peoples' Mission decried the fact that children were growing up in overcrowded homes "where the environment is anything but helpful," and added as an example a mother dying of consumption. Her condition was attributed not to inadequate housing and low wages, but to "a life of drunkenness and sin."[8] The Associated Charities Bureau wrote in 1912 that "the large majority of applications for relief are caused by thriftlessness, mismanagement, unemployment due to incompetence, intemperance, immorality, desertion of the family and domestic quarrels." For this reason, the Associated Charities Bureau concluded that any social assistance should be minimal, because to do otherwise would "simply make it easier for the parents to shirk their responsibilities or lead a dissolute life."[9]

The real issue was less moral failings than poverty-level wages. Most North End residents were working, many for the railways and associated industries, others as builders, or in factories and small shops and stores. Many were seasonal jobs subject to regular layoffs. Blanchard describes "the floating population of workers who spent summers working on railroad construction or on farms who were often unemployed in winter."[10] The winter of 1911–12, for example, was especially difficult: "By the middle of February, the situation of many seasonal workmen in the city was desperate. Unemployed since the beginning of the cold weather, their savings gone, they had problems feeding themselves and their families. The hopelessness these men felt as they went out every day in search of work was appalling."[11]

Perhaps this is a part of the reason so many children worked for wages. Gray observed that: "Child labour was a fact of life in Winnipeg and it was the normal thing for boys when they reached ten years of age to be on the look-out for odd jobs, not to earn spending money but to supplement the family income."[12] Today, by contrast, many North End youth, and especially Aboriginal youth, are not getting jobs in their teen years. They are not a part of the working class, but rather are largely disconnected from the paid labour force, and are thus heading down a path to a different form of poverty.

Winnipeg then, as now, was deeply segregated, a city divided, with the North End cut off from the rest of the city by the vast CPR yards, and distinguished from the rest of the city by its "foreign" character. A 1912 publication described the North End as "practically a district apart from the city," and added that "those who located north of the tracks were not of a desirable character."[13] Winnipeg remains, it will be argued later, a spatially and socially segregated city.

The segregation was, then and now, a product of poverty and extreme inequality. John Marlyn's 1957 novel, *Under the Ribs of Death*, describes the North End of the early twentieth century as "a mean and dirty clutter…a howling chaos…a heap seething with unwashed children, sick men in grey underwear, vast sweating women in vaster petticoats." The lead character, Sandor Hunyadi, a Hungarian immigrant living in the North End, visits Crescentwood, the south end home of the Anglo-Saxon elite who dominated the economic, social and political life of the city: "In a daze he walked down the street. The boulevards ran wide and spacious to the very doors of the houses. And these houses were like palaces, great and stately, surrounded by their own private parks and gardens. On every side there was something to wonder at."[14] Little wonder that Artibise, in his social history of Winnipeg, should conclude that: "Winnipeg in 1914 was a severely divided city, both geographically and socially."[15]

In *Kiss of the Fur Queen*, a novel about two Cree brothers from northern Manitoba who find their way to the Winnipeg of the late 1960s and early 1970s, Tomson Highway similarly describes a socially and spatially divided city. On the north part of Main Street young Jeremiah Okimasis describes what he sees: "Strands of country music—tinny, tawdry, emaciated—oozed through the cracks under the filthy doorways. The doors opened and closed, opened and closed. From their dark maws stumbled men and women, all dark of skin, of hair, of eye, like Jeremiah, all drunk senseless, unlike Jeremiah. Had the music student not looked upon this scene somewhere before? On a great chart with tunnels and caves and forbidden pleasures? He leaned forward to see if he could catch a glimpse, beyond the swinging doors, of horned creatures with three-pronged forks, laughing as they pitched Indian after Indian into the flames."[16]

And juxtaposed to this hell on earth that was North End Winnipeg for newly arrived Aboriginal people in the 1960s, Highway describes the very different establishment, the Centennial Concert Hall, attended by the more well-off of the city's non-Aboriginal population, as "a palace afloat on a nighttime sea, glimmering tantalizingly: the four-storey façade of glass and concrete, giant chandeliers, crimson carpet, swirling silver lettering over its entrance." The chapter closes with the violent death of a young Aboriginal woman, "Evelyn Rose McCrae, long-lost daughter of Mistik Lake," at the hands of a car full of young white men. Her horribly violated body was found the next day "in a ditch on the city's out-skirts."[17] More than forty years later, little in this regard has changed. Indeed, it is likely that it has worsened. Today, there are an estimated 520 missing Aboriginal women across Canada, including seventy-one missing in Manitoba.[18]

Early in the twentieth century, those in the city's south end reacted scornfully and even hatefully to the Eastern European, working-class immigrants of the North End. As Jim Mochoruk and Nancy Kardash write, "The Slavs were the despised 'men in sheepskin coats,' 'dumb hunkies,' 'bohunks,' 'garlic-eaters,' 'Polacks,' 'drunkards'—and on and on; the Germans were the much-hated enemies of the last war; and finally, the Jews faced extreme anti-Semitism, ranging from ethnic slurs, housing covenants which excluded them from certain parts of the city and a quota system which kept their children out of the medical school at University of Manitoba, to actual violence against their persons and property."[19] Such attitudes reinforced the spatial and social segregation of the North End in early twentieth-century Winnipeg, as they do today. Ignorance and scorn directed at the "other" is a constant and cruel feature of Winnipeg's history.

Yet, the North End in the first half of the twentieth century was home to much that was positive. Selkirk Avenue boasted a dazzling variety of stores and shops, whose owners typically spoke several Eastern European languages and made credit available to their North End customers when needed. In 1925 on Selkirk Avenue, in the five blocks between Salter and Parr, there were 128 businesses (today on those blocks there are just over forty if one does not count the pawn shops, thrift stores, tattoo shops, and money marts). On most street corners were small grocery stores, above or behind which lived their owners. Most of these are now gone. On Main Street, between Flora and Stella, across from today's Lord Selkirk Park housing developments, was a thriving public market: "That whole area was just one big market place. The farmers would come with their trucks and wagons and they'd line them up. You could go there before winter… buy your carrots and cucumbers, tomatoes," one North End resident recalled.[20] It too is now gone.

Selkirk Avenue was the heart of the North End. As described in August's "A Social History of Winnipeg's North End," it "was a [hive] of activity. Saturday night was a way of life. People would take their families. The big event was looking at the stores and shopping and chewing sunflower seeds. And they didn't necessarily come in to buy merchandise…. Money they didn't have. Everybody was in the same boat. So a walk down the street with an ice cream cone and a bag of sunflower seeds and walking into a store like Oretzki's was definitely a way to spend an evening."[21]

This scene is a far cry from the media-induced consumerism that characterizes all of Canada today and reaches deep into today's North End, creating a desire for consumption that cannot be satisfied with "an ice cream cone and a bag of sunflower seeds" on a Saturday night. In the absence of employment opportunities, this desire is a major factor in today's problems of gangs, drugs, and violence, which are disproportionately concentrated in the North End and broader inner city.

What is especially significant about the North End early in the century is that, poor as people were, most were working, and in a wide variety of jobs:

> The streets south of Selkirk Avenue were inhabited by working class and lower-middle class families. On Flora Avenue between King and Salter, among other people, there lived three labourers, several caretakers, two clerks, a warehouseman, and a peddler. There were also tradesmen, some with shops on Main: a blacksmith, a printer, a tinsmith, a plumber, and a harness maker. There were three tailors, one of whom, Hyman Gunn, was a manufacturer employing other tailors in his factory on Logan.... On Stella Avenue, the street south of Flora, lived people with a similar mixture of occupations: six labourers, eight clerks, and a number of tradesmen.[22]

Today this neighbourhood is called Lord Selkirk Park, and 2001 census data show that 87.8 percent of residents, almost nine in ten, have incomes below the Statistics Canada Low-Income Cut-Off, revealing the persistence of poverty in the area over a 100-year period. Especially revealing, however, is that in 2001 almost one in four residents of the area were unemployed, four times the rate for Winnipeg as a whole, and the labour force participation rate was slightly more than one in three residents, half the rate for Winnipeg as a whole.[23] This reveals not only that poverty has persisted in this North End neighbourhood, but also that the relationship of the poor to the labour market has changed dramatically. There are still many who are among the working poor today, but a much higher proportion of the poor in Winnipeg's North End and broader inner city today are detached from the labour market, and are not a part of the working class.[24] This is the case also for young people, in particular young Aboriginal people.[25] This structural reality has important cultural consequences, not the least of which is high rates of gang and illegal drug activity, and of violence.

There was a serious drinking problem in Winnipeg early in the twentieth century, and a crime problem as well. But it was of a different scale and character than today. Gray observes that early in the twentieth century "Winnipeg was as crime-ridden a city as there was in Canada, and liquor was at the bottom of it all."[26] It was, he asserts, "one of the most drunken cities in the country," with rates of drinking convictions double those for Ontario and Quebec. Particularly between the CNR station at Main Street and Broadway, and near the CPR station at Main and Higgins, there was a long line of bars and drinking hotels, and "the greatest assemblage of pimps, pickpockets, confidence men, thugs, and sneak thieves in the country....Pickpockets were such a menace that the police department had a special detail which concentrated on 'dips.'" Yet the violence that Gray describes, particularly among youth in the North End, involved, for the most part, fist fights in schoolyards, plus the occasional serious adult beating related to drunkenness—plus, as today, high rates of domestic abuse. But the street violence rooted in the poverty of early twentieth century Winnipeg bears little resemblance to the gangs, drugs, and violence of today.

In the first half of the twentieth century, the North End was a thriving cultural centre, with a remarkably wide range of social, cultural, and educational organizations built largely by ethnic associations. There were newspapers published in many European languages, churches and synagogues, music and drama societies, literary associations, sports clubs, and a wide range of alternative schools that kept alive traditional cultures and languages. There were frequent public speeches, dramatic productions, and musical events. Gray recalls "there was a music teacher in every block in the North End to give the Jewish, Ukrainian, and Polish kids massive degrees of musical instruction weekly."[27] A thriving co-operative sector emerged, meeting the needs of many North End residents.[28] Labour temples were constructed; mutual aid societies created. And radical politics of a bewildering variety of kinds emerged out of the socially and culturally thriving, yet economically disadvantaged, North End.[29]

The result was a real sense of pride about being a North Ender. As Roz Usiskin has described it: "Contrary to middle class, dominant stereotypes which depicted the East European immigrant as 'uncultured,' as suffering from cultural deprivation, many of the North End inhabitants brought with them to the new country an extensive cultural heritage of ancient traditions...[from which] they derived a dignity denied them by the dominant society."[30]

Usiskin's observation draws attention to one of the very important differences between the poverty of then and now. Today, disproportionate numbers of the poor are Aboriginal people in Winnipeg's North End and broader inner city. Their poverty is deepened and made more complex by the fact that Canadian governments deliberately set about to destroy their cultures, and justified doing so on the grounds, the *false* grounds, that Aboriginal people and their cultures were and are inferior to Europeans.

Many Aboriginal people have internalized this false belief. "Aboriginal people start to believe that we are incapable of learning and that the colonizers' degrading images and beliefs about Aboriginal people and our ways of being are true."[31] The result is a deep sense of despair and hopelessness. "Once Aboriginal persons internalize the colonization processes, we feel confused and powerless...We may implode with overwhelming feelings of sadness or explode with feelings of anger. Some try to escape this state through alcohol, drugs and/or other forms of self-abuse."[32]

In Beatrice Culleton Mosionier's emotional novel *In Search of April Raintree*, set, like Tomson Highway's, in the late 1960s and early 1970s, the same anti-Aboriginal racism and brutal violence is depicted, ending with the suicide of April Raintree's Métis sister Cheryl. It is not just that her violent end, and the violence visited more generally upon April and Cheryl Raintree, is the product of the complex and racialized poverty and social exclusion that characterize late twentieth and early twenty-first century Winnipeg. It is also that Aboriginal people, treated with scorn and disdain by the dominant culture, are made to feel shame about their being Aboriginal. April Raintree and Jeremiah Okimasis both seek to abandon that part of their identity, but ultimately cannot. They are Aboriginal. The path open to Sandor Hunyadi, the young Hungarian man from North End Winnipeg earlier in the century, who was able to change identity simply by changing his name, is not open to those who are Aboriginal.

This historic way out of the North End, the acculturation and assimilation chosen by and open to so many descendants of Eastern European immigrants after the Second World War, is today not available to many Aboriginal people. Their appearance alone—that is, the fact that they continue to be visibly Aboriginal, rules out such an option. As Sugrue observes in his historical analysis of the emergence of a new kind of poverty in late twentieth-century Detroit: "To be fully American was to be white."[33] To be other than white, to be African-American or Aboriginal, for example, makes the assimilationist route taken by Sandor Hunyadi and other Eastern European immigrants out of the North End exceptionally difficult. This reality is accentuated today because jobs with which a family can be supported are in dramatically shorter supply due to changes in the global labour market.

The resulting sense of entrapment, of there being no legitimate route out of poverty, can manifest itself in the kinds of violent scenes described so graphically by Highway and Mosionier, and more recently and even more harshly in Sabrino Bernardo's 2007 inner-city Winnipeg novel, *Inner City Girl Like Me*. The dignity that early twentieth-century Eastern European immigrants derived, as described by Usiskin, from "an extensive cultural heritage of ancient traditions," is much less available to Aboriginal people today. This is the result in large part of the deliberate efforts of the Canadian state—via the residential schools and various prohibitions on language retention and cultural and spiritual practices[34]—to destroy their cultures, to systematically remove their "extensive cultural heritage of ancient traditions."

Most of the North End cultural richness of the early twentieth century was unknown to the largely Anglo-Saxon south end of the city; so too is the highly effective rebuilding of Aboriginal cultures currently underway in today's North End. Most appropriately, and necessarily, a major part of an anti-poverty strategy in Winnipeg's North End today is the rebuilding, by Aboriginal people, of a knowledge of and sense of pride in their historic cultures. Yet these initiatives, like the rich cultural practices of Eastern Europeans in the early twentieth century, remain largely unknown beyond the inner city.

Then, as now, the segregation resulted in ignorance, and lack of tolerance. As Artibise has described it: "Many Winnipegers never lived in mixed neighborhoods and thus failed to develop the tolerance which must exist in such areas… many residents escaped the demands of respect for different goals and values."[35] Elsewhere, Artibise observed "Winnipeg's commercial elite had little interaction with other segments of the Winnipeg community."[36] Among Winnipeg's elite, the segregation led not only to ignorance and lack of respect, but also to the callous attitudes that were expressed in public policies that ignored the needs of the North End: "Sheltered in their lavish homes in Armstrong's Point, Fort Rouge and Wellington Crescent, and engaged in a social and business life centred around the Manitoba Club, the Board of Trade and the St. Charles Country Club, the governing elite's callous stance was often the result of ignorance…for the most part they gave little serious thought to the social problems in their midst."[37]

Those in positions of authority looked upon the residents of the North End with condescension and disdain, and "spent only a small fraction of their budgets on such community services as sanitation, health departments or welfare."[38] This was, as Artibise has argued, the result of the "failure of Winnipeg's leadership to develop a mature social conscience."[39] Many are the echoes from the past that can still be heard in the present.

II. Post-Second World War Changes in the North End

After the Second World War large numbers of the descendants of Eastern European immigrants left the North End as part of the continent-wide process of suburbanization.[40] Between 1951 and 1961 the number of Jews in the North End declined by half, from 12,389 to 6,536, and Ukrainians by 10 percent.[41] While just over 2 percent of Jews in Winnipeg lived in the suburbs in 1941, by 1961 just over 44 percent did so—most in West Kildonan, River Heights, or Tuxedo.[42] This process continued for decades, as those who could afford it left for the suburbs. From 1941 to 2001, while the population of Winnipeg grew from 300,000 to 674,000, that of the North End and broader inner city declined from 153,700 to 93,800—from 51.2 percent to 13.9 percent of Winnipeg's total population.[43]

This spatial and social movement was made possible, in part, because the discrimination experienced earlier by those of Eastern European descent was beginning to dissipate. Discrimination did not disappear in the post-Second World War era; it was simply redirected to the next group who moved into the city at the bottom rung of the socio-economic ladder and who, like the Eastern Europeans of the early part of the century, looked and behaved differently. Nevertheless, Artibise has observed "during the 1950s large numbers of non-Anglo-Saxons acquired a relative degree of affluence and were accorded by the charter group increasing degrees of respect and tolerance."[44] Occupations like medicine and law, largely closed to non-Anglo-Saxons throughout the first part of the century, were opened, creating opportunities that were eagerly seized. Thus, many of the North End's most skilled and talented sons and daughters left for the bigger spaces and newer homes of the suburbs.

As they moved, businesses followed. The North End and broader inner city was "hollowed out." This process was fuelled by massive government subsidies for the construction of highways and bridges and other infrastructure to service the new suburban communities, and government support for mortgages for buyers of new homes. By contrast, relatively little public investment was directed at the hollowed-out North End.[45] The result was that those who stayed behind were disproportionately those who could not afford to move to the suburbs; their older homes and neighbourhoods suffered a relative lack of government investment.

As people moved out of the North End, demand for housing fell, driving prices down. Many older homes, their values in decline, were bought by absentee landlords, at least some of whom used them as revenue properties—investing little in maintenance and repair, and cramming in as many renters as possible, often in the form of rooming houses (see Table 15.2). Thus the inner city became an area of cheap housing, which then attracted those with lower incomes in search of housing that they could afford, thus contributing to the further spatial concentration of poverty.

Simultaneously, the thriving commercial life of the North End atrophied. Children chose not to take over the small corner grocery stores that their parents had owned, and live in the back or on the top where many of them had grown up. It is not hard to see why. Even before the post-war exodus, life as a small North End shopkeeper was difficult. Most were poor: too many small stores, not enough local purchasing power, and too much corporate competition. According to a long-time North End resident: "Lots of stores closed. See, we used to have a lot of corner grocery stores....What really influenced the change were the big stores, you know, the Safeways. That's what made the big change. And then of course the malls started. That's what really tore everything apart, that's what broke up the type of community life that you had in the area. The little corner groceries closed down—couldn't compete. They couldn't compete."[46]

The loss of large numbers of skilled, working-age people, and the demise of small-business commercial life, took its toll on the rich social and cultural life of the North End. It too, according to the same North End resident, began to atrophy: "The Halls began to suffer and the organizations suffered as well. There was a Jewish synagogue right over here on McGregor and Magnus, where there is [now] a filling station. And there was a Jewish school right next door. That's gone. People moved and so the churches...began to disappear."[47] The drama and music societies, literary associations and sports clubs, the public speeches, ethnic newspapers and radical politics, all atrophied. The North End changed, and changed dramatically.

Other changes, also the products of broad socio-economic forces, followed in rapid succession. In the late 1960s and early 1970s the process of de-industrialization, a central part of what is now commonly called globalization, began to create a massive shift in the character of the labour market; that is, in the kinds of jobs available to people, in Winnipeg as elsewhere. Industrial jobs—in factories, packinghouses, and warehouses, for example—on which people with relatively low levels of formal education could raise a family, began to disappear, not only to the suburbs but out of the country entirely. This process is still underway. These jobs have increasingly been replaced by service sector jobs, in retail or fast-food restaurants, for example, that are today often called "contingent" jobs,[48] because they are frequently part-time, low-wage, and without benefits, security, or union protections. By 2007, for the first time, retail jobs outnumbered industrial jobs in Canada, a process long underway and not yet over.[49] Large numbers of these are jobs that cannot support a family. This changing character of the labour market has had a dramatic effect on the character of poverty, in Winnipeg and elsewhere.[50]

At precisely the time that suburbanization and globalization were removing jobs and people from the North End and inner city of Winnipeg, "hollowing out" the inner city, Aboriginal people began to move in growing numbers from rural and northern communities to urban centres, especially in Western Canada. Table 15.1 shows the rapid growth in the numbers of Aboriginal people in Winnipeg, starting in the 1960s. In 1971 Aboriginal people represented slightly more than 1 percent of Winnipeg's population; by 2006 they comprised 10 percent of Winnipeg's total population. Evidence suggests a considerable majority are moving in search of better employment opportunities, and improved educational opportunities for themselves and their children.[51]

Table 15.1. Aboriginal People Resident in Winnipeg, 1951–2006

1951	1961	1971	1981	1991	1996	2001	2006
210	1082	4940	16,575	35,150	45,750	55,755	68,380

Source: Census of Canada, various dates.[52]

They arrived just as the good jobs were leaving: for the suburbs, as part of the process of suburbanization; or out of the country altogether, as part of the process of de-industrialization. At the same time, Aboriginal newcomers—like the Eastern European newcomers of the early twentieth century—faced a wall of racism and job discrimination. Newspaper accounts of the time make this evident. Interviews and conversations with Aboriginal people repeatedly cite incidents of job-related discrimination.[53] In the early twenty-first century, a very different employment opportunity structure faces young people with limited levels of formal education. For young Aboriginal people in particular, de-industrialization plus employment discrimination have been a devastating combination. This structural reality has been a crucial causal factor in the rise, in Winnipeg's inner city as elsewhere, of the gangs, drugs, and street-level violence that are an important new feature of persistent poverty in Winnipeg.

This harsh urban reality was worsened by many newcomers' exposure to slum landlords. For example, a 1959 report by the City Welfare Department described a small number of slum landlords accumulating large profits, while incurring repeated housing violations. The report showed what the four landlords—called A, B, C, and D in the *Winnipeg Tribune* account—paid in taxes, and earned in rent, and the numbers of buildings they rented out.

Table 15.2. Taxes Paid and Rent Received by Four North End Winnipeg Slum Landlords, 1959

	Taxes paid	Rent received	Rent-to-taxes ratio	Buildings Owned
A	$7,442	$75,405	10:1	13
B	$3,597	$35,124	10:1	21
C	$7.675	$70,890	9:1	18
D	$2,048	$29,282	15:1	29

Source: *Winnipeg Tribune*, 14 October 1959.

These four landlords collected an amount in rent that was ten times or greater than the annual taxes paid on their many properties. But their rental revenues were not invested in the maintenance of their properties. In 1958 they incurred 388 violations of the Health Act. From 1955 to 1958 they had a total of 1,497 such violations, including 117 for defective walls, floors and ceilings; eighty-six for bedbugs; sixty-six for insufficient plumbing; fifty-four for cockroaches; thirty-eight for insufficient heat and ten for rats. As far as housing was concerned, little had changed since early in the century.

These newcomers were also the targets of racial abuse, as evidenced by a *Winnipeg Tribune* story about Jarvis Avenue, previously near the heart of the Jewish North End and by the 1960s and 1970s home to many newly arriving Aboriginal people.[54] Manley Steiman, City of Winnipeg Health Inspector, "cites Jarvis Avenue itself as being, undoubtedly, the worst street in the entire city."[55] Many houses on Jarvis had been little more than shacks from the beginning of the century; many lots, small as they were, had two or more dwellings squeezed onto them. The *Tribune* story began: "The police, with ponderous legal irony, call it Jarvis Boulevard. Others, with more bitterness, have named it Tomahawk Row." In September 1962, the *Tribune* described a Winnipeg Police Commission report:

> The Report...says the area has been a "problem" for many years. It adds it has become worse recently with the arrival "of more persons of Indian racial origin. The district now appears to have become an Indian and Métis community"...Some 27 single and multiple dwellings are completely occupied by persons of Indian origin...The report says over 100 persons, mostly Indians, have been arrested in the area so far this year.[56]

As had been the case throughout the twentieth century, the most recently arrived, non-Anglo-Saxon inhabitants of Winnipeg's North End were blamed for the area's poverty. Recall the Associated Charities Bureau writing in 1912, referring not to Aboriginal newcomers but to Eastern European immigrants, about their "thriftlessness, mismanagement, unemployment due to incompetence, intemperance, immorality, desertion of the family and domestic quarrels."

Throughout the twentieth century, and continuing to this day, the response to poverty in Winnipeg has been to blame the victim, the "other." The response has been and continues to be to blame those who have most recently arrived in the city and who as a consequence are located socio-economically on the bottom rung of the ladder, and whose appearance and behaviour are different. The poor, whether Eastern European immigrants or Aboriginal people or otherwise, have been constructed simplistically and stereotypically. As Sugrue has described this, referring to the case of Detroit: "To the majority of untutored white observers, visible poverty, overcrowding, and deteriorating houses were signs of individual moral deficiencies, not manifestations of structural inequalities."[57] Causality is attributed to personal characteristics, and to the "otherness," and the "racial-ness," of the poor. To do otherwise would be to open the door to the possibility that the cause might be the capitalist system, or the class-based policies of the state, or both. It has always been more comfortable, and safer, to rely upon stereotypes.

The 1962 report described by the *Winnipeg Tribune* is typical in condemning an entire group, and in making no attempt to *explain* the observed behaviour of some members of the group. No mention is made of the racism that Aboriginal people faced upon arrival in Winnipeg. No mention is made of the activities of avaricious slum landlords. No mention is made of the devastating impact of colonization upon Aboriginal people—that they were stripped of their historic lands, that their economic and political systems were destroyed, that they were pushed onto often distant reserves, subjected to the control of the Indian Act and the Indian Agent, and denied the right to practise their spirituality and their cultures. Perhaps most importantly, no mention was made of the fact that many Aboriginal children were seized by the agents of the state and forced into residential schools where thousands died, and where sickness and various forms of abuse were common.[58] All of these things together constitute a deliberate and systematic attempt to destroy Aboriginal cultures. Aboriginal children in residential schools, for example, were denied the right to speak their languages and were taught to be ashamed of being Aboriginal.

Together, these things done to Aboriginal people are what they now call colonization, and this process of colonization has had devastating effects, which constitute a major part of the explanation for the poverty so many Aboriginal people now experience. None of this was included in the *Winnipeg Tribune* article. The easier and more common approach to such matters is to blame the victim, as was done earlier in the century when it was Eastern European immigrants—the "bohunks," "dumb hunkies," "drunkards" of the time—who struggled with poverty and were subjected to vile and vicious forms of racism.

The common practice, the norm, is to denigrate the histories and cultures of those on the bottom rung of the ladder, whoever they may be at a given time, and to attribute their being on the bottom rung to their cultural and personal failings. Winnipeg has a long and dishonourable history of subjecting the inhabitants of the North End to this kind of racist construction of poverty and its causes.

III. Poverty in Winnipeg Today
The Problems
Poverty persists in Winnipeg's inner city today. Indeed, poverty has become, if anything, deeper and more complex. This can be described with numbers, as below, and these numbers, most relating to income, reveal a serious problem. But the poverty in Winnipeg today is about much more than a shortage of income.

Poverty in today's Winnipeg has been described as "spatially concentrated racialized poverty."[59] It is spatially concentrated in that a much higher proportion of those who live in Winnipeg's inner city, including the North End, are poor than is the case for Winnipeg as a whole, and this spatial concentration grew in the two decades from 1981 to 2001.[60] It is racialized in that a much higher proportion of Aboriginal people are poor compared to the population as a whole.[61] In most inner-city neighbourhoods, there is a very high proportion of Aboriginal people and visible minorities. In five inner-city neighbourhoods examined in a 2005 evaluation of Manitoba's Neighbourhoods Alive! program, it was found that Aboriginal people constituted from 27.5 to 54.9 percent of neighbourhood populations, and that Aboriginal people plus visible minorities comprised a majority in four of the five neighbourhoods—from 51.5 to 66.0 percent—and were 42.5 percent in the fifth neighbourhood.[62]

Table 15.3 shows poverty rates and related indicators in Winnipeg, Winnipeg's inner city, and Lord Selkirk Park, based on 2001 census data. It reveals poverty is concentrated in the inner city, and is particularly concentrated in Lord Selkirk Park, in Winnipeg's North End, where a high proportion of residents are Aboriginal.

Table 15.3. Poverty and Related Indicators 2001: Winnipeg; Winnipeg Inner City; Lord Selkirk Park

Selected Indicator	Lord Selkirk Park	Inner-City	Winnipeg
Population Under 15 Years of Age	33.5%	18.3%	19.1%
Population Over 65 Years of Age	19.0%	13.5%	13.5%
Aboriginal Population as % of Total	54.3%	19.2%	8.6%
Lone-Parent Families (both sexes as % of all families)	47.7%	29.6%	18.5%
Less than high School (adults 20 years of age or older)	67.9%	36.0%	28.2%
Adult Unemployment Rate	23.4%	9.0%	5.7%
Youth (15 - 24) Unemployment Rate	45.5%	13.0%	10.9%
Adult Labour Force Participation	35.8%	63.0%	68.1%
Youth (15 - 24) Labour Force Participation Rate	44.0%	66.4%	71.3%
Median Household Income $	$14,696	$26,362	$43,383
Household Poverty Rate	87.8%	44.1%	24.7%

Source: Statistics Canada.

Children growing up in poor families, often referred to as child poverty, are especially prevalent in Winnipeg. Between 1990 and 2004, Manitoba had the highest child poverty rate of all provinces six times out of sixteen. It was among the three worst provinces every year except 2004. In 1990 the child poverty rate peaked at 30 percent, the worst in Canada; in both 1995 and 1999 the rate was 25 percent, the second-worst in Canada. By 2004, when the national average was 17.7 percent—almost one in every six children—Manitoba's rate of child poverty had dropped to 19.2 percent, almost one in five and the fourth worst in Canada.[63]

High rates of child poverty matter because, as Ross and Roberts have shown, children who grow up in poor families are, on average, less likely to do well in life than are children who grow up in non-poor families.[64] The Canadian Council on Social Development has described the lasting effects of child poverty as follows: "Child poverty is associated with poor health and hygiene, a lack of a nutritious diet, absenteeism from school and low scholastic achievement, behaviourial and mental problems, low housing standards, and in later years few employment opportunities and a persistently low economic status."[65]

The correlation between poverty and levels of educational attainment has been shown to be particularly strong in Winnipeg, where a recent study by the Manitoba Centre for Health Policy concluded that while 81 percent of students living in high socio-economic status (SES) areas graduated high school within five years of leaving Grade 9, only 37 percent of students living in low SES areas did so, and only 22 percent in the North End.[66] The higher the incidence of poverty in a geographic area, the lower the level of educational attainment by young people in that area. We know too that the lower the level of educational attainment, the higher is the risk of future poverty[67] and in this fashion poverty is reproduced across generations, making child poverty a particularly serious problem. It is notable in this regard that in 1911, a survey in the Toronto newspaper, *The Globe*, found that literacy rates were lower in Winnipeg than in any other Canadian city of the time.[68] The close association between poverty and lowered educational attainment has persisted across the decades.

So too have the health inequities described earlier in this chapter. The Manitoba Centre for Health Policy recently reported that residents in Winnipeg's North End and broader inner city had poorer health—a higher incidence of death from heart disease, respiratory disease, cancer, and injury, for example—than residents in the rest of Winnipeg, and that this was related to lower average incomes and higher rates of unemployment in low-income neighbourhoods.[69] A wealth of studies in Canada, the U.S., and the U.K. confirm that today, as in the past, "lower socioeconomic status is associated with poorer health outcomes."

We know too that the incidence of poverty and rates of unemployment are higher, and levels of educational attainment are lower, for Aboriginal people than for the population as a whole;[70] that Aboriginal people are disproportionately concentrated in inner-city neighbourhoods (see Table 15.3); and that the Aboriginal population is younger and growing faster than the population as a whole,[71] creating a form of spatially concentrated racialized poverty in those neighbourhoods that threatens to grow worse with time. A study using 1996 census data found that slightly more than 50 percent of all inner-city Winnipeg households had incomes below the Statistics Canada Low-Income Cut-Off (LICO), and just over 80 percent, or four in every five, of Aboriginal households in Winnipeg's inner city had incomes below the LICO.[72] Issues related to poverty and employment levels in the Aboriginal populations of Saskatchewan and Manitoba are such that Mendelson, in his study of Aboriginal people in Canada's labour market, was led by the evidence to observe that: "To no small degree, the Aboriginal children who are today in Manitoba and Saskatchewan homes, child care centres and schools represent the economic future of the two provinces," (and) "The increasing importance of the Aboriginal workforce to Manitoba and Saskatchewan cannot be exaggerated. There is likely no single more critical economic factor for these provinces."[73]

These various data show that the incidence of poverty and associated problems is high in Manitoba, is particularly high among Aboriginal peoples, and in Winnipeg is spatially concentrated in, although by no means confined to, inner-city neighbourhoods. The problem of spatially concentrated racialized poverty in these neighbourhoods is a function of broad socio-economic and demographic forces. Poverty in Canada as a whole has been persistently high since at least 1980, and reached particularly high levels in the mid-1990s, and although it has since declined somewhat, poverty in Canada is still at the level it was in 1980, almost three decades ago.[74]

The problem of poverty in Winnipeg's inner city, however, is about more than a shortage of income, as important as that is. Many of the poor in Winnipeg's inner city today are detached from the labour market, and from the mainstream national and global economy. This creates a different kind of poverty than that of early twentieth century North End Winnipeg. Then, poverty affected most of the working class, and was simply a given for most workers and their families; now, a much higher proportion of those who are poor are *not* a part of the working class. It is therefore a different *kind* of poverty. As Wilson has argued, referring to the case of American inner cities: "A neighbourhood in which people are poor, but employed, is much different from a neighbourhood in which people are poor and jobless…many of today's problems in America's inner-city ghetto neighbourhoods—crime, family dissolution, welfare, low levels of social organization, and so on—are in major measures related to the disappearance of work."[75] This relative joblessness creates what Wacquant describes as a "new regime of marginality," characterized by the emergence of spatially delineated "zones for the urban outcasts,"[76] where a deep sense of hopelessness sets in.

Early in the twentieth century the North End poor were the underpaid and exploited working class, and as such were an integral part of the economy of the time. This gave them some power, as evidenced for example by the 1919 Winnipeg General Strike. For many in the inner city today, this is not the case. They are disconnected from the mainstream economy, and relatively powerless as a consequence. As former Manitoba attorney general Roland Penner has described it: "The poor are not just the rich without money. The poor are powerless....That's what poverty is all about. It's about powerlessness; about the inability to change the course of one's life."[77]

It is this powerlessness that is the problem, or a major part of the problem, with the poverty of the late twentieth and early twenty-first century in Winnipeg's inner city. The poor are, and feel themselves to be, powerless, unable to change the course of their lives. They are, and feel, trapped. Many of the young among them act out, often in violent and/or self-destructive ways. Many among them feel a lack of self-esteem and of self-confidence; a sense of worthlessness; a lack of hope for the future—hopelessness. It is exceptionally difficult to navigate a complex and harshly competitive society without a sense of self-worth, without a sense of hope and optimism about the future. Colonization, racism, de-industrialization, and related phenomena have eroded that positive psychological sense; they have done and continue to do deep psychological damage, especially but not only to Aboriginal people.

This damage is less a function of personal failings than of broad structural and historical forces. This damage is constantly reinforced by the social and spatial segregation of the poor, and by the repeated recourse to a "blame the poor" form of public discourse, what Wacquant has described as "discourses of demonization."[78]

The kind of poverty that this has produced has recently been described by the Canadian Centre for Policy Alternatives—Manitoba by the use of two metaphors: "One is the notion of a complex web—a web of poverty, racism, drugs, gangs, violence. The other is the notion of a cycle—people caught in a cycle of inter-related problems. Both suggest the idea of people who are trapped, immobilized, unable to escape, destined to struggle with forces against which they cannot win, from which they cannot extricate themselves. The result is despair, resignation, anger, hopelessness, which then reinforce the cycle, and wrap them tighter in the web."[79]

Grassroots Responses

Yet in the case of Winnipeg's inner city this depiction is only partially true. Alongside the despair, the deep sense of hopelessness that so characterizes much of Winnipeg inner-city poverty today, there has emerged a remarkable array of community-based organizations (CBOs) that are creative and effective in combating poverty. Although different in some important respects, they have emerged in much the same empowering, self-help fashion as the vibrant, ethnic-based organizations that breathed such vibrancy into the North End of the early twentieth century. It is not only the existence and form of poverty in Winnipeg today, but the responses of the poor themselves, about which we can say "it's the same, but it's different."

Today's response to inner-city poverty, building gradually as it has over the past thirty years even while poverty has deepened and morphed into its new and more complex form, is a bottom-up, "home-made" community development that takes the form of a multiplicity of relatively small community-based organizations. These CBOs are creative and innovative. The work they do is, for the most part, designed and driven by inner-city people, not outside "experts." In this respect this community development is similar to the vast array of cultural organizations that so enriched the early twentieth-century North End. As was the case then, this work goes largely unseen by those outside the inner city, made invisible by the lenses created by stereotypes and stigma, by ignorance and condescension.

These CBOs include neighbourhood renewal corporations, such as the North End Community Renewal Corporation, the Spence Neighbourhood Association, and the West Broadway Development Corporation; women's organizations, like the North End Women's Resource Centre, the North Point Douglas Women's Centre, and the West Central Women's Resource Centre; family and youth centres such as the Andrews Street Family Centre, Rossbrook House, and Wolseley Family Place. These are but the tip of the iceberg of a rich array of such CBOs.

Working alongside and often in cooperation are distinctly Aboriginal CBOs. Most practice a "holistic" community development that takes some version of the following form.[80] First, Aboriginal community development starts with the individual, and the need to heal from the ongoing damage of colonization and racism; healthy communities require that individuals be healthy and whole. Second, individuals cannot heal without strong and healthy communities, and so this holistic community development focuses simultaneously on building Aboriginal communities, especially by developing a knowledge and appreciation of Aboriginal cultures. Third, this approach requires Aboriginal organizations—created by, and run by and for, Aboriginal people themselves, in a fashion consistent with Aboriginal cultural values. Finally, all of this is rooted in an ideological understanding of the impact of colonization, and the need to de-colonize.

De-colonizing means that Aboriginal people who suffer from the complex form of poverty described above are aware that the root of their problems is less their own personal failings than it is the broad historical forces described by the term colonization. De-colonization means learning to see the causal factors that lie beneath the simplistic, blame-the-victim stereotypes that have always been such a central part of Winnipeg's dominant culture. Knowing this is not intended to produce victims; it is intended to liberate and empower, by making Aboriginal people aware that they themselves are not the problem. It is intended to make a knowledge and appreciation of their rich Aboriginal heritage a source of individual and collective strength and pride. Examples of the many Aboriginal organizations working in this way, or some variant of this way, include the Ma Mawi Wi Chi Itata Centre, Ndinawemaaganag Endawaad, Ka Ni Kanichihk, the Native Women's Transition Centre, and the Urban Circle Training Centre. These are remarkably creative and effective organizations, led by a cadre of Aboriginal people, most of whom were raised poor and who experienced many poverty- and racism-related difficulties, but who have become what has been elsewhere described as "organic intellectuals."[81] By this term is meant people who are deeply knowledgeable about who they are, about how they came to be constructed as they have been by broad historical forces, and about how to build for positive change.

Governments have played an important role in contributing to the funding of these inner-city CBOs. For example, there have been four tri-level (civic, provincial, and federal) urban development agreements since 1980. Despite many weaknesses,[82] these have contributed part of the start-up money for the bottom-up initiatives described above, and the current provincial government's Neighbourhoods Alive! program funds inner-city revitalization efforts, and is effective and successful.[83]

The Limits of Grassroots Responses

Yet the kind and amount of government support that is necessary if today's inner-city poverty is to be defeated is not there. The poverty in Winnipeg's inner city is deeply entrenched, complex, and thoroughly resistant to short-term or uni-dimensional solutions. Its defeat requires public investment on a scale much larger than has been the case to date, undertaken consistently over a long period of time, fifteen or twenty years, and implemented in a much more strategic fashion than has so far been the case. The political will for an undertaking of this scale is simply not there.

This takes us back full circle to the poverty of the North End early in the twentieth century. The North End then, as now, was segregated from the rest of the city, spatially and socially. This promoted ignorance of, and a lack of tolerance for, those who lived there—an intolerance deepened by the different-ness, the other-ness, of the Eastern European residents of the North End. The result was a failure, indeed a refusal, on the part of the city's leaders to invest in the North End. Artibise attributed this to the "failure of Winnipeg's leadership to develop a mature social conscience."[84] Evidence to date suggests that this may still be the case today.

In addition we have experienced, at a national and global level, as well as, albeit to a somewhat lesser extent, at a provincial and civic level, some thirty years of an ideological shift *against* the measures that would be needed to adequately address inner-city poverty in Winnipeg. Some political parties are simply opposed, on ideological grounds, to the degree of government involvement that would be necessary. Others fear that such an expanded government role with its necessarily higher taxes would prompt an electoral backlash from the sprawling suburbs that now encircle, both literally and figuratively, the inner city. None appear to be prepared to play the public education role that would be necessary to counter the "discourse of demonization"[85] that has consistently been directed at the poor these past 100 years, and that so distorts the understanding that is the necessary foundation for solutions.

IV. The Future of Poverty in Winnipeg

Poverty has persisted in Winnipeg for more than 100 years, but it has also changed, especially in the past thirty years, and some of these changes are important. Today, at the start of the twenty-first century, a higher proportion of those who are poor than was the case earlier in the twentieth century are outside of, and detached from, the paid labour force and are thus outside of, and marginalized from, the mainstream of society. In some cases, this detachment has become intergenerational, and thus deeply rooted, contributing to the emergence of norms and values that are also outside of and marginalized from the mainstream of society.

This creates a different kind of poverty than existed earlier in the twentieth century, when poverty was largely a working-class phenomenon, and a function of the appallingly low wages paid by employers. The "jobless poverty" and related social exclusion of today is a major contributing factor in the emergence of a culture of despair and hopelessness that increasingly manifests itself in the prevalence of drugs, gangs, and levels and forms of violence far beyond what prevailed in poor North End neighbourhoods in the first half of the twentieth century. The fact that families, cultures, and communities are now, in some important respects, less strong and resilient than in the early twentieth century is another distinguishing feature of today's poverty. Poverty has persisted in Winnipeg over these many decades, and in some ways—the relentless denigration of the poor, poverty's association with racist attitudes, its spatial concentration in the North End and broader inner city—it remains unchanged. But the separation of large numbers of today's poor from the labour market is the major causal factor in creating changes in the character of poverty that are especially worrisome.

There are those who argue that we are at risk of this new form of spatially concentrated racialized poverty becoming a *permanent* feature of the twenty-first century urban landscape, in Winnipeg and elsewhere.[86] It is now the case, for the first time in human history, that a majority of the world's people live in urban centres, and most of them live in "slums."[87] In some American cases, large swaths of inner cities have been fully abandoned and have been allowed to return to nature, so advanced has the deterioration become. This is dramatically the case, for example, in Detroit, where one can walk for miles in what was once the inner city without seeing another human being.[88] Many inner cities—or in the European case, suburban rings—are plagued by gangs, drugs, and remarkable, deeply troubling levels of violence. These worsening problems, together with persistent racism directed especially, in the case of Winnipeg, at Aboriginal people, add to and reinforce a spatial and social segregation that keeps Winnipeg divided, and prevents serious efforts to find solutions. Thus the problems created by poverty persist, even as they change and, in many important respects, worsen.

These outcomes are a measure of the failure of our society, during a period of 100 years and more, to develop and implement those measures that would eradicate the poverty that has been a constant, albeit changing, feature of Winnipeg's landscape and culture. Rather than develop and implement successful anti-poverty measures, we have collectively chosen to blame the poor themselves. We have chosen to marginalize and exclude the poor, to construct them as the "other," even to demonize them. Even when governments have attempted to address the issue of poverty, they have done so in a partial, time-limited, haphazard fashion.[89] The poor themselves, in the historic North End as in today's inner city, have fashioned many highly effective, locally based organizations and activities that have been creative and effective—but of necessity, given their poverty, too limited to promote the large-scale socio-economic change needed if poverty is to be defeated. That kind of transformation requires a broader societal vision, and a collective commitment to real change. In the absence of such vision and commitment, the poverty that now exists in Winnipeg will not only persist, but worsen and spread, as is happening in many American urban centres and European suburban rings.

Will Winnipeg continue to follow this path? The answer to that question requires an answer to a second question: will governments, federal, provincial and civic, commit to the large-scale, long-term strategic public investment that is the necessary condition for overcoming the new and complex poverty that is now so deeply entrenched in Winnipeg's inner city? At the moment, there is no sign of this happening. Should this not happen, the inner city will continue to spread, and Winnipeg will march inexorably toward a much less attractive future for all. Yet we know that major sea changes occur in politics; we know that in a relatively brief period society, driven by necessity or in some cases by inspired and visionary leadership, can move in very different directions. This is what is now needed to begin to solve Winnipeg's poverty.

Notes

1. Jim Blanchard, *Winnipeg 1912* (Winnipeg: University of Manitoba Press, 2005), 10.
2. Alan Artibise, *Winnipeg: An Illustrated History* (Toronto: Lorimer, 1977), 66.
3. Artibise, *Winnipeg: An Illustrated History*, 104.
4. Alan Artibise, *Winnipeg: A Social History of Urban Growth* (Kingston: McGill-Queen's Press, 1975), 187.
5. Quoted in Alan Artibise, ed., *Gateway City: Documents on the City of Winnipeg 1873–1913* (Winnipeg: The Manitoba Record Society/University of Manitoba Press, 1979), 196.
6. Artibise, *Winnipeg: A Social History of Urban Growth*, 16.
7. James S. Woodsworth, *My Neighbour: A Study of City Conditions; A Plea For Social Service* (Toronto: Missionary Society of the Methodist Church, 1911), 70.
8. Quoted in Artibise, *Gateway City*, 195.
9. Artibise, *Winnipeg: A Social History of Urban Growth*, 188.
10. Blanchard, *Winnipeg 1912*, 47.
11. Ibid.
12. James H. Gray, *The Boy From Winnipeg* (Toronto: MacMillan, 1970), 118.
13. Quoted in Artibise, *Winnipeg: A Social History of Urban Growth*, 160.
14. John Marlyn, *Under the Ribs of Death* (Toronto: McClelland and Stewart, 1957), 64–65. See also Gray, *The Boy From Winnipeg*, 119–120.
15. Artibise, *Winnipeg: A Social History of Urban Growth*, 160.
16. Tomson Highway, *Kiss of the Fur Queen* (Toronto: Doubleday, 1998), 105.
17. Ibid., 106–107.
18. Native Women's Association of Canada, *Voices of Our Sisters in Spirit: A Report to Families and Communities, Second Edition* (Ottawa: Native Women's Association of Canada, March 2009). See also Amnesty International, *Stolen Sisters: Discrimination and Violence against Indigenous Women in Canada* (London: Amnesty International, 2004).
19. Mochoruk, James and Nancy Kardash, *The People's Co-op: The Life and Times of a North End Instituiton* (Halifax: Fernwood, 2000), 5–6.
20. Quoted in Martine August, "A Social History of Winnipeg's North End," unpublished student essay in author's possession, Winnipeg, 2000, 9.
21. Ibid., 20.
22. Blanchard, *Winnipeg 1912*, 205.
23. Statistics Canada, 2001 Census of Canada.

24 Just Incomes Coalition, *Paid to be Poor: Low-Wage Community Inquiry Manitoba 2005* (Winnipeg: Just Incomes Coalition, 2005).
25 Darren Lezubski, Jim Silver, and Errol Black, "High and Rising: The Growth of Poverty in Winnipeg's Inner City," in *Solutions that Work: Fighting Poverty in Winnipeg*, ed. Jim Silver (Halifax: Fernwood, 2000).
26 Gray, *The Boy From Winnipeg*, 8–10.
27 Ibid., 127.
28 Mochoruk and Kardash, *The People's Co-op*.
29 Doug Smith, *Joe Zuken: Citizen and Socialist* (Toronto: James Lorimer and Company), 1990.
30 Roz Usiskin, "Selkirk Avenue Revisited: The Hub of Winnipeg's North End, the Jewish Experience 1905–1950," unpublished paper in author's possession, 18.
31 M. Hart, *Seeking Mino-Pimatisiwin: An Aboriginal Approach to Healing* (Halifax: Fernwood, 2002), 27.
32 Ibid., 27.
33 Thomas J. Sugrue, *The Origins of the Urban Crisis: Race and Inequality in Postwar Detroit* (Princeton: Princeton University Press, 1996), 9.
34 John Milloy, *A National Crime: The Canadian Government and the Residential School System* (Winnipeg: University of Manitoba Press, 1999).
35 Artibise, *Winnipeg: A Social History of Urban Growth*, 173.
36 Artibise, *Gateway City*, 10.
37 Artibise, *Winnipeg: An Illustrated History*, 54.
38 Artibise, *Winnipeg: A Social History of Urban Growth*, 216.
39 Artibise, *Gateway City*, 15.
40 Kenneth Jackson, *Crabgrass Frontier: The Suburbanization of the United States* (New York: Oxford University Press, 1985).
41 Artibise, *Winnipeg: An Illustrated History*, 174.
42 Rosenberg, *A Study of the Growth and Changes in the Distribution of the Jewish Community in Winnipeg*.
43 Lezubski, Silver, and Black, "High and Rising," 30.
44 Artibise, *Winnipeg: An Illustrated History*, 174.
45 Artibise, *Winnipeg: A Social History of Urban Growth*, 216.
46 Quoted in August, "A Social History of Winnipeg's North End," 36–37.
47 Ibid., 39.
48 Gary Teeple, *Globalization and the Decline of Social Reform: Into the Twenty-First Century* (Toronto: Garamond Press, 2000); Dave Broad, *Capitalism Rebooted? Work, Welfare and the New Economy* (Halifax: Fernwood, 2006).
49 Statistics Canada, "Payroll Employment, Earnings and Hours," *The Daily*, 27 August 2008.
50 William Wilson, *The Truly Disadvantaged: The Inner City, The Underclass and Public Policy* (Chicago: University of Chicago Press, 1987); W.J. Wilson, *When Work Disappears: New Implications for Race and Urban Poverty in the Global Economy*, CASE Paper 17 (London: Centre for Analysis of Social Exclusion, London School of Economics, 1998).
51 Probe Research, *Indigenous Voices: INAC Mobility Report* (Winnipeg: Probe Research, 2005).
52 These numbers are not strictly comparable due to changing census definitions. Figures for 1991 and later are for those who self-identify as Aboriginal.

53 Jim Silver, *North End Winnipeg's Lord Selkirk Park Public Housing Developments: History, Problems, Prospects* (Winnipeg: Canadian Centre for Policy Alternatives–Manitoba, 2006).
54 *Winnipeg Tribune*, 25 August 1962.
55 Thomas Yauk, "Residential and Business Relocation from Urban Renewal Areas: A Case Study—The Lord Selkirk Park Experience" (University of Manitoba, Master of City Planning thesis, 1973), 45–46.
56 *Winnipeg Tribune*, September 1962.
57 Sugrue, *Origins of the Urban Crisis*, 9.
58 Milloy, *A National Crime*. See also J.R. Miller, *Shingwauk's Vision: A History of Native Residential Schools* (Toronto: University of Toronto Press, 1996); A. Grant, *No End of Grief: Indian Residential Schools in Canada* (Winnipeg: Pemmican Publications, 1996).
59 Jim Silver, *The Inner Cities of Winnipeg and Saskatoon: A New Form of Development* (Winnipeg: Canadian Centre for Policy Alternatives – Manitoba, 2008).
60 Tom Carter, "Poverty Changes in Winnipeg Neighbourhoods 1981–2001," Research Highlight No. 5, January 2005, http://geography.uwinnipeg.ca/Carter/carter-repository.htm (accessed 1 June 2010).
61 Lezubski, Silver, and Black, "High and Rising."
62 Jino Distasio, M. Dudley, M. Johnson, and K. Sargent, *Neighbourhoods Alive! Community Outcomes Final Report* (Winnipeg: Institute of Urban Studies, 2005), 23.
63 Social Planning Council of Winnipeg, *Manitoba Child and Family Poverty Report Card 2006* (Winnipeg: Social Planning Council of Winnipeg, 2006).
64 D. Ross and P. Roberts, *Income and Child Well-Being: A New Perspective on the Poverty Debate* (Ottawa: Canadian Council on Social Development, 1999), 36.
65 Canadian Council on Social Development, *Countdown '94*, 1.
66 Marni Brownell, Noralou Roos, Randy Fransoo, Anne Guevremont, Leonard MacWilliam, Shelley Derksen, Natalia Dik, Bogdan Bogdanovic, Monica Sirski, *How Do Educational Outcomes Vary With Socioeconomic Status? Key Findings from the Manitoba Child Health Atlas* (Winnipeg: Manitoba Centre for Health Policy, 2004), 5–6.
67 From Jim Silver, "Persistent Poverty and the Promise of Community Solutions," in *Power and Resistance: Critical Thinking about Canadian Social Issues*, 4th ed., ed. Les Samuelson and Wayne Antony (Halifax: Fernwood, 2007), 195.
68 Robin Millar, "Literacy Movement or Campaign? Three Eras of Literacy Initiatives in Manitoba's History," in *Adult Education in Manitoba: Historical Aspects*, ed. D.H. Poonwassie and A. Poonwassie (Mississauga: Canadian Educators Press, 1997), 148.
69 Marni Brownell, L. Lix, O. Ekuma, S. Derksen, S. De Haney, R. Bond, R. Fransoo, L. MacWilliam, and J. Bodnaruk, *Why is the Health Status of Some Manitobans Not Improving? The Widening Gap in the Health Status of Manitobans* (Winnipeg: Manitoba Centre for Health Policy, 2003).
70 Michael Mendelson, *Aboriginal People in Canada's Labour Market: Work and Unemployment, Today and Tomorrow* (Ottawa: Caledon Institute for Social Policy, 2004); Jim Silver, *In Their Own Voices: Building Urban Aboriginal Communities* (Halifax: Fernwood, 2006).
71 Jeremy Hull, "Manitoba in 2006: A Census Snapshot," in *CCPA Review: Economic and Social Trends* (Winnipeg: Canadian Centre for Policy Alternatives–Manitoba, 2008).
72 Lezubski, Silver, and Black, "High and Rising," 39.
73 Mendelson, *Aboriginal People in Canada's Labour Market*, 35 and 38.
74 Silver, "Persistent Poverty and the Promise of Community Solutions," 182–183.

75   Wilson, *When Work Disappears*, 2.
76   Loïc Wacquant, "Territorial Stigmatization in the Age of Advanced Marginality," *Thesis Eleven* 91 (2007): 66 and 68.
77   Quoted in Doug Smith, *In The Public Interest: The First 25 Years of the Public Interest Law Centre* (Winnipeg: Public Interest Law Centre, 2007).
78   Loïc Wacquant, *Urban Outcasts* (Cambridge: Polity Press, 2008), 271.
79   Canadian Centre for Policy Alternatives–Manitoba, *Promise of Investment in Community-Led Renewal: State of the Inner City Report 2005, Part Two: A View From The Neighbourhoods* (Winnipeg: Canadian Centre for Policy Alternatives–Manitoba, 2005).
80   For a fuller description see Silver, *In Their Own Voices*, ch. 5.
81   Silver, *In Their Own Voices*.
82   Jim Silver, *Building on our Strengths: Inner-City Priorities for a Renewed Tri-Level Development Agreement* (Winnipeg: Canadian Centre for Policy Alternatives–Manitoba and Urban Futures Group, 2002).
83   Jim Silver, Molly McCracken, and Kate Sjoberg, *Neighbourhood Renewal Corporations in Winnipeg's Inner City: Practical Activism in a Complex Environment* (Winnipeg: Canadian Centre for Policy Alternatives–Manitoba, 2009).
84   Artibise, *Gateway City*, 15.
85   Loïc Wacquant, *Urban Outcasts*, 271.
86   Ibid.
87   Mike Davis, *Planet of Slums* (London: Verso, 2006).
88   Rebecca Solnit, "Detroit Arcadia: Exploring the Post-American Landscape," *Harper's*, July 2007.
89   Jim Silver and Owen Toews, "Combating Poverty in Winnipeg's Inner City, 1945–1996: Half a Century of Hard-Earned Lessons" *Canadian Journal of Urban Research* 18, 1 (2009).

"Closing the Gap" in Manitoba[1]

Harvey Bostrom

In 2005, a meeting in Kelowna, British Columbia, between First Ministers from Canada's federal, provincial, and territorial governments and national Aboriginal leaders produced the Kelowna Accord—an agreement to reduce disparities in well-being between Aboriginal and non-Aboriginal Canadians. The agreement identified five priority areas: education, health, housing, enhancing economic opportunities, and an engagement with Aboriginal organizations on what were termed relationships and accountability. A commitment was made to take action on these priorities over a ten-year period and to hold a second first ministers conference within two years. At the time the federal government committed itself to spending $5.1 billion on the initiative during the first five years.[2]

In April 2006, the Manitoba cabinet approved the Closing the Gap Implementation Plan, tasking a committee of senior staff from each provincial department with coordinating a ten-year effort to address the socio-economic gaps between Aboriginal and non-Aboriginal people in Manitoba. Working groups were established in the following Kelowna Accord priority areas: education and early childhood; housing and infrastructure; health and well-being; and economic opportunities.

The fifth Kelowna Accord priority speaks to the need to improve relations with First Nation and Métis organizations and improving accountability by establishing measures of progress and outcomes. The Department of Aboriginal and Northern Affairs has the lead role for implementing the relationship priority and works with departments and the working groups to ensure that it is reflected in their practice.

A comprehensive, ten-year plan, Closing the Gap is Manitoba's effort to move forward on the commitments made at Kelowna. At the same time that it moves forward with its Closing the Gap initiative, the provincial government continues to engage both the federal government and the private sector in partnerships and actions that advance these priorities. As a result, in October 2006 Manitoba signed on to the Closing the Gap protocol that had been negotiated between the Assembly of Manitoba Chiefs and the federal government.

Manitoba's Aboriginal Population

Aboriginal people constitute a significant and growing percentage of the Manitoba population. It is a young and growing population that resides in urban centres and throughout every region of the province. In 2006, Aboriginal people accounted for 15.5 percent of the provincial population (175,395 of a total population of 1,133,510). First Nation people made up 57 percent of Manitoba's Aboriginal people, Métis people 41 percent and Inuit people less than 1 percent. From 2001 to 2006, the province's Aboriginal population grew by 16.9 percent (25,350), while the non-Aboriginal population grew by only 0.5 percent (4460). During that period the Métis population grew by 26.4 percent (15,000) and the First Nation population grew by 11.4 percent (10,305). In coming years, the Aboriginal population is expected to grow at four times the rate of the non-Aboriginal population.

The Aboriginal population is considerably younger than the general population: in 2006 the median age of the Aboriginal population was twenty-four, while the median age for the non-Aboriginal population was forty. In Northern Manitoba, 80 percent of the people under the age of thirty-five are Aboriginal.

While Winnipeg's Aboriginal population (63,745) is the largest of any city in Canada and constitutes 10 percent of the city's population, it is important to bear in mind in 2006 a full 50 percent of Aboriginal people did not live in urban centres. There are sixty-three First Nation communities in Manitoba and in 2006, 55 percent of the First Nation population lived on reserve.[3]

The Gap

The existence of a young, growing population spread across the province represents a tremendous opportunity and promise. Young Aboriginal people should be able to look forward to the future with hope and expectation, while the province as whole can expect that the growing Aboriginal community will fill upcoming labour market needs.

But this future is jeopardized by the significant socio-economic gap between Manitoba's Aboriginal and non-Aboriginal population. While this gap has been well documented, the following income, employment, education, housing, child welfare and health statistics provide an overview of the issues that need to be addressed:

- In Manitoba, the 2006 median income for Aboriginal people fifteen years and older was $15,246 while the median income for the comparable non-Aboriginal population was $25,614. While the income gap remains significant, it should be noted that the Aboriginal median income increased by 50 percent from what it was in 1996 ($10,408) while the non-Aboriginal median income increased by 31 percent.
- In 2006, Aboriginal people had an employment rate of 62.6 percent, while the non-Aboriginal employment rate was 85.2 percent. Again, there has been progress in this area: from 1996 to 2006, the Aboriginal employment rate increased by 26 percent.
- There is also considerable variation among Aboriginal groups in terms of both income and employment. The median income for Métis people in 2006 was $20,655 and their employment rate was 76.6 percent. The employment rate for First Nations people reserve was 59.4 percent off reserve and 43.4 percent on reserve.
- The educational attainment levels of Aboriginal people are lower than those of the non-Aboriginal population. In 2006, 41 percent of Manitoba's Aboriginal population between the ages of twenty-five to sixty-four had not completed high school while the rate for the non-Aboriginal population was 17 percent.
- In 2006, 53 percent of Aboriginal people in Manitoba lived in dwellings in need of major repairs.
- In 2006, 30 percent of Aboriginal children in Manitoba aged fourteen and under lived with a lone parent, compared with 15 percent of non-Aboriginal children. In March 2006, 5627 of the 6629 children in care in Manitoba were Aboriginal.
- The life expectancy for First Nations people has been increasing; it is still approximately eight years less than it is for other Manitobans. Aboriginal people also suffer disproportionately higher rates of chronic and communicable diseases and disability.

These are just some of the misery statistics. It is important to recognize that there has been ongoing improvement in a number of areas. For example:

- The university enrolment of Aboriginal people has increased by 77 percent between 2005 and 2008, while college enrollment has increased by 60 percent.
- From 2001 to 2005, the number of employed Aboriginal people increased by 30 percent. Manitoba was tied for the largest decrease in the Aboriginal unemployment rate in Canada.

- The Aboriginal labour force increased from approximately 64,000 to 78,000 from 2001 to 2005.
- The child poverty rate dropped from 19.3 percent in 1999 to 12.4 percent in 2006.
- Since 1999, there have been 1239 low-income people sponsored by various ACCESS programs who have graduated from Manitoba universities. The majority of these graduates would have been Aboriginal people.
- The number of Aboriginal people working for the Manitoba government has doubled during the past decade, increasing from 1000 in 1999 to 2000 in 2009.

The barriers facing Aboriginal people are interconnected: low levels of educational attainment limit employment prospects; low wages limit housing prospects; crowded and unsafe housing increases health problems. All of these factors impact on early childhood development and educational preparedness. These issues are not new to government; indeed the Closing the Gap plan builds on existing provincial government initiatives, some of which have been highly effective. In other cases, it represents a shift to new and different approaches.

Goals

The Closing the Gap strategy has identified the following set of goals:
- an increase in the number of collaboration initiatives/partnerships between the provincial and federal and Aboriginal governments, private sector and Aboriginal organizations;
- an increase in the Aboriginal employment rate;
- a decrease in Aboriginal dependency on social assistance;
- an increase in the education completion rates of Aboriginal people;
- an increase in the participation of Aboriginal people in skilled occupations;
- an increase in Aboriginal business and entrepreneurial activity;
- an increase in the number of single parents participating in labour market training interventions and, subsequently finding jobs; and
- an increase in the average level of income for Aboriginal people and families.

The remainder of this chapter describes the initiatives and approaches that have been taken by the Manitoba Government in the first four Closing the Gap priority areas. It describes not only the work of numerous provincial government departments (most notably Health; Education; Healthy Living, Youth and Seniors; Advanced Education and Literacy; Aboriginal and Northern Affairs; Entrepreneurship, Training and Trade; Family Services and Consumer Affairs) but also cross-departmental committees and agencies, and partnerships with Aboriginal organizations, the non-profit sector, health authorities, school divisions, the private sector, and the federal government. It is also common for initiatives discussed under one heading (education, for example) to have effects in other areas (employment).

This chapter focuses in large measure on the achievements relating to education and youth. Education represents not only a personal achievement for students, but it is the key to closing the gap. For individuals it opens the door to full-time, year-round employment. The creation of a critical mass of educated, employed Aboriginal people has an exponential impact, not only on a person's immediate family but their extended family and their community. The more success we have in this area, the more success we will have in reducing socio-economic problems, increasing employment and entrepreneurial activity, and reducing the misery costs to people, families, and governments. Spending on early childhood, education, and training are evidence-based investments that bear fruit. Having said that, it is important for readers to remember that what follows is a far from complete listing of the initiatives geared toward closing this gap.

Education and Early Childhood
Early Childhood
The Manitoba government has established the Healthy Child Committee of Cabinet, the only standing cabinet committee in Canada dedicated to the well-being of children and youth. The committee is one of Manitoba's primary mechanisms for improving early childhood outcomes and ensuring that children in disadvantaged families fulfill their potential. Healthy Child initiatives include the Triple P Parenting Program, Healthy Baby, and Families.

The Indigenous Positive Parenting Program (often referred to as Indigenous Triple P) is delivered by trained service providers across Manitoba. The Triple P program helps reduce parental stress while ensuring safe and stimulating learning environments for children.

Healthy Baby provides families with financial support and early interventions during pregnancy and the first year of life. Twenty-five percent of the pre-natal benefits provided by the Healthy Baby program are received by women in First Nation communities.

Families First, delivered by regional health authorities, provides home visit support to children in vulnerable families from birth through to kindergarten. The $7.5-million provincial Fetal Alcohol Spectrum Disorder Strategy supports prevention, diagnosis, and diagnosis measures.

Public Schools

In 2007, the employment rate of young Aboriginal people who had finished high school or completed some post-secondary studies was 64.1 percent, virtually identical to the non-Aboriginal rate of 65.9 percent. In other words, the employment prospects of skilled Aboriginals are similar to the prospects of skilled non-Aboriginal people. The success that Aboriginal graduates experience demonstrates the importance of initiatives that keep Aboriginal students in school and ensure that they graduate.

The provincial government's Aboriginal Education Action Plan, established in 2004, takes a comprehensive and strategic approach to keeping Aboriginal children in school and improving graduation rates. Renewed in 2007 as the Aboriginal Education and Employment Plan, it coordinates the activities of three separate departments related to the education, training, employment, and transition to and participation in the labour market. Key focuses include increased high school graduation rates, increased access to post-secondary education, successful labour market participation, and improved research into Aboriginal education and employment.

One example of the kinds of initiatives this plan supports is a federally and provincially funded specific skills training project that will be training 200 Aboriginal people to work in the aerospace industry. The training is being coordinated and provided by Winnipeg's Centre for Aboriginal Human Resource Development (CAHRD). The fact that this agency originated the plan and then arranged for government funding is an example of another heartening development, namely the growth of innovative capacity within the Aboriginal community. It is this capacity that is often the driving force behind the developments described here.

There are serious disparities in the funding and quality of on- and off-reserve education and between schools across the provincial system throughout Canada. The on-reserve schools do not function as part of a divisional system with the wider range of supports that school divisions can supply. In 2006, approximately 60 percent of off-reserve Aboriginal people had graduated from high school, compared to 40 percent on-reserve in Manitoba. The School Improvement Project, a partnership with the federal government and the Assembly of Manitoba Chiefs and led by Manitoba Education provides professional assistance to teachers and administrators in a number of First Nation on-reserve schools. In the spring of 2009, the program was operating on four reserves and the province was offering to expand it to ten more schools, followed by expansion to forty-two schools. The program includes supports in professional development, curriculum, and improving educational outcomes—particularly in literacy, mathematics, and information technology. University College of the North is providing teacher training and mentoring to staff at these schools. Evaluation of the program shows it has led to significant increases in student morale, attendance, and performance. The fact the Manitoba government has chosen to provide services in an area of traditional federal jurisdiction in order to improve the educational attainment levels of First Nations children is an example of the degree to which the Closing the Gap initiative breaks from past practice.

In 2007–2008, the $1-million Bright Future fund was established to enable community organizations and partner schools to implement programming to improve high school graduation rates and increase access to post-secondary education. The program is targeted at prospective students under-represented in post-secondary programs, including Aboriginal people. It includes a homework tutoring program and mentoring and scholarship incentives.

Adult Education

Adult learning centres (ALCs), which provide second chances to those who did not complete high school, receive $14 million in annual provincial funding. In the 2007–08 school year, 7929 learners, nearly half of whom were Aboriginal, were studying at forty-three tuition-free ALCs operating out of eighty-three sites. The ALC model provides training in the literacy and essential skills that many people need if they are going to go on to complete their high school courses. In 2007–08 1172 adults, 42 percent of whom were Aboriginal, completed their high school education in this manner. Four ALCs are registered to offer high school credits on reserves. Manitoba also funds thirty-nine literacy service providers. Thirty percent of the 2500 learners that they serve are Aboriginal.

Training

The Manitoba Government's Technical Vocational Initiative promotes the skilled trades sector as a career path for high school students. In their senior year, students who chose this path are able to gain post-secondary credit in apprenticeship by working in trades. Linked to this is Red River College's five-month-long Introduction to Trades Program, which is offered to Aboriginal people who wish to pursue careers in the trades. The program provides an introduction to eight RRC pre-employment trades.

From 2003 to 2008, the number of Aboriginal people pursuing apprenticeship training increased threefold, reaching 1300 in 2008. More than 20 percent of the people taking apprenticeship training in Manitoba are Aboriginal. Community-based training and apprenticeship training partnerships fostered by the province have been of particular benefit to Aboriginal persons living in the north.

The Hydro Northern Training and Employment Initiative is a $60.3-million partnership between Manitoba, Manitoba Hydro, the federal government, and seven Aboriginal partners. It seeks to ensure that participants have the knowledge and skills to take advantage of the opportunities presented by hydroelectric dam construction, to maximize the employment opportunities of northern Aboriginal people in the construction and related sectors, and lever opportunities related to hydroelectric projects for community capacity building. This five-year program will provide training to more than 1300 northern Aboriginal Manitobans.

Proper assessment of essential skills and prior learning of individual Aboriginal workers can shorten the pathway between training and employment. This can only happen when those skills are properly credited and the training needs met. Igniting the Power Within is a partnership with First Nations and Métis organizations to develop the prior learning accreditation and recognition (PLAR) assessment capability of Aboriginal community counsellors in rural and urban communities. More than 350 individuals have been certified to assess skills and prior learning through this process.

Post-secondary Education

Established in 2005, University College of the North is devoted to community and northern development in northern Manitoba. With campuses in The Pas and Thompson and regional centres in twelve northern communities (nine on reserve), it provides post-secondary education and training in a culturally sensitive and collaborative manner. UCN offers over twenty-five programs, including two degree-path programs, one joint bachelor of nursing program and thirteen diploma programs. UCN's Council of Elders is mandated to promote an environment that respects and embraces Aboriginal and northern cultures and values.

Each year, more Aboriginal people graduate from Manitoba's professional schools than from professional schools in any other province. This is in large measure attributable to the Manitoba government's ACCESS programs, which provides academic, personal, and financial supports to disadvantaged Manitobans taking professional training at the university and college level. There are more than twelve ACCESS programs in existence at various post-secondary institutions in Manitoba. To give one example of the program's impact, of the 150 Aboriginal engineers in Canada, one-third were supported by Manitoba's ACCESS program.

Manitoba also provides a number of scholarships that are targeted to Aboriginal people, including the Helen Betty Osborne Foundation scholarship. In addition, in partnership with the Business Council of Manitoba and the federal government, Manitoba has provided over 852 award scholarships to Aboriginal university students in Manitoba.

Housing and Infrastructure

Safe, affordable housing is essential to the development of healthy and confident families. In the same way, adequate water and sewer systems and reliable transportation links are crucial to remote Aboriginal communities across Manitoba.

Housing

Manitoba had developed HOUSINGFirst, a low-income housing strategy that includes HOMEWorks!, BUILDINGFoundations, Project: A Roof Over Each Bed, and RENOvations. HOMEWorks! is a $104.5-million, three-year program intended to increase housing for low-income Manitobans. It includes funding for the Neeginan Village transitional housing in Winnipeg and a Homelessness and Mental Health Housing Plan. A minimum of $42 million has been committed to Aboriginal off-reserve housing. In addition there is a commitment to develop Aboriginal governance and decision-making processes to oversee the funding of the first year of the strategy. As part of HOMEWorks!, $20.3 million has been allocated to build, rehabilitate or repair 144 housing units in northern Manitoba. This includes $10 million for new low-income housing. Forty new multi-family units will be built in Thompson and The Pas for families attending UCN.

Other initiatives include BUILDINGFoundations, a low-income housing strategy that invests in preventative maintenance and energy efficiency, security enhancement, children's playgrounds, tenant services, and mould prevention and reduction. As part of this initiative, in December 2008, the province committed itself to investing $48 million in renovating Manitoba Housing stock across the province.

The $50-million Affordable Housing Initiative is a five-year joint program between the federal and provincial governments to increase the supply of rental housing, repair existing housing, assist homebuyers with down payments, increase the supply of new homes, and provide rent supplements to tenants.

The Rural and Native Housing Program, another federal and provincial partnership, ensures that lower income families in rural and northern Manitoba do not pay more than 25 percent of their income on housing. It currently includes approximately 1900 single-family rental and homeowner units.

Infrastructure

In addition, the Manitoba government has committed significant resources to improving roads (including winter roads), airports, and water and sewage infrastructure in northern areas. Many small non-reserve Aboriginal communities in northern Manitoba have considerable infrastructure challenges because they do not have a municipal tax base. Historically, this has meant that they have not been able to access federal-provincial infrastructure programs, which typically require the municipality to contribute one-third of the funding. During the past decade, the Manitoba government has quadrupled the infrastructure funding to these communities and agreed to pay for their portion of federal-provincial infrastructure programs.

Also during the previous decade, highway capital funding for northern Manitoba has more than tripled and now accounts for 25 percent of the provincial highway capital budget. Most recently, the province has created the East-Side Road Authority to coordinate the construction of an all-weather road east of Lake Winnipeg to connect remote communities. This will be based on the successful Aboriginal set-aside program developed for the Manitoba Floodway Project.

The province is also working to improve the links between apprenticeship and other training and employment opportunities and community needs. For example, it is providing training for those who will have the responsibility for maintaining local water treatment plants.

Health and Well-being

Improving health and well-being is a critical component of the Closing the Gap initiative. Improvements in early childhood care and education, housing, education, employment, and income are critical to improvements in health. As its name suggests, Healthy Child Manitoba is a health initiative as much as it is an early childhood initiative. The focus of these initiatives is on prevention and measures that address what have come to be called the social determinants of health such as education, income, and housing.

Jurisdictional disputes have the potential to put financing issues ahead of patient interests. This has led the provincial government to adopt what is known as Jordan's Principle, which commits it to ensuring that the needs of children with multiple disabilities not be disrupted or delayed by jurisdictional disputes. The name of Jordan's Principle comes from a young person who died before the jurisdictional disputes around his services could be resolved.

There is also the need for the recognition of culture in the delivery of health services. To do this, and to improve the employment opportunities of Aboriginal people, Aboriginal Human Resources Agreements have been signed with a number of regional health authorities to promote the training, recruitment, and retention of Aboriginal people in health care careers.

The Aboriginal Diabetes Initiative has committed $2.8 million in disease prevention and the promotion of preventative health services. The Island Lake Renal Health and Treatment Unit, established with provincial support in 2005, was the first dialysis unit operated outside a hospital in Manitoba and the first in

Canada located in an isolated reserve community. Another renal treatment unit was established in 2002 at Norway House, with further units in development for Peguis and Berens River First Nations. This program is another example of the provincial government providing services on First Nation reserves.

The Northern Healthy Foods Initiative has improved access to healthy, nutritious foods through increased production, harvesting, and preserving of local foods. Island Lake has incorporated the Northern Healthy Food program into its diabetes prevention program. The initiative has assisted in the purchase of more than 160 freezers, the construction of eight greenhouses, the development of fifteen family-operated goat and chicken operations, and the planting of more than 300 northern vegetable gardens in twenty-eight communities. It is amazing to see an elderly woman in Island Lake walking to her garden with a basin under her arm and a little trowel and digging up the vegetables for that evening's meal. It is just as amazing to discover that in St. Theresa Point there are senior citizens selling the potatoes they have harvested from their gardens.

Economic Development

The enhancement and strengthening of economic opportunities include measures that move Aboriginal people into the workforce, that increase the hiring and continued employment of Aboriginal people, that improve the opportunities of Aboriginal entrepreneurs, and which strengthen the economic position of the Aboriginal community.

Guidance in this area comes from a number of directions, including the multifaceted Strengthening Aboriginal Participation in the Economy (SAPE) plan being coordinated by Aboriginal and Northern Affairs with the input of the Aboriginal community.

The Closing the Gap's economic and income-related initiatives need to be seen in the context of a number of general initiatives intended to address social and economic inequality. These include the reduction and elimination of taxes on persons who can least afford to pay them, including lower-income earners, the elderly, and persons with disabilities. This has been coupled with regular increases in the minimum wage during the past decade.

Moving into the Labour Market

Rewarding Work, introduced in 2007, is a four-year $4.3-million program intended to help social assistance recipients move into the workforce. By providing better access to affordable child care, a job-seekers' allowance, and wage subsidies for social assistance recipients as well as extending the provision of a number of non-insured health benefits, and providing benefits to individuals in training programs, Rewarding Work removes a number of the barriers that in the past have prevented people from participating in the labour force. A special marketAbilities fund supports employment partnerships that assist persons with disabilities in rural and northern areas find and keep sustainable employment.

Finding Work

Manitoba Entrepreneurship, Training and Trade along with First Nation and Métis organizations deliver labour market training programs. Partnerships between training agencies and employers have proven to be very effective in addressing specific skill needs as well as preparing individuals for highly paid employment.

The Partners for Careers placement initiative is funded by the Manitoba government and delivered by friendship centres in ten urban centres. The program has made more than 6000 career placements for Aboriginals since 1997. In addition, Manitoba Employment centres place approximately 1000 people per year, 60 percent of whom are Aboriginal, in jobs in northern Manitoba.

Manitoba Entrepreneurship, Training and Trade also has a sector council initiative that works with major sectors to address skill shortages. Each sector has an Aboriginal Liaison officer who helps the sector identify barriers to Aboriginal participation and develop strategies that will allow them to recruit and retain Aboriginal employees. Similarly, a Northern Employers' Council has been established to link northerners to employers and employment and training opportunities. As part of this initiative, Manitoba is providing $4.5 million for essential skills training.

Manitoba has signed a number of formal Aboriginal Employment Partnership agreements with major employers that focus on hiring and retaining Aboriginal people. One feature of the partnership agreement that IBM entered into with Manitoba is a commitment to support Aboriginal entrepreneurship in the information technology sector.

Creating Opportunities

The Manitoba Government has used a number of large-scale infrastructure projects to create opportunities for Aboriginal communities, Aboriginal entrepreneurs and Aboriginal workers.

The Aboriginal Set-Aside Initiative created opportunities for Aboriginal contractors to participate in the expansion of the Red River Floodway. The total value of the Aboriginal Set-Aside for the Floodway project was $60 million. As a result, more than 500 people were employed on twenty contracts. This set-aside model is going to be employed in other major projects, including the construction of the road on the east side of Lake Winnipeg.

Manitoba Hydro's latest generating station is being developed by Wuskwatim Power Limited Partnership (WPLP), a partnership between Manitoba Hydro and the Nisichawayasihk Cree Nation (NCN). The $1.3-billion project is expected to provide almost 800 jobs over its six-year construction span. First consideration in hiring is being given to qualified workers from Aboriginal communities close to the construction site as well as people from northern Manitoba communities. The partnership agreement dealt not only with the economics of the project, but the scope of the project. As a result, heritage sites were protected as part of the development agreement.

One has to visit the site to really get a sense of the significance of the way the Wuskwatim project is being developed. When you are there, you can see that, unlike any previous northern Hydro development project, this is truly an Aboriginal job site being run by a company that has been jointly set up by Manitoba Hydro and a First Nation. The site and the contracts associated with the projects are jointly managed. It is evident from the spirit of the people on the job site that this is a unique and dynamic project. The community people working there obviously feel very much a player in the process of what is happening. The Wuskwatim model will be employed in other upcoming projects such the Keeyask generating station.

Development Strategies and Supports

A significant barrier facing Aboriginal people is the availability of equity capital to secure business loans. In 2007 the Manitoba government established a $20-million Economic Development Fund for First Nation people. The province is currently working with the federal government and the Manitoba Métis Federation to establish a Métis Economic Development strategy. Work is under way to transfer more than 1.2 million acres of Crown land in Manitoba to First Nations in fulfillment of treaty land entitlement obligations. This land can serve as the basis of future cultural economic developments.

For Aboriginal people attempting to establish a business, the availability of mentorship and access to networks can be crucial. The Aboriginal Chamber of Commerce, established earlier this decade with the support of the Premier's Economic Advisory Council, promotes Aboriginal business and entrepreneurial development through networking with the private sector and lobbying efforts with the government. The Manitoba Procurement Program offers Aboriginal businesses the opportunity to provide goods and services to government agencies.

Conclusion

The Kelowna Accord was a historic national agreement for all parties to close the gap in well-being between Aboriginal and non-Aboriginal Canadians. Manitoba was the first province to move forward on the Kelowna Accord with an implementation plan. Manitoba continues to champion the Kelowna Accord priorities and seeks to strategically engage the federal government in existing and future partnerships with First Nation and Métis peoples, as well as the private sector. Federal action is necessary, particularly to address reserve education outcomes.

The Manitoba government is making impressive unprecedented progress on a wide range of fronts, particularly in education, training, and employment. Success for individuals in these areas means corresponding improvements in health, housing, and the educational outcomes of all family members. Experience demonstrates the importance of all parties working together to achieve greater success.

At the time of this report, there remains an unacceptable gap in socio-economic circumstances. Only through a concerted effort and engagement of all parties will we be successful in closing that gap. Manitoba can play an important role in this province, and nationally, as a leading agent of positive change. Now is the time to close the gap in Canada.

Notes

1   This chapter is adapted from a speech delivered by Harvey Bostrom to the Manitoba Politics, Government and Policy Conference, 22 November 2008.

2   A copy of the final agreement of the Kelowna Accord can be found at http://www.scics.gc.ca/cinfo05/800044004_e.pdf.

3   These figures taken from Statistics Canada, "2006 Aboriginal Population Profile – Manitoba," http://www12.statcan.gc.ca/census-recensement/2006/dp-pd/prof/92-594/details/page.cfm?Lang=E&Geo1=PR&Code1=46&Geo2=PR&Code2=01&Data=Count&SearchText=Manitoba&SearchType=Begins&SearchPR=01&B1=All&GeoLevel=&GeoCode=46 (accessed 20 February 2010). See also Statistics Canada's profile of Winnipeg at http://www12.statcan.gc.ca/census-recensement/2006/dp-pd/prof/92-594/details/page.cfm?Lang=E&Geo1=CMA&Code1=602__&Geo2=PR&Code2=46&Data=Count&SearchText=Winnipeg&SearchType=Begins&SearchPR=01&B1=All&GeoLevel=&GeoCode=602.

The Role of Aboriginal Political Organizations in the Policy Process[1]

Irene Linklater[2]

Introduction

The Assembly of Manitoba Chiefs (AMC)[3] conducts advocacy work so that it can improve the lives of First Nations people in Manitoba. To begin this discussion, it is important to identify the role of First Nations leadership in terms of how it creates policy as decision-makers. This is an important distinction, as one must understand the co-existence, independence, and interdependence of the First Nation chiefs and councils as autonomous First Nation governments representing their citizens and how this relates to the mandate of the Assembly of Manitoba Chiefs as a political organization. The latter represents a decision-making political body formed as unified collective leadership on common issues joined in unity to assert, protect, and advocate the inherent, treaty, and Aboriginal rights of First Nations peoples.[4]

There are sixty-three First Nation governments affiliated with the AMC, with the majority being descendants of the numbered treaties: Treaty No. 1 of 1871, Treaty No. 2 of 1872, Treaty No. 3 of 1873, Treaty No. 4 of 1874, Treaty No. 5 of 1875, Treaty No. 6 of 1876 and Treaty No. 10 in 1906. The five Dakota Nations in Manitoba are not recognized by Canada as being part of the treaties, but they hold the same legal entitlements.

In accordance with the AMC Constitution, the grand chief is the spokesperson, elected by the chiefs of the sixty-three First Nation leaders representing the communities situated in Manitoba and each voting chief is elected by the citizens of their respective First Nations. The AMC is comprised of the political office and the secretariat that serves the affiliated First Nations. There are two other Manitoba First Nation political advocacy organizations that work in concert with the AMC—the Manitoba Keewatinook Ininew Okimowin (MKO), which represents northern Manitoba First Nations,[5] and the Southern Chiefs Organization, which represents First Nations in the southern portion of the province.[6] These organizations work collaboratively in various forums and technical arrangements on research and policy review, including the Intergovernmental Committee on Manitoba First Nations Health described later in this chapter.

The Secretariat's primary functions include:

- Providing administrative services to the Political Office, Executive Council, Chiefs Committees, and Chiefs in Assembly
- Managing the flow of communication in delivering key messages and preparing annual reports, committee business and leadership decision-making process, as well as developing briefings, research, and reports
- Facilitating the implementation of the First Nation's agenda through community-connected research, program and policy review, and development.[7] This includes partnering with governments in research, program, and policy development on key policy sectors including: Child and Family Services, economic development, employment equity, education, the environment, gaming, health, and housing, among others.

A major area of concern for First Nations is the changes in authority for the federal departments of Indian and Northern Affairs Canada (INAC) and the First Nation and Inuit Health Branch (FNIHB) for on-reserve programs and services that link program and services eligibility to residency, membership, and registration. The amendments to the 1985 Indian Act served to eliminate aspects of gender and other discrimination and provided First Nation governments a measure of control in determining membership. However, this brought forth other problems. Bill C-31 may have eliminated some areas of discrimination, but it created other aspects of inequity and inequality. The citizenship/membership categories posing the greatest concern for First Nations are the 6(1) and 6(2) provisions, which prescribe the loss of status after two generations of non-First Nation parents. Being registered as 6(1) gives an individual fewer rights than 6(2) registrations since the member is not permitted to pass on their band status to their child unless the other parent is also a registered Indian. Another area of discrimination is where children of brothers and sisters who married non-Indians prior to 1985 are treated differently for registration eligibility. A study commissioned by INAC in 2002 concluded that overall, First Nations populations both on- and off-reserve will dramatically decrease due to lack of eligibility for Indian registration and membership.[8] This loss of citizens to the First Nations is a major challenge, as it impacts the vision of First Nations' self-determination and to honouring the spirit and intent of the treaties forged with the Crown.

According to a second study in 2006, Clatworthy noted that as a result of the Indian Act changes on membership and registration, "[t]hose who lack registration entitlement and consequently membership status are expected to form about one in every eight individuals within one generation. This segment of the population is expected to account for about one in every four individuals within two generations and about one in every three individuals within three generations."[9] This research is at the technical level and will require sound strategic groundwork to facilitate action that safeguards citizens and indigenous nationhood.

It is for these reasons that the AMC, as part of the collective national political voice it carries through the Assembly of First Nations (AFN), supported several Chiefs in Assembly resolutions since 2001 for Canada to recognize First Nations control of determining citizenship. In 2007, Canada's Department of Indian and Northern Affairs received a mandate to partner with the AFN to "explore all aspects of the issues that arise in respect of registration, membership, First Nations identity and citizenship, including options for future reform in these areas, in response to the direction from First Nations."[10]

Research and Policy

I will now turn to the research and policy developments of the organization. The majority of the political organization's core operations are funded by the federal department of Indian and Northern Affairs Canada, though that includes projects and research project funding from Health Canada—First Nations and Inuit Health and Canadian Heritage. Funding is also received from the provincial government for operations and research projects, including from the Departments of Aboriginal and Northern Affairs and Manitoba Health. Other sources of AMC funding include the Winnipeg Regional Health Authority (for patient advocacy) and as well the Winnipeg Partnership Authority, which supports the E.A.G.L.E. Urban Transition Centre located at 286 Smith Street in Winnipeg.

Other partnerships in research and public education to advance First Nations rights and priorities include the co-establishment in 2001 with the University of Manitoba of the Manitoba First Nation Centre for Aboriginal Health Research. Through the AMC Health Information Governance Committee, this special research partnership supports research between First Nations and academic researchers, for example, developing a Manitoba First Nations Health Report Card and research into men's and women's health as well as promoting First Nations access to quality cancer care. As well, AMC has contracted the evaluation on the ongoing Maternal Child Health-Manitoba First Nations Strengthening Families program.[11] Most of all, the work of the AMC is strengthened through the community First Nations representatives who share their traditions, knowledge, and expertise at the community, regional, and national initiatives to the numerous joint working groups, tables, committees, and task forces to bring positive change to the communities and to the nation-to-nation and government-to-government relationships.

A constant reactive measure to legal, legislative, and policy developments by other governments that impact First Nations directly has been the state of affairs for much too long. It is important that First Nations are equipped to be proactive and stay alert to the ever-changing provincial, national, and international landscape in assessing how new developments impact First Nations from both policy and legal perspectives. Despite some incredible research accomplishments and agreement reached at the technical and political level, the achievements are sometimes short-lived, since in many instances the research findings are not translated into policy or are not deemed relevant by the policy makers. There is a communication gap often faced at the technical, senior official, and political levels that must be bridged. Some say the researcher needs to speak the language of the policy makers.[12] For First Nations, it is an additional responsibility as the first hurdle is to cross the cultural divide that exists between the First Nation and other partners. These partners bring their different cultures, languages, and values, leading to difficulties in transcending understanding of mutual priorities to creation of institutions.

The political office, with support from the Secretariat, also provides advice on other key issues relating specifically to AMC's mandate. This includes matters relating to, among others:

- Treaties
- Section 35 Aboriginal and treaty rights
- Human rights and related issues such as citizenship and matrimonial property
- The Canadian Human Rights Museum
- Leadership council—Common Election Code
- First Nation languages
- Residential school survivors
- Lands and resources
- Land claims, treaty land entitlement
- Justice and policing

The major focus of most reviews of existing policies or joint policy review initiatives is to create a policy and operational framework by which First Nations could assume control over the matter at issue and governance functions within the context of federal or provincial policy. In this context, the initiatives focus on policy and operational reform rather than legislative changes to the Indian Act or recognition of First Nations to take back responsibility. Nonetheless, First Nations continue to pursue the creation of a framework for greater First Nation control and support strengthening First Nation governments over all matters within the areas directly impacting First Nations, including areas currently administered under the Indian Act.

Related to this is the establishment of the Manitoba Leadership Council, which is mandated by AMC resolution to reform the current First Nation leadership selection and term of office system. The First Nations' current election system and term are governed by the Indian Act or by custom codes. Both of these systems present challenges to governance stability as well as being able to sustain economic development by the community and effective representative political organizations, due to most chiefs and councils having a two-year term of office and individual election dates. The goal of this initiative is to work jointly with the federal Department of Indian and Northern Affairs on joint research of other electoral systems and to propose options for a Common Election Code framework for leadership review and decision-making. The two components are for longer terms of office and a common election date. Three options have been developed, all of which involve a specific amendment to the Indian Act from a revision to relevant provisions of the existing legislation, new federal legislation, to a custom code. Political support for this initiative could lead to a broader multi-phased future process that might include but not be limited to the joint development of options and next steps for reform in respect of other key areas affected by the Indian Act and other federal and provincial policies and legislation, and consultation with First Nations on these matters. As well, this will create opportunities to engage in joint political relationship-building, on a nation-to-nation and government-to-government basis, in other areas such as education and training, health, economic development, social issues, justice, natural resources, governance, and perhaps treaties.

Key AMC Policy Areas
Economic Development
A Special Chiefs Assembly on Economic Development was held in May 2007 to generate awareness of economic activity in Manitoba. A number of representatives of government departments, Crown corporations, and private-sector firms

addressed this assembly, with then-premier Gary Doer also speaking to the work of the provincial government. By resolution, the AMC has begun to pursue the concept of a Manitoba First Nation Energy Company. The First Peoples Economic Growth Fund Inc. opened its doors in August 2008. It is designed to meet the developmental gaps experienced by First Nations in Manitoba and to address gaps in six program areas: business plan assistance, skills development, entrepreneur loans, community economic expansion, loans, joint venture investment, and aftercare.

Employment Equity

There are four categories of under-represented groups in the Canadian workforce: women, visible minorities, Aboriginal people, and disabled people. The AMC continues to be engaged in sustaining existing employment equity partnerships. Through increased understanding among the partners and building trust and cooperation, the objective is to lead to the development of employment strategies on training, recruitment, retention, promotion, and accountability. As of 2008, a total of twenty-six partnerships, working relationships, and supports were in place. According to 2007 INAC statistics, by the year 2010 it is estimated that one in four new employees in the labour force will be of Aboriginal descent. The largest growing and youngest Aboriginal youth population in Canada is in Manitoba with a median age of twenty-four.[13] Manitoba-based industries, government, and Crown corporations look to the First Nations community for their labour workforce needs. The challenge for us is to create a resource of trained, available First Nations people to enter and remain in the workforce.

Social Development

In 2002, the Chiefs in Assembly declared that social development includes socioeconomic and cultural elements, and that in order to bring First Nations out of poverty it is fundamental to invest in people and rebuild communities. This requires investing in education, housing, infrastructure, and economic development in order to make improvements to the living conditions of First Nations. The challenge faced by First Nations is to bring about policy changes to have parity, equity or comparability to provincial programs. Action to bring about change to eliminate poverty amongst First Nations requires a concerted collective strategy by all governments that engages First Nations directly.

Health

By 2005 resolution, the AMC Chiefs in Assembly mandated the implementation of the Manitoba First Nations—Health & Wellness Strategy: A 10-Year Plan of

Action and Beyond as well as set up a Chiefs' Task Force on Health to provide direction to health strategies and bring forward recommendations to the leadership at large. One of the promising initiatives is the Intergovernmental Committee on Manitoba First Nations Health (ICMFNH), which is a joint tripartite process[14] consisting of AMC, MKIO, SCO, and representatives of a number of relevant provincial and federal government departments. The committee, established in 2002 following the release of the Commission on the Future of Health Care in Canada (the Romanow Report), seeks to address the high health care service utilization by First Nations peoples; high morbidity rates and co-morbid conditions; separate administrative silos for service delivery; limited funding envelopes for on-reserve services, and jurisdictional ambiguities and disputes.

The committee's goal is to "reduce the prevalence in disorder rates and disease in any area among First Nations where they are higher than provincial or national levels." It is governed by a set of guiding principles, in particular the notions that "the position and perspectives of First Nations (including culture, values, and language) must inform health and social policy development of both federal and provincial governments" and that "all ICMFNH initiatives will promote the capacity of First Nation communities to participate in the health system and decisions affecting their health." Some of the current action items include the Chronic Disease/Diabetes Action Plan, Medical Relocation—Phase II Final Report, First Nation-Primary Health Care Framework, Joint Position Paper on First Nations with Disabilities. As well, the development of a First Nation–Intergovernmental Health Council Proposal is currently underway through community research. It strives to work toward a shared vision including to "provide increased efficiency and effectiveness to facilitate the necessary movement for structural change."

National Aboriginal Health Summit

Hosted by then-premier Gary Doer in 2008 and jointly coordinated with Manitoba, this second summit was a follow-up to the first ministers' meetings with Aboriginal leaders in 2005. The forum consisted of a meeting between provincial, territorial, and federal health and Aboriginal affairs ministers and national Aboriginal leaders, as well as a series of simultaneous workshops on First Nations, Métis, and Inuit health issues. The First Nations priorities focused on three areas:
- Relationship building—To improve/strengthen relationships between First Nations and federal, provincial, and territorial governments and to promote respect and create understanding of responsibilities among all jurisdictions;
- Sustainability—To promote a commitment to sustainability from federal, provincial, and territorial governments to support and provide resources to sustain a health system that respects and protects the inherent and treaty rights

to health and ensures First Nations health and social outcomes are equal to that of Canadians;
- Access to services—To identify innovative ways to provide new investments for new approaches to health care.[15]

Other health research and partnership initiatives at AMC include:

Patient Wait Time Guarantee with Saint Elizabeth Health Care

Research with eight First Nations communities in the areas of prevention, treatment, and care of foot ulcers. The goal is to develop a testable model to form a patient wait-times guarantee for people with diabetic foot ulcers to receive treatment and care.

Manitoba—Regional Longitudinal Health Survey (RHS) Data Collection

This is part of the National RHS and 2008 marked the third collection year. The previous two RHS studies, conducted in 1996 and 2002, were subcontracted to the Manitoba First Nations Centre for Aboriginal Health Research at University of Manitoba. As mandated by resolution, this third round supports research to be carried out according to First Nations OCAP principles (ownership, control, access, and possession of their own data; prior informed consent; and traditional ethical standards). This round of data gathering is under the control of First Nations with an increase in the numbers of First Nations participating. As the AMC's 2008 annual report noted, "AMC has secured technology to utilize its own research server to store the RHS data; with firewalls and measures for privacy and security….The data is separate from AMC as political organization, with virtual servers for each First Nation's data."[16]

Promoting Traditional Ways To Health

This conference was held to promote self-determination as a determinant of health. Key topics included education awareness of traditional foods and medicines, strengths in traditions and traditional lifestyles, as well as indigenous research and documentation. Elders and practitioners in the health fields forged a connection of traditions and new research as the road to the future that will also serve to inform health and social policies.

Conclusion

Indicators of change are slowly emerging. However, these embers need to be fanned so they do not burn out. First, it is necessary to strengthen the political relationships among the First Nations, the general public and within the federal and provincial governments. Second, the importance of language, culture, tradition, values, and identity (identity that is both individual and collective) must be emphasized, with an importance placed upon knowing our histories as a means of becoming tellers of our own history, especially the knowledge of connectedness to the land and environment.

Partnerships on policy review or development with First Nations and other government departments or agencies require a joint agreement of the members of the partnership to the process. There should be engagement of the diverse First Nations' perspectives at the very preliminary stages to ensure that discussions are responsive and reflective of community values, perspectives, experiences, and expectations at every stage. In order to ensure diversity there needs to be inclusion of First Nations youth, elders, women, and men, together with First Nations situated in urban settings in the same categories.

The ICFMNH still has steps to take in its research on the policy implications of the specific issues. It must also research the interplay between the policy areas and governance and its impact on First Nations, including an examination of customary practice issues and how traditional practices have been affected by current legislation, as well as the impact of policies on the individual and communities. Reforms must be consistent and supportive of First Nations right of self-determination and to revitalizing traditional laws to guide changes.

Notes

1. This chapter is adapted from a speech given by Irene Linklater to the Manitoba Politics, Government and Policy Conference, 22 November 2008.
2. This chapter provides a brief overview of the AMC's involvement in research and partnerships related to policies and to identify some areas of focus to establish a proposed research and policy agenda for future work. It is not intended to be a statement of AMC policies or positions in respect of issues presented or to suggest any particular direction for the future design of policy or legislation.
3. The Assembly of Manitoba Chiefs (AMC) Secretariat was created in 1988, though it traces its origins to the creation of the Indian Association of Manitoba (founded in 1947), which was later renamed the Manitoba Indian Brotherhood.
4. The constitution of the AMC and other information is available at http://www.manitobachiefs.com.
5. For more information, see http://www.mkonorth.com
6. For more information, see http://www.scoinc.mb.ca.
7. Annual Reports are available on the AMC website, http://www.manitobachiefs.com.
8. Stewart Clatworthy, *Indian Registration, Membership and Population Change in First Nation Communities,* Four Directions Project Consultants (Winnipeg, 2005).

9   Stewart Clatworthy, "Registration and Membership: Implications for First Nations Communities," presentation to the Aboriginal Policy Research Conference, Ottawa, March 2006.
10 See ARN-INAC Joint Technical Working Group *First Nations Registration (Status) And Membership Research Report* (Ottawa: Indian and Northern Affairs Canada, 2008), http://www.afn.ca.
11 Dr. Kathy Avery Kinew, AMC Annual Report 2008, 95.
12 *"You say 'to-may-to(e)' and I say 'to-mah-to(e)'": Bridging the Communication Gap Between Researchers and Policy-Makers*, CPHI Report on "Moving from Research to Policy: Improving the Health of Canada's Youth," workshop held in Toronto, 19–20 February 2004.
13 Statistics Canada, "2006 Aboriginal Population Profile – Manitoba," http://www12.statcan.gc.ca/census-recensement/2006/dp-pd/prof/92-594/details/page.cfm?Lang=E&Geo1=PR&Code1=46&Geo2=PR&Code2=01&Data=Count&SearchText=Manitoba&SearchType=Begins&SearchPR=01&B1=All&GeoLevel=&GeoCode=46 (accessed 20 February 2010).
14 See http://www.manitobachiefs.com/issue/icfnh.html.
15 "Report on Proceedings: National Aboriginal Health Working Summit," Winnipeg, 3–4 March 2008.
16 AMC, 2008 Annual Report, 92.

Has the Manitoba "Advantage" Worked for Women?[1]

Joan Grace

Introduction

For Canadian women, provincial governments matter. Provinces have constitutional authority over policy areas that significantly influence women's social and economic well-being, and are sites of political debate closer to provincially located policy communities. Moreover, in the Canadian federal system, provincial governments often have room to manoeuvre, apart from federal and other provincial jurisdictions, to develop policies that respond to socio-cultural legacies and unique political realities.[2] Classified as "liberal" welfare states, provincial governments have been important contributors to building Canada's social safety net reinforced by a commitment to social liberalism, which "provided language for the systemically disadvantaged to talk back to the welfare state, and to make claims as citizens."[3]

Yet while at times protecting and advancing women's equality, provincial welfare states have also institutionalized and perpetuated women's systematic discrimination and engendered particular attitudes about women. Early provincial state-building was in part buttressed by a "dominant view of work and family life [which] dictated a strict division of labour between the sexes. Men were expected to earn the market wage to provide for dependents; women were largely confined to the private, domestic sphere, taking care of the 'personal' needs of the family."[4] To be sure, women were "recognized" in emergent welfare states, but largely as members of a gender regime "through the lens of the nuclear family as wives, mothers, and widows...to reinforce a particular family form and model of social reproduction."[5] While many of the most egregiously sexist policies have been repealed and the patriarchal regime has shifted and even muted in some sectors, gendered power relations remain steadfast. Women activists continue to confront a political landscape that is either hostile to feminist policy goals, or simply blasé about women's inequitable treatment and socio-economic situation. As a consequence, women's groups persist to subvert gendered relations of power and along the way reveal why, and why not, state-based actors and governing practices either accept or obstruct their policy objectives. This dynamic is crucial to explore since action or inaction on the part of provincial governments continues to structure women's access to essential public services such as anti-violence initiatives, income security programs, health care, housing, regulated child care, and education. As well, the political priorities of provincial governments can either restrain or advance women's capacity to control their sexual reproduction, their opportunities to participate in political institutions, and their entrance into the paid labour market.[6] For women, it is telling where one lives, and in Manitoba, this is particularly the case.

In a cross-national comparison, women in Manitoba have experienced some of the highest and deepest levels of poverty, particularly so for Aboriginal, disabled, visible minority, and immigrant women. Many women in Manitoba still do not have access to safe abortions, especially in rural and remote areas, and it has been persistently the case that more children than not are without a spot in a regulated child care facility. Yet, women may have an advantage in Manitoba due to the presence of the New Democratic Party (NDP)—a party that has been in power for a decade. As of 2010, Manitoba was one of just two Canadian provinces with a social-democratic political party in government. The presence of an NDP government is of import and interest to feminist policy advocates since it is the Manitoba NDP that has most often espoused a gender equality strategy, and it is the NDP that has articulated a progressive policy platform distinct from its enduring rival, the Progressive Conservative Party.[7] As well, Manitoba's economy has fared relatively well during the last few years, even during the most recent economic crisis, with unemployment rates consistently below the national average. Moreover, it is timely to study the challenges and opportunities which shape women's policy advocacy in a province which has undergone policy and institutional change due to "Third Way" neo-liberalism and state reconfiguration, which have modified conventional understandings of the state's role and the political priorities of the NDP.

To conduct this investigation, this paper analyzes women's movement policy advocacy focusing analytical attention toward the UN Platform for Action

Committee-Manitoba (UNPAC). UNPAC is a well-known and active feminist collective formed by a number of women who attended the United Nations Fourth World Conference on Women in Beijing. UNPAC's objective has been to monitor the implementation of the recommendations of the Beijing Platform for Action. Since then, UNPAC has completed the first stage of a detailed study on women's participation in the Manitoba economy. The second component of this project, gendering the provincial budget, has been underway since 2005. UNPAC is a member of the Manitoba-based Child Care Coalition, and has been a participant in coalitions, such as the national Code Blue for Childcare and the Just Income Coalition, which campaigned for an increase in the provincial minimum wage. UNPAC is also a member of the Canadian Feminist Alliance for International Action (FAFIA), which campaigns to ensure federal and provincial governments honour commitments articulated in international women's and human rights treaties.

As this chapter demonstrates, the particular advocacy strategies employed by UNPAC have had some marginal impact. The NDP provided policy access to UNPAC and made some gestures toward gendering the 2007 provincial budget. UNPAC has also been very successful in engaging in a politics of change amongst the attentive Manitoba public. However, substantive, legislated change has not been forthcoming due to particular aspects of the provincial policy context; the province's political economy and "have not" status within Canadian federalism, and the importance of budgets as a governing instrument of political elites due to the political priorities of the NDP. These obstacles in turn have influenced interactions between the state and the women's movement making it difficult for the feminist equality agenda to take a firm hold in the provincial policy repertoire.

To frame this argument, I look to the work of Lee Ann Banaszak, Karen Beckwith, and Dieter Rucht, who argue that women's movements in North America "face a reconfigured state that offers them opportunities for advancing feminist agendas and that also threatens feminist success."[8] In Canada, an analysis of the political opportunity structure and the "reconfigured state" subsumes both the Manitoba and federal governments and the way in which discourses and policies of neo-liberalism have reoriented social liberalism and restructured state-movement interactions. Changes in governing practices and policy priorities at the federal level have had lasting impacts for provincial governments and for the women's movement in Manitoba. Provincial fiscal transfers from the federal government were dramatically reduced in the mid-1990s, as were funds to women's groups. In turn, relations between the women's movement and the state shifted, as did movement strategies. The interface between the state and the women's movement—each conceived as "sites of struggle"—are understood to be influenced by two broad dynamics. The first dimension is the structures and strategies of the actors, which include institutional arrangements, the issues under dispute, and methods of political persuasion. The second dimension is the policy context, which takes into account the community's political culture, configurations of power, and the forum in which the interaction takes place.[9]

Part I begins with a brief history and overview of women's mobilization in Manitoba to highlight the policy and political priorities of the progressive, feminist women's movement in the province. Part II explores the context of state-movement interaction during the tenure of the NDP. Although analytical energy is directed toward the NDP given that it has been in government for more than a decade, a discussion of the policy context necessarily requires looking to the former Progressive Conservative Party government. Part III offers an in-depth exploration of UNPAC's gender-responsive budget project as a case study of women's policy advocacy, looking to international experiences with gender budgets to assess potentials and perils. Part IV discusses obstacles to change in Manitoba. The conclusion offers a few thoughts on the future of women's policy activism in Manitoba.

I. Women's Organizing in Manitoba—Past to Present

A rich history of women's political activism has animated Manitoba politics. Since the time when Nellie McClung and the Political Equality League held a "Mock Parliament of Women" in January 1914 at the Walker Theatre in Winnipeg as part of their struggle to secure the right to vote, women continued to make a difference. As Judy Rebick reminds us, during the 1970s and 1980s, the second-wave women's movement has been one of the most successful collective politics in Canada, responsible for the creation of women's shelters, rape crisis centres, family law reform, and the entrenchment of women's rights in the Constitution.[10] Manitoba women were sometimes at the centre of these struggles.[11]

It is likely not well-known that the Manitoba Action Committee on the Status of Women (MACSW)—a provincial, umbrella organization at the forefront of women's political activism in the province—was established in 1967 *before* the National Action Committee on the Status of Women was established in 1972. Initially calling itself the Manitoba Volunteer Committee, the group later evolved into the Manitoba Action Committee on the Status of Women in 1971 just after the Royal Commission on the Status of Women (RCSW) reported in 1970. The principle of the original group was to raise "people's consciousness of the current secondary status of women," to educate Manitobans about the recommendations of the RCSW, to receive and exchange information with other groups and to work toward the implementation of the RCSW's recommendations.[12] As the first "action" committee formed in Canada at this time, the original collective had no financial resources, yet possessed a wealth of experience in the women who comprised the group.[13] With funding assistance initially from the Department of the Secretary of State and subsequently from Status of Women Canada, offices were eventually opened across the province in Brandon, Dauphin, Thompson, and Winnipeg. MACSW also reached women outside of Winnipeg in rural and northern communities. They did so by holding occasional conferences, such as the Northern Women's Conference in 1973 and the Women in Rural and Northern Manitoba Conference in 1975, and by reporting events and activities of rural women such as the Portage Farm Women's Organization and the Manitoba Farm Women's Network. As well, a coordinator, located in the Brandon office, was designated to report on rural issues and activities from the late 1980s to early 1990s.

From available archival data, by 1979 membership stood at about 400 individuals. There was also by this time a well-established organizational structure consisting of an executive committee, elected at the annual general meeting, comprising a chairperson, two vice-chairs, a secretary, a treasurer, and representatives from five standing committees (finance, membership, communications, program, and nominations, and up to ten members-at-large). As required, ad hoc "issue committees" were struck which at various times included media monitoring and a labour and education committee.[14]

During the time period of its operation, from 1971 to about 1999, a newsletter was published to inform and co-ordinate the activities of members. MACSW mobilized around a diverse array of issues, ranging from child care, peace and disarmament, highlighting discriminatory aspects of the Indian Act, women's reproductive choice and access to therapeutic abortions (especially when anti-choice forces restricted access in Dauphin and Brandon in the early 1990s), equal pay, pension and family law reform, ending violence against women, free trade, city politics, and women's poverty.[15] Like many groups associated with the English Canadian women's movement, MACSW employed both insider and outsider advocacy strategies, such as giving presentations to legislative committees, staging candidates' debates during elections, and lobbying provincial and federal officials. As well, MACSW engaged in disruptive political action campaigns, and organized a number of conferences such as the Women in Politics and Public Life conference in 1973. Its members also attended conferences organized by other women groups such as the 1981 Women and the Constitution conference held in Ottawa. MACSW was eventually recognized as the main provincial organization that spoke in the media on women's issues and coordinated the "Manitoba women's movement" response to the provincial government on issues of the day and on policy proposals.

MACSW also participated in ad hoc coalitions, one very good example being the Action Coalition on Family Law to formulate a response to the recommendations of the Manitoba Law Reform Commission in the mid-1970s.[16] In the mid-1980s, MACSW was also associated with a group organized to respond to the Meech Lake Accord. This ad hoc group, later renamed the Westman Coalition for Equality Rights in the Meech Lake Accord, was formed in Brandon in April 1988 as a vehicle for rural women to demand that the Meech Lake Accord be amended to guarantee women's equality rights.[17] Later, the Westman Coalition also lobbied for the inclusion of women's rights in the Charlottetown Accord, and in the mid-1990s, MACSW worked with the Manitoba Women's Social Policy Coalition to respond to the federal government's 1994 Social Security Review.

During the late 1980s, the political opportunity structure began to shift with the ascendancy of neo-liberalism and concomitant government restructuring. MACSW's funding, received largely from The Women's Program funded by the federal government and administered through Status of Women Canada, was frozen in 1988 and core funding was cut in 1998 as part of the Liberal government's program review. These government restructuring initiatives contributed to MACSW having to cease operations in 1999. As this chapter argued previously, however, since the demise of MACSW a diverse array of groups and organizations still collectively comprise the women's movement in the province albeit as a less cohesive entity.[18] These groups and organizations can be conceptualized[19] as either institutionalized equality advocates (Manitoba Women's Institute, Provincial Council of Women, Women's Legal Education and Action Fund, Manitoba), as identity-based groups (Mothers of Red Nations, Congress of Black Women, Immigrant Women's Association of Manitoba), as safe space advocates/providers (Fort Garry Women's Resource Centre, Women's Centre, Brandon), or as issue-oriented groups (Child Care Coalition of Manitoba, Women's Health Clinic, UNIFEM, UNPAC).

It is important for groups like UNPAC to step into the breach and organize since conditions for many women in Manitoba remain desperate. In 1999, the year of the election of the NDP government, 19.9 percent of Manitoba women aged eighteen and over were considered poor.[20] Senior, immigrant, and Aboriginal women in Manitoba continue to experience even higher rates of poverty. A persistently high child poverty rate is instructive to analyze since poor children most often reside with poor mothers. In 1989, Manitoba had the highest child poverty rate at 21.8 percent and between 1989 and 2002, the average child poverty rate in Manitoba was 25 percent.[21] By 2004, the situation had only slightly improved with Manitoba experiencing the fourth highest rate of child poverty (19.2 percent) but still above the national average of 17.7 percent.[22] In 2006, however, Manitoba inched slightly up the list, ranking third highest among provinces.[23] The Social Planning Council of Winnipeg further reports that 68 percent of First Nation children under six years old living off-reserve lived in poverty in Manitoba in 2005, the highest percentage of all provinces.[24]

The feminization of poverty is further entrenched by inadequate Manitoba Employment and Income Assistance benefits (welfare assistance)—the majority of recipients of which are individuals with disabilities and mothers living with children.[25] In fact, basic welfare assistance rates have not kept pace with inflation since 1992, and have actually fallen by 15 to 35 percent, in real economic terms. As well, three-quarters of welfare recipients were not able to pay their rental costs from monies received from the province in part because benefit rates for single "employable" individuals have been frozen for more than a decade and have lost 35 percent of their purchasing power.[26]

Economic security and independence have also been jeopardized relative to men's due in part to women's low-wage employment in the service sector.[27] Moreover, many women still do not have access to much-needed affordable and regulated child care to take up paid employment. According to the Child Care Coalition, access to child care is fundamental to alleviating poverty while also promoting women's equality, but in Manitoba only 14.5 percent of children aged zero to twelve are in a regulated child care space, while the number of spaces in licensed family child care homes has fallen.[28]

Regarding health and human security, women also do not have full access to therapeutic abortions, with under-service being particularly acute in northern and rural locations.[29] The health care needs of women have also been put at risk, particularly after the curtailment of some services due to hospital bed closures, shortened hospital stays, and the introduction of user fees and a lack of medical professionals.[30] The Canadian Council on Social Development (CCSD) recently reported that nearly one Canadian woman in three is victimized in her home, and documented that immigrant women were particularly vulnerable to violence and abuse due to language barriers in reporting and seeking help.[31] A report released in 2008 by Statistics Canada on family violence reiterates this situation, reporting that 83 percent of victims of spousal abuse are women, noting that violent offences towards women are higher in the Western provinces and territories.[32] Aboriginal women experience some of the highest rates of violence.[33]

II. Women's Policy Advocacy and the Manitoba "Advantage"

How have Manitoba governments responded to the situation of women? Since the ascendancy of neo-liberalism, at its zenith by the mid- to late 1990s under federal Liberal governments and a Progressive Conservative government in

Manitoba, a "politics of marginalization" emerged wherein "feminists were soon disparaged in political debate and in the popular media, and, along with equality seeking groups, labelled as 'special interest groups.'"[34] Propelled by a discourse of economic rationalism, Canadians were informed that reforms were necessary in order to reduce government debts and deficits, pay crippling interest payments and streamline a bloated bureaucracy, which were argued to be threatening economic competitiveness and the financial sustainability of programs.[35] Program retrenchment was also instituted to ease dependency on welfare state programs and to reconfigure citizen expectations of government. Restructuring within Status of Women Canada had profound impact on the women's movement's ability to engage in policy advocacy and to advance an alternative political discourse.

Maureen Baker aptly argues that restructuring social programs and reconfiguring the welfare state were further motivated by federal-provincial politics and the "fear" of Quebec separatism. By encapsulating the rhetoric in economic rationalism, the federal government was able to make unpopular changes such as replacing the Canada Assistance Program (a conditional, matched-funding scheme) with the introduction in 1996 of the Canada Health and Social Transfer (CHST). Provinces, although sometimes cash-strapped to finance social programs within their respective jurisdictions, were given vast room to spend CHST monies in areas of provincial priority.[36] While appealing to provincial authorities who had long demanded less federal intrusion, decentralized decision making to provinces jeopardized the development of much-needed national programs, such as a universal child care system, and put women's policy goals in direct competition for scarce resources at the local level.

In Manitoba, economic rationalism and the ideology of the neo-liberalism were taken up by the Progressive Conservative Party most fervently under the governments of Gary Filmon.[37] During the tenure of the PC government from 1988 to 1999, the Filmon government introduced many measures that were developed to reconfigure state-society relations and Manitobans' expectations of their government. Various forms of alternative services delivery were implemented including the creation of Special Operating Agencies to infuse a private-sector business ethos into government institutional practices and policy development. Contracting out was conducted in the health care sector and in family services.[38] In 1994, a welfare fraud line was created, followed up by extensive welfare reforms which began in 1996 to "further reduce welfare dependency and ensure all Manitobans capable of working find jobs, or provide community services in exchange for income assistance."[39] As well, the Filmon government implemented an economic strategy which included deficit reduction and capitalizing on open export markets made available through the Canada-U.S. Free Trade Agreement.[40]

This strategy was at the heart of the PCs' neo-liberal policy agenda representing a dramatic shift away from Keynesianism to a new fiscal paradigm.[41]

However, the transition from postwar social liberalism to late twentieth century neo-liberalism has generated a neo-liberal consensus across the political spectrum and amongst a wide array of political elites. As we have argued previously, during the 1999 election the NDP presented itself to Manitobans as a political party that would advance traditional social democratic political priorities (i.e., ending "hallway medicine") while also ensuring affordable and efficient government.[42] Gary Doer presented to voters "clear and simple" policy pledges, a style of governance characterized as "pragmatic idealism" by the NDP because it offered a set of concrete promises to voters and a positive electoral alternative.[43] Framed this way, the NDP has been willing to implement a centre-right agenda consisting of tax reductions, maintaining workfare programs, and many of the privatization initiatives of the previous government.

Balancing between these ideological positions, however, the NDP has made some attempt to advance social inclusion. The NDP has consistently supported not-for-profit health care, abolished the welfare fraud line set up by the Filmon government[44] and implemented a tuition freeze that was sustained over a nine-year period. As well, it was one of the first provinces to eliminate the clawback of the National Child Benefit, developed a five-year child care plan,[45] substantially increased the minimum wage, provided funding to Jane's Clinic, a stand-alone abortion clinic, and developed initiatives such as the Neighbourhood's Alive! Program to encourage economic development in Winnipeg's inner city. The NDP has also kept in place a two-pronged women's policy machinery—the Women's Directorate within the bureaucratic hierarchy to facilitate a gender voice within the policy process, and the Manitoba Women's Advisory Council, an arm's-length agency whose board is staffed by representatives from various identity and ethnic-national communities, and that works closely with women and communities across the province.

While these initiatives are commendable, the overall policy context in the province is significantly influenced by the government's priority of encouraging Manitoba's global economic competitiveness. Just three years in office, the minister of finance promoted what was termed the "Manitoba Advantage," which characterized the province as the place for Canadians to live and work and as the environment to conduct business. The Manitoba Advantage casts the province as family-friendly, due to the availability of affordable housing; a province with a dynamic economy because of its diversification (aerospace, food processing, financial services and transportation, health products, and research), and the ideal location for industry due to some of the lowest hydroelectricity rates in the world; a central location which is ideal as a mid-continental trade corridor (with a 24-hour airport); a cost-competitive locale because of affordable office and land costs, and a province with an abundance of natural resources and the only deep-water port on the Prairies.[46] In the government's performance reporting to Manitobans released in 2005, the NDP government reported that GDP growth averaged 2.5 percent between 2000 to 2004, well above an average of 1.8 percent annual growth during the 1990s. As well, it noted that unemployment rates had steadily been below the national average and that personal disposable income since 1999 had increased by 16.7 percent.[47]

The performance document made only cursory mention of the government's continued efforts to promote women's equality, and there has been no public recognition since of consistently high poverty rates and concomitant social hardships experienced by many Manitobans, nor certainly the development of anti-poverty strategies like those in Ontario, Newfoundland, or Nova Scotia. In most government policy pronouncements and programming that have a direct impact on the lives of women, the issue is generally framed around supporting families or addressing the needs of children in crisis.[48] In the wake of moderate and often non-gendered responses from the NDP (and sometimes outright neglect by federal governments since the late 1980s) activists within the province and across the country have expanded their advocacy strategies and relocated their politics.[49] We now turn to a discussion of The UN Platform for Action Committee—Manitoba, which is part of a movement to rescale political advocacy by connecting the local with the global.

III. UNPAC, Women's Equality, and Gender Budgets

In 1985, a number of Manitoba women organized into a group called the UN Decade for Women in preparation for participation in the Third World Conference on Women scheduled to be held in Nairobi. The UN Platform for Action Committee–Manitoba (UNPAC) is the reincarnation of that group formed in 1995 for the clear purpose of lobbying the Manitoba and federal governments to implement the Platform for Action, a document which outlines various legislative and institutional measures to advance women's equality. The Platform for Action was one of the outcomes of the United Nations Fourth World Conference on Women held in Beijing. Since mobilizing, UNPAC has utilized a number of movement strategies to lobby politicians and educate women and Manitobans on the lived realities of women in the province. Although much of their work takes place in Manitoba, they campaign and participate in meetings at the international level and lobby federal policy makers.

UNPAC has also been very productive in generating its own data and informational materials for education and advocacy purposes. A large component of the data has been derived from UNPAC's own internal work, such as its review on the implementation of the Platform for Action. As well, from 2001 to 2003 UNPAC undertook a comprehensive study of the economic situation of women in Manitoba. The "Women and Economy" project received funding from Status of Women Canada, producing a plethora of quite detailed information and statistics on women's participation and experiences in the labour market and economy. This project produced two printed volumes and a video titled *Banging the Door Down: Women and the Economy*. In 2004, UNPAC launched its most recent campaign, the Gender Budget Project, as the second part of their Women and Economy study. The project aims to advance women's economic literacy and security by "demystifying the provincial budget for women in Manitoba while encouraging broader participation in the budget process" in an effort to compel the provincial government to "create a more gender responsive budget."[50] As Jennifer deGroot and Shauna MacKinnon have put it, gendering budgeting is important since "men and women are not equal beneficiaries of public spending" yet it is women who most often depend on the "equalizing role of government."[51]

Members of UNPAC methodically planned their gender budget campaign. They knew many Manitoba women would not have experience with government consultations, nor know much about the often complex details of government budgets and the administrative processes associated with developing public sector budgets. UNPAC organizers, too, educated themselves on gender budgets, having talked and met with women in other countries who had either advocated gender budgets or had participated in implementing gender budgets. UNPAC also was aware that the concept of a "gender budget" would not be well-known. As a consequence, a communication and consultation strategy was devised to educate women on gender budgets, to encourage their participation, to get the attention of the media and to persuade the provincial government that gender budgets were a worthwhile exercise for women and for Manitobans. The following section provides some definitional structure to the concept of gender budgets, along with experiences in other countries, to provide a fuller understanding of this particular strategy of change. Elements of UNPAC's project are integrated into this discussion.

Why Gender Budgeting?
Gender-responsive budgets are a "way to assess the impact of government revenue and expenditure on women and men, girls and boys"[52] but are not about "dividing budgets 50-50" to create separate budgets. Rather, they are tools to

ensure "that government budgets are allocated in an equitable way so that the most pressing needs of individuals and groups are satisfied."[53] There are a number of ways gender budgeting can be undertaken, ranging from conducting a gender-disaggregated public expenditure incidence analysis or undertaking a gender analysis on women's time use within both the private and public spheres of their lives.[54]

To understand why women's groups like UNPAC have struggled to have budgets gendered, it is crucial to conceptualize or think about budgets as a policy statement.[55] Indeed, the budget is arguably the most significant government policy instrument and policy output since it "reflects the social and economic priorities of a government, [and] the monetary embodiment of its political commitment to specific policies and programmes."[56] Yet a budget is much more—it reflects the "values of a country—who it values, whose work it values and who it rewards...and who and what and whose work it doesn't."[57] What government leaders value and the choices they make through budgets, however, are often taken to be gender-neutral or gender-blind. As Diane Elson argues, speaking specifically in the British context: "The way in which the National Budget is usually formulated ignores the different, socially determined roles, responsibilities, and capabilities of men and women. These differences are generally structured in such a way as to leave women in an unequal position in relation to men in their community, with less economic, social and political power."[58]

Why? Because, as Elson further elaborates, gender-blind budgets do not account for women's contribution to the macro-economy, either because of the absence of gender-disaggregated data (or incomplete statistics, as she puts it) or because the macro-economy does not take into account the productive aspects of women's so-called "unproductive" unpaid work in the domestic sphere.[59] A gender budget reveals the so-called "hidden economy" of women's unpaid work in the domestic realms for calculation (along with the output of the formal realm of paid work) into determinations—for example, of contributions to the gross domestic product, or even more precise measures of what constitutes "unemployment."[60] This would mean, for example, a gender analysis of fiscal policies such as taxation.[61] Moreover, if "both" economies are calculated into budget decisions, policies, and programs that support women's equality would have a better chance of being developed and of being properly funded. These could include tax incentives for work in the home, income maintenance programs, or universal child care. As well, gender budgeting would analyze provincial and federal government surpluses and federal transfer payments to provinces to determine from a gender perspective where this money is and is not spent.[62]

Gender-responsive budgets, however, are not just about addressing women's economic inequality. They have potentially much broader consequences for women's citizenship and for good governance. First, and most basically, it is argued that gender-responsive budgets contribute to better efficiencies in the policy-making process.[63] Policy issues are framed in gender terms leading to policy outcomes having a better chance of meeting intended objectives. Second, gender budgets facilitate more robust accountability and transparency of government action or inaction.[64] For example, a gender-responsive budget can be an effective tool to track the progress of a government's commitment to women's equality. It can, for example, provide better assessment information to women's groups, due to the increase in gender-disaggregated data produced by government departments. The Australian experience is instructive, indicating that women's budget statements became a way to monitor the inputs and outputs of government that would often go unnoticed by "traditional government budgets" that focus on aggregate financial data and financial accounting.[65]

Finally, gender budgets are about demystifying budgets and educating women on the particular elements of a budget, both in terms of revenue and expenditure, and more importantly, why women themselves must be part of the process. Participation facilitates the process of having women's lived realities integrated into budget decisions and spending allocations. The inclusion of civil society in the budget process is part of a larger agenda, Isabella Bakker argues, to "democratize" macro-economic policy making, a process that is generally the domain of economists and other experts in the bureaucracy.[66] Indeed, the technical aspects of macro-economic policies "disguises their social content," which leads to policies being "enacted without a context of institutional structures and power relations among economically differentiated social groups."[67]

The education aspect of gender budgets is a predominant feature of UNPAC's gender budget project. To cast a wide net, UNPAC held several workshops across the province to encourage women to take part in the province's budget consultations. Moreover, from early 2005 through to 2007, UNPAC conducted forty-six day-long workshops across the province attended by more than 500 women.[68] Workshops were held in northern and rural Manitoba, and in Winnipeg. At the workshops, participants were educated about budgets and learned why they are important measures to address women's policy needs. UNPAC also set up an online budget survey on their web page for interested individuals who were not able to attend a workshop, or attend one of the province's budget consultations.

Budget priorities generated from these workshops were synthesized by UNPAC and presented to the minister of finance. Issues presented included the need for affordable housing, child care, health care, accessible public transportation, as well as employment and work issues such as women's unpaid care giving, low wages, and difficulties re-entering the paid labour market. Revenue suggestions were also compiled which generally advocated that the province increase taxes (e.g., for high-income earners and corporations), create new taxes (e.g., lottery-winning tax, inheritance tax), or reduce/re-evaluate government spending (e.g., examine wages of upper management) in order to shore up the government's overall general revenue base.

To summarize, gender-responsive budgets have many potentials. As one of the most important policy instruments, gender budgets can provoke within civil society, among political authorities and public administrators, an awareness of why it is crucial to think about policy problems and program outputs through a diversity lens that puts gender relations and the realities of women at the centre of the analysis. The process, it is hoped, results in public policies that have actual benefits for women, and along the way, shifts thinking amongst policy developers to mainstream gender into government decision making. Gender budgeting is in the end about realigning state practices to generate comprehensive transformation within government public policy processes. Once this is achieved, policy outcomes can substantively address women's particular requirements as a result of a broad, sustained commitment to equality, rather than by a policy-by-policy response and through incremental change.

Gender Budgeting Around the World

It is said that gender-sensitive budgeting has been implemented in at least fifty countries.[69] International organizations such as the United Nations Development Fund for Women (UNIFEM) was one of the early women's organizations to advocate for gender mainstreaming and gender budgets, likely because the initial impetus sprang from analyzing women's plight in developing countries. In 1995, the Commonwealth Secretariat instituted its Commonwealth Plan of Action on Gender and Development[70] and a Gender Budget Initiative. At the UN Fourth World Conference on Women in Beijing during the same year, the resultant Platform for Action reiterated the need for gender budgets as a way to advance women's equality. Gender budgeting has since been promoted by women's groups in South Africa, Uganda, Tanzania, Scotland, Switzerland, and the United Kingdom.[71]

However, gender-responsive budgets were actually pioneered in Australia in 1984. The Australian "women's budget program" was a government-driven exercise begun by a Labour Party government, then led by Bob Hawke, on the heels of an economic and social reform election platform.[72] The exercise lasted for the full twelve years Labour was in office. In the 1980s and 1990s, all of the Australian states and two territories introduced similar experiments.[73] And there were some positive outputs. The women's budget program facilitated the quantitative analysis of government expenditures targeted to women and increased awareness of the need for gender analysis during policy and budget development which also produced much-needed gender-disaggregated data in order to properly assess policy and program inequities between men and women.[74]

There are two broad approaches to developing a gender-responsive budget. The first is the "inside government" approach, which is largely directed by politicians and bureaucrats. This was the approach used in Australia and has the benefit of being spearheaded by those who actually have institutional and political power to determine elements of the budget. As well, advocates within government, such as a women's policy agency, are available to policy makers to guide the process and share knowledge from the local women's group to ensure that the best possible gender budget system is put in place. The second method is referred to as the "outside of government" approach, since it is civil society groups that are at the forefront of advocating and sometimes developing their own gender budget. This approach has been taken in Britain and by Scotland's devolved government, and is the method used by UNPAC. The externally developed gender budget is a process that is best at marshalling women's groups so that they can be educated about the budget, take part in the process, and ultimately ensure the end product fits with preferred objectives. As well, groups outside of government can autonomously monitor government implementation of gender budgets and maintain movement activism.

UNPAC has been innovative in this regard, not only with holding their workshops and providing detailed information on their web page, but by creating the character of Femme Fiscale—a person of unknown identity—who is outfitted from head to toe in vivid red, yellow, and green "caped-crusader" garb, complete with large, dark sunglasses. Femme Fiscale, in all her glory and tenacity, made her first appearance at the provincial legislature on the 6 March 2006 budget day as Manitoba's "superheroine." By using her "POV or point of view" goggles, Femme Fiscale assessed whether the government had lived up to spending commitments in child care and housing, and posed questions to the government during the media scrum. In April 2007, Femme Fiscale once again attended budget day, along with the Golden Boy (another person of unknown identity dressed head to toe in gold) taking "his head out of the clouds" to support efforts of the caped crusader. UNPAC has also produced eight postcards and a comic strip featuring the efforts of the Femme Fiscale superheroine—both available on-line. This political theatre did garner some media attention, and was a rather effective tool in focussing attention on gender issues on budget day.

Ultimately, however, the efforts of UNPAC were only marginally successful. The 2007 budget (unlike the 2006 budget) had a dedicated section on women's poverty, noting that women are more likely than men to be impoverished and experience poverty for a longer period of time.[75] However, in its entirety, the section is only three short paragraphs, and after a brief mention of women's poverty in Canada the section further notes that the female portion of Manitoba's low-income population dropped from 59.6 percent in 1980 to 52.2 percent in 2003.[76] There is no substantive discussion on why women are poor in Manitoba, the causes of women's poverty, or any mention that poverty is experienced quite differently among women *in Manitoba*. Moreover, UNPAC was unsuccessful in shifting government budgeting practices. Not even a basic gender-based analysis was applied (which would have disaggregated data on women's experiences in poverty, such as looking at senior women or lone parents). Remarkably, budget makers did not explicate or use any of the data or information generated or collected by UNPAC. From a social movement vantage point, however, UNPAC did engage hundreds of women in the budget consultation process, often in their own communities, producing a grassroots, democratically generated list of budget priorities. Along the way, and with this data in hand, UNPAC educated many women, policy makers, and the provincial government on the purpose and potentials of gender budgets.

IV. Challenge and Change in Manitoba

Due to the presence of the NDP, UNPAC attained a measure of success. Empirically demonstrated, parties on the left of the political spectrum tend to more often support the objectives of feminism. In Manitoba, women have had this to their advantage. In any case, governing parties of all political stripes are not generally interested in instituting long-term initiatives like gender budgets. They often seek immediate political payoffs from programs that have quick results, such as more money in the pockets to taxpayers by way of tax cuts or marginal funding increases to programs. Or, as Himmelweit has pointed out regarding the Women's Budget Group's experience in Britain, governments are more apt to institute small changes to existing programs that go part way to attend to women because it costs less, rather than creating new programs or implementing program and institutional changes that are required of a substantive gender budget system.[77] We saw this take place in Manitoba with the marginal mention of women and poverty in the 2007 budget.

The Australian, British, and Manitoban experiences demonstrate there are a number of serious challenges to ensuring the development and sustained implementation of a gender budget. First, gender budgets are vulnerable to shifts in the policy context, the health of the economy and partisan ideology. This was the case in both Australia and Britain and has also been the experience in Manitoba. In Australia, gender budgets did not head off neo-conservative ideas or neo-liberal policies[78] that eventually came to pervade the governing ethos, which put an end to Women's Budget Statements at the federal level.[79] In Britain, the Women's Budget Group did not have the attention of government until the Labour Party, under Tony Blair, was elected in 1997, after years of advocating for gender budgeting to resistant Conservative governments.[80] In Manitoba, the NDP's predilection toward "Third Way" politics has meant that only marginal changes to its policy repertoire have taken place, and again, that is generally framed as assisting children and families. Indeed, the 2008 budget did not specifically mention women's poverty, reverting to a discourse of supporting "strong families" through improvements to housing and protecting children.

One of the more intractable barriers has to do with the political realities of governing. Premiers and finance ministers carefully guard control over spending and revenue decisions, since fiscal management is often an easy focus of the Official Opposition, given that economic matters easily resonate with taxpayers and the media. Indeed, developing the budget involves many actors, many of whom have conflicting priorities. The provincial government confronts pressure from the business lobby and taxpayer lobbies to keep the fiscal house in order, which is juxtaposed to women's groups who seek program development and higher funding commitments. This barrier can be undercut somewhat if the political jurisdiction is undergoing some sort of comprehensive change. This was the case in Scotland, wherein an organized women's group called Engendered used the creation of a Scottish parliament and devolution of powers from London as a way to interject the need for the development of a gender budget *as part and parcel* of that process of political change.[81] This type or depth of system change in Manitoba, however, is unlikely to take place. Manitoba's political culture tends toward pragmatism and given the recent economic crisis, the NDP may have to make some tough budgetary decisions in the coming years.

As well, in the Manitoba context we must consider the dynamics of intergovernmental relations. The provincial government may be hesitant to conduct substantive gender budget analysis on the revenue side, given that it is a highly contested political process in Canada often due to difficult, and sometimes unpredictable, federal-provincial negotiations over levels of transfer payments. Provincial politicians and intergovernmental officials may not have a clear picture of the amount of monies to be transferred to Manitoba in any given year, nor may they be willing to approach the federal government for more monies to meet gender budget initiatives while also attempting to increase funding for more broadly popular policy sectors such as health. And although Manitoba's economy has been fairly strong during recent years, Manitoba's status as a have-not province has meant that transfer payments constitute a significant revenue base for the Manitoba government.[82]

As important as these political challenges are, there are also significant institutional barriers to the development and sustainability of gender budgets. The Australian experience indicates that the presence of a strong women's policy agency was crucial as an insider advocate to gain support for a gender budget, and then to provide momentum and policy expertise to sustain the process.[83] The presence of women's policy agencies can also provide an important link with community-based groups. In Manitoba, while there are two functioning women's policy agencies, they are not in a position of influence within the bureaucratic setting, nor do they have significant resources to sustain gender budget advocacy. And although UNPAC did meet with the minister for the status of women, there is no indication in any documentation produced by the Women's Directorate or the Advisory Council that they have advocated gender budgeting to the provincial government.

Experiences with gender budgets in both Australia and Britain clearly demonstrate that policy learning through a gender lens is a slow, incremental process largely because of the administrative setting and the types of policy analysis tools that would have to be employed by public administrators.[84] In Australia, for example, gender analysis of policies, the least time-consuming method of gender budgeting, were generally conducted more often than more substantive time-use analyses or assessments and accounting of women's unpaid work.[85] This is arguably due to the fact that instituting remarkably different tools of analysis—such as those that would be best for gender budgeting—take time to develop to fit the institutional and program specifics of the jurisdiction. Moreover, there would have to be rather dramatic organizational development to integrate new thinking and practices into public administration practices—a process best implemented on a department-to-department basis.

Conclusion

As challenging as these political and institutional constraints are, gender budgets are worth pursuing. They are compelling tools to transform political and institutional practices since budget decisions are made at the centre of the power hierarchy. Gender budgets can dramatically advance women's socio-economic independence and, at the same time, engender good governance.

Government involvement is but one component of a successful gender budget. UNPAC's workshops and the education of many Manitoba women on intricacies of budgets as an equality policy objective are not to be underplayed. Important social movement learning took place with so many women engaged in a process that is generally the domain of political elites and finance officials. However, as this study has also demonstrated, gender budgets are vulnerable to shifts in the political priorities of governments and to the realities of the budget process and a policy context significantly influenced by the reconfiguration of the welfare state. Although there have been moments of policy change, and the NDP has attempted to balance between tepid social democracy with a neo-liberal economic rationality, change has been at the margins, making it all the more important for groups like UNPAC to pressure the NDP to make the "Manitoba Advantage" work for women.

Notes

1. The author appreciates financial support from the Social Sciences and Humanities Research Council under Standard Research Grants Program No. 410-2004-0849. My thanks to Susan Prentice for providing comments on an earlier draft.
2. Michael Burgess, *Comparative Federalism: Theory and Practice* (London: Routledge, 2006), 15.
3. Janine Brodie, "We Are All Equal Now: Contemporary Gender Politics in Canada," *Feminist Theory* 9 (2008): 151.
4. Isabella Bakker and Katherine Scott, "From the Postwar to the Post-Liberal Keynesian Welfare State," in *Understanding Canada: Building on the New Canadian Political Economy*, ed. Wallace Clement (Kingston: McGill-Queen's University Press, 1997), 289.
5. Brodie, "We Are All Equal Now," 150.
6. Janine Brodie, ed., *Women and Canadian Public Policy* (Toronto: Harcourt Brace, 1996); Julia O'Connor, Ann Shola Orloff, and Sheila Shaver, *States, Markets, Families: Gender, Liberalism and Social Policy in Australia, Canada, Great Britain and the United States* (Cambridge: Cambridge University Press, 1999).
7. Joan Grace, "Challenges and Opportunities in Manitoba: The Social Democratic 'Promise' and Women's Equality," in *Challenges and Perils: Social Democracy in Neoliberal Times*, ed. William K. Carroll and R.S. Ratner (Halifax: Fernwood, 2005).
8. Lee Ann Banaszak, Karen Beckwith, and Dieter Rucht, "When Power Relocates: Interactive Changes in Women's Movements and States," in *Women's Movements Facing the Reconfigured State*, ed. Lee Ann Banaszak, Karen Beckwith, and Dieter Rucht (Cambridge: Cambridge University Press, 2003), 3.
9. Banaszak, Beckwith, and Rucht, "When Power Relocates," 16–19.
10. Judy Rebick, *Ten Thousand Roses* (Toronto: Penguin, 2005).
11. Berenice B. Sisler, *Partnership of Equals: The Struggle for the Reform of Family Law in Manitoba* (Winnipeg: Watson and Dwyer Publishing, 1995); Ustun Reinart, "Three Major Strands in the Women's Movement in Manitoba, 1965–1985," in *The Political Economy of Manitoba*, ed. Jim Silver and Jeremy Hull (Regina: Canadian Plains Research Centre, 1990).
12. Manitoba Action Committee on the Status of Women, *Action* 4, 1 (March 1976): 1 and 3.
13. Sisler, *Partnership of Equals*, 19 and 27.
14. Manitoba Action Committee on the Status of Women, *Three-Year Plan, 1979–1981* (1979).

15 Personal interview with Liz Sarin, former member of MACSW (Dauphin) held on 30 July 2003; Personal interview with Jennifer Howard, former staff member of MACSW (Brandon), held on 6 August 2003.

16 Manitoba Action Committee on the Status of Women, *Action* 4, 2 (March 1976): 1. For an in-depth account of the Action Coalition on Family Law, see Berenice B. Sisler, *A Partnership of Equals*.

17 Manitoba Action Committee on the Status of Women, *Action* (1988): 17. "Westman" refers to Western Manitoba.

18 Joan Grace, *In for the Long Haul, Women's Organizations in Manitoba* (Winnipeg: Canadian Centre for Policy Alternatives–Manitoba, 2005).

19 Although some of these groups articulate a pronounced feminist agenda, all advocate for the advancement of women's equality. This list is a representative sample for heuristic purposes. See Grace, *In for the Long Haul*, for a further explanation of the categorization.

20 Lissa Donner, *Including Gender in Health Planning: A Guide for Regional Health Authorities* (Winnipeg: Prairie Women's Health Centre of Excellence, 2000).

21 Social Planning Council of Winnipeg, *15 Years and Counting...Manitoba's Child Poverty Report Card* (Winnipeg: Social Planning Council of Winnipeg, 2004), http://www.spcw.mb.ca.

22 Social Planning Council of Winnipeg, *Manitoba Child and Family Poverty Report Card 2006* (Winnipeg, Social Planning Council of Winnipeg, 2006), 2 and 3.

23 Social Planning Council of Winnipeg, *Manitoba Child and Family Poverty Report Card 2008* (Winnipeg, Social Planning Council of Winnipeg, 2008), 1.

24 Ibid., 5.

25 Social Planning Council of Winnipeg, *Raise the Rates: PAC Fact Sheet* (Winnipeg: Social Planning Council of Winnipeg, 2007), http://www.spcw.mb.ca.

26 Ibid.

27 UNPAC, *Women and the Economy: A Resource Book – Book One and Book Two* (Winnipeg: UN Platform for Action Committee–Manitoba, 2003).

28 Child Care Coalition of Manitoba, "Provincial Budget 2008: 'Major Disappointment,'" news release, 2008, http://action.web.ca/home/ccmanitoba.

29 Molly McCracken, "Manitoba Women Have Access To Abortions...As Long As They Have Time Or Money," Canadian Centre for Policy Alternatives, "Manitoba Fast Facts," 23 September 2002.

30 Barbara J. Payne, Karen R. Grant, Cheryl Christian, and David M. Gregory, "Blurring the Boundaries: Women's Caring Work and Manitoba Health Care Reform," *Centre of Excellence for Women's Health Research Bulletin* 3,1 (2002): 11–13.

31 Canadian Council on Social Development, *Nowhere to Turn? Responding to Partner Violence Against Immigrant and Visible Minority Women*, 2004, http://www.ccsd.ca/pubs/2004/nowhere.

32 Statistics Canada, *Family Violence in Canada: A Statistical Report*, Catalogue No. 85-224-X (Ottawa: Statistics Canada, 2008), 6 and 16.

33 On the issue of domestic violence see Jane E. Ursel, *Report on Domestic Violence Policies and Their Impact on Aboriginal People*, submitted to the Aboriginal Justice Implementation Commission (Winnipeg: RESOLVE Manitoba, 21 February 2001); and Federal-Provincial-Territorial Ministers Responsible for the Status of Women, *Assessing Violence Against Women: A Statistical Profile*, 2002, 14, http://www.gov.mb.ca/wd (accessed 13 May 2004).

34 Brodie, "We Are All Equal Now," 155; Janine Brodie, "Restructuring and the Politics of Marginalization," in *Women and Political Representation in Canada*, ed. Manon Tremblay and Caroline Andrew (Ottawa: University of Ottawa Press, 1998); Sylvia Bashevkin,

Women and the Defensive: Living Through Conservative Times (Toronto: University of Toronto Press, 1998).

35 Maureen Baker, *The Restructuring of the Canadian Welfare State: Ideology and Policy*, SPRC Discussion Paper No. 77 (Montreal: Social Policy Research Centre, 1997), 1.

36 Baker, *The Restructuring of the Canadian Welfare State*, 1–2 and 12–16.

37 It is the case, however, that due to fiscal pressures during the mid-1980s, the NDP government of Howard Pawley instituted "program adjustments" designed in part to reduce dependence on federal transfer payments and to facilitate provincial government efficiencies. See L.R. Jones, "Fiscal Restraint Management and Budget Control in Canadian Provincial Governments," *Canadian Public Administration* 29, 2 (June 1986).

38 Wayne Antony, Sid Frankel, Dick Henley, Dennis Lewycky, Gregg Olsen, Tara Rudy, Todd Scarth, and Jon Young, *Fragile Recovery: The State of Public Services in Manitoba* (Winnipeg: Canadian Centre for Policy Alternatives–Manitoba, 2003).

39 Manitoba Government, "Work Requirements for Able-Bodied Recipients," news release, 17 June 1999.

40 Errol Black and Jim Silver, *A Flawed Economic Experiment: The New Political Economy of Manitoba* (Winnipeg: Canadian Centre for Policy Alternatives–Manitoba, 1999).

41 Alex Netherton, "Paradigm and Shift: A Sketch of Manitoba Politics," in *The Provincial State in Canada: Politics in the Provinces and Territories*, ed. Keith Brownsey and Michael Howlett (Peterborough: Broadview Press, 2001), 225.

42 Grace, "Challenges and Opportunities in Manitoba."

43 Helen Fallding and Paul Samyn, "Doer offers up recipe for NDP success," *Winnipeg Free Press*, 24 November 2001, A4.

44 Manitoba Government, "'Fraud Line' Discontinued," news release, 20 April 2000.

45 Susan Prentice, "Manitoba's Childcare Regime: Social Liberalism In Flux," *Canadian Journal of Sociology* 29, 2 (2004).

46 Manitoba Government, *The Manitoba Advantage* (Winnipeg: Government of Manitoba, 2002).

47 Manitoba Government, *Province of Manitoba: 2005 Annual Report for the Year Ended March 31* (Winnipeg: Government of Manitoba, 2005), 15 and 20.

48 Grace, "Challenges and Opportunities in Manitoba."

49 Melissa Haussman and Birgit Sauer, "Introduction: Women's Movements and State Restructuring in the 1990s," in *Gendering the State in the Age of Globalization: Women's Movements and State Feminism in Postindustrial Democracies*, ed. Melissa Haussman and Birgit Sauer (Lanham, MD: Rowman and Littlefield Publishers, 2007), 1–5.

50 UNPAC, *Gender Budget Project*, 2008, http://www.unpac.ca/gender/project.

51 Jennifer deGroot and Shauna Mackinnon, "We Need A Gender Sensitive Budget for Manitoba," *CCPA Review* 5, 2 (2005): 3.

52 Debbie Budlender and Guy Hewitt, *Engendering Budgets: A Practitioners' Guide to Understanding and Implementing Gender-Responsive Budgets* (London: Commonwealth Secretariat, 2003), 5–6.

53 Budlender and Hewitt, *Engendering Budgets*, 5–6.

54 UNIFEM, *Gender Budget Initiatives*, brochures, 2000, http://www.unifem.org.

55 Ibid., 1.

56 Ibid.

57 Budlender and Hewitt, *Engendering Budgets*, 6.

58 Diane Elson, *Gender Budget Initiatives: Background Papers* (London: Commonwealth Secretariat, 1999), 3.

59 Ibid., 3.
60 Susan Himmelweit, "Making Policymakers More Gender Aware: Experiences and Reflections from the Women's Budget Group in the United Kingdom," *Journal of Women, Politics and Policy* 27 (2002).
61 Canadian Feminist Alliance for International Action, *Canada's Commitment to Equality: A Gender Analysis of the Last Ten Federal Budgets, 1995–2004* (2005).
62 Ibid.
63 Himmelweit, "Making Policymakers More Gender Aware."
64 Budlender and Hewitt, *Engendering Budgets*; Isabella Bakker, "Fiscal Policy, Accountability and Voice: The Example of Gender Responsive Budget Initiatives," *Human Development Office Occasional Paper* (New York: United Nations Development Programme), 2002.
65 Rhonda Sharp and Ray Broomhill, "Budgeting for Equality: The Australian Experience," *Feminist Economics* 8, 1 (2002): 36.
66 Bakker, "Fiscal Policy, Accountability and Voice," 6.
67 Ibid.
68 UNPAC, *Annual Report 2006–2007*, http://www.unpac.ca.
69 Budlender and Hewitt, "Engendering Budgets," 7–8. In 1993, the Canadian branch of the Women's International League for Peace and Freedom developed a gender budget. See also Debbie Budlender, Diane Elson, Guy Hewitt, and Tanni Mukhopadhyay, *Gender Budgets Make Sense* (London: Commonwealth Secretariat, 2002), 147. In 2005, the Canadian Feminist Alliance for International Action (FAFIA) published an extensive gender analysis of federal budgets. See Canadian Feminist Alliance for International Action, *Canada's Commitment to Equality: A Gender Analysis of the Last Ten Federal Budgets (1995–2004)*, written by Armine Yalnizyan.
70 Debbie Budlender et al., *Gender Budgets Make Sense*, 7.
71 Sharp and Broomhill, "Budgeting for Equality," 27-28; UNIFEM, *Gender Budget Initiatives*, 1.
72 Sharp and Broomhill, "Budgeting for Equality," 27.
73 Ibid.
74 Ibid., 33–36.
75 Manitoba Government, *Budget Paper E: Reducing Poverty in Manitoba* (Winnipeg: Government of Manitoba, 2007), E4.
76 Ibid.
77 Himmelweit, "Making Policymakers More Gender Aware," 94
78 Sharp and Broomhill, "Budgeting for Equality," 42.
79 Marian Sawer, "Australia: The Mandarin Approach to Gender Budgets," in *Gender Budgets Make More Cents: Country Studies and Good Practice*, ed. Debbie Budlender and Guy Hewitt (London: Commonwealth Secretariat, 2002), 63. During the timeframe of her study, Marian Sawer relates that gender audits of budgets still took place at the state and territorial levels.
80 Himmelweit, "Making Policymakers More Gender Aware," 85.
81 Ailsa McKay, Rona Fitzgerald, Angela O'Hagan, and Morag Gillespie, "Scotland: Using Political Change to Advance Gender Issues," in *Gender Budgets Make More Cents: Country Studies and Good Practice*, ed. Debbie Budlender and Guy Hewitt (London: Commonwealth Secretariat, 2002).
82 Manitoba Government, *Province of Manitoba 2005 Annual Report*, 39.
83 Sharp and Broomhill, "Budgeting for Equality," 29.
84 Ibid., 33.
85 Ibid., 35.

Health Care Policy in Manitoba: The Past, Present, and Future of Regional Health Authorities

Paul G. Thomas

I. Introduction

In political, policy, and financial terms, health care is one of the top two or three issues on the wide-ranging and shifting discussion agenda of Manitoba society and on the more limited and more stable institutional agenda of the provincial government. The importance and prominence of health issues reflect the scope of the impact of health policy making that takes place on the national, provincial, regional, institutional, and individual provider level within a complicated multi-tiered system that involves a large number of linked domains of disease prevention, care provision, and research. To state that the health care system is complicated, turbulent, and difficult to change in a planned, comprehensive manner is an understatement.

Health care is expensive. The government of Manitoba now spends nearly 50 percent of its total budget on all forms of health care. On a per-person basis more public health dollars are spent in Manitoba than any other province ($3,690.54 per capita in Manitoba, versus a Canadian average of $3,195. 86).[1] Annual spending increases on health care in Manitoba have been running in the 5 to 8 percent range (6.5 percent in the 2008–09 budget), a trend which some commentators believe is unsustainable over the long term. In addition to this public spending, significant amounts of private spending by institutions and individuals occur in the health field.

Despite these large public and private investments, one controversial study conducted in 2006 rated Manitoba last among all the provinces in the overall quality of its health care system based upon selected indicators of health status, health outcomes, and health care utilization and performance.[2] In Manitoba's case, the categories of health status and health care utilization and performance were identified as particularly in need of improvement. It is important to point out that the "basket of health services" provided in Manitoba is one of the most inclusive in the country, particularly in terms of home care, personal care home, and pharmacare. Also, among the ten provinces, Manitoba has a combination of the oldest, sickest, and most geographically isolated populations. Critics, however, tend to ignore such comparisons and charge that Manitoba has done the worst job in terms of the prevention of illness, has performed the worst in terms of treatment, has an inefficient system, or some combination of all these factors.[3]

Among services provided by governments, health care is probably the most personal, emotional, and politically sensitive. In surveys asking citizens to rank issues in terms of importance, health care is almost invariably near the top of the list, often being ranked first in terms of importance. Most Manitobans do not have accurate and in-depth knowledge of the health care system. This lack of knowledge does not, however, prevent three-quarters of respondents in opinion surveys from saying they have lost some or a great deal of trust and confidence in the health care system, especially in its capacity to meet their future needs. At the same time, however, a satisfaction survey conducted in 2005 reported that 87.5 percent of Manitobans rated the services received as excellent or good, which compared to a Canadian average of 85.2 percent.[4] The surveys seem somewhat contradictory in part because they capture perceptions and opinions regarding different dimensions of performance of the health care system. They also reflect the tendency for some respondents to base their general assessments of the health care system on their ideological preference for the current or more mixed model of financing and service delivery rather than on their own experience. Another source of weak public trust and confidence is the prevailing negative stereotype of the system that arises from political controversies and sensational media coverage that focus mainly on "horror stories" of individual tragedies, examples of system breakdowns, and perceptions of widespread inefficiencies.

The complexities of the health care system, its steadily rising costs without seeming limits, its emotional "life-and-death" consequences and the prevalence of the public perception that it is broken and needs to be fixed, all combine to create enormous challenges in terms of "governance," "political management," and "public management." Each of these terms, however, requires a brief explanation.

Governance has become a fashionable phrase that refers to a dispersed, collective, and dynamic process of direction-setting within society. In the field of health, governance involves multiple institutions and actors on the national, provincial, regional, and local level. More than governments and public health authorities of various kinds are involved, influential roles are played by private actors such as professional associations, drug companies, medical technology firms, and international bodies. In a decentralized, collaborative, and sometimes conflict-bound process of ongoing interaction, governments seek to achieve agreement on goals and the means to achieve them, cope with pressures for change, uncertainty and controversy, mobilize consent, and support and ensure that policies and programs are implemented in an efficient and effective manner. In short, governance involves both politics and governing of the management of health care.

Political management is a broad term, which refers to a wide range of activities involved with politics and governing. The field includes election planning and managing, fundraising, polling and focus groups, strategic research, issue identification and problem definition, the search for agreement on policy responses, the arrangements for decision making efforts to mobilize consent and support for actions, providing direction and guidance to ensure the implementation of policies and decisions, and monitoring to obtain feedback and to avoid politically embarrassing surprises. Part science, craft, and art, political management is becoming an increasingly professionalized activity that reflects the preoccupation of political leaders with managing the agenda of public life by using the new political "technologies" (polling, focus groups, the Internet, direct mail, etc.) to gain an advantage in relation to their political opponents. In office, political parties are generally anxious to appear to govern on the basis of a consensus and to avoid "mistakes" which are damaging to their reputation for effective and ethical performance. In the case of health care, even seemingly trivial matters can become the focal point for political controversy.

Political management is different from, but overlaps and intersects with, so-called "public management," which usually refers to the actual formulation and implementation of public policy. As such, public management is usually seen to focus mainly on the role of public bureaucracies and the functional approaches and techniques they use in supporting government decision-making and the delivery of programs. However, public management also covers the shared world of politicians and senior public servants, a world which increasingly involves third parties in the form of advocacy/interest groups, other orders/levels of "government," and for-profit/not-for-profit organizations involved with the production/delivery of programs and services. In an interdependent world of "joined up" governing, there is no neat separation or "bright line" which can be drawn between politics, policy governing and management. Decisions made in all four domains of activity reverberate throughout the political, policy, and management processes in unpredictable ways and have potential consequences for actors on different levels and in different domains. Health care policy making and delivery illustrates this point dramatically.

This chapter examines the past, present, and future of Regional Health Authorities (RHAs) in Manitoba. It will be argued that the original creation of the RHA system, its current operations, and its future directions will be affected as much by "politics" on several levels as by "rational" planning and management. Launched with considerable fanfare back in 1996–97, Manitoba's experience with devolved, regionalized health care policy making and delivery has been moderately successful, but not without its disappointments and problems. Regionalization could not possibly transform the wider environment, pressures, cultures, incentives, and behaviours which shape the overall performance of the health care system. Looking to the future, it seems likely that the current RHA arrangements will undergo further changes based on a blend of politics, policy, and management considerations.

Based on this integrating theme, the chapter proceeds as follows. First, the concept of regionalization is explained. Second, the historical background to the adoption of the regional model is examined briefly. After the adoption of universal, prepaid medical insurance in 1968 in Manitoba, the next major policy change in the health field was the passage of legislation establishing RHAs in November 1996. The "official" policy aims and "unofficial" political aims of embarking on regionalization are discussed. Third, the chapter examines the territorial boundaries and size of Manitoba's eleven RHAs, the authority delegated to them, their governance structures and processes, and their relationships with the communities they serve. RHA boards and executives are intermediary bodies which sit between the regional communities and the provincial government, which has ultimate authority over their role and the scope of their activities. Accordingly, a fourth section analyzes the relationships between the minister of health and her department and the RHA boards and executives in terms of policy direction, control, monitoring, and accountability. In formal legal and policy terms, RHAs are subordinate and accountable to Manitoba Health, but in informal political terms they are more accurately described as quasi-subordinate because of the cultural norms of regional control and responsiveness to regional needs. A final section of the paper discusses the future of Manitoba's RHAs. There is a beginning trend within several provinces towards the reduction of the number of RHAs, and the concluding section analyzes the likelihood of this and other types of changes to the RHA system in Manitoba.

II. The Concept of Regionalization: Some Initial Thoughts

Regionalization was a major structural reform to health care systems across Canada which began in the 1990s and was gradually adopted, with some variation, in all provinces. RHAs can best be described as semi-autonomous health care organizations that are delegated, on the basis of provincial legislation, specified responsibilities, authority, and funding from the provincial government to provide a range of health services within a defined geographic region.

Although regionalization has been implemented in all provinces, the year of implementation, the process of implementation, and the governance arrangements of the regional health systems across the country vary significantly.[5] The reasons behind regionalization may have been essentially the same, but no two provinces have an identical model of regional health care. A major explanation for the differences is the basic social and economic facts of each province. A province such as Manitoba—with slightly more than one million people, with 60 percent of the population living in Winnipeg, with vast sparsely populated rural and northern regions, with a relatively small economy and serious budgetary constraints, and with a diverse society that includes a growing Aboriginal population—faces different health-care challenges than a larger, more affluent, and homogeneous province like Alberta. The historical traditions and policy cultures of provinces can also differ greatly. These differences can be seen in the drastic action of the Alberta government in May 2008 to replace its nine RHA boards with a single "super board" for the entire province, something not likely to be tried in Manitoba where the differences among local communities and the insistence on regional autonomy would cause a political backlash to such a centralizing move.[6] The Manitoba political and policy cultures favour moderate, pragmatic, and limited change.

The balance between provincial centralization and regional decentralization within the health care systems across the country varies by province and over time. Given the importance and sensitivity of health issues it is not surprising that provincial governments are hesitant to empower RHAs so completely they could establish policy and set delivery standards completely independently. Under the Constitution, health care is not assigned exclusively to one order of government, but provincial governments have primary responsibility. Over time Canadians have become conditioned to think of provincial governments as being in "charge" of the health care system. This means that when Manitobans have concerns or complaints about the accessibility, cost, safety, and quality of health care, they are more likely to blame provincial authorities than RHAs.

"Semi-autonomous" is probably the most accurate label to apply to RHAs because provincial governments insist on controlling the number of RHAs; their size (territory and population); their governance structures and processes; the scope and content of their programming; their operational and capital funding; the acquisition of certain types of health and information technology; and, in most provinces, the recruitment and remuneration of physicians and nurses so that both province-wide and individual RHA needs are met. In addition, many provincial health departments develop broad health policy strategies (e.g., on diabetes, immunization, tobacco, etc.) which RHAs are expected to deliver according to their local needs.

In a multi-tiered health care system, defining and delineating the roles of RHAs in a simple diagram does not begin to capture the complex, multi-faceted nature of the regionalization process. Table 19.1 provides a simplified overview of the key responsibilities and actors in the Canadian health care system. Responsibilities are shared across levels of government, among institutions and with different groups of actors. Decisions and actions taken on one level and in one domain have impacts elsewhere in the system.

Within provinces there is both a formal and informal dimension to the provincial-regional relationship. The nature of that relationship varies among RHAs based upon their capacity and performance, as issues come and go on the health care agenda, and as trust relationships strengthen or weaken in response to events. Simple diagrams of formal relationships of direction, control, and accountability need to be supplemented by knowledge of the submerged culture of shared understandings and expectations, the unwritten "rules of the game," and the human factor of people in positions of responsibility coping with difficult challenges by searching for agreement on aims and means. These initial thoughts about the complexity of regionalization as a formal structure, a process, and a set of shared cultural understandings provide the starting point for the examination of the Manitoba experience.

III. The Origins of RHAs in Manitoba

No comprehensive history of the evolution of Manitoba's health care system has been written. Table 19.2 sets forth some of the key events and legislation from the passage to the Public Health Act in 1893 down to the passage of the Regional Health Authorities Act in 1997. While all the developments listed in the chart are significant, two fundamental decisions were made at the national level, with the adoption of hospital insurance in 1957 and medical care insurance in 1967. Manitoba passed legislation to enter these programs and to receive federal funding in 1954 and 1968 respectively. Of course, there needed to be decisions and actions anticipating and implementing these two fundamental policy decisions to provide citizens with universal access to hospitals and physicians. Targeting federal funding at hospitals and fee-for-service physicians created a bias in provincial health systems towards a curative, rather than a preventive, approach to health-care delivery. Provincial systems grew rapidly during the 1960s and 1970s, reflecting the relatively good financial situation of governments, the perceived benefits of modern medicine, the increased number and diversity of health professionals and the rising expectations/demands of the public. Rapid growth led to problems of inadequate planning, fragmentation, and poor coordination and inefficiencies.

Regionalization was seen as part of the answer to these problems. The concept had been around for decades and had been recommended in the Hall Report of 1964, which set the stage for the introduction of medical care insurance.[7] During the late 1980s and early 1990s, commissions or task forces in six provinces investigated the strains and challenges facing the health care system and all came out in favour of regionalization.[8] Manitoba was not among the provinces that launched an arm's-length, in-depth investigation of its health care system at that time. Instead the Manitoba Health Advisory Network was created in 1990 to "engage leading persons from all parts of the health services system in the development of policy recommendations to improve health services and our ability to deliver those services within our financial limits."[9] In addition to this high-level advisory network, the provincial government created the Urban Hospital Council, Regional Mental Health Councils, and the Westman Integrated Strategy for Health, which involved twenty-three different health-care facilities in western Manitoba. The latter was described as potentially providing a regional model that could be applied across Manitoba. The publication in May 1992 of "Quality Health for Manitobans—The Action Plan" by the Progressive Conservative government of the day represented a philosophical shift that paved the way towards regionalization, the concept of "centres of excellence," and better balance between health promotion and the treatment of illnesses.

IV. Debating the Regional Model in Manitoba

Apart from Ontario, Manitoba was one of the last provinces to establish a system of RHAs (see Table 19.2). The Progressive Conservative government of then-premier Gary Filmon introduced the legislation to establish the RHA system in the fall of 1996. The cases for and against regionalization within Manitoba were very similar to the debates that took place in other provinces. Recognizing the likelihood of resistance to devolution by the existing hospital boards and by physicians, then-minister of health Jim McCrae and other proponents of regionalization tended to "oversell" its benefits given the fact a structural change would not transform the incentive systems, cultures, power relationships, and nature of the tasks to be performed in a dispersed health care system with many potential veto points. It also needs to be recognized that there were both "official" and "unofficial" aims of regionalization. In the space available, only a brief itemization of the arguments for regionalization can be presented without much elaboration:

- to increase responsiveness to local needs by avoiding centralized "top-down" direction by Manitoba Health;
- to match responsibility, capacity, and accountability on a regional level to encourage planning within budgetary limits;
- to overcome the problem of "silos" of funding (for hospitals, physicians, home care, etc.) and to promote the integration of services across a wider continuum of care;
- by basing health care decision making closer to local communities, encouraging a greater focus on so-called "upstream" strategies of health promotion and prevention;
- to balance the power of health care professionals by promoting more meaningful public participation and more appropriate governance over management on a regional basis;
- to "de-politicize" the provision of health care by adoption of the "steering-versus-rowing" distinction, leaving provincial authorities to set broad policy and allowing local boards and executives to make operational decisions free of partisan considerations.[10]

The underlying premise behind these arguments is that the health care system is more effective when a broader range of health services falls under a single governance and financial structure. Fragmentation, duplication, gaps in services, competition, and inefficiencies will be avoided or at least minimized when authority and money is consolidated in the hands of regional health authorities who are *accountable* to the minister of health and *responsive* to their communities.

In the debates launching regionalization in Manitoba, the potential "downsides" of devolution were not featured as prominently because it seemed to be an "idea whose time had come." The criticisms were as follows:

- regionalization represented a disguised form of "offloading" of financial responsibility for a "voracious" health care system that was consuming an ever-growing percentage of the provincial budget;
- there would be a blurring of accountability as the minister of health could escape blame for access problems or poor quality services;
- unless there was a "rethinking" of the role and a "downsizing" of Manitoba Health, regionalization would mean another "layer of bureaucracy" and additional administrative costs within a system already facing financial stress;

- unless Manitoba Health could develop the means to "steer by remote control," there could be weaker central policy direction, an inability to coordinate service provision, a loss of the bargaining power of central purchasing, and difficulty in recruiting specialized talent;
- it is difficult to draw the boundaries of RHAS so as to optimize efficiency, effectiveness and equity on the one hand versus accessibility to services, citizen engagement, and responsiveness to local communities on the other, especially in rural and northern RHAS;
- the concern was that devolution would be more rhetorical and symbolic than it was substantive and real.

The multiple, broad, formal, and informal aims of regionalization make it difficult to develop valid, reliable, and consistent evaluative criteria to measure the "success" of the RHAS. Separating the impacts of regionalization from other developments taking place within Manitoba's dynamic health care system is impossible except in a subjective and impressionistic manner. Finally, Manitoba started with twelve RHAS in 1998 and has since dropped to eleven. These RHAS vary greatly in size, capacity, challenges, and accomplishments. Drawing an overall judgement on whether regionalization has worked as intended is therefore very difficult.

V. Transition to Regionalization

While regionalization is usually described as a form of devolution from the provincial level, it was in fact as much a consolidation of roles and programs previously performed by hospital boards and community-based organizations. Prior to regionalization there were more than 100 boards responsible for various components of the health care system, such as hospitals, nursing homes, home care, community health, and ambulance services. There was very little coherent policy direction in this non-system, which was dominated by the values and interests of the physicians. Standards of care varied widely across local communities. There was very little accountability on the part of institutions and providers for safety, quality, and efficiency of care provision.

The main aims of regionalization were to bring coherence to an unwieldy, inefficient, and fragmented system by unifying planning and management at the regional level and by promoting changes in programs and the integration of services to meet regional needs and priorities. This could not happen overnight. When the RHA model was being established, there was talk of a "transition" period following which presumably there would be stable, well-defined, and predictable relationships among the various institutions and actors. In practice, however, regionalization became more an ongoing experiment to find a balanced, middle way between provincial direction and control and semi-autonomous RHAs that were responsive to local communities.

It took several years for the original twelve RHAs to be established and for them to take over the functions previously performed by hundreds of local bodies. Some RHAs made progress more quickly than others. Slightly more than ten years have passed since the process began, which is not long in terms of the life of an organization. RHAs may not be in their "infancy," but they are still probably best described as "less than fully matured as organizations." If there have been growing pains, it has been partly because of the pressures for change, the shifts in provincial direction, and the number of times the relatively young regional system has been examined to determine if it needs to be changed. This lack of stability needs to be recognized in any balanced assessment of the success of regionalization in Manitoba.

In the space available here, only selective aspects of the multi-dimensional process of regionalization can be examined. The general focus will be on the governance of the RHA system, with analysis presented of the legal roles of the RHAs, their boundaries and populations, the roles of their boards of directors, their planning efforts, their engagements with citizens, and their multiple relationships with the provincial governments. It is recognized that the discussion to follow omits any in-depth analysis of the programming and service delivery efforts of the RHAs and the impacts of those activities on the health of regional communities.

VI. The Legislated Roles of RHAS

RHAs are required to assess the health needs of their region on an ongoing basis, to protect and to promote the health of their residents, to develop and to deliver quality programs and services, and to manage their budget allocations. They are required to periodically conduct community health assessments, to prepare health plans for the region, and to submit strategic plans for the corporation. All of these documents, along with the annual budget submission of the RHA, are subject in principle to review by the minister of health and the Department of Health and Healthy Living. The minister of health has important prerogatives in relation to the RHAs. Under the RHA Act, she is given the general duty to promote, protect, and preserve health, which pinpoints responsibility and accountability for the overall performance of the health care system in a single visible and politically accountable individual. In support of this responsibility, the minister can establish provincial objectives and priorities, can issue binding directives to RHAs, can withhold funding for non-compliance, can arrange outside of the RHA structure for the delivery of health services, and can appoint an official administrator if there is a serious breakdown at the RHA level. The boundaries of RHAs are determined by the cabinet on the basis of regulation, not legislation that would require approval by the legislature.

In summary, RHAS operate on the basis of delegated authority and there is no ambiguity about where ultimate responsibility and accountability resides: it is with the minister of health and her cabinet colleagues, including the premier. This is in keeping with the principles of collective and individual ministerial responsibility within a cabinet-parliamentary system. It makes the minister of health the focal point of accountability for the performance of the health system. The formal, legal framework for the creation, direction, control, and accountability for RHAS is the obvious starting point for any understanding of the regionalization process, but it does not come close to telling the whole story. A later section in this chapter examines the dynamics of the provincial-RHA relationship in more depth.

VII. The Scope of RHA Authority

RHAS are non-profit corporations. They are subject to the Canada Health Act, which requires comprehensiveness, universality, portability, accessibility, and public administration in the provision of health services. The scope of service provision as set forth in The Regional Health Authorities Act includes hospitals, long-term care, home care, mental health, public health, medical services, nursing services, medical laboratories, diagnostic imaging, and emergency services. Significantly, the employment and remuneration of physicians is outside of the scope of RHAS. Most physicians are independent contractors (to the provincial government) rather than employees of RHAS or individual institutions. This fundamental fact limits the potential for integration of services at the regional level. Without any control over physician compensation, engaging them in reforms—for example in primary care—has been a struggle for the RHAS. As one former chief executive officer observed to the writer, "working with the docs is the mother of all challenges in political management."

The complexity of the portfolio of institutions and programs within Manitoba's eleven RHAS varies widely. With a budget of $2 billion and over 28,000 employees, the WRHA operates or funds over 200 health service faculties and programs, including two tertiary hospitals, four community hospitals, four long-term care centres, thirty-five personal care homes, and twenty community health offices.[11] In pursuit of service integration, the WRHA has established three access centres and a fourth is planned. Contrast this with South Eastman RHA, which has a budget of $72 million, employs 1,200 people and operates four hospitals, seven personal care homes, and six community services centres.[12] The significance of such differences in terms of governance are discussed allow.

VIII. RHA Boundaries and Populations

Manitoba began its regionalization process with twelve RHAs in 1997–98. In April 2000 the "Health Care Management and Financial Review" report to the ministers of finance and health recommended that the number of RHAs be reviewed to determine whether mergers would improve patient services and save money.[13] At this point, the RHA experiment was barely underway. Based upon this recommendation, the New Democratic Party government (which had replaced the Progressive Conservatives in the 1999 provincial election) passed legislation in 2002 that merged two RHAs outside of Winnipeg (Marquette and South Westman, to form Assiniboine). Within Winnipeg two boards existed initially—the Winnipeg Hospital Authority to oversee and fund hospitals and the Winnipeg Community and Long Term Care Authority to oversee and fund community and long-term care facilities. Within the hospital sector, the government proposed in 1999 to have one chief executive officer (CEO) to lead hospitals city-wide and, in the process, to have one employer. There would be clinical program teams to coordinate service delivery across all Winnipeg hospitals. Hospital boards would be retained, but they would be restricted to defining institutional missions, conducting fundraising, and sponsoring research. Winnipeg's largest teaching hospital, the Health Sciences Centre (HSC) agreed to the merger plan, but the four faith-based facilities resisted. As a compromise, they were allowed to retain their boards and corporate identities, appoint their own respective CEOs and remain separate employers, while pledging cooperation with the WRHA and the clinical program management model. In July 2000, legislation was passed to incorporate the HSC into the WRHA. Subsequently the Deer Lodge Hospital and Victoria Hospital (which was run by the Victorian Order of Nurses) were incorporated into the WRHA. These steps to streamline the RHA system were explained as a way to integrate services, reduce bureaucracy, and to save money. They were also disruptive and provoked a backlash from hospital boards, administrators, and program staff who were loyal to their "home" institutions.

Currently there are eleven RHAs. In 2006–07, 62.9 percent of funds spent by the provincial Departments of Health and Healthy Living were actually delivered through RHAs. This compared to 19.2 percent spent on medical matters (including physician remuneration), 6.0 percent spent on pharmacare, and 2.6 percent spent on departmental administration.[14]

The population differences among RHAs and the vast territory covered by many of them is a striking feature of Manitoba's regionalization arrangements. It creates a set of challenges not found in most provinces. No other province features as dominant a presence as the WRHA, which has approximately 60 percent of the provincial population (more than 700,000) within its boundaries and accounts for nearly 50 percent of the health spending authorized by Manitoba Health and Healthy Living. Furthermore, many residents of other RHAS come to Winnipeg to receive specialized services not available in their home region. In terms of policy and administrative capacity, the WRHA has a significant advantage over other RHAS (with the possible exception of the Brandon RHA) in terms of having the professional staff to develop new policy and managerial approaches and to respond to provincial initiatives. To its credit, the WRHA has often contributed staff support to assist with the development of programs in the rural RHAS, most recently in the field of patient safety. More will be said about the significance of the dominant position of the WRHA for the future of RHAS in the concluding section.

IX. The Role of RHA Boards

Members of RHA boards have always been appointed by the minister of health. In principle, there is an open nomination process for RHA boards. There is an information page and nomination form posted on the department's website and on most RHA websites. Any resident of the region can nominate board members for a term of three years, with eligibility for one re-appointment. The CEO and anyone who provides professional advice to the RHA for remuneration are ineligible to serve on boards, but other care providers can serve. The officially stated qualifications for board membership include commitment, time, leadership, communications, planning, legal, financial, and human resource skills. Informally, the minister takes into account where the individual resides in the region, connections to interest groups, and past association with the governing party. A glance at the backgrounds of board members across the eleven RHAS reveals they are exemplary citizens, many having extensive records of community and public service. The fact that board stipends have not been adjusted since the inception of regionalization means there is a significant component of volunteerism involved in serving on boards, especially given the large volume and complicated and serious nature of the work.

The 2008 report of the Manitoba Health Authority External Review Committee found the board appointment process problematic on several grounds: it lacks transparency, it does not ensure a proper mix of skills, there is no succession planning, appointments are sometimes made without consulting the board chair or the CEO, and non-performing board chairs and members are not held accountable. Appointment by the minister on geographic grounds, links to interest groups, and association with the governing party is seen to lead to potential role conflicts for board members. Do members see themselves primarily as *trustees* of the long-term health needs of their region, as *representatives* of parts or segments of the region, as *facilitators* of democratic citizen participation in setting directions and priorities for the region, or as *agents* of the minister in terms of her policy priorities for the region? A survey of RHA board members conducted by the Office of the Auditor General (OAG) in 2002 reported that most members saw themselves primarily representing patients. Representing the minister was seen as one of their least important responsibilities. "Governing" management was ranked in the middle of their duties in terms of importance. There may have been an inclination for board members to provide a "correct" response by putting patient interests first, but it is also the case that service on the board probably leads members to identify with community needs and the institution itself.

Of necessity, RHA boards must rely heavily on the CEO and other managers to identify issues, conduct planning, engage in policy formulation, provide information, and implement policy. This dependence is encouraged by the adoption by most RHA boards of the "policy-governance" model made popular by the management guru John Carver. According to Carver, the key role of a board is "to set policy as the value or perspective that underlines actions."[15] Its role should not involve looking over the shoulder of management or giving advice on management matters. Based upon Carver's "policy vs. operations" dichotomy, boards should avoid meddling in matters best left to the professional managers of the corporation. It is claimed that this policy-governance model simultaneously creates more authoritative boards and more empowered management because it clarifies the relationships between the key players. The 2008 report of the RHA review committee strongly endorsed the Carver model without any discussion of the complications of applying a model derived principally from the private sector firm in the very different context of Manitoba's RHAs. Three brief comments need to be made. First, RHA boards and executives are subject to formal, binding policy directives issued by the minister of health. They are also influenced by informal pressures from the minister and the department—what might be called "dinnertime" directives to the board chairs and CEOs because they are often transmitted privately over meals. Secondly, even at the RHA level, the distinction between "policy" and "operations" is often not clear because in the sensitive and emotional field of health service delivery the "means" by which policies are implemented are almost as important as the "aims" of policies. Often it is the "means" (e.g., which hospital to close, where to locate offices, etc.) that generate the most public reaction and the greatest attention from the minister and the department. Third, it can be argued that management issues can serve as useful "windows" into the operations of RHAs and even provide the "conceptual handles" by which board members can better grasp the broad, complicated policy issues presented to them by management. Based on these considerations, it can be argued that not all board attention and involvement with operational matters can be seen as "destructive meddling"; it could be seen instead as "constructive meddling" which supports the board's trustee and representative roles.

A key figure in ensuring the boards find the appropriate balance between "destructive" and "constructive" meddling and operate effectively is the chair of the RHA board. Again, analogies to the chairs of private corporate boards are inexact for two reasons. First, RHA board chairs are appointed by the minister, not the board itself. Second, the CEO of a private firm plays a major role in communicating with "shareholders" whereas in the case of RHAs the board chair is the link with the minister who is the key "stakeholder" who controls the fate of the RHA. In addition to liaison with the minister, the board chair should ensure there is a positive and productive board culture. This involves planning the board agenda, ensuring that the board focuses on strategic decisions and manages risks, presiding at meetings, encouraging the use of the knowledge and skills of all board members and ensuring there are processes for assessing and improving the effectiveness of the board. Relationships with the CEO are crucial in performing the leadership role of the board chair. Without going into detail here, the balance to be struck involves independent scrutiny of executive performance based upon valid, reliable, and balanced information and support for the CEO in terms of understanding the challenges faced by management and providing constructive advice.

The WHRA board has rejected the "Carver board" model mainly for the reasons given above. The emerging preferred model for health board governance has been described as "generative governance" because it moves beyond structures and formal procedures to focus more on building trust on many levels and the promotion of honest discussion of risks, failures, learning, and problem solving. In the fall/winter of 2008–2009, the WHRA board embarked on a governance reform process with the assistance of an outside consultant. It dealt with a range of topics: strategy, stakeholder relationships, board committees, physician leadership, quality, and safety and accountability. The lessons learned from the WHRA reforms may be useful to other boards across the province.

X. Planning and Budgeting

One of the aims of regionalization was to promote a shift to a population-based and preventative approach to the planning of health services based on the assessment of regional health needs and citizen input. These aims are reflected in the requirement that RHAs conduct Community Health Assessments (CHAS), develop a five-year strategic plan (SP), produce an annual health plan (AHP), and integrate these documents with their operational and capital spending budget submissions to Manitoba Health and Healthy Living. Each of these components of the planning and budgeting framework will be examined briefly.

The objective of the CHAs is to identify community health strengths and needs, examine the determinants of health, and establish priorities and objectives for the future. One of the methods for gathering information is through community input, about which more is said below. The Manitoba Centre for Health Policy (MCHP) has been working for several years with "The Need to Know Team," consisting of representatives of the RHAs and Manitoba Health and Healthy Living, to produce data to guide assessments and planning.[16] Additional data are derived from Manitoba Health and Healthy Living, Health Canada, the census, surveys, and community consultations. The CHA process concludes with a written report posted on the websites of the RHA and submitted to Manitoba Health and Healthy Living for review. Taking place once every five years, the CHA is an intensive and time-consuming exercise. It is seen by the RHAs as a valuable basis for identifying needs, for setting policy and program priorities, for allocating resources, and for gaining community consent and support for actions. RHA boards and executives are less certain whether CHAs are used by the department to guide budgetary allocations.

Each RHA is required to produce a five-year Strategic Plan, based in part on their CHA but focused more on the institutions, programs, staffing, and budgets required to meet future regional needs. This is difficult given the complicated, dynamic, and dispersed nature of regional health systems. A key issue is the recruitment and retention of health professionals, especially of physicians and nurses. The health human resources shortages across the country are a major obstacle. The RHAs have only limited tools of their own to plan their professional staffing, as remuneration of physicians is in provincial hands. With foreign-trained physicians heavily relied upon in rural Manitoba, there is both competition among RHAs as well as high rates of physician turnover.

The budget process is examined below, but the fact that there is no multi-year funding for RHAs also limits the capacity to plan for the longer term. Requests for new programs or capital projects will sometimes arise outside of the planning process and the political pressures to accede to these requests can move decision making away from a planned, needs-based model. It is not clear from the available evidence how seriously the minister and the department treat strategic plans as guides to regional needs, as a basis for setting regional budgets, and as an accountability mechanism. RHA officials point out that closures or modifications to care facilities, particularly hospitals, are the most politically explosive issues they face. Loss of a hospital is now seen as the equivalent to the loss of a grain elevator in earlier decades in terms of the future of local communities. Even when the RHA boards make tough choices in their proposed plans to change their delivery structures (based upon efficiency or patient safety considerations), they believe the provincial government lacks the political will to approve the decision because of the feared backlash. For example, the Assiniboine RHA has developed plans to rationalize the hospital and other services in its region but has never found provincial officials were ready to make the tough choices. Some RHA officials point out with frustration that Manitoba Health and Healthy Living does not produce and publish its own strategic plan. In fairness to the department, it does comply with the provincial financial management system of strategic program objectives, estimates preparation, performance measures, and published annual reports.

Based upon their CHAS, RHAS prepare ongoing health service plans which must comply with content requirements set down by the Accountability Support branch within the Administration, Finance and Accountability Division of Manitoba Health and Healthy Living. "Performance deliverables" are a part of the planning and budgeting transactions conducted between the RHAS and the department. To enhance the communication of expectations and to receive feedback on its support services to the RHAS, the Accountability and Support branch participates in a Regional Health Authorities of Manitoba (RHAM) Planning and CHA Network. In 2006–2007 the branch also began discussions with the RHAS on updated framework for performance reporting.[17] While regional health service plans are produced for budgeting and accountability purposes, they are not released publicly for fear of how communities will react to the potential closure or changed use of faculties, especially hospitals.

This brings us to one of the most frequent complaints about the RHA system; namely, that medium-range planning and multi-year budgeting have not been integrated. This was the conclusion of the Health Care Financial Management and Accountability Review report (Webster Report) in April 2000 and of the Report of the Manitoba Regional Health Authority External Review Committee in February 2008. Each year RHAS are required to submit balanced operating budgets based on the funding allocation letter sent out after the provincial budget has been approved by the legislature. This means that firm budgets are not set until RHAS are several months into their fiscal year. Since annual appropriations are a key convention of cabinet-parliamentary government, there seems to be no possibility of multi-year funding commitments to the RHAS.

The Webster Report issued in 2000 recommended that RHAS establish small contingency funds to provide a cushion against unforeseen reductions in provincial transfers and/or increased demands for services. In fact, over the past eight years many RHAS have run operating deficits, which, though small, have forced them to find lines of credit from banks or seek special funding from the department. All requests for new initiatives at the RHAS level must be made through their annual health plan submission, which means they attract greater scrutiny in the department and in the central budgetary process of the government. A lack of transparency and objective criteria to guide budgetary allocations has led several RHAs to have serious concerns about the fairness of the process. In October 2007, the Manitoba Centre for Health Policy released a preliminary report on a "made-in-Manitoba" funding allocation methodology which would combine quantitative and qualitative data to enable the department to "slice" the "health spending pie" more fairly than in the past.[18] A more objective and transparent approach to setting RHA budgets will reduce the potential for real or perceived favouritism. However, there will still be complaints that particular RHAs have not made the tough budgetary choices to consolidate facilities or to pursue other efficiencies.

XI. Citizen Input at the RHA Level

The 2008 report of the external review community argues that the boards and CEOs of the RHAs should be "accountable" in two directions: to the minister and the department and to the citizens of their communities. Whether this notion of "dual accountability" is accurate and appropriate depends on how the phrase is understood. Elsewhere, I have argued that accountability has become a cliché and is acquiring an ever-expanding meaning.[19] Ideally, the term should be restricted to a formal relationship in which responsibility, authority, and funding is delegated to another organization answerable for successful performance and subject to sanctions for deficient performance—and in the best of all possible worlds, receive recognition and rewards for superior performance.

The RHAs are clearly accountable to the minister of health who, as noted earlier, has such important prerogatives as appointing the chairs and members of boards, reviewing RHA plans, issuing policy directives, establishing funding levels, and putting nonperforming RHAs under departmental supervision. By contrast, the RHA boards and executives are only "answerable" and presumed to be "responsive" to their communities. The community does not have the formal authority to impose penalties or to bestow rewards on the leadership of the RHAs. Performance shortcomings can be the subject of complaints to the minister and department and there can be negative publicity campaigns. However, the RHA boards cannot be changed through elections, nor are they required to approach the local community for their finances. Staff of the RHA cannot be hired, promoted, or dismissed by the community. In summary, RHA boards and executives are formally and directly *accountable* to the minister and only *answerable* and *responsive* to their communities. While this is an accurate legal interpretation, in practice a 2003 survey of RHA board members revealed they felt most "accountable" to the citizens of their community.

The Regional Health Authorities Act requires the creation of District Health Advisory Councils (DHCs) unless the minister approves otherwise. In some regions, these councils are referred to as Community Health Advisory Councils (CHAC). The number and level of activity of these councils varies significantly across the eleven regions, but all RHA's have made some effort to engage their citizens in discussions of health needs, priorities for health services, and their satisfaction with existing services. The Community Health Assessments is the major occasion on which advisory councils are consulted, but RHA boards may also seek advice on specific health care issues. The examples of the WRHA and the South Eastman Regional Health Authority (SERHA) illustrate how the regions adopt consultative mechanisms based on the character of the region. Serving the people of Winnipeg and some adjacent municipalities, the WRHA has invested significantly in achieving meaningful citizen input. Six CHACs have been created, each representing two community areas. Each CHAC has up to fifteen members, nine of whom are community representatives and six of whom are WRHA employees. The councils are provided with a dedicated WRHA staff person and their minutes and advice are posted on the WRHA website. In preparing for the 2009 CHA, the Research and Evaluation Unit at the WRHA first drafted a sophisticated research paper on community involvement in health assessment and then followed up with a more operational paper, both of which documents were posted on the WRHA website.[20] In the field of patient safety, the WRHA established an advisory group to increase patient input into the reduction of adverse events. Regular polling is done by the authority to track changing public perceptions of how well community needs are being met and whether patients and families have the information they need to use the system more easily.

SERHA is a rural authority which has a budget of $72 million and 1,200 employees compared to the $1.8 billion budget and 28,000 employees in the WRHA. The board of SERHA seeks advice from two groups: four District Health Advisory Committees (Central, Northern, Southern, and Western) and a provider advisory committee. Each group is provided with a board and a staff liaison contact. In connection with its CHA, South Eastman was one of eight rural RHAs which took part in a telephone survey designed by the Community Health Assessment Network which took place November–December 2003. In addition, qualitative data were gathered from focus groups, key informant groups, and roundtables across the region.

Evaluating Manitoba's experiences with citizen participation in RHAs has to take account of the different challenges in the various regions. Blanket judgements are inappropriate. The 2008 review committee surveyed members of the advisory councils and found some level of dissatisfaction in terms of meaningful input into the most pressing issues seen to be facing the region.[21] Difficulties of the recruitment of members, the travel involved, and the cost of attending advisory councils were mentioned as practical obstacles to participation in rural regions. More philosophically, it can be observed that the regions as they exist really transcend communities as usually understood and that is why the component of CHACS/DHCS were incorporated into the regional model. It must be remembered that adoption of the regional model was meant to overcome the fragmentation, parochialism, and provider (mainly physician) dominance of the old hospital- and community-based boards. The debates over the success of RHAS as vehicles for meaningful citizen involvement also reflect differing opinions over the requisite knowledge and skills to engage in health planning and service provision decision-making. The traditional assumption that health care providers and administrators have the expert knowledge and the best interest of the patient in mind has clashed increasingly with a decline in public deference towards health professionals, with an insistence on more transparency and accountability and with more demands there be opportunities for citizen input.[22] While public opinion research tells us people like to be consulted, it also suggests the majority still prefer to have decisions on health care made by experts.

XII. Summing Up the Provincial-RHA Relationship

The committee which reviewed Manitoba's RHA system in 2007–08 after a decade of operation concluded that health care decision making, services, and effectiveness could be improved if RHA boards and executives were given more autonomy and control over defining and achieving outcomes for their communities. According to the committee, too much of the scrutiny and accountability requirements by Manitoba Health and Healthy Living focused on narrow financial and process requirements and not enough on insisting that RHAS set targets in terms of health outcomes and report on demonstrated results.[23] The review committee quoted RHA officials as saying that the major strategic decisions, like the closure of facilities, were ultimately made at the provincial level and that even more operational decisions were hemmed in by a web of rules, procedures, and reporting requirements set by the department.

Ministers of health and the department insist they have a responsibility to the public to ensure the programs and services delivered are meeting the needs of the population and are of acceptable quality. Monitoring is meant to provide the assurance that reasonable levels of performance are achieved relative to expectations and available resources. Also, knowing how well the health system is performing is seen as necessary to ensure learning about what works. Manitoba Health and Healthy Living has an extensive array of mechanisms to steer, monitor, and require that corrective action be taken. Mention has already been made of the minister's prerogative to appoint boards, to issue policy directives, to review community health assessments, health plans, strategic plans, budgets, and annual reports. Provincial policy strategies have been developed on many topics, such as diabetes, women's health, and patient safety, and RHAs are expected to contribute to the accomplishment of the aims of those policies. The department has entered into performance agreements with particular RHAs with specified "deliverables" being a key feature. Critical incident reporting within RHA facilities became mandatory in 2007 and reports on adverse events must be filed with the department.

In the worst-case scenario, the minister can take over the delivery of health services in a region. In 2003–04 the minister required that two communities within the Assiniboine Regional Health Authority cease their attempts to recruit physicians. Pointing to the loss of thirty-six of the forty-three physicians recruited in the preceding four years, the minister ordered a review of the RHA to be conducted by the executive director of the Regional Health Associations of Manitoba and to be assisted by the Office of Rural and Northern Health.[24] In 2007 when allegations of financial mismanagement in the Burntwood Regional Health Authority arose, the minister put the RHA under departmental supervision and appointed two retired CEOs to run its affairs on an interim basis.[25] The response to such breakdowns has often been to add new accountability requirements and/or to increase the scrutiny exercised by the department.

The political sensitivity of health issues means officials in Manitoba Health and Healthy Living are concerned to ensure, if at all possible, there are no surprises that could embarrass the minister and the government. Moreover, for many decades prior to regionalization, departmental staff spent much of their time negotiating contracts and processing claims. Logically, under regionalization the volume of such transactional activity should have declined and the department would adopt a more strategic orientation of system-wide planning, policy direction, standards setting, monitoring, and evaluation. To some extent, this change in the orientation has happened, at least in terms of the rhetoric of departmental spokespersons. The devolution and consolidation involved with the creation of RHAs after 1997 meant the withdrawal of the department from the direct management of service delivery. Staff levels in the department dropped from 2500 in 1997 down to 1100 in 2007. The reduction reflected fewer transactions, but also budgetary restraint and downsizing within the provincial government. Vacancy management programs applying to the entire public service made it hard for the department to obtain new appointments. The departure of a significant number of managers to work at the RHAs, especially the WRHA, meant that Manitoba Health lacked adequate capacity to perform its new roles of policy planning, coordination, standard setting, monitoring and risk management.

The department has undergone several internal reorganizations to reflect and promote its new orientation. For example, in 2003–04 one of the five functional areas of the department was "Regional Programs and Services" and its role was defined as developing the capabilities of the RHA. As of 2007, the organization chart for the department showed an assistant deputy minister leading a "Regional Affairs" division and the role was defined more in terms of partnerships and collaboration with RHAs. Changing the departmental culture to reflect the new relationships with the RHAs has been a slower, more problematic process. The frequent turnover of ministers and deputy ministers during the first decade of regionalization has not helped in terms of creating a new departmental mindset. Finally, there is the fact the eleven RHAs have widely varied capacities to run their own affairs and to comply with provincial policy directives, care standards, and management requirements. The WRHA dwarfs all other RHAs in terms of the population served (700,000) and the depth of its expertise. With its responsibility for tertiary care throughout the province, the WRHA might be more accurately seen as a health authority for the whole province. It is also the case that the WRHA has often contributed staff support to assist smaller rural RHAs adopt provincially mandated policies and programs. The WRHA has a different relationship than other RHAs with the minister of health and her department, which is not surprising given that Winnipeg is the population, economic, health, and political centre of the province. Often the premier and the minister of health turn to the WRHA rather than Manitoba Health and Healthy Living for advice and the implementation of responses to hot issues of the day. This might be seen as a reversal of the formal lines of responsibility and accountability in which the WRHA is presumed to take direction and to report to the department. However, Manitoba Health and Healthy Living cannot compete with the WRHA in terms of its resources and expertise. Of the department's budget of approximately $4 billion, only $66 million is allocated to departmental salaries and operating expenses. In 2006–07, it had a full-time staff of approximately 1100, but 410 worked at the Selkirk Mental Hospital, 148 in the field of public health, and 124 in running the insured benefits program.[26] In other words, there was limited "in house" capacity to perform the strategic oversight functions that the regional model presumed for the department. Any plan for the future of regionalization must take into serious consideration the dominating presence of the WRHA and the limited surveillance capacity of Manitoba Health and Healthy Living.

XIII. Conclusions and the Future

On the tenth anniversary in 2007 of the creation of the RHA system, the government of Manitoba appointed a three-person committee to review the structures, programs, and impacts of regionalization. Released on 14 February 2008, the committee report concluded there had been significant benefits from regionalization, but further improvements were necessary and possible if the RHAs were granted more autonomy from provincial process and financial control.[27] In return for more freedom to plan and to design programs to suit the needs of their regions, RHAs should be held more strictly accountable by Manitoba Health for specifying targets of improved health and reporting on progress towards them. The committee used the management buzzword "empowerment" to describe what it saw as a necessary fundamental change to the status of RHAs. The report provided a reasonably comprehensive and informative assessment of the structures, processes, programs, and impacts of regionalization. Unfortunately the report was long on diagnosis and short on prescriptions. The committee announced at the start of its report (p. 7) that it would leave the "how" of its recommendations up to the appropriate authorities within the health field. The failure to consider the practical matters of feasibility and implementation meant that, no matter how sophisticated the analysis and the presentation of the findings, there was less likelihood that the review committee's report would provide a basis for action.

The feasibility of recommendations involves a number of factors: the available evidence and knowledge to support proposals, the plausibility of the presumed linkage between proposed actions and anticipated outcomes, the capacity or the potential to build the capacity within organizations to deliver the changes, the reactions of key stakeholder groups, and the willingness and capacity of politicians to explain and to gain support for the proposed changes. On the matter of political feasibility, I believe the review committee's integrating theme of "empowering" the RHAs and making them accountable for performance within their regions was a "political non-starter" for several reasons. First, the RHA Act enshrines the principle of ministerial responsibility for the overall performance of the health care system, and the act provides for the delegation of authority to RHA boards, but makes the boards and executives of authorities subject to ministerial direction, control and oversight.

Second, even after a decade of experience with RHAs, there is limited public awareness of the boards and almost no tradition of the public seeking to hold boards accountable for the performance of regional health institutions. Instead, it is more common to look to the minister and department of health to resolve problems when they arise. By one estimate there were more than 10,000 contacts annually with the office of the minister of health.[28]

Third, the sensitivity of health issues and the intense political dynamic surrounding them means that opposition parties in the legislature, interest groups, health care unions, the media, and the general public lay the blame for tragedies, mismanagement, and inefficiencies on the minister and the government. Even though the minister may not have direct and complete control, she is expected to prevent problems and to deal decisively with them when they arise. In political terms, it is not satisfactory for ministers to declare that the RHAs are in charge because she will still pay a political price in terms of the loss of her reputation and in the worst case the loss of her job. Given the insistence on error-free health care and on blaming, it is not surprising ministers of health and the provincial government will insist on retaining the authority to set policy direction and to exercise a significant measure of control and to hold RHAs accountable.

The review committee called for a clarification of the respective roles of the province and the RHAs and more transparency in the processes of accountability for results. It might be possible to delineate roles somewhat more clearly and publicly in order to focus responsibility and accountability for different levels of policy making, decision making, and programming activity. Manitoba Health and Healthy Living published a document ("Achieving Accountability") in 1999, which mapped the accountability relationships in very general terms. It would be more helpful, however, to develop a matrix designating the institution responsible—either exclusively, primarily, or on a shared basis—for policies, decisions, resource allocations, and activities. This might clarify the responsibility/accountability relationships somewhat, but parts of the health care system are interdependent, and decisions made on one level or in one domain have consequences (often unforeseen) elsewhere, so there is no possibility of a neat, linear diagram which perfectly captures the complex relationships in the real world.

As noted previously, there is no shortage of monitoring and accountability mechanisms. Multiple accountability processes may end up blurring more than clarifying the accountability picture and certainly they add to the burden of compliance on RHAs, especially smaller rural organizations. To encourage the shift, which the review committee recommended, from the process-based model of accountability to a results-based model, a performance council with representatives of the department and the RHAs could be established to review existing accountability requirements in terms of potential streamlining and to seek consensus on a meaningful performance measurement framework which would identify strategic issues and indicators of achievement.

The devolution of more authority and influence to RHAs involves further complications beyond the politicization of health care. Regionalization emphasized planned, evidence-based, integrated service delivery and the achievement of economies of scale. This emphasis on professionally driven effective and efficient health care clashed with the other aims of the active representation of citizen voices, encouraging responsiveness to local needs, and promoting accessibility and equity in terms of services. The external review committee concluded that RHA boards were uneven in the performance of their governance roles and in their encouragement of citizen engagement. It called for more provincial monitoring of boards. It is easy to be hyper-critical of RHA boards given the challenges they face: provincial control over policy and resources; the difficulty of the issues faced; the power of the health professions, especially physicians; the expectations and demands of the communities and their leaders; and in rural areas especially the distances involved, the disparities among communities, and the lack of volunteers who can give time to a challenging, poorly paid job. The review report did not give enough recognition to the ingenuity and efforts of RHAs, including pooling resources and sharing "best practices" to cope with these challenges.

Notably, the review committee did not call for any changes to the boundaries of the existing eleven RHAs. Stability would enable current programs within the individual RHAs to achieve their impacts and would allow for the emergence of greater regional consciousness. Amalgamations of RHAs might occur in the future when the benefits of increased effectiveness of care delivery and efficiency of administration could be demonstrated. While Manitoba's RHAs will, for now, be spared the disruption of consolidation, the trend in other provinces has been in that direction. In 2001 British Columbia went from fifty-two to five RHAs. In 2002, Saskatchewan reduced the number of RHAs from thirty-two to twelve. As Canada's smallest province, PEI did away entirely with its five RHAs and recentralized authority in the health department. New Brunswick replaced its nine RHAs in 2008 with just two boards, one for English-language and one for French-language services. In 2008 Alberta replaced its nine RHAs with one province-wide "superboard." The rallying cry behind these consolidations was the reduction of bureaucracy and the promotion of efficiency in cash-strapped provincial health systems.

Similar arguments have been made by opposition parties in the legislature and by other critics of regionalization. The WRHA, in particular, has been a popular target for criticism, which is not surprising given its size, visibility, and reputation for influence with the provincial government. There are no definitive studies which identify the optimum size of health authorities in terms of geography, population served, and organizational capacity in order to achieve the desired balance between citizen involvement and responsiveness to local needs versus system-wide planning, service integration, and effective programming and the achievement of economies of scale. Even though the review committee concluded that the administrative costs of RHAs were reasonable (at approximately 4 percent of budgets), this evidence is not likely to deter opposition parties and other critics from attacking what they see as excessive executive salaries and overhead costs in a health system already under severe strain.

On 18 August 2008 the leader of the Progressive Conservatives was quoted as saying Manitoba should consider following Alberta's example and centralize some functions back into the hands of the provincial health department while recreating the community boards that help run individual hospitals and other community health bodies.[29] The minister of health defended the RHA structure as having delivered significant benefits. Any move to drastically recentralize functions and abolish boards would clearly be disruptive. On the other hand, the demonstration effect of the streamlining steps in other provinces will put pressure on the government of Manitoba to consider similar moves. Manitoba's geography and population distribution pose serious challenges to any drastic consolidation. It might be possible to reduce to five or six the number of RHAs, but in order to avoid a political backlash there would have to be more meaningful citizen input into the fate and operation of health facilities within individual communities.

This chapter has assessed regionalization mainly from a governance perspective. It has not attempted to evaluate the substance of health care reform brought in under the umbrella of the RHA system. The benefits of revised structures were oversold when regionalization was introduced. Regionalization could never be a panacea for dealing with the challenges involved with reforming primary care, health human resource shortages, healthier aging, patient safety, service integration, and so on. By reducing fragmentation and by enabling more coherence in policy making and implementation, the RHA system has produced some significant benefits, such as moves towards a wellness model, more focus on safety and quality, preliminary steps towards service integration, some limited reductions in acute-care facilities, and increased responsiveness to local needs. The fact that progress has been slow and less than complete is not mainly the fault of regionalization per se. Remuneration of physicians remains a provincial responsibility and primary care operates largely autonomously from the RHAs. This might change slightly as primary health care reform proceeds. Pharmacare spending on medications is a provincial program and that is not likely to change.

The problems with regionalization also reflect the "stop-and-go" policy leadership and funding leadership from the provincial and the national government. The complicated, multi-tiered nature of the Canadian health care system (which is actually thirteen provincial/territorial systems) means that there are many potential points of resistance to reform. Finding a political consensus on the future of a publicly financed health care system in which there are multiple stakeholders is the real challenge. None of the institutions and actors involved acts simply on the basis of self-interest, but it would be a mistake to think that self-interest is not part of their motivation. Elected politicians, public servants in the health department, regional health boards and executives, health professionals and unions, patients, and the citizens in various regions can have perspectives on what actions qualify as reform and will lead to improved health outcomes. The political management of change will continue to be a crucial part of health care reform.

Table 19.1. Key Responsibilities in Canadian Health Care

	Policy Development	Service Planning	Funding	Direct Service Delivery	Regulation and Redress	Performance and Outcome Evaluation and Reporting
Federal Government	✓	✓	✓	✓ (limited)	✓	✓
Provincial/ Territorial Governments	✓	✓	✓	✓ (limited)	✓	✓
Regional Health Authorities	✓	✓		✓		✓
Health Care Facilities				✓		✓
Health Professionals				✓		
Regulators	✓				✓	
Safety/Quality Agencies						✓

Table 19.2. Manitoba: Key Events and Acts

- Public Health Act in Manitoba (1893)
- Establishment of a Department of Health and Public Welfare (1928)
- Changes to the Municipal Act and the Public Health Act (1954)
- The Hospitals Act (1958)
- The Hospital Services Insurance Act (1962)
- Manitoba Hospital Services Plan implemented including the establishment of the Manitoba Hospital Commission
- Reorganization of provincial health and social services administration (1961)
- Medical Care Insurance Act (1968)
- Comprehensive medical services became insured (1 April 1969)
- Manitoba Health Services Commission established (1 July 1969)
- Amendments to the Municipal Act (1970)
- District Health and Social Services Act (1975)
- Regional Health Authorities Act (1997)

Table 19.3. Dates RHAs were established

Province/Territory	Date RHAs Established
British Columbia	1997
Alberta	1994
Saskatchewan	1992
Manitoba	1997
Ontario	2004–2005
Québec	1989–1992
Nova Scotia	1996
New Brunswick	1992
Prince Edward Island	1993 and 1994
Newfoundland	1994
Yukon	—
Northwest Territories	1988–1997
Nunavut	—

Notes

1. This figure combines provincial and federal spending. See Canadian Institute for Health Information, National Health Expenditure Trends, 1975–2006 (Ottawa: 2007).
2. Conn Hamilton, *Healthy Provinces, Healthy Canadians: A Provincial Benchmarking Report* (Ottawa: Conference Board, 2006).
3. Dr. Jon Gerrard, "Delivering the Care You Need When You Need It," Manitoba Liberal Submission to the Regional Health Authority External Review Committee, September 2007.
4. Report of the Manitoba Regional Health Authority External Review Committee (Winnipeg: Manitoba Health and Healthy Living, February 2008), 21.
5. Steven Lewis and Denise Kouri, "Regionalization: Making Sense of the Canadian Experience," *Healthcare Papers* 5, 1 (2004): 12–13.
6. Alberta Government, news release, "One Provincial board to govern Alberta's health system," 15 May 2008; Jodie Sinnema, "Former Health CEOs pocket millions; Disbanding regional boards will cost taxpayers at least $12 million in executive payouts," *Edmonton Journal*, 9 October 2008.
7. Linette McNamara-Paetz, "Can Regionalization Live Up to Its Economic Reputation?" *Health Law Review* 3 (1996): 2–8; Ken Rasmussen, "Regionalization and Collaborative Government: A New Direction for Health System Governance," in *Federalism, Democracy and Health Policy in Canada*, ed. Duane Adams (Kingston: Institute of Intergovernmental Relations/McGill-Queens University Press, 2001), 239–270.
8. Gregory Marchildon and Elias Massialos, *Health Systems in Transition: Canada* (Toronto: University of Toronto Press, 2006), 109.
9. Manitoba Health, *Quality Health for Manitobans: The Action Plan* (Winnipeg: May 1992), 11.
10. An excellent summary of the pros and cons of regionalization is contained in Colleen M. Flood and Duncan Sinclair, "Steering and Rowing in Health Care: The Devolution Option?" paper prepared for the Role of Government Panel in Ontario, 2003. An abridged version of the paper appears in *Healthcare Quarterly* 8, 1 (2005): 54–59.
11. See the Winnipeg Regional Health Authority website (http://www.wrha.mb.ca).
12. See South Eastman Regional Health Authority website (http://www.sehealth.mb.ca)
13. Gordon Webster, *Health Care Financial Management and Accountability Review, Report to Ministers of Health and Finance* (Winnipeg: April 2000), 19.
14. Manitoba Health and Healthy Living, Presentation on Regional Health Authorities, 2007.
15. John Carver, "A Theory of Governing the Public's Business: Redesigning the jobs of boards, councils and commissions," *Public Management Review* 3, 1 (2001): 53–71.
16. Manitoba Centre for Health Policy, *What Works? A First Look at Evaluating Manitoba's Regional Health Programs and Policies at the Population Health Level* (Winnipeg: March 2008).
17. Manitoba Health and Healthy Living, Annual Report, 2006–2007, 15.
18. Manitoba Centre for Health Policy, *Allocating Funds for Healthcare in Manitoba Regional Health Authorities: A First Step—Population-Based Funding* (Winnipeg: October 2007).
19. Paul G. Thomas, "The Swirling Meanings and Practices of Accountability in Canadian Government," in *Power, Professionalism and Public Service: Essays in Honour of Kenneth Kernaghan*, ed. K. Rasmussen and D. Siegel (Toronto: University of Toronto Press, 2008), 43–75.

20 See "WRHA Community Health Assessment 2009: Purpose, Objectives, Philosophy and Approach, Concept Paper" (January, 2007) and "Operationalizing the Redesign of the WRHA Community Health Assessment Process" (January 2008), http://www.wrha.mb.ca.
21 Report of the Manitoba Regional Health Authority External Review Committee, February 2008, ch. 7.
22 Paul G. Thomas, "The Swirling Meanings and Practices of Accountability."
23 External Review Committee, 2008.
24 Hansard debates, 27 November 2003.
25 Minister of Health, press release.
26 Manitoba Health and Healthy Living, Annual Report, 2006–2007.
27 External Review Committee, 2008.
28 Interview with ministerial assistant to Minister of Health.
29 Mary Agnes Welch, "Fix or kill health boards, Tories say," *Winnipeg Free Press*, 18 August 2008.

Questions of Allocation: Resources and Degrees Awarded at the University of Manitoba, 1998-2005[1]

Rodney A. Clifton

Introduction

The forces of transparency and accountability that are transforming the Canadian economy and society are slowly beginning to transform Canadian universities.[2] In many colleges and universities, students increasingly complain about rising tuition fees, administrators are concerned about uncertain revenues, parents question the quality of their children's education, and new universities based on computer technology and online courses and programs are rapidly overtaking universities built with bricks and mortar.[3] These forces, of course, are affecting specific universities, such as the University of Manitoba (U of M), which is the largest university in the province with about 70 percent of the university students and more than 75 percent of the faculty members in the province.[4]

At the same time, many university presidents, deans, and directors have claimed their universities are underfunded. Given the economic situation in Manitoba between 2006 and 2009, university administrators in this province claimed that they needed more resources to properly serve their students, particularly their undergraduate students.[5] More specifically, in answering a question about funding for the U of M, Dr. Emőke Szathmáry, the past president of the University of Manitoba, said something that she had repeated many times throughout her term: "Were more revenue available universities could...meet the costs of providing a proper education to their students."[6] In the United States, Richard Vedder notes that similar words have echoed across North America by many university presidents, deans, and professors.[7]

Nevertheless, before deciding on how many more resources, basically money and personnel, faculties and schools deserve, university administrators, professors, students, and citizens need to know the answer to four questions. First, what resources have been given to the University of Manitoba during the last few years? Second, how have these resources been dispersed to the faculties and schools? Third, how many students have graduated with degrees in this period of time? Finally, what is the relative cost of each degree awarded in each of the schools and faculties? Fortunately, the University of Manitoba is one of the few Canadian universities that publishes data that can be used to answer these questions.

Table 20.1. Expenditures at the University of Manitoba, 1998 and 2005 ($ x 1000)

Source	1998	2005	Increase $	Percentage
Academic Salaries in Faculties and Schools	84,033.8	114,851.0	30,817.2	36.7
Support Staff Salaries in Faculties and Schools	19,259.5	30,229.4	10,969.9	57.0
Other Expenditures	113,516.6	165,218.1	51,701.5	45.5
Net Operating Expenditures	216,809.9	310,298.5	93,488.6	43.1

Source: University of Manitoba (1998, 85); University of Manitoba (2005, 121).

I. Resource Allocation and Degrees Awarded in the University from 1998 to 2005

By examining data from the University of Manitoba's Institutional Statistics reports, summarized in Table 20.1, we see that from 1998 to 2005 (data that were available in 2009), the operating funds for the University of Manitoba increased from $216,809,900 to $310,298,500, an increase of 43.1 percent, while over the same period, the consumer price index (CPI) increased by 17.2 percent. Thus, the operating expenditures at the University of Manitoba increased by more than 2.5 times the CPI. Interestingly, the expenditures on academic salaries, both hiring new professors and increasing the current professors' salaries, increased by 36.7 percent, the least amount (2.1 times the CPI), while the expenditures on administrative and support staff increased by 57.0 percent, the greatest amount (3.3 times the CPI). Other expenditures (libraries, equipment, etc.) increased by 45.5 percent (2.6 times the CPI). Not surprisingly, Vedder also notes that the administrative costs at U.S. universities have increased much faster than other expenditures.[8]

Table 20.2 reports that the number of degrees awarded increased by only 13.5 percent from 4,136 in 1998 to 4,696 in 2005 with obvious random variation over the intervening years; undergraduate degrees increased by 14.0 percent and graduate degrees increased by 10.9 percent. In other words, during these seven years, the University of Manitoba received $93 million more in operating funds, but increased its graduation rate by only 560 students. To put these figures into a more meaningful perspective, the $93 million increase in operating funds represents about $80 from each person residing in the province, with a cost for each new degree awarded to students at about $130,000.

Table 20.2. Degrees Awarded by Faculties and Schools at the University of Manitoba, 1998 to 2005

Degrees Awarded	1998	1999	2000	2001	2002	2003	2004	2005	Increase No.	(%)
Undergraduate	3514	3611	3348	3538	3643	3730	4009	4006	492	14.0
Graduate	622	598	535	554	550	548	617	690	68	10.9
Total	4136	4009	3883	4092	4193	4278	4626	4696	560	13.5

Source: University of Manitoba.[9]

Essentially, these data suggest that the University of Manitoba has been treated quite favourably by the provincial government—and by extension, citizens, parents, and students—but that there is a rather weak relationship between the money received and the number of students graduating from the university programs. Again, Richard Vedder says: "Very little of the additional financial support recently given to...universities has actually been used to reduce the cost of undergraduate instruction."[10] The data reported in Tables 20.1 and 20.2, in fact, support Vedder's claim, but they do not tell what happened within the faculties and schools. The next step is to examine changes in both expenditures and degrees awarded to students within the various faculties and schools.

Table 20.3. Increases in Academic and Support Staff Expenditures ($ x 1000) in Faculties and Schools, 1998 and 2005

Faculties/Schools	1998	2005	Increases $	Increases (%)
Agricultural and Food Sciences	7,842.2	9,751.3	1,909.1	24.3
Architecture	3,004.4	3,952.0	947.6	31.5
Art, School of	1,373.6	1,978.1	604.5	44.0
Arts	20,529.4	24,113.6	3,584.2	17.5
Business, I.H. Asper School of	5,041.8	8,368.1	3,326.3	66.0
Dentistry and Dental Hygiene	5,290.0	8,717.7	3,427.7	64.8
Education	4,746.8	5,891.5	1,144.7	24.1
Engineering	6,840.7	9,469.2	2,628.5	38.4
Environment, Earth and Resources		4,822.6		
Human Ecology	2,307.1	2,466.9	159.8	6.9
Law	2,053.6	3,008.0	954.4	46.5
Medicine and Medical Rehab.	17,022.5	24,411.4	7,388.9	43.4
Music	1,382.9	2,577.9	1,195.0	86.4
Nursing	4,114.7	6,648.2	2,533.5	61.6
Pharmacy	1,056.3	1,952.0	895.7	84.8
Phys. Education/Rec. Studies	1,443.1	2,084.2	641.1	44.4
Science	17,044.4	19,963.8	2,919.4	17.1
Social Work	1,758.3	4,206.2	2,447.9	139.2
Total	102,851.8	144,382.7	36,708.3	35.6

Source: University of Manitoba.[11]

II. Resource Allocation and Degrees Awarded in the Faculties and Schools

Data on the increases in the academic and support staff expenditures for seventeen of the eighteen faculties and schools in the university in both 1998 and 2005 are presented in Table 20.3. During this period, the faculty of Environment, Earth, and Resources was created from resources that were reallocated from both Arts and Science, and this is why Table 20.3 does not report expenditures for this faculty in 1998 or the increase in expenditures from 1998 to 2005. Nevertheless, examining the percentage increases in resources spent on faculty members and support staff in the other seventeen faculties and schools illustrates that there is substantial variation, from a low of a 6.9 percent increase for Human Ecology to a high of a 139.2 percent increase for Social Work—with virtually no increases for the two core faculties, the Faculty of Arts (17.5 percent) and the Faculty of Science (17.1 percent) when the CPI (17.2 percent) is taken into consideration.

Table 20.4 presents the number of degrees awarded in the seventeen faculties and schools in both 1998 and 2005. Of course, trends for the intervening years were also examined to ensure that the data reported in this table were not anomalous. The number of undergraduate, graduate, and the total number of degrees awarded are reported separately, but I use the total number of degrees awarded even though it may be inappropriate to equally weight undergraduate and graduate degrees. The two columns of figures on the right-hand side of the table represent the changes in the total number of degrees awarded in the faculties and schools and the percentage changes from 1998 to 2005.

As noted previously, the total number of degrees awarded by the University of Manitoba increased by 13.5 percent between 1998 and 2005, but these data show that the overall trend masks substantial variation between the seventeen faculties and schools. Nursing, for example, increased the number of degrees awarded from 176 to 394, an increase of almost 124 percent; Arts increased the number of degrees awarded by 249, slightly more than 30 percent; while Social Work increased the number of degrees awarded by thirty-three, about 27 percent. On the other hand, Engineering decreased the number of undergraduate degrees awarded from 241 in 1998 to 154 in 2005 while increasing the number of graduate degrees from sixty-three to ninety. Similarly, Agricultural and Food Sciences decreased the number of undergraduate degrees awarded from 166 to ninety-two while increasing the number of graduate degrees from forty-three to forty-seven.

The question becomes: How do the financial resources in each faculty and school relate to the number of students who graduate? Table 20.5 presents the percentage increase in the expenditure for both academic and support staff—the input that administrators consider crucial because they argue that they need more money to educate more students, as well as the percentage changes in the number of degrees awarded, which is the output they should consider crucial. This table illustrates, on the one hand, that Agricultural and Food Sciences increased its expenditures on academic and support staff funding by 24.3 percent, and decreased the degrees awarded by 33.5 percent, while Engineering increased its expenditures on faculty and staff by 38.4 percent, and decreased the degrees awarded by 19.7 percent. On the other hand, the Faculty of Arts increased its expenditures on academic and support staff salaries by 17.5 percent and increased the number of degrees awarded by slightly more than 30 percent, Music increased its expenditures by 86.4 percent, and increased the number of degrees awarded by only 24.2 percent, while Social Work increased its expenditure by 139.2 percent and increased the degrees awarded by only 27.1 percent.

Table 20.4. Changes in the Number of Degrees Awarded in Faculties and Schools, 1998 and 2005

Faculties/Schools	1998 Under-graduate	1998 Graduate	1998 Total	2005 Under-graduate	2005 Graduate	2005 Total	Changes No.	Changes (%)
Agricultural and Food Sciences	166	43	209	92	47	139	-70	-33.5
Architecture	94	72	166	84	47	131	-35	-21.1
Art, School of	47	0	47	67	0	67	20	42.6
Arts	728	93	821	954	116	1070	249	30.3
Business, I.H. Asper School of	385	43	428	468	51	519	91	21.1
Dentistry and Dental Hygiene	49	7	56	61	7	68	12	21.1
Education	513	79	592	508	67	575	-17	-2.9
Engineering	241	63	304	154	90	244	-60	-19.7
Environment, Earth and Resources				78	23	101		
Human Ecology	125	14	139	85	18	103	-36	-25.9
Law	80	0	80	84	5	89	9	11.3
Medicine and Medical Rehab.	156	55	211	167	87	254	43	20.4
Music	33	0	33	36	5	41	8	24.2
Nursing	164	12	176	374	20	394	218	123.9
Pharmacy	49	3	52	45	9	54	2	3.8
Phys. Education/Rec. Studies	109	8	117	98	11	109	-8	-0.7
Science	485	56	541	491	59	550	9	0.2
Social Work	90	32	122	137	18	155	33	27.1
Total	3514	580	4094	3983	680	4663	569	13.9

Table 20.5. Percentage Increases in Academic and Support Staff Expenditures and Percentage Changes in the Number Degrees Awarded in Faculties and Schools, 1998 and 2005

Faculties/Schools	Increases in Academic and Support Staff Expenditures (%)	Change in Degrees Awarded (%)
Agricultural and Food Sciences	24.3	-33.5
Architecture	31.5	-21.1
Art, School of	44.0	42.6
Arts	17.5	30.3
Business, I.H. Asper School of	66.0	21.1
Dentistry and Dental Hygiene	64.8	21.1
Education	24.1	-2.9
Engineering	38.4	-19.7
Environment, Earth and Resources		
Human Ecology	6.9	-25.9
Law	46.5	11.3
Medicine and Medical Rehab.	43.4	20.4
Music	86.4	24.2
Nursing	61.6	123.9
Pharmacy	84.8	3.8
Phys. Education/Rec. Studies	44.4	-0.7
Science	17.1	0.2
Social Work	139.2	27.1
Total	40.9	13.9

Finally, Figure 20.1 illustrates the cost, using only the academic and support staff salaries, of each academic degree awarded in the seventeen faculties and schools in both 1998 and 2005. These are organized from the least expensive, Education, at slightly more than $10,000 in 2005, to the most expensive, Dentistry, at slightly more than $128,000. This figure illustrates that there is almost a thirteen-fold difference between faculties and schools in the cost of the degrees they award when only the salary of faculty members and support staff are included in the calculations. Surprisingly, only two faculties—Nursing and Arts—decreased the costs of awarding degrees during the seven-year period. In all likelihood, Nursing has become cheaper because it was established in the late 1990s, with relatively high startup costs and relatively few students and its costs decreased as more students enrolled and then graduated from the faculty. But, Arts seems to have become slightly more efficient during the seven-year period.

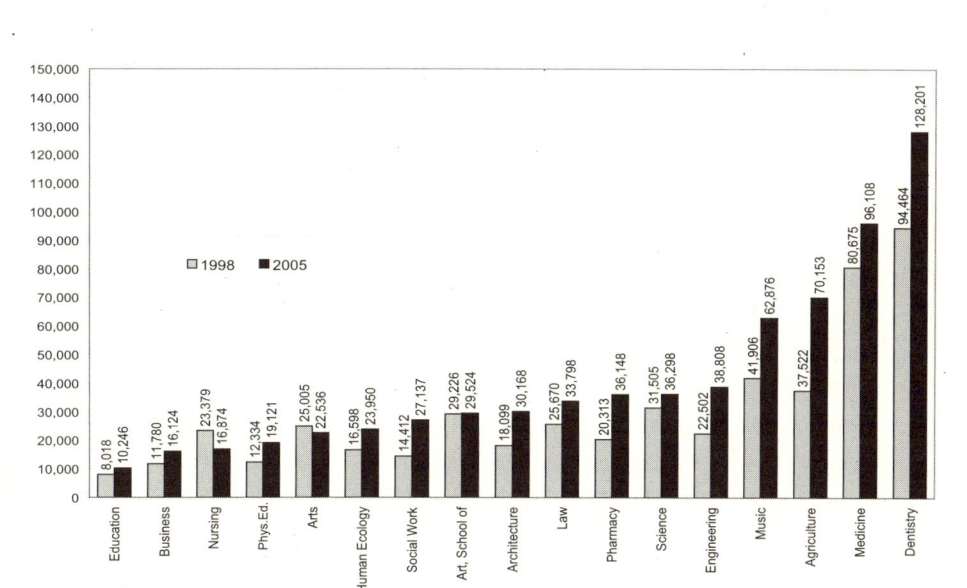

Figure 20.1. Academic and Support Staff Expenditures per Academic Degree Awarded in Faculties and Schools, 1998 and 2005

Equally obvious, the data show that during this period, a few faculties and schools have been highly supported while other faculties and schools have not been supported to the same extent. On the one hand, Dentistry increased its expenditures per degree awarded by $33,737, Agriculture increased its expenditure by $32,631, Music increased its expenditure by $20,970, Education increased its expenditure by only $2,228, and the School of Art increased its expenditure by only $298 per degree awarded. On the other hand, Nursing decreased its expenditure by $6,505 and Arts decreased its expenditure by $2,469. The obvious conclusion is that for the seventeen faculties and schools there is virtually *no* relationship between changes in the expenditures on academic and support staff salaries and changes in the number of degrees awarded. In other words, more money spent on increasing the number of faculty and support staff and/or increasing their salaries did not necessarily mean that more students graduated with degrees from the faculties and schools at the University of Manitoba between 1998 and 2005.

III. Is There an Explanation?

For citizens and students, specifically because they pay for the university, it is important to ask: why has efficiency and productivity not improved in all the faculties and schools at the University of Manitoba? Except for four faculties and schools, Nursing, Art, Arts, and Sciences, it took more rather than fewer resources to educate a fixed number of students during the seven-year period even though there were substantial advances in technology to support teaching and the administration of educational programs. The reason for the lack of a relationship between the costs of faculty and support staff and the number of degrees awarded seems to be quite simple to understand. Increasingly decisions are part of the "self-governance ethos" of universities, where professors, department heads, and deans participate on committees that make institutional policies for the allocation of resources, but often these people are insulated from the consequences of their decisions. In other words, deans, department heads, and faculty members seem to be able to increase their resources and at the same time decrease their graduation rates, essentially of undergraduate students, without facing the same consequences that private businesses would face if they made similar decisions. This may be the reason why the faculties of Engineering and Agricultural and Food Sciences could shift resources from teaching a relatively large number of undergraduate students to teaching graduate students while they received increasing resources to pay for faculty members and support staff. In this respect, the economist Thomas Sowell explained similar findings in the words of a science professor at the University of Michigan, who bluntly said: "Every minute I spend in an undergraduate classroom is costing me money and prestige."[12] In addition, at the University of Manitoba substantial funds have been spent on non-instructional objectives, such as increasing the number of administrators and/or increasing their salaries, purchasing a golf course, and constructing new buildings.[13]

From a theoretical perspective, self-governance at universities produces what economists call "rent-seeking," which is the increased use of resources provided by citizens and students who are weakly, if at all, represented by the administrative structure, all without increasing the number of students who receive degrees.[14] Rent-seeking is, in fact, quite common in large publicly funded organizations, like universities, but the type illustrated by these data represents a special variety. In the late 1960s, Robert Merton Sr., the eminent American sociologist, pointed out that senior scientists in research teams are much more likely to receive important awards, such as Nobel prizes, than their junior colleagues, even though the junior collaborators conducted much of the groundbreaking research.[15] Merton called this phenomenon "the Matthew effect" from the parable of the talents in St. Matthew's Gospel: "For unto every one that hath shall be given, and he shall have abundance: but from him that hath not shall be taken away even that which he hath."[16]

Consequently, at least between 1998 and 2005, the highly supported faculties and schools at the University of Manitoba—Dentistry, Agriculture, Music,

Engineering—have been able to engage in this type of rent-seeking that gives them advantages in comparison with the less-supported faculties and schools—Nursing, Arts, the School of Art, Education, Business, Sciences. Given this trend, can the University of Manitoba spend the money it receives—more than $450 million as of 2008—to serve the needs of students, particularly undergraduate students, better? Obviously, the answer is "yes."

IV. What Can Be Done?

What is the problem with a university taking money from the provincial government, in the form of block grants, and from students, in the form of tuition fees, and distributing it differentially to faculties and schools? The most important problem is that university administrators often ask for increased funding—grants from the government and tuition fees from the students—under the guise that the money will be distributed to students on the principle of universalism; that is, all students will be treated equally because they are all equally deserving. The clearest example of this principle has been recently expressed by Harvey Weingarten, the past president of the University of Calgary, in response to the question: "What is the biggest challenge facing universities in Canada?" He said: "If you look at the funding in Canadian public universities relative to public universities in the United States, we are really underfunded. The average gap is about $5,000 per student per year. That's huge. Imagine what a university could do if it had another $5,000 for every student to spend every year."[17] Of course, many other university administrators have made similar claims that more money would advantage all students irrespective of their faculty or school.

Not surprisingly, there are simple policies and procedures that would help university administrators act on the principle of universalism, equalizing resources for students, decreasing the cost in some faculties, and ensuring that more students successfully graduate with degrees—assuming, of course, that senior university administrators and faculty members actually want such policies and procedures. In this respect, I outline three policies that would begin realigning the resources distributed to the faculties and schools at the University of Manitoba so that students would be treated more fairly and more of them would complete degrees. Specifically, I suggest ways of rationally increasing the cost-effectiveness of the university before the impending external budget and accountability pressures from the government actually force the university to change.[18] Of course, I recognize that these policies still need to be developed in further detail before they could be implemented.

First, the procedures for allocating funds that presently advantage the faculties and schools that have been successful rent-seekers need to be changed so that the less successful faculties and schools can fairly compete with them. Foremost, professors, department heads, and deans who are possibly advantaged by decisions must not sit on committees that make decisions about the allocation of funds. In this respect, a truly independent body, the board of governors, for example, should make budgetary decisions for the faculties and schools. In addition, independent auditors must carefully examine the relevant information provided by the faculties and schools before the board uses that information as a justification for providing funds to the various units. Furthermore, the criteria for the board of governors' decisions and the data from the faculties and schools should be published so that all faculty members, students, and, in fact, all citizens in the province can easily see the way the resources have been allocated.

Of course, receiving and publishing good information does not necessarily mean that the board will make good decisions. But receiving poor quality information, unaudited, from self-interested deans and department heads, almost guarantees poor decisions will be made. Such procedures are used at investment firms where rent-seeking may potentially have serious negative effects on the viability of the business. If universities are serious about transparency and accountability, similar procedures will begin to be used by more institutions.

Second, students should be empowered by requiring they pay the same proportion of the cost of their education directly to the faculties and schools in which they are enrolled and not to the central administrators of the university to be distributed in ways that are unrelated to the cost of their education. Specifically, the students' tuition fees should pay about 40 percent of the cost of the salaries of the academic and support staff in the faculties and schools in which they are enrolled. The reason for selecting this percentage is because universities and faculty members often claim that about 40 percent of faculty members' time is spent on teaching and supervising students.[19] As such, the tuition fees for students in the Faculty of Education would be the lowest on campus, while the fees for students in the Faculty of Medicine would be almost ten times higher and the fees for students in the Faculty of Dentistry would be about thirteen times higher than their present amount. Of course, the tuition fees would be supplemented by the existing scholarships and needs-based bursaries and loans.

Essentially, this policy would make the students' fees contingent on the costs of delivering the educational programs within the faculties and schools. Just as important, the policy would also allow students to compare their fees within and between universities, and consequently they could more easily comparatively shop for courses and programs across faculties and schools and even across universities. If this happened, faculties, schools, and the university itself would suffer serious consequences if students did not enrol or if they dropped out before completing their degrees. For this reason, all the faculties and schools would be forced to keep their tuition fees as low as possible, enrolling as many students—particularly undergraduate students—as possible, while delivering high-quality educational programs. This would be especially true if students could substitute relatively expensive in-class courses for relative cheap online courses.

If this policy were implemented, Agricultural and Food Sciences and Engineering, for example, would have more difficulty replacing a relatively large number of undergraduate students with many fewer graduate students because their tuition revenue would decrease substantially unless they substantially increased the tuition fees paid by the graduate students. As expected, both present and potential students in highly subsidized faculties and schools—Dentistry, Medicine, Agriculture, and Music—for example, would probably object to this proposition because their tuition fees would increase to better reflect the true costs of the salaries of the faculty members and support staff responsible for delivering their academic programs. As a result, these students would probably put pressure on their administrators to reduce the costs without decreasing the quality of the programs. The students in the other faculties and schools, however, would pay less because they would not be subsidizing the students in the advantaged faculties and schools.

Finally, academic units should receive funds from the block grants provided by the provincial government, in part, on both the percentage of students who graduate with degrees and the cost of the tuition fees students pay within their specific faculties and schools. In other words, faculties and schools should receive internal funds based on their graduation rates, or changes in the graduation rates, of the students in their faculties. At present, only about 56 percent of University of Manitoba undergraduate students graduate with degrees within six years.[20] Assuming that a faculty or school graduated 80 percent of its students within six years, then the faculty or school would receive more internal funds than a faculty that graduated only 40 percent of its students. Another part of the internal funds should be negatively related to the tuition fees paid by the students. In other words, the higher the tuition fees paid by students—or increases in tuition fees over time—the lower the grants received by the faculties and schools. If tuition fees increased, the funds would decrease; if tuition fees decreased, the funds would increase. This policy would encourage faculties and schools to be more careful in admitting ill-prepared and/or unmotivated students and more concerned about graduating the students they admit.

Essentially, these three policies would provide incentives for faculties and schools to keep the cost of degrees low and the quality of the educational programs high—especially the costs of undergraduate programs in which about

85 percent of the students at the University of Manitoba are enrolled. Economists tell us that incentives, such as the ones created by these policies, matter. For this reason, the three policies I outlined would increase the incentives for all university administrators, support staff, and faculty members to value teaching, particularly teaching undergraduate students, more than they do at present. Specifically, the objective of these policies would be to produce transparent information from faculties and schools, and then to reward administrators, support staff, and faculty members for cutting costs and focussing resources on graduating more students, particularly undergraduates, from good quality programs in the shortest possible time. In this process, the students would be treated as price-conscious customers and the faculties and schools, and the university in total, would be forced to make cost-saving reforms, which would increase their efficiency and productivity in first enrolling and then graduating students.

Even with these three policies, the University of Manitoba would still serve its two most important functions, creating new knowledge and passing it on to the next generation. In all likelihood, these two functions would become even more important, but the administrative and educational structures in the faculties and schools would probably change so that both the creation of new knowledge and the education of students would be conducted more effectively. Calling students "price-conscious customers" would probably provoke a strong negative reaction from faculty members and administrators. Nevertheless, it is necessary to think of students as customers because in the future they are likely to be paying for a larger proportion of their education and the pressures for accountability, transparency, and efficiency are not going to disappear soon. In fact, these pressures are probably going to increase. For this reason, policies that produce incentives for reducing the cost of educating both undergraduate and graduate students while maintaining or improving the quality of the programs must be seriously considered.

Notes

1 I would like to thank John Stapleton, my friend and colleague, for his advice and suggestions on previous drafts of this article.

2 Canadian Council on Learning, *Post-secondary Education in Canada: Strategies for Success* (Ottawa: Canadian Council on Learning, 2007). See also James E. Cote and Anton L. Allahar, *Ivory Tower Blues: A University System in Crisis* (Toronto: University of Toronto Press, 2007); Derek Hum, "Tenure and Pay Structures in Canadian Universities," *Research Monographs in Higher Education no. 4* (Winnipeg: Centre for Higher Education Resarch and Development, 1998); David Laidler, ed., *Renovating the Ivory Tower: Canadian*

Universities and the Knowledge Economy (Toronto: C.D. Howe Institute, 2002); Mary Agnes Welch, "Presidential Perks," *Winnipeg Free Press*, 23 August 2008, A5.

3   See Rodney Clifton, *What Can Be Done About the Underfunding of Canadian Universities?* (Winnipeg, Frontier Centre for Public Policy, 2003); Rodney Clifton, "Is the tuition freeze at the University of Manitoba reasonable?" *Fraser Forum*, 17–20 March 2007; Rodney Clifton, "More bean counters needed," *Winnipeg Free Press*, 13 June 2007, A15; Rodney Clifton and Hymie Rubenstein, *Collegial Models for Enhancing the Performance of University Professors* (Vancouver: The Fraser Institute, 2002); Rodney Clifton and Michael Zwaagstra, *Questionable Graduate Programs for Teachers and Administrators* (Winnipeg: Frontier Centre for Public Policy, 2008); Julie Guard, "Top-down bosses top up: Executive pay raises at U of M wildly out of line with staff increases, *Winnipeg Free Press*, 25 October 2007, A15; Payam Pakravan, *The Future Is Not What It Used To Be: Re-examining Provincial Post-Secondary Funding Mechanisms in Canada*, (Toronto: C.D. Howe Institute, 2006); Thomas Sowell, *Inside American Education: The Decline, the Deception, The Dogmas* (New York: The Free Press, 1993); Richard Vedder, *Going Broke by Degrees: Why College Costs too Much* (Washington: The AEI Press, 2004).

4   Manitoba Education, Citizenship and Youth, A Statistical Profile of Education and Training in Manitoba 2000–01 to 2004–05 (Winnipeg: Manitoba Education, Citizenship and Youth), 5–6.

5   See, for example, James Blatz, "NDP's tuition freeze downgrades quality of education," *Winnipeg Free Press*, 21 January 2007, B4; Scott Forbes, "Falling short: Tuition freeze and underfunding are strangling our universities," *Winnipeg Free Press*, 17 December 2006, B4; Jessica Werb, "Q and A: An Interview With Harvey Weingarten," *Canadian University Report*, 2009, 12.

6   Emőke Szathmáry, "Let the U of M manage its finances: The era of being able to live off student volume has ended," *The Bulletin*, 2 November 2006, 4.

7   Vedder, *Going Broke by Degrees*, xviii.

8   Ibid., 44.

9   University of Manitoba, *1998–99 Institutional Statistics*, 47; University of Manitoba, *2005–2006 Institutional Statistics*, 64.

10 Vedder, *Going Broke by Degrees*, xviii.

11 University of Manitoba, *1998–99 Institutional Statistics*, 85; University of Manitoba, *2004–2005 Institutional Statistics*, 121.

12 Sowell, *Inside American Education*, 205.

13 See, for example, Guard, "Top-down-bosses top up," A15.

14 See Anne Krueger, "The Political Economy of the Rent-Seeking Society," *American Economic Review* 64 (1974): 291–303.

15 Robert Merton Sr., "The Matthew Effect in Science," *Science* 159 (1968), 56–63.

16 Matthew 25:29. Cited in Merton, "The Matthew Effect in Science."

17 Werb, "Q and A: An Interview With Harvey Weingarten," 12

18 See, for example, Clifton, *What Can Be Done About the Underfunding of Canadian Universities?* Clifton and Rubenstein, *Collegial Models for Enhancing the Performance of University Professors*; Cote and Allahar, *Ivory Tower Blues*; Laidler, *Renovating the Ivory Tower*; Pakravan, *The Future is Not What It Used To Be*; Sowell, *Inside American Education*; Vedder, *Going Broke by Degrees*.

19 Vedder, *Going Broke by Degrees*, 169.

20 University of Manitoba, *2004–2005 Institutional Statistics*, 74.

CONTRIBUTORS

Christopher Adams is the Vice-President of Research and Client Services with Probe Research Inc., a Winnipeg-based market research company. He is also an Adjunct Professor at the University of Winnipeg where he teaches in the fields of politics and public administration, as well as an Adjunct Professor at the I.H. Asper School of Business, where he teaches research methods courses in the MBA program. He is the author of *Politics in Manitoba: Parties, Leaders, and Voters* (University of Manitoba Press, 2008).

Paul Barber is a graduate in political science (before they changed the name to political studies) from the University of Manitoba, where he was for a time active in the Liberal Party. He is a Senior Intergovernmental Affairs Specialist in the Ontario Department of Intergovernmental Affairs, which included participation in the negotiations that led to the Charlottetown Accord. He has also worked for the government of Manitoba as well as a television producer for CBC current affairs programs in Winnipeg and Toronto.

Harvey Bostrom has served as the Deputy Minister of Manitoba Aboriginal and Northern Affairs since 2001. He has been with the Government of Manitoba as a senior public servant for more than twenty years, working in various capacities including Special Advisor on Aboriginal issues, and Director of the Native Affairs Secretariat. He also served for eight years as the MLA for Rupertsland (1973–1981), during which time he was a cabinet minister in the Schreyer Government. He held two portfolios as Minister of Cooperative Development and Minister of Renewable Resources and Transportation Services.

Curtis Brown is a Duff Roblin Scholar at the University of Manitoba, graduating in 2010 with a Master of Arts in Political Studies. A former political reporter and editor with the *Brandon Sun* and *Winnipeg Free Press*, he continues to contribute political commentary to these newspapers and to his independent blog, *Endless Spin Cycle*. He currently works in the market research industry with Probe Research Inc. in Winnipeg.

Rod Clifton, BEd, MEd (Alberta), PhD (Toronto), FilDr (Stockholm) is a Professor in the Faculty of Education and a Senior Fellow at St. John's College, University of Manitoba. His research pertains to sociology of education, post-secondary education and educational policy, He has published more than 150 articles and written or co-written six books on these subjects, including *Socioeconomic Status, Attitudes, and Educational Performances: A Comparison of Students in England and New Zealand, Authority in Classrooms, Crosscurrents: Contemporary Canadian Educational Issues*, and *Recent Social Trends in Canada, 1960-2000*. He is also a recipient of a Spencer Fellowship from the International Association for the Evaluation of Educational Achievement as well as many other research awards.

James Eldridge's career as a Manitoba public servant spans four decades under seven premiers—Weir, Schreyer, Lyon, Pawley, Filmon, Doer, and Selinger. He is currently the Manitoba government's Special Advisor on Intergovernmental Relations, having served as Clerk of the Executive Council and in a number of other roles mostly pertaining to intergovernmental affairs. He has been honoured with a number of awards, including the Lieutenant-Governor's Medal for Excellence in Public Administration in Manitoba, and currently serves on the boards of the Canada West Foundation, the Queen's Institute of Intergovernmental Relations, and the Order of Manitoba Advisory Council.

Gerald Friesen is a Professor of History at the University of Manitoba. He is the author of several books, including *The Canadian Prairies: A History* (1984) and *Citizens and Nation: An Essay on History, Communication, and Culture* (2000). His most recent book, co-written with Royden Loewen, is titled *Immigrants in Prairie Cities: A Century of Canadian Cultural Diversity* (2009).

Jean Friesen is a Professor of History at the University of Manitoba. She received her PhD in History from the University of British Columbia and is the author of *Magnificent Gifts: The Treaties of Canada with the Indians of the Northwest, 1869-76*. She served as the MLA for Wolseley from 1990 to 2003 and later served as Manitoba's Deputy Premier and Minister of Intergovernmental Affairs from 1999 to 2003.

Joan Grace is an Associate Professor in the University of Winnipeg's Department of Politics, where she teaches courses on Canadian politics, women and politics, and social movements/collective action. She holds a PhD in political science from McMaster University, a Master's of Public Administration from the University of

Manitoba/University of Winnipeg, and BA (Hons) in political science from the University of Victoria. Her research interests include women's political and policy advocacy, women's relationship to the state, and the role and influence of institutions in public policy development.

Kerri Holland is currently pursuing a PhD in Political Science from the University of Alberta. She became a Duff Roblin Fellow in 2006 and received her MA degree from the University of Manitoba in 2007. Her research largely focuses on Canadian agriculture and rural policy, intergovernmental affairs, and interest group activity.

Derek Hum is a Professor of Economics at the University of Manitoba and Adjunct Professor, School of Public Policy, Simon Fraser University. He is a graduate of Mount Allison University, Oxford University and University of Toronto and a former Rhodes Scholar. Trained in Mathematics, Economics, and Political Science, he is also an acknowledged expert in social policy. He was formerly research director of a large-scale experimental test of guaranteed income in Canada. He has published widely in economics, sociology, and public policy, including seven books and more than one hundred articles and essays.

Irene Linklater is a citizen of the Anishinabe Nation and a residential school survivor. She is an advocate for First Nations self-determination and treaties and inherent rights preservation and promotion of First Nations culture, language, and values. A lawyer by training who has taught at the universities of Ottawa and Winnipeg and Red River College, she currently serves as executive director of the Assembly of Manitoba Chiefs and represents the organization on the Intergovernmental Committee on Manitoba First Nations Health and Treaties Relations Commission (Manitoba).

Frances Russell is a Winnipeg-based freelance journalist and author. Her career spans more than forty years and includes stints as a reporter and political columnist with the *Winnipeg Tribune*, the *Vancouver Sun*, the *Globe and Mail*, United Press International, and the *Winnipeg Free Press*—to which she continues to contribute a weekly column. She has also written two award-winning non-ficiton books: *Mistehay Sakahegan—The Great Lake*, and *The Canadian Crucible—Manitoba's Role in Canada's Great Divide*. She is married with one son and two grandsons.

Kelly Saunders is a political studies professor at Brandon University. She is a graduate of the Master's and PhD program at the University of Manitoba. She worked as an assistant to the Minister of Justice in the Progressive Conservative government of Gary Filmon.

Jim Silver is Chair of the Politics Department and Co-Director of the Urban and Inner-City Studies program at the University of Winnipeg. He has written extensively on inner-city issues, especially but not only in Winnipeg. He is the author of *In Their Own Voices: Building Urban Aboriginal Communities* (2006), and co-editor, with John Loxley and Kathleen Sexsmith, of *Doing Community Economic Development* (2007).

Wayne Simpson is a Professor of Economics at the University of Manitoba. He is a graduate of the University of Saskatchewan and the London School of Economics. He is a specialist in labour economics, applied microeconomics, quantitative methods, and social policy. In addition to writing more than forty peer-reviewed articles for economics and policy journals, he is also the author of *Urban Structure and the Labour Market: Analysis of Worker Mobility, Commuting and Underemployment in Cities* (1992) and co-author (with D. Hum) of *Income Maintenance, Work Effort and the Canadian Mincome Experiment* (1991), and *Maintaining a Competitive Workforce* (1996).

Paul G. Thomas was the Duff Roblin Professor of Government at St. John's College, University of Manitoba, where he taught political studies and public administration from 1969 (after completing his PhD at the University of Toronto) until his recent retirement in 2010. He is a recipient of the Order of Manitoba and has numerous other citations for his contributions to the field of public administration. In addition to authoring more than 100 journal articles and book chapters, Prof. Thomas is also well-known for his contributions to public life, including as chairman of the Manitoba Telephone System's Board of Directors, the Review and Implementation Committee for the Report of the Manitoba Pediatric Cardiac Surgery Inquest, the Manitoba Institute for Patient Safety, and the Regional Planning Advisory Committee (which made recommendations regarding Manitoba's Capital Region).

Paul Vogt currently serves as Manitoba's Clerk of the Executive Council, a position he has held since 2005. Previously, he served as policy secretary to the provincial cabinet from 1999 to 2005, moving to that position after working as research director for the New Democratic Party caucus. Mr. Vogt is a graduate of the University of Manitoba and has undertaken graduate studies at Oxford and Princeton. He has also taught courses in political studies, economics and philosophy as a sessional instructor at the universities of Winnipeg and Manitoba.

Jared Wesley is an Assistant Professor in the Department of Political Studies at the University of Manitoba. A former Duff Roblin Scholar when he completed his MA at the University of Manitoba, he later graduated with a PhD at the University of Calgary. His research focuses on political parties in Manitoba and other Canadian provinces. His work has been published in the *Canadian Journal of Political Science* and several edited volumes.

Nelson Wiseman was born in Bucharest and emigrated from Israel to Canada with his family at the age of six. Politically socialized in North End Winnipeg, he is a graduate of the University of Manitoba, where he served as president of the campus NDP and vice-president of the University of Manitoba Students' Union, and completed his graduate studies at the University of Toronto. He is a specialist in Canadian government and politics at the University of Toronto and author of several books, including *Social Democracy in Manitoba* (1981) and *In Search of Canadian Political Culture* (2007).